Fluency with Information Technology

Skills, Concepts, and Capabilities

Preliminary Edition

Lawrence Snyder
University of Washington, Seattle

"In which the secrets of computers and networks are revealed, in English, with no math, and starting at the very beginning."

Boston San Francisco New York
London Toronto Sydney Tokyo Singapore Madrid
Mexico City Munich Paris Cape Town Hong Kong Montreal

Executive Editor: Susan Hartman Sullivan
Associate Editor: Galia Shokry
Executive Marketing Manager: Michael Hirsch
Managing Editor: Pat Mahtani
Production Supervisor: Vicki Hochstedler
Cover Design: Regina Hagen Kolenda
Text Design: Vicki Hochstedler
Design Manager: Regina Hagen Kolenda
Composition: Vicki Hochstedler
Copyeditor: Margaret Hill
Proofreader: Helen Maggie Carr
Prepress and Manufacturing: Caroline Fell

Access the latest information about Addison-Wesley titles from our World Wide Web Site: http://www.aw.com/cs

Library of Congress Cataloging-in-Publication Data
Snyder, Lawrence.
Fluency with information technology : skills, concepts, and capabilities / Lawrence Snyder.— Preliminary ed.
p. cm.
ISBN 0-321-12201-1
1. Information technology. I. Title.

T58.5 .S645 2003
004—dc21

2002026034

ISBN 0-321-12201-1

3 4 5 6 7 8 9 10—PA—040302

For Julie Ann, Dan, and Dave

Acknowledgments

Many people have contributed to this work. First to be thanked are my collaborators in the creation of the Fluency concept, the NRC Committee on Computer Literacy—Al Aho, Marcia Linn, Arnie Packer, Allen Tucker, Jeff Ullman, and Andy van Dam. Special thanks go to Herb Lin of the NRC staff who assisted throughout the Fluency effort, tirelessly and in his usual great good humor. Two enthusiastic supporters of Fluency— Bill Wulf of the National Academy of Engineering and John Cherniavski of the National Science Foundation—have continually supported this effort in more ways than I am aware. It has been a pleasure to know and work with this team.

As the material was developed for this book, many have contributed: Ken Yasuhara and Brian Bannon, teaching assistants on the first offering of CSE100, contributed in innumerable ways and injected a needed dose of practicality into my ideas. Grace Whiteaker, Alan Borning, and Batya Friedman have been generous with their ideas regarding Fluency. Martin Dickey of CSE and Mark Donovan of UWired have been constant sources of support. The original offerings of CSE100 benefited greatly from contributions by Nana Lowell, Anne Zald, Mike Eisenberg, and Fred Videon. Frank Tompa was extremely helpful with the *OED* material.

I am particularly grateful for the keen insights and valuable feedback from the reviewers of this project: Robert M. Aiken, Temple University; Anne Condon, University of British Columbia; Nicholas Cravotta, University of California, Berkeley; Gordon Davies, Open University; Peter J. Denning, George Mason University; John P. Dougherty, Haverford College; Philip East, University of Northern Iowa; Michael B. Eisenberg, University of Washington; Robert S. Fenchel, University of Wisconsin, Madison; Esther Grassian, UCLA College Library; Raymond Greenlaw, Armstrong Atlantic State University; A. J. Hurst, Monash University, Australia; Doris K. Lidtke, Towson University; Wen Liu, ITT Technical Institute; Jim McKeown, Dakota State University; David R. Musicant, Carleton College; Laurie J. Patterson, University of North Carolina, Wilmington; John Rosenberg, Monash University, Australia; Robert T. Ross, California Polytechnic State University; Robert J. Shive, Jr., Millsaps College; and Mark Urban-Lurain, Michigan State University.

The Fluency material has been a topic of discussion with many international colleagues. Discussions with Hans Hinterberger, John Rosenberg, and John Hirsch have been especially valuable in critiquing the material from an overseas perspective. Other helpful international commentary came from Anne Condon, Hannes Jonsson,

Jerg Nievergelt, Clark Thomberson, Barbara Thomberson, Ewan Tempero, and Kazuo Iwama.

Among the many thoughtful computer users who have either generously described their misunderstandings about IT or patiently listened to my explanations about IT, I wish to thank Esther Snyder, Helene Fowler, Judy Watson, Brendan Healey, Victory Grund, Shelley Burr, Ken Burr, and Noelle Lamb.

It is my great pleasure to thank my editors, Susan Hartman Sulllivan and Mary Clare McEwing. Susan's excellent judgment and insight, coupled with her enthusiasm for this book, have kept me focused amid a multitude of distractions. Mary Clare has been an excellent colleague. Her high standards for literate presentation have taken on the beast of technological jargon and style and been victorious. The day-to-day exchange of bytes and tastes with her has been a particular joy to me. Others of the Addison-Wesley team to whom I owe thanks are Michael Hirsch, Regina Kolenda, Kim Ellwood, Galia Shobry, and Lesly Hershman. Thanks especially to Vicki Hochstedler for her patience in working across a dozen time zones.

Finally, my wife Julie, and sons, Dan and Dave, have been patient, encouraging, and, most important, a continual source of good humor throughout this effort. It is with my deepest appreciation that I thank them for everything.

The names of the people used in the examples are 100% fictitious.

Contents

Preface

The overarching goal of *Fluency with Information Technology* is to give students the experience, knowledge, and capabilities needed to apply information technology effectively throughout their lives. Such an ambitious goal eclipses the more modest objectives of the computer literacy syllabus, which has traditionally focused only on imparting immediately useful skills. Fluency *contains* literacy, but adds problem solving, reasoning, complexity management, and other higher-level thinking processes, as well as a broader coverage of technological topics that prepare students to keep pace with the ever-advancing technology. The result is an intellectually rich curriculum constructed from equal parts of application proficiency, timeless knowledge, and thinking.

The inspiration for *Fluency with Information Technology* comes from a report by the National Research Council, *Being Fluent with Information Technology*.[1] In that study, commissioned by the National Science Foundation, the authors asserted that traditional computer literacy classes do not have the "staying power" necessary for students to keep pace with the rapid changes in information technology (IT). They concluded that the educational "bar needs to be raised" if students' knowledge is to evolve and adapt. The recommended alternative, dubbed *fluency with information technology,* or *FIT*, described a tripartite formulation of skills, concepts, and capabilities wrapped around a project-oriented delivery mechanism that assures the content is fully integrated. *Fluency with Information Technology* is designed to implement the Fluency proposal as outlined in the NRC study.

To present an overview of *Fluency*'s content and the rationale for its approach, consider the following four topics:

- Tripartite Content
- Projects as a Delivery Medium
- Debate about Programming
- Lifelong Learning

[1] *Being Fluent with Information Technology*, National Academy Press, 1999. [The author chaired the NRC's Committee on Computer Literacy that produced this report.]

Tripartite Content

The NRC's *Being Fluent* report asserted that to be successful, IT education must prepare students to adapt to an ever-changing IT landscape. It envisioned them engaged in a process of lifelong learning, adapting to and exploiting the new opportunities presented by the perfectly malleable media of information, computers, and networks. In order to launch the lifelong learning process students should be taught three different types of content—Skills, Concepts, and Capabilities.

> *Skills* refers to proficiency with contemporary computer applications such as email, word processing, Web searching, and so on. Skills make the technology immediately useful to students and ground their learning of the other content in practical experience. The Skills component approximates traditional computer literacy topics, and is time varying. As students arrive at college knowing say, browsing, it is dropped from the curriculum and a new application can be added instead.
>
> *Concepts* refers to the fundamental knowledge underpinning IT, such as how a computer works, digital representation of information, assessing information authenticity, and the like. Concepts provide the principles on which students will build new understanding as IT evolves. The Concepts component has been selected carefully from the curricula of the underlying IT disciplines, and is essentially timeless.
>
> *Capabilities* refers to higher-level thinking processes such as problem solving, reasoning, complexity management, troubleshooting, and so on. Capabilities embody modes of thinking that are essential to exploiting IT, but they apply in many other situations as well. The Capabilities component is a standard element of all education, of course, but it is essential to the effective use of IT, making it an explicit focus of *Fluency with Information Technology.*

For each component the NRC report listed ten recommended items. These are shown in the following table.

The NRC's list of top 10 Skills, Concepts and Capabilities.

Fluency with Information Technology		
Skills	**Concepts**	**Capabilities**
Set up a personal computer	Fundamentals of computers	Engage in sustained reasoning
Use basic operating system facilities	Organization of information systems	Manage complexity
Use a word processor to create a document	Fundamentals of networks	Test a solution
Use a graphics or artwork package to manipulate an image	Digital representation of information	Find problems in a faulty use of IT
Connect a computer to the Internet	Structuring information	Navigate a collection and assess the quality of the information
Use the Internet to locate information	Modeling and abstraction	Collaborate using IT
Use a computer to communicate with others	Algorithmic thinking and programming	Communicate using IT about IT
Use a spreadsheet to model a simple process	Universality	Expect the unexpected
Use a database to access information	Limitations of Information Technology	Anticipate technological change
Use online help and instructional materials	Social impact of computers and technology	Think abstractly about Information Technology

Projects as a Delivery Medium

The Skills, Concepts, and Capabilities represent different kinds of knowledge that are co-equal in their contribution to IT Fluency. They span separate dimensions of understanding. Rather than attempting to teach them separately, however, the NRC report recommends the material be integrated using a project-centric approach. *Fluency with Information Technology* adopts this technique.

The overall strategy is to focus the Skills instruction in the lab, the Concepts instruction in standard lecture material, and the Capabilities instruction in lecture/lab demonstrations. The projects are the opportunity to use the three kinds of knowledge for a specific purpose. They illustrate IT as it is often applied in practice—to solve information-processing tasks of a substantial nature involving non-obvious complexities.

A project is a multiweek assignment to achieve a specific IT goal. For example, create a database to track patient testing for a walk-in Drug and HIV Testing Clinic, and give a presentation to convince an audience that patient privacy has been preserved. (The NRC report lists a series of projects.[2]) Students, who can work in groups as appropriate, will employ a variety of Skills such as using a database, Web searching and presentation facilities. They will rely on their understanding of Concepts such as database keys, table structure, and the Join query operator. They will use Capabilities such as reasoning, debugging, complexity management, testing, and others. The Fluency components will be applied together to produce the final result, leading to an integrated understanding of IT and preparing for significant "real-life" applications of IT.

Debate about Programming

Since the advent of computer literacy syllabi nearly three decades ago, there has been debate as to whether non-specialists should be taught programming. Rational arguments have been offered on both sides, and thoughtful, well-intentioned adherents espouse each point of view. The NRC's study received strong input on both sides of the issue, but in the final report the definition of Fluency specifies "algorithmic thinking and programming" as one of the ten essential Concepts. The topic is sufficiently controversial that the original rationale and the strategy used in *Fluency with Information Technology* should be reviewed.

The NRC committee's report acknowledges the dilemma about programming in the opening to a long discussion[3] as to why programming was, in fact, finally included:

> Algorithmic thinking is a valuable ability for many educated people, yet programming—the act of expressing an algorithm in a specific form to solve a problem—is widely seen as the purview of the specialist. Algorithmic thinking and programming were listed together as a concept because they are very closely related forms of the same phenomenon.

The discussion makes clear that the committee is *not* claiming one must be a professional programmer to be Fluent. Its intentions are much more limited. The committee defines a modest set of basic programming ideas—variable, conditional, iteration, and so on—that are sufficient for programming's role in the Fluency context. Programming's role, as the report makes clear, is to support algorithmic thinking, reasoning, debugging, and other components of Fluency. The recommended programming concepts are essential to this use, but are insufficient to produce a practicing programmer. Thus, the committee might have more precisely specified, "algorithmic thinking and related programming concepts essential to algorithm specification."

---

[2] *Being Fluent*, Appendix A.

[3] Ibid., pp. 41–48.

Since the report recommends only a handful of basic programming concepts, *Fluency with Information Technology* treats only that set. Nevertheless, the perception that programming is a difficult and intellectually challenging topic suitable only for "techies" raises the question of whether even this small set of concepts can be taught to a general student population. Moreover, since programming is usually taught to students with a strong mathematics background, one wonders if it isn't hopeless to expect "non-techie" students to learn it. The answer, based on the experience of teaching from early drafts of *Fluency with Information Technology,* is that it *can* be done and the students find it rewarding.

Specifically, the considerations that lead to success are three in number. First, programming must be taught in a patient, accessible way. The general student population does not find it intuitive, and so needs more complete explanations than would be given to a "techie" audience. Second, the programs must be non-intimidating and be applied to problems of interest to the class. Students expect to find programming terrible, and are amazed when they have early success on an interesting problem. Third, the "mathematical reasoning" expectations assumed in standard programming classes must be replaced with an expectation of "reasoning" ability only. This is sufficient. Programming is purely a reasoning activity and is within the ability level of college students. It relies only incidentally on mathematics. Similar success has been observed in related situations[4].

With a clear understanding of the report's intent regarding programming, and evidence that *Fluency's* gentler treatment makes programming accessible to the general student population, the final concern is whether including programming in the Fluency curriculum is worthwhile. This is an obvious concern because the amount of programming is too limited to produce programmers, and the time might be better spent on some other content. Without long-term studies it is impossible to say definitively, but there is some evidence that the answer will be "yes." First, the report's claim that programming knowledge facilitates other aspects of Fluency seems correct. From comprehending the Fetch/Execute Cycle to debugging, programming knowledge can be observed to assist students in understanding and to deepen their level of comprehension. Second, the inclusion of programming assures that the course is a substantive, ideas-based course. It is an intellectually challenging class equivalent to other "science classes," but without a heavy reliance on mathematics. Students report the class "is intellectually challenging" and that it "expanded my thinking." Third, succeeding with programming is an intellectual achievement that aids a student's confidence as a computer user. Confident users are the goal of Fluency, and in the limited cases studied so far, the goal has been reached.

LIFELONG LEARNING

The students registering for a Fluency with Information Technology course can have a variety of expectations, which rarely include the course's actual objectives. Some are expecting to learn the popular computer applications and Web skills. Others, who already know these skills, are expecting an easy class and a good grade. For both of these groups a classic literacy course would fulfill their needs with less effort. For students with broader, less specific goals, Fluency is likely a better choice because it prepares students to use computers today and to be effective IT users forever through lifelong learning.

To appreciate the magnitude of the task of teaching the essential IT knowledge for life, consider that as a "product" a college education has an expected useful lifetime

[4] Ibid., Appendix B.

of 55 years for men, based on a life expectancy of 77 years, and slightly longer for women. From that perspective what should the Class of '44 (the students graduating 55 years prior to the publication of the *Being Fluent* report) have been taught, given the following facts:

- The first electronic computer would not be completed for two more years.
- The first computer network would be created for their 25th reunion.
- The term *personal computer* would take 35 years to be invented.
- The World Wide Web would be effectively a half-century away.

Clearly, more wonders from IT can be expected, and predicting what they will be is hopeless. Focusing on fundamental principles, foundational ideas, and higher-level thinking skills is the key to preparing graduates for the task of keeping pace with future developments. Thus, the committee has emphasized a fundamentals-rich approach.

Will the *Being Fluent* report's recommendations achieve the desired goal of launching lifelong learning? The question cannot be answered definitively before long-term studies are complete, so anecdotes must suffice. There are those (non-technical) people who are proficient computer users and make effective use of the technology based entirely on their own understanding and the new knowledge they are able to teach themselves. The common thread among the handful of people of my acquaintance who meet this definition of Fluent Citizen is that they learned the fundamentals of Information Technology, especially programming. Then, once they began using personal computers to solve some personally relevant problem, they continued steadily and incrementally to expand their knowledge. Their success became an incentive to apply IT more broadly and provided the confidence to believe that accomplishing the goal was within their grasp. This is Fluency, and it is the goal of *Fluency with Information Technology*.

A Word to Students about *Fluency with Information Technology*

Fluency with information technology is a somewhat unusual subject, making this a somewhat unusual textbook. There are three things I think you should know about using *Fluency With Information Technology:*

- Part of the Fluency content comes from labs, and is not described in this book.
- Though you must spend significant time in the lab, the "book learning" part is the most important.
- Read this book with a computer at hand.

Let me amplify on this advice.

Of the three kinds of knowledge defining Fluency—Skills, Concepts and Capabilities—the skills are the most likely to change. Writing about a software system in a textbook is useless to students if the software changes before the book is printed. Keeping such information current is nearly impossible. But it's also true that learning skills is best done on a computer in a lab using contemporary applications. You can use the latest and greatest software installed, and there is usually someone nearby to whom you can ask questions when you get stuck. Consequently, almost all of the skills in the Fluency curriculum will be learned in the lab, not with this book. What *can* be taught in a book is *how to learn* a new application, since there are guidelines about learning new software. These principles are the subject of Chapter 3. So, *Fluency with Information Technology* does treat skills, but it does so at a more general level than for any particular computer software system. I do expect that you will be learning skills in the lab, so the chapters of the book assume more and more familiarity with computer applications as they progress.

Though the skills are taught in the lab, the concepts and capabilities are the subject of this book. They are the more important material, since they are the foundations on which you will learn. It's easy to be distracted by the "hands on" part of Fluency, because it can be fun, active, and practically useful in your other classes. But don't forget to read the book. The book explains the complex parts of Fluency in a patient, understandable way, enabling you to apply them in the lab. It is always easiest and fastest to read about the concepts first before attempting a project or assignment. I know it's obvious advice, but so many ignore it for too long.

In writing this book on my laptop I obviously had a computer always available to explore the Web or test out an example. To get the most out of the text you too will need a computer for about half of the content. As you read you should "follow along online," often reproducing the running example so that you can watch active aspects of it that cannot be printed in a book. Every section in which I intend for you to have a computer available while reading will be clearly marked by a computer icon, .

Finally, good luck! Writing this book has truly been a pleasure. I hope reading it is equally enjoyable.

Fluency with Information Technology

The Master said: "To learn something and then put it into practice at the right time. Is this not a joy?"

—The Analects of Confucius

PART I

Becoming Skilled at Information Technology

CHAPTER 1

The Context of Information Technology

Learning Objectives

- Understand two reasons why knowing the right term is essential.
- Recall familiar terms for computer components.
- Be introduced to some basic computer terms.
- Understand how buttons are created and "clicked."
- Appreciate that the world of the computer screen is completely synthetic.
- Comprehend a few "idea" terms of IT.
- Become familiar with the book's glossary.

At the dawn of the twenty-first century, the world is irreversibly dependent on computers and networks. Instead of the dire predictions of 40 years ago about computers enslaving people, we find that information technology (IT) expands our world. By typing our address and that of our friend, we can receive driving instructions and a map of the route between the two houses. It's possible to write a term paper using resources from libraries around the world. Scientists can design drugs using supercomputers to model the interactions with other compounds. Though IT has eliminated some jobs, as predicted, it has made many other jobs less tedious, and it has created many high-quality "knowledge worker" professions. For better or worse, information technology is here to stay. The rational response is to become informed about IT and to apply it to full advantage. Those are the goals of this book.

The goal of Chapter 1 is to set the context for learning more about information technology. The process begins with an explanation of what constitutes information technology, recognizing two strong incentives for studying IT and sketching the purpose of becoming Fluent. Next we explore the concept of scale of change and the idea of a factor of improvement. These ideas emerge in our discussions of the mile run and the speed of flight. Armed with those two concepts, we consider how rapidly computers have advanced and we challenge ourselves to comprehend the scale of improvement. Another objective is to assess five fundamental changes that seem to be emerging from the widespread application of IT. Though the list is not exhaustive nor are the changes all favorable, they are indicative of ways in which our world is irreversibly changing due to IT. Next we speculate on the potential for future advances. Finally, we consider what we need to know to become Fluent and take advantage of all that information technology offers.

FLUENCY WITH INFORMATION TECHNOLOGY

Information technology (IT) is a broad term that encompasses computers, networks, online information resources, software and applications, digital media, and other related forms of information and technology. Virtually everything we encounter when sitting down to a personal computer is included in that definition, but there is much more. Indeed, most technology and resources derived from the invention of the electronic computer and the discovery of digitization are also included. Among the few forms of computer-derived technology that will not be included here are such things as the application of computers to control disk brakes on cars or the use of computer technology in thermometers. In those cases, a computer is used not for its information processing capacity—the feature of interest here—but as a shortcut for implementing a device that could be built out of standard (noncomputer) electronics. The key is information, its representation, and processing.

IT is not computer science, computer engineering, library science, electrical engineering, business data management, communications, nor any of a long list of other established disciplines. But it includes some content from all of them. Information technology is concerned with information—its representation, structure and organization, processing, transmission, distribution, and so on—and the technologies implementing those activities—computers, networks, software, search engines, data encryption processes, and so on. Just as you cannot read the newspaper passively, ignorant of factors like writer's bias, limitations on sources, fact versus opinion, you cannot expect to use electronic information passively. Moreover, unlike newspapers, information technologies are interactive. You can direct how the information is located, processed, validated, managed, and so on. To perform those tasks effectively, you must understand a few fundamentals from the established disciplines that make up IT. We can't and won't become experts in any of these fields, but we will familiarize ourselves with the vocabulary of each and some of the principal ideas.

Fluency implies that we are conversant with the language, in control and able to synthesize it effectively to express ourselves. Fluency, in that sense, is the goal of this book relative to the language of information technology. But, unlike natural language, which changes very slowly and thus allows us to attain the state of fluency, information technology is rapidly changing. It is not possible in such circumstances to attain a complete and lasting understanding of IT because the available technology and resources are quickly replaced with newer, different technologies and resources. Thus Fluency with information technology is a process of life-long learning in which you steadily add to your knowledge of IT, building on your present knowledge and acquiring facility with the new advances. This book provides the foundation for Fluency with information technology that will enable you to "keep up" with the advances. It is your responsibility to keep pace with IT as it ever expands and becomes potentially more useful to those who understand how to use it.

To appreciate how dramatically IT has changed the world in the last half century, let's begin by considering the scale of different forms of change.

The Scale of Change

When Moroccan miler Hicham El Guerrouj broke the world record on July 7, 1999, reports trumpeted that he "smashed," "eclipsed," and "shattered" the world's record. He had run a mile in an astonishing 3 minutes, 43.13 seconds, an impressive 1.26 seconds faster than the record set six years earlier by Noureddine Moreceli of Algeria. The verbs were not hyperbole. People around the world truly marveled at El Guerrouj's accomplishment. It was an auspicious achievement for the new century and millennium that were about to arrive.

To put El Guerrouj's run into perspective, notice that 45 years had passed since Englishman Roger Bannister attracted world attention as the first man in recorded history to run a mile in less than 4 minutes. His time was 3:59.4. In 45 years, the world's best runners improved the time for the mile by an astonishing 16.27 seconds. As a rate, that represents an improvement from 15.038 miles per hour to 16.134 miles per hour, or just over 7%. Given that Bannister's world-class time was the starting point, an improvement in human performance of that magnitude justifies our admiration.

How do these world champions compare to average people? Most healthy people in their early 20s—the age group of the world record setters—can run a mile in 7.5 minutes. This number was chosen because it covers the ability of a majority of the people in the age range, and because it is approximately twice the time El Guerrouj required. This factor-of-2 difference is a rough rule of thumb for the performance gap between an average person and a world champion for most physical strength activities such as running, swimming, jumping, and pole vaulting. The factor-of-2 rule tells us that no matter how hard most people try at physical activities, their performance can improve by at most twice. Of course, most of us can only dream of achieving even a portion of that factor-of-2 improvement. Nevertheless, the factor-of-2 human standard of improvement is an important benchmark.

The point of looking closely at El Guerrouj's performance is to calibrate our expectations about other performance improvements. As a second calibration point that could help us assess how computers have advanced, consider the speed improvements in aircraft.

Flyer 1, the aircraft that Orville and Wilbur Wright flew at Kitty Hawk, North Carolina, went so slowly that the brother who wasn't piloting it could run alongside as it flew a few feet above the ground. The brothers' first flight covered a distance of 120 feet in 12 seconds, and the fourth flight covered 852 feet in 57 seconds. When wind speed was taken into consideration, the Wrights reported that Flyer 1 flew at roughly 10 miles per hour.

Among modern aircraft we should probably accept the SR-71 Blackbird, a reconnaissance aircraft, as the fastest. Reports are vague about its maximum speed,[1] but NASA asserts that it flies at least 2200 mph, or more than three times the speed of sound. The exact speed is not so important, however, because we are interested in the magnitude of improvement in aircraft performance—defined here to be speed. Our estimate is that the SR-71 is an impressive 220 times faster than Flyer 1. Naturally, the factor-of-2 human performance improvements pale when compared to this factor-of-220 scale of advancement.

Notice that this discussion of scale of change focused on describing the amount of improvement between two rates. There is a difference between expressing improvement as a *percentage* and expressing improvement by a *factor*. A factor of improve-

---

[1] www.dfrc.nasa.gov/PAO/PAIS/HTML/FS-030-DFRC.html

ment is found by dividing the faster rate by the slower rate. So, to find El Guerrouj's improvement over Bannister's, divide their rates (16.134 / 15.038) to get 1.07. Percentages are a closely related computation found by dividing the amount of change by the slower rate—(16.134 – 15.038) / 15.038 = 0.07—and multiplying by 100. This added complexity confuses matters for the magnitudes of change of interest to us, so we adopt the simpler factor of improvement method.

The Scale of Advance for Computers

It is standard for the news media to report on the speed improvements of computers, increases in their memory capacity, or miniaturizations of transistors on silicon chips. We quickly lose track of how much improvement this is comparatively. Is the news reporting a 1.07 factor of improvement, a factor-of-2 improvement, or a factor-of-220 improvement over last week's performance? For perspective, we examine how computers have advanced and relate the improvement to that of the mile run and the increase in aircraft speed.

The speeds of the very earliest computers are difficult to quantify, but the UNIVAC I, the first commercial computer unveiled in 1951 and current when Bannister set his record, operated at a rate of nearly 100,000 addition operations per second. By comparison, a typical PC today—say, the portable IBM ThinkPad—can perform additions at 500,000,000 per second or so. This factor-of-5000 advance truly eclipses the performance improvements of our previous cases. But, consider this—the ThinkPad is no record setter. It's the sort of computer a college student can buy on a moderate budget. Engineering workstations easily achieve a billion adds per second, boosting us to the factor-of-10,000 range of advancement. In the realm of championship performance, an Intel computer called ASCI Red, built specifically for Sandia National Laboratory, held the world record for computer speed when El Guerrouj set his record. ASCI Red ran at an astonishing 2.1 trillion floating-point operations per second.[2] Compared to the UNIVAC I, ASCI Red is a factor of 21 million times faster!

Perhaps no other phenomenon in human experience has improved so dramatically. In roughly the same time period that human performance improved by a factor of 1.07 as measured by the mile run, computer performance improved by a factor of 21,000,000. Can we comprehend such a huge factor of improvement, or even the raw speed of ASCI Red? Most of us can appreciate the 7% improvement of El Guerrouj's run over Bannister's, and probably the factor-of-2 improvement in average versus world champion performance. Those feats are within the range of our imagination. But factors of improvement in the thousands or millions cease to be comprehensible. As proof, notice that if El Guerrouj had improved on Bannister by a factor of 21,000,000, he'd have run the mile in 11.4 microseconds. That's 11.4 millionths of a second. What does that mean?

- Human visual perception is so slow that El Guerrouj could run 3000 miles at that rate before anyone could even notice he had moved.
- The sound would still be "inside" the starting gun 11.4 microseconds after the trigger was pulled.
- Light travels only twice as fast.

We must accept the fact that both the raw power of today's computers and their improvement over the last half-century are virtually incomprehensible.

[2] Floating-point operations are decimal arithmetic operations and are *more* complicated than the additions that were used to measure the speed of the UNIVAC I.

Why have improvements in computer performance been so staggering? The explanation lies in the fact that, unlike most other phenomena such as aircraft speed, for which a limited number of parameters can be improved (for example, increasing engine thrust and reducing drag), computers have been improved along several dimensions. For example, better architecture and enhanced circuit designs, tremendously improved technology (vacuum tubes to silicon chips), and advanced parallel processing have all contributed to achieving ASCI Red's performance. And, though it doesn't appear in these raw speed numbers, the programs and software run on modern computers are much more advanced, meaning that problems are solved even faster than the improvements in the raw horsepower would imply. All these features have contributed to the computers we use every day.

So computers are fast and have been getting faster. But have they made any real difference?

> **Faster Still.** ASCI Red was the fastest of its day, but its day has passed. Several computers have eclipsed its performance, and better designs continue to emerge. For the latest speed tests, see `www.netlib.org/benchmark/top500.html`.

The Changes IT Brings

The enormous hype surrounding personal computers, the World Wide Web, electronic commerce, and other so called "benefits" of information technology leaves the skeptic wondering if anything has actually changed for the better with information technology. The evidence of impact always seems to be given in anecdotal form—an article on the number of new computers added to the Internet, for example, or an anecdote about a grandmother sending email to her grandchildren. It's interesting data, but what has changed qualitatively?

Though different commentators focus on different aspects of the Information Age, the following five changes appear to illustrate the fundamental effects of IT:

1. Nowhere is remote.
2. Connecting with others.
3. Revised human relationships.
4. English as a universal language.
5. Enhanced freedom of speech and of assembly.

Let's consider each in turn.

Nowhere Is Remote

In the past, centers of commerce, learning, and government justly claimed a distinctive difference from more remote places in the world based on the ready access to information. But today, because of information technology, nowhere is remote any longer. For instance, comparing New York, New York, and Unalakleet, Alaska, in terms of a resident's access to information, we see few differences: To find a Prague subway map for vacation planning we might have gone to the New York Public Library in the past, but both places are the same now in terms of information access because the best, up-to-date map is available online from the Prague subway system. To get a quote from the NASDAQ stock exchange, both places are equivalent. And to find out what people think "about them Mets," it's possible either to listen to NYC radio online or join a sports chatroom of other fans.

Differences still remain, of course. For example, the entire holdings of the New York Public Library will not soon be online, so scholars and others will continue to visit the library in person. But the vast amount of information people want or need is available electronically from the nearest net connection. It's as easy to read the *Sydney Morning Herald* in Sydney, Nova Scotia, as it is in Sydney, New South Wales, and unlike distributing a physical copy of the paper, readers can peruse it electronically at the same time on both sides of the world.

It may be that the claim "nowhere is remote" is backwards. Perhaps everywhere is remote in the sense of being equidistant from most information sources. Employees now take advantage of that fact because in many companies, information workers can choose to telecommute. Though they may be at home, physically remote from their employer, they are electronically at the same distance as if sitting in the office. Telecommuting is obviously attractive to the employee, but the employer may see advantages, too. A worker may be more productive in a bathrobe and fuzzy slippers than choked by a power tie and fuming from a terrible commute. One consequence of the telecommuting option may be that people will choose to live in remote places that are picturesque or idyllic in some other ways. That might ease the population burden on already congested cities, but raise the burden elsewhere. One day, Port Douglas, Australia; Banff, Canada; or Hania, Greece, may be overcrowded.

Connecting with Others

Though there seem to be no studies to quantify it, the anecdotal evidence is that people keep in closer, more frequent contact with friends and family across the country or in foreign lands via the Internet, than by telephone or mail. The advantages are the generally lower cost of email compared to the telephone and its faster speed compared to letters. You can email friends or family to find out what they are having for dinner, if you're interested. Such an inquiry might not be worth a phone call, especially considering that time differences complicate long-distance telephonic communication because both parties must be connected simultaneously. The Internet gives everyone the option of treating email as a message by reading it later or as a conversation by being online and answering it immediately, or some mixture of the two strategies.

A very interesting opportunity derived from World Wide Web technology is the possibility of "meeting people passively." By creating a Web page describing our interests, hobbies, free-time activities, and other descriptive information, we are publishing a passive advertisement that can be read from anywhere in the world. Most important, the Web page can be seen by "Web search engines"—programs that cruise the Internet, archiving the pages on which various descriptive terms appear. Suppose you list as an interest growing bonsai trees from *Sequoia sempervirens.* If someone else also interested in Sequoia bonsai asks a Web search engine to look for pages containing information about that topic, your page may be found. The searcher can contact the Web page owner, and a friendship or collaboration based on this shared interest may blossom. In this way, people can become acquainted with others sharing similar interests without ever meeting face-to-face. Historically this has only been possible via international organizations through which membership associates people. The benefit of passive meeting is that it can be based on extremely narrow interests or specialties that would not support a society. And associations of this form can form rapidly—a whole interest group could form around an event that is unfolding, such as a typhoon or election.

Revised Human Relationships

Not all aspects of information technology are self-evidently good. A possible dark side is that time spent in using a computer displaces other activities. In cases where the activities are substitutable—writing a novel with a computer rather than a typewriter—the impact may be very small, except possibly increased productivity. But if people spend time with a computer surfing the Web, playing games, or engaging in other activities that displace standard social interaction, the outcome may be less desirable. Recent preliminary studies from Carnegie-Mellon and Stanford Universities seem to document a decline in social interactions after people become intensive computer users. Claims were even made for an "increase in depression." The topic is complicated and further study is required, but the "displacement effect" of using computers is undoubtedly a potential risk.

As an example of how the problem can quickly become complicated, notice that one activity that might occupy a person's time online is participating in chatrooms or sending email to friends and family. Isn't this simply a modern form of social interaction? Possibly, but possibly not. Maybe we know our electronic acquaintances only superficially compared to our in-the-flesh friends. On the other hand, maybe the possibility of keeping in close e-contact with family or meeting others passively who have similar interests is more rewarding than our face-to-face acquaintances. Clearly, IT is neither black nor white, and it is probably not even a uniform shade of gray.

English as a Universal Language

Since the end of World War II, there have been growing indications that English may become the de facto universal language. Doubtless many reasons exist for this shift, including the huge influence of U.S. culture, and the dominance of science and technology in English-speaking countries since that war. English is not yet the universal language, of course, but it is the leading candidate at the moment. IT is giving its adoption a huge push.

Microsoft Windows is available in German and French editions, of course, but perhaps the driving force behind people's desire to read and understand English is the World Wide Web. Most Web pages are in English, and when they are multilingual, English is usually among the alternative forms. English is also widely used for e-commerce. The bias toward English motivates more postings in English, reinforcing English's status as the language of IT. Fluent English speakers have greater access to IT's benefits. Of course, computer translation can convert from English to another language, but so far the translations have not been very faithful, and they are available for only a few very widely spoken languages. There will likely be no translators for most of the world's languages.

Interestingly, it seems that adopting English as a universal language for purposes of IT interaction could have little effect on other natural languages. In non–English-speaking countries, English would be taught as a second language and the population would be bilingual. This is already the case in many countries. There is no real jeopardy to the mother tongue because it is used in most other aspects of daily life.

Enhanced Freedom of Speech and of Assembly

As noted previously, posting a Web page is a means of identifying ourselves. We can state who we are (or think we are) and what we believe in. The Web page can be viewed from anywhere and located by content via a Web search engine. Most important, it is not subject to any editorial oversight or significant restrictions. Such an unfettered, worldwide communication medium presents an unprecedented degree of freedom of speech, previously available only to those who owned broadcast channels or printing presses. It allows political expression, artistic expression within the limits of the medium, and any form of self-promotion (including shameless). As with freedoms generally, free speech on the World Wide Web can be abused, leading to hate propaganda or instructions on building bombs. The opportunity for *unmediated* expression to such a large audience, however, would seem to be a fundamentally new benefit of IT.

The corollary to free speech on the Internet is that it also promotes freer association. Like-minded people are soon attracted to one another by the content searching facilities of Web search engines. Once connected, they can communicate via email or form chatrooms and newsgroups. They are electronically close regardless of how far apart they are in physical space. Unlike ham radio, which relies on broadcast to connect a group, email can be private. Electronic assembly, though completely conventional in terms of being a basis for association, is unique in overcoming the problems of place and time for bringing people together.

IT's Future

The progress of information technology to date has been breathtaking, and the effects on our world are significant and largely beneficial. What will the future bring?

Though the technology has become spectacularly more powerful over the past four decades, there is good reason to expect continued improvement. Silicon microchips are the ubiquitous semiconductor technology of today's information technology. The Semiconductor Industry Association publishes a Roadmap describing anticipated advances in this type of electronics. Their predictions indicate continued progress for at least another decade. But on the flip side, consider that present-day computers are already grossly underutilized—even when the user is busy at work, the computer's processor is idle most of the time. Do we really need much faster computers? Probably not. Personal computers are already powerful enough for the standard applications like sending email and word processing. But progress can take many forms, and the ever-smaller size of powerful computer chips brings new opportunities. Most people expect that the chief impact of future technological improvements will come in the realm of "ubiquitous computing"—computers available everywhere, embedded into other systems and very specialized. Our reliance on computers is certain to increase.

> **Not So Fast.** Because computers eclipse human performance, it is essential for applications involving sound or motion to be slowed to match human perception. This means that when the computer is playing audio or video it is mostly idle, waiting to output the next sound or motion change. This is why the computer can word-process your term paper while playing an audio CD. It goes at your rate . . . not too fast.

Though hardware will continue to get better, it is in software—the applications that solve our problems—that the changes to our lives are sure to be the most dramatic. But it is hard to predict the future capabilities introduced through software. Such "tools" to process information, unfettered by the physical constraints of weight, friction, power requirements, and so on that limit mechanical systems, encourage almost unlimited invention. With human creativity as the primary ingredient, amazing new applications can be anticipated. Certainly many imaginative people will think of ways to transform information in completely unexpected ways. Their ingenuity will doubtless benefit us all.

Finally, we can expect that more and more of the information that people want to use will be available digitally. Today most information is created in electronic form, making it easy to access and process. But representing information digitally is a recent development. A large proportion of mankind's records—books, papers, manuscripts, music, art, sounds—exist in physical form only. These are being digitized steadily. Eventually most of the information that people want to access will be available online.

The task now is to become Fluent so as to enjoy the inevitable advancements.

FLUENCY WITH INFORMATION TECHNOLOGY

Information technology already has significant value to individuals, and the prospects for greater benefits are excellent. So how does one benefit from IT now and in the future? Become Fluent. What do we mean by *Fluent*? People Fluent with Information Technology (FIT) use computers, networks, and information resources effectively, and they know when and how to acquire new IT knowledge as their needs and/or the technology change.

Fluency requires the acquisition of three kinds of knowledge:

Contemporary Skills: Knowing how to use a suite of today's most popular computer applications (e.g., email)

Fundamental Concepts: Understanding the ideas underpinning IT (e.g., organization of a computer)

Intellectual Capabilities: Thinking at an abstract level about IT (e.g., ability to engage in sustained reasoning)

These three kinds of knowledge enable you to apply IT today (skills), to comprehend how effectively you are using IT and whether new technology can help (capabilities), and to acquire new IT knowledge as it evolves (concepts). Fluency lets you use IT now and in the future by establishing a basic understanding of contemporary systems and then giving you the foundations on which to learn more through a process of lifelong learning. This is an adaptive strategy that allows a person's understanding to grow and evolve as the technology changes.

This book is dedicated to teaching the skills, concepts, and capabilities needed for Fluency. Much of the skills information is taught in the lab in a hands-on way because that's the best process for learning computer applications, both the specifics of a given vendor's application and the general ideas applicable to all of the vendor's software for that task. Nevertheless, in some places (Chapters 3–5) the text covers major ideas behind certain computer applications. Whether these are concepts or skills is debatable, but the information is essential to the effective use of computers. The text contains many chapters dealing with fundamental concepts, including how the Internet works (Chapter 4), how computers work (Chapter 9), what algorithms are (Chapter 11), database basics (Chapter 14), and so forth. This book covers effectively every concept that "everyone should know" about computers. And that material turns out to be quite interesting. But the capabilities are the most fascinating material. These are the higher-level thinking abilities that are essential for IT but valuable in almost every other aspect of school and everyday life. We'll introduce the key ideas of troubleshooting and debugging so that when things go wrong, you can extract yourself from the mess. Such knowledge is fundamental to using computers, but it's also handy when your car won't start. The same goes for reasoning, problem solving, finding and assessing the quality of information, and so forth. The capabilities—you'll develop your technique here, and improve your facility with them throughout life—are perhaps the greatest long-term value of studying Fluency. Anyone can teach you a computer application; you need to invest some effort in learning how to think well.

This book has four parts:

Part I deals with getting started using computers, the Internet, and information resources. This terrific topic lets us browse the World Wide Web finding neat stuff and call doing it "homework"!

Part II explains the key concepts every computer user needs to know to be in control: How to instruct a computer to do your work, why some of the things computers do are so marvelous (and so bizarre!), and what can be done when . . . well, when things go wrong.

Part III introduces eCommerce and databases and how to harness their power for your everyday use. It also covers the social impact of computers, including netiquette—electronic etiquette—and privacy.

Part IV is all about how people and computers solve problems. Such information helps with everything from giving driving directions to making glitzy Web pages. It is also filled with ideas you have probably not thought about such as how Deep Blue beat Kasparaov at chess and whether a computer can create art.

Summary

We have set the context for our study of information technology. The concepts of *scale of change* and *factor of improvement* were introduced and illustrated using human performance in the mile run, mechanical performance in aircraft speed, and electronic/computational performance in the speed at which computers can do addition operations. Computers have advanced at a staggering rate. This improvement in technology—computers and networks—is bringing fundamental changes, including making information widely available, allowing people to interact in ways not previously possible and enhancing our freedoms. English is getting a boost as a universal language as a result. And there are also downsides—time spent with a computer in some instances reduces time that might be spent in regular interpersonal interactions. IT's effects are largely, but not completely, positive. We learned that more advancement can be anticipated. The key components of Fluency with Information Technology were outlined—skills, concepts, and capabilities. Presenting this information is the goal of this book, a task that has been divided into four parts. And though the skills will be taught largely in the lab with some coverage in the book, the text focuses mainly on the concepts and capabilities.

Exercises

1. What is information technology? What does it encompass?
2. What is *scale of change*?
3. What is *factor of improvement*?
4. For the period 1954–1999, what was the factor of improvement for the mile run?
5. If something improves by 100%, by what factor has it improved?
6. What are five fundamental changes that have emerged as a result of information technology?

7. Concerning the "Nowhere Is Remote" change, what property of information technology enabled the advancement?

8. Concerning the "Connecting with Others" change, what property of information technology enabled the advancement?

9. Can you think of other ways besides limiting direct personal contact that IT is having a negative effect on people or institutions?

10. What aspect of IT has encouraged the widespread use of English?

11. What does it mean to say the Web provides "unmediated" forms of expression?

12. Using the World Wide Web, find some rate that has changed greatly (more than 7%) between 1954 and 1999.

13. In what other ways does information technology enhance our freedoms?

14. Discuss the ways in which information technology is or could be personally relevant to you.

15. Are there other forms of human performance besides sports activities in which the "factor-of-2 rule" between the best of a champion and the best of the "normal" person applies?

CHAPTER 2

Terms of Endearment—Defining IT

Learning Objectives

- Understand two reasons why knowing the right term is essential.
- Recall familiar terms for computer components.
- Be introduced to some basic computer terms.
- Understand how buttons are created and "clicked."
- Appreciate that the world of the computer screen is completely synthetic.
- Comprehend a few "idea" terms of IT.
- Become familiar with the book's glossary.

Information technology has been created by people who are notorious for using acronyms, jargon, and everyday words in unusual ways. Acronyms like WYSIWYG (pronounced *WHIZ·zee·wig*), which is an abbreviation for "what you see is what you get," convey nothing to the uninitiated. Jargon like "click around" for navigating through an application or a series of Web pages tends to make sense only after you have actually done it. And an everyday term like *window,* originally used to convey the basic idea of a portal to the computer, may now no longer be an apt metaphor for the sophisticated computer concept. It is not surprising, therefore, that people coming across such terms for the first time are confused. But is such technospeak any more arcane to the uninitiated than, say, medical terms—who is bilirubin? Or musical terms—does a hemi-demi-semi-quaver vibrate? Technology, like medicine and music, does make sense, after all, with a little explanation and thought.

In this chapter, we start to tame the jargon beast. The first goal is to understand why learning the right terms is essential to any new endeavor, especially IT. Next we ask a series of simple questions such as "Where's the Start button?" as a means of achieving our second goal, a review of familiar terminology. But, for almost every familiar term, there is a new word and an associated idea that is essential to our study of IT. So, the third goal is to introduce about 25 new words for the physical or computational aspects of the computer. These are mostly terms you have already heard, so finding out exactly what they mean in context will help them quickly become part of your everyday vocabulary. Along the way we explain basic ideas like how buttons come to be shown on the screen and how they can be clicked. This discussion should demystify how the computer's virtual world works and informally introduce the basic ideas of process and algorithm that will be used throughout our subsequent study. Finally, the most ambitious goal is to introduce the "idea" terms of IT, words like *abstraction* and *generalization.* These are the deepest and most fundamental terms of the chapter, and devoting a few minutes to comprehending them will pay dividends throughout the remainder of our Fluency study. The chapter closes with guidelines on how to find out more about IT terms. At completion, IT should be much more intelligible, and less "*jargonic.*"

Just the Right Word

Why has information technology adopted so many strange terms? Because an enormous number of new ideas, concepts, devices, and so forth, have been invented for IT. These phenomena had to be named by their creators in order to describe them and explain them to others. Acronyms are common because as engineers and scientists develop ideas, they often abbreviate them with the letters of the concept's description. The abbreviation sticks, and if the concept is important, its use extends beyond the laboratory. For example, when engineers invented the "small computer system interface," they abbreviated it SCSI. When SCSI moved out of the lab, people began to pronounce it *skuzzy* rather than saying S-C-S-I. The result of naming-by-abbreviation is a multitude of terms that commentators invariably deride as "alphabet soup," but which turn out to be reasonably intelligible if you take a moment to find out what they stand for. For example, ROM is the acronym for "read-only memory." Even without knowing much about computers, you can guess that it is a special type of memory that cannot be written to, which is right.

> **Just Right.** Using exactly the right word at the right time is one hallmark of an educated person. Perhaps the best term to learn to use well is *le mot juste* [*mo·joost*], a French phrase that has become part of English and means the right word or precise phrasing.

There are two important reasons for using *le mot juste*. First, understanding the terminology is fundamental to learning any new subject. The new ideas and concepts of a field are named by unfamiliar terms or familiar words used in new ways. In learning what these new words mean, we learn the ideas and concepts that they stand for. Our brains seem to be organized so that when we give a thing or idea a name, we seem to remember it more easily. So, for example, the concept in ice hockey when the puck crosses the blue lines without a player touching it is called *icing*. It's a feature of hockey that we might not even notice amid all the passing and slap shots. By knowing this new definition for the familiar word *icing,* we are alerted to watch for the situation, increasing our understanding and enjoyment of the game. Precision in using the terms translates to precision in understanding the ideas because we need to know when and when not to use the new word. Eventually these words cease to be isolated elements of a vocabulary and become an integrated set of ideas in our mind. At that point, we understand the subject and use the right word without even thinking about it.

The second reason for knowing and using the right word is to communicate with others. They understand the terms, and if we use them properly, they understand us. Using universally understood terminology enables us to ask questions and get help from others—something everyone starting out in a field needs to do. In information technology, using the right word to get help is especially critical because we must often get help "remotely" by sending email, phoning, or using an online help facility. In all of these cases, we must be precise and articulate about our problem because no one will be by our side to help us describe it. If we cannot say accurately what's wrong, we won't be successful in getting help. Indeed, a goal of Fluency is to be able to get help from such resources. The ability to use *le mot juste* makes us self-reliant.

With the motivations of speeding our understanding of IT and becoming self-reliant, let's start out by learning a few basic terms. We could learn vocabulary by reading a computer dictionary, of course, but that's waaay too boring. Rather, we introduce the basic terminology by answering some of the nagging questions about IT that have unexpected answers.

WHERE'S THE START BUTTON?

Most computers remain "on" all of the time, which is why *screen savers* were invented. Screen savers—animations such as a kitten prancing around the screen or a changing geometric design—are programs that sleep when the computer is in use but wake up after a few minutes of idleness. They "save the screen" because computers, when idle, display a single, unchanging image. There is a risk that the single image could be "burned into the screen"; that is, it could permanently change the phosphorous surface of the screen creating a "ghost" of the image that interferes with viewing other images. The continuously changing image avoids the possibility of burn-in. You can activate a computer that is running a screen saver by moving or clicking the mouse, or by pressing any key.

If computers are usually on, why bother to learn where the Start button is? Because sometimes they are off, and as we will see later, we occasionally need to *cycle power*, that is, turn the computer off and then back on. Knowing where to look for the power button requires recognizing the different organizations of a computer.

Two Basic Organizations: Monolithic or Component

Some computers are sold as components with separate monitor, computer and hard drive, speakers, and other devices. Many desktop PCs are organized this way. The alternative like an iMac or a laptop is a monolithic package with all devices bundled together. The component approach gives consumers the greatest flexibility because they can mix and match component parts to fit their needs. At the other extreme, the all-in-one monolithic design provides greater simplicity because manufacturers decide for consumers which components will form a balanced, effective system. There are economies of scale when a single configuration of parts is packaged together and sold as a unit. Laptops are monolithic, of course, because it is inconvenient to carry around multiple parts. Expect to use both.

In the monolithic design, the power switch (⏻) is on the chassis, or for Macs, frequently on the keyboard. For component systems, the power switch is usually on a separate box near the display containing the CD and/or floppy disk drives. Most displays also have a power switch, but turning that off usually turns off only the monitor.

The Monitor

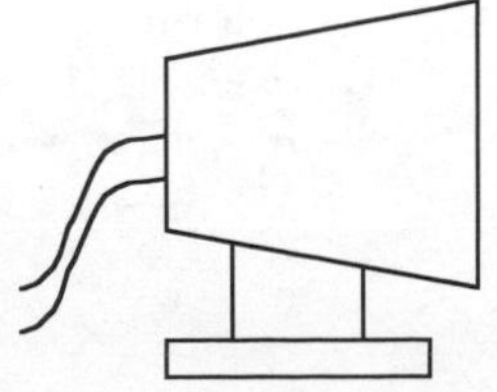

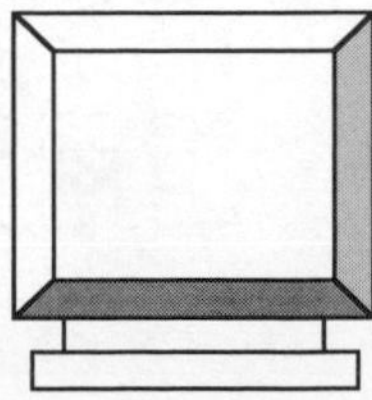

The *monitor* is a video screen that displays images like a TV. But there are many differences. Unlike passive TVs, computers are interactive, so the monitor becomes more like a blackboard where information generated by both the computer and the user is displayed to facilitate human-computer communication. Modern monitors are *bit-mapped*, meaning that they display information stored in (the bits of) the computer's memory. TVs generally display images live or from recorded tape, captured with a camera. The big, bulky monitors are *cathode ray tubes*, abbreviated CRT, whereas the slim, flat displays are *liquid crystal displays* (LCD).

To emphasize the contrast between TVs and computers, notice that television is restricted to filming "reality" with a camera, that is, it shows the images *recorded* through the camera's lens. But a computer *creates* the images it displays in its memory; they don't have to exist in physical reality. This is why we can create what we call *virtual reality*. The "special effects" seen on TV are created on a computer and combined with the video signal.

Cables

The components and the computer must be connected to receive or send signals, of course, and they must be connected to an electrical power source. For power-hungry devices like monitors, separate cables are usually used, which is why there is a separate power switch. For simple devices like the keyboard or mouse, the signal and power wires are combined into a single cable. To assist with connecting cables, the computer's sockets and the cable's plugs are often labeled with icons. So, we simply match icons.

Computer component plugs fit into their sockets in only one orientation. After determining the orientation, insert the plug into the socket gently at first to assure that the pins—the stiff wires making the connections—align and do not become bent. Once the plug is inserted, *seat* it by pushing it in firmly.

Power Rules. When connecting computer components, make the power connection last, and when disconnecting, remove the power connection first. Briefly, **P.I.L.P.O.F.—plug-in last, pull-out first.**

Notice that connectors like the "RGB" cable on a monitor are usually held in place by screws or a clasp, which should be tightened after the cable is seated.

RGB

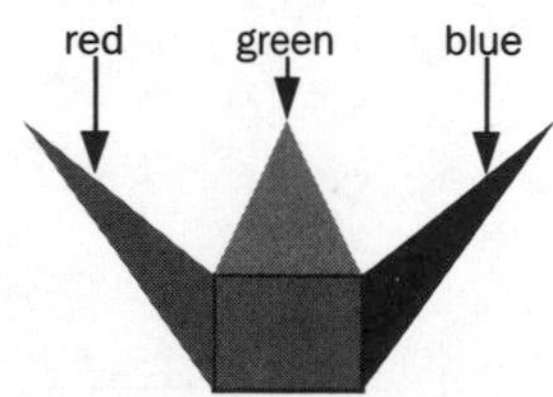

Combining different proportions of Red, Green, and Blue light produces the colors displayed on a computer monitor. The computer directs the monitor to display the right proportions of light via signals sent through the RGB cable. Any color can be created with some combination of intensities of these three elemental colors. In computer applications, selecting a color from a palette is specifying the proportions of these three colors of light.

Pixel

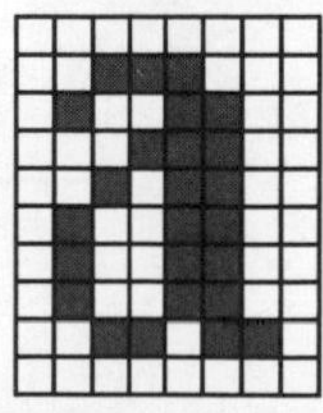

The monitor's screen is divided into a grid of small units called *picture elements*, or *pixels*. The dot on an *i* is a rough guide to the size of a pixel for a small (10-point) font size. The computer displays information on the screen by drawing each pixel the color required for the intended figure or image. The size of the grid in pixels—for example, 1024 × 768 is typical for a laptop—is important when choosing a monitor because the more pixels in each row and column, the higher the resolution of the image on the screen, that is, the smoother and crisper it can be.

The conclusion from this discussion of monitors, colors, and pixels is that the computer must first create in its memory everything displayed on the screen, pixel by pixel. For computer-animated movies like *Toy Story,* creating images of dancing toys is extremely difficult. But the "reality" that we see on the screen when we use a computer is considerably easier to generate, as we now demonstrate.

Pressing a Virtual Button

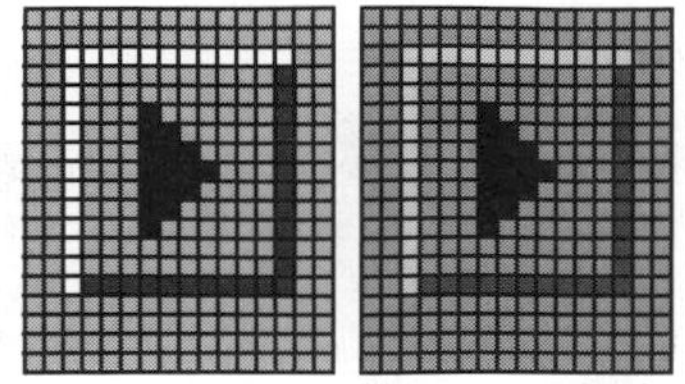

It is a simple matter to color the screen's pixels to produce a figure that looks like a believable button. On a medium gray background, color the top and left sides of a rectangle white and the bottom and right sides black. This makes the interior of the rectangle appear to project from the surface because the white seems to be highlights and the dark seems to be shadows from a light source at the upper left. (If the figure doesn't look much like a button, view it from a distance.) There is nothing special about the medium gray/white/black combination except that it gives the lighted/shadowed effect. Other colors work, too. And, using colors with less contrast, it is possible to give the button a different "feel," for example, less metallic, as shown on the right.

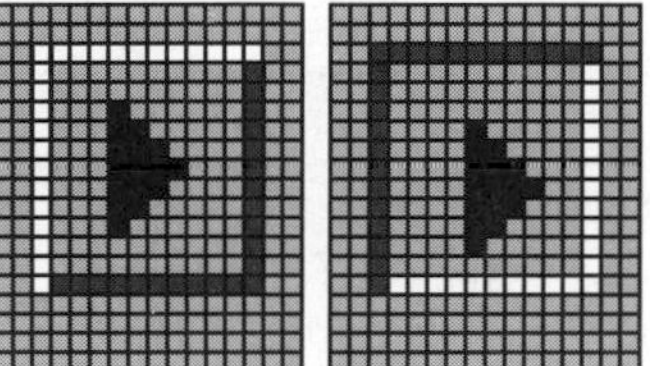

To show the button pressed in can be achieved by reversing the black and white colors and translating the icon one position down and to the right. To *translate* a figure means to move it, unchanged, to a new position. Because our brains assume that the light source's position remains unchanged, the reversal of the colors changes the highlights and shadows to make the interior of the rectangle appear to be inward from the surface. The translation of the icon creates the appearance of motion by the difference in position of the two images. Our eyes notice, completing the illusion that the button is depressed. Observe, however, that the translation of the icon down and to the right is not really an accurate motion for a button that moves straight into the plane of the screen. But accuracy is less important than is the cue to our brains that there is motion.

It must be emphasized that there is no button anywhere inside the computer. The bits of the computer's memory have been set so that when they are displayed on the screen, the pixels appear to be a picture of a button. The computer can change the bits when necessary so that the next time they are displayed, the button looks as if it has been pushed in. Adding a "click" sound makes the illusion even more real. But there is still no button.

If there is only a picture of a button, how can we "click" it with the mouse? It's a good question, which can be answered without becoming too technical.

Of course, the place to begin is with the mouse pointer. It is a white arrow point with a black border and, like the button, must be created by the computer. When the mouse is moved, the computer finds out in which direction it is moving and redraws the pointer translated a short distance in that direction. By repeatedly redrawing the pointer in new positions that are redisplayed rapidly, the computer produces the illusion that the pointer moves smoothly across the screen. It's the same idea as cartoon flipbooks or motion pictures: A series of still pictures, progressively different, displayed rapidly creates motion. The frequency of display is called the *refresh rate*, and like motion picture frames, is typically 30 times per second. At that rate, the human eye perceives the sequence of still frames as smooth motion.

As the mouse pointer moves across the screen, the computer keeps track of which pixel is at the point of the arrow. In Figure 2.1 the computer records the position by the row and column coordinates, since the pixel grid resembles graph paper. So (141, 1003) in Figure 2.1(a) means that the point pixel is in the 141st pixel row from the top

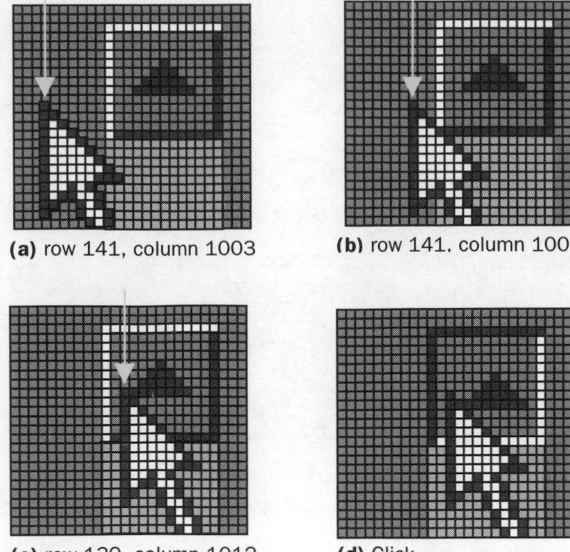

Figure 2.1. Mouse pointer moving toward, and then clicking, a button; the coordinates of the point of the pointer are given by their row, column positions.

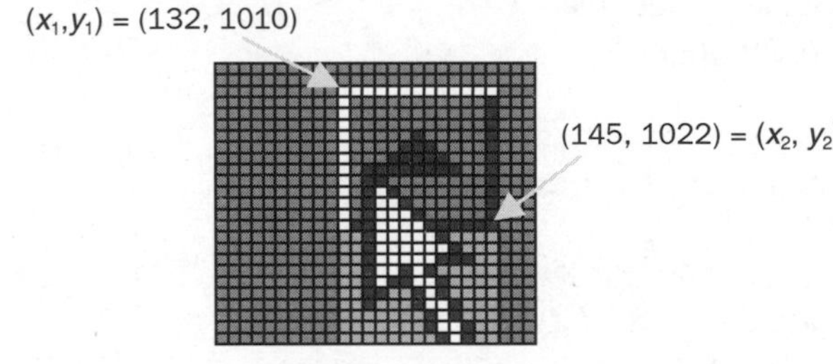

Figure 2.2. A button's location is completely determined by the positions of its upper-left and lower-right corners.

of the screen and at the 1003rd pixel column from the left side of the screen. With each new position, the coordinates are updated. When the mouse is clicked, Figure 2.1(d), the computer determines which button the mouse pointer is over, and then redraws the button to look pushed in.

How does the computer know which button, if any, the mouse pointer is over? It keeps a list of every button drawn on the screen, recording the coordinates of the button's upper left and lower right corners. So, in Figure 2.1, the button would have its upper left corner at pixel (132, 1010) and its lower right corner at pixel (145, 1022) (see Figure 2.2). The two corners, call them (x_1, y_1) and (x_2, y_2), completely determine the position of the rectangle that defines the button: the top row of white pixels is in row x_1, the left side column of white pixels is in column y_1, the bottom row of black pixels is in row x_2, and the right side column of black pixels is in column y_2.

Now, if the mouse pointer's point has a row coordinate between x_1 and x_2, the pointer is somewhere between the top and bottom of the button, though it may be to the left or right of the button. But if the pointer's point also has a column coordinate between y_1 and y_2, the pointer is between the left and right sides of the button; that is, it is somewhere on the button. So, for each button with coordinates (x_1, y_1) and (x_2, y_2), the computer tests whether

$$x_1 < \text{row coordinate of mouse pointer point} < x_2$$

and

$$y_1 < \text{column coordinate of mouse pointer point} < y_2$$

are *both* true. If so, the mouse pointer's point is over that button, and the button is redrawn in the "clicked configuration." Also the software is told that the user just clicked on the button, so it can perform the action corresponding to the button.

Creating the button and generating the mouse pointer may seem like a lot of work, but the metaphor of pressing a button to cause an action is so suggestive to us that going to the trouble facilitates our work.

Where Is the Computer?

This may seem like an odd question to ask, but doing so is instructive. When speaking informally, most of us refer to the monitor sitting on a desk as "the computer." Technically speaking, we're usually wrong. For monolithic organization the computer, that is, the part that actually does the computing, *is* inside the same unit as thc monitor. So for laptops or iMacs we're right. But for component systems, the computer is not in the monitor unit, but rather in a separate box that is often on the floor below the desk or somewhere else nearby. Referring to the monitor as the computer is not so much a mistake as an acknowledgment that the monitor is our interface to the computer, wherever it may physically be. Indeed, it doesn't much matter where the microprocessor chip is except when things go wrong.

In the component approach, the computer and many of its associated peripheral components (for example, hard disk, floppy disk drive, and CD drive) are packaged together in a box that is called the *processor box*, though it often has a fancy marketing name, for example, minitower, that has no technical meaning. For the monolithic approach, of course, the associated disks and drives are in the same package as the monitor. It's as if the monitor were attached to the processor box, so everything in this section applies.

Motherboard

Inside the processor box is the *motherboard*, a printed circuit board containing most of the circuitry of a personal computer system. The name comes from the fact that smaller printed circuit boards, occasionally called *daughter boards*, but more often called *cards*, are plugged into the motherboard to provide additional functionality. A motherboard is impressive to look at with all of its fine wire patterns, colorful resistors, economy of space, and so forth. (Ask your computer dealer to show you one rather than inspecting the one in your computer and risking harm to it.) Of the many parts on this PC board,[1] only the microprocessor chip and the memory are of interest to us at the moment.

Microprocessor

The *microprocessor*, located on the motherboard, is the part of a personal computer system that computes. The microprocessor is involved in every activity of the system, everything from making the mouse pointer appear to move around the screen to locating information stored on the hard disk. In essence, the microprocessor is the "smart" component of the system, causing engineers to describe the other parts of a computer as "dumb." It is surprisingly easy for a computer to be "smart," as will become clear as our study proceeds. Eventually, we will even ask, "Can a computer think?"

The "micro" part of microprocessor is archaic and by now inaccurate. The term *microprocessor* was adopted around 1980 when the prevailing small computers were called minicomputers, and it was first possible to fit all of the circuitry for a computer on a single silicon chip. These were technically computer processors, but they were small and primitive compared to the reigning mainframes and minicomputers of the day, hence the appellation *micro*processor. But the performance improvements came so rapidly that in a few years microprocessors were more powerful than the largest computers of 1980. Today they are fast, highly optimized, loaded with features, and extremely sophisticated. In fact, microprocessors spend most of their time doing nothing, just waiting for us. Because there is nothing "micro" about today's microprocessors, we will simply use the proper term *processor* for the remainder of this book.

Memory

The *memory* of a computer is where a program and data are located while the program is running. For example, when you are using a word processor, the word processing program and the document being edited are stored in the memory. (When they're not in memory, programs and data are stored on the hard disk; see below.) Computer memory is also called *RAM*, short for *Random Access Memory*. The basic unit of memory is a *byte*, which will be described in Chapter 8. Today's personal

[1] This "PC" is an abbreviation for "printed circuit," and it predates "PC" used for "personal computer" by decades.

computers have millions of bytes of RAM memory, or *megabytes*, from the Latin prefix *mega-* for million.

There are two basic ways to locate and retrieve, that is, access, information: *sequential* and *random*. Information stored sequentially is arranged in a line, requiring that to access a specific item, all items stored before it must be skipped. Cassette tapes, VCR tapes, and so on are examples of sequential access. Random access means that any item can be retrieved directly. Dictionary entries, library books, and numbers in a phonebook are examples of random access. Random access is faster than sequential access, as anyone wanting to listen to the last track on a cassette tape well knows.

Hard Disk

Though the *hard disk* is not technically part of a computer—it is a high-capacity, persistent storage peripheral device, as explained in Chapter 9— it is so fundamental to multipurpose computer systems that it's helpful to think of it as a basic part. The hard disk is also referred to as the *hard drive* and was once simply known as a *disk* before floppy disks became popular and forced everyone to be more explicit. The hard disk stores programs and data while they are not in immediate use by a computer. Disks are made from an iron compound that can be magnetized. Because the magnetism persists even when the power is off, the encoded information is stable; that is, it is still there when the power comes back on. Thus a disk is said to be permanent or persistent storage. A hard disk is usually located in the same box as the processor because without access to permanent storage, the processor is crippled.

The hard disk looks like a rusty phonograph record with an arm that can sweep across it. The "popping" or "clicking" sound we sometimes hear emanating from a computer is the arm moving rapidly back and forth as it accesses information on various tracks of the disk.

A successful computer user must understand an important difference between the RAM memory and the hard disk memory. Today's RAM is made from integrated circuit (IC) technology, informally called *microchips*. One property of IC memory is that it is *volatile*, meaning that the information is lost when the power is turned off. Hard disks are nonvolatile. They keep their magnetized information without power, like cassettes and VCR tapes. So all of the information that must be permanently saved must be on the hard disk. The practical point is to *save* your work periodically, which in effect moves it from the RAM to the disk. This minimizes the amount of work that will be lost if the computer crashes, that is, fails, for some reason. A crash requires the computer to be restarted, which may require that the power be cycled. When the power goes off, the information in the volatile RAM is lost, but the information saved on the nonvolatile disk will be reloaded when the computer restarts.

How Soft Is Software?

The term *hardware* predated computers by centuries, referring to metal components like hinges used in construction. There was no need for the word *software* until computers were invented.

Software

Software is a collective term for programs. Computers are *hardware*, of course, and software gets its name by contrast with hardware. But what does it mean for software to be "soft"? Things that a computer does that are implemented with wires and transistors on the processor chip are hardware. Multiplication is an example. Things that a computer does by following instructions are software. Figuring income taxes is an example. The difference between "hard" and "soft" is like the difference between an inherent ability like coughing and a learned ability like reading. Inherent abilities are "built in" biologically, and they're impossible to change. Learned abilities can be easily changed and extended. We can change from reading English to reading French, *n'est-ce pas*? A computer cannot change how it multiplies, but one minute a computer can be following the instructions to figure U.S. income tax, and the next moment it can be following instructions to compute Canadian income tax.

Computers don't *learn* to perform soft operations, of course, as we learn to read. Rather they are simply given the instructions and told to follow them.

There is an intermediate situation, called *firmware*, in which instructions are incorporated into hardware.

The Hard Reality. The inflexibility of hardware as compared with software was dramatically illustrated in 1994 when a bug was discovered in the divide circuits of Intel's Pentium processor. Though the wrong answers were rare and tiny, the error had to be fixed. If divide had been implemented in software, as had been the usual approach in computing's early years, Intel could have sent everyone a simple patch for $1 or $2. But hardware cannot be changed, so the Pentium chips had to be recalled at the cost of millions of dollars.

Algorithms and Programs

An *algorithm* is a precise and systematic method for producing a specified result. *Process* is a synonym for "systematic method." Familiar algorithms include the elementary arithmetic operations of addition, subtraction, multiplication, and division; the process for sending a greeting card to a parent; and the method for finding a number in the telephone book. The method derived in the last section for determining when a mouse pointer is over a button is an algorithm. Because an algorithm's instructions are written down for some other agent to follow, usually a computer, precision is essential so that the agent is successful and can handle any eventuality.

Though we are sometimes taught algorithms, like the arithmetic algorithms, we figure out many algorithms on our own, like finding phone numbers. In Chapter 10, we will introduce *algorithmic thinking*, the act of thinking up algorithms. The act of writing out the steps of an algorithm is *programming*, and *programs* are simply algorithms written in a specific programming language for a specific set of conditions.

In common terminology, we request that a computer perform some operation or service for us by asking it to *run* a program. This is literally what we are asking when we click on an application like Netscape. We are saying, "Run the program from the Netscape company to assist in browsing the Internet." "Run" *is* a correct term that has been used since the invention of computers. But the preferred term is *execute* because it emphasizes an important property of computing.

Execute

A computer *executes* a program when it performs instructions. The idea the word *execute* conveys is that of an agent following a set of orders precisely and literally. Indeed, computer pioneers used the word *orders* for what we now call instructions. The orders direct the computer to act in a specific way and in no other. Like most situations where orders are given, the faithful agent is *not* supposed to think. There is no possibility for optional or independent behavior. "Following instructions literally" is what computers do when they run programs, and it is that aspect that makes *execute* a preferred term.

In addition to *run* and *execute*, *interpret* is also a correct term for what a computer is doing when it is following a program's instructions. However, the important nuance that "interpret" suggests will be explained in Chapter 9.

Finally, the term *booting* means to start a computer and *rebooting* means to restart it. Because booting most often comes in response to a catastrophic error or crash, you might guess that the term is motivated by frustration—we want to kick the computer like a football. But booting comes from bootstrap. Computers were originally started by an operator who manually entered a few instructions into the computer's empty memory using console pushbuttons. They directed the computer to read in a few more instructions from punch cards, say, giving the nearly empty memory a primitive operating system. This operating system could then read in the instructions of the real operating system from magnetic tape similar to that used for a VCR. Finally, the computer was able to start doing useful work. This incremental process was called *bootstrapping* by analogy to "pulling yourself up by your bootstraps" because the computer essentially started itself. Today this process is permanently resident in the boot ROM.

THE WORDS FOR IDEAS

Though understanding the physical components of IT—monitors, motherboards, and megabytes—seems critical to successfully applying IT, we will not be so concerned with them. Rather, we will make greatest use of *concept* words such as those in this section.

One of the most important "idea" words used in this book is the verb *to abstract*. It has several meanings. In British mysteries, *to abstract* means *to remove*, as in purloin: "The thief abstracted the pearl necklace while the jeweler looked at the diamond ring." The meanings of *to abstract* encountered in information technology share the idea of removal, but the thing being removed is not physical. The intangible thing being removed is an idea or a process, and it is extracted from some form of information.

Abstract

To *abstract* is to remove the essential concept, idea, or process from a specific situation. The removed concept is usually expressed in another more succinct and usually more general form, called an *abstraction*.

We are familiar with abstraction in this sense. Parables and fables, which teach life lessons in the form of stories, require us to abstract the essential point of the story. When we are told about a fox who repeatedly fails to reach a bunch of grapes and so dismisses them as being sour, we abstract an idea from the story: People make excuses when they try but fail to attain something. The concept is one of frustration derived from failure changing our view of the desirability of the goal.

Notice two key points illustrated by abstracting from the story. First, many but not all of the specifics of the story are irrelevant to the concept. In the process of abstracting, we must make a judgment as to which details of the story are relevant and which are irrelevant. The "grapes" and the "fox" are unimportant, but "failure" is crucial to the point. Making such distinctions is essential to understanding the point of a story, and it is critical to abstraction generally. Second, the idea—we call it the *abstraction*—applies to a range of situations. That's the point of repeating the parable, of course, to convey a concept that applies to many situations.

A closely related process is to recognize the common, essential idea in two or more specific situations. Recognizing the similarity of many situations is what causes us to formulate parables, rules of thumb, aphorisms, and maxims.

Generalize

To generalize is to formulate an idea, concept, or process that abstracts two or more specific situations. The formulation is called a *generalization.*

For example, when one friend says, "There were no good seats left anyhow," after waiting in line for four hours without getting concert tickets, and another friend says, "The test was totally unfair," after partying rather than studying the night before the exam, we generalize the cases to a common underlying idea: Sour grapes. The situations are not the same, nor are they very parallel. But they both embody criticism based on frustration derived from failure.

Operationally Attuned

Another term related to extracting concepts and processes refers to being aware of a gadget's operation. To be *operationally attuned* is to apply our knowledge of how a device or system works as an aid to simplifying its use.

In our daily lives, we use hundreds of devices, systems, and processes. For some, like the ignition on the car, we quickly learn which way to turn the key because it turns in only one direction. We give no thought to how it works. Our use becomes habitual. Other gadgets, however, have more leeway, and for them it helps to be attuned to their operation. A trivial example is a deadbolt lock, which moves a metal bar from the door to the door frame to lock the door. Thinking how the lock works can remind us whether the door is locked or not. Referring to Figure 2.3, we notice the orientation of the knob used to set the lock. By visualizing the internal works of the lock, we can imagine that the top of the knob is attached to the bar. When the knob is pointing left, the bar must be positioned to the left, that is, unlocked. When the knob is positioned to the right, it is locked.[2] Recognizing these facts means that at a distance we can see if the door is locked or unlocked. It's not a major simplification to our lives, but it might save us from getting up off the sofa and trying the door to see if it's locked.

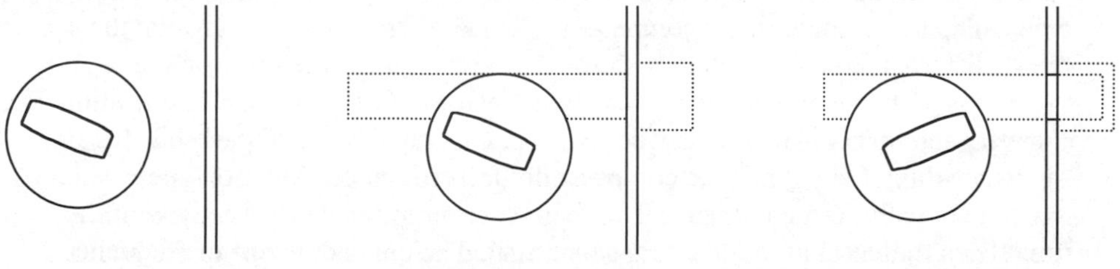

(a) (b) (c)

Figure 2.3. Deadbolt lock. (a) The external view. (b) Internal components, unlocked. (c) Internal components, locked. Thinking about how the deadbolt works allows us to see at a glance whether the door is locked or not.

The term *operationally attuned* has been introduced here to emphasize that thinking about how information technology works greatly simplifies its use. We don't expect to be experts on all of IT—no one can be. But by asking ourselves, "How does this

[2] Not all deadbolt locks are this simple, nor are they all installed right side up. Your lock's operation may vary.

work?" and using the insights derived by thinking about the answer, we are likely to be more successful at applying IT. Our Fluency study will focus on learning enough to answer the "How does this work?" questions. Chapter 3 fully illustrates the idea of being operationally attuned in IT.

Finally, *mnemonic* is one rather unusual term that sees regular duty in IT, but is used in other fields as well. The silent *m* implies that it's a word with an unusual past.

Mnemonic

A *mnemonic* is an aid to remembering. The reminder can take many forms, often using pronounceable words or phrases. North Americans remember the five Great Lakes with HOMES—Huron, Ontario, Michigan, Erie, and Superior. We've mentioned PILPOF—plug-in last, pull-out first—for when to connect and disconnect power cables.

There are many details about IT that we need to know only occasionally, like when to connect power. They're not worth memorizing, but they're an inconvenience to look up. So, if we can think of some mnemonic that helps us recall the details when they are needed, we simplify our use of the technology.

Word Search

We have introduced some basic IT terminology, both for physical things like the motherboard and for logical things like abstraction. The acquisition of new terms is not over, however. All of the chapters of this book introduce new terms when new ideas are introduced. Learning and remembering the terms help the learning and remembering of the ideas. As an aid, all of the new terms have been collected together in the glossary at the end of the book. Consult the glossary when a term slips your mind. In addition to the glossary in this book, there are several good online glossaries, and it's probably wise to locate one with your Web browser and bookmark it, that is, save its URL. (Whoops, have we defined *URL* yet? No, but we will in Chapter 4. Meanwhile, check the glossary to find out what it's an acronym for.)

The only remaining task is to define the first acronym mentioned in the chapter, *WYSIWYG*. Recall that it stands for "What you see is what you get." To understand the term, recall that the computer creates for us the virtual world we see on our screen. The representation the computer uses to keep track of the things on the screen is very different from the picture it shows us. For example, the text you are reading was stored in the computer as one very long line of letters, numbers, punctuation, and other characters, but it was displayed to me as a nicely formatted page like the one you are reading. Only when the computer processes its representation does the text look like a nicely formatted page. The original text editors worked only with the computer's representation, that is, the long string. Users had to edit the sequence of characters directly, and they had to *imagine* what it would look like printed out. Eventually text editing systems were programmed to show the user the page as it would appear when printed, enabling the user to change the text in terms of the way it would be seen. This property was described as "what you see is what you get" or WYSIWYG. Text editors with the WYSIWYG property became known as *word processors*.

Summary

In this chapter we have focused on learning IT terms in context. We started by recognizing that knowing and using *le mot juste* is essential in IT for two reasons. Our brains seem to organize knowledge around terminology, so as we learn the words, we learn the ideas. Also, knowing the right terms allows us to get help when things inevitably go wrong. Then we organized our tour through the basic terminology of computers using basic questions like "Where is the Start button," and "How soft is software." These questions enabled us to recall basic terms that were probably already familiar—monitor, screen saver, RAM, software, and so on. Mixed in with these discussions were new words that perhaps you didn't know—sequential access, volatile, motherboard, and so on. You will use some of these terms, like *software,* daily. Others, like *volatile,* you may never use. But the concept that it names—information is lost when power is removed—is critical to your everyday use of IT, making the term a secure site to anchor practical advice: Save your work regularly. In addition to the familiar words and the new words for tangible things, we added a brief list of "idea" words, the most important of which is *to abstract.* These words and the ideas they embody will be used throughout our study of IT. Finally, we mentioned that terms will be continually introduced, motivating a brief advertisement for the glossary at the end of the book.

Midway through the chapter, we explained how the buttons of a computer application are constructed and clicked. We learned the practical information of how to color pixels so they appear to be buttons, how the mouse pointer moves around on the screen, how the computer knows when the pointer is on the button, and how the button is changed to appear to be depressed. The most important point was that this metaphorically meaningful world doesn't exist but was created inside the computer with software to simplify our use of IT. It is a theme that will recur throughout our Fluency study.

EXERCISES

1. Explain why the information technology field has developed so much jargon.
2. Define the French term *le mot juste.*
3. What are the two reasons why we need to learn the vocabulary of IT?
4. What is the purpose of a screen saver?
5. Distinguish between a computer's monitor and a TV.
6. ⏻ is the icon for what?
7. What is the rule describing when to connect a computer's power cable to the electricity?
8. When cabling computer components, what are the two clues used to indicate which cable connects to which socket?
9. Using the monitor of your computer or a computer in the lab, determine the size of the pixel grid required to represent an *a* in Times Roman font at 10 points and at 24 points.
10. Describe the difference of the pixels displayed for a button in its normal position and a button that has been "pressed."
11. Using an application from your computer or a computer in the lab that does *not* create buttons with the *exact* "light line/dark line" technique discussed in this chapter, describe how you think the colors are controlled to give the appearance of a button.
12. Using simple drawing tools, perhaps within a word processor, make a simple button from triangles, squares, and lines.

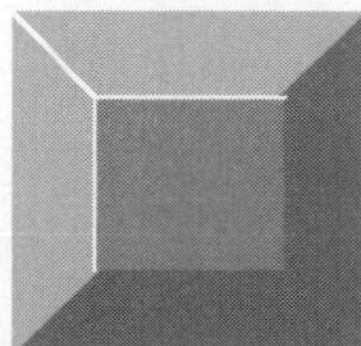

13. There is one subtlety about the mouse pointer motion. The computer must save the screen image where the pointer will be drawn before drawing the white and

black pixels of the pointer. This is so that when the pointer moves to a new position, the background at the old position can be restored to its original image. This enables the pointer to appear to slide *over* objects on the screen. Describe how it would be possible to make a mouse pointer appear to move *under* text.

14. Describe in words the algorithm for determining whether a "clicked" mouse is over a button.

15. Suppose that on a computer screen a mouse is moved horizontally a thousand pixels in a third of a second. How many pixels apart will the successive mouse pointer images be?

16. Explain the difference between hardware and software. How is firmware related to hardware and software?

CHAPTER 3

What the Digerati Know

Learning Objectives

- Learn to teach yourself new applications.
- Acquire the skills of experienced users.
    - Appreciate that software exploits consistent interfaces.
    - Learn to expect feedback from applications.
    - Comprehend that nothing breaks when mistakes are made.
    - Learn to explore and try new applications.
- Understand that process follows function.
- Learn the basics of text searching, including the Placeholder Technique.
- Learn to think abstractly about technology.

Perhaps the most uncomfortable aspect of being an inexperienced computer user is the nagging suspicion that everyone but you innately knows how to use technology. They appear to know automatically what to do in any situation. Perhaps, you conjecture, they have all come from the same alien planet that computers have.

Of course, the reality is that experienced users don't have any innate understanding of how to use computers. Through experience, however, they have acquired a certain kind of knowledge that allows them to figure out what to do in a reasonably directed way. Most do not "know" this information explicitly—it is not usually taught. They just acquire it through experience. But, in this chapter, some secrets of the Digerati[1] will be revealed, enabling anyone to "join the club."

The major goal for this chapter is to demonstrate how to think about technology abstractly. This will be accomplished by questioning how we learn technical skills and by considering what the creators of technology expect from us as users. By asking these questions, we will better understand how to make a computer do what we want it to do. The five subsidiary goals are to understand (1) that computer systems exploit consistent interfaces, standard metaphors, and common operations; (2) that computer systems always give feedback while they are working; (3) that using a computer system erroneously will not break it; (4) that the best way to acquire basic proficiency with new computer software is to try it out, expecting to make mistakes; and (5) that asking questions of other computer users is not evidence of being a dummy, but proof of an inquiring mind. These ideas enable us to learn new software quickly. A key abstract idea about software is that it is constrained by fundamental laws of nature. This deep concept has implications for our everyday software usage. Finally, we demonstrate how the laws influence basic text searching, enabling us to learn it abstractly without considering any specific vendor's software. Such knowledge transcends any specific system and makes us versatile users. We, too, can become one of the Digerati.

Using Technology

Human beings know innately how to chew, cough, stand, blink, smile, and so forth. They do not innately know how to ride a bicycle, drive an automobile, operate a food processor, or start a lawn mower. For any tool more complicated than a stick, a person requires some amount of explanation as to how it works and possibly some training in its use. Parents teach their children how to ride bicycles, driver's training classes explain to teenagers how to operate an automobile safely, and most products come with an owner's manual explaining how the product works and its range of application.

Some tools such as portable CD players are so intuitive that most people living in a technological society find their operation "obvious." There's no need to look at the owner's manual. For example, given a CD and the player and having seen one in use or having had experience with related technologies like cassette tapes or vinyl records, it is simple to infer how to operate the gadget. We can guess what the controls do based on what operations the device should be capable of performing. (Without this knowledge, the icons on the buttons would probably make little sense.) And it is even likely that most people can recover from faulty guesses about the operation. For example, if we should load the CD upside-down, trying the other orientation is a likely response.

The claim that portable CD players are so intuitive that people living in a technological society can without assistance figure them out does not contradict the fact that humans have no innate understanding of technology. A person from a primitive society who has never seen a device for playing recorded sound would probably not figure it out without instruction, much less find it intuitive. Rather, the intuitive operation of a CD player emphasizes two facts about technology:

- Our experience using (related) devices found in our technological society guides us in what to expect.

[1] *Digerati* is a recently coined word for those knowledgeable in IT, analogous to *literati.*

- Designers try to create products that are so intuitive that with experience and reasoning we can infer their operation.

These two facts are key to success with IT.

A Perfect Interface

On certain Apple Macintosh computers, when a user loads an audio CD into the computer's CD drive, the graphic user interface (GUI) shown in Figure 3.1 appears on the screen. A GUI, pronounced *gooey,* is the medium by which users interact with programs running on a personal computer. The reason that this GUI appears on the screen is that the Macintosh's operating system, noting that a CD has just been inserted into the drive and recognizing that it is an audio CD, assumes the user wants to listen to it. So, it starts the software that plays audio CDs, presents the GUI to the user to find out what he or she wants to play, and waits for a response.

Figure 3.1. Graphic user interface for one version of an Apple Macintosh audio CD player.

As first time users of this software, we look at the GUI wondering what the software does and how to use it. There is an online user's manual, but we will not need it. The graphic user interface tells the whole story. The GUI presents to us a completely familiar picture of a "physical" CD player, complete with digital readout in green LCD numerals, "metallic" buttons with the standard icons, and other recognizable characteristics. No physical CD player looks exactly like this one—for example, the CD slot has the wrong proportions—but it is so similar to real CD players that anyone who has seen one recognizes this image immediately. Recognizing the similarity, we guess that pressing the button with the Play icon will cause the computer to play the CD. But because this is a GUI, it is not possible to "press" a button literally. The action analogous to "pressing" for a computer is "clicking" with the mouse. We know this from experience. Clicking on the button with the icon for Play starts the CD playing. That success is to us confirming data that the analogy of the GUI to a physical CD player is correct, and from then on we have a basic idea of how to operate the software. We needed no lessons; no one had to help us.

The use of the physical analogy to guide the user in understanding how to operate the CD player software may seem obvious, but it illustrates a basic idea of present-day consumer software. Like anyone who invents a new tool, software designers are confronted with the problem of teaching users how to operate their inventions. They can and do write manuals explaining all of the software's slick features, but products are much more successful if users can figure them out without resorting to studying the manual. So, software designers, like physical CD player designers, try to pick easy-to-understand interfaces to their software. Rather than choosing a GUI design that requires explanation, the designer(s) predicted that an analogy with the familiar physical device would be intuitive. To make the analogy unambiguous, they invested

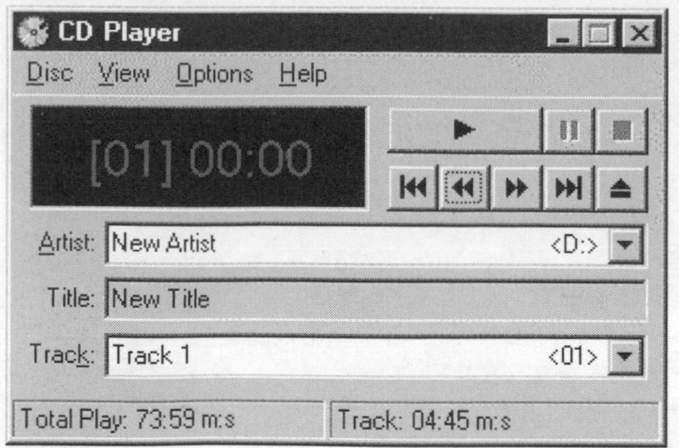

Figure 3.2. Audio CD player GUI for the Windows operating system.

considerable effort to enhance the similarity by using LCD numerals,[2] "metallic" buttons, the standard button icons, a "slot" for the CD (which plays no role but to support the metaphor), slider volume control, and so forth. There can be little doubt that that decision was correct. Those of us who have used a CD player before know how this software works, at least its basics. (The Microsoft Windows operating system audio CD player for the same software generation also leverages some of these features of the physical analogy, as shown in Figure 3.2.)

Summarizing, it is in a software designer's interest to make the GUI simple and intuitive enough for us to figure out on our own. Though they do not always succeed as brilliantly as the designer(s) of the Macintosh audio CD GUI, we should expect as users that the software has been well crafted and that we can "brain out" how it works. That expectation is the basis on which we confront every piece of new software.

Buttons and Windows

It is clear from a physical analogy how to play a CD with the audio CD player GUIs, but there is more to this software than just the seven standard buttons: Play, Stop, Eject, Last Track, Next Track, Forward, Backward. How are we supposed to know about those other features? Some of them, like Shuffle, can also be inferred from our knowledge of physical CD players and the fact that the button is realistic. But, we figure out the other aspects of this software based on standard metaphors used in virtually all consumer software GUIs. Most have suggestive graphic forms, and we see them in the audio CD player. Once we become familiar with these metaphors, computer interaction quickly becomes intuitive.

The following basic metaphors are by now universal—they are no longer unique to Apple, which introduced them in consumer software, or Microsoft, which gave them the widest distribution. They generally have a consistent meaning though sometimes slightly different graphic forms.

Command Buttons

As shown in Figures 3.1 and 3.2, command buttons take various graphic forms. At a minimum, they are rendered as a 3D rectangle, usually highlighted and with an icon or text centered on the button, as explained in Chapter 2. This text label indicates the command to be performed. To invoke the command—that is, to tell the software to perform the operation shown on the label—we are expected to "press" the button by clicking on it with the mouse. (A click is sufficient; it is not necessary or advisable to press down on the mouse button for a sustained interval.) We then get feedback indicating that the button has clicked, usually in the form of a color, shadow, or highlight change; some text/icon change; or other indicators, including an audible "click." (Some people think such indicators are obsessive attempts at realism, but some form of feedback is essential to effective computer use, as explained below.)

[2] Amazingly, the LCD numerals even have the "shadow" characteristic of "unilluminated" segments that would make up a physical LCD digit display, though they may not be visible in the Figure 3.1 screen shot.

Slider Control

The volume control in Figure 3.1 (on the right) illustrates a slider control. Slider controls set a value from a "continuous" range, such as volume. To move the slider, place the mouse pointer on the slider, hold down the mouse (left) button, and move in the intended direction of change. The most common instances of sliders are the scroll bars in a window display, usually shown at the right and bottom of the window. When the window is not large enough to display all of the information in the horizontal or vertical direction, a scroll bar is shown for each orientation in which information has been clipped. The "continuous" range is the length of the information in that dimension. So, for a document in a word processor, the length is the number of lines in the document, and the width is the length of the (maximum) line. Often the size of the slider of the scroll bar is scaled to indicate what proportion of that dimension is displayed. Thus, if the slider occupies half of the length of the "slot," about half of the information is displayed; if the slider is 1/10 of the length of the "slot," about 1/10 of the information is shown. There are usually directional triangles (▼▲) at one or both ends of the scroll bar; clicking on them moves the slider one "unit" in the chosen direction.

Triangle Pointers

To reduce complexity and clutter in a GUI, it is common to hide information that can be displayed on demand. The presence of hidden information is indicated by a triangle "pointing" to it. Clicking on the triangle reveals the information. Such triangles (▼▲)are visible in Figure 3.1 (below the Normal button) and Figure 3.2 (at the ends of the Artist and Track text boxes). Clicking on the triangle pointer in Figure 3.1, for example, results in Figure 3.3. Notice that now the direction of the pointer is reversed. Clicking on that triangle again hides the information.

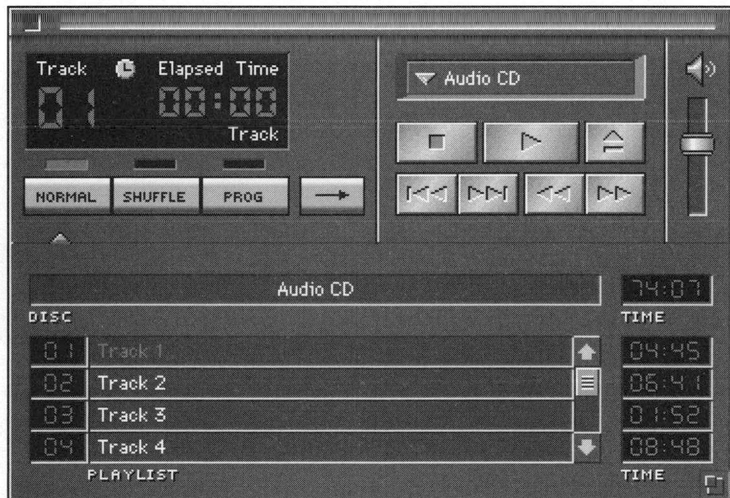

Figure 3.3. Audio CD GUI displaying the hidden title and track

Close

Any open window can be closed, and most GUIs provide a way to do it with a click. On the Macintosh (Figure 3.1), clicking on the empty box in the upper-left corner closes the window, whereas on Windows systems (Figure 3.2), clicking on the button in the upper-right corner with an X on it closes the window. A Windows application terminates when its main (or only) window is closed, but if just subwindows are closed, the application generally continues running.

This list is only a sampling of metaphors to illustrate the concept. There are many others, and beginning users should familiarize themselves with them quickly. The point of listing some here is to emphasize that computer applications have many operations in common, and software designers purposely present a consistent interface in order to leverage the user's knowledge and experience. Accordingly, experienced users look for metaphors, and when they recognize the recurring use of a new metaphor, they add it to their repertoire.

Mac or PC? Is the Macintosh better than the PC or vice versa? The question usually ignites a pointless religious war. Listening to the battle, many wrongly conclude that the other system must be very different and difficult to use. In fact, the two systems are much more alike than they are different, sharing the concepts of this chapter and much, much more. Any competent user of one can quickly and easily pick up the idiosyncrasies of the other. And *every* Fluent user should.

Menus

The primary way in which the functionality of sophisticated software applications is presented to users is through menu choices. Menus list the operations that the software is capable of performing. A menu groups operations by similar function. Menus are either listed across the top of a window, in which case they are *pull-down* or *drop-down* menus, or they appear wherever the mouse is pointing when a mouse button is clicked, in which case they are *pop-up* menus. Both menu types work the same way.

Pulling down or popping up a menu reveals a list of operations. Sliding the mouse down the list causes the items to be highlighted as it passes over them, and clicking or releasing the mouse button selects a menu item. If the software has sufficient information to perform the selected operation, it does so immediately and the window closes. If not, you are queried further. A window opens to request the additional information. Answering these questions may necessitate further queries. Eventually the command will be fully specified and can be performed. Throughout the dialog it is always possible to abort the operation. While viewing the menu, simply move your cursor away from the menu. While answering questions in a window, Cancel is always one of the command button choices, enabling you to change your mind without penalty. That is, clicking on Cancel is generally equivalent to never having looked at the menu in the first place, no matter how much information has been entered.

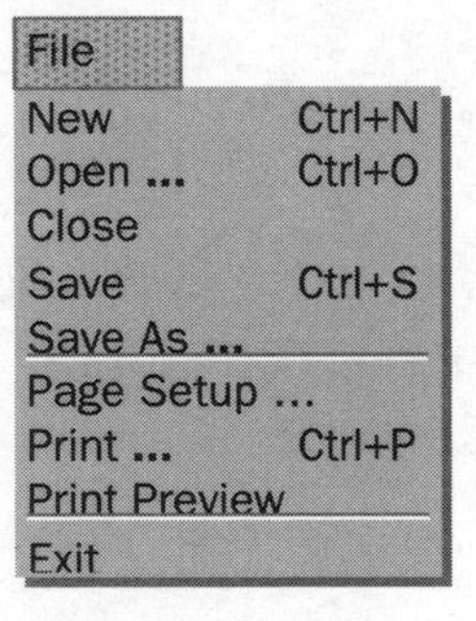

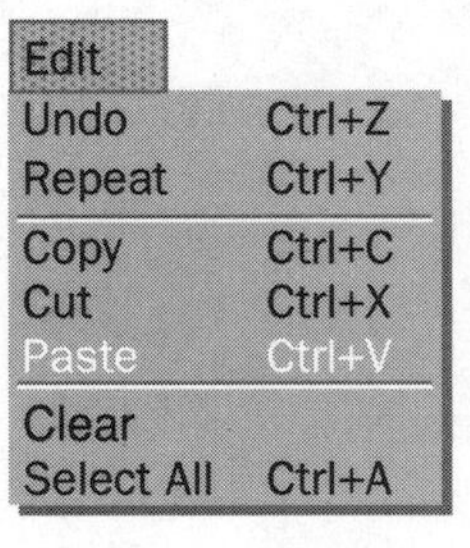

Figure 3.4. Generic File and Edit menus.

Menus in contemporary consumer software convey more information that just the item list. They also indicate the availability of the operations, further input, and shortcuts for each item. Refer to Figure 3.4. as you read these descriptions.

Availability

Unlike restaurant menus that are printed and reused, occasionally requiring the server to indicate that certain items are not available, GUI menus are created each time they are opened. Accordingly, they specify exactly which operations are available. (An operation may not apply in every context. For example, Paste is not available if nothing has been Cut or Copyed.) Operations that are available are generally shown in solid color, whereas those that are unavailable are shown in a lighter color or "gray," as shown for the Paste operation in Figure 3.4. Unavailable items are not highlighted as the cursor passes over them, and, of course, they cannot be selected.

Further Input

Certain operations require further specification or additional input. Menu items requiring further specification indicate this need with a triangle pointer (▶) at the right end of the entry. Selecting such an item pops up a window with the additional choices. Making a selection causes the operation to be performed unless it requires still more selections. Menu items indicate their need for additional input with an ellipsis (. . .) following their name. Selecting the item opens a dialog window for specifying the necessary input. For example, in Figure 3.4, Open has an ellipsis because it requires the name of the file to open.

Shortcuts

Sometimes it is more convenient to type a keyboard character than to point and click with the mouse. Accordingly, some menu items have keyboard characters bound to them, indicated by showing the character combination that selects the item. For example, in Microsoft Windows, the menu choice Copy is bound to Ctrl C and Paste is bound to Ctrl V. (Like the shift key, the control key [Ctrl] is held down while typing the associated character. Though the character is shown as a capital, pressing the shift key is not correct.) A character combination is required so that the operating system can distinguish between the menu choice and a plain character. The Macintosh uses Command C and Command V for these operations, that is, the same letters.[3] Notice the consistency between different operating systems. Shortcuts are not very important for a casual user, but they are extremely handy for those using a single application intensively. The shortcut key combination can be set or changed in most systems.

Menu entries can be further embellished. For example, Windows includes an icon as a visual cue for some operations.

Standard Functionality

There is a standard set of operations that almost all personal computer applications should be expected to perform simply because they process information. That is, regardless of whether the information is text or spreadsheets or circuit diagrams or digitized photographs, the fact that it is information stored in a computer implies that certain capabilities should be available in the software. For example, the information should be printable. It should be possible to save the information to a file, open a file containing the saved information, create a new instance, and so on. Accordingly, the user should expect to find all of these facilities in almost every software application.

To assist users, the standard operations are grouped—usually with other operations specific to the application—into two menus labeled: File and Edit. Generally the operations under the File menu apply to whole instances of the information being processed by an application. For example, in word processing the instance is the entire document being processed, so File menu items treat a whole document. Expect the following items under the File menu:

New Create a "blank" instance of the information.

Open Locate a file in permanent storage containing an instance of the information and read it in.

Close Terminate processing of the current instance, but remain available to process other instances, for example, a document newly created with New or retrieved with Open.

Save Write the current instance to permanent storage, for example, the hard disk or floppy disk, using the previously specified name and location.

[3] The Command key is labeled with the so called "clover" symbol, ⌘.

Save As Write the current instance to permanent storage with a new name or location.

Page Setup Specify how the printing should appear on paper; changes to the setup are rare.

Print Print a copy of the current instance of the information.

Print Preview Display the information instance as it will appear on the printout.

Exit or Quit Terminate the entire application.

Notice the ellipses in the File menu of Figure 3.4, indicating that further information is required in some cases; shortcut information is also shown. Lines further subdivide the operations.

The Edit operations generally allow you to make changes within an instance. They often involve selection and cursor placement. The operations are performed in a standard sequence: Select-Cut/Copy-Indicate-Paste-Revise. Selection identifies the information to be moved or replicated. Selection is usually accomplished by moving the cursor to a particular position in the instance and while holding down either the mouse button or keyboard keys, moving the cursor to the new position. All information "between" the two positions is selected. Highlighting of some form, usually color reversal, demarcates the selection. If the information is to be moved, it must be removed from its present position with the Cut command; otherwise, Copy saves the selected information. Next, the new location for the information is indicated in preparation for pasting it into position, though in many applications the Indicate step is skipped and the pasted information is placed in a standard position. The Paste operation is next, causing the information to be copied from temporary memory into the indicated position. Because a copy is made, it can be pasted again and again. Often, revisions or repositioning are required to complete the editing operation.

Expect the following facilities under the Edit menu:

Undo Cancel the most recent editing change, returning the instance to its previous form.

Repeat Apply the most recent editing change again.

Copy Retain a copy of the selected information in temporary storage in preparation for pasting.

Cut Remove the selected information and save it in temporary storage in preparation for pasting it.

Paste Insert the information saved in the temporary storage by Cut or Copy into the instance; it is placed either at the indicated (cursor) position or at a standard position depending on the application.

Clear Delete the selected information.

Select All Make the selection be the entire instance.

In addition to the basic editing commands, Undo and Repeat are usually included. These commands are extremely valuable. Undo is not always available because not all operations are reversible.

Often additional shortcuts are available with the software, and users who work with an application intensively are advised to learn about them to make the software even more convenient. For example, a "double click"—two clicks with the (left) mouse button in rapid succession—is often a synonym for Open when that operation is applicable.

> **Be Selective.** New users are often confused when a desired operation of a menu is not available, i.e., it is shown in gray. Frequently this is because the operation requires that something be selected and currently nothing is. So, for example, the computer cannot perform Copy until you have specified what you want copied.

To complete this section, notice that New under the File menu creates a "blank" instance. What is "blank information"? To understand this fundamental idea, observe that all information is grouped into *types*, based on its characteristic properties. So, photographs—digital images—are a type of information, and among the several properties of every image is its length and width in pixels. Monthly calendars are a type of information having properties such as the number of days, year, and day of the week on which the first falls. Text documents are another type, and the length in characters is one property. Any given piece of information—image, month, or document—is an *instance* of its type. Your term paper is an instance of the document type of information; June 2002 is an instance of calendar type information. To store or process information of a given type, the computer sets up a structure to record all of the properties and store its content. A "new" or "blank" instance is simply the structure without any properties or content filled in. As an example, imagine a blank monthly calendar—seven columns of squares headed with the days of the week, a place to enter the month name, and so on. That's a "New" month, ready to receive its content.

FEEDBACK

A computer is the user's assistant, ready to do whatever it is commanded to do. It is natural that when any assistant performs an operation, he, she, or it should report back to the person who made the request regarding the status of its execution. This is especially true when the assistant is a computer (and therefore not very clever) because the person needs to know that the task was done and when to give the next command. Accordingly, a user interface will always provide feedback to the user on "what's happenin'."

Feedback takes a variety of forms, depending on what operation a user has commanded. If the operation can be performed instantaneously, that is, so fast that a human would not have to wait for its completion, the user interface will simply indicate that the operation is complete. When there are editing changes to the information instance, the evidence of completion is that the revision is visible. When this is not evident—say, when one clicks on a button—then there is some other indication provided, for example, highlighting, shading, graying, or some other color change, or underlining.

The most common form of feedback with which all users are familiar is the indication that the computer is continuing to perform a time-consuming operation. As the operation is being carried out, the cursor is replaced with an icon suggestive of elapsing time. On Windows systems, the icon is an hourglass, and on Macintosh systems, it is a wristwatch with a hand advancing. Applications can also provide custom feedback. Claris software uses a circle divided into quarters, two white and two black that "revolves" because the coloring is continually reversed. The file transfer application Fetch converts the cursor into a running dog. In cases where the completion time can be predicted reasonably accurately, applications show a meter as a bar that is "filled" as the operation progresses. Often these displays carry a time estimate for when 100% will be reached. Finally, when an operation is processing a series of inputs, the "completion count" is incremented or decremented as inputs are processed, and often a final dialog box is displayed stating that the overall operation is finished.

Following Protocol. Our normal interactive use of computers alternates between our commanding the computer to do something and its doing it. If it can't finish immediately, it gives feedback showing the operation is in progress. If it's done, the effects of the command will be visible. Be attuned to this protocol. Notice the effect the command had. If nothing seems to be happening, the computer is waiting for you to give a command.

"Clicking Around"

When the Digerati encounter new software, they expect a consistent interface. They expect that basic metaphors are in use, that standard operations are available, and that feedback is provided. They automatically look for these essential components of the interface and begin exploring. The purpose of the exploration is to learn what the software can do.

The act of exploring a user interface will be called *clicking around.* It involves noting the basic facilities presented by the GUI and checking each menu to see what operations are available. So, for example, on seeing a slider bar, the experienced user's response is to slide it to see what happens. On the Mac audio CD GUI shown in Figure 3.1, sliding the slider up and down causes—in accordance with the feedback principle—the speaker icon shown above it to have more-and-larger or fewer-and-smaller white arcs to its right. The user guesses these arcs indicate more or less sound being emitted by the speaker. If the CD is playing, the user will also notice that the volume increases or decreases. Either way, the user rightly guesses that this is volume control.

Fast Start. When using software for the first time, take a minute—it rarely takes more time—to study the graphics presented by the GUI. Open each window to see what operations are available. Determine the purpose of icons and controls. Many applications have a "Balloon help" or "What's this?" help facility giving a short explanation of icons and controls when the cursor is placed on them.

"Clicking around" is the act of figuring out what operations are available with a software application without reading the manual or being instructed by someone else. Manuals describing software are notoriously tedious to read and difficult to use. But "clicking around" is not suggested as a means of making them obsolete. Manuals—they're mostly online and called Help—are necessary and useful. Rather, "clicking around" exploits the facts that (a) we come to the new software with technological experience, and (b) software designers try to build on that knowledge by using metaphors that are available with other tools, that is, a consistent interface. When the new software works as the last software did, we already "know" how to use it. The manual is usually needed only to understand advanced features or subtleties of operation. Ironically, then, the manual is most useful for sophisticated users, not beginners.

Returning to the audio CD GUI of Figure 3.1, when we clicked on the down triangle, we revealed the track list shown in Figure 3.3. As new users of this software, we may not find it immediately obvious what the list is for, especially if the physical CD players we are familiar with do not have a play list. But, by "clicking around," we notice either that "Track 1" can be selected like text or that the cursor when moved across the text changes into the "I-beam" text editing cursor. Both indicate the possibility of adding text. Or, perhaps, we just guess that listing off the tracks wouldn't have required a large text box reading "Track 1" and so on, and so there must be some other purpose for it. No matter how "clicking around" cues us, we discover that we can edit the entries. We infer from the editing capability that we can customize the title and songs on each track. And doing so results in Figure 3.5.

Figure 3.5. Customized Audio CD GUI.

"Clicking around" is exploration and as such is not guaranteed to lead the user to all features of the software. It may be necessary to experiment and test repeatedly, or give up and try again later. But the technique will usually yield results. And if it doesn't, the software product designer has undoubtedly failed to some extent.

"Blazing Away"

After familiarizing ourselves with a software application by "clicking around," the next step is to try it out. This will be called *blazing away.* The term is intended to connote the idea of a user trying out features assertively, that is, exploring features even without a clear idea of what they will do. "Blazing away" can be difficult for beginning users because they fear that something will break if they make a mistake. A fundamental rule of information processing is: **Nothing will break!** If you make a mistake, the software is not going to screech and grind to a halt and then plop onto the floor with a clunk. When a mistake is made, the software may "crash" or "become wedged" or "deadlock" or enter some other unsavory configuration, but nothing will actually break. Most of the time, nothing happens. The software catches the error without actually performing the erroneous operation and displays a diagnostic message. By paying attention to the diagnostics, you quickly learn what's legal and what isn't. Therefore, "blazing away" can be an effective way to learn about the system even if you make mistakes.

Of course, asserting that nothing will break is not the same as asserting that it's impossible to get into a horrendous mess by "blazing away." Getting into an incomprehensible mess is often very easy. Beginners and experts alike do it all the time. The difference between the two groups is that the experts know the corollary to the fundamental rule of information technology: **When stuck, start over.** So the best response to a mess is to start over. That may mean exiting the software. It may mean rebooting the computer. It may simply mean "undoing" a series of edits and repeating them. The simple point is that the mess has no value. It does not have to be straightened out because it didn't cost anything to create in the first place, except for the time expended. Because that time will be chalked up to "experience" or "user training," there is no harm in throwing the mess out. Thus an experienced user who is "blazing away" on a new software system will probably exit the software and restart the application repeatedly. Each time, when asked whether the instance should be saved, he or she will reply "No."

Getting Out More. Starting over is so characteristic of computer users—it is called *getting out and getting back in*—that it's become the subject of some geek humor: A mechanical engineer, an electrical engineer, and a computer engineer are camped at Mt. Rainier. In the morning, they pack up to leave, and get into their car, but it doesn't start. The ME says, "The starter motor is broken, but I can fix it," and he gets out of the car. The EE says, "No way. It's the battery, but I know what to do," and she gets out of the car. The CE says while getting out of the car, "Now, let's get back in."

Usually, we are working with new software to achieve a particular goal, so it pays to focus on getting that task done. This means that we should "blaze away" on those operations that will contribute to completing the task. It is not necessary to become an expert, only to achieve the goal. Indeed, it is common for Fluent users to know only the rudiments of the software systems they use infrequently. And, because they are not regular users, they invariably forget how the systems work and have to "click around" and "blaze away" all over again.

It is obvious that if you are "blazing away" and will probably throw away your efforts when you get into trouble, it is best not to spend too much time creating complex inputs. Thus experienced users who are "blazing away" invest the minimal amount of effort required to explore the system. For example, if the software asks for text input and provides space for several paragraphs or pages, experienced users "blazing away" will enter, "Test text." and continue exploring. Once they understand the system, they can focus on using the software productively.

THE SHIFT PARADIGM

"Clicking around" and "blazing away" are unquestionably the first steps when learning new software because you are very likely to be successful without using any resources beyond your own observation and reasoning skills. And, if you do need to know about some very specific aspect of the software, you can always consult the manual or online help. However, these two extremes do not necessarily cover all of the possibilities. Complicated software systems usually have some features in between. Such features are generally nonobvious, advanced, or specialized to the particular software application. They are GUI features that most of us would not think to look for, and they provide capabilities that many of us do not even recognize we need.

An example of such a nonobvious feature is the use of the shift key in selection operations. Suppose we want to perform the task of selecting the red and green circles of the stoplight in Figure 3.6a so that we can change their color, but not the yellow circle. Clicking on the red circle selects it (3.6b), as shown by the small boxes bounding the circle. Clicking on the green circle selects it and deselects the red circle (3.6c). Dragging the cursor across the red to the green selects all the circles (3.6d). But, how to select just red and green without the yellow? The problem is that when we select something (e.g., the green circle), anything that is already selected (e.g., the

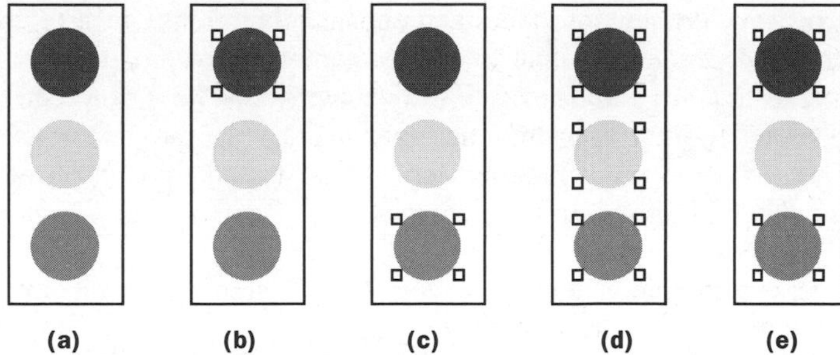

Figure 3.6. Examples of selection.

red circle) becomes deselected automatically. We need some way to bypass that automatic protocol.

The solution is to select the first item (e.g., the red circle) and then hold down the shift key while selecting the second item (e.g., the green circle). The use of shift during a selection has come to mean "continue selecting everything that is already selected" rather than deselecting. So, because the red circle is already selected when the green is clicked-with-shift, the two become selected, completing the task.

The click-with-shift or shift-select operation, meaning "continue to select the item(s) already selected," is a common feature in commercial software, although the exact interpretation of multiply selected items differs with different applications.[4] Without knowing about shift-select, however, it is unlikely that most of us would discover it by "clicking around" or "blazing away." We would not think to try it. We might not even realize that we need the feature in the first place. So, how do we learn about this kind of feature?

The options include taking a course on the specific software or actually reading the user's manual. Perhaps the best alternative, though, is to watch other users when they are using the software. As you watch someone using an application that you are also familiar with, it should be possible to follow what he or she is doing, though it might seem very fast. If you observe an operation that you cannot explain, ask what the person did. Rather than thinking you're a dummy, most people are eager to show off their know-how. Many an obscure feature, trick, or shortcut is learned while looking over the shoulder of an experienced user, so it pays to pay attention.

Toggling shift-select. Generally shift-select results in the selection of one or more additional items because the click is applied to an unselected item. But, what happens when shift-select is applied to an item that is already selected? It deselects that item only while leaving all other items selected. This property of changing to the opposite state—selecting if not selected, deselecting if selected—is called *toggling*. It is a convenient feature that arises in many situations.

An Application of Fundamental Principles

A theme of this chapter is that computer systems are very similar because the designers of software want users to figure out on their own how a system works based on prior experience. To assist this self-instruction process, designers employ consistent interfaces and suggestive metaphors. Designers could be extremely

[4] Notice that for text, shift-select usually results in the selection of all of the text between the cursor's previous position and its new position; it is not usually possible to select disconnected sequences of text.

creative thinking up wild new interfaces and unusual operations. Such GUIs might be quite interesting and very cool, rather like video games with a practical purpose, but it might take years to learn and be effective with such tools. Few of us can devote so much time to being productive. Rather, designers exploit the fact that consistency and familiarity promote rapid comprehension. In this way, the power of the computer is available quickly with little investment in learning.

But a much deeper principle is at work here as well. Designers are not simply limited by good sense to develop software that behaves in a consistent way. They are also constrained by laws of nature. Logic imposes limits on what information can be recorded or what operations can be computed. The laws governing information and computation are complex, beyond our introductory textbook, but they are nevertheless as fundamental as those that dictate the structure of the atom from the fundamental forces.

Even without understanding any of the fundamental laws governing IT, we can draw an important conclusion from the knowledge that they exist: The task—*not* the specific software implementation—dictates the behavior of a solution. We should expect similarity in software for similar tasks, not only because easy-to-learn metaphors are used, but also because they perform the same basic functions. We describe this property as *process follows function*, which is analogous to the design maxim *form follows function.*

So, for example, word processors provide a similar set of capabilities and perform their operations in a similar way regardless of what software company created them. The differences (and there are always differences, often substantial differences) influence the look, feel, and convenience of software, but they are rarely essential to the core task. Word Perfect, Word, Apple Works, Simple Text, BBText, and a dozen other systems all provide a core set of operations on a linear stream of text characters. That basic capability implies that users must be able to move a cursor around the text, to select a range of text characters, and to create, copy, insert, and delete characters. They must be able to create an "empty" file of text—systems use the term *new*—as well as save it, name it, display it, and print it. All of those features are fundamental to text processing—they were not invented by the software companies.

Similarly, commonalities exist among browser programs, among spreadsheet programs, among drawing programs, and so on. When we learn to use an application from one software vendor, we acquire both the core operations for that task and the specific features and idiosyncracies peculiar to that vendor's product. When we use software for the same task from a different vendor, we should look for and expect to recognize immediately the core operations. They may have a different look and feel in the second vendor's software, but the basic functionality must be there.

The existence of common core operations across programs for the same task is liberating in at least three ways.

- When new versions of software are released, our expectation should be that we will learn them very quickly because not only must they still have the core functions, but they'll probably also have most of the same vendor features and idiosyncrasies.
- When we are provided with another vendor's software for an application we know well, we should expect to use it immediately at least in a rudimentary way because the core capabilities should all be present and we can rely on those basic operations.
- When we are frustrated by a vendor's software, perhaps because it's buggy or suffers feature-bloat (too many useless features), we should stop complaining

and try another vendor's system. Learning the new system will be quick, and someone who shared our frustration may have done a better job. (It would seem that when users "vote" by buying better software, rather than accepting what they are given, overall software quality should improve.)

In summary, because the function dictates how a process must work, different software implementations must share basic core characteristics. Computer users should not feel tied to a particular software system that they learned years ago, but rather should experiment with new systems because they already know the basic functional behavior.

SEARCHING PRINCIPLES

The concept that process follows function has another advantage besides liberating us from a particular vendor's application program. It enables us to learn abstractly or generically how to use software without reference to any specific software system. Of course, we must focus only on the fundamental processing behavior rather than on the "bells and whistles" of the GUI, but learning in this way has the advantage that our knowledge applies to any implementation. We illustrate this form of knowledge by studying text searching.

Many applications include the ability to search text. Often called *find*, it's found in word processors, browsers (to look through the text of the current page), email readers, operating systems, and so on. *Find* is typically available under the Edit menu because locating text is often the first step in modifying it. In cases where modification doesn't make sense—say, when looking through a file structure in an operating system—*find* may be listed under the File menu or as a "top level" application. The shortcut for *find*—Command F for Macs and Ctrl F for Windows—is standard with most applications

The things to be searched for are called *tokens*. Most often the tokens are simply the letters, numbers, and special symbols like @ and & from the keyboard, which will be collectively known as *characters*. However, sometimes we search composite items, such as dates, that we want to treat in their entirety. In such cases, the date would be the token, not the letters and digits from which it's composed. For the purposes of searching, tokens form a sequence, called the *text*, and the tokens to be found are called the *search string*. An obvious property of the search string is that it can be composed of any tokens that could occur in the text. That is, if the text can contain peculiar, unprintable characters like tab, the search string must be allowed to specify such characters.

To illustrate, suppose the search string is "`content`" and the text of interest is a sentence from Martin Luther King's *I Have a Dream* speech:

```
I have a dream that my four little children will one day
live in a nation where they will not be judged by the color
of their skin, but by the content of their character.
```

Searching begins at the beginning or at the current "place," which is at the current cursor position if there is a cursor. Though computers use many ingenious ways to search text, the easiest one to understand is to think of "sliding" the search string along the text, comparing at each position to see if there is a token match. Of course, to do the match simply requires looking at corresponding token pairs to see if they are the same.

```
I have a dream . . .
content
```

(Notice that spaces are characters, too.) If there is a match, then the process stops because the search string has been found. But, if there is no match, slide the search string one position along and repeat.

If the search string is not found when the end of the text is reached, the search stops and is unsuccessful. Search facilities typically give the option to continue searching from the beginning of the text if the search did not start there. If so, the search terminates where it began if the search string is not found.

Character searching is easy, but to be completely successful, we must be operationally attuned. One complication is that the characters stored in a computer are case sensitive, meaning that the uppercase letters, e.g., *R,* and lowercase letters, *r,* are different. Accordingly, a match occurs only when the letters *and* the case are identical. A case-sensitive search for "`unalienable rights`" fails on Jefferson's most famous sentence from the *Declaration of Independence*:

```
We hold these truths to be self-evident, that all men are
created equal, that they are endowed by their Creator with
certain unalienable Rights, that among these are Life, Liberty
and the pursuit of Happiness.
```

To find "`unalienable rights`" in a text that uses the original capitalization requires that we ignore the case. Search facilities can be case sensitive if case is important to other aspects of the application. So, word processors are typically case sensitive, whereas operating systems may not be. If the search is case sensitive, the user will have the option to ignore case.

Characters are stored in the computer as one continuous sequence. The characters are of two types: The keyboard characters that we type, and possibly formatting information added by the software application. Because every system uses a different method to denote the formatting information and because it is usually irrelevant to the search anyhow, we will show the formatting information here using tags. *Tags* are abbreviations in paired angle brackets, e.g., `<Ital>`, that describe additional information about the characters, in this case, that they should be printed in italics. Tags generally come in pairs so that they can enclose text like parentheses. The second of the pair is like the first, except with a slash(/) or backslash(\) in it.[5] For example, to specify that the word "Enter" should be printed in italics, a software application might represent it as `<Ital>Enter<\Ital>`. The application won't show this formatting information to the user, but it's there.

For example, the balcony scene from Shakespeare's *Romeo and Juliet* appears in print as

[5] Tags arise repeatedly in our study, so backslash (\) will be adopted here for the tags of our generic application to distinguish them from later uses in HTML, the OED digitization, and XML.

SCENE II. *Capulet's orchard.*

Enter Romeo.

Romeo. He jests at scars that never felt a wound.

[Juliet appears above at a window.

But, soft ! what light through yonder window breaks?
It is the east, and Juliet is the sun.

but it might be stored in the computer as

```
SCENE·II.·♦<Ital>Capulet's·orchard.<\Ital>↵↵<Center><Ital>Enter<
\Ital>Romeo.<\Center>↵↵<Ital>Romeo.<\Ital>♦He·jests·at·scars·tha
t·never·felt·a·wound.↵<Right>[<Ital>Juliet·appears·above·at·a·wi
ndow.<\Ital><\Right>↵But,··soft·!·what·light·through·yonder·wind
ow·breaks?·↵It·is·the·east,·and·Juliet·is·the·sun.↵
```

The word processor's tags surround the italic text (`<Ital>`, `<\Ital>`), and the text to be centered (`<Center>`, `<\Center>`) or right justified (`<Right>`, `<\Right>`). The user typed the remaining characters, and they are the ones of interest now. These remaining characters include the visible text as well as nonprinting formatting characters: spaces (·), tabs (♦), and new lines (↵). Because these characters control formatting and have no printable form, there is no standard for how they are displayed; for example, new-line is the paragraph symbol (¶) in some systems. Users can ask that all the characters they type be displayed

```
SCENE·II.  ·♦    Capulet's·orchard.↵
↵
                           Enter·Romeo.↵
↵
Romeo.♦   He·jests·at·scars·that·never·felt·a·wound.↵
                                          [Juliet·appears·above·at·a·window.
↵
But,··soft·!·what·light·through·yonder·window·breaks?↵
It·is·the·east,·and·Juliet·is·the·sun.↵
```

and because the effects of the formatting are shown, it is easy to see where the nonprinted formatting characters are. During a search, the software's formatting tags are generally ignored, but all of the characters typed by the user are considered. Some systems do allow tags to be searched by providing a means to specify that the searched text be formatted in a particular way, for example, italic.

Complications arise when we think of search strings as having a meaning more complex than tokens. For example, we often look for words, though the tokens are characters. The problem is that the software searches for token sequences, not the more complex objects that we may have in mind. For example, searches for the search string "`you`" in President John Kennedy's inaugural address turn up five hits:

```
And so my follow Americans: Ask not what
your country will do for you—ask what you
can do for  your country.

My fellow citizens of the world: Ask not
what America will do for you, but what
together we can do for the freedom of man.
```

Of the five hits, only three are the actual word being sought; the other two hits *contain* the search string. To avoid finding "`your`", we can search for "`·you·`" because words in text processing systems are generally surrounded by spaces.

However, that search discovers *no* hits in this situation. There are no instances of "·you·" in the quote. The five occurrences of "you" are terminated by "r", hyphen, new-line, "r", and comma, respectively. The "you" at the end of the second line probably should have had a space between it and new-line, but the typist omitted it and the omission's not visible. Because looking for each occurrence of the word "you" and avoiding "your" would require checking for all of the possible starting and terminating punctuation characters as well as blank, it is probably better to give up on finding the exact word matches, and simply ignore the cases where the search string is embedded in another word. If the search facility is part of the system where "words are primitive," e.g., a word processor, the ability to search for words will be available. Such cases are equivalent to changing the tokens from characters to words.

A related problem for characters-as-tokens searches concerns multiword search strings. The words of a multiword string are separated by spaces, but if the number of spaces in the search string differs from the number in the text being searched, no match will be found. For example, the search string "That's·one·small·step·for·a·man" will not be found in the quote

```
That's·one·small·step·for·a··man,·one·giant·leap·for·mankind.
```

from Neil Armstrong's remarks on stepping onto the surface of the moon because there are two spaces between "a" and "man" in the text. We could be scrupulous about separating words by only one space when we type, but others often produce the text we search, and they might not be. For that reason it is a good tactic to limit the use of multiword searches by looking instead for single words that apply to the context. For example, looking for "leap" or "mankind" might work because they were probably not used again while Armstrong was on the moon.

In summary, searching is the process of locating a sequence of tokens, the search string, in a longer sequence of tokens, the text. Character searches are usually restricted to the characters the user has typed, though other characters may be present. User-typed characters can include nonprintable formatting characters like new-line. Search algorithms look for token sequences, and the tokens—for example, characters—are often more primitive than what we can construct from them—for example, words. To be successful, we must formulate search strings so that the tokens on which they match find all the situations of interest.

SUBSTITUTION

Search-and-replace, also known as *substitution*, is a combination of searching and editing to make corrections in documents, and because the first step is to search, it is usually coupled with *find*. The string replacing the search string is called the *replacement string*. Though substitution can apply to a single occurrence of the search string in the text, there is little advantage of search-and-replace over simply searching and editing the occurrence directly. The real power of substitution comes from applying it to all occurrences of the search string. For example, if you write a paper in which you refer to the "west coast," but forget that regions of a country are usually capitalized, it is a simple matter to search for all occurrences of "west coast" and replace them with "West Coast".

Because substitution can be a powerful tool that we want to learn to use effectively, we express it using a left pointing arrow (←) between the search string and the replacement string. The capitalization example is expressed as

```
west coast ← West Coast
```

Such an expression can be read, “west coast *is replaced by* West Coast” or “West Coast *substitutes for* west coast.” Another example is

```
Norma Jeane Mortensen ← Marilyn Monroe
```

describing her 1946 name change when she signed her first movie contract.

We emphasize that the arrow is only a *notation* that will allow us to discuss substitutions. When using an application some GUI will specify a replacement, see Figure 3.7. The two text windows of the GUI correspond to the information on each side of the arrow. Find is the left side of the arrow, and Replace is the right side. Typing the arrow is not appropriate in applications. It’s only for use here.

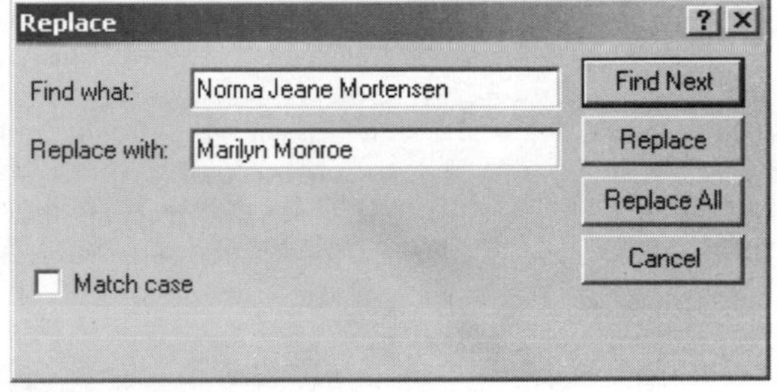

Figure 3.7. Example GUI for Find/Replace as it occurs in an application.

In the last section, we noted that multiple spaces separating words in a text complicates searching for multiword strings. Substitution can fix the “multiple spaces in a document problem”: Simply collapse double spaces to single spaces. That is, if the search string is “· ·” and the replacement string is “·”, a universal substitution results in all pairs of spaces becoming single spaces. Expressed using the arrow notation, the “two spaces are replaced by one ” substitution is

```
·· ← ·
```

Of course, every place where there are double spaces they will be reduced, including the end of sentences where we might want double spaces. Such cases can be fixed with substitutions of the form

```
.· ←.··
?· ←?··
!· ←!··
```

which will restore the sentence terminating double blanks following the three punctuation characters. Performing multiple transformations on text is a valuable technique.

A frequent instance when text must be transformed by several substitutions is when text is imported into a document from another source. It is common for the formatting to be messed up during conversion from the source document to the target document. For example, you find the Articles from the UN’s Universal Declaration of Human Rights:

> **Article 1** All human beings are born free and equal in dignity and rights. They are endowed with reason and conscience and should act towards one another in a spirit of brotherhood.
>
> **Article 2** Everyone is entitled to all the rights and freedoms set forth in this Declaration, without distinction of any kind, such as race, color, sex, language, religion, political, or other opinion, national or social origin, property, birth or other status.
>
> Furthermore, no distinction shall be made on the basis of political, jurisdictional or international status of the country or territory to which a person belongs, whether it be independent, trust, non-self-governing, or under any other limitation of sovereignty.
>
> **Article 3** Everyone has the right to life, liberty and security of person.

But when you copy the first three articles and paste them into your document, they come out looking this way:

        Article 1 All human beings are born free and equal in dignity and
rights. They are endowed with reason and
        conscience and should act towards one another in a spirit
of brotherhood.

        Article 2 Everyone is entitled to all the rights and freedoms set forth
 in this Declaration, without distinction of any
        kind, such as race, color, sex, language, religion, political
or other opinion, national or social origin,
        property, birth or other status.

        Furthermore, no distinction shall be made on the basis of
political, jurisdictional or international status of
        the country or territory to which a person belongs, whether
it be independent, trust, non-self-governing,
        or under any other limitation of sovereignty.

        Article 3 Everyone has the right to life, liberty and security of person.

It's a mess. Displaying the text with the formatting characters reveals:

········Article·1··All·human·beings·are·born·free·and·equal·in·dignity·and·↵
rights.·They·are·endowed·with·reason·and·↵
········conscience·and·should·act·towards·one·another·in·a·spirit·↵
of·brotherhood.·↵
↵
········Article·2··Everyone·is·entitled·to·all·the·rights·and·freedoms·set·forth↵
·in·this·Declaration,·without·distinction·of·any↵
········kind,·such·as·race,·color,·sex,·language,·religion,·political·↵
or·other·opinion,·national·or·social·origin,·↵
········property,·birth·or·other·status.··↵
↵
········Furthermore,·no·distinction·shall·be·made·on·the·basis·of·↵
political,·jurisdictional·or·international·status·of·↵
········the·country·or·territory·to·which·a·person·belongs,·whether·↵
it·be·independent,·trust,·non-self-governing,·↵
········or·under·any·other·limitation·of·sovereignty.·↵
↵
········Article·3··Everyone·has·the·right·to·life,·liberty·and·security·of·person.·↵

we see that extra space and new-line characters have been inserted in the process of incorporating the text into your document.

Clearly, removing the groups of eight leading blanks is simple: Replace them with nothing. When writing the substitution expression, we express "nothing" with the Greek letter epsilon, referred to as the *empty string*, that is, the string with no letters.[6]

········ ← ε

Removing the leading blanks was easy because they occur only at the beginning of the lines and nowhere else. Correcting the new-line characters is more of a problem.

We want to eliminate the new-lines that have been inserted within a paragraph and keep the paired new-lines that separate the paragraphs. But, eliminating single new-lines

↵ ← ε

[6] Notice that epsilon is used only for writing out substitution expressions for ourselves. In the Find-and-Replace facility of an application as in Figure 3.7, simply leave the replacement string empty.

will eliminate all the new-lines! How can we keep the paired new-lines but remove the single occurrences?

An easy strategy, known as the *Placeholder Technique*, solves such problems. It begins by substituting a placeholder character for every occurrence of the string we want to keep, that is, the pairs. We pick # as the placeholder on the assumption that it doesn't appear anywhere else in the document, but any unused character or character string will work. The substitution expression is

```
↵↵ ← #
```

Our text without the leading blanks and double new-lines now looks as follows:

```
Article·1·All·human·beings·are·born·free·and·equal·in·dignity·and·↵
rights.·They·are·endowed·with·reason·and·↵
conscience·and·should·act·towards·one·another·in·a·spirit·↵
of·brotherhood.#Article·2··Everyone·is·entitled·to·all·the·rights·and·freedoms·set·forth·↵
in·this·Declaration,·without·distinction·of·any↵
kind,·such·as·race,·color,·sex,·language,·religion,·political·↵
or·other·opinion,·national·or·social·origin,·↵
property,·birth·or·other·status.·#Furthermore,·no·distinction·shall·be·made·on·the·basis·of·↵
political,·jurisdictional·or·international·status·of·↵
the·country·or·territory·to·which·a·person·belongs,·whether·↵
it·be·independent,·trust,·non-self-governing,·↵
or·under·any·other·limitation·of·sovereignty.#Article·3··Everyone·has·the·right·to·life,·liberty·and·security·of·person.
```

The new-lines that remain are the ones to be removed, implying the need for another replacement by nothing

```
↵ ← ε
```

The resulting text has no instances of ↵ left:

```
Article·1·All·human·beings·are·born·free·and·equal·in·dignity·and·rights.·They·are·endowe
d·with·reason·and·conscience·and·should·act·towards·one·another·in·a·spirit·of·brotherh
ood.#·Article·2··Everyone·is·entitled·to·all·the·rights·and·freedoms·set·forth·in·this·Declar
ation,·without·distinction·of·any·kind,·such·as·race,·color,·sex,·language,·religion,·political
··or·other·opinion,·national·or·social·origin,·property,·birth·or·other·status.··#Furthermore,·
no·distinction·shall·be·made·on·the·basis·of·political,·jurisdictional·or·international·status
·of·the·country·or·territory·to·which·a·person·belongs,·whether·it·be·independent,·trust,·no
n-self-governing,·or·under·any·other·limitation·of·sovereignty.#Article·3··Everyone·has·the·
right·to·life,·liberty·and·security·of·person.
```

Finally, replace the placeholder with the desired character string

```
# ← ↵↵
```

Except for the bold form of **Article**, the result looks like the original document with only new-line pairs and no singletons. One final replacement

Article ← **Article**

completes the task.

To summarize, the Placeholder Technique is used to remove short search strings that are part of longer strings that we want to keep intact. If we removed the short strings directly, we'd trash the longer strings. The idea is to change the longer strings into the placeholder temporarily. Of course, a single placeholder character can replace the long strings because all we're keeping track of is where the longer string is located.

With the longer strings replaced by the placeholder, it is safe to remove the short strings. Once they are gone, the placeholder can be replaced by the longer string, and our desired result is achieved. The substitution expressions,

LongStringsContainingInstance(s)OfAShortString ← *Placeholder*
ShortString ← ε
Placeholder ← *LongStringsContainingInstance(s)OfAShortString*

summarize the idea.

THINKING OF IT ABSTRACTLY

We began this chapter promising to reveal some secrets known to expert computer users. And we have. Now, it is not so miraculous that the Digerati appear to know how to use software they have never seen before.

Then we observed that application software systems are constrained to behave in certain ways by the functionality they provide. Process follows function was our description of it. So, creating and editing keyboard input implies a small set of basic operations that all editing and word processing systems must have. Commonalties exist among browsers, among spreadsheets, and so forth. This recognition implies that when we learn a specific system for a specific task, we are learning both its core operations, common to all systems, as well as the superficial "bells and whistles" of its GUI. So, once we've learned one vendor's software for a task, we should expect to use another's for the same task without much difficulty, despite myriad differences evident in the "bells and whistles." Our introduction to the core concepts underlying searching and substitution illustrated the point: We learned the basics without regard to any specific implementation. In addition, we acquired useful computational skills, for example, the *Placeholder Technique*.

But the chapter's topic really concerned information technology more abstractly. We considered how people learn technology generally, and information technology specifically. Appreciating that no one knows how to use technology innately, we concluded that users must be trained to use each new tool. The best case is when the training is simply a user's previous experience with technology. In such cases, the technology is "perfectly intuitive"; that is, it operates exactly the way users expect. Software designers try for "perfectly intuitive" software through consistency, using standard metaphors, providing standard operations, and so on. Therefore, having considered the "training problem" for information technology, we inferred that one way to proceed would be to explore, for example, "click around." This deduction from the abstract to the specific shaped our expectations, guided our response to the technology, and put us in control. The larger lesson of this chapter, then, is to think about information technology abstractly.

Thus, as members of the Digerati, we will think about IT abstractly, and we're likely to ask such questions as

"What do I have to learn about this software to do my task?"

"What does the designer of this software expect me to know?"

"What does the designer expect me to do?"

"What metaphor is the software presenting to me?"

"What additional information does this software need to do its task?"

"Have I seen these core operations in other software?"

When we think about IT in terms of our personal or workplace needs, we may ask questions such as

> "Is there information technology that I am not now using that could help me with my task?"
>
> "Am I more or less productive using this technological solution for my task?"
>
> "Can I customize the technology I'm using to make myself more productive?"
>
> "Have I assessed my uses of IT recently?"

These and similar questions speak to our application of IT to achieve the work and pleasure goals of our lives. IT, being a means rather than an end, should be continually assessed to assure that it is fulfilling those needs as they and IT change and evolve.

Summary

This chapter began by thinking about how people learn to use technology. The conclusion was that they must either be taught technology or figure it out. We found that we can figure out software because designers use consistent interfaces, suggestive metaphors, standard functionality, and so on. We admired how the "perfect GUI" was perfectly intuitive. These features allow us to apply our previous experience to learn new applications, just like the Digerati. We learned that in computer systems, nothing will break when we make mistakes, so we should explore a new application by "clicking around." Further, we should try it out by "blazing away," knowing that we will mess up; when we do we will throw away our work by exiting and starting over—*getting out and getting back in.*

Exploration is not the only technique, however. Some aspects of a new application, like the shift-select are not likely to be discovered, so we expect to watch other users, and to ask questions. You're not a dummy if you ask, only if you don't. The last obervation relative to learning applications—*process follows function*—indicates that although software systems for a given task might look superficially different, there are basic operations that they must have in common. Thus, if we look past the "flash" of the GUI to these core operations, we can adapt easily to another vendor's software for the task. To demonstrate such core features we studied searching and substitution, which are available with many applications. The study culminated in using the Placeholder Technique for restructuring text. Finally, the chapter concluded with a discussion of thinking abstractly about technology. As individuals with goals to accomplish and with technology at hand, we must continually consider whether the technology we are using is helping us, whether we can be more productive with the technology we use, and whether we need to expand our uses of technology.

Exercises

1. How do people learn to use technology?
2. All consumer computers come with a "calculator" application. Find the calculator application on your computer and list the GUI features that contribute to helping people use it.
3. The audio CD players of Figures 3.1 and 3.2 are from the same generation operating systems. Compare and contrast the two designs in terms of aiding the user in understanding how it operates.
4. Describe, in words, the standard icons for the following operations: Cut, Copy, Paste, Print, Save, Search, and Help.

5. What are the shortcuts for the standard operations: New, Open, Save, Print, Cut, Copy, Paste, Undo, and Exit?

6. Using your favorite browser as an example, list ways in which it gives feedback about its operation.

7. Why is no feedback shown for any calculator operation?

8. Describe the operations you would perform when "clicking around" a new application.

9. What is the "fundamental rule of information technology," as described in this chapter? What is its corollary?

10. Locate a new application on your computer or the lab's computer and "click around." List ten icons you discover, noting which are new and which you've seen before. Compare the standard operations given in Figure 3.4 with those of the application, noting which are available and any differences in shortcuts.

11. In the stoplight example in the text the goal was to change the color of only the red and green lights. Explain how this result can be achieved by changing the red and green lights at the same time, but without using select-with-shift.

12. Using the application chosen in Exercise 10, spend 20 minutes "blazing away." Begin with a "new" instance and attempt to use the application successfully. Try to accomplish as much as possible. Print your final result.

13. A fundamental conclusion, described as "process follows function," can be drawn from the fact that information technology is governed by laws of nature. What is it?

14. If you are a PC user, locate a Macintosh. If you are a Mac user, locate a Windows PC. Explore the machine, looking under the "Start" or Apple menus. Check out the control panels. Start up your usual Web browser if it is resident on the machine, or another browser if it is not. List ten differences and ten similarities that you note.

15. The basic operation of a text searcher is "match the search string to the current position in the text; if there is a match, stop and report the search string found; otherwise, move the search string one position right and repeat." How many times would that basic operation be performed to find "content" in Martin Luther King's *I Have a Dream* speech?

16. Find a new word processor, possibly on the machine used in Exercise 14. Enter the following text, including all formatting as shown:

    To see the world in a grain of sand,
    And heaven in a wild flower,
    Hold infinity in the palm of your
        hand,
    And eternity in an hour.
                William Blake, *Auguries*
                of Innocence

    The font is Bookman Old Style, 12 pt.; the lines are 3 inches wide with an additional half inch more overhang. The author and source are right justified. After the text, write a paragraph (Times Roman font, 10 point, normal spacing and margins) about the similarities and differences of the new word processor versus your usual word processor. Print the document.

17. What happens when we apply the · · ← · replacement to · · · ·? Try this out on your text editor.

CHAPTER 4

Making the Connection

Learning Objectives

- Know how the Internet aids access to information.
- Learn the basic concepts of Internet routing.
- Understand the concept of physical/logical separation.
- Appreciate how Web pages are represented.
- Learn the basics of HTML tags and attributes.
- Become acquainted with the process of Web design.
- Understand how links work and how to structure the files.

Computers alone are useful. Computers connected together are even more useful. Proof of this came dramatically in the mid-1990s when the Internet, long available to scientists and researchers, became generally available to the public through Internet Service Providers (ISPs). For the first time, people could conveniently and inexpensively connect their computers to the Internet and thereby connect to all other computers attached to the Internet. They could send email and surf the Web from home. This convenient access to volumes of information, eCommerce, chatrooms, and other capabilities greatly expanded the benefits people derived from computers.

A skeptic might wonder whether all of the excitement and frenzy surrounding the wide access to the Internet is anything more than hype. After all, for a hundred years, average citizens in developed countries have had access to great repositories of information in the form of libraries, have been able to communicate with each other via telephones or the post, and have enjoyed the benefits of complex retail commerce. There have been wire services to bring the news from distant locales and broadcast media such as newspapers, radio, and television to convey that news widely. Has anything actually changed? Very definitely.

This chapter begins by considering how connecting computers together with the Internet has changed our access to information. Three of the most significant effects—convenience, immediacy, and economy—are identified. With the impact established, a taxonomy of communication gives the terminology needed to place the Internet among the other more traditional forms of communication. Next comes a series of topics designed to give a sense of how the Internet works without technical details: naming computers, packets, and the TCP/IP protocol, Ethernet and the Party Protocol, and connecting your computer to the Internet. These topics are described by analogy to everyday experience, bypassing the complicated technicalities. A significant concept that emerges is that of a logical/physical separation. This idea is illustrated by the Internet's domain name system (DNS). The concept pervades information technologies. Next the World Wide Web is defined and the role of HTML is explained. A brief tour of HTML presents the essence of the notation in two brief sections. By the end of that introduction, you will be able to create a respectable Web page. Subsequent sections add the familiar blue links and images. Appendix A covers lists, tables, and numerical colors—the last three topics needed to give a working knowledge of HTML.

Internet. The Internet is the totality of all of the wires, fibers, switches, routers, satellite links, and other hardware for transporting information between named computers. The present-day Internet is the commercial descendant of the ARPANet, developed in the late 1960s for the U.S. Defense Department's Advanced Research Projects Agency. Although ARPANet's original purpose was primarily to support remote login—access to a remote computer via a local computer—researchers quickly began to use it for email.

Connecting Computers Together

Several obvious advantages stem from connecting computers together, including convenience, immediacy, and economy.

Convenience. If you need information that would previously have been available at the library, it is more convenient to sit at your computer than to go to the library. If the information is available only at a distant library, it is even more convenient to sit at your computer—or even at a computer at a local library—than to go to the distant location. The convenience is proportionately greater as the distance increases between the user and the site where the information is stored. In the extreme, there is a convenience to accessing information at a distant site even if you intend to go there: Vacation planners access information from the destination before they leave. Similarly, online banking is more convenient than physically going to the bank because it's available when the physical bank is closed.

Immediacy. Information that must be printed and physically transported can become stale or out of date. Online information moves at electronic speeds and so can be kept current. Though the advantage of electronic transmission previously gave an immediacy advantage to radio and television over newspapers and magazines, the immediacy benefits of the Internet apply to keeping information current at all sources, not just a small number of broadcast sources.

Economy. Though computers require a substantial fixed investment and a continuing cost to connect to the Internet, these costs are shared over many applications and are generally independent of the amount of use. The personal computer system performs all of the "home office" tasks from figuring taxes to homework reports. But it can also be a means for communication, replacing long-distance telephone charges; a source of news, replacing newspapers and some forms of radio and cable; a tool for investing, reducing brokerage charges; a resource for many forms of entertainment, and so on. When used extensively, a computer connected to the Internet is generally inexpensive.

Though these advancements considered alone are really incremental improvements on previously available capabilities like newspapers and phones, their collective effect is significant in allowing people to be location independent. Telecommuting is now possible for many jobs. People living in remote parts of the world can access the World Wide Web's store of information as easily as citizens of world capitals can. Electronic commerce allows companies to access a global market with potential customers coming from anywhere. These are significant changes to the status quo.

> **Spamming**. Spam is unsolicited email. Spam is often sent by people promoting get-rich-quick schemes. Spam email once had subject lines like "Earn Big $$$," but spammers have become more subtle, choosing innocuous subject lines to snare readers. The term is widely believed to derive from a *Monty Python* skit in which the word *spam* was chanted by Vikings to drown out restaurant conversation; that is, unwanted input harms legitimate communication. State legislatures have attempted to outlaw spam.

Communicating

To explain what is fundamental about the Internet, it is necessary to explain some basic vocabulary of communication.

Communication between two entities, be they people or computers, can be separated into two broad classes: synchronous and asynchronous. *Synchronous communication* requires both the sender and the receiver to be active at the same moment in time. A telephone conversation is an example of synchronous communication because both parties to the conversation must perform one of the two parts of the transmission—sending (talking) or receiving (listening)—during the same moment in time. In *asynchronous communication,* the sending and the receiving are separated in time. A postcard is an example of asynchronous communication because it is written at one time and read sometime later. An answering machine or voice mail make telephones asynchronous in the sense that the caller leaves a message that the receiver listens to later. Email is asynchronous.

Another property of communication concerns the number of receivers. A single sender and many receivers constitutes *broadcast communication.* Radio and television are examples of broadcast communication, of course. The term *multicast* is also used when there are many receivers, but the intended recipients do not constitute the whole population. Magazines, generally being specialized to a topic, are an example of multicast communication. The opposite of broadcasting and multicasting is *point-to-point communication.* Telephone communication is point-to-point. The property of broadcast *versus* point-to-point communication is separate from the property of synchronous *versus* asynchronous communication.

A fundamental feature of the Internet is that it provides a general communication "fabric" linking all computers connected to it. Facilities include point-to-point asynchronous communication. Postal connections have always provided this capability, too, but the Internet provides it at electronic speeds. In fact, the speed is sufficiently fast that it can approximate synchronous communication, if desired. That is, two or more people can have a conversation by the rapid exchange of asynchronous messages. Instant messaging is an example. It offers a facility traditionally provided by the telephone. Multicasting is possible based on multiple active links to a Web page, enabling small to modest size groups to communicate via chatrooms. Finally, because it is possible to post a Web page that can be accessed by anyone, the Internet offers a form of broadcasting that compares with radio or television. In essence, Internetworking provides a single medium that can be applied in multiple ways to rival different established forms of communication. Reducing to a single universal medium is both more efficient and more flexible.

A corollary to the universality property of the Internet is that it becomes more effective with each additional computer added to it. That is, if x computers are already attached to the Internet, adding one more computer results in x potential new connections—that computer with each of the original machines.

THE MEDIUM OF THE MESSAGE

How does the Internet transmit information such as email messages and Web pages? Very complex and sophisticated technologies are used to implement today's Internet, but the underlying idea is extremely simple.

The Name Game

To begin, observe that the Internet implements point-to-point communication. When anything is sent point to point, whether it's a phone conversation, a letter, or furniture, the destination address for the recipient is required. For computers to exchange information over the Internet, they must have unique addresses, called *IP addresses*. The *IP* abbreviates *Internet Protocol*. An IP address is a sequence of four numbers separated by dots. For example, the IP address of the computer on which I am typing this sentence is `128.95.1.207`, and the machine to which my email is usually sent is `128.95.1.4`. Although the range of each of these numbers (0–255) allows for billions of Internet addresses, IP addresses are actually in short supply.

If, in order to send email to our friends, we needed to know the four number IP addresses of their computers, email would be very annoying and uncivilized. Instead, the Internet provides for human-readable symbolic names for computers based on a hierarchy of *domains*. A domain is a related set of networked computers. So, for example, the name of my computer, `spiff.cs.washington.edu`, reveals in its structure the domains of which it is a member. Pulling apart the name, my computer (`spiff`) is a member of the Computer Science and Engineering Department domain (`cs`), which is part of the University of Washington domain (`washington`), which is part of the educational domain (`edu`). This is a hierarchy of domains because each is a member of a larger domain. Another of my computers, `tracer.cs.washington.edu`, has a name with a similar structure, so it is apparently a member of the same domains. As might be expected of a hierarchy, other departments at the University of Washington, such as Astronomy (`astro.washington.edu`) have names that are peers of `cs` within the `washington` domain, and other schools (`princeton.edu`) have names that are peers with `washington` within the `edu` domain. The fact that these names are symbolic and meaningful to humans makes them easier to read than numbers, and the fact that they are hierarchical makes them easier to remember.

> **Where It's @.** Email addresses, for example, `president@whitehouse.gov`, have a specific structure. The portion to the right of the `@` is the *destination address*, and it has domain structure. It is processed by the sending computer. The information to the left of `@` is the user ID, and it is processed by the receiving computer.

How do the convenient domain names like `spiff.cs.washington.edu` get converted into the IP addresses `128.95.1.207` that computers need? By the DNS. The *Domain Name System* translates the hierarchical, human readable names into the four number IP addresses. This allows both people and computers to use their preferred scheme. Every Internet host (computer connected to the Internet) knows the IP address of its nearest Domain Name Server, a computer that keeps a list of the symbolic name/IP address correspondences. Whenever a computer is told by a user to send information to some destination, which will be given by the hierarchical symbolic name, it asks the DNS to look up the corresponding IP address. It then uses that IP address to send the information to the specified site. The DNS servers use elaborate mechanisms to keep their information up to date dynamically, making the existence of IP addresses almost invisible to users.

The `.edu` domain for educational institutions is one of several *top-level domain* designators. The others are `.com`, for commercial enterprises, `.org` for organizations, `.net` for networks, `.mil` for the military, and `.gov` for governments. These all apply to organizations in the United States. There are also a set of two-letter country designators that are reasonably mnemonic: `.ca` (Canada), `.uk` (United Kingdom), `.fr` (France), `.de` (Germany, as in Deutschland), `.es` (Spain, as in España), `.us` (United States), and so on. These allow domain names to be grouped by their country of origin. The punctuation character—it is always pronounced *dot*—simply separates the levels of the domains, and was chosen to be easy to type and say. (See Table 4.1.)

Following Protocol

Having figured out how a computer addresses the destination computer to which it must send information, we still need to describe how the information is actually sent. The process uses a mechanism called TCP/IP, abbreviating Transmission Control Protocol/Internet Protocol. It sounds technical, and is. But in concept it is easy.

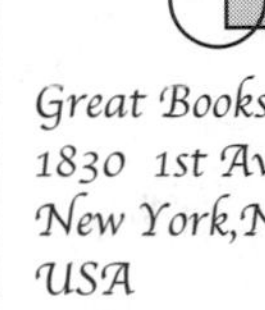

#1 Chapter 1:
It was a dark and stormy night. Rain pelted the glass as Sir Bulwer-Lytton dozed restlessly.

Great Books
1830 1st Ave
New York, NY
USA

To explain how TCP/IP works, we repeat an analogy used by Vincent Cerf, one of the pioneers of IP: Sending a message, say, an email message, is like sending your novel from Tahiti to your publisher in New York City using only postcards. How could that be done? Begin by breaking up the novel into small units, only a few sentences in length, so that each unit fits in the space available on a postcard. Each postcard is numbered to indicate where in the sentence sequence of the novel its sentences belong, and each postcard has the publisher's address written on it. As the postcards are completed, they are dropped into a mailbox. The postal service in Tahiti will send them to the publisher, but the cards will not be kept together, nor will they all take the same route to the publisher. Some postcards may go west, via Hong Kong, when an airplane with capacity to carry mail is headed in that direction. Others may go east, via Los Angeles, when there is an aircraft headed in that direction. From either city there are multiple routes to New York City. Eventually the postcards arrive at the publisher, who uses the sequence numbers to order the postcards and reconstruct the novel.

The concepts underlying TCP/IP are now clear using Cerf's postcard analogy. Transmission of any amount of information, including a whole novel, can be implemented by breaking it into a sequence of small fixed-size segments. An *IP packet*, which corresponds to the postcard, has a fixed capacity, a destination IP address, and a sequence number. IP packets are filled in order and assigned sequence numbers. The packets are transmitted over the Internet independently using whatever route is available. At the destination, they are reordered by sequence number to assemble the information.

Table 4.1. Top-level Country Domain Abbreviations

AF Afghanistan
AL Albania
DZ Algeria
AS American Samoa
AD Andorra
AO Angola
AI Anguilla
AQ Antarctica
AG Antigua & Barbuda
AR Argentina
AM Armenia
AW Aruba
AU Australia
AT Austria
AZ Azerbaijan
BS Bahamas
BH Bahrain
BD Bangladesh
BB Barbados
BY Belarus
BE Belgium
BZ Belize
BJ Benin
BM Bermuda
BT Bhutan
BO Bolivia
BA Bosnia & Herzegovina
BW Botswana
BV Bouvet Island
BR Brazil
IO British Indian Ocean Territory
BN Brunei Darussalam
BG Bulgaria
BF Burkina Faso
BI Burundi
KH Cambodia
CM Cameroon
CA Canada
CV Cape Verde
KY Cayman Islands
CF Central African Republic
TD Chad
CL Chile
CN China
CX Christmas Island
CC Cocos (Keeling) Islands
CO Colombia
KM Comoros
CG Congo
CK Cook Islands
CR Costa Rica
CI Cote d'Ivoire
HR Croatia (local name: Hrvatska)
CU Cuba
CY Cyprus
CZ Czech Republic
DK Denmark
DJ Djibouti
DM Dominica
DO Dominican Republic
TP East Timor
EC Ecuador
EG Egypt
SV El Salvador
GQ Equatorial Guinea
ER Eritrea
EE Estonia
ET Ethiopia
FK Falkland Islands (Malvinas)
FO Faroe Islands
FJ Fiji
FI Finland
FR France
FX France, Metropolitan
GF French Guiana
PF French Polynesia
TF French Southern Territories
GA Gabon
GM Gambia
GE Georgia
DE Germany
GH Ghana
GI Gibraltar
GR Greece
GL Greenland
GD Grenada
GP Guadeloupe
GU Guam
GT Guatemala
GN Guinea
GW Guinea-Bissau
GY Guyana
HT Haiti
HM Heard & McDonald Islands
HN Honduras
HK Hong Kong
HU Hungary
IS Iceland
IN India
ID Indonesia
IR Iran (Islamic Republic of)
IQ Iraq
IE Ireland
IL Israel
IT Italy
JM Jamaica
JP Japan
JO Jordan
KZ Kazakhstan
KE Kenya
KI Kiribati
KP Korea, Democratic People's Republic of
KR Korea, Republic of
KW Kuwait
KG Kyrgyzstan
LA Lao People's Democratic Republic
LV Latvia
LB Lebanon
LS Lesotho
LR Liberia
LY Libyan Arab Jamahiriya
LI Liechtenstein
LT Lithuania
LU Luxembourg
MO Macau
MK Macedonia, the former Yugoslav Republic of
MG Madagascar
MW Malawi
MY Malaysia
MV Maldives
ML Mali
MT Malta
MH Marshall Islands
MQ Martinique
MR Mauritania
MU Mauritius
YT Mayotte
MX Mexico
FM Micronesia,
MD Moldova, Republic of
MC Monaco
MN Mongolia
MS Montserrat
MA Morocco
MZ Mozambique
MM Myanmar
NA Namibia
NR Nauru
NP Nepal
NL Netherlands
NC New Caledonia
NZ New Zealand
NI Nicaragua
NE Niger
NG Nigeria
NU Niue
NF Norfolk Island
MP Northern Mariana Islands
NO Norway
OM Oman
PK Pakistan
PW Palau
PA Panama
PG Papua New Guinea
PY Paraguay
PE Peru
PH Philippines
PN Pitcairn
PL Poland
PT Portugal
PR Puerto Rico
QA Qatar
RE Reunion
RO Romania
RU Russian Federation
RW Rwanda
KN Saint Kitts & Nevis
LC Saint Lucia
VC Saint Vincent & the Grenadines
WS Samoa
SM San Marino
ST Sao Tome & Principe
SA Saudi Arabia
SN Senegal
SC Seychelles
SL Sierra Leone
SG Singapore
SK Slovakia (Slovak Republic)
SI Slovenia
SB Solomon Islands
SO Somalia
ZA South Africa
GS South Georgia & South Sandwiches
ES Spain
LK Sri Lanka
SH St. Helena
PM St. Pierre & Miquelon
SD Sudan
SR Suriname
SJ Svalbard & Jan Mayen Islands
SZ Swaziland
SE Sweden
CH Switzerland
SY Syrian Arab Republic
TW Taiwan, Province of China
TJ Tajikistan
TZ Tanzania, United Republic of
TH Thailand
TG Togo
TK Tokelau
TO Tonga
TT Trinidad & Tobago
TN Tunisia
TR Turkey
TM Turkmenistan
TC Turks & Caicos Islands
TV Tuvalu
UG Uganda
UA Ukraine
AE United Arab Emirates
GB United Kingdom
US United States
UM United States Minor Outlying Islands
UY Uruguay
UZ Uzbekistan
VU Vanuatu
VA Vatican City State
VE Venezuela
VN Vietnam
VG Virgin Islands
VI Virgin Islands (U.S.)
WF Wallis & Futuna Islands
EH Western Sahara
YE Yemen
YU Yugoslavia
ZR Zaire
ZM Zambia
ZW Zimbabwe

It is beyond our goals here to understand the engineering design decisions that lead to TCP/IP, but it is possible to see some of its advantages. For example, it is natural to assume that IP packets would take a single path to their destinations like telephone calls, but they do not. By allowing each packet to take a different route, congestion and service interruptions do not unnecessarily delay transmissions. Returning to the postcard analogy, if sending the first postcard via Hong Kong implied that all subsequent postcards were also sent via Hong Kong, a typhoon could disrupt or delay delivery. If the typhoon prevented aircraft from flying between Tahiti and Hong Kong, a protocol requiring all postcards to take the same route to the destination would delay transmission of the novel. But permitting postcards to take any available route allows the transmission to continue via Los Angeles when a typhoon delays flights to Hong Kong. As a result, all of the novel might be delivered via LA before airline service is restored between Tahiti and Hong Kong.

The Wires

Although Cerf's analogy makes a reasonable case for communication with postcards, the Internet uses electrical, electronic, and optical means. The original ARPANet was implemented using long-distance telephone lines, and the Internet continues to rely on telephone carriers for long-distance connections. However, as the Internet's capacity needs have escalated and as new technologies such as fiber optics and satellite communication have matured, separate facilities dedicated just to the Internet have come online. Because the TCP/IP protocol describes exactly how IP packets are structured and how they are to be handled, the actual technology used to move the packets is only of economic and engineering concern to the carrier. The computers at each end of the communication do not know or care what medium is used because they simply send and receive IP packets. Indeed, it is often the case that a given document transmission will rely on multiple technologies as its packets move through the Internet.

Ironically, with the growth of Internet capacity, telephone companies are finding it beneficial to send telephone conversations over the Internet. The speech is digitized, stuffed into IP packets at the phone company at the speaker's end, sent over the Internet, unpacked at the phone company at the listener's end, and converted back to analog form acceptable to a phone set. The universality of an IP packet makes this possible, and suggests that the Internet is fast becoming the universal information carrier.

Closer to Home

The Internet is termed a *wide area network (WAN)*, having been designed to send information between two locations widely separated and not directly connected. In our postcard analogy, Tahiti and New York City are not directly connected; that is, there is no single airline flight that goes between Tahiti and the Big Apple. Consequently, each postcard is carried on a sequence of airline flights to reach New York City. Analogously, the Internet is a collection of point-to-point channels and packets that must visit a sequence of computers to reach their destination. In networking terminology, packets take several *hops* to be delivered.

When computers are proximate enough to be linked by a single cable or pair of wires, the interconnection is referred to as a *local area network*. The dominant technology for *local area networks (LAN)* is Ethernet technology. It is appropriate for connecting all the computers in a lab or building. Ethernet uses a radically different approach than the Internet, but it is equally easy to understand.

The physical setup for an Ethernet network is a wire, wire pair, or fiber, depending on the technology, called the *channel*, and winding past a set of computers. Engineers "tap" the channel to connect a computer, allowing it to send a signal, that is, drive an electronic pulse or light flash onto the channel. All computers connected to the channel can detect the signal, including the sender. Thus the channel supports broadcast communication.

Party Protocol

To understand how an Ethernet works, consider another analogy. A group of friends is standing around at a party telling stories. While someone is telling a story, everyone is listening. The speaker is broadcasting to the group. When the story is over, there may be a momentary pause while they wait for someone to start the next story. But how do the revelers decide who tells the next story? There is no plan or agreement as to who should speak next. Typically someone just begins talking, "I remember the time. . . ." If no one else begins talking, that speaker gets the floor and continues telling the story to completion. When the end of the story is detected, there may be a pause, and someone else will start talking. If two or more people begin talking after the pause, they will detect that others are speaking and immediately stop. There is a pause while everyone waits for someone to go ahead. Assuming speakers tend to wait a random amount of time, someone will begin talking and take the floor. It is possible that two or more speakers will again start at the same time, detect the situation, stop, and wait a random amount of time. Eventually some single person begins telling another story.

In this analogy we have assumed a peer relationship for the partygoers; that is, there is no differential stature nor does anyone have an especially loud or soft voice. Even so, the system, as described, isn't fair, because it favors the least deferential person who waits the least amount of time at the end of a story. Of course, we all know such people!

The concepts underlying Ethernet are clear from the storytelling analogy. When the channel is in use, as when someone is telling a story, all of the computers listen to it. Unlike storytelling, however, only one computer typically keeps the information transmitted, that is, this broadcast medium is being used to implement point-to-point communication. The completion of the transmission will be indicated by a pause, when no computer is sending signals and the channel is quiet. A computer wanting to transmit starts to send signals and simultaneously starts to listen to the channel to detect what is being transmitted on the channel. If it is exactly the information the computer sent, the computer must be the only one sending, and it completes its transmission. If not, its signals are being mixed in with signals from one or more other computers. It detects that the data is garbled, and so it stops sending immediately. The other computer(s) will stop, too. Each machine pauses for a random amount of time. The computer that waits the shortest amount of time begins sending, and if there are no conflicting computers, it proceeds. If not, it repeats the protocol.

Big Difference. The Internet uses a point-to-point network to implement point-to-point communication. An Ethernet LAN uses a broadcast network to implement point-to-point communication between attached machines. The difference is that with the Internet multiple communications can take place at once over different wires, but with the Ethernet LAN only one communication can take place at a time. The limitation is usually not a problem because LANs usually carry much less traffic.

Making the Connection

How are computers actually connected to the Internet? Today there are two basic methods:

1. Connections via an Internet Service Provider (ISP)
2. Connections via a campus or enterprise network

It is typical to use both kinds of connections in one day, depending on where you are working. Consider each approach.

Connections via ISP. As the name implies, Internet Service Providers sell connections to the Internet. Examples of ISPs are `AOL.com` and `Earthlink.net`, but there are thousands. Connecting via ISPs is common for home users. Here's how such a connection usually works. Users plug in their computer to the telephone system just as they would connect an extension telephone. Then the computer's modem, which is generally built into modern personal computers, can dial up the ISP and establish a connection. This operation is similar to a fax machine dialing another fax machine. The modems—there is one at each end of the telephone connection—enable the home computer to talk to the ISP's computer so that they can send and receive information from the Internet. For example, when surfing around the World Wide Web and clicking on a remote link, that is, referring to a page stored on a distant computer, the address of the requested page is sent from the home computer to the ISP's computer, across the Internet to the remote computer, which then transmits the Web page across the Internet into the computer at the ISP. From there, the pages are transmitted via the phone line to the home computer for display on the screen.

Connections via LAN. The other primary way to connect to the Internet is as a user of a larger networked organization such as a school, business, or governmental unit. In this case, the organization's system administrators have connected the computers using various local area network (LAN) facilities. The Ethernet technology mentioned earlier is an example of a local area network. These local networks support interoffice communication within the organization, but they also connect to the Internet by a gateway, which is a portal to the Internet. Information from a distant Web site would be sent across the Internet, through the gateway to the organization's LAN, and across the LAN to the user's computer.

With either technique, the user is sending and receiving information transparently across the Internet.

THE WORLD WIDE WEB

Some of the computers connected to the Internet are *Web servers*, computers programmed to send files to browsers running on other computers connected to the Internet. Collectively these Web servers and their files are the *World Wide Web*. From this explanation it's clear that

- The files are Web pages, though other kinds of files are included.
- The World Wide Web and the Internet are different: The Internet is the totality of wires and switches connecting named computers, whereas the WWW is a subset of those computers (servers) and their files.
- Requesting a Web page, say, `http://www.cs.washington.edu/education/courses/100`, causes the browser to ask for the file from a Web server computer. The Web page address, known as a *Universal Resource Locator*, or *URL*, must specify which computer (that's the IP address `www.cs.washington.edu`), and it must specify which file (that's the sequence following the address, `/education/courses/100`). Because there are different ways to send files, the request must also specify how to send it (that's the `http:` part).
- When it requests a file our browser is a client of the Web server, and a Web server can serve many clients at once, as we learn in Chapter 15.

When described in these technical terms, the WWW doesn't seem like much. And technically, it's not. What makes the World Wide Web so significant is the information embodied in the files and the ability of the client and server computers to process it. In Chapter 5, we will concern ourselves with the content of the WWW, and in Chapter 15 we will consider its application to business. In the remainder of this chapter we consider how Web pages are represented and processed.

> ***WWW* Is Not Short for *World Wide Web:*** As everyone correctly assumes, WWW *abbreviates* World Wide Web, but it is not *short* for World Wide Web. In fact, it's long. *World Wide Web* is only three syllables, whereas *WWW* is nine. A brief way to say *WWW* would be "dub, dub, dub."

The first and perhaps most important point about the World Wide Web is that the Web server does not store pages in the form that we see them on our screens. Rather, Web pages are stored as a *description* of how they should appear on the screen. When the Web browser receives the description file, known as the *source*, it creates the image that you see. Two advantages to storing and transmitting the source rather than the image itself are first, that it usually requires less data to be transmitted, and second, the browser, using the description, can more easily adapt it to the peculiarities of your computer. For example, it is easier to shrink or expand the image from its description than it is to shrink or expand the image itself. Though browsers show the image, they always give the option of seeing the description, too. Look under View and find Source or Page Source. Figure 4.1 on page 67 shows a simple Web page and its source.

To describe how a Web page should look, we most frequently use the famed HTML, or *hypertext markup language*. Markup languages, long a staple of publishing and graphic design, describe the layout features of a document, such as width of margins, font, whether text is left justified or centered, italic, bold, where images and figures go, and so on. Hypertext began as an experiment to break away from the linearity of documents—normal text is arranged in a sequence. The legacy of hypertext is the (usually blue) highlighted links of Web pages that allow us to keep our place but optionally jump to somewhere else and return, allowing a document to have a more complex structure. Hypertext got its name in the late 1960s from Theodore Nelson, though in his *Literary Machines* Nelson credits the seminal idea to computer pioneer Vannevar Bush. Combining the two ideas enabled construct-on-the-fly nonlinear documents, ideal for the dynamic and highly interconnected Internet. The World Wide Web was born.

> **Colliding Ideas.** HTML, a markup language incorporating hypertext, was invented in 1990 by Tim Berners-Lee while at CERN, the European Laboratory for Particle Physics.

Marking Up with HTML

The basics of HTML are straightforward. In essence, the words that will appear on the Web page are simply surrounded by formatting tags describing how they should appear. Recall from Chapter 3 that *tags* are words or abbreviations enclosed in angle brackets, < and >, like `<title>`, and that a tag generally has a companion tag that includes a "/", like `</title>`. This pair—perhaps it's a *tag team*!—surrounds the text to be formatted like parentheses. Thus the title, which every HTML Web page has, would be written as

```
<title>Tiger Woods, Masters Champion</title>
```

These two tags can be read as "begin title" and "end title." The title is shown on the title bar of the browser when the page is being displayed (see the very top of the window where the close button is). In HTML, the tags are not case sensitive, but the actual text is. Thus, in this example, `<TITLE>`, `<Title>`, or any other mix of lower- and uppercase could have been used, but each word in the title will be displayed as shown beginning with a capital letter.

HTML has tags for indicating bold text, `<b>` and `</b>`, for indicating italic text, `<i>` and `</i>`, and for indicating a paragraph, `<p>` and `</p>`. Multiple types of formatting can be specified, such as italic bold text, simply by "nesting" the tags, as in

```
<b><i>Veni, Vidi, Vici!</i></b>
```

which produces

Veni, Vidi, Vici!

and is equivalent to a version in which the italic specification encloses the bold specification,

```
<i><b>Veni, Vidi, Vici!</b></i>
```

That is, the ordering doesn't matter. The key point is to ensure that the tags are properly nested. All the tags between a starting tag and its corresponding ending tag must match. So, in this last Caesarian quote, for example, between the starting `<i>` tag and its corresponding ending tag `</i>` all the tags, which is just the bold pair, match.

A few tags are not paired and so do not have a "/" ending form. An example is the horizontal rule tag, `<hr>`, which displays a horizontal line. Another example is break `<br>`, which continues the text on the next line and is useful for ending each line of an address. Such singleton tags perform an operation that doesn't apply across multiple characters, and so needn't bracket anything.

An HTML Web page file begins with the `<html>` tag, ends with the `</html>` tag, and has the following structure

```
<html>
      <head>

       preliminary material goes here

      </head>
      <body>

       the main content of the page goes here

      </body>
</html>
```

The section bounded by `<head>` and `</head>` contains preliminary material like the title, and the section bounded by `<body>` and `</body>` contains the actual content of the page. *This form must always be followed, and all of these tags are required.*

While we are giving absolute, ignore-at-your-own-peril style rules about a Web page's form, it is important to offer a caution about text editors. HTML must be written using basic ASCII characters, defined in Chapter 8, but they're generally the characters from the keyboard. As we learned in Chapter 3, standard word processors (e.g., Claris

Works, WordPerfect, and Word) produce files of such characters, but they also include special formatting information that browsers do not like. For that reason, it is *essential* that the HTML be written using a primitive text editor such as NotePad (Windows), Simple Text (Mac), BBText (Windows, Mac, UNIX), or the like. Then, always be sure that when saving the file, it is saved using `Text` format. These precautions—using a simple text editor and always saving with `Text` format—assure that the HTML file will be comprehensible to Web browsers. Also, always assure that the file name ends with the `.html` extension, so that the browser knows it's reading an HTML document.

There's not very much to HTML. By the end of the next section, we will have created a respectable Web page—our first!

> **Compose and Check.** To write HTML effectively, compose the text first and then format it. A productive way to work is with two windows open, the editor and the browser. After specifying a small number of HTML formatting tags in the editor, *save* them and then check the result with the browser by *reloading* the source.

Structuring Text

Because documents have headings and subheadings and even finer levels of structure, HTML provides several levels of heading tags, beginning with the highest, level one headings, `<h1>` and `</h1>`, and proceeding through level two, `<h2>` and `</h2>`, all the way to level eight, `<h8>` and `</h8>`. The headings automatically display the material in large font on a new line. For example,

```
<h1>Pope</h1> <h2>Cardinal</h2> <h3>Archbishop</h3>
```

would print as

Pope
Cardinal
Archbishop

The heading levels should be used in numerical order with no level being skipped, though they need not start at 1. Notice that the headings are bold and their strength, that is, how bold they are, decreases as the level increases.

Notice as well that although the HTML text was run together on one line, it displayed in a formatted form, illustrating the main idea that the HTML source instructs the browser to produce the formatted image based on the meanings of the tags, not on how the source instructions look. Though the source's form is unimportant, it is nevertheless customary to write HTML in a structured way as an aid to *human* understanding. There is no prescribed form, but the example might have been written with indenting to emphasize the levels

```
<h1>Pope</h1>
 <h2>Cardinal</h2>
   <h3>Archbishop</h3>
```

The two forms produce the identical result. Computer experts describe such source formatting as *white space*, inserted for readability. In HTML, white space is ignored. That is, any sequence of white space characters—spaces, tabs, and new-lines—are reduced to a single space by the browser before it begins processing the HTML. The only exception is *preformatted* information contained within `<pre>` and `</pre>` tags, which is displayed literally.

The fact that white space is ignored is crucial to the display of paragraphs. All text within paragraph tags, <p> and </p>, is treated as a paragraph, and any sequence of white space characters collapses to a single space. Thus

```
<p>  <b>Xeno's Paradox: </b>
Achilles and a turtle were to run a race. Achilles could
run twice as fast as the turtle.  The turtle,
being a slower runner, got a 10 meter head start, whereupon
Achilles started and ran the 10 meter distance.  At that
moment the turtle was 5 meters further.  When Achilles had run
that distance the turtle had gone another 2.5 meters,
and so forth. Paradoxically, the turtle always remained ahead.  </p>
```

would appear as

> **Xeno's Paradox:** Achilles and a turtle were to run a race. Achilles could run twice as fast as the turtle. The turtle, being a slower runner, got a 10 meter head start, whereupon Achilles started and ran the 10 meter distance. At that moment the turtle was 5 meters further. When Achilles had run that distance the turtle had gone another 2.5 meters, and so forth. Paradoxically, the turtle always remained ahead.

The width of the line is determined by the width of the browser window. Of course, a narrower or wider browser window results in a paragraph with different line breaks, explaining why HTML ignores white space and simply adapts the paragraph's formatting to the space available. Table 4.2 summarizes the basic HTML tags.

Table 4.2. Basic HTML Tags

Start Tag	End Tag	Meaning	Required
<html>	</html>	HTML document; first and last tags in an HTML file	✔
<title>	</title>	Title bar text; describes page	✔
<head>	</head>	Preliminary material, e.g., title, at start of page	✔
<body>	</body>	The main part of the page	✔
<p>	</p>	Paragraph, can use align attribute	
<hr>		Underline (horiz. rule), can use width and size attributes	
<h1> . . . <h8>	</h1> . . . </h8>	Headings, 8 levels, use in order, can use align attribute	
<b>	</b>	Bold	
<i>	</i>	Italic	
<a href="*fn*">	</a>	Anchor reference, *fn* must be a pathname to html file	
<img src="*fn*">		Image source ref., *fn* must be pathname to .jpg or .gif file	
 		Break, continue text on a new line	

Notice that there would be a problem if our Web page had to show a mathematical relationship such as $0 < p > r$ because the browser would misinterpret < p > as a paragraph tag. To display angle brackets, we use an *escape* symbol, the ampersand (&), followed by an abbreviation: < displays as <, > displays as >, and & displays as &. The latter is necessary because the escape symbol needs an escape, too, to avoid confusion. So, the mathematical relationship would be written in HTML as

```
<i>0 &lt p &gt r</i>
```

Letters with accent marks also use the escape. The general form is an ampersand followed by the letter—case matters here—followed by the name of the accent mark. So, for example, é displays as é, È displays as È, ñ displays as ñ and `ö` displays as ö. Table 4.3 contains a list of a few useful special symbols for some Western European languages. A full list is given at

`www.ics.uci.edu/pub/ietf/html/rfc1866.txt.`

Though most properties of text are easily specified by a single key term or abbreviation, some properties such as how to align text require more information. For example, we must specify left, centered, or right justification. Such information is specified inside the tag's brackets using *attributes*. Attributes, which are generally optional, appear inside the angle brackets. For example, paragraphs and headings have an `align` attribute specifying whether the text should be left justified, centered, or right justified. The attribute follows the tag word, separated by a space, and has an equal sign separating it from the value being specified in double quotes. Thus,

```
<p align = "center"> <b>Winston Churchill once observed:</b>  </p>
<p> If at 20 you are not liberal, you have no heart. </p>
<p align = "right"> If at 40 you are not conservative, you have no mind.</p>
```

would display as

Winston Churchill once observed:

If at 20 you are not liberal, you have no heart.

If at 40 you are not conservative, you have no mind.

Notice that when no alignment attribute is specified as in the second line with the tag `<p>`, the default of left justified applies, implying that it is an optional attribute.

Table 4.3. Special Symbols Occurring in Western European Languages

à	à	á	á	â	â	ã	ã	ä	ä	å	å
ç	ç	è	è	é	é	ê	ê	ë	ë	ì	ì
í	í	î	î	ï	ï	ñ	ñ	ò	ò	ó	ó
ô	ô	õ	õ	ö	ö	ø	ø	ù	ù	ú	ú
û	û	ü	ü		For capitals, make the letter following the & uppercase.						

Note: Terminate each with a semicolon (;).

The horizontal rule tag, `<hr>`, mentioned earlier, further illustrates attributes: One attribute, `width`, specifies how wide the line should be as a percentage of the browser window's width; another attribute, `size`, specifies how thick the line should be. Thus `<hr width="50%" size=1>` displays a horizontal line that occupies half of the horizontal width and is the minimum thickness as in

---

The default size is 2. Experiment to find the size that works best for your application. Notice that the width specification is enclosed in quotation marks, whereas the size specification is not. This has been done only for illustration purposes, since HTML does not require the quotes around the attribute values if a browser can figure out what is intended. But, the advice is, don't take chances—put quotes around anything following an equal sign.

Though we have introduced only a few HTML tags so far, it is already possible to create Web pages, as shown in Figure 4.1. Analyze the HTML shown and notice the following points:

- The title is shown on the title bar of the browser window.
- The alignment attribute has been used in the level 1 heading to center the heading.
- The level 2 headings are left justified because that is the default.

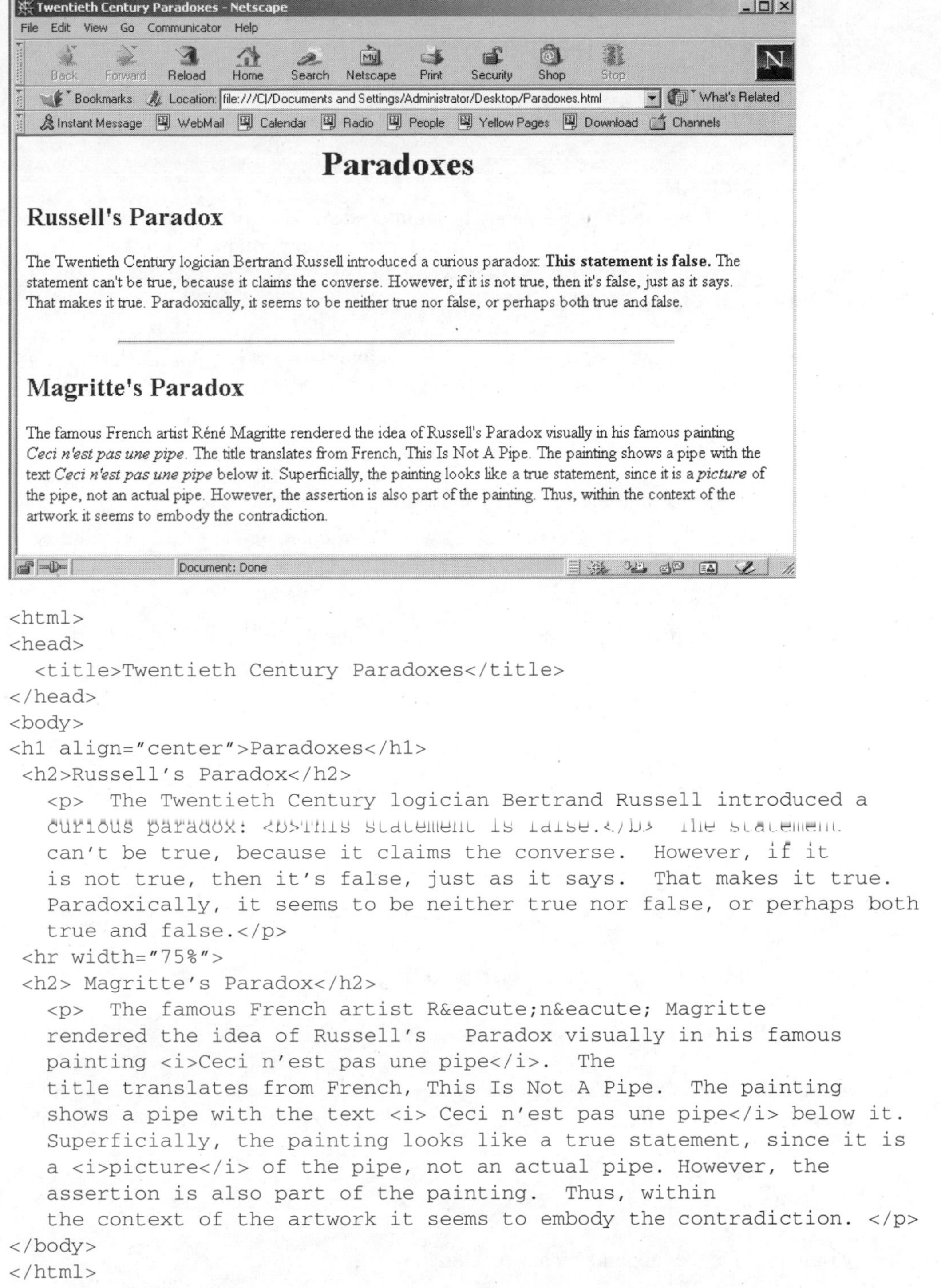
Twentieth Century Paradoxes - Netscape
File Edit View Go Communicator Help
Back Forward Reload Home Search Netscape Print Security Shop Stop
Bookmarks Location: file:///C|/Documents and Settings/Administrator/Desktop/Paradoxes.html
What's Related
Instant Message WebMail Calendar Radio People Yellow Pages Download Channels
Paradoxes
Russell's Paradox
The Twentieth Century logician Bertrand Russell introduced a curious paradox: This statement is false. The statement can't be true, because it claims the converse. However, if it is not true, then it's false, just as it says. That makes it true. Paradoxically, it seems to be neither true nor false, or perhaps both true and false.
Magritte's Paradox
The famous French artist Réné Magritte rendered the idea of Russell's Paradox visually in his famous painting Ceci n'est pas une pipe. The title translates from French, This Is Not A Pipe. The painting shows a pipe with the text Ceci n'est pas une pipe below it. Superficially, the painting looks like a true statement, since it is a picture of the pipe, not an actual pipe. However, the assertion is also part of the painting. Thus, within the context of the artwork it seems to embody the contradiction.
Document: Done

```
<html>
<head>
  <title>Twentieth Century Paradoxes</title>
</head>
<body>
<h1 align="center">Paradoxes</h1>
 <h2>Russell's Paradox</h2>
   <p>  The Twentieth Century logician Bertrand Russell introduced a
   curious paradox: <b>This statement is false.</b>  The statement
   can't be true, because it claims the converse.  However, if it
   is not true, then it's false, just as it says.  That makes it true.
   Paradoxically, it seems to be neither true nor false, or perhaps both
   true and false.</p>
 <hr width="75%">
 <h2> Magritte's Paradox</h2>
   <p>  The famous French artist R&eacute;n&eacute; Magritte
   rendered the idea of Russell's   Paradox visually in his famous
   painting <i>Ceci n'est pas une pipe</i>.  The
   title translates from French, This Is Not A Pipe.  The painting
   shows a pipe with the text <i> Ceci n'est pas une pipe</i> below it.
   Superficially, the painting looks like a true statement, since it is
   a <i>picture</i> of the pipe, not an actual pipe. However, the
   assertion is also part of the painting.  Thus, within
   the context of the artwork it seems to embody the contradiction. </p>
</body>
</html>
```

Figure 4.1. HTML source and corresponding Web page resulting from its interpretation by a browser.

- The statement of Russell's Paradox is in bold.
- The HTML source paragraphs are indented further than the <h2> heading lines for readability.
- The line separating the two paragraphs is three-quarters the width of the browser window.
- Acute accents are used in Magritte's first name.

- The French phrase from the painting is italicized.
- The word *picture* is italicized for emphasis.

It's a reasonably attractive page for a first attempt.

HYPERTEXT ANCHORS

The example shown in Figure 4.1 may be an interesting Web page, but it doesn't use hypertext very effectively. It would be more informative, perhaps, if it linked to biographies of Russell and Magritte. Also, it would be easier to comprehend if it showed Magritte's painting or linked to it. In this section we consider how to make hyperlinks.

In concept, a hyperlink to another Web page has two parts, the text in the current document that is highlighted, known as the *anchor*, and the address of the other Web page, known as the *reference*. Both parts of the hyperlink are specified in the anchor tag, constructed as follows:

- Begin with <a making sure to include the space after the a.
- Specify the hyperlink reference by href="*filename*" making sure to include the double quotes.
- Close the tag with >.
- Specify the anchor text, which will be highlighted when it is displayed by the browser.
- Terminate the hyperlink with the </a>.

Thus, if www.bios.com/bios/sci/russell.html were a Web biography of Bertrand Russell, we would anchor it to his last name on our Web page with the anchor tag

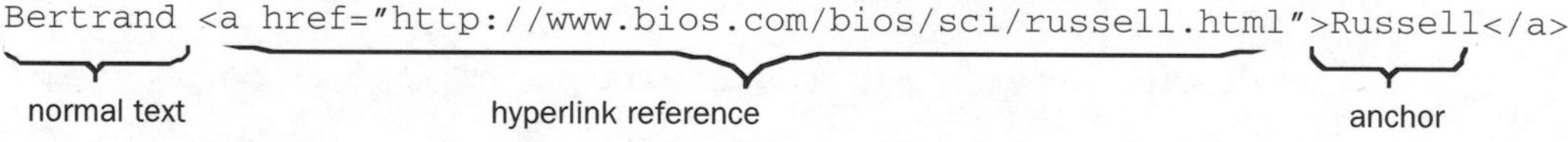

which would be displayed with his last name highlighted as

Bertrand Russell

to indicate the presence of a hyperlink. When the browser displays the page and the user clicks on Russell, the browser downloads the page given in the href. As another example, if Magritte's biography were at the same site, the text

```
<a href="http://www.bios.com/bios/art/magritte.html">Magritte</a>
```

would provide the link and anchor for him.

In the anchor tag examples just given, the hyperlink reference is an entire URL because the Web browser needs the exact description of how to find the page. As noted before, the URL contains an IP address, www.bios.com in this case, and a path to the file. It is important to be able to read such paths as they work their way down in the directory (folder) hierarchy. From the two examples, we infer that at the mythical Bios Company site, many or all of the biographies have been grouped together in a directory called bios. It is a good guess that the scientists, including logicians like Russell, are grouped together in the directory called sci and the artists are grouped together under the directory called art. Within these directories are the individual biography files, russell.html and magritte.html. The slash "/" separates levels in the directory hierarchy and "crossing a slash" moves lower in the hierarchy. Such complete URLs are known as *absolute pathnames,* and they are appropriate for referencing pages at other sites of the WWW.

However, it is common for a Web site to have a main (home) page at the top of a whole hierarchy of pages. The Bios Company site is an example. Because these pages will all be stored in the same or subsidiary directories of the site, anchor tags referencing local pages can be given as *relative pathnames* that describe how to find the referenced file from the position of the current file. Relative pathnames are much more flexible, so using them is preferable for any pages stored at the same site (IP address) as the page containing the anchor tag.

For example, suppose that with the Paradoxes page, we have written our own biographies for Russell and Magritte. If the files are named `russellbio.html` and `magrittebio.html` and they are in the same directory as the Paradoxes page, the anchor tags of the Paradoxes page simply become

```
<a href="russellbio.html">Russell</a>
```

and

```
<a href="magrittebio.html">Magritte</a>
```

If in the directory of the Paradoxes page we create a directory, `biographies`, that contains their two profiles, the anchor for Russell becomes

```
<a href="biographies/russellbio.html">Russell</a>
```

because we must say how to navigate to the file from the Paradoxes page's location. Of course, using relative pathnames implies that the files for the pages must be kept together with a fixed structure, but that's the easiest solution anyway.

The only remaining problem with relative pathnames is how to refer to directories higher up in the hierarchy. The technique, which is inherited from the UNIX operating system, is to refer to the next outer level of the hierarchy as "`..`", which is read "dot dot". Thus, if we imagine that the directory structure has the form

```
mypages
  biographies
    russellbio.html
    magrittebio.html
  coolstuff
    paradoxes.html
```

then, in `paradoxes.html`, the Russell biography anchor would be referred to as

```
<a href="../biographies/russellbio.html">Russell</a>
```

because the biography is not in the same directory (`coolstuff`) as `paradoxes.html`, but requires that we go up to the next higher level to `mypages`. It's possible to cascade a sequence of dot dots, so that each successive pair causes the browser to move up higher in the hierarchy. Thus

```
<a href="../../buddypages/dumbjokes/knockknock.html">
```

would move up to the directory containing the directory containing the page, then through the `buddypages` and `dumbjokes` directories, and down to the actual HTML page.

IMAGINE IMAGES

Pictures are worth a thousand words, as the saying goes, so incorporating them into the HTML document contributes substantially to a page's content. The mechanism for including pictures is to use a tag, of course, but not an anchor tag because we don't want to *refer* to the picture, but to *incorporate* it directly into the page. (Whenever we would *prefer* to refer to it, anchor tags are appropriate.) An image tag, which shares some structural similarities with anchors, specifies a file containing an image. The image tag format is

```
<img src="filename">
```

where SRC stands for "source" and the *filename* is specified using the same rules for absolute and relative pathnames as given for anchors. So, for example, if Magritte's painting is stored in a file, `pipe.jpg`, in the same directory as the Paradoxes page, we can incorporate its image with a relative pathname

```
<img src="pipe.jpg">
```

which locates the image and includes it in the document.

Images are encoded in a variety of formats, two of which—GIF (pronounced with either a hard or soft *g*) and JPEG (pronounced *JAY·peg*)—are important for Web pages. GIF, Graphics Interchange Format, is best for cartoons and simple images. JPEG, named for the Joint Photographic Experts Group, is the format best suited to high-resolution photographs and complex artwork. To tell the browser which format has been used to encode the image, the filename should have the proper extension, `.gif`, `.jpg`, or `.jpeg`.

The big question is, "Where does the image go on the Web page?"

To understand how images are placed, observe that HTML lays out text in the browser window *left-to-right, top-to-bottom*, just as Latin alphabet–based languages are written. If the image is the same size or smaller than the letters, it can be placed inline just like a letter at the point where the image tag occurs in the HTML. For example, to insert a small image in the text simply results in its being drawn in place. This is convenient for placing icons or smiley faces in the text. If the image is larger than the letters it is dropped in the text in the same way, but the line spacing is increased to separate it from the adjacent lines. Thus the HTML default rule: *Images are inserted in the page at the point where the tag is specified in the HTML, and the text is aligned with the bottom of the image*. Using the align attribute in the image tag can change the text to be aligned with the top of the image (`align="top"`) or be centered (`align="middle"`) in the image. In all cases, the "bottom" (default), "center," and "top" alignments apply only to the line of text in which the image has been inserted.

Another common and visually pleasing way to incorporate images in text is for the text to flow around them, either by having the image right justified with the text flowing along the left, or vice versa. To cause the text to flow around the image, use the align attribute in the image tag with value "right" or "left." This forces the *image* to the right or left of the browser window, and then the text will continue to be laid out left-to-right, top-to-bottom, in the remaining space; that is, it will flow around the image. Finally to display an image by itself without any text on either side of it, simply enclose the image tag within paragraph tags, which separates it from the paragraphs above and below it. Optionally, the *paragraph* can be centered to center the image.

Returning to the question of how to handle the image of Magritte's painting in the Paradoxes page, perhaps the most pleasing solution is to right-justify it and let the paragraph flow around it. Such would be accomplished by writing

```
<img src="pipe.jpg" align="right">
```

assuming the picture is not so large as to take all or most of the window, preventing the text from flowing naturally. To specify how large the picture should be, use the `height` and `width` attributes in the image tag. The size is given in pixels. Thus,

```
<img src="pipe.jpg" align="right" height="100" width="240">
```

specifies an image that would be about one quarter of the width of a thousand-pixel screen. If the natural size of the image is different from what has been specified, the browser shrinks or stretches it to fit in the allotted space. (The natural size of an image would be the truest size to use. It can be found by checking the Properties or the Info of the image file.)

Images can also be used to fill in a background as tiled copies of the image, a small image copied over and over to give a pattern to the background. Images used in this way are best if they are bland, low contrast, and in a uniform tonal range. Special collections of suitable pictures and graphics are widely available, such as one that gives the page a look of linen paper. The image is specified as the `background` attribute of the body tag as in

```
<body background="filename">
```

where the *filename* has the same path properties as anchors.

Finally, color can be used for both the background and text. To use a solid color rather than an image for the background, use the `bgcolor` attribute of the body tag. The color can be specified either numerically, as explained in the appendix to this chapter, or using a small set of predefined color terms, as in

```
<body bgcolor="silver">
```

The body tag attribute `text` can be used to give the entire document's text a specific color, as in

```
<body text="aqua">
```

The text can be changed using the font tag with the color attribute. So, to make Russell's Paradox red, write

```
<b><font color="red">This statement is false.</font></b>
```

The basic color list is given in Table 4.4.

With the information learned in the last two sections it is possible to enhance the Web page of Figure 4.1. The result is shown in Figure 4.2. Notice the local pathnames to our own biographical profiles of Russell and Magritte, the background and text colors, the change of color for the font for the headings, and of course, the image.

> **Get Organized.** It is advisable to keep a Web page's image files together in a separate directory. This reduces the clutter. Thus, the reference to an image might be: `This_Pages_Pix/picture1.jpg`.

Table 4.4. Table of Standard HTML Colors

black	silver	white	gray
red	fuchsia	maroon	purple
blue	navy	aqua	teal
lime	green	yellow	olive

HTML Wrap-up

We revealed the not-so-well-kept secret that Web pages are stored and transmitted in an encoded form before a browser translates them into the image viewed on the screen. HTML is the most widely used form of encoding. HTML has a simple structure in which the text to be displayed is surrounded by tags indicating the details of how the text should be formatted. With a dozen basic tags and a dozen attributes to go with them, we were able to create an interesting and attractive Web page.

In learning HTML, we have seen specifically how a Web page is encoded and understood its physical form. Though HTML has more exotic features than those presented here and the other Web languages strive for even greater sophistication, they are all variations on the same theme: Tags surround all objects that appear on the page, the context is set by specifying global properties of the page (e.g., `<body bgcolor="white">`), and each individual feature of the format is specified locally (e.g., `<i>Isn't it?!</i>`). It's so easy, even a computer could do it!

Indeed, that's what happens most of the time. Web authors most often do not write HTML directly, but rather use Web authoring tools, such as Macromedia Dreamweaver, or standard text editors like Microsoft Word, or the Composer feature of Netscape. They construct the page as it should look on the screen using a WYSIWYG Web authoring program, and then the computer generates the HTML. And in this application we see another instance of the logical/physical separation provided by software. The screen image, the logical form, is the version that the designer manipulates, whereas the HTML, the physical form, is generated by the tool for computer manipulation. Web authoring tools, in the same fashion as the DNS, separate us from the physical form by translating from the logical to the physical. It's a powerful idea.

Paradoxes
Russell's Paradox
The Twentieth Century logician Bertrand Russell introduced a curious paradox: This statement is false. The statement can't be true, because it claims the converse. However, if it is not true, then it's false, just as it says. That makes it true. Paradoxically, it seems to be neither true nor false, or perhaps both true and false.
Magritte's Paradox
The famous French artist Réné Magritte rendered the idea of Russell's Paradox visually in his famous painting Ceci n'est pas une pipe. The title translates from French, This Is Not A Pipe. The painting shows a pipe with the text Ceci n'est pas une pipe below it. Superficially, the painting looks like a true statement, since it is a picture of the pipe, not an actual pipe. However, the assertion is also part of the painting. Thus, within the context of the artwork it seems to embody the paradox.
Ceci n'est pas une pipe.

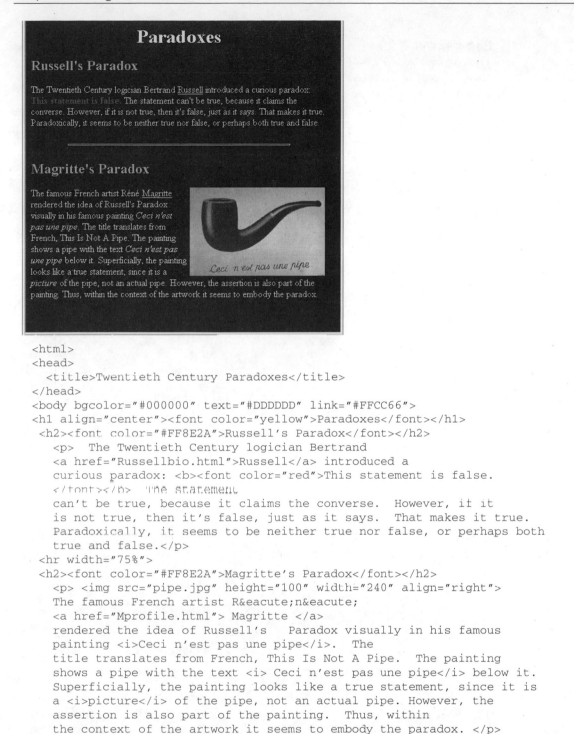

```
<html>
<head>
  <title>Twentieth Century Paradoxes</title>
</head>
<body bgcolor="#000000" text="#DDDDDD" link="#FFCC66">
<h1 align="center"><font color="yellow">Paradoxes</font></h1>
 <h2><font color="#FF8E2A">Russell's Paradox</font></h2>
   <p>  The Twentieth Century logician Bertrand
   <a href="Russellbio.html">Russell</a> introduced a
   curious paradox: <b><font color="red">This statement is false.
   </font></b>  The statement
   can't be true, because it claims the converse.  However, if it
   is not true, then it's false, just as it says.  That makes it true.
   Paradoxically, it seems to be neither true nor false, or perhaps both
   true and false.</p>
 <hr width="75%">
 <h2><font color="#FF8E2A">Magritte's Paradox</font></h2>
   <p> <img src="pipe.jpg" height="100" width="240" align="right">
   The famous French artist R&eacute;n&eacute;
   <a href="Mprofile.html"> Magritte </a>
   rendered the idea of Russell's   Paradox visually in his famous
   painting <i>Ceci n'est pas une pipe</i>.  The
   title translates from French, This Is Not A Pipe.  The painting
   shows a pipe with the text <i> Ceci n'est pas une pipe</i> below it.
   Superficially, the painting looks like a true statement, since it is
   a <i>picture</i> of the pipe, not an actual pipe. However, the
   assertion is also part of the painting.  Thus, within
   the context of the artwork it seems to embody the paradox. </p>
</body>
</html>
```

Figure 4.2. Completed Web page and the corresponding HTML source. (The numerical color specifications are described in Appendix A.)

SUMMARY

The chapter opened with a discussion of the convenience, immediacy, and economy advantages of networked computers. Next the basic types of communication were presented, including point-to-point, multicast, and broadcast, as well as synchronous and asynchronous communication. These were connected to familiar communication situations—telephones are synchronous, point-to-point. There followed an overview of networking, including IP addresses, domains, the postcard analogy for IP packets, wide area versus local area networks, Ethernet and the party protocol, ISPs, and enterprise networks. From there we explained the difference between the Internet and the World Wide Web, terms that are commonly confused. Web pages were explained and the idea of tags for formatting text was recalled. A working set of HTML tags was introduced, followed by an explanation of links and anchors and how they use absolute and relative pathnames. Images and their two formatting schemes—JPG and GIF—were introduced; the placement of images explained. A full example illustrated the ideas of the chapter. Finally, we noted that although HTML is straightforward for us to program, it is most common to build Web pages with Web authoring tools, programs that give a WYSIWYG interface to the author, and then automatically create the HTML when the page design is complete. Expect to use both approaches.

EXERCISES

1. What is the Internet?
2. List three benefits to connecting computers together.
3. Distinguish between synchronous and asynchronous communication.
4. What does "IP" stand for and what is an IP address?
5. What is a domain?
6. What is the proper description of `.com` in networking terminology?
7. What does "DNS" stand for? What does it do?
8. Compare an IP packet to a postcard.
9. Write a page-long message to a relative—say, a parent or a grandparent, whom you have not seen recently. Transfer it to two or more postcards as in Cerf's analogy for IP, and mail them to the relative. This assignment has no Fluency goal; it's simply a thoughtful thing to do!
10. What is the difference between the Ethernet and the Internet in terms of capacity to carry point-to-point communications?
11. What is the World Wide Web?
12. What is hypertext?
13. What is a Web page's source?
14. What four tags are required of all HTML files?
15. What is white space?
16. Why use a primitive text editor to write HTML programs? What format should the file be written in?
17. Create a Web page with an h1 heading and three paragraphs. One paragraph is to be left justified, one centered, and one right justified. Print the page. Next resize the window and notice how the formatting changes and print that result.

CHAPTER 5

Searching for Truth

Learning Objectives

- ♦ Know how to find sources of information.
- ♦ Understand the hierarchical organization of information repositories.
- ♦ Learn how Web search engines work.
- ♦ Learn guidelines for making effective queries.
- ♦ Become effective at forming good queries.
- ♦ Understand the risks of using an information source.
- ♦ Learn to evaluate the authenticity of Web information.

A well-known joke tells of a man out for an evening walk. He meets a drunk who is under a streetlight on his hands and knees. "What are you doing?" asks the man. "Looking for my car key," replies the drunk. "You lost it here?" asks the man in conversation as he begins to help the drunk look. "No, I lost it by the tavern." "Then why are you looking over here?" "The light's better," said the drunk. The principle lampooned in the joke—that the best place to look for something is where it's likely to be found—is crucial when searching for information.

In this chapter we discuss the principles that underlie searching for and evaluating information. The first goal is to explore the principle that to find anything requires looking where it will be found. Historically, libraries have housed well-organized archives, collections, and diverse information resources that are good places to look. Now many of those resources are available in electronic form, motivating an update to the "visit the library" advice: Log in to the library. The second goal is to understand how information is organized for the purposes of searching and to recognize its hierarchical structure as we encounter information sources. Of course, using a computer to perform a search greatly extends our reach, so the next goal is to understand how search engines work, how they organize the information they store, and how to interpret the results of a search. The next objective is to formulate effective searches because asking the right question is a variation of looking in the right place. But finding information and finding truthful, accurate, insightful information are two different things. So, the next goal is to understand what types of deceptive information lurk on the Internet, and how to recognize authoritative sources. Finally, we test our understanding by assessing whether a Web page is true or fictional.

Searching in All the Right Places

Ask a reference librarian where to find a *Scientific American*–type article on black holes and the reply will invariably be "*Scientific American*." Yet, many of us ask such questions because we don't think about where to look for the information we want. Or if we think about it, we're not very rational or insightful about our search strategies. Reference librarians are, and we can emulate them, becoming more effective and independent information gatherers. To do so, we must approach the task of finding information rationally and creatively.

The first step in applying the principle of "look in the right place" is to know the potential "places," that is, to know sources where the information we want may be found. Like *Scientific American*, many sources are obvious and familiar if we think about them:

- To find tax information, the federal (IRS) or state tax offices are a source.
- To locate Liverpool, the Beatles' hometown, from London, consult a map of the United Kingdom.
- To find out how many shares of stock IBM has outstanding, check their annual report.

Many of the questions we want answers to have an obvious source. Of course, we don't have to find paper copies of these documents; they're all online at `irs.gov`, `mapquest.com`, and `ibm.com`, respectively.

One advantage that research librarians have over most of us, however, is that they know about many more information sources than we do. Their advantage can be our advantage when we recognize that libraries remain substantial information resources despite the growth of the Internet. Specifically most college and university libraries and many large public libraries provide access not only to the online catalogue of their own collections, but also to a wide array of other information resources. These libraries are just a "click away" from us all.

For example, the University of Washington's Libraries, `www.lib.washington.edu`, links to the "Top 20 Databases," as shown in the list on the next page, as well as the catalogs for theirs and the Library of Congress' collection. Though many of these resources are commercial databases that UW subscribes to and therefore are restricted to UW students and faculty, your library probably provides you access to similar collections. A quick glance at the resources in that list indicates a wide variety of specialized information that is online-accessible and electronically searchable. Checking these sources is a quick and easy way to get information for the topics these databases cover.

In addition to the catalogs and databases just discussed, the UW Library homepage provides links to Reference Tools. These links are classified into various groups, also listed on the next page.

UW Libraries Catalog

ABI/INFORM global: business and management periodicals

Agricola: articles and book chapters from the National Agriculture Library

Aquatic sciences & fisheries abstracts ASFA: marine/brackish/freshwater biology, commerce, engineering, etc., literature

BIOSIS previews: life sciences literature

Books in print: books from North American publishers

Britannica online: searchable encyclopedia

Current Contents: search ® citations and tables of contents from science, social science, arts, and humanities

Electronic Journals list:

Engineering village 2: Compendex, CRC Press, Patent Office, Techstreet abstracts

ERIC: education citations covering over 750 professional journals

Expanded academic index: indexing and abstracting of 1500 scholarly journals

GeoRef: geology literature, including North America (back to 1785) and elsewhere (back to 1933)

INSPEC: indexes and abstracts, conference proceedings in physical sciences, EE and CS

LEXIS-NEXIS: full-text newspaper and other popular literature archive

MEDLINE: citations and indexes from 3,900 journals in biomedicine

MLA: modern language literature bibliographic information

OCLC WorldCat: world library holdings

PsycINFO: scholarly literature for medicine, psychiatry, nursing, sociology, education, etc.

Research libraries complete: general interest literature from humanities, social science, and science periodicals

Web of science citations database: science citations, and social science citation index, 1980–present

UW Libraries List of Links

Biographical Info	Financial Aid & Grants
Bookstores	Geographic Info
Calculators	Libraries
Career Info	News
Consumer Info	Seattle Info
Dictionaries	Statistical Info
Directories	Telephone Directories
Dissertations	Universities Elsewhere
Educational Info	UW Info
Electronic Journals	Web Tools
Encyclopedias	Writing Guides

A-Z List of Reference Tools

The last entry—the entire list of tools—is an impressive compilation of 223 research resources, including a list of Nobel Prize winners. There are links to the Canadian

Yellow Pages, the *Oxford English Dictionary,* the Catholic Encyclopedia (1917 edition), the Blue Book of Car Prices, a Middle English Dictionary, and the World Flag Database. Many questions of burning interest can be answered by locating the right link on the list and following it.

The point is not that UW's librarians provide a unique resource (though they've done a nice job), but just the opposite. Libraries generally provide a huge array of online facilities that are well organized and authoritative. For example, the Chicago Public Library, `www.chipublib.org`, has similar resources listed on its Virtual Libraries page, and the Library of Congress, `www.loc.gov/library/` has extensive online collections and services for researchers. These resources are free and unrestricted. So, to find out information, go (electronically) to the library.

Finally, it must be emphasized that the online digital library is not yet a substitute for going to the physical library and checking out paper books and journals. Despite the billions of Web pages and the rapid move to digital documents, *most of the valuable information typically found in a library is not online*. Most of mankind's pre-1985 knowledge is not yet digitized. Further, in some cases where paper documents have been digitized, the online version is incomplete; missing footnotes, references, and appendices; and often having unreadable equations. So, the best place to begin tracking down information is to look at the online library, but don't be surprised if the information you need is not yet digital.

THE HIERARCHY

To assist us in finding information, librarians, archivists, Web-page designers, and others who organize documents and files impose a structure on them. The structure is created by classifying all of the information into a few separate groups based on broad, inclusive categories. We are familiar with this approach from guessing games such as 20 Questions. The terms are best when they describe natural classifications that are familiar to the searcher. When searchers pick the term most descriptive of the kind of information they seek, they focus attention on the relevant part of the collection and eliminate large portions of the rest of it from further consideration. Of course, the information in each group is also classified into subgroups in the same way using broad terms that are descriptive of information of that type. And so on, until the groups are small enough that the searcher can realistically look through the whole group if necessary.

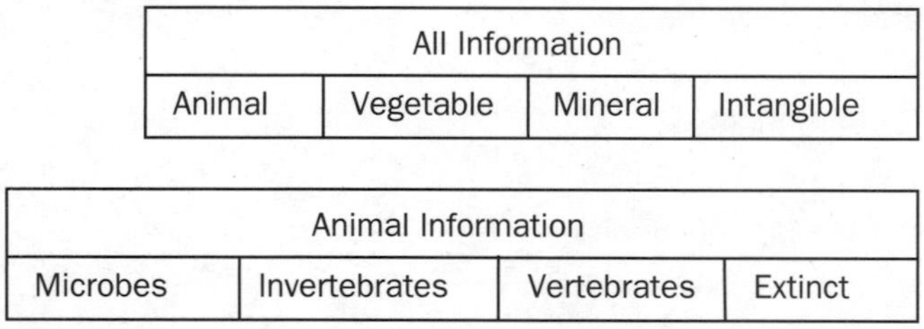

All Information			
Animal	Vegetable	Mineral	Intangible

Animal Information			
Microbes	Invertebrates	Vertebrates	Extinct

Table 5.1. The biological classification of human beings, *Homo sapiens.*

Taxonomic Level	Name of Classification
Kingdom	*Animalia*
Phylum	*Chordata*
Subphylum	*Vertebrata*
Class	*Mammalia*
Order	*Primates*
Family	*Hominoidea*
Genus	*Homo*
Species	*Sapiens*

Such an index structure is called a *hierarchy,* and as we shall see in a moment, it is commonly abstracted as a tree. The most famous instance of such a classificational hierarchy is the so-called tree of life, the biological taxonomy of organisms. It is too large to display as a stylized tree, but Table 5.1 shows the layers of classification for human beings, from the first (highest) classification—kingdom—to the last (lowest)—species. Hierarchies are a rational way to organize information, so we find them everywhere. Further, they are an intuitive way to organize information, so we don't often consciously notice them. Our goal for the remainder of this section is to recognize hierarchies when we see them. Being aware of the hierarchical structure can speed our discovery of information.

For example, consider the National Public Radio Web site, `www.npr.org` shown in Figure 5.1. We might visit this site to find audio information about the current news. Its structure, typical of many homepages, applies hierarchical organization repeatedly, but that structure is sometimes apparent, and sometimes not.

Looking at the NPR Programming pull-down menu (Figure 5.2), we find a list of all of National Public Radio's programs. From the scroll bar on the right we infer that we are not seeing all of the entries, and judging from the size of the slider, the visible portion represents only about 20% of the whole list. The first item (highlighted) is the entire (alphabetized) list of NPR Programs, but after that we notice category terms—Most Requested, NPR News—set off by horizontal lines. Below these are the NPR programs in that category. What we are looking at is a one-level hierarchy of NPR's programming. They have chosen five categories into which to divide their programs:

- Most Requested
- NPR News
- Talk
- Music
- Additional Programming

Figure 5.3 shows the hierarchy drawn as a tree. The tree is drawn on its side with the "root" to the left and the "leaves" to the right. Hierarchy trees are often drawn sideways in English because it's more convenient to write text that way. Alternatively, they are drawn upside down, with the root at the top. Either way the important part is not the orientation, but the branching metaphor.

Hierarchies are so widespread that it is not surprising that there is a series of conventions regarding their design and terminology:

- The convention of drawing hierarchy trees with the root at the top motivates the common phrases like "going up in the hierarchy" and "down in the hierarchy." Such directional terms are relative to the root being drawn at the top. Thus "going up" means the classifications become more inclusive, whereas "going down" means they become more specific or restrictive.
- The greater-than symbol is a suggestive and commonly seen notation for going down in a hierarchy through levels of classification:

  Classification 1 > Classification 2 > . . . > Classification *n*

- We call NPR's Programming menu a one-level hierarchy because there is only one level of "branching." Counting levels of a hierarchy can be a little confusing sometimes with all of the lines, but it is easy if we keep two points in mind. First, any collection will have a root—its name. Second, any collection will have leaves—the things themselves. Because they exist without any hierarchy, the root and leaves must not count as levels of the hierarchy. When we eliminate the root and leaves from Figure 5.3, the result is the one level of classification.

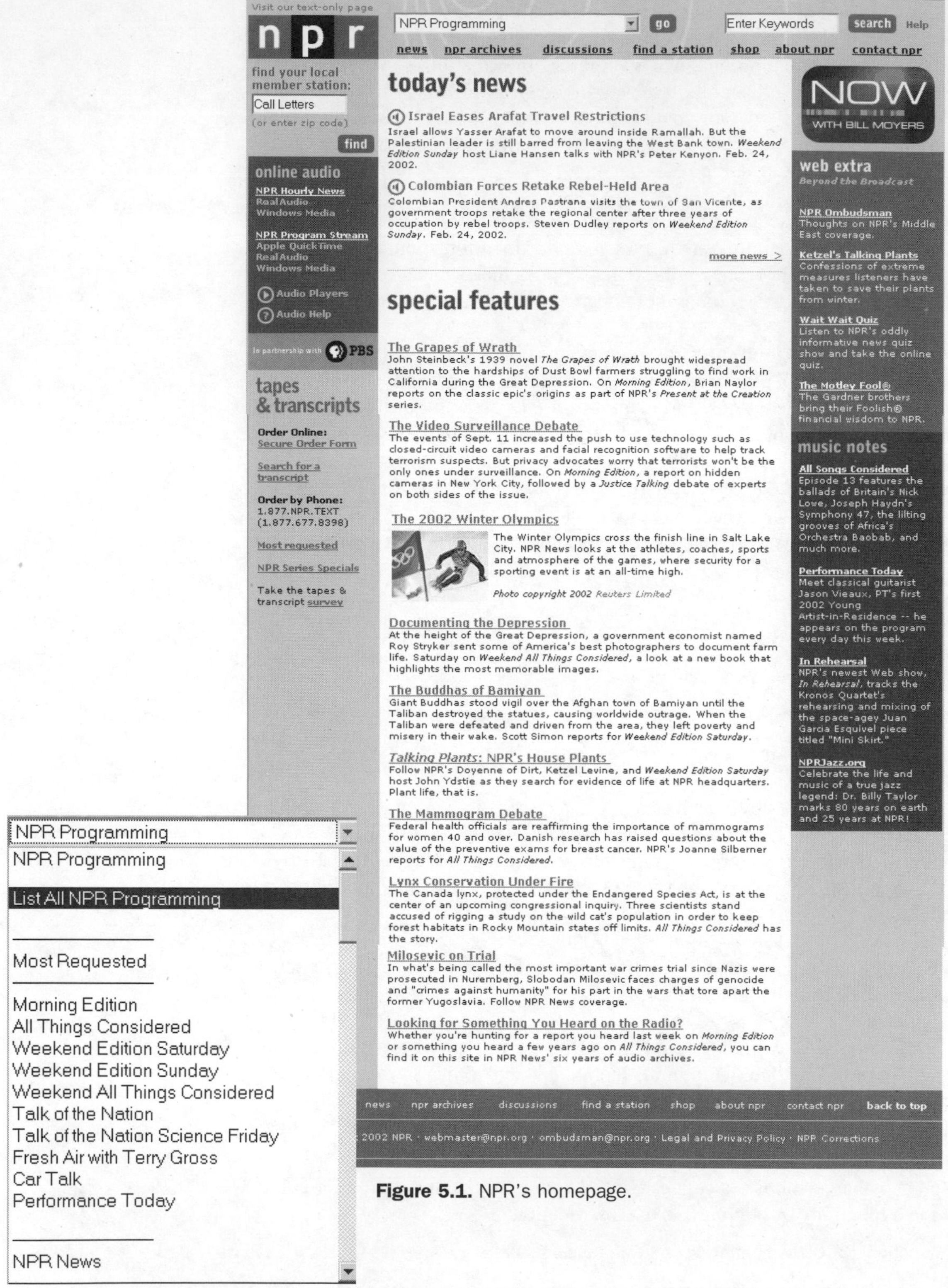

Figure 5.1. NPR's homepage.

Figure 5.2. The start of the NPR Programming pull-down menu.

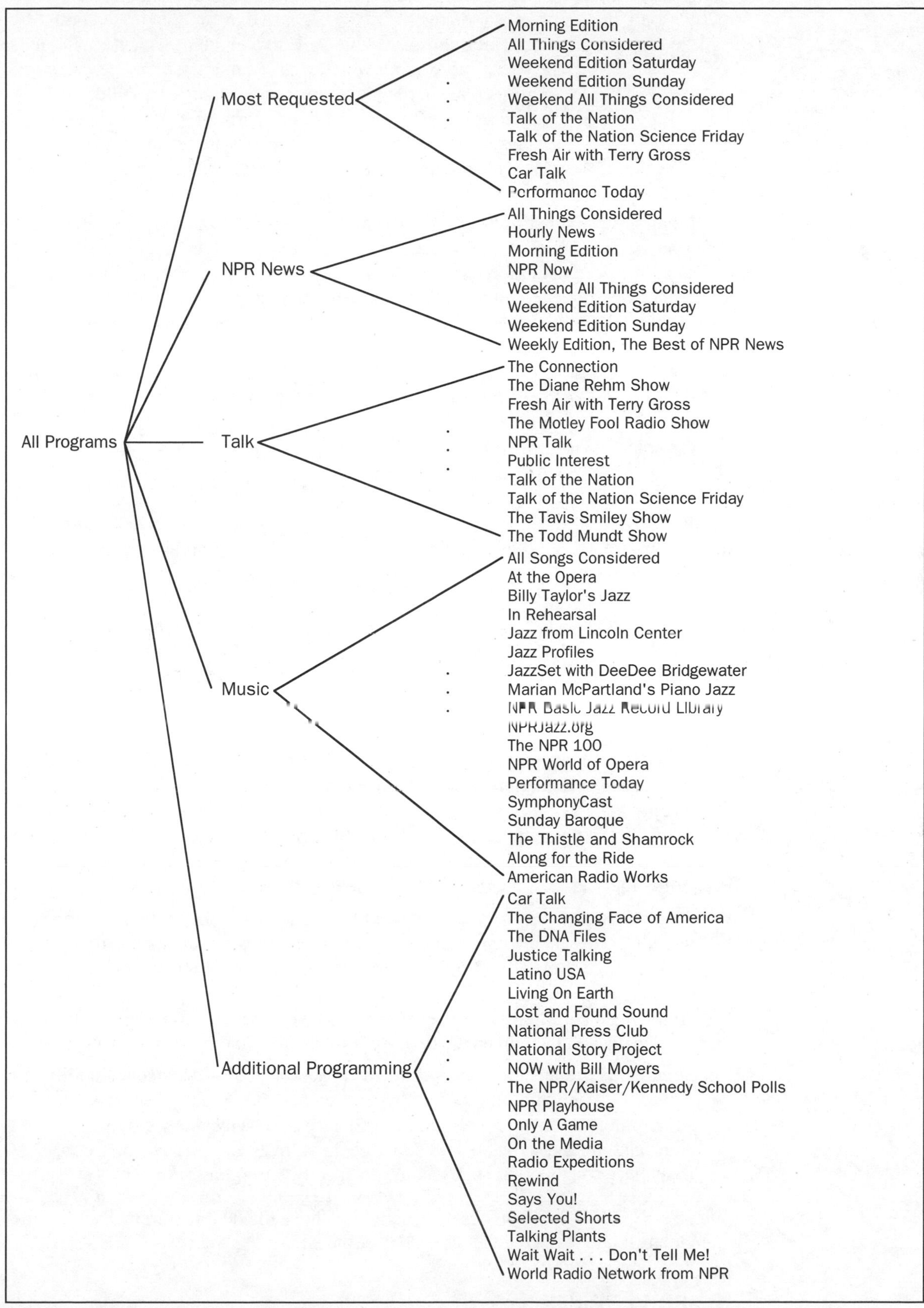

Figure 5.3. Hierarchy tree for NPR Programming; lines have been removed to reduce clutter.

- Notice that in the NPR menu example, the programs listed are not unique. That is, some programs appear on the list twice because they are mentioned both in the Most Requested, and then are also in their own category such as News, for example, All Things Considered. When every leaf appears once in the hierarchy, the groupings are called *partitionings*. The tree of life is a partitioning because every species is listed once. When the leaves are repeated, groupings "overlap," meaning that an item can be reached by selecting more than one category. There is no "proper" way to classify information.

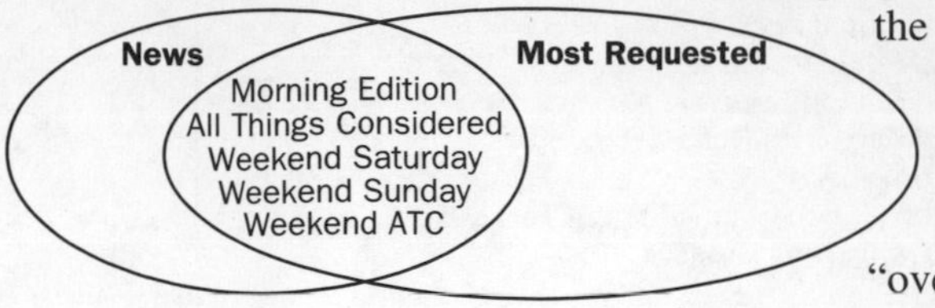

News
Most Requested
Morning Edition
All Things Considered
Weekend Saturday
Weekend Sunday
Weekend ATC

- Finally, the number of layers of a hierarchy need not be the same for all leaves. That is, the number of classifications between a leaf and its root need not be the same for every leaf. Some groupings might require more levels of division to reduce the group to a manageable size. For example, we could imagine further dividing the Music category of Figure 5.3 into, say, three groups: Jazz, Classical, and Other. Then the music programs would be reached by two levels of classification, whereas other programs would be reached by only one. A program like Performance Today can be reached by two different paths—a single level through Most Requested, or a double level through Music > Classical. When asked how many levels there are in a hierarchy, the expected answer when levels vary is the maximum.

So, the NPR Web page designers have applied hierarchy to assist us in finding our favorite programs. But they and other Web designers use hierarchy in a more fundamental way.

The NPR homepage itself can be seen as the top-level classification for the whole NPR Web site. That is, all of the information that the NPR site can present to us must be organized for our successful navigation, not just the Web pages for the individual programs. So, when we look at the NPR page, we should notice how the information is organized. The page has three basic kinds of information:

- *Classifications* are the roots of hierarchies that organize large volumes of similar types of information. Examples include the row of links listing News, NPR Archives, Discussions, Find a Station, Shop, and About NPR. Contact Us is in this list of Classifications, but it is really a Single Link. Notice that these Classifications are also listed at the bottom of the page, and some are available from other places, for example, more news > links to News.
- *Topic Clusters* refers to a set of related links on a particular theme. Examples include Today's News, which shows two of about twenty items listed on another page (News), and Special Features, which highlights features from other NPR programming. They are not there for navigational purposes, but for "immediate consumption." They are available elsewhere at the site, but have been placed on the homepage to make it interesting and immediately useful.
- *Single Links* connect to very specialized pages, such as downloads of audio player software, order forms for buying merchandise, and the hourly news stream. Single Links provide specialized access to pages that are either "unusual" for the sight, such as software downloads and surveys, or are frequently sought after, such as links to specific programs or the news stream.

Such a structure is common because many sites have the dual requirements of immediate interest and access to the remainder of the site.

SEARCH ENGINES

A *search engine* is a collection of computer programs designed to assist users in finding information on the World Wide Web. Though programs for text searching existed long before the WWW, the explosion of Web-based digital information and its distribution across the planet necessitated the invention of search engines. No one organizes the information posted on the WWW, so it is necessary for programs to look around to find out what's out there and to impose a structure on it. It's a big task. What do search engines do?

A search engine is composed of two basic parts: A *crawler* and a *query processor*. The crawler visits sites on the Internet, discovering Web pages and building an *index* to the Web's content. The query processor looks up user-submitted keywords in the index and reports back which Web pages the crawler has found to be associated with those words. Popular search engines include Alta Vista, Excite, InfoSeek, Google, and Yahoo! We will use the Google search engine as our example here.

When the crawler visits a Web page, its first action is to identify all the links to other Web pages on that page. It checks in its records to see if it has visited those other pages recently, and if not, it adds them to its "To Do" list of pages that must be crawled. Thus crawlers find the pages to look at by noting the links in the pages they've already seen. (Google also allows Web page authors to submit their pages to be crawled.)

> **Shortsightedness**. Search engines crawl only a fraction (substantially less than half) of the Web because it is growing so fast that there are always new pages not yet visited. Also, if no page points to a given page, it never gets on a search engine's To Do list. And many pages are behind "firewalls," barriers requiring authorization such as passwords that search engines can't cross.

Another action the crawler does is to record in an index the keywords used on a page. The words can appear in either the title or the body of the page. For example, the HTML homepage for the Hot Dang! Thai restaurant (`www.hotdang.com`) might have the title tag

```
<title> Hot Dang! Restaurant, Cuisine of Siam </title>
```

so, in the index, the crawler would associate the keywords "hot," "dang," "restaurant," "cuisine," and "siam" with the `www.hotdang.com` URL. Small, unspecific words like "of" are ignored. Crawlers also ignore case.

Google pioneered the idea of including keywords from the *anchor* (that highlighted text associated with a link) in the index also. That is, the words of the highlighted text of a link *pointing to a page* are included among the descriptive terms for the target page. For example, if your Web page referenced the Hot Dang! Restaurant with the text

```
...my favorite <a href="http://www.hotdang.com"> Thai restaurants </a>...
```

Thai restaurants would be the highlighted anchor and the terms "Thai" and "restaurants" would be included by Google as keywords associated with `www.hotdang.com`. Anchors improve a search engine's effectiveness at finding relevant pages because they are often more descriptive of the page than the page's own content. For example, the Hot Dang! restaurant's motto is "Cuisine of Siam" so the page may not actually say that it's a Thai restaurant. But your anchor does.

The query processor of a search engine receives keywords from a user and looks them up in the index to find the URLs of pages associated with those keywords. So, for example, when a user asks for "Thai restaurants," all of the URLs associated with those words will be reported back. If Google had crawled your page, the query processor will return `www.hotdang.com` among its responses to the "Thai restaurants" query because your anchor connected "Thai" and "restaurants" with the Hot Dang! site.

Notice that in this case the Google crawler might not have crawled the Hot Dang! restaurant's site yet, that is, it is still on the To Do list. Nevertheless, it will know that the site is somehow connected with the terms "Thai" and "restaurants" based on the anchor from your page. If Google had crawled the Hot Dang! site, the query processor would also return `www.hotdang.com` among the responses to the "Thai cuisine" query because "Thai" is in your anchor and "cuisine" is in the restaurant's title.

It is important to give the query processor the right terms to look up so that it finds the intended information. In the next sections, we will explain how to formulate good queries. But even assuming that the query specifies exactly the right terms, there could be hundreds or thousands of relevant URLs, or "hits." For example, suppose someone in your hometown of Dallas queries "Thai restaurants in Dallas Texas." There could be a huge list of hits, including (presumably) the homepages for all Thai restaurants, but also your homepage because it uses those words, too. But your page has nothing to do with Thai restaurants, except for your comment of liking Hot Dang! If the search engine just returns an unordered list of all hits, the user would have to click through the whole list looking at pages that could be completely irrelevant. We need more help from the search engine!

Google pioneered another concept called the PageRank that enables it to order the hits by their importance to the user. (Of course, it cannot have any clue, really, as to what you are looking for.) PageRank is Google's guess as to how important a page is. It computes the PageRank by noting that if many pages link to a page, it must be a more important page than one that fewer sites reference. As the Google inventors describe it, if page A links to page B, consider the link as a vote by A for B. So, for example, because your page links to `www.hotdang.com`, it "votes" for the restaurant. If many sites vote, it must be of greater interest, so the search engine lists the pages with higher PageRank first. Google also takes into account whether the page "voting" is itself highly ranked. For example, if a restaurant reviewer has a page that many people link to, and the reviewer's page links to Hot Dang! Google treats that link as a more significant vote than yours, assuming fewer pages link to your homepage. Thus Google would probably list `www.hotdang.com` before your page in the list of hits resulting from the query. Page ranking is highly successful in identifying the pages of greater interest, but, of course, fame isn't everything.

> **Yea or Nay, It's Still a Vote.** PageRank's concept of one page voting for another exactly captures the purpose of citing Hot Dang! as a favorite Thai restaurant. But, if the citation had been a complaint about food poisoning with the purpose of discouraging others from going, Google would still count it as a vote for the restaurant's page.

ASK THE RIGHT QUESTION

Perhaps the best advice to someone looking for information is "Ask the right question." The question of interest is our request to a search engine, "What pages are associated with the following terms . . .?" Getting the right answer back requires that we know how the search engine will use the terms and thoughtful consideration of the choice of terms. In this section, we consider how to make effective queries based on universal searching principles. All searching facilities have slight syntactic variations.

> **Peculiarities.** Most search facilities explain their rules in a link near the search window called "Advanced" or "Hints" or some similar term. Start with the "usual" syntax of this section, but if the results are unsatisfactory, check for differences.

The first point to understand is that text-searching facilities generally consider each word separately. Though most English speakers interpret "Thai restaurants" as a single noun phrase, most search facilities consider it as two independent words. We can ask the search facility to look for the exact phrase by placing quotation marks around it, as in

```
"Thai restaurants"
```

which has the effect of binding the words together.

But, the problem with using the exact-phrase quotes is that the match must be perfect, ignoring spaces and case. Exact matching causes information in other forms to be missed. So, among the text occurrences that would *not* match are

```
Thai restaurant
restaurants featuring Thai cuisine
Thai and Asian restaurants
```

and others, though these are probably of interest to anyone querying on "Thai restaurants." The problem is that an exact match is too stringent of a requirement for a comprehensive search. It is for this reason that search facilities treat the words as separate and allow them to occur anywhere. It is best to limit the use of exact match quotes to phrases like titles,

```
"Crime and Punishment"
```

where the form is agreed upon and consistent. Notice that quoting part of a phrase, say "Tale of Two Cities" is a safe solution when we cannot remember whether it's "The Tale of Two Cities" or "A Tale of Two Cities."

Thus the words are treated independently, which immediately raises the question of whether the search should pick pages with both of the words "Thai" and "restaurants" (the intention) or pages with just one of them? If it's just one of the words, pages referring to "Thai vacations" and pages referring to "steak restaurants" would also be hits. Intending both, but asking for either results in an enormous number of irrelevant hits.

To control how the query processor interprets our requests, we are explicit about how the words should be processed. This is possible using *logical operators* to specify what we mean. The three logical operators used in searching are AND, OR, and NOT, and as a common rule they are written using all capital letters to distinguish them from the keywords. Recall that search facilities usually ignore case, so there is no need to capitalize any keywords. Capitalizing the connectives makes them stand out. AND and OR are the most commonly used logical operators in searching, and they are *infix operators*, meaning that they are placed between keywords. AND means *both*. OR means *either or both*. So, for example, the phrase

```
Thai AND restaurants
```

finds pages with both words appearing in any position; that is, they may not be together in the given order. The query

```
Thai OR Siam
```

finds pages with either word, including pages where they both appear. Of course, we could write expressions that include both operators, but we risk ambiguity. For example, does

```
Thai OR Siam AND restaurants
```

mean either a page containing the words *Thai* and *restaurants* or *Siam* and *restaurants* or a page containing either the word *Thai* or the two words *Siam* and *restaurants.* The former is what we intend. The latter would hit on pages about "Thai vacations." Because the query is ambiguous, there is no way of guessing how the search facility will interpret it. Therefore, we include parentheses as we do when we write algebra formulas. Specially,

```
(Thai OR Siam) AND restaurants
```

achieves the desired goal of looking for pages that must have *restaurants* and also either *Thai* or *Siam.*

We can use NOT to exclude pages with the given word. NOT is a prefix operator, meaning that it precedes the word to be excluded. So, to exclude from the Thai restaurant search any page connected with the word *review,* we would write

```
Thai AND restaurants AND NOT review
```

Notice that the AND is required to indicate that three conditions must be met: matching *Thai,* matching *restaurants,* not matching *review.* Most often, NOT is used to restrict a search when we recognize a pattern of unintended interpretations.

So far, we have assumed the simplest case where the search facility offers only a single window for expressing the query. The Google Advanced Search page (recommended) provides multiple windows to simplify expressing the logical relationships among the search words of a query. Figure 5.4 shows the GUI of the Advanced Search and each of the windows. There are separate windows for AND words, exact phrases, OR words, and NOT words. In this case, Google saves us from having to type the logical operators.[1] All we need to do is list the search words, separated by blanks, in the appropriate window. Notice that if more than one window is filled in, the page must fulfill the requirements of all windows together.

Mispellings. Correct spelling is obviously essential to effective searching. Search engines typically spell-check submitted terms, and either use the correct spelling when it's obvious—e.g., Mandela for Mandella—or ask if you intend another word. But it cannot guess you've erred if you mistype producing a legal word, for example, trail for trial. It pays to be careful.

Getting Close

To be effective at searching, pick meaningful and specific keywords. Choosing the right words is sometimes trivial, as when you're looking for data on ibuprofen, because the term is so unique it has few alternative uses. At other times, choosing the right words is very difficult, as when you're looking for information on the fuel efficiency of new cars because the obvious terms—gas mileage, cars—are extremely common. In any event, thinking for a few moments about a search strategy to pinpoint the desired information repays the effort manyfold.

[1] Though most of the searches illustrated in this book use Google, queries will always be written using the logical operators.

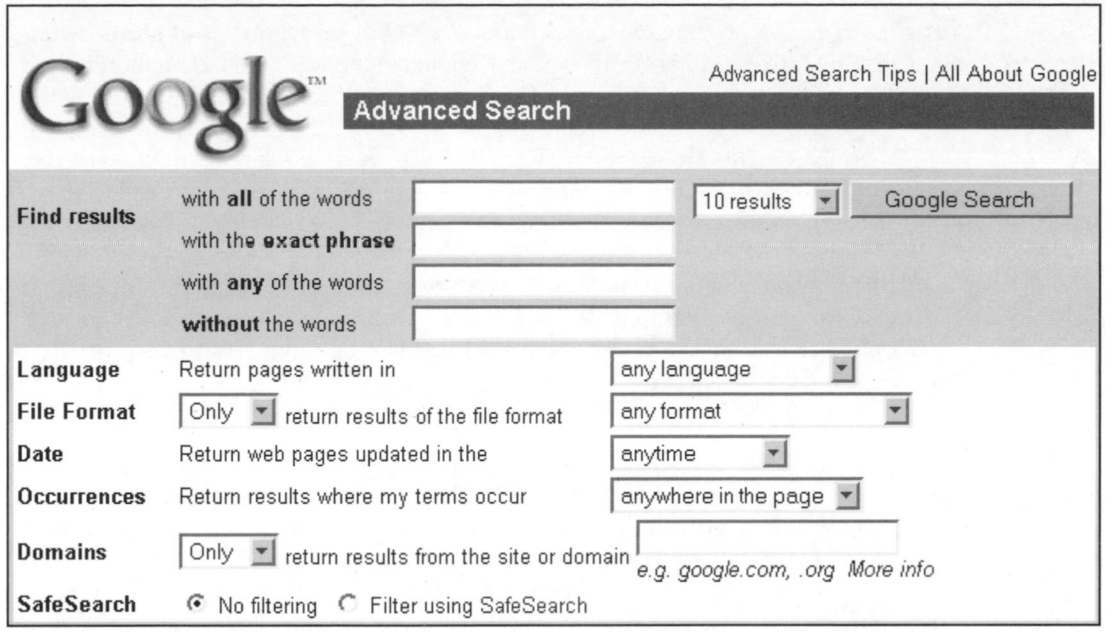

Figure 5.4. Google advanced search GUI.

A recommended process for formulating a search is as follows:

1. *Be clear about what sort of page you seek.* Ask yourself whether you want a source page from a company or organization, for example, the Hot Dang! restaurant, or whether you want a reference page that points to a collection of similar pages, for example, the restaurant reviewer's page, or perhaps a resource page that compiles information related to the topic, for example, a guide to Thai spices. Thinking clearly about the kind of page sought helps to direct the search toward that page.
2. *Postulate the type of organization that might publish the page you seek.* Is the information likely to come from a company, a government agency, an educational institution, some specialized organization, or a source in another country? This could enable you to figure out a direct address for the site, and avoid the search all together. If it's possible to guess a likely URL, for example, `www.hotdang.com`, then try it! The advantage of predicting the kind of organization is that even without guessing the URL, it is possible to limit the search by the domain suffix, that is, the "dot com" part of a domain name. (See Figure 5.4.)
3. *Formulate a list of specific terms that must appear on the pages you seek.* The goal is to find a combination of words that will appear on the desired pages, but appear on the fewest number of other pages. Certainly, you must include words that describe the category, for example, *Thai* and *restaurant.* But there can be many thousands of pages containing the category words, including your own homepage! So, AND-in, that is, include, limiting words such as

   - Location specific words such as *Dallas* AND *Texas*
   - Time-specific words such as *Monday* because businesses often give the times they're open
   - Activity specific words such as *entrées*
   - Specialty terms such as *phad* because every Thai restaurant probably serves Phad Thai

   The pages we seek have many specific properties, each with their characteristic terms. With some thought, we can think up those terms.

4. *Assess the results.* Before looking at each returned page, check the results to determine how effective the search was. Be alert for two types of errors: being too inclusive and not being inclusive enough. One way to be too inclusive is to have a consistent type of match that wasn't anticipated. For example, all the pages discussing vacationing in Thailand probably describe the restaurants because tourists are interested. Requerying with a NOT keyword, for example, `NOT vacation`, can eliminate these. The other error, not being inclusive enough, is somewhat more subtle to recognize. For example, by requiring "Monday" in a search, we might have eliminated all of the restaurants that post their business hours, "Tuesday–Sunday" because they're closed on Monday. So, we must be alert to what we are not finding among the pages and consider whether some of the keywords that we've required should be dropped in another query.

5. *Consider a two-pass strategy.* Because of the difficulty of getting the search terms just right, it is probably best when using the Google search engine to employ a "two-pass" strategy, in which a broad topic search is performed first followed by (one or more) search-within-results queries to pinpoint the desired page. Google provides the ability to further limit the hits already found through additional keywords. (See Figure 5.5.) This search-within-results capability allows us to capture the pages within the category and then try various ways of limiting the search until we find what we are looking for. If we overly limit the search, we simply Back out to the point where the current list of hits is still inclusive enough. Notice that the terms in the search-within-results window are further AND terms; that is, they are required on the page. However, we can force the absence of a term, say, vacation, by writing a minus sign before it like this: –vacation.

Finding the Needle: Narrowing the search to the right page is the primary task, but finding the actual information can require further searching within the page. Remember that browsers have a word-search facility, Find, under the Edit menu. To search within a page, use Find.

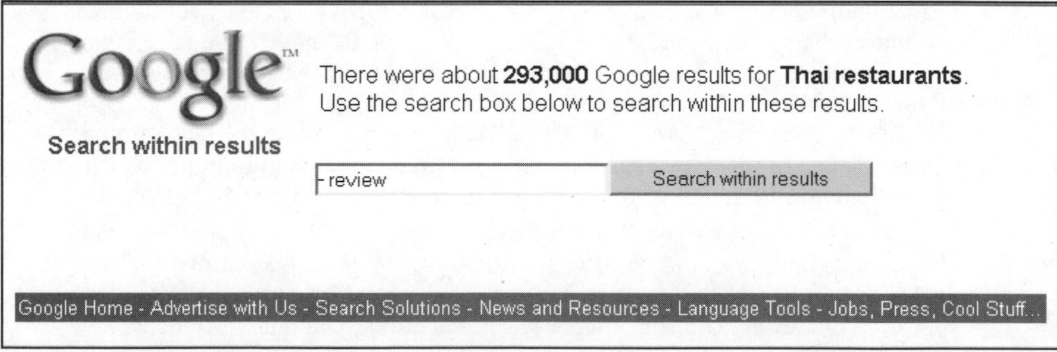

Figure 5.5. Restricting the Thai restaurants by eliminating any page containing *review.*

Using the principles just outlined, imagine that you plan to go windsurfing and need a sailboard. You are thinking of going to Hood River, Oregon, where the Hood joins the Columbia, a famous windsurfing area. You're flying, so you will need to rent equipment when you arrive. Your queries yield

sailboards	9180 hits
sailboards AND oregon	342 hits
sailboards AND oregon AND "hood river"	151 hits
sailboards AND oregon AND "hood river" AND rental	23 hits

which generally include the shops and tourist facilities pages you are seeking.

In summary, successful searches result from well-thought-out queries based on specific terms. It is wiser to spend time formulating precise queries, possibly querying several times or searching through results to pinpoint the few pages of interest, than it is to check many potentially worthless pages resulting from unspecific searches.

TRUTH OR FICTION?

In Chapter 1 we noted that an increased exercise of freedom of speech is a fundamental change wrought by the World Wide Web. It is possible in most countries of the world to publish anything on the WWW, unmediated by companies or governments. This was claimed to be a benefit, and it surely is. But, like all freedoms, this one carries with it some important responsibilities—not so much for the speaker in this case, but for the reader or listener. Because anyone can publish anything on the World Wide Web, it is possible, in fact likely, to encounter false, misleading, deceptive, self-serving, slanderous, or simply disgusting content. It is essential that we be continually vigilant and always ask, "*Is this page legitimate, true, and correct?*" In this section we consider whether the pages we've found in our search are legitimate, true, and correct.

The first evidence that a Web page is legitimate or authoritative is the organization that publishes it. We believe that health information from the Centers for Disease Control, the World Health Organization, or the American Medical Association is the best that can be found. These respected organizations seek to publish current and correct information, so it is reasonable to trust their pages. Of course, much of the information they publish is based on science, and over time new discoveries might occasionally invalidate something, implying that it wasn't true. But, worrying about such problems begs a pointless philosophical discussion about the *nature of truth*. It can be assumed that respected organizations publish the best information available. We're unlikely to find better

Checking the organization that publishes the information seems like overkill. After all, if the Web site's domain name is `ama-assn.org`, it claims to be the AMA page, and it's giving out medical information, it must be the American Medical Association, right? In fact, it is. But, just because a page purports to be from a certain organization and the URL *seems* plausible, it isn't necessarily true. Domain names are not checked. Anyone could have reserved the domain name `ama-assn.org` and publish bogus health information. You must be wary.

To emphasize that sites are not always what they appear to be, consider the hoax perpetrated from the site `www.gatt.org`. The URL looks like it is related to the General Agreement on Tariffs and Trade, or GATT as it's known, the free-trade agreement of the 1990s. The site looks like the official publication of the World Trade Organization (WTO), the free-trade group that followed on from the GATT treaty. The page shows photographs of Michael Moore, WTO President, quotes him, and posts WTO-related news. However, the site is actually run by an anti-free-trade organization known as the Yes Men. As retold in the January 7, 2001, *New York Times*, organizers of a meeting of international trade lawyers in Salzburg, Austria, sent mail to `www.gatt.org` inviting WTO President Moore to speak at their meeting. From `www.gatt.org` came an email reply declining on behalf of Mr. Moore, but offering (a fictitious) speaker, Dr. Andreas Bichlbauer, as a substitute. The meeting organizers accepted Dr. Bichlbauer who came to their October 2000 meeting and gave a very offensive speech critical of Italians and Americans. The perpetrators of the hoax even claimed that a WTO protestor threw a crème pie at Dr. Bichlbauer. They further perpetuated the deception by claiming that the pie had contained a *bacillus,* Bichlbauer had taken ill and been hospitalized, and ultimately died.

The whole hoax, which was a considerable embarrassment, began when someone assumed that `www.gatt.org` was a legitimate WTO site.

How can one find out if a site is legitimate? A two-step process can help:

1. The InterNIC site `www.internic.net/whois.html` lists what company assigned the IP address (i.e. domain). Type in the domain name, such as `company.com`. Included in the returned InterNIC information about the domain is a site called a `WhoIs Server` maintained by the company that assigned the address. That site will give the identity of the domain's owner.
2. Go to the `WhoIs Server` site and type in the domain name or IP address again. The information returned is the owner's name and physical address.

When checking a Web site, remember to pull the IP address out of the URL.

Elaborate deceptions like the `gatt.org` hoax are rare, though there have been others. Most people don't have the money, time, or motivation to be so deceptive. A more likely situation is that information found on the Web is unintentionally wrong or simply fictional. In the first category is information such as "urban legends"—stories like alligators living in the New York City sewer system—that people pass along as true, although they don't have primary evidence or an authoritative basis for believing it. They heard it through a friend of a friend. Urban myths are harmless, but other hearsay information, e.g., "my neighbor's recipe for homemade bubblegum," may not be. In the second category, fictional Web sites, the purpose of the site is to entertain. April Fools' Day pages, alien spaceships visiting Seattle's Space Needle, and reports of one-ton squirrels fall into this category. They are fun. Every year National Public Radio, for example, broadcasts a fictitious news story on the program "All Things Considered." It is best to approach Web pages with a healthy amount of skepticism.

What cues can alert a reader to misinformation? In a recent survey, Internet users thought that the believability of a site was enhanced by features such as

- **Physical Existence.** The site provided a street address, phone, and legal email address.
- **Expertise.** The site's authors listed references, citations, or credentials, and there were links to related sites.
- **Clarity.** The site was well organized, easy to use, and provided site searching facilities.
- **Currency.** The site had been recently updated.
- **Professionalism.** The site's grammar, spelling, punctuation, and so forth, were correct; all links worked.

Certainly, sites that fail on any of these criteria should be scrutinized closely, but having these characteristics does not guarantee that the site is legitimate. No such definitive list can exist because a site trying to be deceptive can take care to appear to have these features. If you have doubts, check it out. If the site gives a street address, look it up using `mapquest.com`; if it doesn't exist, maybe you should be more suspicious. If it's a business, can you find the business in the online phone directory or yellow pages? If the author gives credentials, citations, or other links, check them out, too. By verifying, you can have the confidence that the information you are getting is the best possible.

Finally, if the information has any importance to you, do not take a single source's word for it. Find other sources that confirm or support the information. After all, it is very easy to use the Internet to find information, so it's equally easy to use it to confirm information. Ask yourself, if this information were true, what other source could directly or indirectly confirm it? Verifying is like solving a mystery given a good clue, making it fun to track down. But, we must be thoughtful about what information we accept as supporting the topic. For example, we cannot count the number of sites referencing information as proof that it's true because by that reasoning the alligators in the sewer urban legend would seem to be supported by the 2050 hits on `alligator AND sewer`. A better approach is to find sites that speak directly to the topic, such as `urbanlegends.about.com/science/urbanlegends/mbody.htm`.

Burmese Mountain Dog Page

To test our ability to assess a site, suppose we have found `lme.mnsu.edu/akcj3/bmd.html`, a site describing the Burmese Mountain Dog of Burma. (See Figure 5.6.) The page is authoritative looking. It has been posted by someone claiming DVM credentials, probably meaning Doctor of Veterinary Medicine. There are photographs, links to the American Kennel Club, and so on. The page seems completely legitimate and meets most of the criteria the Internet users have listed as indicating authenticity. If we ask Google to find `Burmese AND mountain AND dog`, we get 2350 hits. Many people would probably accept the page as truthful.

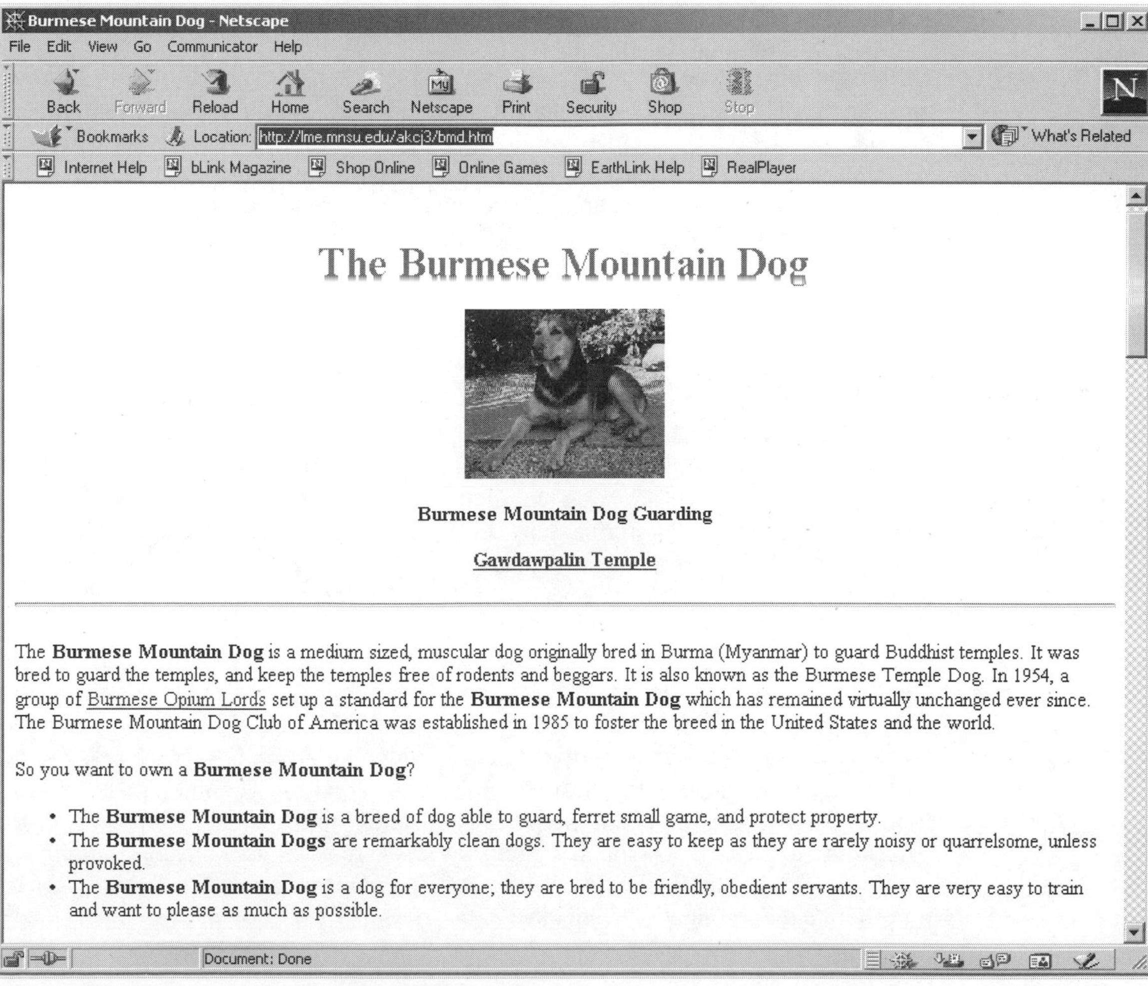

Figure 5.6. Web page for the Burmese Mountain Dog.

Because the page has a link to the American Kennel Club, `akc.org`, which lists all breeds the Club recognizes, it's possible to check out the Burmese Mountain Dog. In the AKC's list of breeds, we find that there is no Burmese Mountain Dog, though there is a Bernese Mountain Dog, named for Berne, Switzerland. What gives? First, we ask if `akc.org` is legitimately using the InterNIC WhoIs service, and find it is. Next, we check `lme.mnsu.edu` and find it is the Library Media Education department of Mankato State University in Minnesota. This is somewhat of a surprise. A university is usually a reliable place to get information, but we would expect it to come not from Library Media, but perhaps, from the Department of Veterinary Medicine. Accepting that the AKC is giving correct information about the Bernese Mountain Dog, we conclude that either the Burmese page is a fake or the Burmese Mountain Dog is not yet a recognized breed.

One curiosity is that there are so many hits on Burmese Mountain Dog, but when we ask Google to look up `bernese AND mountain AND dog` we get 17,800 hits, so the Burmese is less popular. When we look at the two dogs, we notice that they look very similar. The main difference is that the Bernese has a white chest, while the Burnese has a dark chest with a brown V. Such a striking similarity suggests that someone has made a comparison, so we check for pages citing both. Checking `bernese AND burmese AND mountain AND dog` yields only 175 hits. A phrase displayed by Google,

> It's Bernese, Burmese is a cat

suggests two points: Many of these pages must be listing both cats and dogs, and there *is* a Burmese cat. (Removing cat (`-cat`) yields only 35 hits.) The other possibility is people may be mispronouncing or misspelling Bernese as Burmese. A quick look at several of the pages validates this guess. Some personal pages show a photo of what the AKC calls a Bernese Mountain Dog, but they call it a Burmese Mountain Dog. Another page makes a point of saying it's from Berne rather than Burma. So, we conjecture that the original page is fiction, and return to it to admire how authentic it seems.

SUMMARY

The secret to finding the information we're looking for is to look in the right place. Though the Internet is a valuable resource, the first place to look for many types of information is not the Internet, but the library. The online resources at large public and university libraries are extensive. Libraries not only have a high likelihood of providing the needed information in digital form; they also connect us with the archives of "pre-digital" information—the millions of books, journals, and manuscripts that still exist only in paper form. In many situations the best information is accessible only through these paper documents. We can expect to rely heavily on traditional documents for years to come.

Unlike a library where we can enlist the help of a reference librarian, we must rely on software and ourselves to search the Internet effectively. Effective searching requires that we formulate queries using the logical operators of AND, OR, and NOT, and specific terms to pinpoint the information we seek. Once we've found the information, we must assess its authoritativeness and validity to avoid being duped or misled. Checking out the organization that publishes it is essential, including checking the credentials of the "authorities" that have written the information. Finally, we need to corroborate the information from other sources when the information is important.

EXERCISES

1. Where would you find a *National Geographic*–type article on Uruguay?
2. What WWW sites would you consult to find the following information?

   a. How many transistors are there on the Intel Pentium III microchip?
   b. What is the principal headline in today's *New York Times*?
   c. Is the Louvre closed on New Year's Day?
3. Explain how to find out in what year Nelson Mandela won the Nobel Peace Prize.
4. How might you find out whether Winston Churchill was born in the nineteenth or twentieth century?
5. List twenty-five items that can be found in a refrigerator. Classify, that is, find descriptive terms to partition these items into (a) two groups, (b) three groups, (c) four groups, and (d) five groups.
6. Go to the National Public Radio homepage (`www.npr.org`) and follow the top-level link to Archive. On that page selection windows are provided for four types of information. Find and list ten stories that aired on the program *All Things Considered* on your birthday in the year 2000.
7. Analogous to Figure 5.3, sketch how the NPR's Archive is structured as a hierarchy.
8. Compare the BBC homepage (`www.bbc.co.uk`) to NPR's homepage as was done in the text. Specifically, identify Classifications, Topic Clusters, and Single Links.
9. Find the Web page for a college or university of your choice and list the top-level classifications they have chosen for their information, and for each, list the second-level classifications.
10. Formulate a query to rent scuba equipment on the Florida Keys, say, Key West. How many hits does Google get for each term as the terms become more specific?
11. Who owns `npr.org`?
12. Using the research facilities of the Internet, find out notables who share your birthday.

CHAPTER 6

To Search and Research

Learning Objectives

- Understand the advantages and limitations of the WWW for research.
- Learn to find characteristic terms to narrow a search.
- Apply and refine searching methods learned earlier.
- Apply and refine information assessment techniques learned earlier.
- Learn when to use primary and secondary sources.
- Experience the pleasure of curiosity-driven research.

We're all curious, and the IT knowledge we've developed so far is sufficient to track down the answers to questions we wonder about. Usually such questions are just simple factual problems: "Is the Colorado ski area Telluride named after the chemical element Tellurium?" With a few clicks we find the answer, perhaps mention it to a friend, and that's that. The World Wide Web has enabled us to answer the question while it's fresh in our mind without visiting the library. In the past, an insignificant matter like the origin of a ski area's name would probably not have justified the trip. However, now, with the speed and convenience of the WWW, we can easily add to our store of useless facts and amaze our friends.

But information technology embodies a more fundamental opportunity to satisfy our curiosity and fulfill our needs to communicate than indicated by that simple example. It allows us to find out about substantial topics that interest us and probe deeply wherever our curiosity leads us. It's called *curiosity-driven research*. In recent centuries, an educated person who was curious about a topic would consult a book. The advantages of books are that they are generally authoritative, having been carefully researched by the author, usually well written, and permanent. Their disadvantages are that they contain only the information the author selects, thereby reflecting one point of view; they frequently take years to produce, thus limiting immediacy; they are static; and despite so many titles, they cover only a limited number of topics. Books remain excellent sources of information. But the fact is, a book exists because someone else was curious about a topic, researched it, and interpreted the findings. With the World Wide Web, our curiosity can pick the topic, we can do our own research, and we can impose our own interpretation on the findings.

In this chapter we demonstrate curiosity-driven research using the WWW. This activity provides a forum in which to summarize ideas introduced in Part I. A principal goal is to explore the limits of the research that can be performed on the WWW because not everything is in digital form yet, and not everything in digital form is worth viewing. Another goal is to enjoy a tour through the life and mind of an amazing individual, R. Buckminster Fuller, who described himself as both an engineer and a poet. The topic requires the use of various information resources. Finally, we will explore how to fill in the gaps in our knowledge. Though the case study runs to many pages in order to fulfill the foregoing learning objectives, it represents the search/research activity of a single interesting and enjoyable evening. The conclusion is that curiosity-driven research is recreation, more interesting and rewarding than watching another rerun of *Friends*.

Student Aid. Curiosity-driven research can be a random process, as various discoveries pique our interest. It appears even more aimless when it's someone else's curiosity doing the driving. Though I explain completely the motivation for the path we take, it's still possible to lose the thread of the research. If that happens, check the summary of the entire effort at the end of this chapter.

GETTING STARTED

Curiosity-driven research usually begins with little more than a name or word we've heard or read. We wonder about it, but often we have too little information initially to implement an informed search with a search engine. In the present case we wonder about R. Buckminster Fuller, who is a man with a reasonably distinctive name. Even so, performing a Google search on

```
Buckminster AND Fuller
```

produces at least 26,800 hits, way too many to consider. Limiting the search to biographies

```
Buckminster AND Fuller AND biography
```

reduces the hit count to 1600, which is still too many. So, we must gather some initial information from another source to be able to formulate an effective search-engine search. For the specific case at hand, we exploit the fact that biographies of famous people are online. Other topics will require different resources.

After going electronically to a convenient library, we find among its research links a list of sourccs for biographies, including

Biography.com	www.biography.com/search/
Biographical Dictionary	www.s9.com/biography/
Britannica Lives	www.eb.com/people/
Lives, the Biography Resource	amillionlives.com

and we try the first one. Our choice is arbitrary because we have no basis for selecting one resource over another, but if we were to use biographies repeatedly, it would be wise to shop around. The completeness and quality of the entries vary. Biography.com claims a database of "25,000 personalities." The response to the `Buckminster Fuller` search request is successful and is shown in Figure 6.1.

Fuller, R(ichard) Buckminster	**1895–1983**
Inventor, designer, poet, futurist; born in Milton, Massachusetts (great-nephew of Margaret Fuller). Leaving Harvard early, he largely educated himself while working at industrial jobs and serving in the U.S. Navy during World War I. One of the century's most original minds, he free-lanced his talents, solving problems of human shelter, nutrition, transportation, environmental pollution, and decreasing world resources, developing over 2,000 patents in the process. He developed the Dymaxion ("dynamic and maximum efficiency") House in 1927, and the Dymaxion streamlined, omni-directional car in 1932. Fuller wrote some 25 books, notably *Nine Chains to the Moon* (1938), *Utopia or Oblivion* (1969), *Operating Manual for Spaceship Earth* (1969), and *Critical Path* (1981). An enthusiastic educationist, he held a chair at Southern Illinois University (1959–75), and in 1962 became professor of poetry at Harvard. In his later decades he was a popular public lecturer, promoting a global strategy of seeking to do more with less through technology. His inventions include the 1927 Dymaxion House, the 1933 Dymaxion Car and, foremost, the 1947 geodesic dome. He has the distinction of having both his names used for a scientific entity, the "fullerene" (also known as a "buckyball"), a form of carbon whose molecule resembles his geodesic dome.	

Figure 6.1. Biography.com's biography of Buckminster Fuller.

Reading Fuller's biography immediately raises interesting questions. The first line mentions that he is the great-nephew of Margaret Fuller. Who's she? Because we're at a biography site, our immediate response is to look her up. Her Biography.com entry is shown in Figure 6.2. Reading her biography, we note that both of them chose to go by their middle names! More substantive parallels in their lives also exist: They were both largely self-taught, they were both intellectually gifted, and they were both concerned about making the world a better place—she through her feminist writings and he through his inventions. Her tragic shipwreck death with her new husband and young child reminds us that Buckminster Fuller's profile doesn't mention if he was married or had children. So, we seek more biographical information. We could check the other three biography sites, but having achieved our original goal of finding basic information to guide a Google search, we do that.

In the first biography, the term *Dymaxion,* perhaps a term Fuller thought up, is mentioned as a name of both a house and a car that he invented. Surely any biography will mention these inventions, so we search on

```
Buckminster AND Fuller AND biography AND Dymaxion
```

which reduces the hits from more than 1600, when only "biography" is included, to a manageable 149.[1]

Early in the list of hits is another biography from About.com shown in Figure 6.3. Reading this biography reveals something researchers encounter all the time: Different sources differ. Whereas the previous biography had described his departure from Harvard as "leaving," this one says he was "expelled." Though we could track down whether he left or was expelled, we will leave it unresolved for now. Instead, we

[1] Interestingly, "Buckminster" and "Dymaxion" are so unusual and so descriptive of this one person that his last name is unnecessary! Searching on `Buckminster AND Dymaxion AND biography` hits 149 times.

savor the irony that he eventually became Professor of Poetry at Harvard, an outstanding accomplishment for one who apparently didn't graduate from any place. Despite this position and so many honorary degrees, he obviously didn't take himself too seriously, based on his self-description, *Guinea Pig B*.

Fuller, (Sarah) Margaret	**1810 – 1850**
Feminist, literary critic; born in Cambridgeport, Mass. Her father, Timothy Fuller, was a prominent Massachusetts lawyer-politician who, disappointed that his child was not a boy, educated her rigorously in the classical curriculum of the day. Not until age 14 did she get to attend a school for two years (1824–26) and then she returned to Cambridge and her course of reading. Her intellectual precociousness gained her the acquaintance of various Cambridge intellectuals but her assertive and intense manner put many people off. Her father moved the family to a farm in Groton, Mass. (1833), and she found herself isolated and forced to help educate her siblings and run the household for her ailing mother. From 1836 to 1837, after visiting Ralph Waldo Emerson in Concord, she taught for Bronson Alcott in Boston, and then at a school in Providence, R.I. All the while she continued to enlarge both her intellectual accomplishments and personal acquaintances. Moving to Jamaica Plain, a suburb of Boston, in 1840, she conducted her famous "Conversations" (1840–44), discussion groups that attracted many prominent people from all around Boston. In 1840, she also joined Emerson and others to found the *Dial*, a journal devoted to the transcendentalist views; she became a contributor from the first issue and its editor (1840–42). Her first book, based on a trip through the Midwest (1840–42), was *Summer on the Lakes* (1844) and this led to her being invited by Horace Greeley to be literary critic at the *New York Tribune* in 1844. She published her feminist classic, *Woman in the Nineteenth Century* (1845). In addition to writing a solid body of critical reviews and essays, she became active in various social reform movements. In 1846 she went to Europe as a foreign correspondent for the *Tribune*. In England and France she was treated as a serious intellectual and got to meet many prominent people. She went on to Italy in 1847 where she met Giovanni Angelo, the Marchese d'Ossoli, ten years younger and of liberal principles; they became lovers and married in 1849, but their son was born in 1848. Involved in the Roman revolution of 1848, she and her husband fled to Florence in 1849. They sailed for the U.S.A. in 1850 but the ship ran aground in a storm off Fire Island, N.Y., and Margaret's and her husband's bodies were never found.	

Figure 6.2. The Biography.com entry for Margaret Fuller, RBF's great-aunt.

The second paragraph emphasizes how he overcame his despair at the death of his daughter, turned his thoughts away from suicide—his life was not his to throw away—and proceeded to see what he could do "on behalf of humanity." He actually worked on the problem of world hunger, a problem most people dismiss as not solvable. His philosophy of treating life as an experiment in "what the little, penniless, unknown individual might be able to do effectively on behalf of all humanity" is inspiring! We need to know more.

Perhaps before going any further we ought to find out what Fuller looks like. To locate some photographs, we use Google's image search facility. Entering `Buckminster Fuller` yields nearly 500 images, files (`.jpg` and `.gif`) from pages associated with those words. They're not all of RBF—some people have named their cats Buckminster Fuller—but there is a wide range of interesting images of Fuller. Three images from later in life, shown in Figure 6.4, reveal an intense man who also seems grandfatherly, the sort of guy who might give you the keys to the Dymaxion car for the weekend.

Place of Birth: Milton, Massachusetts

Education: Expelled from Harvard University during freshman year

Awards: 44 honorary doctoral degrees, Gold Medal of the American Institute of Architects, Gold Medal of the Royal Institute of British Architects and dozens of other honors. Nominated for Nobel Peace Prize.

Selected Works:

1932: The portable Dymaxion house manufactured

1934: The Dymaxion car

1938: Nine Chains to the Moon

1949: Developed the Geodesic Dome

1967: US Pavilion at Expo '67, Montreal, Canada

1969: Operating Manual for Spaceship Earth

1970: Approaching the Benign Environment

Standing only 5'2" tall, Buckminster Fuller loomed over the twentieth century. Admirers affectionately call him *Bucky*, but the name he gave himself was *Guinea Pig B.* His life, he said, was an experiment.

When he was 32, Buckminster Fuller's life seemed hopeless. He was bankrupt and without a job. He was grief stricken over the death of his first child and he had a wife and a newborn to support. Drinking heavily, he contemplated suicide. Instead, he decided that his life was not his to throw away: It belonged to the universe. He embarked on "an experiment to discover what the little, penniless, unknown individual might be able to do effectively on behalf of all humanity."

To this end, Buckminster Fuller spent the next half-century searching for "ways of doing more with less" so that all people could be fed and sheltered. Although he never obtained a degree in architecture, he was an architect and engineer who designed revolutionary structures. His famous Dymaxion House was a pre-fabricated, pole-supported dwelling. His Dymaxion car was a streamlined, three-wheeled vehicle with the engine in the rear. His Dymaxion Air-Ocean Map projected a spherical world as a flat surface with no visible distortion.

But Fuller is perhaps most famous for his creation of the geodesic dome—a remarkable, sphere-like structure based on theories of "energetic-synergetic geometry," which he developed during WWII. Efficient and economical, the geodesic dome was widely hailed as a possible solution to world housing shortages.

During his lifetime, Buckminster Fuller wrote 28 books and was awarded 25 United States patents. Although his Dymaxion car never caught on and his design for geodesic domes is rarely used for residential dwellings, Fuller made his mark in areas of architecture, mathematics, philosophy, religion, urban development, and design.

Figure 6.3. About.com's biography of R. Buckminster Fuller.

We won't take the time to look through all of these images, nor will we follow all of the links from the About.com biography (Figure 6.5) now. But we might want to check these out later. And we have no idea how we will use the information we will discover. So, we should acquire the habit of *bookmarking* all of the sites we visit, or in the case of the specific pictures we just found, to *save* a copy locally on our computer. These links will allow us to review information we've found and perhaps use it for other purposes. We may decide to send it to someone, or print it, or more typically, just reread it.

Online Research Methodology. Whenever you use the WWW for research, bookmark every site you visit (deleting them later is trivial) and record the keywords of all searches—both search engine and site searches—in a notebook file. With this information, you can revisit the sites and reconstruct the searches you used. You never know when you'll need them.

Figure 6.4. R. Buckminster Fuller.

PRIMARY SOURCES

To find out more about Fuller's philosophy and personal life, we decide to do another search on the exact phrase `"Guinea Pig B"`—a name so distinctive there cannot be any others. Recall that Google allows for a search of an exact phrase, which in this case yields 200 hits. When we revise the search to `Buckminster AND "Guinea Pig B"`–the count drops to 99. This list is a goldmine of specific information about Fuller, and we will return to it.

The first hit for the `Buckminster AND "Guinea Pig B"` search is a page from WNET New York City's public television station for a documentary they produced on Fuller's life titled *Thinking Out Loud*. The *Guinea Pig B* page from this site is shown in Figure 6.6.

Buckminster Fuller: Biography Fast facts about the life and works of Buckminster Fuller, affectionately known as "Bucky."

Buckminster Fuller: Quotes A compendium of quotes and excerpts from Fuller's most famous writings.

What is a Geodesic Dome? From our architecture glossary, illustration and definition of the geodesic dome, conceived by Buckminster Fuller.

Build A Geodesic Dome Model Step-by-step instructions, with diagrams, from Trevor Blake.

Spaceship Earth Facts and photo for the famous dome at Disney Epcot, which is built according to Buckminster Fuller's principles.

Buckminster Fuller: Inventions An extensive collection of resources, illustrations and links, from your Guide to Inventors.

Buckminster Fuller: Net Links Best Buckminster Fuller sites on the Web, selected by your Guide.

Geodesic Domes: Net Links Best Geodesic Dome sites on the Web, selected by your Guide.

Figure 6.5. Additional links from About.com's biography of R. Buckminster Fuller.

The WNET page shows us a new photograph of RBF, cites a recent book about him, and quotes a small excerpt. This is all useful, but the links at the bottom of the page, to four essays, are perhaps more valuable. (See Figures 6.7, 6.8, 6.9, and 6.10.)

> *Who Was R. Buckminster Fuller?*, by E. J. Applewhite, author and Fuller collaborator.
>
> *Experience and Experiencing*, by Allegra Fuller Snyder, Bucky's daughter.
>
> *Life, Facts and Artifacts*, by Bonnie Goldstein DeVarco, archivist and senior researcher on *Buckminster Fuller: Thinking Out Loud*.
>
> *Dare To Be Naïve*, by Sarah Feldman. An overview of Fuller's life.

From the list we note that one of Fuller's children was a daughter, Allegra, who apparently married someone named Snyder.[2]

The importance of these essays is that they are extremely reliable sources of information. Applewhite as a collaborator and Snyder as Fuller's daughter write from direct personal experience. They are known as *primary sources*. Such information is

Guinea Pig B

Some Perspectives on Buckminster Fuller

Guinea Pig B is a name Bucky gave himself, to signify that his life was an experiment.

Excerpted from <u>BuckyWorks: Buckminster Fuller's Ideas for Today</u> by James T. Baldwin:

His alternative to politics was radical and deeply subversive. If we are designed like other animals to be a success, then nature must have provided enough of everything needed for all to live a healthy existence. People living well would have little interest in fighting and destruction. Bucky decided that reliable information and efficient design could identify and fairly distribute the Earth's resources, bringing a good life to all. Developing that information and putting it to work would be the mission of Guinea Pig B.

Reused by permission of the publisher, John Wiley & Sons, Inc.

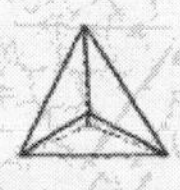

Who Was R. Buckminster Fuller? by E.J. Applewhite, author and Fuller collaborator.

Experience and Experiencing by Allegra Fuller Snyder, Bucky's daughter.

Life, Facts & Artifacts by Bonnie Goldstein DeVarco, archivist and senior researcher on "Buckminster Fuller: Thinking Out Loud."

Dare To Be Naive by Sarah Feldman. An overview of Fuller's life.

Figure 6.6. WNET's Guinea Pig B page.

[2] No relation to the author.

to be preferred for several reasons. First and foremost, the information presented is actual experience and personal impressions. Thus the information is unbiased, except to the degree that any data a person gathers from experience is subject to that person's ability to perceive it and convey it to others. As primary sources, they are not subject to the distortion or omission that can come when someone else reports information from a primary source, making it a secondary source. If someone reports from that, creating a tertiary source, further distortion and omission are possible. Using primary sources allows us to formulate our own impression and point of view on the subject.

Who Was R. Buckminster Fuller?
by E. J. Applewhite

Buckminster Fuller had one of the most fascinating and original minds of his century. Born in 1895 in Milton, Massachusetts, he was the latest—if not the last—of the New England Transcendentalists. Like the transcendentalists, Fuller rejected the established religious and political notions of the past and adhered to an idealistic system of thought based on the essential unity of the natural world and the use of experiment and intuition as a means of understanding it. But, departing from the pattern of his New England predecessors, he proposed that only an understanding of technology in the deepest sense would afford humans a proper guide to individual conduct and the eventual salvation of society. Industrial and scientific technology, despite their disruption of established habits and values, was not a blight on the landscape, but in fact for Fuller they have a redeeming humanitarian role.

Fuller rejected the conventional disciplines of the universities by ignoring them. In their place he imposed his own self-discipline and his own novel way of thinking in a deliberate attempt—as poets and artists do—to change his generation's perception of the world. To this end he created the term Spaceship Earth to convince all his fellow passengers that they would have to work together as the crew of a ship. His was an earnest, even compulsive, program to convince his listeners that humans had a function in universe. Humans have a destiny to serve as "local problem solvers" converting their experience to the highest advantage of others.

Fuller's favorite method of teaching—in the tradition of all great teachers since the Greek philosophers—was lecturing to large and youthful audiences. Though his penchant for talking for hours on end was notorious, he really regarded all communication as a two-way street, and he was remarkably sensitive to individual reactions—well beyond those in the front row. He tuned his always extemporaneous discourse to the rate he could see it being absorbed and digested. In the 1960s and 70s a generation seized on his prescription that there was no need to "earn a living"—often disregarding the other side of the coin: the need for individual initiative in "doing what needs to be done." In this spirit he advanced "design science" as the solution for worldwide social and ecological problems.

Fuller was an architect, though he never got a degree and in fact didn't even get a license until he was awarded one as an honor when he was in his late 60s. This did not prevent him from designing the geodesic dome: the only kind of building that can be set on the ground as a complete structure—and with no limiting dimension. The strength of the frame actually increases in ratio to its size, enclosing the largest volume of space with the least area of surface. This was his virtuoso invention, and he said it illustrated his strategy of "starting with wholes" rather than parts.

He was also a poet, philosopher, inventor and mathematician, as documented amply in many other web sites on the net.

America has been in the middle of a love-hate affair with technology—and Fuller is right in the middle of it. He introduced not only a unique rationale for technology, but an esthetic of it. Likewise his synergetic geometry bears for Fuller an imperative with an ethical content for humans to reappraise their relationship to the physical universe. Manifest together as design science, they offer the prospect of a kind of secular salvation.

Figure 6.7. Applewhite essay from the WNET "Guinea Pig B" site.

DeVarco's essay is almost as valuable to us because it is based on information from the archive of Fuller's papers and artifacts, which DeVarco described as "approximately 90,000 pounds of personal history." Fuller produced this information, so it is a primary source. As an archivist and researcher, DeVarco can be presumed to be scrupulously accurate and reliable. Though her essay is not technically a primary source, we can trust it.

Like DeVarco's essay, Feldman's essay relied on the Fuller archive for its information and so is potentially an excellent resource. As researchers, however, we wonder who she is. Her title or relationship to Fuller is not stated with the essay. For example, is she a scholar with academic credentials and so can be presumed to make every attempt to be accurate, or does she write advertising copy for used car companies and is accustomed, perhaps, to embellishing the facts? We look her up in Biography.com, but she's not there. We go to the WNET Web site and search their site for her name. We get a link to her bio, which reads

> **Sarah Feldman**
> Sarah Feldman is the National Project Director for the National Teacher Training Institute (NTTI) at Thirteen/WNET New York. She is also a content developer and writer for Thirteen's wNetStation and wNetSchool, and other online venues. She taught second grade in the South Bronx and Harlem.

As a director at a national teacher training institute, content developer, and writer with access to the Fuller archive, Feldman sounds extremely reliable and so we can be confident that her essay is, also.

Experience and Experiencing
by Allegra Fuller Snyder

When I was asked to contribute to this volume I wondered where I would start. Writing about one's father is a challenging, almost overwhelming, task—particularly if one has not confronted that presence in writing before. I have written about many other subjects, but not about Bucky.

My father was a warm, concerned and sharing father. As focused as he was on his own work he nevertheless included me in his experiences and experiencing. I remember with great clarity when I was about four years old. I was sick in bed and he was taking care of me. He sat down on the bed beside me, with his pencil in hand, and told me, through wonderful free-hand drawings, a Goldilocks story. I was Goldilocks and with his pencil he transported me, not to the Bear's house, but to universe, to help me understand something of Einstein's Theory of Relativity. What he was telling me was neither remote nor abstract. I was in a newly perceived universe. I was experiencing my father's thoughts and he was experiencing his own thinking as he communicated with me. It was exciting. We were sharing something together and I felt very warm and close to him in that experience. Something of this episode was later remembered in a book called *Tetrascroll.*

. . .

By experiencing I mean involving one's whole self, not being present at, or observing, something, but "doing" that thing. I remember how my father always loved to wash dishes. I had a perfectly good dishwasher, a piece of excellent technology, but he preferred to get his hands wet, to rinse, soap and stack the dishes in just the right way. (Technology, from my father's point of view, was always an extension and enrichment of experience not a substitute for experience.)

He loved our island in Maine because it was a physically involving place. We have no fresh water, except cistern-caught rain and well water, which has to be drawn or pumped and then hauled; kerosene and candles for light, a fire in the hearth for heat. Each of these basic requirements involves physical action to produce the needed results. . . . And then, of course, there was sailing, which he loved, where the dialog between nature and human action is so dynamic.

At the heart of each one of these actions, was the sense of the "special case" that would lead to a generalized principle. Any experience would become a "special case," the doorway to larger comprehensivity. When you were around him you were aware how sensitive he was to the smallest experience. His focus could zero in on a pebble on the beach, a twig or flower along a path. Each became the stepping stone to the largest whole.

> "The human brain apprehends and stores each sense reported bit of information regarding each special case experience. Only special case experiences are recallable from the memory bank."

Apprehended, a word Bucky used a great deal, suggests the "fingertip" experience. Remember, Bucky said, "Questions . . . must be answered only in terms of experience . . . Hearsaids, beliefs, axioms, superstitions, guesses, opinions were and are all excluded as (my) answer resources."

Bucky didn't use the word feeling often but he quotes this wonderful e.e. cummings thought at the beginning of his book "Critical Path." I believe what cummings meant by feel and feeling relates to Bucky's experience and experiencing.

> "A lot of people think or believe or know they feel (experience)—but that's thinking or believing or knowing; not feeling (experiencing). Almost anybody can learn to think or believe or know, but not a single human being can be taught to feel (experience). Why? Because whenever you think or you believe or you know, you're a lot of other people: but the moment you feel (experience), you're nobody-but-yourself. To be nobody-but-yourself—in a world which is doing its best, night and day, to make you everybody else— means to fight the hardest battle which any human being can fight; and never stop fighting."

That was the scenario of Bucky's life—to fight the hardest battle which any human being can fight; and never stop fighting.

Intuition, imagination, all relate to and are a part of experience. Let me turn for a moment to Bucky's own words on these matters. (What follows are drawn from E.J. Applewhite's wonderful Synergetics Dictionary.)

> Intuition is practically physical, the kind of supersensitivity that a child has. Imagination. Image-ination involves rearranging the "furniture" of remembered experience as retrieved from the brain bank.

Speaking with an audience he would say, "All that I can really give you I must always identify by experience." One of his great gifts as a speaker was the fact that he made you experience his ideas and carried you along with the connection between your experience and his experience. "Information is experience. Experience is information."

He then goes on to really explore the essence of experience.

> Thinking is inherently exclusive. Experience, which comes before thinking, is inherently inclusive. Experience is complex consciousness of being, of self, co-existing with all the non-self. Re-experienced consciousness is re-cognition. Recognitions generate identifications. Re-cognition of within self rhythms, of heart beatings or other identities, generate a matrix continuum of time consciousness upon which, like blank music lines, are superimposed all the observances by self of the non-self occurrences. Experience is inherently discontinuous and islanded and each special experience represents a complex of generalized principles operative in special or limited size modulated realization. Experience is finite; it can be stored, studied, directed; it can be turned, with conscious effort to human advantage. (This means that) evolution pivots on the conscious, selective use of cumulative human experience. Universe is the coordinate integral of all experience."

Where or how does experience continue to be a part of the picture when, as Bucky pointed out,

> "At the dawning of the twentieth century, without warning to humanity, the physical technology of Earthians' affairs was shifted over from a brain-sensed reality into a reality apprehended only by instruments."

His response is that invisibility can be "understood and coped with only by experience-educated mind." Let me turn again, for a moment, to my own work in hopes of clarifying this very important point. It is my observation that dance is most significant in societies that are least literate, where they have had no need for a tool to document the spoken word, and it is least significant in societies, such as our own, where literacy, rather than knowledge and understanding, is set up as the criteria of education and cultivation. Since I have learned a very great deal from understanding dance, what does this tell me? The written word was and is an extraordinary technological tool but it was the first step in the separation of knowledge from experience. It extended knowledge, in time and space, but away from self, and made invisible, and often forgotten, the source of knowledge, the reason for knowledge. There are trade-offs in the process of literacy which I think are very important to examine. Literacy allows detachment, lack of involvement, sometimes, and most important of all, irresponsibility to the essential understanding and retention knowledge. Physical-conceptualization is deeper and more lasting as a learning process, and the individual is propelled into a sense of responsibility by that process, that, I think, is why Bucky said invisibility can be "understood and coped with only by experience-educated mind."

From my perception of reality, and orientation to life, all of the above suggests that in order to really understand Bucky's work, you must, in essence, be a dancer yourself. You must understand your body and experience as a way of knowing. In a functional way the ideas need to be embodied in your own thinking/experiencing. Bucky was at his most essential Buckyness when he burst into his wonderful clogging dance. Bucky was a dancer in the way I understand dance, as a way of knowing, and his understanding of universe was through his dancing in his mind.

Figure 6.8. Essay excerpt by Allegra Fuller Snyder from the WNET "Guinea Pig B" site.

Life, Facts and Artifacts

by Bonnie Goldstein DeVarco

[*Bonnie Goldstein DeVarco presents a fascinating account of Fuller's archive—he saved everything! Much of the content concerns specifics of the archive that are somewhat tangential to our interest. But two paragraphs stand out in her section on Ephemeralization, quoted here.*—LS]

EPHEMERALIZATION

Although the tactile pleasures of sorting through the physical artifacts of Bucky's life brings a dimension all its own to the discovery of who he was and who he shared his life with, almost the same could be done with the same body of materials available on a computer screen-from drawings, letters and manuscripts to "ephemerabilia," at the touch of a fingertip. In hundreds of letters spanning well over half a century, the love story of Bucky and Anne is told. Anne's letters carry a lilting youthful quality that punctuates even the most fatuous groupings of correspondence to be found in the Chronofile* boxes. Her handwriting is like a beautiful victorian stenciled wallpaper and her ardent and boundless devotion gives life to the saying that behind every great man is a great woman. It is no wonder he personally deemed his most famous geodesic dome, at the 1967 Montreal Exposition, his "Taj Majal to Anne" in honor of their 50th anniversary.

The letters of sculptor Isamu Noguchi, Bucky's lifelong friend, span decades and flavor the correspondence files with Asian subtlety, each page an artwork in and of itself, all on sheer white rice paper written with a brown fountain pen, always poignant, always aesthetically disarming. And how affecting it is to see in a letter to his mother bound into the 1928 Chronofile volume, Fuller's youthful discovery of his Great Aunt Margaret Fuller's thought and its parallels to his own as he writes, "I have been reading much by Margaret Fuller lately. I was astonished to find that some things I have been writing myself are about identical to things I find in her writings. I am terribly interested and am astounded fully that I should have grown to this age and never have read anything of her or grandfather Fuller's."

*RBF kept his correspondence and other documents in a bound file in time order called the Chronfile.

Figure 6.9. Excerpt from DeVarco's essay at the WNET "Guinea Pig B" site.

Dare to Be Naïve

by Sarah Feldman

Jobless, without savings or prospects, with a wife and newborn daughter to support, suicidal and drinking heavily, in 1927 Richard Buckminster Fuller had little reason to be optimistic about the future. R. Buckminster Fuller—or "Bucky," as he's affectionately known—transformed that low point in his life into a catalyst for transforming our planet's future and as well as his own. A mathematical genius, environmentalist, architect, cartographer, poet, and an engineer of rare foresight and a philosopher of unique insight, Fuller was born in 1895 but can be truly considered a 21st century man.

Renouncing personal success and financial gain, at age 32 Fuller set out to "search for the principles governing the universe and help advance the evolution of humanity in accordance with them." Central to his mission were the ideas that 1) he had to divest himself of false ideas and "unlearn" everything he could not verify through his own experience, and 2) human nature—and nature itself—could not be reformed and therefore it was the environment—and our response to it—that must be changed. Fuller entered into a two-year period of total seclusion, and began working on design solutions to what he inferred to be mankind's central problems.

With his goal of "finding ways of doing more with less to the end that all people—everywhere—can have more and more," Fuller began designing a series of revolutionary structures. The most famous of these was the pre-fabricated, pole-suspended single-unit dwelling Dymaxion House. (The term Dymaxion was derived from the words "dynamic," "maximum," and "ion.") In 1933, he developed the three-wheeled, rear engine, streamlined Dymaxion Car. Unfortunately, though the car performed well, negative publicity resulting from a fatal accident halted its production. Fuller's designs tended to be based a geometry that used triangles, circles and tetrahedrons more than the traditional planes and rectangles. His Dymaxion Air-Ocean Map, which projected a spherical world as a flat surface with no visible distortion, brought him to the attention of the scientific community in 1943, and his map was the first cartographic projection of the world to ever be granted a U.S. patent.

In 1947 and 1948, Fuller's study of geodesics, "the most economical momentary relationship among a plurality of points and events," led him to his most famous invention, the geodesic dome. A hemispherical structure composed of flat, triangular panels, the domes were inexpensive to produce, lightweight yet strong space-efficient buildings. The geodesic dome combines the sphere, the most efficient container of volume per square foot, with the tetrahedron, which provides the greatest strength for the least volume of weight. Its design allows the dome to withstand winds of 210 mph, while at the same time it is light and easily transportable. Today, Fuller's geodesic domes can be found in varying sizes in countries all over the world, from Casablanca to Baton Rouge. Recognized as a landmark achievement in design and architecture, Fuller's dome was described in 1964 by Time magazine as "a kind of benchmark of the universe, what seventeenth century mystic Jakob Boehme might call 'a signature of God.'" In 1959 he joined the faculty of Southern Illinois University in Carbondale and used that as a base of operations for what Fuller called his "toings and froings." For the next two decades, Fuller globe-trotted and lectured and consulted on a variety of projects. During this period of upheaval and great change, Fuller's ideas and work in such areas as ecology, conservation, education and environmental design found an enthusiastic audience among young people all over the world. After a stint at the University Science Center in Philadelphia, in 1972 the non-profit Design Science Institute was formed in Washington, DC to perpetuate Fuller's ideas and designs.

A self-proclaimed "apolitical," Fuller maintained there was "no difference between left and the right." Nevertheless, he admitted he struggled to "dare to be naive," and retained an optimistic faith that "an omni-integrated, freely intercirculating, omni-literate world society" was within our grasp. A prolific writer, Fuller's magnum opus is undoubtedly "Synergetics: Explorations in the Geometry of Thinking," on which he collaborated with E.J. Applewhite in 1975. The work is considered a major intellectual achievement in its examinations of language, thought and the universe.

Though he only stood 5'2" tall, R. Buckminster Fuller looms large over the 20th century. Though a man of incredible intellect and vision, many of "Bucky's" fans remain most impressed by the man's awe-inspiring humility—and his abiding love for his planet and his fellow human beings. "Above all," said Fuller, "I was motivated in 1927 and ever since by the most mysterious drive we ever experience—that of love. I don't think there's any influence upon my life that compares with . . . love."

R. Buckminster Fuller
July 12, 1895–July 1, 1983

Figure 6.10. Sarah Feldman essay from WNET's "Guinea Pig B" site.

To summarize, we found four essays (Figures 6.7 through 6.10) about RBF and assessed the potential quality of their information. We have found it to be either from primary sources or from researchers who relied on the Fuller archive. This is excellent information, and we will take the time to read it. Notice that we are not implying that secondary or tertiary sources should not be used—we just used two from Biography.com and an About.com profile. They were unsigned biographical sketches that presumably relied on generally available information about Fuller. We assumed they are accurate, though we noted an apparent discrepancy—one says Fuller left Harvard and the other says he was expelled. The point is that the two biographies fulfilled our needs for a quick introduction. Now, with the desire to find out accurate information about Fuller's life and philosophy, we go to the source(s) ourselves.

Reading the essays gives us extraordinary insight into Buckminster Fuller. He believed, according to Applewhite, that technology is not the "problem" but rather the "solution," and understanding technology deeply is the key to individual behavior as well as "saving" society. Snyder's essay emphasized how he only trusted his direct experience as he sought to overcome the bias of conventional wisdom that he believed prevented effective thinking. He sought to do more with less. Feldman quotes Fuller's assertion that he turned his life around in 1927 motivated by love, the greatest influence on his life, and DeVarco quotes his description of the Montreal geodesic dome as the "Taj Mahal to Anne." It is a personal story of a deep thinker. The geodesic structure was his "virtuoso invention" [Applewhite] and *Synergetics*, a "major intellectual achievement," was his magnum opus [Feldman].

Details emerge. Snyder describes her father's departure from Harvard as "dismissed," a synonym for "expelled"—settling that question. Feldman says that Dymaxion stands for "dynamic," "maximum," and "ion," a somewhat more plausible assertion than the "dynamic with maximum efficiency" that we learned in the first biography. Fuller was a walker, according to Snyder; he loved to sail, and he liked to live a more primitive life on their island in Maine.

While thinking about this complex man, we cruise the WNET site and discover a page with two short video clips of Fuller. This is also primary information. Though downloading them takes a few moments, they show Fuller describing in his own words some of his most radical ideas. In one he says,

> *This is the* real *news of the last century. It is highly feasible to take care of all of humanity at a higher standard of living than anybody has ever experienced or dreamt of, to do so without having anybody profit at the expense of another . . . so that everybody can enjoy the whole earth . . . and it can all be done by 1985.*

In the video clip we not only hear what he has to say, but we see the emphasis of his gestures and hear the conviction in his voice. There is a tone here, perhaps, an urging as if he intends to imply also, "not only *can* we raise humanity's standard of living, we should." In this way the spoken word is more powerful than its written equivalent. This digitized information has given us valuable insight.

ULTIMATE SOURCES: CHRONFILE AND *EVERYTHING I KNOW*

Recall that the WNET page was the first item in a Google search with the terms `Buckminster AND "Guinea Pig B"`. Having mined that page reasonably completely, we return to the next item, which is a link to the Buckminster Fuller Institute. The page is shown in Figure 6.11.

The BFI chronology of Fuller's life is very interesting, ending with the amazing fact: *Anne* [his wife] *and Bucky died within 36 hours of one another one week before their 67th wedding anniversary!* If this page is what it appears to be—a site associated with the Fuller estate—the information is doubtless authoritative. Mindful, however, of the hoaxes perpetrated by sites that are not what they appear to be, we take the precaution to check to see who owns the `bfi.org` domain. Recall that the process of finding out who owns a domain, which takes less than a minute, was explained in Chapter 5. After a few clicks, our expectations are confirmed: The site is owned by the Buckminster Fuller Institute of Santa Barbara, California.

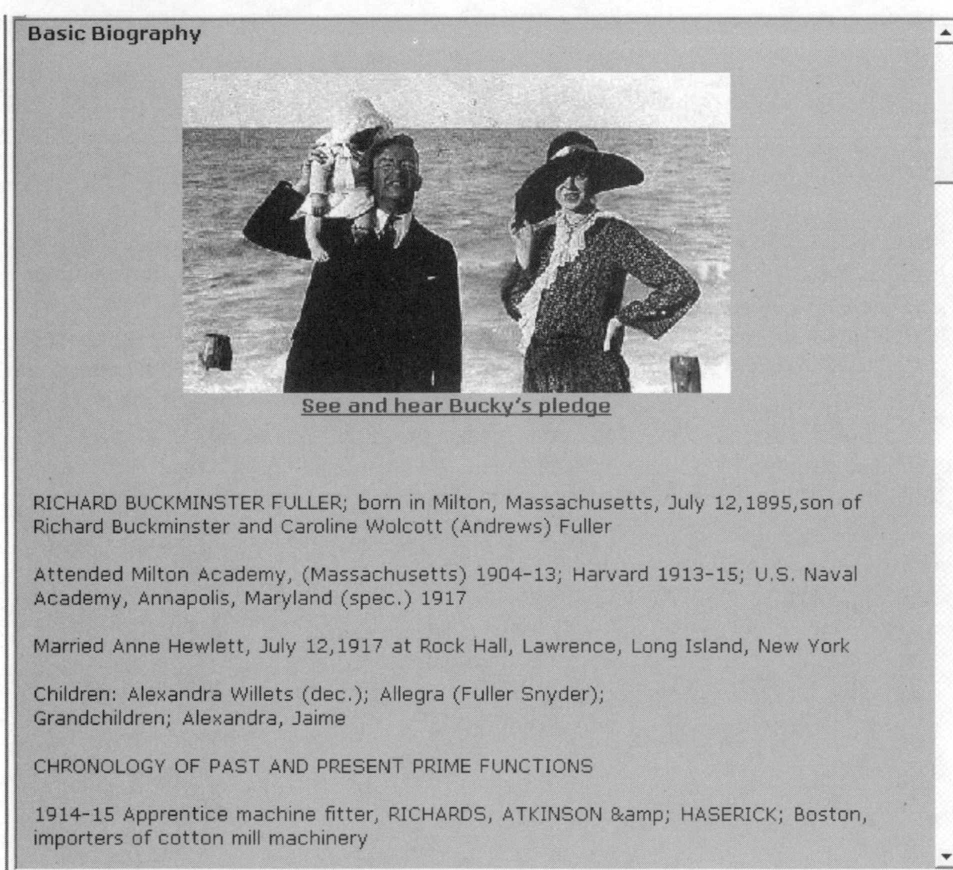

Figure 6.11. Buckminster Fuller Institute chronology of his life.

Clicking around the site, we find a tremendous amount of authoritative information, including Chronfile information, copies of whole books by Fuller, and 42 hours' worth of Fuller recordings from 1975 titled *Everything I Know*. This huge archive of online information is divided into twelve parts, each of which is further subdivided into paragraph-size units called clips. We listen to a few minutes to get an idea of what *Everything I Know* is like. It's interesting, of course, and we notice from its description that it includes deep, abstract ideas as well as personal anecdotes. Though we're interested in the deep ideas, the personal details are interesting, too. What, we wonder, does he say about Allegra and his relationship to her?

If the archive were composed of 42 hours of audio clips only, we would probably have to listen to most of it to find out. However, JoAnne Ishimine has transcribed the entire reminiscence. This allows it to be searched, and so we can make a site search for `Allegra`. Among the hits is a citation in Volume 12 of the *Everything I Know* transcripts where Fuller mentions how Allegra loves to dance and then relays a conversation they had.

> And, when she was twelve, she said "Daddy," we were living in New York at that time, she said "Daddy, you were brought up in Boston with the custom that it is ill mannered for men to make gestures that the man who is properly cultivated is well in possession of his movements, and he just doesn't even move his head, he just talks and sits very motionless, beautifully disciplined to do that." And she said, "I'll tell you, I don't know if I really am a dancer, but whatever I am, my body wants to talk all the time." And she said, "Daddy, I like your ideas very, very much and I want them to prevail, but I think you are frustrating your ideas by your disciplining yourself to sit motionless. I think if you'd just let yourself go things would happen way better for you." She was used to my having a lot of hard luck, nobody was paying any attention to me in those days. And so she seemed so wise that I think I did everything I could to free myself up. . . . But she did make it perfectly clear, a child does move comfortably and uses his body, so I began to let myself do [*sic*] I am utterly unaware of the motions, I assure you, but I have had moving pictures taken of me I've seen myself when I've been giving a lecture and I'm practically going all over the stage like a ballet dancer.

Certainly, the fact that he is an animated speaker is evident in the lectures we watched from the WNET *Thinking Out Loud* program.

Bookmarking the *Everything I Know* archive is essential because it is a rich resource of Fuller information expressed in his own words. When his ideas pique our interest, we can return to the archives.

Surfing the BFI Site

Looking around the site, we quickly come across Fuller's Dymaxion Map—the surface of the globe projected onto an icosahedron that produces a minimal-distortion flat map. Thinking of an icosahedron inside the earth and imagining the earth's curved surface shrinking down onto the icosahedron's faces gives the idea of the projection. Unfolding the icosahedron as shown in Figure 6.12 yields the flat map. An animation by Chris Rywalt (`www.westnet.com%7Ecrywald/unfold.html`) is available, and watching the earth unfold a few times gives a good idea of how it works. One important aspect of this minimal-distortion map is that the continents are shown in realistic proportion to one another. The particular unfolding shown has the property that the continents form one essentially contiguous island in a single sea. It's Fuller's schematic diagram for Spaceship Earth.

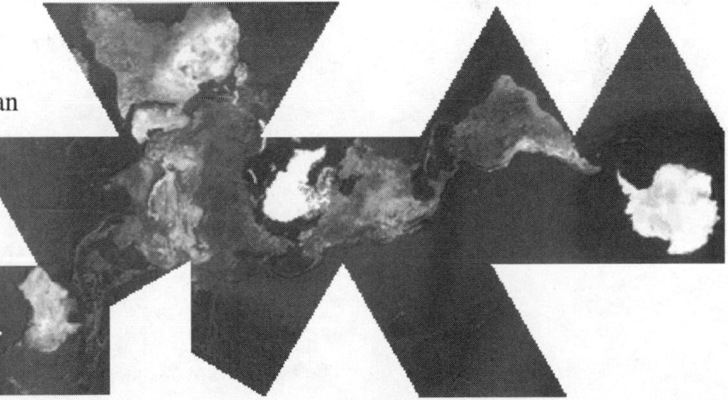

Figure 6.12. Dymaxion map of Earth.

There is something confusing here. Fuller invented the geodesic dome, as we knew before we started. It's his "virtuoso invention." And he invented the Dymaxion Map. The map page emphasizes that the map projects the globe onto an icosahedron. Remembering the geodesic dome of the Montreal Expo 67, we remember it as smoother than an icosahedron. What's the difference? Are they the same? Are they the same idea? If not, how is a geodesic dome related to an icosahedron?

To answer these questions, our first impulse might be to search the local BFI site because it may be the best place to find information about geodesics and the map's projection. Or, maybe we might think to try a Google search on `difference AND icosahedron AND geodesic`. But, if we reflect on the question before starting to search, we notice that answering it could be as easy as finding out the two definitions. The best place to find definitions is in a dictionary, of course, so, despite being at the Buckminster Fuller Institute site and having bookmarked a dozen other related sites, we click up an online dictionary. Again, if we cannot remember the site name for an online dictionary, we could go to our favorite library's research or reference page to find a link to one.

It's Not Rocket Science. The two principles at work here are (1) consider what kind of information will answer the question, and (2) look where that type of information may be found. The question may be answerable simply by knowing the meaning of the two words. And, giving the meanings of words is the purpose of a dictionary.

The online dictionaries give the following definitions:

geodesic, *n*: The shortest line between two points on any mathematically defined surface.

icosahedron, *n*: A 20-sided polyhedron.

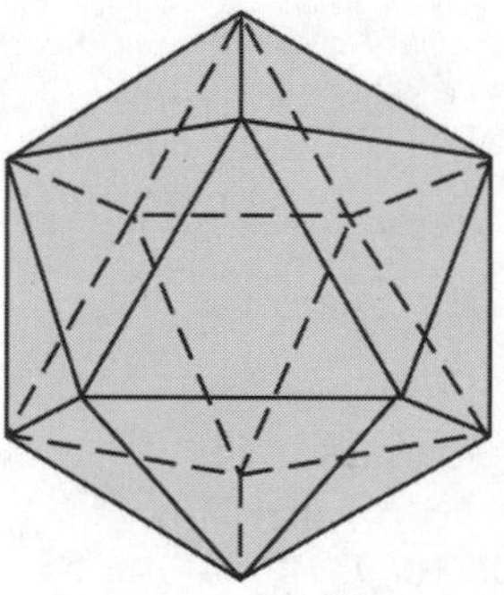

Obviously these are not the same. The icosahedron is a solid, whereas a geodesic is a line. But, this doesn't really explain how a geodesic dome differs from an icosahedron because the definition we found is for "geodesic" in its noun form, and when we refer to the "geodesic dome," we use it as an adjective. Looking further in the dictionary we find

geodesic, *adj:* Made of light straight structural elements mostly in tension <a *geodesic* dome>.

geodesic dome, *n:* A domed or vaulted structure of lightweight straight elements that form interlocking polygons.

These definitions help. The icosahedron has just 20 sides, which are triangles, and no matter how large it is—even the size of the earth—it must still have 20 sides. The geodesic dome apparently has any number of sides. From the picture of the Expo dome we can discern first, that the sides are also triangles, and, second, that they appear to be interlocking hexagons. That is, the triangles of one hexagon can be grouped to be parts of other adjacent hexagons. Viewing the icosahedron, we see the triangles forming interlocking pentagons, and because the geodesic definition requires only "straight elements that form interlocking *poly*gons," we conclude that an icosahedron is a geodesic solid. It's no surprise that Fuller came up with both the map idea and the dome idea.

We could begin learning about geodesic structures, where we would find that the geometry is quite complex, that the interlocking polygons can be combinations of pentagons and hexagons, and that it is possible to build a model using pipe cleaners and plastic straws. But we're more interested in the man than the engineering, so we push on probing the information from the `"Guinea Pig B"` search.

Completing the Picture

Our search to this point has been extremely successful. It has revealed a complex and productive man, whose profile as "one of the most original thinkers of the 20th century" is definitely supported by our research. He was scrupulously rational, tenderly sensitive, and used "both sides of his brain." The primary sources available to us have been extensive and rich, including textual, photographic, audio, video, and animated. Indeed, the volume of information is so extensive it overwhelms us—we've studied only a tiny fraction of it.

Our problem at this point is two-fold. First, there is a question of coverage. Though we've studied a lot of information, we have done so haphazardly. What is missing in our understanding of Fuller? Second, there seems to be no organization in our thinking. At the moment it is just an unordered collection of facts. One way to solve both problems is to check some *secondary* sources. Though it's always best to gather information from primary sources so we can interpret it for ourselves without the biases of others, secondary sources have their value. Secondary sources can

- Represent a more thorough investigation of the topic—certainly more thorough than ours to this point—and therefore enable us to fill in gaps
- Impose structure on the information, which can help us organize it.
- Provide other authors' interpretations, which will differ from our views, of course, but typically they offer insights we have not thought of.

As always, we need to check out the sources.

From the results of the `Buckminster AND "Guinea Pig B"` search we find a 3000-word biography by Kirby Urner, who maintains the Synergetics Web page. (From his homepage we find that Urner is a writer and curriculum developer from Portland, OR.) The biography excerpted in Figure 6.13 organizes some of the information that we've found independently and amplifies on Fuller's Navy days. It also reveals that Fuller was involved in controversies regarding the independence of his ideas, with Ken Snelson, Alexander Graham Bell, and Walter Bauersfield. These controversies are subjects we've not yet encountered.

A 20th Century Philosopher

by Kirby Urner

Originally posted: May 11, 1998; Last updated: June 19, 2000

R. Buckminster Fuller (b. July 12, 1895, d. July 1, 1983) is perhaps most easily pigeonholed as the last of the New England Transcendentalists, although Fuller himself always resisted being pigeon-holed.

His philosophy is centered around the human potential to overcome whatever "reflex conditioning" might have entrapped our humanity in counterproductive scenarios.
His focus on "intuition" as coming from the mind, which is beyond the realm of

brain-banked experiences, is what most clearly puts him in the transcendentalist tradition, along with a host of New England mannerisms and a life-long base of operations on Bear Island in Maine—now his grave site and that of his wife, Anne Hewlett Fuller.

Also, his great aunt, Margaret Fuller Osoli (1810–1850), was one of the first to publish the writings of Emerson and Thoreau in her magazine The Dial and her writings made an impact on the young Fuller early in his intellectual career.

Although the family had a four-generation tradition of sending its sons to Harvard, Fuller was too much the wild romantic to settle in and was expelled for treating an entire New York dance troupe to champagne on his own tab. The family sentenced him to hard labor in a Canadian cotton mill, where he sobered up quite a bit, but he still didn't like Harvard upon giving it a second try and was again expelled. He later returned to Harvard as the Charles Eliot Norton Professor of Poetry (1962).

Given his nautical background as a boy messing about with boats around Bear Island, Fuller was attracted to the navy, and managed to achieve a command with family assistance (1917). His marriage to Anne Hewlett was in grand military style. His native genius as an inventive soul was recognized (he developed a winch for rescuing pilots downed over water) and this led to an appointment at the Annapolis Naval Academy (1918).

At Annapolis, under the tutelage of retired admirals, Fuller felt very much at home, and began to germinate his "Great Pirates" narrative, wherein the big picture thinking then offered to young officers was a culmination of a long tradition of "thinking globally, acting locally" on the part of high seas figures, many of them pirates, and many of them lost to history because operating invisibly, over the horizon from those who kept the historical accounts (mostly landlubbers).

A few years after his honorable discharge, Fuller attempted to make money using his father-in-law's invention, a morterless brick building system, but failed in this enterprise (1926). This failure, which led to joblessness in Chicago, coupled with the trauma of losing his first child Alexandra to prolonged illness in 1922, pushed Fuller to the brink in 1927. He considered suicide but, as he put it, resolved to commit 'egocide' instead, and turn the rest of his life into an experiment about what kind of positive difference the 'little individual' could make on the world stage. He called himself 'Guinea Pig B' (B for Bucky) and resolved to do his own thinking, starting over from scratch. Hugh Kenner likens this to Descartes' resolve to shut himself in a room until he'd discerned God's truth—a kind of archetypal commitment to a solitary journey.

. . .

It was over this concept of 'tensegrity' that early divisions over the issue of Fuller's character and integrity came to the foreground. Ken Snelson, a star pupil at Black Mountain College (1948), at first enchanted by Bucky's spell, became highly disillusioned when it appeared that Fuller planned to abscond with the "tensegrity" idea without properly crediting his student.

Fuller's reputation for egomania and improperly seizing upon others' ideas as his own may be traced to this Fuller-Snelson split, and led many to question whether the geodesic dome, widely credited to Fuller (who took out a number of patents around the idea) was another case in point. Walter Bauresfeld had hit on the same strategy in 1922, for use in constructing planetaria. Alexander Graham Bell had also made extensive use of the octet truss circa 1907, another one of Fuller's key concepts (also patented).

Fuller's own archives, maintained since his death in 1983 by the Buckminster Fuller Institute (BFI) and his estate (EBF), details his side of the story and he seems to have died with a clear conscience regarding these matters—realizing they would remain bones of contention. . . .

Figure 6.13. Excerpt from Kirby Urner's biography of R. Buckminster Fuller. `www.grunch.net/synergetics/bio.html`

The Snelson controversy concerns discoveries that Fuller called tensegrity, for *tension integrity*. Ken Snelson, a sculptor (`www.grunch.net/snelson/`) recalls his version of its history in an email to the *International Journal of Space Structures* in response to their request for information for a planned special issue on tensegrity (`www.grunch.net/snelson/rmoto.html`). The events unfold at Black Mountain College in North Carolina in the summer of 1949. Snelson, who had been captivated by Fuller at Black Mountain the previous summer, had spent an aimless year building models or artworks (he couldn't decide whether he was an engineer or an artist) that used geometrical ideas he learned from Fuller. Snelson takes up the story:

> When we got together again in June I brought with me the plywood X-Piece (shown). When I showed him the sculpture, it was clear from his reaction that he hadn't understood it from the photos I had sent. He was quite struck with it, holding it in his hands, turning it over, studying it for a very long moment. He then asked if I might allow him to keep it. It hadn't been my intention to part with it, but I gave it to him, partly because I felt relieved that he wasn't angry that I had employed geometry (Buckminster Fuller's geometry) in making art. That original small sculpture disappeared from his apartment, so he told me at the end of the summer.
>
> Next day he said he had given a lot of thought to my "X-column" structure and had determined that the configuration was wrong. Rather than the X-module for compression members, they should be shaped like the central angles of a tetrahedron, that is, like spokes radiating from the gravitational center, to the vertices of a tetrahedron. Of course the irony was that I had already used that tetrahedral form in my moving sculpture, and rejected it in favor of the kite-like X modules because they permitted growth along all three axes, a true space-filling system, rather than only along a single linear axis. Those were not yet the years when students easily contradicted their elders, let alone their professors.
>
> Next day I went into town and purchased metal telescoping curtain rods in order to build the "correct" structure for Bucky. I felt a little wistful but not at all suspicious of his motive as he had his picture taken, triumphantly holding the new structure I had built.

Fuller said in a letter to Snelson that he mentioned Snelson's role in speeches, but never in print, according to Snelson. When in 1959 Fuller's tensegrity ideas were displayed at the Museum of Modern Art in New York City, Snelson, knowing the curator, forced Fuller to admit publicly that Snelson had contributed.

Searching at the Buckminster Fuller Institute for `Snelson`, we quickly find Fuller's recollection of the incident in *Everything I Know*, Vol. 8, though he incorrectly places it in 1958–59:

> Then in the second summer at Black Mountain, Ken showed me a sculpture that he had made, and, in an abstract world of sculpture, and what he had made was a-a tensegrity structure. And he had a structural member out here two structural members out here, that were not touching the base, and they were being held together held they were in tension. And I explained to Ken that this was a tensegrity. Man, I had found, had only developed tensegrity structure in wire wheels and in universal joints. Universal joints where he had a steel shaft, and the reason for needing a universal joint because you were changing the angle of the drive, and you had two shafts, and each one of them came to three arm points like this, tetrahedronally like this. . . . In other words it was a tensional interconnection. So man had used tensegrity in this drive shaft of the universal joints. He had also made it with the wire wheel where he had an island of compression as the hub, and an atoll of compression at the rim, and the whole thing was tensionally cohered. So this is the only place I found that man actually had tensegrity. So when Ken Snelson showed me this little extension thing he did it was really just an arbitrary form, he saw that you could do it, but he was just, as I say, an artistic form or something startling to look at. And I said, "Ken, that really is the tensegrity and it's what I'm looking for because what you've done I can see relates to

> the octahedron and this gives me a clue of how this goes together in all the energetic geometry.
>
> So Ken opened up my eyes to the way to go into the geometry.

Fuller clearly sees Snelson as having contributed in the form of an artwork one more instance of tensegrity to the two that Fuller already knew. He seems not to be particularly defensive in his explanation.

He is similarly at peace with the fact that Alexander Graham Bell independently invented the octet truss—a key tensegrity structure. Fuller explains as he answers questions in an interview (`www.grunch.net/synergetics/docs/bellnote.html`):

> **Q.** It seems to me that Bell's tetrahedron, which he developed while working on kites, is very like your geodesic structure?
> **A.** Exactly the same.
>
> **Q.** When you developed your structures, did you know about the work of Alexander Graham Bell?
> **A.** I did not. I was astonished to learn about it later. It is the way nature behaves, so we both discovered nature. It isn't something you invent. You discover. I had the great advantage of being allowed to look through all of his notes in Washington at the National Geographic [Society]. His grandson had me admitted to his beautiful notebooks and I found where he comes to the actual discovering of it. The thing he was interested in was how to make a stronger airplane wing. He was probably taken with Langley [aviation pioneer Samuel Pierpont Langley] and all the others and he was trying to understand how he might do something better. And he comes to discovering omni-triangulation. I call it the octahedron-tetrahedron truss. Then of course he went right on with his kites but I knew absolutely nothing about it until I had discovered the same thing myself.

The Bell case seems to be a pure instance of independent discovery.[3] We skip tracking down the Bauersfield's claim.

Overall, Snelson's criticism of Fuller mutes the rah-rah enthusiasm of the many sites we have found. RBF has a rock-solid reputation still, but even the finest diamonds have tiny imperfections.

Finally, in terms of filling out our profile of Fuller, there is the repeated mention of buckminsterfullerenes. What are they? The first biography we read ends with the statement

> He has the distinction of having both his names used for a scientific entity, the "fullerene" (also known as a "bucky-ball"), a form of carbon whose molecule resembles his geodesic dome.

It's a carbon molecule, and we can assume that Fuller didn't discover it because scientists typically don't name discoveries after themselves. But to find more, we ask Google to search on `buckminsterfullerene` and find a host of useful links. From a *Scientific American* link we find a page from the State University of New York at Stony Brook, `sbchem.sunysb.edu/msl/fullerene.html`, showing images of the molecule and we see that the structure fulfills the "interlocking polygons" requirement of the geodesic dome definition (Figure 6.14). The next link,

[3] According to archivist DeVarco, on two different occasions Bell's descendants gave Fuller octet truss models that Bell had made. So, they apparently harbor no disagreement with this view.

www.msu.edu/~hungerf9/bucky1.html, is to Michigan State University's Nanotechnology Laboratory, which provides a succinct definition:

> **Buckminsterfullerene**, C_{60}, the third allotrope of Carbon, was discovered in 1985 by Robert Curl, Harold Kroto, and Richard Smalley. Using laser evaporation of graphite they found C_n clusters (where n>20 and even) of which the most common were found to be C_{60} and C_{70}. For this discovery they were awarded the 1996 Nobel Prize in Chemistry.

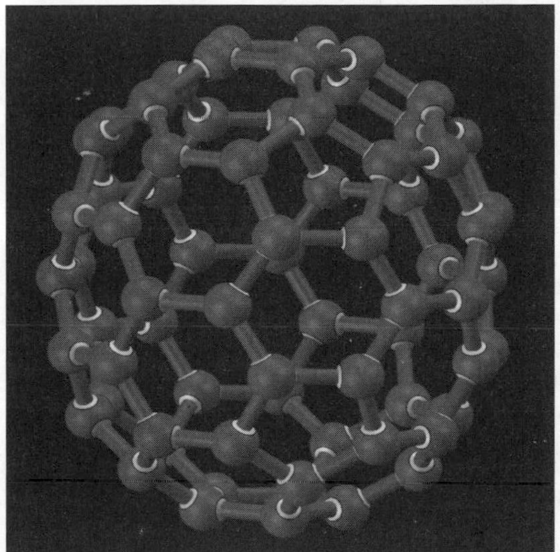

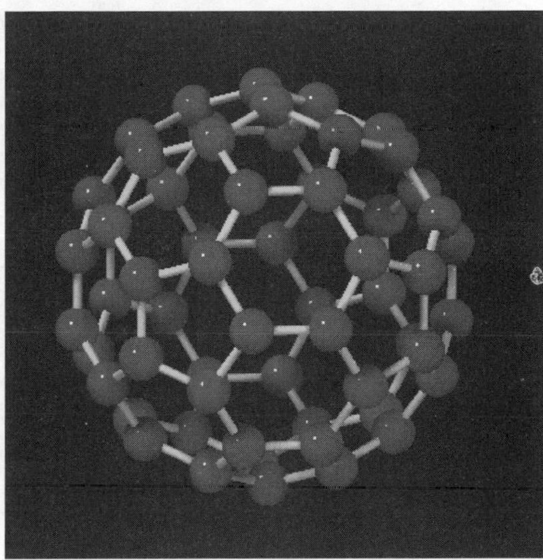

Figure 6.14. Graphic rendering of buckminsterfullerenes, buckey-balls, C_{60} and C_{70}, respectively.

Checking the online dictionary to find that *allotrope* means "structural form of" (differentiating bucky-balls from graphite and diamond forms of carbon), we've answered the question: A fullerene is a stable molecule of Carbon composed of 60 or 70 atoms in the shape of a geodesic sphere. However, the discovery of fullerenes piques our curiosity, and we decide to go to the Nobel Prize site to learn more about the discovery.

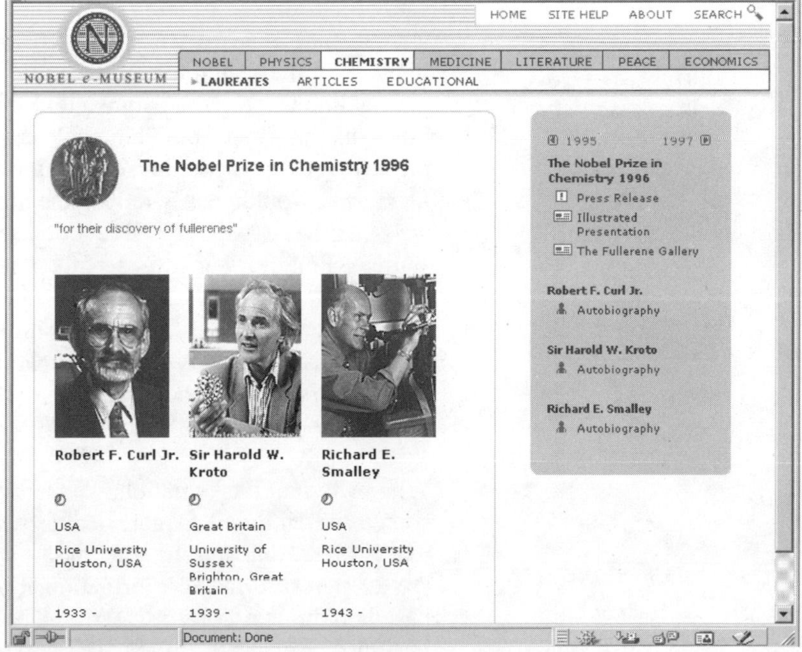

Figure 6.15. The Nobel Prize site for the discovery of the buckminsterfullerene.

Recalling that all countries have a country extension, and that Sweden is the home of the Nobel Prize, we correctly guess at the site www.nobel.se. There we click chemistry > laureates > 1996 to find the page shown in Figure 6.15. From there we can read the "illustrated presentation" explaining the apparatus and experiment that Curl, Kroto, and Smalley used to produce bucky-balls and win the prize. As it happens, C_{60} has the exact structure of a soccer ball: 12 pentagons and 20 hexagons.

Of course, the mention of soccer gets us to wondering how the Ajax Amsterdam team is doing, so we click up. . . .

Wrap-Up

We explored Buckminster Fuller's life only because he was an interesting person. Being finished, at least for the moment, we can put the computer to sleep and get some sleep ourselves. But often the next step is to use the information from an investigation for some other purpose, say, to write a report. In that case, it is best before turning off the computer to create a summary file containing

- Bookmarks from the sites visited—they can be copied from the browser as a group
- Notebook entries of the search terms used with the search engines
- Brief notes on the your impressions—interesting discoveries, most useful sites, why you looked up specific topics, and so forth

This collected information represents the record of your research, and it will be your source material for writing the report. The purpose of writing down your impressions immediately is that they are ephemeral. The amazement of new discoveries wears off, you forget points, and time changes your perspective on the content. Though it is important to have the perspective of time to digest what you've learned and to organize it in your mind, the excitement of learning something new gives a fresh quality to your notes that will not be available later.

SUMMARY

The goal of this chapter has been to illustrate curiosity-driven research using the WWW, and we have been quite successful (see a summary of our efforts at the end of the chapter, following the exercises). The two dominant features of this tour through Buckminster Fuller's life were the process by which we found the information and the methods by which we determined whether the information was authoritative. Additionally, we sought to use the "right" source for the type of information sought.

In terms of the search for information, the emphasis was on learning enough to ask the right question. To do so, we took a quick look at a brief biography, learned that Fuller had invented something called a Dymaxion house and car, and concluded from the term's uniqueness that searching for biographical information containing *Dymaxion* would greatly reduce the hits. It did, tremendously. Similarly, searching on `"Guinea Pig B"` led to a rich set of links composed largely of primary sources. Finally, "buckminsterfullerene" with its narrow technical meaning led us to the essential information without additional qualification. Further, we avoided trying a Web search each time we sought information, but rather consulted a likely source directly based on the type of information sought—dictionary, biography database, WNET personnel, Nobel Prize page. The strategy effectively eliminated any "aimless wandering" around the Web.

When we found information, we were always concerned with its authoritativeness. In some cases, it didn't matter, such as when we checked the short biography to find words like *Dymaxion.* In other cases, we sought primary sources, knowing that they are the purest forms of information about a topic because they report information based on direct experience. With respect to secondary sources, we preferred signed to unsigned works. When the page was signed, we checked the credentials of the author. Secondary sources were valuable both because they could fill in gaps in our knowledge and could show us how others interpreted the same information. Our goal was to learn as much as possible from primary sources so that we could interpret the information ourselves, and then to read secondary sources for further elaboration. This strategy enables us to distinguish other people's opinions from the facts.

Finally, we began the chapter by noting that the Web is better in many ways than reading a book on a particular topic, and it is. In a brief amount of time we have consulted primary data from Fuller, his colleagues, and family. We have relied on short biographies, archived photographs, film clips, audio clips, the dictionary, animations, and a broad collection of other types of reference material. The multimedia resources especially have given us the opportunity to form our own impressions, unmediated by others. Computer searches, including global searches with Google, site searches, and page searching have sped our discovery of information. We have sampled various authors' essays on Fuller. Further, the links provided by people who have found the material before us have connected us to information we might not have known existed. Truly we have discovered Buckminster Fuller based on our own curiosity.

EXERCISES

1. Spend 15 minutes playing *Stump the Crawler*: Find pairs of English nouns, for example, *depreciation* and *organdy,* whose AND query (`depreciation AND organdy`) in Google returns the fewest number of hits. The goal is to find pairs that have zero hits. Report your five best (fewest hits) pairs.
2. What is a primary source in the context of biography?
3. What advantages do primary sources have over other sources?
4. Under what circumstances was the term *Dymaxion* coined, and what does it stand for? [Hint: The question is not answered in the chapter, but requires information from the WWW.]
5. For Norman Borlaug, the Nobel Prize–winning agronomist, find a specifying term (playing the role Dymaxion played in the Fuller search) for a Google query that limits the search enough that `www.theatlantic.com/issues/97jan/borlaug/borlaug.htm` is listed in the first ten hits.
6. For Edward R. Murrow, the CBS journalist, find a specifying term for a Google query that limits the search to less that 1% of the hits that `Edward AND Murrow` receives.
7. With respect to Edward R. Murrow, explain the significance of the transcript located at `www.indiana.edu/~ivieweb/murrow.htm`.
8. Using Google alone, find out what performance of Beethoven's Ninth Symphony was probably the most significant for the conductor and composer Leonard Bernstein.

THE BUCKMINSTER FULLER RESEARCH PATH

The listing below describes the research path followed in this chapter. Most lines represent an access to a WWW document, image, audio or film clip, and so on. Indenting indicates subsidiary actions.

- Begin with a Google search because "Buckminster" is a distinctive name
  - Fail—too many hits
- Restart by checking online biography sites to find some characterizing term
  - Succeed—find "dymaxion"
  - Learn basic facts about RBF's life, including that he is related to Margaret Fuller
      - Check online biography of Margaret Fuller—19th C feminist thinker, died in shipwreck
- Check Google for further biographical material using "dymaxion"; select a highly ranked biography
  - Find that he called himself "Guinea Pig B," a characterizing, personal term
  - Discover his "little, penniless, and unknown individual" quote and his dream of helping humanity
- Check Google for photos to find out what he looks like
- Check Google using "Guinea Pig B"
  - Find WNET site and four essays: Applewhite, Snyder, DeVarco, Feldman
      - Assess sources—Applewhite and Snyder are primary, DeVarco is archivist
    - Check on Feldman, first at biography site, then WNET personnel; writer with access to papers
      - Read Applewhite's essay for professional assessment—great intellect, creative, influential
      - Read Snyder's essay for profile of RBF as father—warm, loving, deeply believed in primary experience
      - Read Feldman's essay—threads facts together with personal aspects of his success, tragedy, family
      - Read DeVarco's essay—the "ephemera" of RBF's life; he called Expo dome Taj Majal
      - Summarize our impressions of essays
      - View video clip; Fuller passionately argues world hunger/housing woes can be eliminated by 1985
  - Visit Buckminster Fuller Institute site
      - Check BFI's authenticity
      - Review Basic Chronology—married to Anne; 2 children, one died; many jobs, many awards
      - Discover *Everything I Know*—42 hours of audio
    - Listen to Fuller describe Allegra's asking him to become more animated
      - Discover dymaxion map on icosahedron and watch animation
      - View the Montreal Expo geodesic dome
      - Wonder how icosahedron and geodesic dome relate
    - Check dictionaries for definitions—unsatisfactory
    - Check dictionaries further and interpret definitions relative to map and Expo dome
  - Assess how complete our knowledge of Fuller is—decide to read another biography
      - Check the Kirby Umer biography found in the Guinea Pig B search
    - Check out Umer
    - Discover there is controversy on originality of Fuller's ideas: Snelson, Bell, Bauersfield
      - Check Ken Snelson, the sculptor
      - Check the *Journal of Space Structures* page giving Snelson's view of discovery
      - Return to BFI's site and *Everything I Know* for Fuller's view; he acknowledges it
      - Check an interview with Fuller regarding independent discovery with Bell; he acknowledges it
  - Conclude our knowledge of Fuller is reasonably complete and balanced
- Wonder what a buckminsterfullerene is, and use Google to find citations
  - Find through *Scientific American* graphic renderings of C_{60} and C_{70}—geodesic spheres, not domes
  - Find a definition and the discoverer's names from SUNY Stonybrook
      - Look up *allotrope* in the dictionary and infer the difference from graphite and diamonds
  - Wonder about the discoverers of bucky-balls
      - Navigate Nobel site and find short biographies of the discoverers

PART II

Digitization and Algorithms

CHAPTER 7

To Err Is Human . . .

Learning Objectives

- Understand the importance of precision in IT.
- Learn the different ways IT systems can fail.
- Learn to watch yourself debug, to be objective, and to be rational in your analysis.
- Know the principles of debugging.
- Apply the principles to faulty IT.
- Develop confidence and courage in your debugging abilities.

A widely known epigram, often prominently displayed on or near the computers of new users, transforms the biblical truism, "To err is human; to forgive is divine," to

> "To err is human, but to really foul things up takes a computer."

One of a computer's defining characteristics—and perhaps for many the source of its greatest frustration—is that it does exactly what it is told to do, but nothing more. Because it will literally follow each instruction "to the letter" and continually check itself, it operates essentially perfectly. So, in truth, the computer doesn't foul things up at all. We humans—those of us who write the software and those of us who use it—are not perfect, of course. And that combination *does* have the potential for really fouling things up. Our response to recognizing our own fallibility is to learn how to discover what's wrong and to extricate ourselves from our difficulties. Learning debugging techniques—the subject of this chapter—is perhaps the best way to deal successfully with mistakes and errors, and to avoid the foul-ups in the first place.

The first goal of this chapter is to recognize that the greatest, most consistent source of problems is our lack of precision. The demonic feature of computers is that they never get what we mean, only what we say. Accordingly we must say exactly what we mean. The next objective is to understand what debugging is in modern IT systems. We then introduce the debugging process using a college student/parent scenario. This allows us the opportunity to kibitz about the process during the student/parent interaction. The next goal is to extract from the story the principles of debugging. The principles do not yield a mechanical procedure guaranteeing success, but rather are a reliable set of guidelines that can be effective. We then apply the principles to the task of debugging a faulty Web page design. This detective work will not reveal *who*dunit because we're the most likely "perps," but rather *what*dunit. The final objective is to illustrate debugging a system when we have no idea how it works.

Precision

When using information technology, we must be precise. The standards of accuracy in IT are extremely high, transcending many people's usual level of precision. In normal conversation, for example, when giving telephone numbers, many North Americans will say "Oh" rather than "Zero," as in Five-Five-Five-Oh-Oh-One-Two for 555-0012. Of course, the listener knows that phone numbers are all numeric, and simply makes the mental conversion. A computer does not know that fact about phone numbers unless it has been specifically programmed to know it and to make the substitution. So, if we type "Oh" for "Zero," a computer would simply accept the input as given and attempt to use it literally. But the letters are different (bit sequences) to a computer.

> **Merrily Mistaken**. Occasionally we purposely exploit this confusion, as in Canada's alternating letter-numeral postal code for Santa Claus, H0H 0H0.

The "Oh" for "Zero" substitution has probably been adopted by North Americans because it is easier to say, having only one syllable. (Other English speakers use *naught.*) It is a verbal simplification and probably not the sort of error we would make if we were asked to type a phone number into a database system or modem software. And, even if it were, the software would catch the error, because such systems *have* been programmed to know that phone numbers are all numeric. Rather than converting "Oh" to "Zero," however, they usually just object to being given nonnumeric input. But there are many cases in which the problem is more insidious and the computer cannot offer assistance.

Exactly How Accurate Is "Precise"?

New email or Web users quickly have the experience of typing an incorrect email address or URL. A common error is to confuse "Oh" and "Zero," or "El" and "One," though there are many other mistakes new users can make. If computers can catch mistakes like "Oh" for "Zero" in modem software or databases, why can't they catch them in email addresses and URLs? The reason is simple: Whereas "Oh" and "El" are illegal in all phone numbers, they are not illegal in all email addresses or URLs. For example, `flo@exisp.com` and `f10@exisp.com` could both be legitimate email addresses. If the software made "Zero" for "Oh" and "One" for "El" substitutions, poor Flo would never get any email. So, computers must necessarily accept the letters or numbers as given for email addresses or URLs. Corrections are not possible. Users must be scrupulously accurate when entering such information.

Be Sensitive. Be alert to case sensitivity—the distinction between lower- and uppercase—in email addresses and URLs. Computers distinguish between *C* and *c* in some cases, and in others they have been programmed to ignore case. For example, case does not matter in Internet domain names—`flo@exisp.com` and `flo@ExISP.COM` are the same—because case is normalized for DNS lookup. But frequently the "local" information in URLs, that is, the text after "/" symbols is case sensitive because it is processed by the destination Web server. So, `www.exisp.com/flo/home/` and `www.exisp.com/FLO/HOME/` may be different. In fact, flo, Flo, fLo, flO, FLo, FlO, fLO, and FLO are potentially all different. When in doubt, assume that case matters.

The general principle operating is this: Call the kinds of inputs just discussed *field inputs* because they are the sorts of information that are entered into boxes on forms, that are used for names, code numbers, user IDs, files, folder names, and so on. All such field inputs are governed by some *lexical structure*, rules that specify the legal forms for the input fields. The lexical structure imposes limitations on what symbols can be used in specific positions, possibly how many symbols can be used (i.e., a length limit), and possibly restrictions on legal punctuation symbols. Lexical constraints can be extremely restrictive. For example, the lexical structure for inputting course grades is limited to at most two symbols: the first symbol must be chosen from {A, B, C, D, F} and the second symbol must be chosen from {+, -, ƀ}. (The ƀ denotes *blank*.) So, A+ is OK, but C++ is wrong. Lexical constraints can be loose, too, allowing any sequence of symbols of any length. Computers generally check to see that the lexical constraints are met, preventing lexical errors. But, if the lexical structure permits both alternatives of a commonly confused symbol, no check can be made. Both alternatives are legal as in UserIDs. Precision is essential.

Spacing Out. The ƀ will represent blank or space. This notation solves the problem that spaces must be given a visual form in some cases so that we know that they're there. "Product dots," ·, are used by word processors (Chapter 3), but when they are easily confused with other symbols, we use ƀ to represent blank.

Clearly, then, computers are not being perverse. They simply follow directions, as they must do. Because it is essential to be scrupulously accurate when supplying any input to a computer, we can avoid considerable grief by being as exact as we possibly can be. It is obviously faster and less frustrating to enter information exactly than to be sloppy, have to find the mistake, and enter it correctly later.

Debugging

Debugging is the act of figuring out why a faulty process or system doesn't work properly. The term, which is synonymous with *troubleshooting,* is most commonly applied to computer or communication systems, especially software, but the techniques are the same whether the systems are mechanical, architectural, business, or otherwise. People engage in debugging all the time. When their cars don't start, they deduce that the battery is dead or there is no fuel in the tank. Though debugging is logical reasoning applied to a faulty mechanism and is usually "learned from experience" throughout life, there are principles and effective strategies associated with it that we should acquire. Knowing these techniques takes on greater importance in information technology because a major part of using IT systems is figuring out why things are not working properly.

A Bug's Life. Admiral Grace Murray Hopper, a computer pioneer, coined the term *bug* for a glitch in a computer system while she was working on the Harvard Mark I. When the Mark II computer got a moth jammed in one of its relays (electro-mechanical switches), bringing the machine down, technicians taped the bug into the machine's logbook (Figure 7.1).

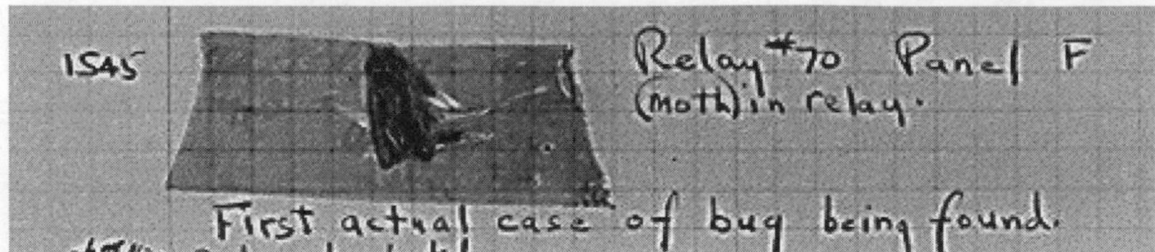

Figure 7.1. The Harvard Mark II logbook noting "First actual case of bug being found," from the Smithsonian Institution.

The goal of this section is to take an objective look at debugging as preparation for our intense use of computers and IT applications. To have a situation in which to discuss debugging, consider the following scenario:

> *Sophomoric Humor*—You and your friends have made a video spoofing college life. You showed it to your cluster in the dorm, and everyone thought it was hilariously funny. You sent a copy to your parents, hardly able to wait to hear their praise of your cleverness, but you heard nothing. Eventually you phoned them to ask if they got the tape, and they replied, "Yes. We tried it in the VCR player, but something's wrong." Your impulse is to say, "You're pathetic. Fix it!" but you ask brightly, "What was wrong?"

In a moment we'll debug your folks and their VCR system, but first, what about debugging generally?

The first point to notice is that debugging an information system is slightly different than most debugging in everyday life, for example, figuring out why a car won't start. Faults and failures in everyday life usually involve correct, working systems with a broken or worn-out part. That is, the system is properly designed and constructed, but some part failed. The car's dead battery keeps it from starting. When the part is replaced, the system works. The analogy in information systems is when we have entered wrong data or wrong configuration information in a working system. When it's corrected, the system works. But another possibility with information systems is that they have a *logical design error*. An analogy in car design would be if the backup lights, which should only illuminate when the car is in reverse gear, come on when stepping on the brakes. This would be a design or construction error. In software, such logical errors are quite possible even in commercial software, and users must be aware that a correct, working system cannot be relied upon. Despite that fact, a "correct, working system" will always be our initial hypothesis.

A second aspect of debugging information systems is that *we* are generally part of the problem. In information systems we command the computer to perform specific activities, and present it with many inputs. When these inputs get the computer into an erroneous state despite our belief that they should have achieved our intended result, the two possibilities—wrong data or erroneous command—involve us. Our commands or data led to the problem, and so we'll have to fix it or our goals will not be achieved. Computers cannot debug themselves, though they do detect and correct low-level errors such as memory errors. The two types of mistakes are treated differently.

When our wrong data creates an error, the two usual causes are either that we *understand* the system and just goofed up, or that we *don't understand* the system and goofed up. In the first case, we merely go back to a logically stable place, for example, begin afresh, and navigate through the data entry again, being more careful. Typically, in these cases, we have some vague idea where the mistake might have occurred, and fixing it is easy. In the second case where we don't understand the system, the problem is almost certainly *our* conceptual error. In such cases, debugging will rely more on the how-to-learn-a-new-system guidelines given in Chapter 3 than on the debugging guidelines here, though debugging principles will probably be needed, too. Of course, the situation is not always so neatly divided. Often we *think* we understand the system, but don't. Such cases then become indistinguishable from the logical error cases, but the logical error is with our understanding.

When a command is at fault, we must debug the system, even if we didn't make the system. This will involve the steps outlined in this chapter, but it will also require precision in typing and thinking to avoid introducing more errors. Introducing new errors simply makes the problem worse, usually much worse, so it is generally good advice to rivet our attention on debugging the immediate problem, postponing distractions and side concerns until later.

Finally, not only is the computer unable to debug itself, we can't debug it directly, either. That is, failures are internal to the computer, either in the data stored or the logic of the software. To get diagnostic information, we have to ask the computer to report what data it has stored, to run the faulty software, and so forth. We are one step removed from the failure and the causes and will need the computer to help us find the problem.

Work Around. Though the 1960s slogan "If you're not part of the solution, you're part of the problem" may still apply in social issues, the modern version for IT is: "If it's not part of the solution, it can't be a problem." That is, if you can find a solution without using a problem (faulty) part of the system, you've achieved your goal. This idea of bypassing an error with an alternative approach is called a *workaround.* Workarounds are essential when you are using commercial software. Bugs in commercial systems are usually not fixed until the next version, so bypassing errors is essential.

Tracking Down a Bug

Returning to the problem of why your parents haven't watched your videotape, we assess the situation. What you know is that your parents have tried the videotape in their VCR player—which you're very familiar with, having spent most of last break watching movies on it—and it didn't play the tape. That's all the information you have, plus the fact that there's a bug somewhere.

Debugging is solving a mystery, and just as we watch detectives solve mysteries in whodunits, we should watch ourselves solving the mystery when debugging. Why? Because doing so will probably direct us to a solution faster than if we aimlessly "try stuff." By deliberately asking questions such as, "Do I need more clues (inputs)?" "Are my clues reliable?" "What is the hypothesis to explain the problem?" we will likely avoid distractions and irrelevancies, and discover a resolution more swiftly.

The first step in debugging is to *verify that the problem is reproducible*. Computers are deterministic, which means that they will do exactly the same thing every time if given the same input. But there is a tiny possibility that a one-time transient glitch caused the problem, so start by determining if the problem can be re-created.

You ask your folks,

"Can you try the tape again?"

And, as the scenario unfolds, your parents report that there is nothing showing on the TV.

The next step is to *be sure that you know exactly what the problem is*. Agatha Christie mysteries usually have a dead body, making the problem clear. The mystery is who murdered the person, not why the dead person failed to show up for work the next morning. But in information technology, a sequence of subsidiary operations may take place following an error, and eliminating them is essential. For example, the reason there are no mailing labels coming out of the printer may be due to a printer problem, but it could be a problem with the word processor or database that is sending the labels to the printer, or it could be that the file containing the addresses is empty; that is, there are no addresses to print. We don't want to be debugging the printer when the problem is an empty file. So, determining the exact problem is critical.

Your parents should be a little more explicit about the problem. You patiently ask,

"What's on the screen?"
"Nothing."
"Is it black nothing? or blue nothing? or snow nothing?"
"Snow."

A standard next step is to *check all of the "obvious" sources of error*. Of course, if the error were all that obvious, you wouldn't be in the midst of debugging. . . . you'd have fixed the problem and be on your way. What constitutes an obvious source of error depends on the problem being debugged, naturally, but checking inputs, connections, and links, and so on is standard.

Ask your parents to check all of the obvious causes. Is there power to the VCR? (The TV obviously has power.)

"Yes."

Is the tape in the machine (it couldn't be upside down because the drive mechanism doesn't allow that)?

"Yes."

Is the tape rewound?

"Yes."

Have they "clicked" Play?

"Yes."

Is the tape advancing?

"Sounds like it."
"What happens?"
"Snow reigns."

Clearly the VCR is pretty much as you left it. Except it isn't playing your hilarious tape.

It's now time to apply a basic strategy of debugging, to *isolate the problem by partitioning the operation into those parts that are working and those that are not*. The strategy will necessitate formulating a hypothesis of where the problem is located, and possibly gathering additional data. At this point nothing should be taken for granted. Limit the number of untested assumptions you make. The error could be anywhere. The goal is to eliminate as many possibilities as you can, or equivalently, to focus in on the specific, failing part.

In the case of your parents' VCR, the system is composed of two basic units, the TV and the VCR player. The data, which is on the tape, is read by the player and transmitted to the TV for display. You ask yourself, can either of them be eliminated from consideration? If the VCR were OK and the TV were faulty, the TV probably wouldn't show regular programs.

"Do you get normal TV programs?"
"Define normal."
"You know what I mean . . . ABC?"
"Yes."

So, if the TV is OK, the VCR must be broken, though it seems from the earlier diagnostics that it is working mechanically; that is, the videotape is running through it. So, if it's OK, what other parts are there? There's the cable connecting the VCR to the TV.

"Are the TV and VCR connected?"
"Didn't look, but it's the way it's always been."

So, they're connected as you left them when you left for college. And there are no other parts.

Everything seems to check out. This is a common situation in debugging. You analyze the problem, perhaps getting additional data and conclude that everything is OK. Except it's not. There is a bug somewhere. Though it is natural to become frustrated, the constructive response is to review your analysis. You've made some assumptions, gathered data, made some tests, interpreted the results, and made some deductions. Ask yourself, "Is there a wrong assumption?" "Am I misunderstanding what the data means?" "Did I make a wrong deduction?" A good way to proceed is to *step through the process from beginning to end, comparing what should be happening with what is happening*. It's important at this point to think objectively about the process.

So, starting from the beginning, you ask your parents to put in a different tape.

"OK, we put in the tape of your sister's wedding, but it's the same thing. Snow."

You know that tape works. You had to sit through the whole two tedious hours of it last summer.

"Is it rewound?"
"Yes. Just did it."
"When you clicked on Rewind, was the screen blue and the letters R-E-W displayed?"

This is a prediction you make about how the TV–VCR system is supposed to operate based on your experience with it.

"No, it's still snow."

At this point you have a prediction that is inconsistent with an observation. That's what you're looking for. Why would the VCR not be telling the TV that it is rewinding the tape? Possibly because they're not connected.

"Can you check if the cable from the VCR is plugged into the back of the TV?"

And at this point you know that they're not connected. As you're waiting for your parents to verify that the cable is not connected to the back of the TV, you recall last summer when the Women's World Cup Soccer final was on. How a bunch of your friends came over to watch the game and you carried the TV out to the patio. Everyone sat around eating pizza and cheering. It was late when you carried the TV back into the house, and you postponed plugging in the VCR cable until morning. And forgot. When you left for college they were still unconnected.

"Nope, the cable wasn't plugged into the TV. It's working now. How'd you figure that out?"
"Got lucky, I guess. Hope you like the video."
"We're sitting down to watch it right now."

Debugging Recap

The key point of the debugging illustration is not that debugging occasionally reveals embarrassing errors, but rather that there is a semi-organized process to follow to find out what's wrong when an error is discovered. The key points were

- Verify that the error is reproducible.
- Determine exactly what the problem is.
- Eliminate the "obvious" causes.
- Partition the process, separating out the parts that work from the part that does not.
- When you reach a dead end, reassess the information you have, trying to identify what mistake you are making.

Work through the process from start to finish, making predictions of what should happen and verifying that the predictions are fulfilled.

This is not a recipe, but it is a useful set of guidelines. Debugging requires tough, logical reasoning to determine what's wrong. But, it's possible to do, and though it is not as entertaining as deducing whodunit from the few clues Agatha Christie reveals, there is a certain satisfaction to figuring it out.

Closer Examination. Socrates said, "The unexamined life is not worth living." In debugging it is enough to examine our debugging process as it progresses.

Butterflies and Bugs: Debugging HTML

To illustrate the debugging principles in action, we develop a small table in HTML. The result we intend is shown in Figure 7.2. The HTML code we've written is shown in Figure 7.3 together with Netscape's interpretation of that text. Obviously, we're not getting the right output, so there is an error somewhere. We could study the HTML very, very closely and "brain out" where the error is, or we could use the debugging strategy. It is recommended that you follow along online.[1]

Butterflies Only -- No Bugs

Food 'n' Foto

Name	Larval Diet	Picture
Behr's Metalmark	Buckwheat	
Bog Copper	Cranberries	
Satyr Comma	Nettles	

Figure 7.2. The intended HTML table.

As we begin the out-of-body experience of watching ourselves debugging the HTML, we recall that the first step is to be sure the error is reproducible. So, we close Netscape and reopen our file using a "fresh" copy of that browser. Unfortunately the results are the same. In fact, Internet Explorer produces the same result, so it is definitely a problem with our HTML.

[1] The file is `www.aw.com/snyder/Chapter7/butterfly.html`

The next step is to identify the problem. In the case of debugging HTML, identifying the problem is straightforward: Just look at the page. In this case we have a table with no pictures and nine columns, so there are apparently two bugs here. There could be more, but we focus on these, guessing that problems like the caption, which is supposed to be centered over the table, is centered over the broken table and will be in the right location when the table is right. So, we focus on the two problems: too many columns and missing images.

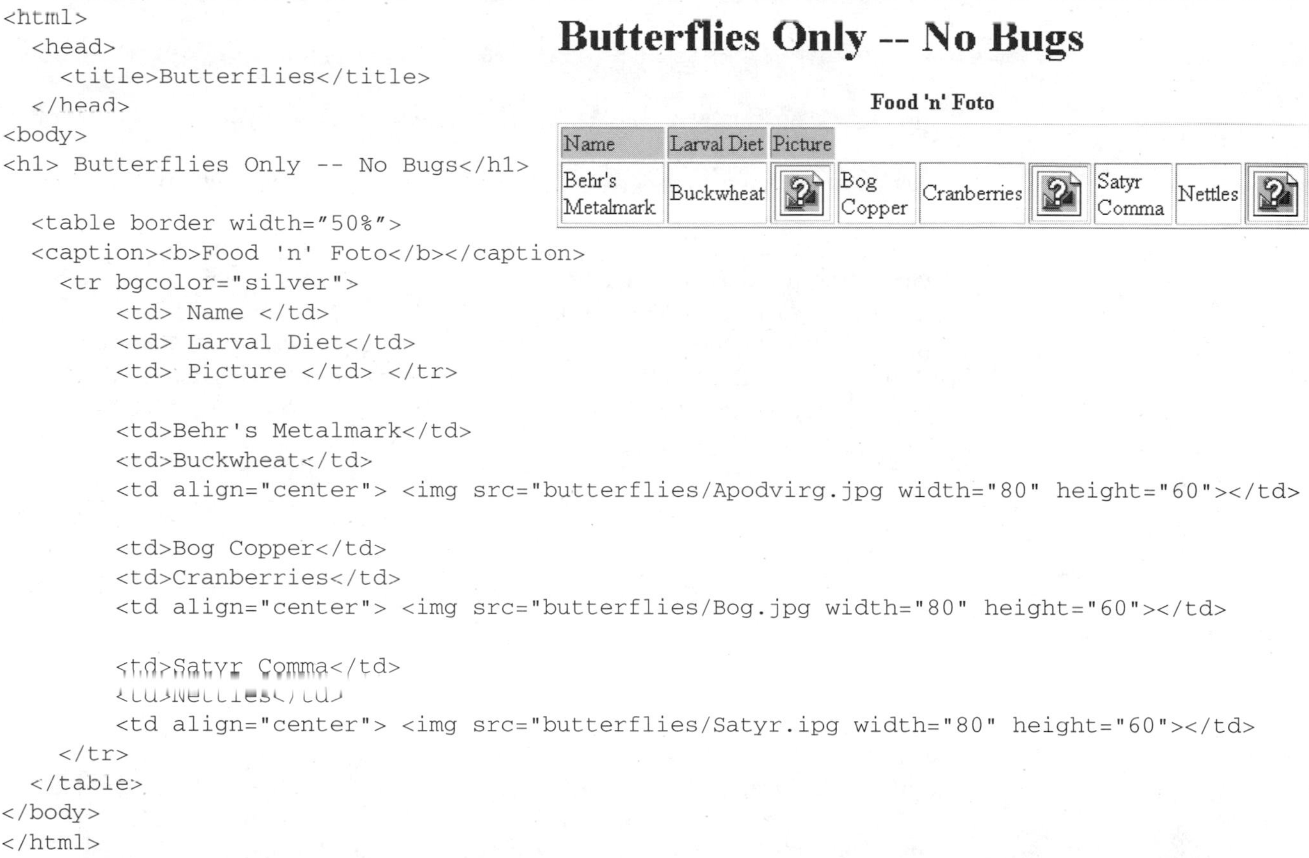

```
<html>
  <head>
    <title>Butterflies</title>
  </head>
<body>
<h1> Butterflies Only -- No Bugs</h1>

  <table border width="50%">
  <caption><b>Food 'n' Foto</b></caption>
    <tr bgcolor="silver">
        <td> Name </td>
        <td> Larval Diet</td>
        <td> Picture </td> </tr>

        <td>Behr's Metalmark</td>
        <td>Buckwheat</td>
        <td align="center"> <img src="butterflies/Apodvirg.jpg width="80" height="60"></td>

        <td>Bog Copper</td>
        <td>Cranberries</td>
        <td align="center"> <img src="butterflies/Bog.jpg width="80" height="60"></td>

        <td>Satyr Comma</td>
        <td>Nettles</td>
        <td align="center"> <img src="butterflies/Satyr.ipg width="80" height="60"></td>
    </tr>
  </table>
</body>
</html>
```


Figure 7.3. Faulty HTML text and its rendering in a browser.

Once the problem has been identified, look for the "obvious" errors. The most obvious HTML error is to forget to close a tag, that is, forget the matching "slash-tag." Inspecting the HTML, however, indicates that every tag is matched. However, we do get lucky. In reviewing the HTML text we notice that our triples of cell data are not all surrounded by the row tags `<tr>` and `</tr>`. Row tags bracket the heading row—the silver background of the heading proves that. But the others are not. Surrounding them with row tags produces the result in Figure 7.4, a definite improvement. As conjectured, the caption is centered over the table. Notice that although we described the problem as too many columns, the actual bug was too few rows.

With one bug swatted, we focus on why there are no pictures. Another obvious error in HTML is to get the relative pathnames wrong, and when checking our `butterflies` directory (Figure 7.5), we notice that we have indeed made another mistake. The names are capitalized in the HTML and they are lowercase in the directory. Though we may not

Butterflies Only -- No Bugs

Food 'n' Foto

Name	Larval Diet	Picture
Behr's Metalmark	Buckwheat	
Bog Copper	Cranberries	
Satyr Comma	Nettles	

Figure 7.4. Page with row tags added.

Figure 7.5. Files in the `butterflies` folder.

know whether case matters for this computer, we make the change anyway. And when we try out the revised page, it looks no different from Figure 7.4. Apparently the change didn't hurt the program, but it didn't help either. There must be a different error. Because the relative pathname directs the browser into a directory to find the file, it could still be wrong. Removing the indirection—that is, the use of the subdirectory to store the images—may help. So, we move the butterfly images into the same directory as the HTML for our page, and rewrite the `<img . . .>` tags to eliminate the `butterflies/` directory level. The table data for the Metalmark becomes

```
<td align="center"> <img src="apodvirg.jpg width="80" height="60"></td>
```

But there is no improvement. What else is there to check?

Having run out of obvious errors and with everything checking out, it is time to move on to the next step of debugging, which is to partition the system to focus on the faulty parts. Again, HTML is relatively easy because the page indicates visually where the error must be. In the present case, the error almost certainly must be in the `<img . . .>` tags. Ignoring the rest of the HTML, we carefully analyze that text, using the `View > Page Source` feature of the Web browser. The source display shows, using color and different fonts, how the browser interprets our HTML. Netscape displays the line as

```
<td align="center"> <img src="apodvirg.jpg width="80" height="60"></td>
```

whereas Internet Explore shows it as

```
<td align="center"> <img src="apodvirg.jpg width="80" height="60"></td>
```

Our simplified relative pathname attribute is visible, but its coloring is strange. The browser indicates that the filename (dark gray) includes the word `width`, which is wrong. We then notice that there is no closing quote mark after the filename. With no closed quote, the pathname spills into the `width` specification. Fixing only this line produces the result in Figure 7.6. The fact that this row is improved indicates that this is the fix, so we change the other two lines, producing the result in Figure 7.7. Isolating our attention on the `<img . . .>` tags has helped, but apparently not quite enough.

We observe that although the addition of a closed quote didn't display the Satyr Comma's image, it did change the spacing, based on a comparison of Figures 7.6 and 7.7. So, the quote was the problem, and we infer that perhaps there is something wrong with the file. The fact that the thumbnail is visible (Figure 7.5) is evidence to the contrary, but it is not airtight. Occasionally one form of a file is OK, while another is not. One debugging strategy is to run an experiment, so we can try to use the `satyr.jpg` file in another application. And it works fine. What can the problem be?

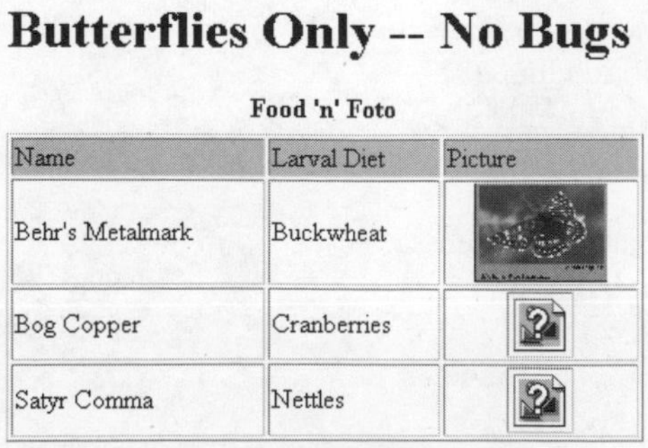

Butterflies Only -- No Bugs

Food 'n' Foto

Name	Larval Diet	Picture
Behr's Metalmark	Buckwheat	
Bog Copper	Cranberries	
Satyr Comma	Nettles	

Figure 7.6. The result of revising one row of HTML.

Butterflies Only -- No Bugs

Food 'n' Foto

Name	Larval Diet	Picture
Behr's Metalmark	Buckwheat	
Bog Copper	Cranberries	
Satyr Comma	Nettles	

Figure 7.7. The result of including quotes after all pathnames.

Reviewing our performance in the investigation: We have corrected the capitalization, so that can't be a problem. We have changed the relative pathnames so they don't involve the directory `butterflies`, and that works, as evidenced by the two pictures that do display. We have fixed the quote, and that has restored the size of the table cell to match in all cases. We have checked the Satyr Comma image file and it works in another application. Basically the HTML should work. We must be making a wrong assumption or misconstruing the evidence.

Focusing on the `<img . . .>` tag must be the right strategy. We assumed that the "quotation mark fix" corrected the names for each file. That's certainly right for the first two butterflies, and we thought it was right for the Satyr Comma, based on the fact that it fixed the table spacing. But maybe not. Reviewing the third image tag using the browser's Source View,

```
<td align="center"> <img src="satyr.ipg" width="80" height="60"> </td>
```

we see that indeed all of the parameters to the attributes (blue) are interpreted correctly. However, there is a microscopic mistake: The file extension has been written `ipg` rather than `jpg`. It's not particularly visible in Figure 7.3, but it's there. So, we had jumped to conclusions about the "quotation mark fix." It helped, but it didn't eliminate the third `<img . . .>` tag from consideration. When we correct the extension, the result is shown in Figure 7.8. This solves the problem, but when we compare to the goal page, we notice there is still a small difference.

The column headings are not correct. Reviewing the figures, we see that it's obvious this has been a problem the whole time. It just wasn't particularly noticeable, given the other problems. And thinking about it, it's clear what the problem is. Tables in HTML should have a *table heading* tag, `<th>` and `</th>`, rather than a table data tag. Correcting that detail produces the identical result to our goal page, completing the debugging task. The column headings are now bold and centered. We revise the text to restore the relative pathnames to use the `butterflies` subdirectory, as originally intended.

Butterflies Only -- No Bugs

Food 'n' Foto

Name	Larval Diet	Picture
Behr's Metalmark	Buckwheat	
Bog Copper	Cranberries	
Satyr Comma	Nettles	

Butterflies Only -- No Bugs

Food 'n' Foto

Name	**Larval Diet**	**Picture**
Behr's Metalmark	Buckwheat	
Bog Copper	Cranberries	
Satyr Comma	Nettles	

Figure 7.8. The corrected file extension page, left, and the goal page, right.

Debugging Postmortem

The bugs in the HTML text have been crushed. In the process we made a series of conjectures, tried a variety of modifications to the program, ran a couple of experiments, and drew various conclusions. How did we do? Certainly the result turned out fine.

For the record, we made the following modifications to the HTML in the process of producing the final result:

1. Enclosed the table rows with `<tr> </tr>` tags.
2. Corrected the capitalization of the file names.
3. Simplified the pathnames to avoid the complexity of referring to the `butterflies` subdirectory.
4. Corrected the quotation mark problem.
5. Corrected the file extension problem for the Satyr Comma.
6. Fixed the `<th> </th>` tags for the first row.
7. Restored the pathnames to allow the images to be kept in the `butterflies` directory.

Of these seven changes, only 1, 4, 5, and 6 were necessary to fix the program. The other changes were not required: Change 2 was not needed because the filenames are not case sensitive, change 3 was not needed because there was no problem with the relative pathnames, and change 7 reversed change 3. The unnecessary changes were introduced in connection with incorrect conjectures about the cause of the error. Making changes that are unnecessary is quite typical because making incorrect conjectures is also quite typical. Luckily these changes were benign—they didn't make the situation worse—but it is possible to introduce additional errors when following the wrong logical path.

When we originally described the errors, we thought we had two: Too many columns and no pictures. In fact, we had four errors:

1. Too many columns, which was actually not enough rows
2. No pictures because of a consistent error of leaving out the closing quote
3. No Satyr Comma picture because of a mistyped extension
4. Wrong heading tags

Error 3 was hidden by error 2, and we simply didn't notice error 4 initially. One error hidden by another is also typical. Though the hidden error didn't interact with the other errors here, it often happens. Interacting errors can be very difficult to track down because they can create data that is very confusing when interpreted as coming from the apparent error. For that reason, we must always remember that multiple errors could be causing the observed problems.

Notice that the most effective technique applied during our debugging exercise was to use the browser Source View feature. Seeing the color- and font-coded HTML source indicated how the browser interpreted our page. This revealed an error and then confirmed that it had been corrected. In general, one of the most powerful debugging techniques is to find ways for the computer to indicate the meaning of the information it stores or the effects of the commands it executes. Having it say how it's interpreting the instructions can separate the case in which we tell it to do the wrong thing from the case in which we command it correctly, but the computer is doing it wrong. This is an important distinction for finding the bug.

Finally, the errors in the HTML code were—with the exception of forgetting the row tags—quite tiny: three missing quotation marks, a wrong character in the file extension, and a wrong character in table heading tags. Of the 582 non-space characters in the original file, the 27 = 3(4 + 5) row tags and 3 quotes represent a 5% addition. The four character corrections are less than 1%. But as we've seen, a single missing or erroneous character can ruin the HTML source. The conclusion: We must be extremely precise.

More Than Meets the Eye

Though debugging HTML is possible because we know and write HTML, we don't create most computer systems, and they are extremely complex, beyond our comprehension. A standard personal computer and its software are more complex in several ways than the (noncomputer parts of the) Space Shuttle. As users we have no idea how something so complex works, so how is it possible to troubleshoot a system we do not understand?

Of course, we cannot debug software and information systems at the detailed implementational level used by programmers or engineers. If there is a fundamental, conceptual error in the system, users probably won't find it. But we don't have to. Before we ever come in contact with a system, it has been extensively tested. This testing doesn't eliminate all errors, but it probably means that the "standard operations" used by "average" users have been run through their paces many times. They should be bug-free, and we should depend on the software.

> **Putting It To the Test.** As noted in Chapter 3, "getting out and getting back in" often works to resolve a faulty application. The reason this tends to work is related to how software is tested. Beginning with a fresh configuration, the testing proceeds "forward" into the application, with the common operations receiving the most attention. So the most stable portion of a system is the part that is reachable from an initial configuration using the basic operations.

To illustrate debugging a system without understanding it, consider a classic debugging scenario: You attempt to print a document and nothing comes out of the printer. Conceptually this situation is similar to the videotape example discussed earlier. Like the VCR/TV system, the computer/printer system is connected by a cable, there is a mechanical component, the flow of information is from one device to the other, and the system has worked in the past. The printing problem is solved just as the videotape problem was solved: Reproduce the error, understand the problem, and check the obvious causes. These include checking the printer's control panel, the paper, the cartridges, the cable connections, the file to be printed, the installation of the printer driver (the correct printer dialog window comes up when the print command is issued), whether others can print if this is a shared printer, and whether you can print another document. When this familiar drill has not solved the problem, you may think it's time to ask for help. You've already gone further than most users, so this wouldn't be embarrassing, but you can do more. Specifically you should proceed with the next step in the debugging strategy, *trying to isolate the problem.* But this is daunting because you don't really understand how printing works. Not to worry. It's still possible to make progress.

Having printed before, you know your computer is configured correctly. You try printing a simple document like a text file in hopes of reducing the complexity of the situation. But it's the same story: The printer driver's dialog window comes up asking how many copies you want, and so forth—you reply `1`, click Print, the machine appears to compute for a moment, but when you check the printer, nothing's there. What could be happening to your output?

Thinking through what you guess to be the process, you speculate that when you click Print, the printer driver must convert the file into the form suitable for the printer. Because the computer runs briefly after you click Print, it's a safe bet that it's doing something like a conversion. Then your computer must send the converted file to the printer. Does it go? Surely, if the computer tried to send the file to the printer and the printer didn't acknowledge getting it, the computer would tell you to plug in the printer. Or would it? Suppose you unplugged the printer from the computer and tried again to print. You run this experiment and the behavior is identical. The printer *couldn't* even receive the converted file, and there were no complaints. What's happening? Where is the file?

Perhaps the computer is saving the converted file. Why? Shouldn't it print if it's told to print? This is a little odd because it's not asking you to plug in the printer. Could the other files you tried to print be waiting too, even though the printer was plugged in earlier? So, you start looking around for the stranded file(s). You locate the printer driver's printing monitor (START > Settings > Printers on the PC; among the active programs on the Mac). When you open up this monitor, what you find is a list of all the files you've tried to print recently. They're not printing—they're just listed.

What you have discovered is the "print queue" for your machine. You didn't know that computers have print queues, but they apparently do. Not being a computer engineer you don't know why they have them, either. But it's obvious that your printing is stalled in the queue. As described in Chapter 3 under "Click Around," you explore the monitor application, discovering that the queue is "turned off" or possibly "wedged." (The actual description for "turned off" varies from system to system; for the PC it is Use Printer Offline, which is set under File; for Macs the Print Queue button is configured to Start Print Queue; shared printers are different still.) Though machines are different, the situation is the same: The computer's settings tell it to queue your converted files rather than trying to print them immediately. How it got into this state may never be discovered. The best approach is to cancel or move to trash all of the jobs in the queue using the facilities of the monitor because there are probably many duplicates, and restart the queue. That is, configure it so that it is attempting to print your files rather than queuing them. Your printing problem may be solved! Or have you forgotten to recable your printer?

Sleep on It. One observation that professionals make about debugging is that, when a bug is not yielding to their best efforts, it's good to take a break. Whether our mind continues to work on the problem subconsciously or if it's simply that returning to a task refreshed tends to clarify our thinking, getting away briefly helps.

Summarizing the situation, you have debugged the printing operation despite its complexity and your admitted lack of knowledge about printing. A key assumption was that the software is correct. You discovered that computers use a print queue to stage jobs for the printer, though it's a mystery why. The queue can become stopped or stalled or otherwise deactivated, but by invoking the print monitor it can be restarted. The process of locating the problem was just the standard debugging strategy applied with a certain amount of courage and common sense. The results were successful. Though there are obviously many potential problems that will not yield to this approach—that actually require some technical knowledge—the assumption should always be that the standard debugging strategy will work. When it's been fully applied without producing a solution, it's time to call Tech Support.

SUMMARY

This chapter began by emphasizing why being precise is so important when using computers. The standard of precision is higher than in most other human endeavors, but being careful and exact smoothes our use of computers. Next we considered the nature of debugging, what it is and why we need to know how to do it. Then we introduced the basic strategy of debugging by helping virtual parents watch their college student's video spoofing college life. That situation allowed us to discuss the whys and hows of debugging. The principles that form the debugging strategy were abstracted into a tidy list in preparation for demonstrating their use in debugging a Web page. The Web page yielded to the strategy directly, thanks largely to the Source view of the document that revealed how the computer was interpreting it. In the postmortem to that effort, we noted that debugging involves both correct and incorrect conjectures about the cause of a problem. Acting on incorrect conjectures can result in unnecessary changes, or worse, harmful changes. Finally, we emphasized that it is possible to debug the operation of a sophisticated system like a computer's printing facility without understanding exactly how it works. This effort uses the standard strategy applied with common sense and courage.

EXERCISES

1. What is debugging?
2. Who coined the term *bug* for a computer glitch?
3. What insect was jokingly called the "first bug"? (Answering this question correctly was worth $1M on a recent TV game show.)
4. How does debugging information systems differ from debugging experiences in everyday life?
5. Why should you "watch yourself" debug, and what should you be watching for?
6. Describe the steps in the debugging process, and briefly explain each step.
7. Why partition a system during debugging?
8. What should be done when you reach a dead end?
9. Why work through the process step by step?
10. Find a small HTML file and print it out. Then make one or a few small errors in it, making it produce a visually wrong output. Find a partner in class, and ask them to debug it. Write a brief report on your partner's application of debugging principles to locate the bug(s). Comment on whether they "watched themselves debug." (Of course, your partner's participation obligates you to debug for your partner.)
11. Why, when debugging the Web page, did we make unnecessary changes to the HTML?

CHAPTER 8

Bits and the "Why" of Bytes

Learning Objectives

- Learn that digitizing represents things by symbols.
- Understand how symbols are formed from patterns.
- Know how the "escape" technique extends encodings.
- Understand how physical and logical worlds connect.
- Learn how the presence and absence of a physical phenomenon encodes information.
- Become familiar with the 8-bit ASCII encoding.
- Appreciate the problems of digitizing the *OED* so a computer can assist in using it.
- Understand how tags specify metadata.

Perhaps one of the most widely known facts about computers and networks is that they record and transmit information in *bits* and *bytes*. Without knowing anything more than basic English, we can guess that whatever bits are they probably represent little pieces of information. But what are bytes? And why is "byte" spelled with a *y*? In this chapter we confirm that bits do represent little pieces of information, we define what bytes are, and by the very end we explain the mysterious use of *y*. But the chapter is much more fundamental than even these basic concepts. It describes how the building blocks of bits and bytes—the atoms and molecules of information—combine to form our virtual world of computation, information, and communication. (Multimedia is covered in Chapter 11.) We even explain how information exists when there is nothing, as when Sherlock Holmes solves the mystery using the information that "the dog didn't bark in the night."

The first objective of this chapter is to establish that digitizing doesn't require digits—any set of symbols will do. Next we explore encoding information using dice, with the objective of learning how pattern sequences can create symbols and symbols can represent information. With these foundational ideas of encoding in mind, our goal is to learn the fundamental patterns on which all information technology is built: the presence and absence of a phenomenon. Called the *PandA* encoding here, this meeting of the physical and logical worlds forms the foundation of information technology. Using our understanding of this fundamental idea, we define bits, bytes, and ASCII. And finally, we describe the digitization of the *Oxford English Dictionary* (*OED*) and show how metadata is added to the content to enable a computer to manipulate it to our advantage.

DIALING FOR $$$

The dictionary definition of *to digitize* is to represent information with digits. In normal conversation, *digit* means the ten Arabic numerals 0 through 9. Thus digitizing uses whole numbers to stand for things. This familiar process represents Americans by Social Security numbers, telephones as phone numbers, and books as ISBN numbers. Such digital representations have probably been used since numerals were invented. Though familiar, this sense of *digitize* is much too narrow for the digital world of information technology.

One limiting aspect of the conventional definition of *digitize* is that it calls for the use of the ten digits. The result is a whole number, but in many cases the numerical property is inessential and of little use. The benefit of numbers is that they quantify things and enable arithmetic to be performed. But Social Security numbers, phone numbers, and ISBN numbers are not quantities. You are not better than someone else is if you have a larger telephone number. Nor is it meaningful to multiply two ISBN numbers together. Thus, when there is no particular need for the quantifying properties of numbers, there is no need to use the digits. But what is the alternative?

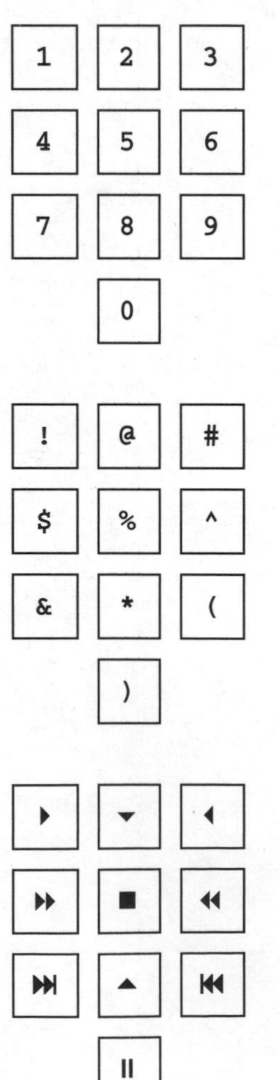

Figure 8.1. Three symbol assignments for a telephone keypad.

Digitizing in information technology can use any appropriate symbols. For example, the North American telephone number 888 555 1212 could be represented as *** %%% !@!@. This encoding, rather than using {1, 2, 3, 4, 5, 6, 7, 8, 9, 0}, uses the symbol set {!, @, #, $, %, ^, &, *, (,)} These symbols are simply the uppercase characters on a keyboard corresponding to the digits, that is, the numerals typed with the shift key pressed. Alternatively, the symbol set { ▶, ▼, ◀, ▶▶, ■, ◀◀, ▶▶|, ▲, |◀◀, II } results in the phone number being represented as ▲▲▲ ■■■ ▶▼▶▼. This could be called the *player* encoding because it uses the standard symbols from tape and disc players. These representations work just as well as the digits as long as the telephone keypad is relabeled, as shown in Figure 8.1. The reason the encoding works is that the only role for a phone number's digits is to specify the sequence of keys to press to "dial" a specific phone line. Any encoding of unique symbols will work for that purpose as long as the keypad is labeled properly.

One practical advantage of the use of digits over other less familiar alternative representations is that digits have short names. The characters used in the preceding alternate representations have verbose standard names. Imagine speaking a phone number "asterisk asterisk exclamation point closing parenthesis exclamation point . . ." In fact, as information technology has adopted representations involving these symbols, they are acquiring shorter names. For example, exclamation point is widely pronounced *bang* by computer professionals; asterisk is pronounced *star,* and so forth. The alternative to saying "eight eight eight five five five one two one two" might be "star star star cent cent cent bang at bang at," which is just as brief. So, the advantage of brevity is not limited to digits.

One other apparent advantage of digits for encoding information like telephone numbers is that the items can be listed in numerical order. This feature is rarely used for the kinds of information discussed here; for example, telephone books are ordered by the name of the person to whom the phone line is assigned rather than by the number. But, sometimes ordering items is useful, as in a list of books by ISBN. To order information when symbols other than digits are used, we need to agree on an ordering for the basic symbols. This is called the *collating sequence*. In the same way, the digits are ordered

0 < 1 < 2 < 3 < 4 < 5 < 6 < 7 < 8 < 9

the player symbols could be ordered

⏸ < ▶ < ▼ < ◀ < ⏩ < ■ < ⏪ < ⏭ < ▲ < ⏮

Then, two coded phone numbers can be ordered based on which has the larger first symbol, or if the first symbol matches, which has the larger second symbol, or if the first two symbols match, which has the larger third symbol, and so on. For example,

▲ ⏸ ⏸ ■ ■ ■ ▶ ▼ ▶ ▼ < ▲ ▲ ▲ ■ ■ ■ ▶ ▼ ▶ ▼

So digitizing means *representing information by symbols*—not just the ten digit symbols. But which symbols would be best? Before answering that question, we should consider how the choice of symbols interacts with the things being encoded.

Encoding with Dice

Because information can be digitized using any symbols, consider a representation based on dice. A single die has six sides, and it will be the patterns on the sides of the dice that will be used for this digital representation.[1] Consider representing the Latin alphabet with dice.

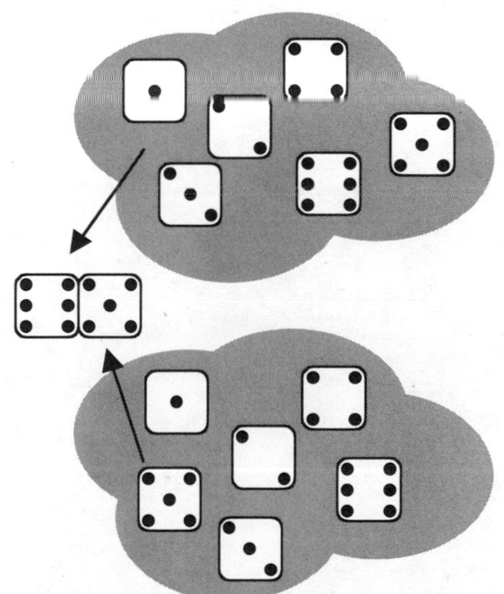

Figure 8.2. Pairing two dice patterns results in 36 = 6 × 6 possible pattern sequences.

With 26 letters in the alphabet, but only six different patterns on a die, there are more letters to represent than there are patterns available. This is typical. So we use multiple patterns to represent each letter. How many will be required? Two dice patterns together produce $6 \times 6 = 36$ different pattern sequences because each of the six patterns of one die can be associated with each of the six different patterns of the other die. (See Figure 8.2.) Three dice can define $6 \times 6 \times 6 = 216$ different pattern sequences because there are six choices for the first position, six for the second position, and six for the last. More generally, *n* dice together can produce 6^n different pattern sequences. If instead of six there is some other number *m* of basic patterns, a sequence of *n* of them produces m^n different pattern sequences.[2]

Returning to the problem of digitizing the alphabet, we can agree to call each of the pattern sequences produced by pairing two dice a *symbol*. Then we can associate these dice-pair symbols with the letters simply by listing them off:

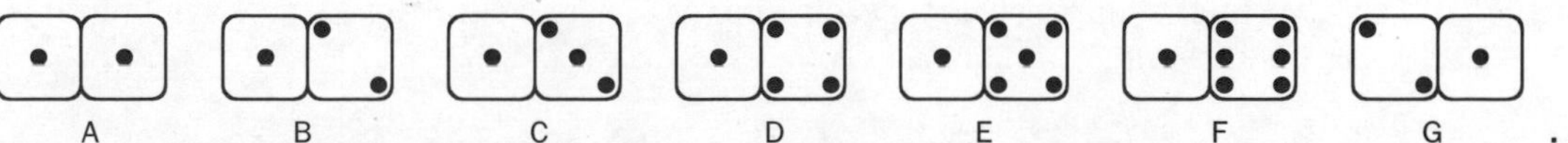

[1] The patterns can be interpreted as numbers, of course, but for the moment we ignore that property.

[2] Recall that m^n means $m \times m \times \ldots \times m$, i.e., *n* copies of *m* multiplied together.

It helps to be orderly about associating the letters with the symbols to make it easier to remember the encoding. In fact, because two dice form the symbols, the simplest way to present the association between the symbols and the values they encode (letters) is illustrated in Figure 8.3. The table is structured so that the pattern along the left side of the table is the first component of the symbol and the pattern along the top is the second. This makes the digitizing process easy:

- *Encode a Letter.* To find the symbol representing a given letter, find the letter in the table and use the pattern of the row as the left half of the symbol and the pattern of the column as the right half.
- *Decode a Symbol.* To find the letter represented by a given symbol, find the row corresponding to the left half of the symbol and the column corresponding to the right half; the letter is at the intersection of the row and column.

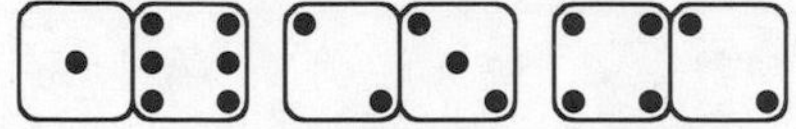

Verify that "FIT" is represented by the three symbols shown.

The representation has associated 26 of the symbols with the Latin letters, leaving 10 positions unassigned. If the information to be digitized is composed only of letters, the representation is complete, because a symbol is associated with each letter. But this rarely happens. A slightly more common situation is that the information is composed of at least letters and numerals; many automobile license plates are restricted to those 36 characters. In such cases, assigning the Arabic numerals to the unassigned symbols of Figure 8.3, for example, would complete the digitization, as shown in Figure 8.4(a). But the most typical situation is that the textual information to be digitized includes more than letters and numerals; it also includes punctuation symbols. The inclusion of punctuation complicates the dice pair representation because it implies the need for more symbols than are available with pairs of dice. Anyone inventing a digitization confronts the problem of deciding which items are the most important to represent.

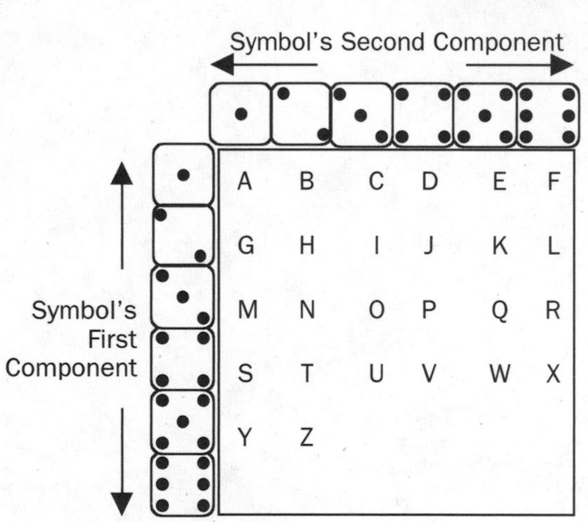

Figure 8.3. Initial Assignment of Letters to the Dice-Pair Symbols

Perhaps the most important character is the space character because it is essential for *delimiting* letter sequences, that is, separating words. We cannot use spacing in the digitization (that is, in our arrangement of dice-pairs) to indicate word separations in the text because we have no control over how the digital form will be used. For example, using the Figure 8.4(a) digitization, two people could communicate in a noisy environment with a pair of dice by spelling out words one letter at a time. But with only one pair of dice there is no way to "separate the pairs" to indicate the end of a word. The point is that the digitization must encode all the information, and the spaces separating words are part of the information. So space must be assigned to some symbol. The nine remaining symbols are not sufficient for the digits, so they will be used for punctuation characters. A representation of this type is shown in Figure 8.4(b).

Figure 8.4(b) has the advantage of representing space and other punctuation, but it doesn't represent the numerals. In some cases, this might not be a serious restriction because it might be possible to circumvent the need for these unrepresented characters. For example, the two people communicating in a noisy environment with a pair of dice might simply spell out each numeral. There would be no single symbol for zero, for example, but it could be presented as

But solutions such as spelling out numerals are a limitation imposed by the digital representation of the information, and they are to be avoided if at all possible. Though it appears that we need to use dice triples, there is an alternative.

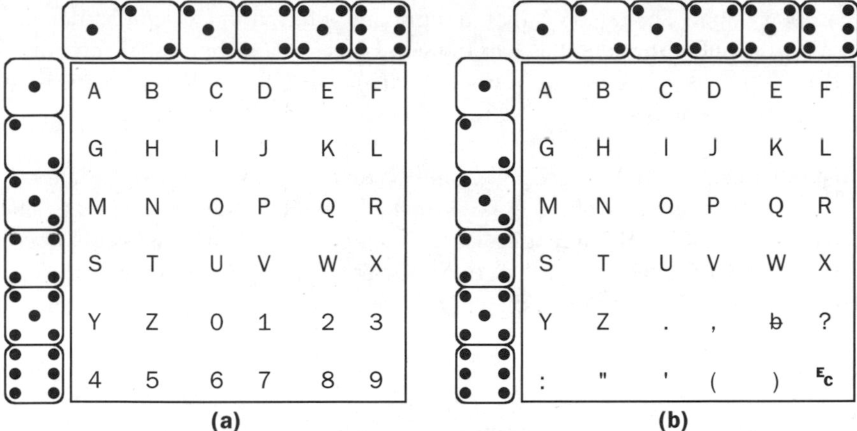

Figure 8.4. Two Complete Dice-Pair Representations.
Note: ƀ indicates a space.

In Figure 8.2(b) the boxcars symbol (double sixes) has been assigned an unfamiliar character, Ec. This character, which is not a letter, numeral, or punctuation character, will be called *escape*. It has been included to illustrate how to extend a representation. Because escape does not correspond to any legal character, it will never be encountered in the normal process of digitizing text. So it can be used to indicate that the digitization is "escaping from the basic representation" and applying a secondary representation. In this way, more symbols can be represented because pairing escape with another symbol doubles the number of representations at the expense of a slightly longer representation for some characters.

To illustrate the idea, encode the numerals by pairing the escape symbol with each of the symbols used for the first ten letters of the alphabet, A through J. Each escape-letter symbol pair, that is, four dice, is matched to a numeral. Thus the symbol pair

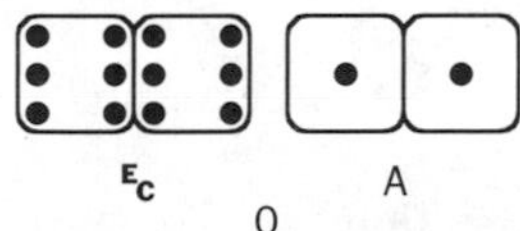

which is escape-A, corresponds to 0. Escape-B corresponds to 1, and so on. Notice that the escape symbol precedes the letter for each occurrence of a digit. So, 10 is represented as

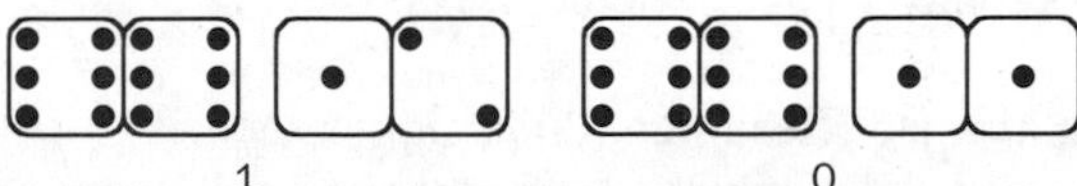

There can be no "group discount" for a sequence of digits in which escape would precede only the first digit because the decoder would not know when the last digit had been encountered. So, a ten-digit number requires twenty symbols in this dice-pair encoding extended by escape.

> **Shifty**. The escape technique is familiar. The shift keys (and control) are used as an escape for the keyboard.

Using this escape approach allows for 35 basic symbol assignments because the Ec takes up the boxcars symbol. But, it gives an equal number of two-symbol assignments. These secondary assignments should probably be assigned to the less frequently used values because the encoding is less efficient. Of course, the idea can be continued because $^{E}_{C}{}^{E}_{C}$. could also be treated as another escape. A double escape could be used to define a second alternate assignment of values to symbols, but this approach is typically not adopted because there are other more sophisticated ways to use the escape symbol. The lesson is that in digitizing information, do not associate all symbols with legal information as was done in Figure 8.4(a), but rather reserve one symbol to serve as an escape, as in Figure 8.4(b). The availability of escape gives flexibility to a representation.

Notice that when the 36 symbols created from two dice didn't suffice for the letters, numerals, and punctuation, we could have adopted three dice pattern sequences. That would have produced $6^3 = 216$ symbols. The advantage is that numerals would have been encoded with three dice rather than four. The disadvantage is that the letters would have been encoded with three dice rather than two. If numerals make up less than half of the values we wish to encode, our "two plus escape" uses fewer dice than the "triples" solution.

Summarizing, the process of digitizing involves associating symbols with values, which in the case of text are the keyboard characters. The method of constructing symbols—combining base patterns—creates a fixed-size set of symbols. The symbol set must be large enough to represent each value, but it is also desirable for each symbol to be associated with a value. Reserving one symbol for escape allows the encoding to be extended to handle exceptional cases.

The PandA Representation

The six base patterns of a die are familiar, but not fundamental. The fundamental patterns from which we construct the symbols of information technology derive from the confluence of the physical and the logical worlds. In the physical world, the most fundamental exposition of information is the presence or absence of a physical phenomenon:

- Does matter occupy a particular place in space, or not?
- Is light detected at a particular place, or not?
- Is magnetism sensed at a particular place, or not?

The same goes for pressure, charge, flow, and so on. In many cases, the phenomena exhibit a continuous range of values enabling them to encode analog information, discussed in Chapter 11. From a digital information perspective, the amount of a phenomenon is not important as long as it is reliably detected. The important part is only whether there is some or none; whether it is present or absent.

In the logical world, true and false reign. Propositions such as "*Rain implies wet streets*" can be expressed and combined with other propositions such as "*The streets are not wet*" to draw conclusions such as "*It is not raining*." Logic is the foundation of reasoning, and it is also the foundation of computation. *By unifying* true *and* false *with the* presence *and* absence *of a phenomenon, the physical world can be used to implement the logical world to produce information technology.* In this section, we make that unification.

PandA is the name we use for the two fundamental patterns of digital information based on the presence and absence of a phenomenon. *PandA* is mnemonic for "presence and absence." A key property of the PandA representation is that it is black and white; that is, the phenomenon is either present or it is not; the logic is either *true* or *false*. Such a formulation is said to be *discrete*, meaning "distinct" or "separable"; it is not possible to transform one value into the other by continuous gradations. There is no gray.

The PandA encoding has just two basic patterns—Present and Absent—making it a *binary system*. The names Present and Absent are not specific to any particular representation, so it is customary to adopt alternate names that are appropriate to the encoding and also convey the discrete, black-and-white nature of the two patterns. (See Table 8.1.) The assignment of these names to the two patterns is arbitrary in the sense that there is no law that says that in all cases and forever and ever On means "Present" and Off means "Absent." We could agree to assign the names the other way, and engineers deep into a design often do. The associations given in the table seem reasonable, however, and they are probably the associations that occur most frequently. But the entries are only names for the two patterns.

Table 8.1. Possible Interpretations of the Two PandA Patterns

Present	Absent
On	Off
Yes	No
1	0
True	False
+	–
Black	White
For	Against
Yang	Yin
...	...
Lisa	Bart

A second aspect of the PandA encoding, besides the alternative patterns, is the unit that can assume the different patterns. In the dice representation, the unit was the top of a single die, which was capable of assuming any of six patterns. In the PandA representation, the unit is a specific place in space and time where the presence or absence of the phenomenon can be set and detected. The unit is known as a *bit*, which is capable of assuming either of the two PandA patterns, Present or Absent. *Bit* is a contraction for "binary digit," and was originally adopted because early computer designers interpreted the two patterns as 1 and 0, the digits of the binary number system. Though bit sequences can be interpreted as binary numbers, the key idea is that bits form symbols, not that bits form (binary) numbers. Encoding numbers is a particularly useful application of symbols, but the idea is more general.

The patterns are called the *states* of the bit when they are part of a storage medium in the physical world. To illustrate bits in the physical world, consider the magnetic encoding of information as might be used on tapes, floppy disks, or hard disks. Like audiocassette tapes, these media are constructed out of a material containing iron that can be magnetized. Figure 8.5 shows a sequence of positions, some of which are positively magnetized and some of which are not. Each position is capable of representing a bit because it can be configured into both states, positively magnetized or not, corresponding to the two PandA patterns.[3] Specifically the sixteen positions shown in Figure 8.5 encode the sixteen bits

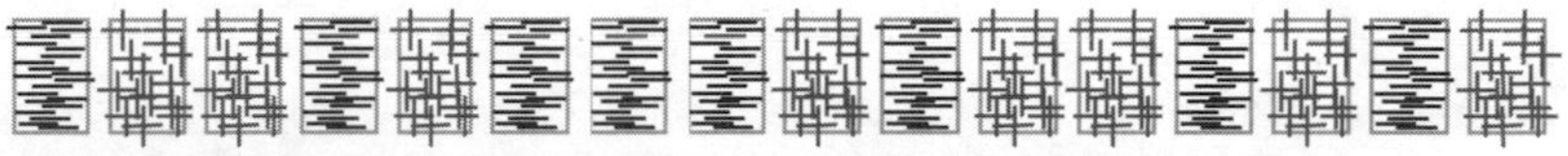

Figure 8.5. Schematic diagram of a sequence of bit positions on a magnetic medium. The boxes illustrate a position where magnetism may be set and sensed; pluses (gray) indicate magnetism of positive polarity, interpreted as "present" and minuses (black) indicate magnetism of negative polarity, interpreted as absent.

absent-present-present-absent-present-absent-absent-absent-present-absent-present-present-absent-present-absent-present

or, more economically,

0110 1000 1011 0101

[3] The use of physical phenomena to represent information sometimes poses problems because there might be more than two alternatives. For example, a magnetic material might not be magnetized at all, or it could be magnetized with positive polarity or negative polarity; that is, there seem to be three possibilities. In such situations, engineers adopt one state such as positive polarity to mean "present" and all other states to mean "absent."

It is obvious why computer scientists and engineers prefer the names 1 and 0 to Present and Absent, even when the information being encoded is not numbers. Ones and zeros are simpler to read, write, and say.

Digital Man. The first person to apply the term *digital* to computers was George Stibitz, a Bell Labs mathematician. While consulting for the U.S. military, he observed that "pulsed" computing devices would be better described as digital because they represent information in discrete units.

Inside the computer the memory is arranged in a very long sequence of bits. In an analogous way, a sidewalk can serve as a memory. Imagine a sidewalk made of a line of square paving stones (pavers) that has initially been swept clean, and agree that a stone on a paver corresponds to 1 and the absence of a stone corresponds to 0. Sidewalk memory encodes information just as computer memory does. But, it is not as economical of space!

The bits can be set to write information into the memory, and they can be sensed to read the information out of the memory. To write a 1 the phenomenon must be made to be present, for example, put a stone on a paver. To write a zero, the phenomenon must be made to be absent, for example, sweep the paver clean. To determine what information is stored at a specific position, sense whether the phenomenon is present or absent. So, if a stone is detected on a paver, the phenomenon is present (1); otherwise, it is absent (0).

There are innumerable other ways to encode two states using physical phenomena, of course. Remaining just in the world of pavers, we could use stones on all pavers but use white stones and black stones to distinguish the two states. Or, we could use multiple stones per paver, using a majority of white stones for one state and a minority of white as the other state, being careful that the total number of stones is always odd. Or we could use a single stone on each paver, placing it the center of the paver for one state and off center for the other state. And so forth. These are all instances of the PandA encodings, provided the "phenomenon" is chosen properly: Presence of white, presence of majority of white, presence of a centered stone.

No Barking. Sherlock Holmes used one bit of information to solve the *Mystery of Silver Blaze*, which concerns the disappearance of a prize racehorse. In the vicinity of the stable during the night [place and time], the phenomenon [barking watchdog] was not detected [absent], implying to Holmes the perpetrator was known to the dog, and implicating Simpson, the owner. Though we are impressed with Holmes's deductions, the concept of information being represented by a dog not barking is straightforward.

Table 8.2. Number of Symbols When the Number of Possible Patterns is Two

n	2^n	Symbols
1	2^1	2
2	2^2	4
3	2^3	8
4	2^4	16
5	2^5	32
6	2^6	64
7	2^7	128
8	2^8	256
9	2^9	512
10	2^{10}	1024

As with the sides of a die, the two bit patterns alone provide a limited resource for digitizing information. If the information being encoded has only two alternative values—that is, it's binary information such as votes (*aye*, *nay*), personality types (*A*, *B*), Mariners baseball games (*win, loss*)—the two patterns of a single bit suffice as the symbols to represent the two alternative values. But most often the information to be digitized has more than two alternatives, so, like dice, the two patterns must be combined into composite sequences to create the necessary symbols. As we learned in the last section, if there are $m = 2$ patterns, as the PandA representation has, grouped into n-length sequences, 2^n symbols can be produced. So, Table 8.2 relates the length of the bit sequence to the number of possible symbols.

The sixteen symbols of $n = 4$ length bit sequences are shown in Table 8.3.

The PandA encoding is the fundamental representation of information. By grouping bits together, it is possible to produce enough symbols to represent any number of values. By creating symbols using the two PandA patterns, it is possible to record and transform information using resources from the physical world. Information and computation exist in a completely abstract form without a physical implementation, but the miracle of information technology is that it can be made tangible. With machines and networks doing the work, our lives are simplified.

Coincidence? Though *bit* means "small piece" in English, the word's technical definition is a contraction. Of course, bits represent small pieces of information, suggesting the choice may not have been coincidental.

Table 8.3. The Basic PandA Encoding of length four Symbols and the Associated Bits

Sixteen Symbols of the 4-Bit PandA Representation					
Symbol	**Binary**	**Physical Bits**	**Symbol**	**Binary**	**Physical Bits**
AAAA	0000		PAAA	1000	
AAAP	0001		PAAP	1001	
AAPA	0010		PAPA	1010	
AAPP	0011		PAPP	1011	
APAA	0100		PPAA	1100	
APAP	0101		PPAP	1101	
APPA	0110		PPPA	1110	
APPP	0111		PPPP	1111	

The Hex Explained

Before applying the PandA representation to text, let's pause briefly to resolve a mystery from Chapter 4. Recall that when we specified custom colors in HTML—<font color="#FF8E2A"> as shown in Figure 4.2—the specification used hex digits, short for hexadecimal, or base 16. We didn't explain hex at the time but simply gave Table A.1, enabling us to convert back and forth between decimal and hexadecimal.

The motivation for using hexadecimal is as follows. When we specify a color, we must give the proper bit sequence for the RGB. The bit sequence might be given in 0s and 1s,

```
<font color="#111111111001100011100010101 0"> Illegal HTML tag
```

but that's tedious and error prone. Computer professionals long ago realized that they needed a more efficient way to specify bit sequences than the literal 0s and 1s, and so have adopted hexadecimal. The digits of hex are 0, 1, . . . , 9, A, B, C, D, E, F. Because there are 16 of them, they can be represented perfectly by the sixteen symbols of 4-bit sequences. In Table 8.3, the first column is associated with hex digits 0 through 7 and the second column with hex digits 8 through F. That is, bit sequence 0000 corresponds to hex 0, 0001 corresponds to hex 1, and so forth, up to the bit sequence 1111, which corresponds to hex F. (This is simply a numeric interpretation of the bits, which will be explained Chapter 11.)

Because each hex digit corresponds to a 4-bit sequence, and vice versa, it is possible to translate between hex and bits easily. Given hex, write down the associated groups of four bits. Given a sequence of bits, group them into sequences of four, and write down the associated hex digit. Thus,

```
0010 1011 1010 1101 = 2BAD
```

What is ABE8 BEEF as a bit sequence?

So, in HTML when we specify white as `"#FFFFFF"`, we are effectively setting each bit of the RGB specification bits to 1.

Text: A Basic Application of the PandA Representation

The two earliest uses of the PandA representation were to encode numbers and keyboard characters. These two applications remain extremely important, though now representations for sound, images, video, and other types of information are almost as significant. In this section text is encoded; numbers are encoded in Chapter 11.

As noted in the last section, the number of bits determines the number of symbols available for representing values: n bits in sequence yield 2^n symbols. And as we've learned, it is difficult to decide which characters to represent, because the more characters encoded, the more symbols required. Latin letters, Arabic numerals, and about a dozen punctuation characters are essential for digitizing English text. It is convenient to have capital and small letters, and the basic arithmetic symbols like +, -, *, /, =. But, where should the line be drawn? Should characters not required for English, but useful in other languages like German (ö), French (é), Spanish (ñ), and Norwegian (ø) be included? What about Czech, Greek, Arabic, Thai, or Cantonese? Should other languages' punctuation be included, like French (« ») and Spanish (¿)? Should arithmetic symbols include degrees (°), pi (π), relational symbols (≤), equivalence (≡), for all (∀)? What about business symbols: ¢, £, ¥, ©, ®, ...? What about unprintable characters like backspace and new-line? Should there be a symbol for smiley faces (☺)? Some of these questions are easier to answer than others. Though the goal is to keep the list small so that it requires fewer bits for the representation, doing so at the expense of not being able to represent critical characters would be a mistake.

The 26 capital and 26 small Latin letters, the ten Arabic numerals, a basic set of 20 punctuation characters (including blank), five arithmetic characters, and three non-printable characters (new-line, tab, backspace) can be represented with 90 symbols. Such a set would be sufficient for English and the keys on a basic computer keyboard. To produce 90 distinct symbols requires 7 bits because six bits yields only $2^6 = 64$ symbols. Seven bits produce $2^7 = 128$ symbols, so the 90 different values underutilize the 7-bit symbols. Luckily some special control characters must also be represented. The control characters are used for data transmission and other engineering purposes. They are assigned to the remainder of the 7-bit symbols.

An early and still widely used 7-bit code for the characters is ASCII, pronounced *AS·key*. The acronym stands for "American Standard Code for Information Interchange." The advantages of a "standard" are numerous: Computer parts built by different manufacturers can connect together; computers can transmit data to other computers; programs that create data can store it so that different programs can process it later; and so forth. In all cases, there must be an agreement as to which character is associated with which symbol (bit sequence).

As the name implies, ASCII was developed in the United States. But by the mid-1960s, it became clear that 7-bit ASCII was not sufficient because it could not fully represent text from languages other than English. So IBM, the dominant computer manufacturer at the time, decided to adopt the next larger set of symbols, the 8-bit symbols, as the standard for character representation. Eight bits produce $2^8 = 256$ symbols, enough to encode English and the Western European languages, their punctuation symbols, and a large set of other useful characters. The enhancement to ASCII resulting from the move to 8-bits was Extended ASCII, shown in Table 8.4. This widely used representation has the original ASCII as the "first half" of the representation; that is, 7-bit ASCII is the 8-bit ASCII representation with the first bit set to 0. Though Extended ASCII does not handle all natural languages, it is sufficient to handle many languages derived from the Latin alphabet. Handling other languages is solved in two ways: Revising Extended ASCII to recode "the second half" for different characters; and to use the escape mechanism mentioned earlier, yielding a 16-bit encoding.

Table 8.4. ASCII, The American Standard Code for Information Interchange

ASCII	0	0	0	0	0	0	0	0	1	1	1	1	1	1	1	1
	0	0	0	0	1	1	1	1	0	0	0	0	1	1	1	1
	0	0	1	1	0	0	1	1	0	0	1	1	0	0	1	1
	0	1	0	1	0	1	0	1	0	1	0	1	0	1	0	1
0000	NU	SH	SX	EX	ET	EQ	AK	BL	BS	HT	LF	VT	FF	CR	SO	SI
0001	DL	D1	D2	D3	D4	NK	SY	EB	CN	EM	SB	EC	FS	GS	RS	US
0010		!	"	#	$	%	&	'	(	)	*	+	,	-	.	/
0011	0	1	2	3	4	5	6	7	8	9	:	;	<	=	>	?
0100	@	A	B	C	D	E	F	G	H	I	J	K	L	M	N	O
0101	P	Q	R	S	T	U	V	W	X	Y	Z	[	\	]	^	_
0110	`	a	b	c	d	e	f	g	h	i	j	k	l	m	n	o
0111	p	q	r	s	t	u	v	w	x	y	z	{	|	}	~	DT
1000	80	81	82	83	IN	NL	SS	ES	HS	HJ	VS	PD	PU	RI	S2	S3
1001	DC	P1	P2	SE	CC	MW	SP	EP	98	99	9A	CS	ST	OS	PM	AP
1010	A0	¡	¢	£	¤	¥	¦	§	¨	©	♀	«	¬	-	®	¯
1011	°	±	²	³	´	µ	¶	·	¸	¹	♂	»	¼	½	¾	¿
1100	À	Á	Â	Ã	Ä	Å	Æ	Ç	È	É	Ê	Ë	Ì	Í	Î	Ï
1101	Ð	Ñ	Ò	Ó	Ô	Õ	Ö	×	Ø	Ù	Ú	Û	Ü	Ý	Þ	ß
1110	à	á	â	ã	ä	å	æ	ç	è	é	ê	ë	ì	í	î	ï
1111	ð	ñ	ò	ó	ô	õ	ö	÷	ø	ù	ú	û	ü	ý	þ	ÿ

Note: The original 7-bit ASCII is the top half of the table; the whole table is known as Extended ASCII (ISO/IEC8859-1). The 8-bit symbol for a letter is the four row bits followed by the four column bits, e.g., female (♀) = 10101010, while male (♂) = 10111010. Characters shown as two small letters are control symbols used to encode nonprintable information, e.g., BS = 00001000 is backspace. The bottom half of the table is largely devoted to characters derived from the Latin alphabet and required by Western European languages, including Icelandic's eth (Ð) and thorn (þ).

IBM's move to 8-bits was bold because they adopted the more generous representation at a time when computer memory and storage were extremely expensive. IBM anointed 8-bit sequences with a special name, *byte*, and they adopted it as a standard unit for computer memory. Bytes remain the standard unit of memory, and their "8-ness" permeates many aspects of computers. For example, recent computers have been "32-bit machines," meaning their datapaths (size of information processed by most instructions) is four bytes.

> **The Ultimate.** Though ASCII and its "recoded variations" are widely used, the more complete solution is a 16-bit representation, called *Unicode*. With 65,536 symbols, Unicode is sufficient to handle all languages.

With the ASCII encoding defined, return to the phone number, `888 555 1212`, whose representation concerned us at the start of the chapter. How would a computer represent this phone number in its memory? As mentioned, this is not really a number in the sense that we do not expect to perform arithmetic on it. Rather, it is a keying sequence for a telephone's keypad represented by numerals; it is not necessary, or even desirable, to represent the phone number as a numerical quantity. Because each of the numerals has a representation in ASCII, express the phone number by encoding each digit. The encoding is easy: Find each numeral in Table 8.4, and write down the bit sequence from its row, followed by the bit sequence from its column. Accordingly the phone number 888 555 1212 in ASCII is

```
0011 1000   0011 1000   0011 1000   0011 0101   0011 0101   0011 0101
0011 0001   0011 0010   0011 0001   0011 0010
```

which can easily be verified. This is exactly how computers represent phone numbers. The encoding seems somewhat redundant because each byte has the same left half: 0011. The numbers repeat because all of the numerals are located on the 0011 row of the ASCII table. If only phone numbers were to be represented, fewer bits could be used, of course. But there is little reason to be so economical, so we adopt the standard ASCII.

> **Two bits, four bits . . .** The term *byte* has motivated some to call 4 bits, that is, half a byte, a *nibble*.

Notice that we have streamed all of the digits of the phone number together, even though when we write them for ourselves we usually insert spaces between the area code and exchange code, and between the exchange code and the number. The computer doesn't care, but it might matter to users. However, it is easy to add these separators and other punctuation. Demonstrate this by encoding the phone number in ASCII as: (888) 555-1212. (Notice that there is a space before the first 5.)

Finally, although we usually try to construct efficient representations (shortest symbol sequences for a given number of letters) to minimize the amount of memory required to store and transmit text, not all letter representations seek minimality. Indeed, the code for the letters used in radio communication is purposely inefficient in this sense, so that representations are distinctive when spoken amid noise. The NATO broadcast alphabet, shown in Table 8.5, encodes letters as words as a replacement for their standard spoken names. For example, Mike and November replace the difficult-to-distinguish "em" and "en." The more distinctive encoding improves the chances letters will be recognized when spoken under less-than-ideal situations. The digits retain their usual names, except "nine," which is frequently replaced by "niner."

Table 8.5. NATO Broadcast Alphabet Designed Not to Be Minimal

A Alpha	G Golf	M Mike	S Sierra	Y Yankee
B Bravo	H Hotel	N November	T Tango	Z Zulu
C Charlie	I Indian	O Oscar	U Uniform	
D Delta	J Juliet	P Papa	V Victor	
E Echo	K Kilo	Q Quebec	W Whiskey	
F Foxtrot	L Lima	R Romeo	X X-ray	

It's Greek to Me. There are dozens of phonetic alphabets for English and many other languages. The NATO alphabet, standard for air traffic control, begins with "alpha," raising the question, What is the first letter of the Greek phonetic alphabet? Alexandros.

The *Oxford English Dictionary*

Representations like ASCII allow computers to store books and other documents. But, what good is there in storing a book in a computer? Computers can print books, of course, or display them on the monitor, but printing was a mature technology long before the invention of computers.[4] Computers cannot understand the content of the books. Nor does it seem possible to compute on books. Or does it? What might a computation on a book involve? Possibly counting up the total number of words, counting the number of occurrences of each of the words, or listing the page numbers where interesting words are found, that is, forming an index or concordance. Searching—looking for specific words or phrases in the book—is another example of a computation performed on text. To complete our understanding of the textual aspects of digitizing information, we consider the digitization of the *Oxford English Dictionary*.

The *Oxford English Dictionary* is the definitive reference for every English word's meaning, etymology, and usage. Because it is so comprehensive, the *OED* is truly monumental. The printed version comprises 20 volumes, weighs 150 pounds, and fills 4 feet of shelf space. The goal of producing a complete listing of all English words was set in 1857 by the Philological Society of London. It was expected at that time that the completed dictionary would have 6,400 pages in four volumes. By 1884, with the list completed only up to **ant,** it became clear to James Murray, the lexicographer in charge, that the effort was much more ambitious than originally thought. The first edition, completed in 1928, long after Murray's death, filled 15,490 pages and contained 252,200 entries. In 1984 the conversion of the *OED* to digital form was started.

How would we go about digitizing a dictionary? First, of course, a representation of the letters of the Latin alphabet is needed, for example, ASCII. But the 90 or so standard letters of 7-bit ASCII are not enough. About 750 different characters are used in the *OED*, including the special characters giving pronunciation and the characters from non-English languages required to explain derivations. For these characters the "escape technique" described earlier is used to represent the non-ASCII characters inside the computer. But how can we type 750 different characters? No keyboard has so many keys. The answer is to use the escape technique again. That is, a character is reserved to flag places where one of the non-ASCII characters is needed; the reserved

[4] In fairness, computers can revise the format of a book very quickly—its font style, font size, pagination, and so on—compared to traditional printing methods. Large print versions for the visually impaired are a good application of this feature.

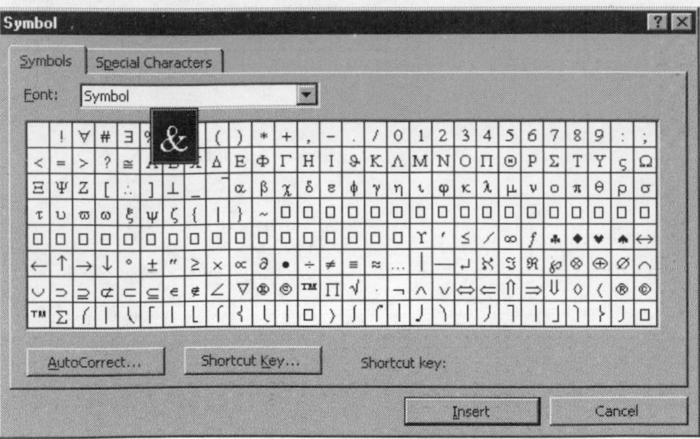

Figure 8.6. A selection table for special symbols, an alternative to the escape technique.

character is **&**. An agreed-upon name for the non-ASCII character follows the reserved character, for example, **&infinity**. Then wherever the character (∞) is needed, the escape sequence (**&infinity**) is typed where the character is to appear. This is the same technique used later in HTML for accented words, as we saw in Chapter 4. (See Table 8.6 for a partial list for the *OED*.) The software of the text processor recognizes the escape character and then reads the following name. In this way, it knows which character to enter into the file. The escape character that the computer uses in the file may be different. Further, because the *OED* has 750 special characters, two bytes will follow the escape character in the internal representation. Word processors could also use this technique for typing unusual characters, but typically they give users a table of letter alternatives from which to choose. (See Figure 8.6.) As with HTML the escape technique implies that the escape character cannot be typed directly when it is needed; that is, there must be an escape for ampersand (**&** is at the start of row 3 in Table 8.6).

Table 8.6. Escape Sequences for Some Symbols Used in the Digital Form of the *OED*

&41	&278	&380	&Aacu	&aacu	â
&acu	&AE	&Ae	&ae	à	&alpha
&	&ang	ä	&b1	&Beta	&beta
&breve	&Ccdil	&ccdil	&cdil	&dag	°
&div	&dollar	&dubh	&Eacu	&eacu	&Edh
&edh	è	&epsilon	&Eth	&fata	&frown
&ge	&hash	&ia	&Iacu	&iacu	&ib
&ic	&id	&ie	&ig	&ih	&ii
&index	&infinity	&iota	&iq	&isub	ï
&Kappa	&lambda	&le	&lenis	&lm	&mac
&min	&mu	&Mu	&ng	&Nu	&nu
&Oacu	&oacu	&Obar	&obar	ô	&OE
&Oe	&oe	&omicron	&ope	ö	&p
&pa	&Page	&page	&paln	&pm	&pp
&ppp	&pstlg	&rdot	&reva	&revc	&revope
&revr	&revv	&rfa	&schwa	&schwax	§
&sh	&shti	&shtu	&shty	&sm	&smm
&sqrt	&sylab	&Th	&th	&theta	&tilde
×	&trli	&Uacu	&uacu	ü	&vb
&Yacu	&yacu	&ygh	&Ygh	&zh	

Given an internal-to-the-computer representation for the 750 characters and a way to type each one, we could in principle type the entire *OED* into a text document. That would take a person about 120 years. But the result might be unsatisfactory without a little more planning. To see why, imagine that the entire dictionary is one continuous string of characters from **A** through the end of the definition for **Zyxt**, the last word in English. Now, suppose we would like to look up the definition for the verb **set**, which is distinguished by being the word with the longest entry in the *OED*. The searching software—as described in Chapter 3—would look for **set** and no doubt find it thousands of times. This is because **set** is part of many words like **beset**, **cassette**, and **settle**, and **set** is used in many definitions, for example, "*match-point* in tennis is the final score ending the present game, set and match." The first of these problems—separating the occurrences of **s-e-t** within words from the word itself—is easily solved by ignoring all occurrences that do not have a punctuation character or space before and after the **s-e-t**. The software can do that. But among the thousands of true occurrences of **set** is the verb definition, the single place in the dictionary that we are looking for. The software processing the text file, unable to understand the dictionary's contents, would have no clue which one that is.

Human readers of the dictionary are assisted by typesetters who start each definition on a new line with the defined word printed in bold typeface. For the software, the solution is to *tag* the different parts of the dictionary's text so that when the word is found, the software will know how each occurrence is used. The tags are not formatting tags as used in word processors or HTML, but a special set of tags developed for the *OED*. For example, <hw> is the *OED*'s tag for a *headword*, which is the lexicographic terminology for the word being defined. As usual, because tags surround the text like parentheses, there is a closing *headword* tag, </hw>. Thus the place in the *OED* where the verb **set** is defined appears in the text file of the dictionary as

```
<hw>set</hw>
```

Other tags label the pronunciation <pr>, phonetic notations <ph>, the parts of speech <ps>, the homonym number, which distinguishes different headwords that sound the same <hm>, and so forth. There are also tags to group items, such as <e> to surround an entire entry and <hg> to surround a head group, that is, all of the information at the start of a definition. Because the first entry for the verb **set** in the *OED* begins

set (sɛt), *v.*[1]

giving the word being defined, the pronunciation, the part of speech, and the homonym number, we expect it must be tagged as

```
<e><hg><hw>set</hw> <pr><ph>s&epsilont</ph></pr>, <ps>v</ps>. <hm>1</hm></hg>
```

Notice the use of the escape code (**&epsilon**) for the epsilon character in the pronunciation. Also, the </e> is not shown because it must be at the very end of the entry.

Of course, the tags are not printed. They are included only to specify the *metadata*, the structural features of the text. They tell the computer what part of the dictionary it's looking at. But in fact, tags are very useful in conveying formatting information. For example, the boldface type used for headwords can be automatically applied when the dictionary is printed based on the <hw> tag. Similarly for the Italics typeface in the part of speech. The parentheses surrounding the pronunciation and the superscript for the homonym number are also generated automatically. But it must be emphasized that the tags describe the structure, not how to print it, as with HTML.

Figure 8.7 shows the entry for **byte** together with its representation, as it actually appears in the file of the online *OED*. At first the internal form looks very cluttered, but by comparing it with the printed form, it is possible to make sense out of the tags. Using the tags allows the software to determine the role of each word of the definition. So, for example, to find the definition and examples of usage for the word **byte**, the searching software should look first for

```
<hw>byte</hw>
```

and once found, display all of the information for the **byte** entry, that is, all of the information between <e> and </e>. The tags indicate to the software which occurrence of *byte* is in the definition of *byte,* and also the extent of the definition. Using tags enables the software to intelligently help the user.

byte (baIt). *Computers*. [Arbitrary, prob. influenced by bit *sb.*[4] and bite *sb.*] A group of eight consecutive bits operated on as a unit in a computer.

> **1964** ***Blaauw*** & ***Brooks*** in *IBM Systems Jrnl.* III. 122 An 8-bit unit of information is fundamental to most of the formats [of the System/360]. A consecutive group of *n* such units constitutes a field of length *n*. Fixed-length fields of length one, two, four, and eight are termed bytes, halfwords, words, and double words respectively. **1964** *IBM Jrnl. Res. & Developm.* VIII. 97/1 When a byte of data appears from an I/O device, the CPU is seized, dumped, used and restored. **1967** ***P. A. Stark*** *Digital Computer Programming* xix. 351 The normal operations in fixed point are done on four bytes at a time. **1968** *Dataweek* 24 Jan. 1/1 Tape reading and writing is at from 34,160 to 192,000 bytes per second.

```
<e><hg><hw>byte</hw> <pr><ph>baIt</ph></pr></hg>. <la>Computers
</la>. <etym>Arbitrary, prob. influenced by <xr><x>bit</x></xr>
 <ps>n.<hm>4</hm></ps>and <xr><x>bite</x> <ps>n.</ps></xr></ety
m> <s4>A group of eight consecutive bits operated on as a unit
 in a computer.</s4> <qp><q><qd>1964</qd><a>Blaauw</a> &amp. <
a>Brooks</a> <bib>in</bib> <w>IBM Systems Jrnl.</w> <lc>III. 1
22</lc> <qt>An 8-bit unit of information is fundamental to most
 of the formats <ed>of the System/360</ed>.&es.A consecutive gr
oup of <i>n</i> such units constitutes a field of length <i>n</
i>.&es.Fixed-length fields of length one, two, four, and eight
are termed bytes, halfwords, words, and double words respective
ly. </qt></q><q><qd>1964</qd> <w>IBM Jrnl. Res. &amp. Developm.
</w> <lc>VIII. 97/1</lc> <qt>When a byte of data appears from a
n I/O device, the CPU is seized, dumped, used and restored.</qt
></q> <q><qd>1967</qd> <a>P. A. Stark</a> <w>Digital Computer P
rogramming</w> <lc>xix. 351</lc> <qt>The normal operations in f
ixed point are done on four bytes at a time.</qt></q><q><qd>1968
</qd> <w>Dataweek</w> <lc>24 Jan. 1/1</lc> <qt>Tape reading and
 writing is at from 34,160 to 192,000 bytes per second.</qt></q
></qp></e>
```

Figure 8.7. The *OED* entry for the word *byte* together with the representation of the entry as it exists in the digital form.

> **Price Tag.** The tag characters are included with the content characters, and so increase the size of the file compared with plain text. The entry for *byte* is 841 characters, but the tagged code is 1204, an almost 50% increase.

Returning to the problem of locating the definition for the verb **set**, its clear that all the computer need do is to search the text for the character sequence `<hw>set</hw>`, which will be a **set** definition. Locating the part of speech within the entry and testing to see if it indicates a verb. So, although the computer still doesn't understand a single word of the dictionary, it can help us locate information because the information has been structured.

As informative as the *OED* definition is, it doesn't answer that nagging question: Why is *byte* spelled with a *y*? To understand the charming nature of the answer, it's necessary to know that computer memory is subject to errors 0 ← 1 or 1 ← 0, caused by such things as cosmic rays. Really. Such errors are rare, but frequent enough to be a legitimate concern to computer engineers, who devote considerable attention to detecting and correcting memory errors. They often add additional bits to the memory for the purpose of detecting errors, for example, a ninth bit per byte. So, why is *byte* spelled with a *y*? The answer comes from Werner Buchholz, the inventor of the concept and the term. In the late 1950s Buchholz was the project manager and architect for the IBM supercomputer, called *Stretch*. For that machine, he explained to me,

"We needed a word for a quantity of memory between a bit and a word.[5] It seemed that after 'bit' comes 'bite.' But we changed the 'i' to a 'y' so that a typist couldn't accidentally change 'byte' into 'bit' by the single error of dropping the 'e'." No single change to *byte* can create *bit,* and vice versa. So concerned with memory errors were the engineers that Buchholz invented an error-detecting name for memory!

SUMMARY

The chapter began by establishing that digitizing doesn't require digits—any symbols will do. Using dice as a source of patterns, we considered problems posed by encoding keyboard characters. These problems were solved by making sequences of dice, assigning a special escape symbol, and deciding not to encode certain characters. With this principle firmly established, we introduced the PandA encoding, the fundamental representation of information based on the presence and absence of a physical phenomenon. Key properties of the two PandA patterns are that they are discrete, they form the basic unit of a bit, and their names—most often 1 and 0—are arbitrary and could instead be any of a set of opposing symbols. The term *bit* is a contraction for binary digit, but bits are used more generally than simply representing numbers, though that remains an important application. Next, 7-bit ASCII was introduced and cited as an early, and still useful, assignment of bit sequences (symbols) to keyboard characters. The standard Extended ASCII, however, is now the basic assignment of characters to bytes. Once there is an encoding for keyboard characters, it is possible to apply it to tasks such as encoding the *Oxford English Dictionary.* There, we learned that the use of tags associates metadata with every part of the *OED.* Using that data, a computer can easily assist us in finding words and other information because every part of every entry has been identified. Finally, we resolved the mystery of the *y* in *byte.*

EXERCISES

1. What is the standard definition of *digitize* and how is it expanded for IT?
2. What North American telephone number is: ▲ ‖ ‖ ◀ ◀ ■ ▲ ⏮ ‖ ‖ ?
3. Using the collating sequence for the "player" encoding of phone numbers, is ▲ ‖ ‖ ◀ ▼ ▶ ‖ ▼ ▲ ▲ smaller or larger than ▲ ‖ ‖ ■ ■ ■ ▶ ▼ ▶ ▼?
4. Write the approximate value of π (3.1416) using the dice encoding of Figure 8.4(b).
5. What message does the following dice sequence encode?

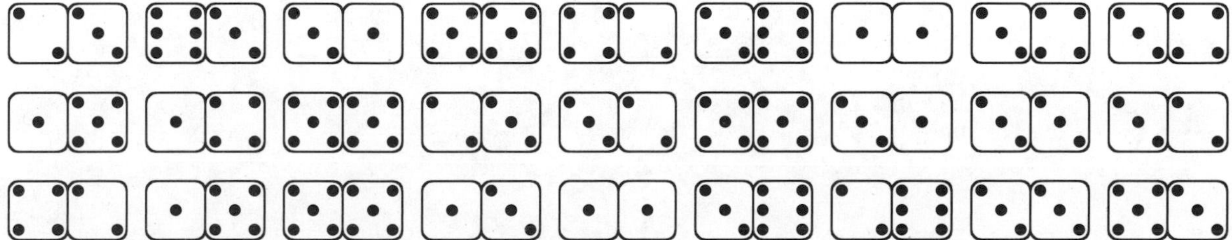

6. Explain why the "two dice plus escape" encoding uses the same number of dice as the "triple dice" encoding when half the values to be encoded are numerals.
7. What does *discrete* mean in the context of information technology?

[5] A "word" of computer memory is typically the amount required to represent computer instructions and the "usual" integer numbers. On modern computers a word is 32 bits.

8. What is *PandA* mnemonic for, and what does PandA name?
9. Think of five PandA representations using water glasses.
10. You bought a mosaic coffee table in Santorini, Greece, last summer and while listening to a boring story about your friend's visit home, you notice the table is eight tiles across, which could be the bits of a byte. Starting at the left end, what ASCII message did the Greeks encode, using the obvious PandA encoding?

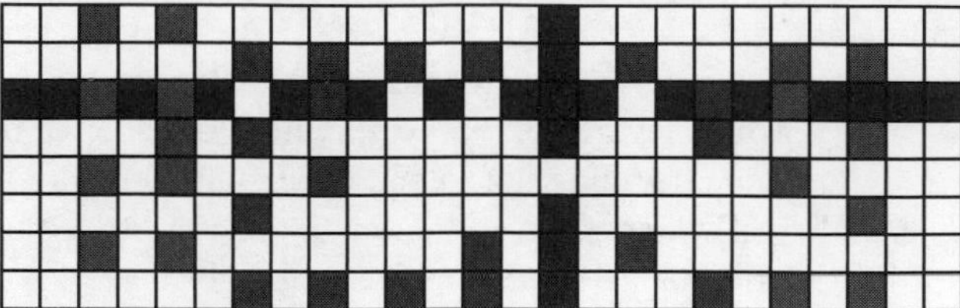

11. What is a *bit* and how was the word created?
12. How many symbols could 15-bit sequences encode?
13. What is ABE8 BEEF as a bit sequence?
14. What is 8-bit ASCII?
15. Encode (888) 555-1212 in Extended ASCII, including punctuation.
16. Represent the letters of the sentence "THE APPLE LOGO HAS A BYTE MISSING" with the broadcast code (ignore spaces in all cases) and then represent the result with ASCII. How many bytes are required for each?

Chapter 9

Computer Basics

Learning Objectives

- Understand the Fetch/Execute Cycle's operation.
- Learn the five components of a computer.
- Learn the roles of the components in instruction execution.
- Understand the role of the Program Counter.
- Know how clock speed relates to instruction execution and machine performance.
- Understand the two key features of integrated circuits.
- Learn how complex tasks are translated into primitive instructions.
- Know the function of an operating system.

This chapter introduces two topics—computers and integrated circuits (ICs)—that rank among the top technological achievements of all time. Naturally they are both complex and sophisticated topics, so difficult in fact that a Ph.D. degree is not sufficient training to understand current practice fully. Making today's computers and chips each requires the cooperative effort of a diverse team of specialists. If completely understanding either topic is at the limit of an expert's ability, what hope is there for nonspecialists to understand any of it?

Both topics are based on easy-to-understand ideas. What makes the technology so sophisticated and complex is pushing the basic ideas to their limit, and that is definitely beyond our needs and preparation. But why even learn the basics of computer operation? Because the same basic processes of instruction interpretation used by computers arise repeatedly throughout information technology. Web browsers process our HTML using instruction interpretation that mirrors computer operation. Spreadsheet applications use the same principles. You are even an instruction interpreter when you prepare your income taxes. This idea is fundamental to processing information and a key concept of IT.

The first learning objective of this chapter is to understand the components of the Fetch/Execute Cycle, the instruction interpreter, and their role. An analogy will help make the details of this process clear. Next, we describe the parts of a computer, their arrangement, and briefly what each does. The next objective is to outline how these parts can accomplish instruction interpretation. This is illustrated by a detailed example that reveals that computers operate in a straightforward manner. Next we explain the "big idea"—there are actually two of them—behind integrated circuits. Finally, there is a discussion of software and operating systems to fill out the picture.

World Domination. During the 1950s and 1960s, as computers were leaving the lab and entering business, there was concern in the popular press as to whether "computers would take over the world." The concern was founded on their prodigious capabilities that eclipsed human performance, for example, adding 100,000 numbers in a second. Grim, 1984-type scenarios of tyrannical computers were predicted. When it eventually happened—when life as people knew it relied irrevocably on computers—no one apparently noticed.

What Do Computers Do?

Before dissecting a computer, consider what a computer actually does. The obvious answer, "It computes," does not say very much to those of us accustomed to using modern information processing applications. These applications—Web searching, email, word processing—are very complex and sophisticated. Their complexity is achieved by piling layers and layers of powerful software on the basic processing capabilities of the computer's hardware, obscuring its intrinsic characteristics. Beneath all of this software is the basic computer. What is it doing?

As a definition, *computers* deterministically perform or execute instructions to process information. A synonym for *computer* would be "instruction execution engine." The most important aspect of this definition is that the computer is doing what it is told—following instructions—so evidently someone or something else must have decided what those instructions should do. This is where the programmer comes in. Programmers formulate the instructions that computers follow. Consequently everything that computers do was planned for them by programmers. The computer simply does the work by performing the instructions. If the instructions do not achieve a desired result, it's certainly not the computer's fault.

No Fault. How often have we heard "It was a computer error," as an explanation for a billing or other clerical mistake? As we've often said, true computer errors are extremely rare. A better explanation would be "There was a billing system error caused perhaps by one of the many people who worked on the software, installed and configured the system, entered the data, or modified and manipulated the database; it could be the result of fraud, data transmission or network errors, or failed checkpoint recovery; oh, . . . and there's a tiny chance it was a computer error." Said more briefly, "It probably wasn't a computer error."

A second key feature of the definition is the term *deterministically*. This means that when it comes time for the computer to determine which instruction to execute next, it is required by its construction to execute a specific instruction based only on the program and the data that it has been given. There are no alternatives, no options. It will execute one and only one next instruction, logically determined by a specific, unvarying process. As a result compared to people, computers are very stolid:

- Computers have no imagination nor creativity.
- Computers have no intuition.
- Computers are literal, with no sense of irony, subtlety, proportion, decorum. . . .
- Computers don't joke or have a sense of humor.
- Computers are not vindictive, cruel,[1] thoughtless. . . .
- Computers are not purposeful.
- Computers have no free will.

They only execute instructions. Deterministically. One consequence of determinism is that rerunning a program with the same data produces exactly the same result every time.

Following Instructions—The Fetch/Execute Cycle

Calling a computer an "instruction execution engine" conveys the idea of a device cycling through a series of operations, performing an instruction on each revolution, and that's pretty much the idea. Computers implement in hardware a process called the *Fetch/Execute Cycle*. Intuitively, the Fetch/Execute Cycle is the sequence of actions of getting the next instruction, figuring out what to do, gathering the data needed to do it, doing it, saving the result, and repeating. It's a simple process, but repeating it hundreds of millions of times a second can accomplish a lot.

The five steps of the Fetch/Execute Cycle have been assigned names, and because these operations are repeated in a never-ending sequence, they are often written with an arrow from the last step to the first showing the cycle. The step names suggest the operations described in the last paragraph. But there is a little more to the Fetch/Execute Cycle than is implied by our simple deconstruction of instruction execution. What is an instruction like? How is the next instruction located? When instructions and data are fetched, where are they fetched from, and where do they go to?

```
Instruction Fetch (IF)
Instruction Decode (ID)
Data Fetch (DF)
Instruction Execution (EX)
Result Return (RR)
```

To simplify answering these questions, consider an analogy based on the person who opens the mail at the Nenana Ice Classic, a lottery run by the town of Nenana, Alaska (pop. 449). People worldwide buy $2 tickets to guess the exact minute when the ice will break up on the town's river, the Tananah, and flow downstream. In 2001, breakup was exactly 1:00 P.M., May 8, and the jackpot, split among eight winners, was $308,500. After competition is closed, but before breakup, the town publishes a thick book listing the names of all the contestants organized by the date and time of their guesses. The process of compiling the data for this book is the analogy for the Fetch/Execute Cycle.

Imagine in the office at Ice Classic Headquarters a table with trays containing a few thousand 3 × 5 cards, each labeled with a month, day, hour, and minute. The card

[1] Admittedly some frustrated users will find these assertions far-fetched.

records the names of contestants guessing that time. For example, the 2001 winners' names would have been listed on the card labeled 5/08-13:00. The cards are filed in time order in several long trays so the card for a given date and time can be easily located. Also, imagine a tray of envelopes.

Hello, Nenana!
I'm sure breakup will be on
**** May 4 at 12:04PM ****
Find $2 enclosed.
Yours, Frost T. Snowman
61 River St.
Circle AK

The Classic volunteer, implementing a human version of the Fetch/Execute Cycle, proceeds as follows: (IF) He or she Fetches the first envelope, opens it, and removes its contents, setting aside the $2 fee in the cash drawer. In essence what comes out of the envelope is an instruction to the volunteer to enter the contestant's name on a particular date and time. (ID) The volunteer Decodes the instruction, determining the contestant's name and the day, hour, and minute that the contestant predicts for breakup. The key part of the Decoding operation is finding the day and time guessed because together they determine which card is required. (DF) The volunteer then fetches the proper card. This Data Fetch operation in effect retrieves the list of the other people, if any, who have already guessed that same day and time. (EX) He or she then Executes the instruction by entering the person's name and address on the card.[2] When the entry has been made, (RR) the card is returned to the proper place in the tray, implementing the human version of the Result Return step of the Fetch/Execute Cycle. The tireless volunteer then picks up another envelope and repeats the process.

The Ice Classic analogy helps to give an intuitive meaning to the steps of the Fetch/Execute Cycle, but to answer the questions raised earlier, we need to know how a computer is organized.

> **No. 1 Computer.** The first computer was designed and built by J. Presper Eckert and John Mauchley of the University of Pennsylvania. Named **ENIAC** for Electronic Numerical Integrator And Calculator and built for the U.S. Army, the machine was constructed using 18,000 vacuum tubes, weighed 30 tons, and filled a room.

ANATOMY OF A COMPUTER

Knowing intuitively how the Fetch/Execute Cycle works, consider now how a computer's parts are arranged to accomplish it. All computers regardless of their implementing technology have five basic parts or subsystems: Memory, Arithmetic/Logic Unit, Control Unit, Input Unit, and Output Unit. These are arranged as shown in Figure 9.1. *Caution:* It is a coincidence that there are five steps to the fetch execute cycle and five subsystems to a computer—they're related, of course, but not one-to-one.

The five components of a computer have the following characteristics.

Memory

Stores both the program, while it is running, and the data on which the program operates. Recall the paver analogy of Chapter 8. In the Ice Classic analogy, the memory for the instructions was the tray of mail and for the data it was the sequence of cards on which the names are written. Important properties of memory are:

[2] If the space is full, the volunteer simply stores the card in a safe place, gets a blank card, labels it with the same month, day, hour, and minute, and begins using it; the cards will be merged later to create the contestants book.

Discrete Locations

Memory is organized as a sequence of discrete locations, like the cards in the Ice Classic analogy. In modern memories, each location is composed of one byte, that is, a sequence of eight bits.

Addresses

Every memory location has an address, like the month/day/hour/minute card labels in the analogy, though computer memory addresses are just whole numbers starting at 0 in sequence.

Values

Memory locations record or store values, like the cards that record the contestants' names.

Finite capacity

A memory location has finite capacity, like the cards, and provision must be made in programming to handle the problem of the locations not having enough capacity.

These properties motivate a commonly used diagram of computer memory:

0	1	2	3	4	5	6	7	8	9	10	11	
100	T	h	a	N	K	$	*	4	ƀ	d	a	...

The key properties of memory are visible in the diagram. The discrete locations are represented as boxes. The address of each location is displayed above it. The value or contents of the memory locations are shown by enclosing them in the boxes.

The one-byte capacity of a memory location is enough to store one character (letter or numeral or punctuation symbol) or a number less than 256. Obviously a single computer memory location would not have enough capacity to store the names of several contestants like the 3 × 5 cards in the analogy. To overcome the small capacity of computer memory locations, a programmer simply uses a block of consecutive memory locations and ignores the fact that they all have separate addresses, that is, the programmer treats the address of the first location as if it were the address of the whole block of memory.

Computer memory is often called *RAM* (random access memory). The modifier "random access" is archaic and simply means that the computer can refer to the memory locations in any order required. (The songs on a cassette tape are not randomly accessed, but are *sequentially accessed* because you have to skip past the first song to play the second song, the next song in sequence.) RAM is sold by the megabyte, abbreviated MB. A large memory is generally preferable to a small memory because there is more space for programs and data.

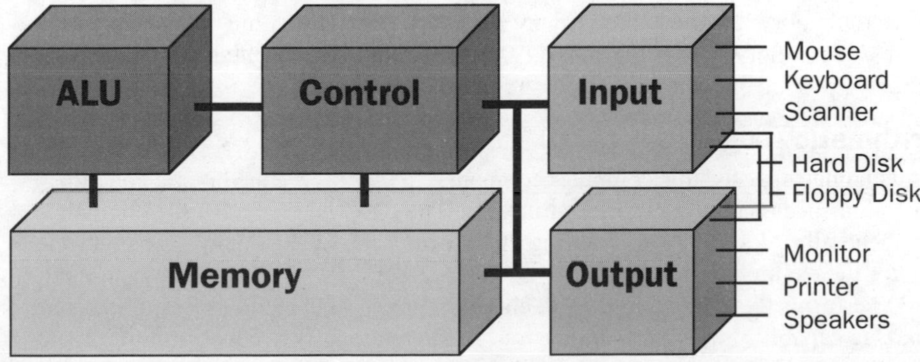

Figure 9.1. The principal components of a computer.

Free Memory. *Mega-* is the Latin prefix for "million," so a megabyte should be a million bytes of memory. In fact, a megabyte is 1,048,576 bytes. Why such an odd even number? Computers need to associate a byte of memory with every address. A million addresses require 20 bits because 19 bits are not enough. But with 20 bits, 2^{20} = 1,048,576 addresses are possible with binary counting. So, to ensure that every 20-bit address has its byte of memory, the extra 48,576 bytes are included "free."

Summarizing these properties informally, memory is like a sequence of labeled containers for information known as locations: The address is the location's number in sequence; the value or the information stored at the location is the container's contents; only so much can fit in each container.

Control

The control component of a computer is a hardware implementation of the Fetch/Execute Cycle. Its circuitry fetches an instruction from memory and performs the other operations of the Cycle on it. In the Ice Classic analogy, the tireless volunteer corresponds to the control.

Computer instructions are more primitive than the "Enter my name . . ." instructions of the Ice Classic analogy. A typical machine instruction has the form

```
ADD 2000, 2080, 4000
```

which appears to be commanding that three numbers, 2000, 2080, and 4000, be added together, but it does not. Rather, the instruction asks that two numbers, the numbers stored in the memory locations 2000 and 2080, be added together, and that the result be stored in the memory location 4000. Thus, to execute this instruction, the Data Fetch step of the Fetch/Execute Cycle must retrieve the two values at memory locations 2000 and 2080, and after they are added, the Result Return step will store the answer in memory location 4000.

A fundamental concept implicit in this discussion of instructions is worthy of further emphasis. The instruction `ADD 2000, 2080 4000` does not command the computer to add together the numbers 2000 and 2080—the answer is 4080 and it is pointless to program a computer to do a task we know the answer to. Rather, the instruction commands the computer to add together the numbers *stored in memory locations* 2000 and 2080, whatever those numbers may be. Because different values could be in those memory locations each time the computer executes the instruction, a different result could be computed each time. The concept is that computer instructions encode the memory addresses of the numbers to be added, not the numbers themselves, and thus refer to the values *indirectly*. The indirection allows a single instruction encoding to combine any two numbers simply by placing the numbers in the referenced memory locations. (See Figure 9.2.) Referring to a value by referring to the address in memory where it is stored is fundamental to a computer's versatilitiy.

Arithmetic/Logic Unit (ALU)

As its name suggests, this computer component performs the arithmetic and other operations necessary to execute instructions. The ALU is the part of the computer that generally "does the work" during the Execute step of the Fetch/Execute Cycle. So, for the example instruction `ADD 2000, 2080, 4000` just discussed, the ALU performs the actual addition. A circuit in the ALU can add two numbers—an amazing capability when you think about it. There are also circuits for multiplying two numbers to implement the MULTIPLY instruction, circuits for comparing two numbers to see which is larger to implement the COMPARE instruction, and so on.

You can think of an ALU as implementing the operation of each machine instruction with a separate circuit, though modern computers are so sophisticated that they can combine the functionality of several instructions into one circuit.

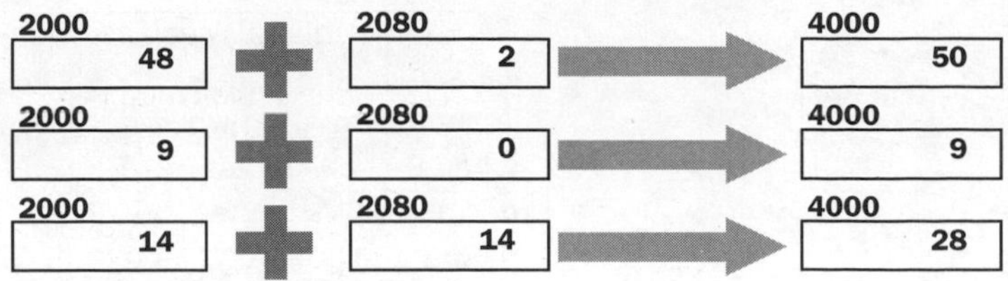

Figure 9.2. Illustration of a single ADD instruction producing different results depending on the contents of the memory locations referenced in the instruction.

In the Ice Classic analogy, the ALU corresponds to the office calculator. The instruction execution in the analogy didn't require any arithmetic because the instruction the volunteer was performing—entering names—entailed writing onto the card. When the volunteer performs the instruction "ADD the amount in the cash drawer to the amount previously received to compute the total receipts," the calculator is used. This distinction implied by our analogy—some instructions use the ALU and others don't—is true for computers. It emphasizes that computers sometimes *transform* information (using the ALU) and sometimes *transfer* information. Both aspects are included in the term *information processing.*

For those instructions that use the ALU, it is now clear what the Data Fetch and Result Return steps of the Fetch/Execute Cycle must do: Data Fetch retrieves from memory the values needed by the ALU to perform operations like `ADD` and `MULTIPLY`. These values are called *operands*, and as we've learned, the instruction specifies the addresses where the data is to be found. The Data Fetch step delivers these values to the ALU. When the ALU completes the operation, producing a sum or product, the Result Return step moves that answer from the ALU to the memory at the address specified in the instruction.

Input Unit and Output Unit

These two components, which are inverses of each other, and so can be conveniently discussed together, are portals through which information moves into and out of a computer. Computers need to input information in order to have data to work on, and they need to output information to report back the results of the computation. A computer without input or output, that is, the memory, control, and ALU sealed in a box, is useless. Indeed, from a philosophical perspective, we might question whether it can even be said to "compute."

As indicated in Figure 9.1, a variety of devices—called *peripherals*—connect to the computer I/O ports providing it with input or receiving its output. As the term *peripherals* implies, these are not considered part of the computer, but rather they are specialized gadgets that encode or decode information between the computer and the physical world. The keyboard encodes the keystrokes we type into binary form for the computer. The monitor decodes information from the computer's memory, displaying it in a visible form on a lighted, color screen. In general, the peripherals handle the physical part of the operation, sending or receiving the binary information the computer uses.

The cable from the peripheral to the computer connects to the Input Unit or the Output Unit. These units handle the communication protocol with the peripherals. As a general rule, think of the Input Unit as depositing information from the peripheral into the memory, and the Output Unit as removing information from the memory and delivering it to the outside world. (The actual details are much more complicated.)

Certain peripherals such as floppy disks and hard disks are used by computers in both capacities, input and output. These are storage devices, where the computer files away information when it is not needed, an output operation, and then retrieves it when it needs the information again, an input operation. The hard disk is the *alpha-peripheral,* being the most aggressively engineered and the device most tightly coupled to the computer. Why? Because although programs and their data must reside in the computer's memory when programs run, they reside on the hard disk the remainder of the time where there is more permanent space. In that sense, the hard disk is an extension of the computer's memory, but typically it has several hundred times more capacity and several thousand times less speed.

Volatility. Contemporary computer memory is made of Integrated Circuit (chip) technology, making it volatile: When the power is removed, the electrical charge encoding the information dissipates, and the information is lost. As mentioned in Chapter 2, volatility is a good feature when we've wedged the computer. Cycling power erases everything, requiring rebooting, and giving a fresh start. It's a bad feature if the computer crashes and we haven't saved our work to disk recently. In Chapter 8, we learned that disks record information magnetically, and because magnetic polarity is stable when the power is off, the information persists.

Most peripheral devices are "dumb" in that all they provide is basic physical translation to or from binary signals. They rely on the computer for any further processing, which is almost always required to make the device function in an "intelligent way." So, as I type the letters of this sentence, signals are sent from the keyboard to the computer indicating which keys my fingers depress. When the computer receives information that *w* has been depressed and that *Shift* is also being depressed at the same moment, the computer converts the *w* keystroke to the intended capitalized *W*. Similarly, keys like *Ctrl* and *Backspace* are just keys to the keyboard. It is the added processing by a piece of software called a *device driver* that gives the keyboard its standard meaning and behavior. Every device requires a device driver to provide this added processing. Naturally, because the device may have very odd characteristics unique to itself, a device driver will be specialized to only one device.

New Toys. Many users are excited about getting a new peripheral such as a printer, scanner, or CD-ROM. They plug it into their computer, but forget that it needs a device driver before it can run. This is partly because computers often come loaded with standardized or popular device drivers, and so users don't know that peripherals need them, or they forget. A floppy or a CD containing the device driver(s) should come with the peripheral, or the driver can be downloaded from the manufacturer's Web site.

In the Ice Classic analogy, the output device is the printing company in Fairbanks that prints and binds the List of Contestants. When all of the entries have been received, the data for the List will have been recorded in the memory (3×5 cards), once all of the filled-up cards are merged back in. This is not the right form to publish, of course, because the Fairbanks company wants "camera-ready" pages. So, we expect the tireless volunteer to execute the instructions of the device driver, converting the information in memory to the right form for the printing company. This might require the positioning of 6–8 cards on the copier glass, and photocopying the cards in order to create a page that is usable by the printer, maybe including cards with headings for each day. The copier is analogous to the output unit, that is, taking the data from memory and preparing it for transmission to the output device. When the List's pages are done, they are transmitted to the company in Fairbanks to produce the user-readable output.

The PC's PC

The remaining question concerns how a computer determines which instruction to execute next. In the Ice Classic analogy, the volunteer simply removes letters from a tray of mail to get the next "instruction." When processing mail, the order doesn't matter, so any letter will do. In computers, the order in which instructions are executed is critical.

Recall that when the Fetch/Execute Cycle is processing a program, called *instruction interpretation*, the instructions are stored in the memory. Consequently every instruction has an address, which is the address of the memory location of the first byte of the instruction. (Instructions of present-day computers occupy four bytes.) Naturally computers keep track of which instruction to execute next by its address. This address, stored in the Control component of the computer, should probably be called the *next instruction address*, but for historic reasons it is actually known by the curious term, *program counter*, abbreviated, *PC*.

The precise description of the Instruction Fetch step of the Fetch/Execute Cycle is that it transfers the instruction from the memory at the address specified by the Program Counter to the Decoder of the Control component. Once the instruction has been fetched, and while it is being processed by the remaining steps of the Cycle, the computer prepares to process the next instruction. The next instruction is assumed to be the next instruction in sequence. Because instructions occupy four bytes of memory, the next instruction must be located at the memory address PC+4, that is, four bytes further along in sequence than the current instruction. Therefore, the computer adds four to the PC, so that when the Cycle gets around to the Instruction Fetch step again, the PC is "pointing at" the new instruction.

This scheme of executing instructions in sequence seems flawed: Won't the Fetch/Execute Cycle blaze through the memory executing all the instructions, arrive at the last instruction in memory, and "fall off the end of memory" having used up all of the instructions? This possibility is unlikely unless the program has a bug in it. The reason is that computers come with instructions called *branch* and *jump* that change the PC. That is, after the Control has prepared for the next instruction by adding four to the PC, the Execute step in the Fetch/Execute Cycle can reset the PC to a new value. This overrides the selection of the next instruction in sequence and causes the Program Counter to address some other instruction in memory. The next instruction will be fetched from this memory location on the next revolution of the Fetch/Execute Cycle.

Instruction Interpretation Illustrated

To make the idea of interpreting instructions more exact, consider the execution of a typical ADD instruction. The state of affairs just before the Fetch/Execute Cycle starts on this instruction is shown in Figure 9.3. Observe that the memory has been refined to show some of the locations and the PC is visible in the Control Unit.

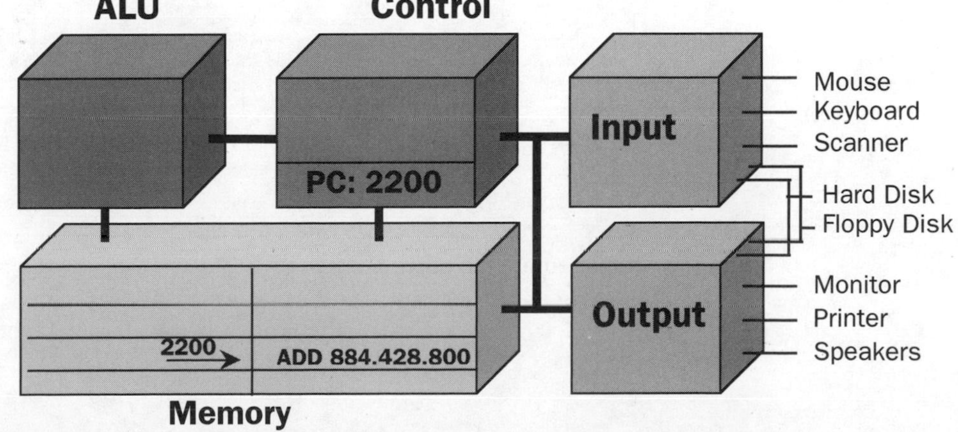

Figure 9.3. Computer configuration prior to executing an ADD instruction.

Instruction execution begins by moving the instruction at the address given by the PC from the Memory Unit to the Control Unit. (See Figure 9.4.) Once that operation is completed, the PC can be readied for fetching the next instruction. For present-day computers whose instructions are four bytes long, 4 is added to the PC. In Figure 9.5, the Instruction Decode step is illustrated. The ALU is set up for the operation in the Execute step. The addresses of the instruction's data, the source operands, are set up to be fetched from memory by the Data Fetch step, and the destination address for the answer is set up for the Result Return step. Figure 9.6 shows the Data Fetch step in which the operand data values are moved into the ALU from the Memory. The Execute step is illustrated in Figure 9.7, and the Result Return is illustrated in Figure 9.8. Once the result is returned, the cycle begins all over again.

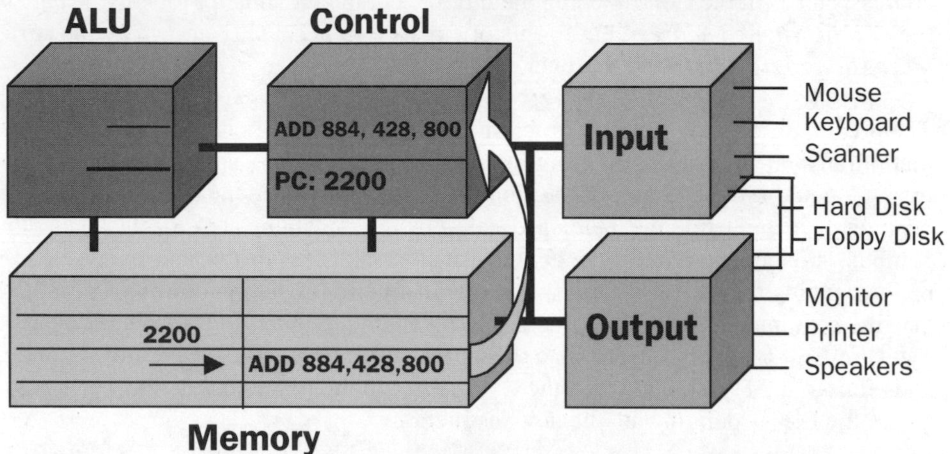

Figure 9.4. Instruction Fetch: Move instruction from memory to the control unit.

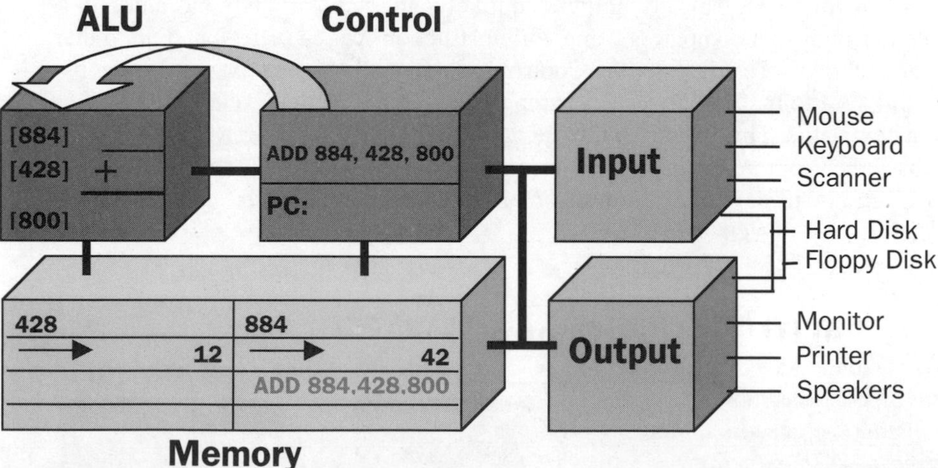

Figure 9.5. Instruction Decode: Pull apart the instruction, set up the operation in the ALU, and compute the source and destination operand addresses.

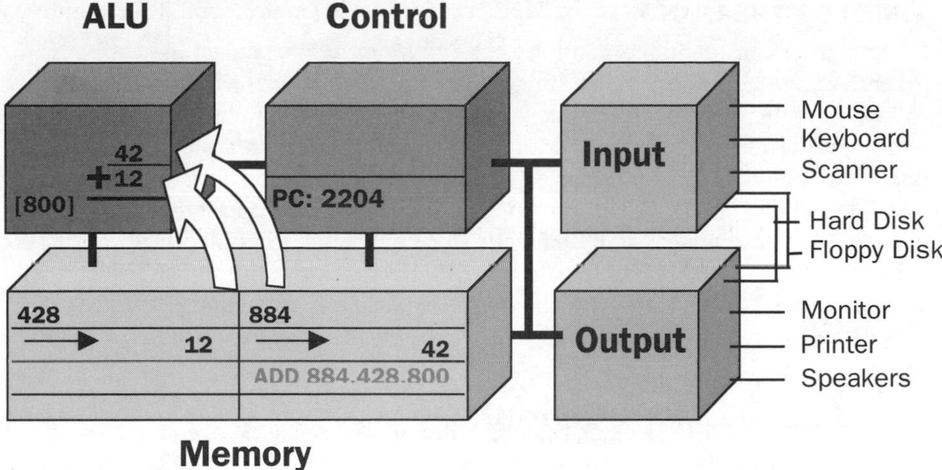

Figure 9.6. Data Fetch: Move the operands from memory to the ALU.

> **Stop!** If the Fetch/Execute Cycle is an infinite loop, how does a computer stop? Early computers actually had Start and Stop buttons, but present computers simply execute an "idle loop" when there's nothing to do. The instructions continually check if there's anything to do, like process a mouse click or keystroke.

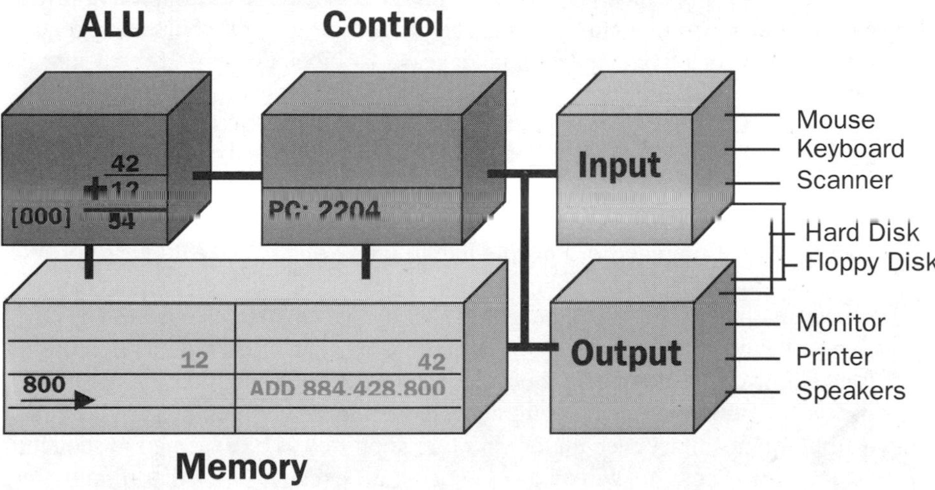

Figure 9.7. Execute. Compute the result of the operation in the ALU.

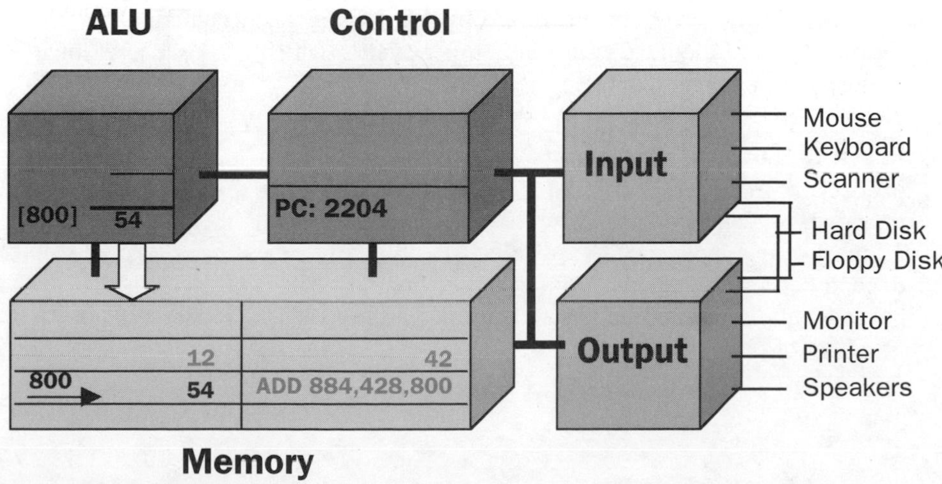

Figure 9.8. Result Return: Store the result from the ALU into the memory at the destination address.

Time for the Clock

Computers are instruction execution engines. We have just studied in detail how the Fetch/Execute Cycle performs a single instruction. With one instruction per cycle it follows that the speed of a computer—the number of instructions executed in a second—is determined by the number of revolutions of the Fetch/Execute Cycle. The rate of the Fetch/Execute Cycle is determined by the computer's *clock*, and it is measured in *megahertz*, or millions (mega) of cycles per second (hertz). Computer clock speeds have increased dramatically in recent years, resulting in speeds of 1000 MHz or more. A 1000 MHz clock ticks a billion (in American English) times per second, which is 1 gigahertz, 1 GHz, in any language. (See Figure 9.9 for terms.) Clock speeds are a prominent feature of computer advertisements, but how important are they?

A computer with a 1 GHz clock has one billionth of a second—one nanosecond—between clock ticks to run the Fetch/Execute Cycle. In that short interval of time, light can travel only about a foot (30 cm.). Is it really possible to perform an add or multiply instruction that fast? No. In truth, modern computers try to *start* an instruction on each clock tick. They pass off the completion to other circuitry in an assembly line fashion. This process, called *pipelining*, frees the fetch unit to start the next instruction before the last one is done. As shown in Figure 9.10, even if the five steps of the Fetch/Execute Cycle take a nanosecond *each*—which is still extremely fast—it is possible to complete one instruction on each clock tick as long as there is enough circuitry for five instructions to be "in process" at once. Completing instructions at that rate keeps up with a starting rate of one per tick. Of course, to execute 1000 instructions in a five-stage pipeline takes 1004 clock cycles—1000 to start each instruction, and four more for the last four steps of the last instruction. So it is not quite true that 1000 instructions are executed in 1000 ticks. But that's probably close enough.

So, should we assume that a computer with a 1 GHz clock executes a billion instructions per second? Computer salespeople like to imply that it's true, but it's not. We said that computers *try* to start an instruction on each clock tick, but there is a long list of reasons—they won't concern us here—why starting one on each tick is not possible. If the computer cannot start instructions on each clock tick, its execution rate falls *below* one billion instructions per second. But the situation is even more complex. Miraculously computer engineers have figured out how to start more than one instruction at a time, even though they are supposed to be executed in sequential order. How this is possible will also not concern us, except to note that if multiple instructions can be started frequently enough, they can make up for not starting instructions at other times. Thus the rate could be *above* one billion per second. It is extremely difficult—even for experts—to figure out how fast a contemporary computer runs. As a result, the one-instruction-per-cycle—which was once a reasonable guideline—is no longer reliable.

> **Speed of Fluency**. This book was written on two new laptops with different processors that seem comparable in most ways except clock speed: One machine's clock is twice as fast as the other's. However, the "slower machine" regularly runs applications faster than the "fast machine," because performance depends on many features: instruction set, memory size and design, other system components, software quality, and so on. The lesson: Clock speed is not a good predictor of performance.

The Importance of Integration

One reason that modern computer clocks can run at GHz rates is that the processor chips are so tiny. Recall that the maximum distance electrical signals can travel in a nanosecond under ideal circumstances is about 1 foot, and to compute, much more has to happen to the signals than simply being transmitted. Early computers, which filled whole rooms, could never have run so fast for several reasons, including that their connected components were separated by distances greater than a foot. So, miniaturization has improved computer performance by allowing for faster clock rates.

1000^1	kilo-	$1024^1 = 2^{10} = 1{,}024$	milli-	1000^{-1}
1000^2	mega-	$1024^2 = 2^{20} = 1{,}048{,}576$	micro-	1000^{-2}
1000^3	giga-	$1024^3 = 2^{30} = 1{,}073{,}741{,}824$	nano-	1000^{-3}
1000^4	tera-	$1024^4 = 2^{40} = 1{,}099{,}511{,}627{,}776$	pico-	1000^{-4}
1000^5	peta-	$1024^5 = 2^{50} = 1{,}125{,}899{,}906{,}842{,}624$	femto-	1000^{-5}
1000^6	exa-	$1024^6 = 2^{60} = 1{,}152{,}921{,}504{,}606{,}846{,}976$	atto-	1000^{-6}
1000^7	zetta-	$1024^7 = 2^{70} = 1{,}180{,}591{,}620{,}717{,}411{,}303{,}424$	zepto-	1000^{-7}
1000^8	yotta-	$1024^8 = 2^{80} = 1{,}208{,}925{,}819{,}614{,}629{,}174{,}706{,}176$	yocto-	1000^{-8}

Figure 9.9. Standard prefixes from the Système International (SI) convention on scientific measurements. Generally a prefix refers to a power of 1000, except when the quantity, for example, memory, is counted in binary; for binary quantities the prefix refers to a power of 1024, which is 2^{10}.

> **Beauty of Prefixes**. Prefixes "change the units" so that very large or small quantities can be expressed with numbers of a reasonable size. A well-known humorous example recalls Helen of Troy from Greek myth "whose face launched 1000 ships." The beauty needed to launch one ship is one-thousandth of Helen's, that is, 0.001 Helen, or 1 MilliHelen.

But the real achievement of microchip technology is not miniaturization, but *integration*. It is impossible to overstate its significance. To appreciate how profound the invention of integrated circuitry is, realize that before integration, computers and other electronic gadgets were built out of discrete parts that were manually wired together. The wires coming out of each transistor (3), resistor (2), capacitor (2), and so on had to be connected to the wires of some other transistor, resistor, capacitor, and so on. Even for printed circuit boards in which the "wiring" is realized by printing metallic strips to connect the components, a person or machine must still "populate" the board with the components one at a time. Any complex system will have hundreds of thousands or millions of these parts and at least twice as many connections, which are expensive and time consuming to construct, error prone, and unreliable. If computers still had to be constructed out of discrete parts, they would still be rare.

> **Cray's Limit**. Seymour Cray, who designed and built more huge computers than anyone else, once commented that there is a "manufacturing complexity limit" of about six million connections. Beyond that a system becomes too complex to produce, test, and maintain. The fact that the Space Shuttle has approximately six million parts may be a confirmation of Cray's limit.

The "big idea" behind integrated circuits has two parts. The first concept is that the active components—transistors, capacitors, and so forth—and the wires that connect them together are all made of a single family of compatible materials by a single (multistep) process. Thus, rather than making two transistors and later connecting them by soldering a pair of their wires together, IC technology places them side by side in the silicon and at some stage in the fabrication process—perhaps while some of the transistor's internal parts are still being constructed—a wire connecting the two will be placed into position. The crux of integration is that the active and connective parts of a circuit are constructed together. Integration saves space (promoting speed), but its most significant advantage is to produce a single monolithic part for the whole system without manual wiring. The resulting "block" of electronics is extremely reliable.

The second concept behind integrated circuits is that the fabrication process uses *photolithography*, a printing process. Here's how it works. Making a chip is like making a sandwich. Start with a layer of silicon, and add layers of materials to build up the transistors, capacitors, wires, and other features of a chip. For example, wires might be made of a layer of aluminum. But the aluminum cannot be smeared over the chip like mayonnaise covers a sandwich; the wires must be electrically separated from each other and must connect to specific places where the active components are located. This is where photolithography comes in. The aluminum smear is covered with a layer of light-sensitive material called a *photoresist*. A mask is placed on the chip. The mask—it's like a photographic negative—shows the pattern of the wires. When light illuminates the mask, it passes through at places to react with the photoresist. The mask is then removed and the changed-by-light resist—and the aluminum it covers—are etched away. The remaining photoresist is also etched away. What remains is the pattern of aluminum corresponding to the pattern on the mask, that is, the wires! The key aspect of photolithography is that the cost and complexity of fabricating a chip is not related to how complex its design is, that is, how complex the pattern is on the mask. Like a page of a newspaper, which costs the same to print five words or 5000 words, the cost of producing integrated circuits is not related to their complexity. Thanks to the photolithographic process, computers and other electronics can be as complicated as we wish.

IC Man. Jack Kilby shared the 2000 Nobel Prize in Physics for his invention of the integrated circuit. Kilby worked for the electronics firm Texas Instruments. New to the staff, Kilby hadn't accrued vacation time, but while the other employees were away on their holidays, he invented integrated circuits.

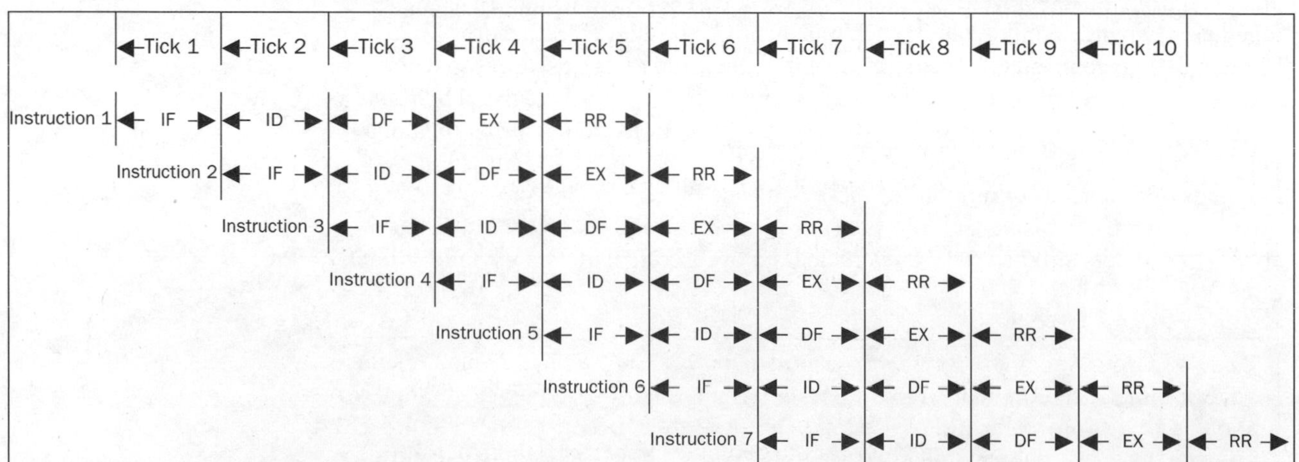

Figure 9.10. Schematic diagram of a pipelined Fetch/Execute Cycle. On each tick, the IF circuit starts a new instruction, and before the time runs out, it passes it along to the ID unit; the ID circuit works on the instruction it receives, finishing just in time to pass it along to the DF circuit, and so on. When the pipeline is filled, five instructions are in progress, and one instruction is completed on each clock tick, making the computer *appear* to be running at the rate of one instruction per clock tick.

LOTS AND LOTS OF SIMPLE OPERATIONS

Computers "know" very few instructions. That is, the decoder hardware in the Controller recognizes, and the ALU can perform, only about 100 or so different instructions. And these few instructions are usually quite redundant. For example, different types of data usually have different kinds of ADD instructions, one for adding bytes, one for adding whole numbers, one for adding "decimal" numbers, and so on. *Everything* that computers do must be reduced to one of these primitive, hardwired instructions. They have no other capabilities.

ADD is a reasonably complex instruction for a computer, and MULTiply and DIVide are at the screaming limit of complexity. Other instructions

- Shift the bits of a word (4 bytes) to the left or right, filling the vacated places with zeros and throwing away the bits that fall off the end. (Where do they go?)
- Compute the logical AND, which tests if pairs of bits are both true (1), and logical OR, which tests if at least one of two bits is true.
- Test if a bit is zero or nonzero, and jump to a different set of instructions based on the outcome.
- Move information around in memory, transferring it between different memory locations.
- Sense the signals from Input/Output devices.

Computer instructions are very primitive. There is no DRAW_A_BUTTON or SPELL_CHECK.

But computers tirelessly perform these simple instructions very fast, and that is the secret of getting them to do tasks that are more interesting than adding two numbers together. If we can figure out how to describe a more complex operation as a sequence of the primitive hardwired instructions, each time we want the more complex operation performed, we simply instruct the computer to follow our sequence of primitive instructions. It will *appear* that the computer knows the more complex operation, especially if it does the sequence blazingly fast. Once we have more complex operations, we can use them to describe still more complex operations and whole tasks. This activity is known as *programming*, of course, and it is the essence of making a computer help us. In later chapters, we describe in detail how to build more complex operations from simpler ones—there's more to it than it sounds. Though few of us will ever be professional programmers, the ability to accomplish complex results by combining simple components is a capability of benefit to us all.

> **Geekettes?** The first programmers, who wrote and ran the programs on the ENIAC, were all women: Kathleen McNulty Mauchly Antonelli, Jean Jennings Bartik, Frances Snyder Holberton, Marlyn Wescoff Meltzer, Frances Bilas Spence, and Ruth Lichterman Teitelbaum. They were recruited from the ranks of *computers*, humans who used mechanical calculators to solve complex mathematical problems prior to the invention of electronic computers.

Think of writing a term paper with a word processor and consider the thousands of operations that a computer performs for you, from recognizing which keyboard key you pressed to spell checking. In order for the computer to perform these actions, each task had to be converted into a sequence of the primitive hardwired instructions because none of these word processing operations is primitive. This is programming, but the programmer's job would be tediously boring if the translation to primitive instructions was performed manually. No one would be a programmer no matter how much he or she was paid.

Fortunately, one "complex" task that computers can be programmed to do is translating complicated operations into the simpler primitive instructions that they understand. Of course, some programmer had to tell the computer how to do this the first time, but thereafter the computer can do the translation for itself. This automatic translation—there are actually several levels of translation—helps keep programming interesting. The only roll for the programmer is to figure out how to do a complex task once. That specification is the *program.* From then on, the computer handles the conversion into more primitive operations that it can understand and then it can perform the task when needed.

Specifically, computers only understand instructions expressed in binary digits. Writing a string of 32 or more 0s and 1s is so tedious that the earliest computer builders developed a symbolic form for instructions called *Assembly Language.* The ADD instruction shown in Figure 9.2 is an example of the symbolic form of the binary machine instruction. The process of converting from assembly instructions to machine instructions is called *Assembling.* But these instructions are still too primitive to be of much use to humans because they typically correspond one to one with binary machine instructions. So, computer scientists invented programming languages like FORTRAN and Basic to allow programmers to express complex tasks easily. Still more expressive languages such as C, C++, and Java have eclipsed these early programming languages. The translation process from a programming language to an assembly language is called *compilation.* Because the programming languages are expressive, a single statement in one of these languages may convert into dozens of assembly instructions, which are then converted into binary machine instructions. Summarizing the process:

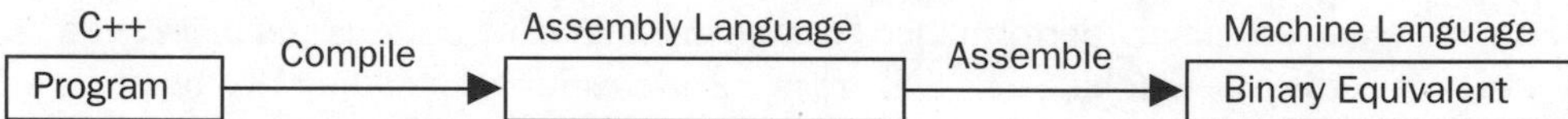

Many programmers work in development environments such as Visual C++ in which they simply combine previously written programs, possibly with small amounts of program written in the programming language. This is an even more powerful way to direct a computer to do a task.

Operating Systems

Three operating systems are in wide use—Windows in its various forms, MacOS, and UNIX in its various forms including Linux. Dozens of others have been created, but these three represent the state of the art. The question is not which one is best—they all have their technical triumphs and tragedies—but why do we have them at all? The answer can be found in the meager list of instructions that are hardwired into computers. None of the operations that a computer needs to start up and keep running is provided for as a basic hardwired instruction. Because processors are so pathetic, programmers must develop a large collection or relatively small but intricate procedures to enable the computer to start and perform useful work. The result is an operating system, leading to the following definition: An *operating system* (OS) is software that extends the hardwired functionality of a processor with general-purpose facilities, enabling it to start up (boot), manage its memory and applications, and interact with its peripheral devices. Being general purpose, these facilities are provided to other software (applications) when they need the functionality. For example, device drivers are considered operating system software, implying that when your word processor prints your term paper, it invokes (runs) the print driver and other operating system components to convey your crisp prose from the computer memory onto paper.

Memory management is a basic service that operating systems provide. When you go to write your term paper, the word processor program is on the hard disk where the operating system put it when the application was installed. The operating system provides some means for you to start the word processor, and when you do so, it locates the start of the program on the hard disk, loads the first part of it into memory, and causes it to begin executing. Most modern computers provide the facilities of virtual memory and demand paging, so that it doesn't much matter where in the memory the OS puts the first part of the program or how much it loads in initially. The computer executes the instructions that are available in memory, and when it tries to execute instructions that are still on the disk, it *page faults*, meaning it stops, waiting for the next page of instructions. A page fault is a hardware "wake up," called an *interrupt*, to the operating system, which may not have been active while the word processing application was running. The operating system determines that the problem is that the needed page is still on the disk, and loads it. Then, the OS causes the computer to resume executing your application. And so it goes, the computer faulting when the next page of instructions or data is not in the memory, the OS fielding the complaint, and loading it in. It happens so fast we don't even notice that the program was only partly available at the beginning.

Printing and managing the memory pages is not the only help your word processor application is getting from the OS. All of the interactions with the monitor—it's a device after all—including menus, scroll bars, and most other features of the GUI. The OS manages the mouse. The mouse pointer is a fiction, of course, so the OS creates it and moves it around on the screen in response to your actions. The operating system determines when the mouse pointer is over a button when you click, and so performs the operations described in Chapter 2. All user software can benefit from having these basic facilities provided so that they need not be implemented repeatedly by each application.

SUMMARY

This chapter has given a simple, but accurate formulation of a computer, including its principal components and the Fetch/Execute Cycle. It mirrors the construction and operation of many early computers built in the days before silicon technology had advanced to the microprocessor stage, that is, before everything in Figure 9.1 fit on a chip. Once silicon technology matured, computer architects—the engineers that design computers—became very aggressive. By exploiting fundamental properties of integrated circuitry they have hybridized the simple structure of Figure 9.1 and further deconstructed the Fetch/Execute Cycle. Today's computers are dramatically more complex than explained here in order to achieve their impressive speeds. But, the abstraction—the logical idea of how a computer is organized and operates—remains as presented.

The chapter began with a simple intuitive explanation for the Fetch/Execute Cycle, the instruction interpretation engine of a computer system. The process repeated forever is one of fetching the next instruction (as indicated by the PC), decoding what operation is to be performed and on what data, retrieving the data, performing the operation, and storing the result back into the memory. This process is hardwired into the Control subsystem, one of the five components of a processor. The Memory, composed of a very long sequence of bytes, each with a consecutive address, stores the program and data while the program is running. The ALU does the actual computing. The Input and Output Units are the interfaces for the peripheral devices attached to the computer. A key point about machine instructions is that their power comes from not referring to the data directly, but rather indirectly. The instructions refer to their operand values by the memory address of the data, not the data itself. Thus an instruction can be repeated many times using different data each time because there is different data in the memory locations each time. Examples illustrated the basics of instruction execution. It was observed that computers have few instructions in their hardware with very simple capabilities. This meager resource is used to build up more complex operations, which are used in turn to build even more complex operations still, and so on, resulting in the powerful capabilities that we associate with computers today. The special family of operations that form the operating system, particularly memory management, illustrated how the more powerful operations are used.

EXERCISES

1. Define what a computer does and give a synonym for *computer.*
2. What is the intuitive description of the five-step process of the Fetch/Execute Cycle?
3. What are the names of five steps of the Fetch/Execute Cycle, and why do they have an arrow from the last to the first?
4. What are the five subsystems of a computer?
5. What are the four properties of computer memory?
6. What does the *Control* subsystem of a computer do?
7. What does *ALU* stand for, and what is its role in a computer?
8. Explain what the machine instruction `ADD 6000, 2080 4104` does.
9. Explain the statement, "Information processing involves both transforming and transferring information."
10. Post Office mail boxes, the type that you can rent as an alternative to having mail delivered to your residence, have often been used as an analogy for computer memory. What are the similarities?
11. How are hard disks and floppy disks distinguished form other input and output devices?
12. What does *PC* abbreviate, of what subsystem of a computer is it a part, and what does it do?
13. How many instructions do modern computers issue per clock tick?
14. It has been claimed that the optimal length for a lecture is 1 microcentury. How many minutes is that?
15. What two aspects of integrated circuitry explain its importance?
16. What is compilation?
17. Explain the role of an operating system.

CHAPTER 10

Algorithmic Thinking

Learning Objectives

- Appreciate that algorithms are a familiar idea.
- Learn the five defining requirements of algorithms.
- Know the importance of language.
- Appreciate the role of context for programs.
- Understand the operation of the *Alphabetize CDs* algorithm by following its execution.
- Understand the anatomy of *Alphabetize CDs*.
- Comprehend the *Beta* Sweep and *Alpha* Sweep abstractions.

An algorithm is a precise, systematic method for producing a specified result. We encounter algorithms as recipes, assembly instructions, driving directions, business processes, nominating procedures, and so on. Algorithms are at the core of processing information, of course, and we've already met several in this book. Three reasons stand out among the motivations to learn more about algorithms. First and foremost, we must often formulate algorithms so that other people or computers can help us achieve our goals. If they are to be successful, the algorithms must "work." This chapter explains how to formulate effective algorithms—precise, systematic methods—so that the intended result (our goal) is achieved. Second, we will find ourselves following algorithms produced by others. Knowing the "dos" and "don'ts" of algorithm design, we can be attentive to the details and alert to errors in other people's directives, and so produce better results. Finally, our study of algorithms will complete the picture begun in Chapter 9 of how computers solve problems. Understanding this process promotes Fluency by making us more productive computer users, more effective debuggers, and more insightful problem solvers.

The overall goals of this chapter are to understand the concept of algorithms and to acquire a basic facility for thinking algorithmically. The strategy for achieving these goals is to begin by reviewing familiar examples of everyday algorithms. Next, the five fundamental requirements of algorithms are introduced, defined, explained, and illustrated. The role of *language* in specifying algorithms is explained and the value of a formal language is recognized. The relationship between algorithms and programs is then discussed, with guidelines—applicable to formulating driving directions—for understanding the role of context in executing algorithms. Next, we create an algorithm for alphabetizing our CD collection. This algorithm, expressed in much greater detail than we are accustomed to—provides a forum for discussing how and why algorithms are structured as they are. We execute the algorithm, that is, we sort a five-slot rack of our favorite CDs, watching the progress of the algorithm. Then, perhaps most important, we analyze the algorithm, identifying properties of its construction that are more abstract than its sequence of operations. The abstractions illustrate key concepts in algorithmic thinking.

Weird Word. *Algorithm*—it seems to be an anagram of logarithm—comes from the name of a famous Arabic textbook author, Abu Ja'far Mohammed ibn Mûsâ al-Khowârizmî, who lived about 825. The end of his name, meaning *native of Khowârism*, today Khiva, has been corrupted over the centuries into *algorithm*.

A Familiar Idea

As defined in Chapter 2, an algorithm is a precise and systematic method for producing a specified result. Algorithms are familiar—we've already seen several of them so far in this book.

- **Recognizing a button click**: Recall from Chapter 2 that after describing how computers draw buttons on the screen, we explained how the button is "clicked." The systematic method described how, when the mouse is clicked, the computer can look through the list of buttons it has drawn on the screen, and for each button, check to see if the current position of the cursor is inside the square defining the button.
- **Placeholder technique**: Recall from Chapter 3 that we described a three-step process to eliminate occurrences of short letter sequences, for example, new-lines, which also occur as parts of longer strings, that is, double new-lines, without also eliminating the occurrences in the longer strings.
- **Effective research process**: Recall from Chapter 6 that we described how to keep track of your research thread while you conduct curiosity-driven research: bookmark each new page, record search terms in a notebook file, and on completion combine these parts with a stream-of-consciousness description of your impressions and thoughts into a summary file.
- **Hex to bits**: Recall from Chapter 8 that we explained the hexadecimal color specification of HTML and then gave algorithms for how to convert back and forth between hexadecimal digits and bits.

Other algorithms were mentioned as well, but these are probably some of the more memorable ones.

We use algorithms every day. The arithmetic operations—addition, subtraction, multiplication, division—we learned in elementary school are algorithms. Making change is an algorithm, as are looking up a number in a telephone book, sending a greeting card to our parents, and balancing a checkbook. Changing a tire is algorithmic, too, being a systematic method to produce a specified result, though in common usage, *algorithm* tends to be applied mostly to information processing activities.

Most of the algorithms we use we were either taught by a patient teacher, like arithmetic, or we figured out for ourselves, like looking up a phone number. Because we are the ones performing the operations, we don't think much about algorithms as an explicit sequence of instructions. We simply *know* what to do. Other algorithms—recipes, assembly instructions for a bicycle, driving directions to a party, or income tax filing rules—are written out for us. Written algorithms are of interest here because we want to be able to think up an algorithm, write it out, and have some other agent—another person or a computer—perform its instructions successfully. It's not a matter to be taken lightly.

In addition to being a systematic method to produce a specified result, the specification of an algorithm must be "precise." The algorithms just mentioned from the earlier chapters, though possibly clear enough to direct a human, were not precise enough for a computer. Computers, as we saw in Chapters 7 and 9, are so clueless and literal that every aspect of a task must be spelled out in detail. To make the algorithm precise enough for a computer requires that we attend to three characteristics of its description:

- **Capability:** Ensure that the computer knows what and how to do the operations.
- **Language:** Ensure that the description is unambiguous.
- **Context:** Minimize the assumptions about the input or execution setting.

These aspects (to be explained momentarily) are crucial to having computers perform algorithms for us. But attending to these issues is also crucial when our algorithms are for other humans. Though we expect people to use their heads and make up for any weaknesses in our descriptions, humans are to some degree clueless and literal, too, when confronted with unfamiliar situations. Accordingly, it's still in our interest to avoid ambiguity, be sure they know what to do, and minimize assumptions no matter who performs the algorithm.

Properties of Algorithms

To ensure that algorithms are sufficiently well specified for a computer to follow and achieve the right result, we require that every algorithm have five essential properties:

- Inputs specified
- Outputs specified
- Definiteness
- Effectiveness
- Finiteness

The Inputs and Outputs specifications are familiar to anyone who has seen a cooking recipe or assembly instructions. The others are less familiar. Definiteness and Effectiveness are implicitly used in recipes. Finiteness may be less relevant to informal cases, but it is fundamental to computing. Consider each in turn.

Inputs specified: The inputs are the data that will be transformed during the computation to produce the output. It is essential to specify the type of the data, amount of data to be expected, and the form that the data will take. In a cooking recipe, it is customary to enumerate the inputs at the beginning, including the list of ingredients (type of inputs), their quantities (amount of input), and their preparation, if any (form of inputs), for example, "1/4 cup onion, minced."

Outputs specified: The outputs are the data resulting from the computation, the intended result. Often the description is embodied in the name of the algorithm, as in "Algorithm to compute a batting average." As with inputs, specifying the outputs generally entails specifying the type, amount, and any structural form of the result. A possible output for certain computations is a statement that there can be no output, that is, that no solution is possible. Cooking recipes specify their outputs, giving the type, quantity, and form of food, for example, "3 dozen 3-inch chocolate chip cookies."

Definiteness: Algorithms must be explicit about how to realize a computation. Definiteness generally entails specifying a particular sequence of operations that instruct how to transform the inputs into the outputs. These instructions involve performing specific actions on specific data. Every detail of each step must be spelled out, including how to handle erroneous cases. Definiteness ensures that if the algorithm is performed at different times or by different execution agents (people or computers) using the same data, the output will be the same. Cooking recipes should be definite, but because they often rely on the judgment, practicality, and experience of the cook, they can be much less definite than computer algorithms and still be successful. And in those cases where they are not definite—"salt and pepper to taste"—the potential for variation may be desirable.

Effectiveness: It must be possible for the agent executing the algorithm to perform its operations mechanically without any further inputs, special talent, clairvoyance, creativity, help from Superman, and so on. Whereas definiteness ensures that the executor knows which operations to do, effectiveness ensures that the executor can do each operation. Examples of ineffectiveness abound: "Add to the total the number of sunny days in Toronto next year," "Enter the amount of income you would have received this year had you worked harder," and "Print the length of the longest run of 9s in the decimal expansion of π."

Finiteness: An algorithm must eventually stop, either with the right output or an indication that no solution is possible. A process that fails to stop is pretty useless because when no answer comes back, we cannot distinguish between continued progress toward an answer and the process being "stuck." Finiteness is not usually an issue for noncomputer algorithms because they typically have no repeated instructions—"Preheat the oven to 375°, place well mixed ingredients into a greased loaf pan, bake for 25 minutes." But as we shall see, computer algorithms often entail repeating instructions with different data. Finiteness becomes an issue because if the algorithm fails to properly specify when to quit the repetition, the executing agent will continue to repeat the instructions forever.

Any process having these properties will be called an algorithm.

Work Without End. "Long" division is an algorithm in which finiteness is important. Divide 3 into 10. As each new digit is added to the quotient, the computation returns to a situation—call it a *state*—in which it has been before. When should the algorithm stop?

```
    3.33. . .
3)10.00
   9
   1.00
     9
     10
      . . .
```

THE LANGUAGE

Algorithms are developed by people, but executed by some other agent. For the agent to know the steps to be performed, the steps must be expressed in some language. The essential requirement of the language is that the person who creates the instructions for the algorithm and the agent that performs them both interpret the instructions identically.

If the algorithm's executing agent is a person, a natural language such as English is used to express the algorithm. Though we usually presume that all speakers understand every utterance of a language alike, it's not true. In fact, it's very likely that no two people understand all utterances of a language the same way. So, an instruction may mean one thing to the algorithm writer and something else to the algorithm executor. Ambiguity is very common in natural languages, of course, but ambiguity is not so much the problem as the fact that natural languages are not very precise. When natural language must be used, as with cooking recipes, writers depend on readers to respect their careful choice of words. Thus *fold in* and *beat* are not synonyms for *stir* in cooking; they are chosen for their specific nuances. Generally a natural language is an extremely difficult medium in which to express algorithms.

If the algorithm's executing agent is a computer, a programming language is used to express the algorithm. Programming languages are called *formal languages*, synthetic notations purposely designed to express algorithms. They are precisely defined. Programming languages are rarely ambiguous, and the precise definition ensures that the programmer and the computer agree as to what the instructions mean. In this way, programmers can be assured that what they tell the computer to do is exactly what it will do. Of course, programmers may make mistakes in formulating algorithms, that is, the algorithms may have bugs in them, but at least programmers can be sure that if the computer does something wrong, the fault is in their formulation of the algorithm, not in how the computer interprets the algorithm.

A *program* is an algorithm that has been customized to solve a specific task under a specific set of circumstances in a specific language. Thus making change—returning money for a purchase for x amount when it is paid for with a larger amount y—is an algorithm, but making change in U.S. dollars is a program. The program uses the "making change" algorithm specialized to the denominations of coins (1¢, 5¢, 10¢, 25¢, 50¢, $1) and paper currency ($1, $2, $5, $10, . . .) of the United States. Making change in New Zealand dollars requires a different program; it also uses the making change algorithm but with the New Zealand coins (5¢, 10¢, 20¢, 50¢, $1, $2) and currency ($5, $10 $20, . . .). From our point of view, whether the method is general (algorithm) or specialized (program) makes no difference. The issues are the same.

CONTEXT

A program can fulfill the five criteria for algorithms and be specified unambiguously, and still not be perfectly reliable because it is sensitive to the context of its use. If it is executed in the wrong context, it does not work properly. For example, forms that request an applicant's *Last Name* assume they are asking for his or her surname, as is the case in the United States. The request achieves the proper result when used by Americans, but perhaps not by citizens of countries like China where the surname is given first. Good algorithm designers minimize the dependence on context and would request *Surname* or *Family Name* rather than *Last Name* and *Given Name* rather than *First Name*.

Consider driving directions, which yield many instances where context matters. For example, the instruction

> From the Limmat River go to Bahnhof Strasse and turn right

seems satisfactory, but it may not be. The "turn right" assumes that the traveler approaches the street from a specific direction. If previous instructions have established a direction of travel, the instruction works. But if there are several points along the river where travel could begin, resulting in arrival at Bahnhof Strasse from different sides of the street—as there are in Zürich—the instruction doesn't work. Turning right will send the traveler north from one direction and south from the other direction.

Guidelines for Travel Directions

- Give the starting point, "From Place de la Concorde. . . ."
- State travel direction, "Going west on Route 66. . . ."
- Give landmarks, especially when turning, "Turn left; a temple (Todai-ji) is visible on the right. . . ."
- Prefer measured distances (2.3 miles) to blocks, cross streets, or traffic lights, which can be ambiguous.
- Include "overshot" tests for difficult turns, "If you cross Via Giuseppi Verdi, you've gone too far."

The context in which to apply the algorithm—the point of departure in this case—has not been taken into consideration. The conditions for a successful application of the algorithm could be expressed as input conditions, but that limits its applicability. A better solution is not to use words like *right* that have interpretations dependent on orientation until that orientation has definitely been established. Terms like *north* that are orientation independent are preferable.

In developing algorithms and programs, it is essential to anticipate such eventualities and to take care that the resulting algorithms work under the widest range of circumstances.

An Algorithm

After much discussion, it's time to give a complete example algorithm. Though most of the algorithms in future chapters will be presented using a programming language to ensure precision, our first algorithms will be given using a stylized form of English.

Imagine that your audio CD collection, which fills an impressively large, slotted rack, is completely disorganized. You've decided that it's time to get your CDs in order, and you want to alphabetize them by the name of the group, the performing musician, or perhaps the composer. How would you go about solving this problem?

A popular solution—this is not an algorithm—is to dump the CDs on the floor in a large pile, and put them back into the rack in order. This requires digging through the pile looking for a CD that would come first in the alphabet. Maybe eventually the *Abba* CD is found and put in the first slot. The next CD in order requires more digging in the pile. After filling up a few slots, the *Aardvark and Joey* CD turns up. This belongs before *Abba*, so the CDs already in the rack must be shifted down one position to make space for it. Later, in another shift, the Beatles CD gets placed *after* the four Beethoven CDs, and so on. The dump-on-the-floor approach is not an algorithm because it is not systematic. What we want is a systematic method that is guaranteed to alphabetize the CDs. To accomplish that task, we use the *Alphabetize CDs* algorithm.

Alphabetizing CDs in a Slotted Rack

Input: An unordered sequence of CDs filling a slotted rack

Output: CDs in the rack in alphabetical order

1. Use the term *Artist_Of* to refer to the name of the group or musician or composer on a given CD.
2. Decide which end of the rack is to be the beginning of the alphabetic sequence. Call the end slot at that end the *Alpha* slot.
3. Call the slot adjacent to the *Alpha* slot the *Beta* slot.
4. If the *Artist_Of* the CD in the *Alpha* slot is later in the alphabet than the *Artist_Of* the CD in the *Beta* slot, interchange the CDs; otherwise, continue on.
5. If there is a slot following the *Beta* slot, begin calling it the *Beta* slot and go to Instruction 4; otherwise, continue on.
6. If there are two or more slots following the *Alpha* slot, begin calling the slot following the *Alpha* slot, *Alpha* and the slot following it the *Beta* slot, and go to Instruction 4; otherwise stop.

How does this algorithm work? The following commentary references Figures 10.1 and 10.2.

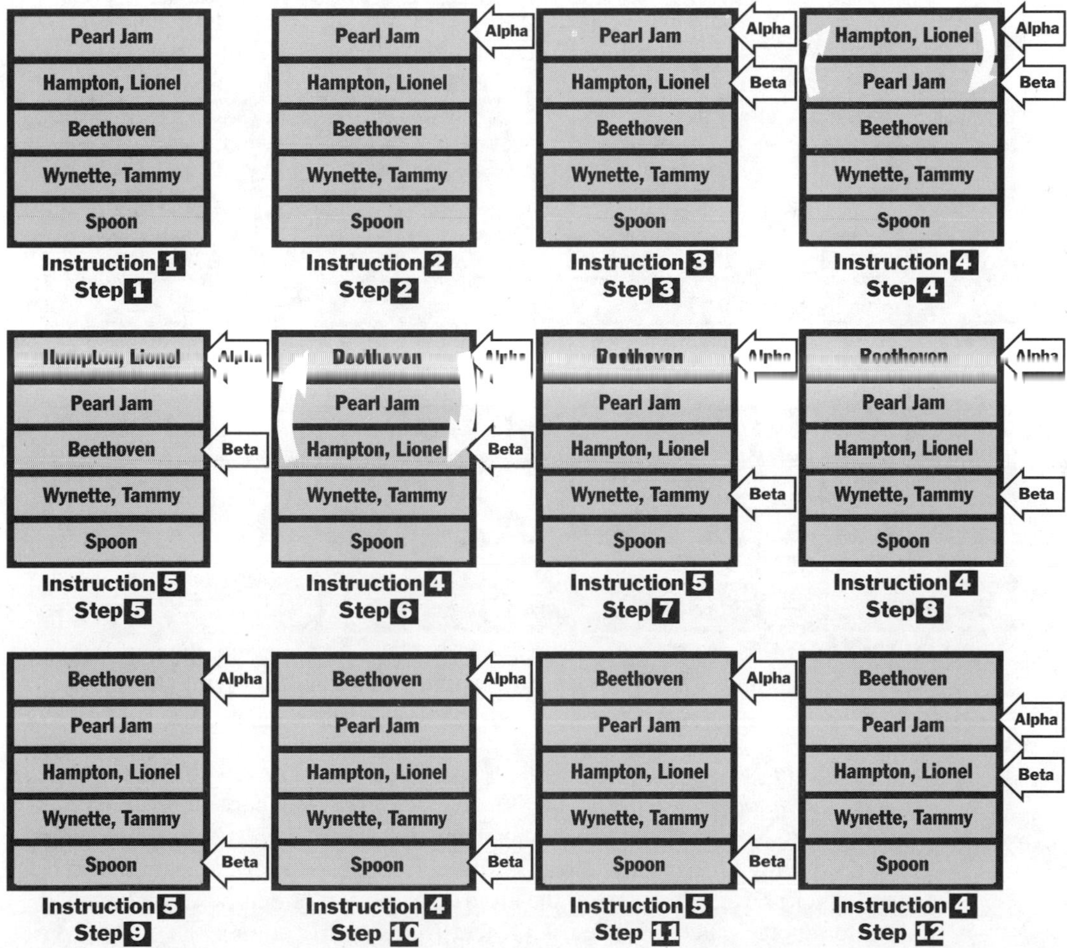

Figure 10.1. The first twelve steps of *Alphabetize CDs*. A snapshot of the CD rack is shown at the completion of each instruction. The pair of numbers in the boxes gives the instruction from the algorithm and step in the overall execution just completed. For example, Instruction 5, Step 9 means "the ninth step of the computation is to perform instruction 5 of the algorithm." Notice how *Beta* sweeps through all of the slots following *Alpha*. After the first eleven steps, the alphabetically earliest CD, Beethoven, is in the Alpha slot.

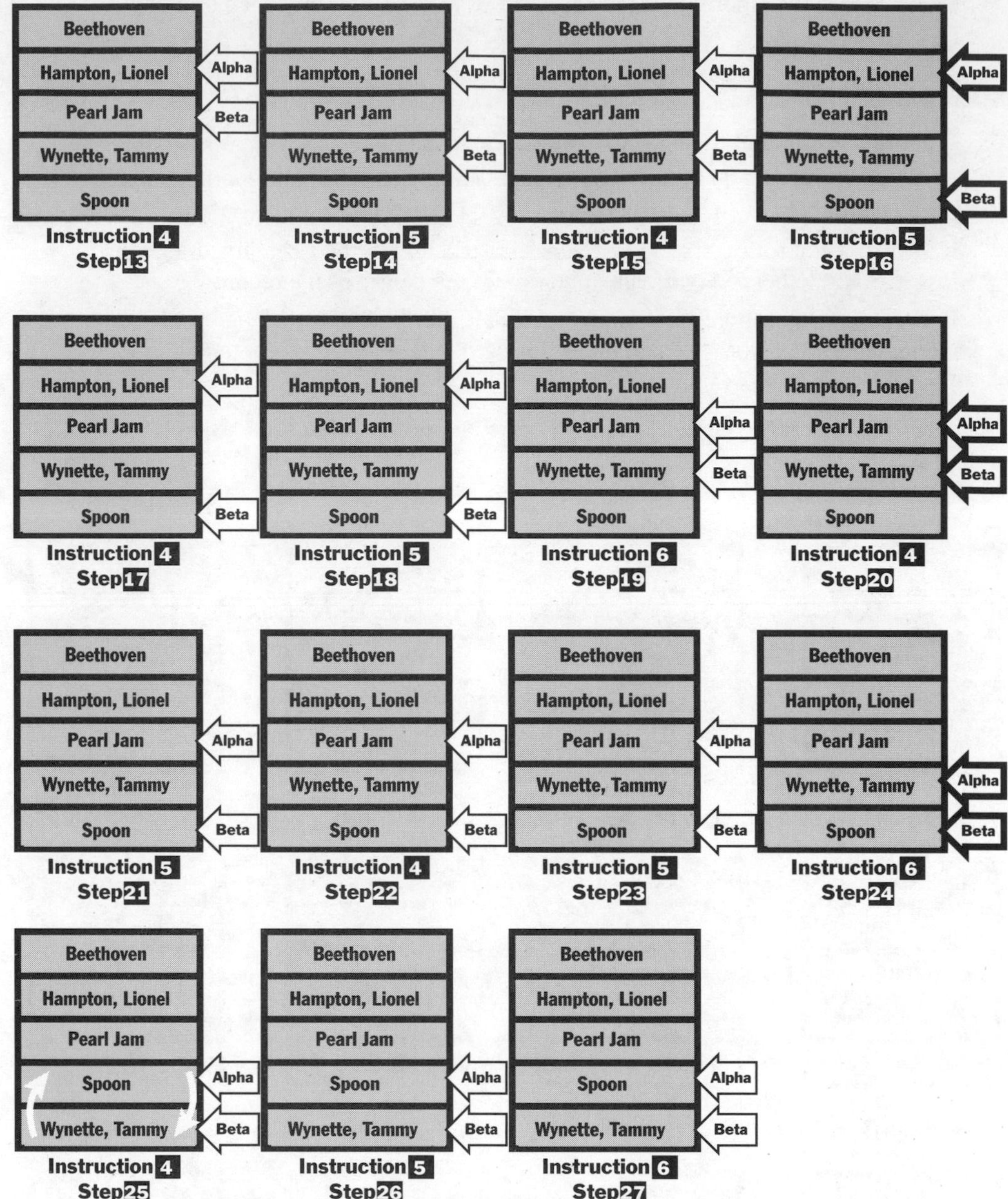

Figure 10.2. Snapshots of the last 15 steps of the *Alphabetize CDs* algorithm.

Instruction 1: *Use the term* Artist_Of *to refer to the name of the group or musician or composer on a given CD.* This instruction gives a name to the operation of locating the name used for alphabetizing. By agreeing to this terminology, we have simplified the specification of Instruction 4 because *Artist_Of* abbreviates the longer phrase "the name of the group or musician or composer that made the recording of," which must be used twice. That simplification is the only purpose of this step, and it could be eliminated at the expense of a wordier Instruction 4.

Instruction 2: *Decide which end of the rack is to be the beginning of the alphabetic sequence. Call the end slot at that end the* Alpha *slot.* The purpose of this instruction is to orient the process so that we know which end of the rack the alphabetization is relative to. It also gives the initial meaning to the word *Alpha*. In the algorithm, *Alpha* refers to slots in the rack. As a result of this instruction, *Alpha* refers to the first slot at the beginning of the to-be-constructed alphabetic sequence, and as the algorithm progresses, it will refer to successive slots in the rack.

Instruction 3: *Call the slot adjacent to the* Alpha *slot the* Beta *slot.* Like Instruction 2, this one assigns the initial meaning to a slot-referencing word, *Beta*. The names *Alpha* and *Beta* have no intrinsic meaning. The programmer needed to refer to slots in the rack by some names, and arbitrarily chose these two.

Instruction 4: *If the* Artist_Of *the CD in the* Alpha *slot is later in the alphabet than the* Artist_Of *the CD in the* Beta *slot, interchange the CDs.* This is the workhorse instruction of the algorithm. It compares the names of the recording artists of two CDs—those in the slots referred to by *Alpha* and *Beta*—and if necessary reorders them so that the CD whose name is earlier in the alphabet is in the *Alpha* slot. It may not be necessary to make an interchange because the CD in the *Alpha* slot may already be the earlier one. But either way, the alphabetically earlier CD is in the *Alpha* slot when this instruction is complete.

Instruction 5: *If there is a slot following the* Beta *slot, begin calling it the* Beta *slot and go to Instruction 4; otherwise, continue on.* This instruction redefines the *Beta* slot to refer to the next slot in sequence, if there is one. With this new definition of *Beta*, Instruction 4 can be reexecuted with the effect of comparing a different pair of CDs. One of the pair, the CD in the *Alpha* slot, participated in the comparison the last time Instruction 4 was executed, but because *Beta* refers to a new slot, the pair is "new." So, the algorithm executor is directed to reexecute Instruction 4. If all slots have been considered, that is, there is no next slot for *Beta* to refer to, the executor is directed to continue on to Instruction 6 rather than returning to Instruction 4.

Instruction 6: *If there are two or more slots following the* Alpha *slot, begin calling the slot following the* Alpha *slot* Alpha *and the slot following it the* Beta *slot, and go to Instruction 4; otherwise, stop.* By the time this instruction is reached the alphabetically earliest CD is in the *Alpha* slot as a result of the collaboration of Instructions 4 and 5. The idea now is to advance *Alpha* to the next slot and to sweep through locating the alphabetically next-earliest CD by repeating the Instructions 4–5 collaboration. *Alpha* is advanced again, the Instructions 4–5 collaboration is repeated again, and so on. On each subsequent arrival at this step, the CDs in slots up to and including *Alpha* will be alphabetized. When there are no longer enough slots to assign one to *Alpha* and the next one to *Beta*, the whole rack has been alphabetized and the algorithm stops.

The *Alphabetize CDs* approach does not dump the CDs on the floor, but rather orders the CDs while they are sitting in the rack. But that is not the property that makes *Alphabetize CDs* into an algorithm; it could be reformulated to work with the CDs spread out on the floor. Rather it is the fact that *Alphabetize CDs* instructs the executor to methodically find the alphabetically first CD, then the next , then the next after that, and so forth until the alphabetically last CD is found. That is, *Alphabetize CDs* is systematic.

Anatomical Analysis of the *Alphabetize CDs* Algorithm

The *Alphabetize CDs* example illustrates the basic properties of algorithms, of course. In specifying *Alphabetize CDs*, the five properties were fulfilled. The Inputs and Outputs were listed. Each instruction was described precisely—or as precisely as English allows—fulfilling the Definiteness requirement. The operations of the algorithm are effective because actions like selecting the adjacent slot and counting to see if there are at least two slots left are obviously simple and doable mechanically. The most complicated operation, the task of determining which of two artists' names is earlier in the alphabet, is also a completely mechanical process. We need only compare the first two letters of the names and the one closer to *A* is the earlier; if the two letters are the same letter, compare the second letters, and so forth. So, our specification satisfies the Effectiveness property. Finally, the specification is finite, though because Instructions 4, 5, and 6 are repeated, this property is not so obvious. However, notice that each time Instruction 4 is repeated, *Alpha* and *Beta* refer to a different pair of slots that has not previously been considered, and because slots can be paired in a rack in only a finite number of different ways, Instruction 4 cannot be repeated forever. Instructions 5 and 6 cannot be repeated forever without repeating Instruction 4 forever. Hence, the specification satisfies the Finiteness property.

But, there are other more interesting aspects of the algorithm.

Structural features: The algorithm contains two instructions, 5 and 6, in which the executor is directed to go back and repeat previously performed instructions. Such instructions create loops in the algorithm. Loops tend to be more obvious when the instructions are given in programming notations other than our original English text; the two-dimensional flowchart form in Figure 10.3 makes the loops very visible. Loops are fundamental to algorithms because they allow parts of the computation to be performed as many times as are necessary to accommodate the number of data items. So, the loops in the *Alphabetize CDs* algorithm repeat instructions as many times as are necessary to sweep through all the slots.

An essential aspect of any loop is that it must contain a *test* to determine whether the instructions are to be repeated again, or not. So, Instruction 5 tests whether there are slots following the *Beta* slot, and if so, Instruction 4 will be repeated; if not, that repetition will end. Instruction 6 tests to determine if there is at least a pair of slots after the *Alpha* slot. If so, it repeats Instructions 4; if not, the repetition ends. These tests enable the loop to complete and ensure the Finiteness property.

Failed Test. Requiring a test to determine when to stop repeating a series of instructions may seem obvious, but some North American shampoo manufacturers give directions: *Wet hair, massage in shampoo, rinse, repeat*, failing the finiteness test. Does the shampoo run out before the shower's hot water?

Notice that if the looping is to continue at Instruction 5, *Beta* is advanced to the next slot. Similarly, Instruction 6 advances *Alpha* to the next slot and resets *Beta* to follow it. These advancements ensure that, on the next test, *Beta* and *Alpha* refer to different positions. If there are no changes between the two consecutive tests, the outcome must be the same, and so the looping would never terminate. Thus it is essential that these advancements take place.

Properties: assumptions are made in specifying *Alphabetize CDs*. First, it is assumed (and stated in the Input specification) that the CD rack is full. This is relevant because the instructions do not handle the case of empty slots in the rack. So, for example, if *Beta* referred to an empty slot, how would Instruction 4 operate? It requires that the *Artist_Of* two CDs be compared, but if one or both of the slots are empty, the executor might not know what to do. The specification is correct as given because it states that it expects a full CD rack as input. But a better solution would explain what to do if the rack is not full. Then the "full" requirement could be dropped.

Another property of the solution—it's a fact, not an assumption—is that when the *Beta* slot is first set in Instruction 3, only one slot is adjacent to *Alpha* because *Alpha* was chosen in Instruction 2 to be an end slot. This ensures that there is a unique slot for *Beta* to refer to, and so the specification is Effective. There is an assumption in the use of the term *following* in Instructions 5 and 6.

Instruction 5 refers to a slot "following" *Beta*, which would mean a slot further from the end chosen in Instruction 2. Similarly, Instruction 6 refers to a pair of slots "following" *Alpha* and also intends that the slots are further from the end chosen in Step 2. But, nowhere in the specification was the term *following* defined. This makes the orientation of the term *following* an assumption. The orientation can be defined and would be defined for a computer to execute this algorithm because it is clueless about concepts like *following*.

Algorithm versus program: The *Alphabetize CDs* example illustrates a well-known algorithm called Exchange Sort. In the *Alphabetize CDs* example, we specialized the Exchange Sorting algorithm to the problem of alphabetizing CDs based on the names of the musicians. A different program based on the Exchange Sort algorithm might alphabetize CDs on their title, and another might alphabetize CDs on the recording company's name (label). The Exchange Sort algorithm can be specialized into programs for alphabetizing books by their authors, ordering books by their ISBNs, ordering canceled checks by date, and so on. The Exchange Sort algorithm embodies the idea of comparing pairs of items chosen in a particular way, exchanging them if they are out of order, and continuing to sweep through the items to locate the next minimal item. When the kind of item is chosen (e.g., CDs) when the criterion for "out of order" is chosen (e.g., not alphabetically ordered by musician's name), when we choose specific names for keeping track of the items we are working with (e.g., *Alpha* and *Beta)*, we have created a program based on the algorithm. The algorithm is a systematic process, and the program is that process formulated for a particular situation. An algorithm contin-

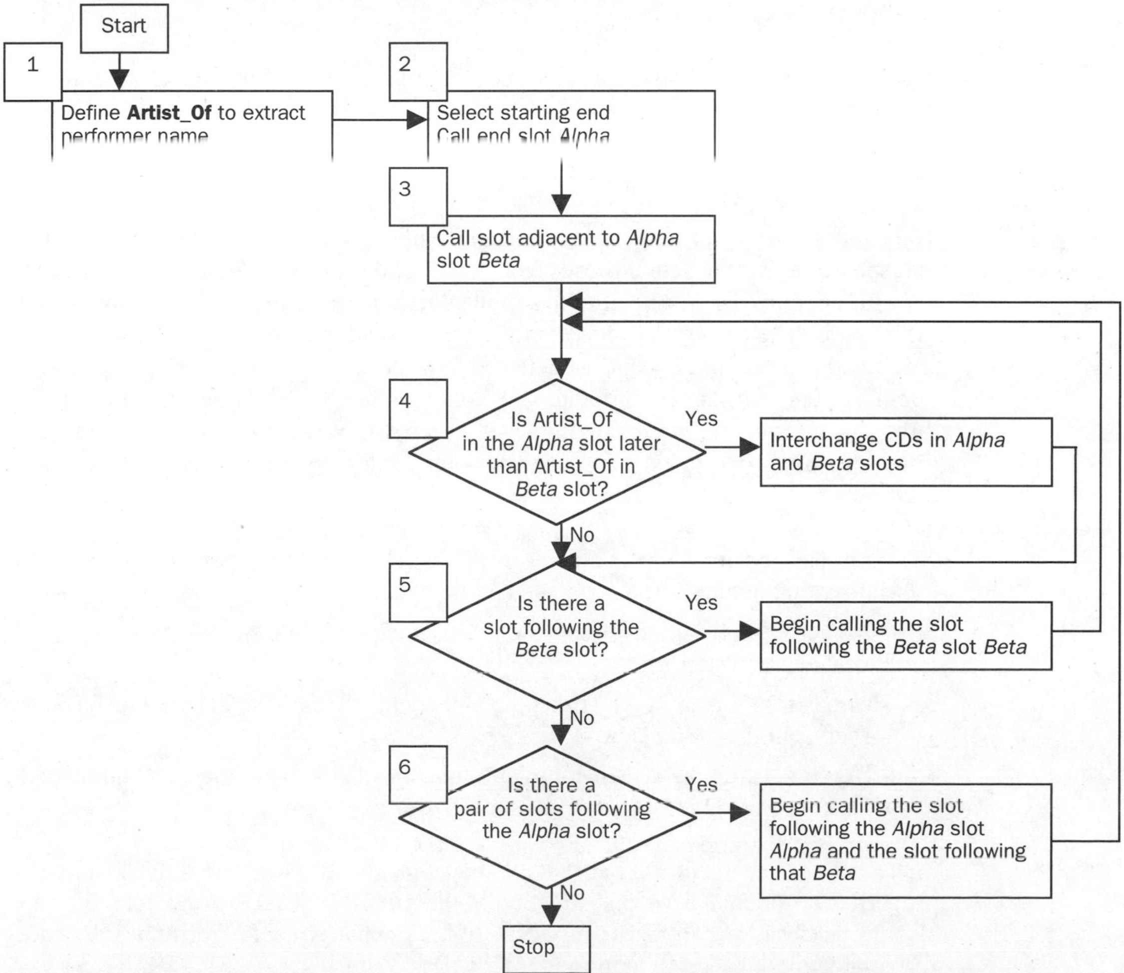

Figure 10.3. Flowchart form of *Alphabetize CDs*. Operations are shown in rectangles; decisions are shown in diamonds. Arrows indicate the sequencing of the operations.

ues to be an algorithm even when it is specialized into a program.

Are there other ways to alphabetize CDs? Absolutely. There are dozens of sorting algorithms, and all of them could be the basis of programs for alphabetizing CDs. Why one algorithm should be preferred over another is the sort of question computer scientists worry about. It need not concern us.

A Great Idea That Didn't Work. Early in the twentieth century, logician A. N. Whitehead and others wanted to codify logic and develop an algorithm to "crunch" logical propositions to determine if they're true or false. Algorithmically testing truth seemed like a good idea, but in 1931 logician Kurt Gödel proved it couldn't be done. Though bad news for Whitehead's plans, Gödel's work led to the scientific foundations of algorithms.

ABSTRACTION

The *Alphabetize CDs* example seems very complicated when described in so much detail, but it is easier to understand than it may first appear. This is because parts of the algorithm's behavior become encapsulated in our minds, and we think of them as a unit rather than as their individual instructions. So, for example, the "*Beta* Sweep" of the Instructions 4–5 collaboration becomes a concept in our minds. That is,

> ***Beta* Sweep:** While *Alpha* points to a fixed slot, *Beta* sweeps through the slots following *Alpha*, comparing each slot's CD with the CD in the *Alpha* slot, and interchanging when necessary.

To acquire this more abstract view of the solution, study the figures and try some examples.

Do not proceed beyond this point without trying your own example!

The idea of encapsulating portions of the algorithm's behavior—not the instructions that specify it, but the actual processing steps that the instructions define—is key to algorithmic thinking. We want to discipline ourselves to think about algorithms in these terms. The encapsulation is an abstraction—recall from Chapter 2 that an *abstraction* is an idea or concept extracted from a specific situation. For example, the "*Beta* Sweep" considers in order all CDs following a specific *Alpha*, tick-tick-ticking through the sequence, interchanging when necessary. When we think of the abstraction of the *Beta* Sweep, we can recognize some of its important properties. The *Beta* Sweep is

1. **Exhaustive**—it considers all CDs from the *Alpha* slot to the end of the rack, ensuring that none is left out.
2. **Non-redundant**—it never considers the same pair of CDs twice, ensuring that the sweep will stop.
3. **Progressive**—at any given time, the alphabetically earliest CD seen so far in this sweep is in the *Alpha* slot.
4. **Effective**—after the sweep completes, the alphabetically earliest CD among all CDs considered in this sweep (including *Alpha*) is in *Alpha*.

These are not general properties that all algorithms have. These are only specific properties of the *Beta* Sweep abstraction of the *Alphabetize CDs* program. (They are also properties of the "inner loop sweep" of the Exchange Sort algorithm if they are formulated more generally not to refer to "CDs," "slots," "*Alpha*," "*Beta*," etc.)

Where did the four properties of the *Beta* Sweep abstraction come from? We observed them in the process of analyzing how the *Alphabetize CD* algorithm works. (They are all mentioned in the discussion of the Anatomical Analysis section.) Though they have been explicitly listed here so we can discuss them, they are examples of the features we should notice about the behavior of an algorithm when studying how it operates. Why? Because collectively these properties will convince us that the algorithm actually works. That it achieves its intended goal of alphabetizing.

To see how the properties of the *Beta* Sweep process imply that the algorithm works, first note that properties 1–3 imply property 4. That is, the *Beta* Sweep process of the algorithm considers all CDs once and keeps the alphabetically earliest in *Alpha* at all times. The net outcome of that behavior after processing all CDs in a sweep is to ensure that the alphabetically earliest CD is in *Alpha*, which is part of the answer.

For the rest of the answer, consider the *Alpha* Sweep abstraction—the process of sweeping through all CDs (but the last) performing the *Beta* Sweep instructions each time. We can explicitly list off properties that we notice about the *Alpha* Sweep abstraction:

1. **Exhaustive**—it considers all CDs from the first to (but not including) the last.
2. **Non-redundant**—no slot is assigned the *Alpha* status more than once, ensuring that the process stops if the *Beta* Sweep stops, and it does by property 2 of the *Beta* Sweep abstraction.
3. **Progressive**—at the completion of each *Beta* Sweep, the alphabetically next earliest CD is in *Alpha*.
4. **Complete**—when the last *Beta* Sweep is completed, the CD in the last slot is later in the alphabet than the CD in the next to last slot because the last *Beta* Sweep involved these last two slots and it is property (3) of the *Beta* Sweep. (Refer to Figure 10.2, Step 25.)
5. **Effective** at alphabetizing the CDs—the alphabetically earliest CD is in the first slot at the end of the first *Beta* Sweep by its property 4 together with the fact that all CDs are considered, and inductively, in every subsequent position for *Alpha*, the *Beta* Sweep assigns the next earliest CD.

Property 5 of the *Alpha* Sweep says this program for the algorithm works. We asserted that it did originally, but noticing these properties of the two abstractions—*Beta* Sweep and *Alpha* Sweep—it is possible to understand *why* it works. When we create computer solutions, knowing why our solution works is the only way to have confidence that the solution does work, achieving our IT goal.

SUMMARY

In this chapter we have introduced one of the most fundamental ideas about thinking. Like finding information and debugging earlier, the value of understanding algorithms transcends our uses in IT. We learned that recipes and other everyday algorithms suffer from the imprecision of the natural language in which they are expressed. The five fundamental properties of algorithms were introduced and explained, and then the role of language in making the specification precise was reviewed. A discussion of being sensitive to context followed. We then presented an algorithm for alphabetizing the audio CDs in a filled rack. This was a six-instruction program that identified two distinguished slots, *Alpha* and *Beta*, and made repeated sweeps over the remaining CDs. Each instruction was explained, as were several of the general properties of the process. It was noted that *Alphabetize CDs* is a program built using a well-known algorithm Exchange Sort. Finally, and most fundamentally, we abstracted the processing of *Alphabetize CDs*, recognizing two coherent behaviors: The *Beta* Sweep and the *Alpha* Sweep. These two abstractions have several properties, and by noting them we could explain why the algorithm produced an alphabetized sequence. Making these sorts of abstractions and inferring properties about them is the essence of algorithmic thinking. With a little practice, algorithmic thinking can become second nature, making us much more effective problem solvers.

Looking to the Future

This chapter has introduced many deep and fundamental ideas. The reward for the reader who has reached this point with an understanding of these concepts is the satisfaction of having seen nearly all of the ideas underlying algorithms and programming. With perhaps two exceptions, every programming idea covered in this book that is relevant to nonspecialists appears in this chapter. All that remains is elaboration and mastery. These are not trivial, of course. But, in terms of encountering completely new phenomena relative to algorithms and programming, there is little left to say.

Because we have invested heavily in understanding these complex ideas, it is worth spending a moment naming some of the concepts seen here that will also appear later. For the record, then, here are some of the phenomena encountered in this chapter that are further elaborated in other chapters. (This list may be a useful reference.)

Variables—*Alpha* and *Beta* are variables in the *Alphabetize CDs* program.

Locations—The slots in the CD rack are analogous to memory locations of a computer.

Values—The CDs are the values stored in the locations.

Function—*Artist_Of* is a function for extracting the name of the group or performer from a value.

Initialization—Instructions 2 and 3 initialize the variables *Alpha* and *Beta*, respectively.

Loops—The Instructions 4–5 sequence is a loop; the Instructions 4–6 sequence is also a loop.

Array—The rack is a (linear) array.

All of these concepts are described in greater detail in later chapters.

Exercises

1. Define algorithm.
2. What is the difference between processes we perform such as doing laundry, and an algorithm for those processes?
3. What are the five properties that an algorithm must possess?
4. Explain the Definiteness property of algorithms.
5. Explain the Effectiveness property of algorithms.
6. Explain the Finiteness property of algorithms and the role of tests.
7. What weaknesses do natural languages such as English have for the purpose of programming?
8. Distinguish between an algorithm and a program.
9. Does the instruction "go downhill" have the same problems as "go right"? Explain.

10. Give travel directions from the Fluency classroom to your favorite off-campus café.

11. A series of repeated instructions requires a test. What does the test test for?

12. What is the purpose of the *Artist_Of*, Step 1, of the *Alphabetize CDs* algorithm?

13. Explain why *Alpha* doesn't have to reference the last slot.

14. Explain in your own words (to someone else in class) the *Beta* Sweep abstraction and its properties.

15. Formulate a version of the Exchange Sort algorithm to alphabetize CDs in a slotted rack, which builds the alphabetized list in the last to first order. That is, your solution produces the same result as *Alphabetize CDs*, but it works from the back end forward.

CHAPTER 11

Sound, Light, and Magic

Learning Objectives

- Understand how RGB color is represented and manipulated.
- Know how to convert between decimal and binary.
- Know how to add binary numbers.
- Understand the concept of "computing on a representation."
- Learn how sound is digitized.
- Know what lossless and lossy compression are.
- Understand basics of optical character recognition.
- Appreciate the techniques of virtual reality and how latency and bandwidth limit them.
- Learn the Bias-free Universal Medium Principle.

A day at college involves so many forms of digital information that few of us notice any longer: There's the email to the folks, the photo attached to email from a friend, MP3 tunes off the Web, the EKG needed to try out for the swim team, the roommate's new DVD movie, the smart ID card from work, and the ever-popular database called the Library Online Catalog. Though these all seem to be way more complex than the digital representations we've seen so far—well, maybe not the email—they are not. As we'll see in this chapter, the common multimedia representations build on the basic ideas we've already seen, being somewhat cleverer and larger, but not really more complex.

We begin by looking more closely at the phenomenon of RGB color, which we've seen several times before. Now, we consider exactly how a color is encoded in bits, resolving some mysteries left over from previous chapters and leading to the idea of manipulating intensities, that is, making the colors darker or lighter. This process—a staple of digital photo software—is little more than arithmetic on binary numbers.

Changing the color of an image and performing other transformations will demonstrate these ideas. Next, we discuss JPEG and MPEG and the need for compression techniques for images and video. The following discussion of virtual reality addresses how effective computers are at creating synthetic worlds. And finally, the whole topic of digital representation is summarized in one basic principle, completing the chapter.

Color Range

When we discussed the binary encoding of keyboard characters to create the ASCII representation, we—and the inventors of ASCII—paid only slight attention to which bit patterns were associated with which characters. It's true that in ASCII the numerals are encoded in numeric order, and the letter sets are roughly in alphabetical order, but the assignment is largely arbitrary. The specifics of the keyboard character encoding don't matter much (as long as everyone agrees on them) because the bytes are used as monolithic units. We rarely manipulate the individual bits that make up the pattern for the characters. For other encodings, however, manipulating the individual bits is essential.

Recall that giving the intensities for the three constituent colors—Red, Green, and Blue (acronymically RGB)—specifies a color on the monitor. Each of the RGB colors is assigned a byte to record the intensity of that color. Are the color intensities assigned as arbitrarily as characters are assigned in ASCII? Not at all. Intensity is a quantity, ranging from 0 (none) through 255 (most intense), in which greater values mean more intensity. Obviously, to change the intensity we want to add to or subtract from the values, implying that our encoding should make it simple to perform arithmetic on the intensities. Accordingly, RGB intensities are encoded as binary numbers.

Binary numbers differ from the familiar decimal numbers by being limited to two digits, 0 and 1, rather than the customary ten digits, 0 through 9. But that is really the only difference because the other features distinguishing binary from decimal derive from that one restriction. For example, in decimal numbers, we use a place value representation, where each "place" represents the next higher power of 10, starting from the right:

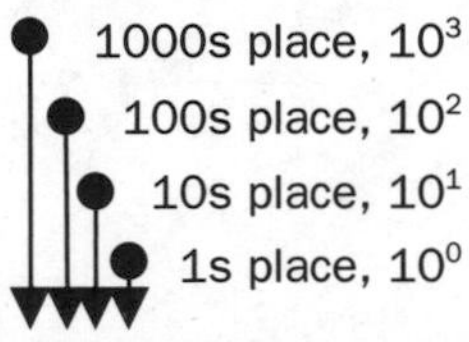

The digit in a place is multiplied by the place value and the results added up. So, in the example, the result is one thousand ten, found by adding $0 \times 1 + 1 \times 10 + 0 \times 100 + 1 \times 1000$.

Binary works in exactly the same way except that the base of the power is not 10 but 2:

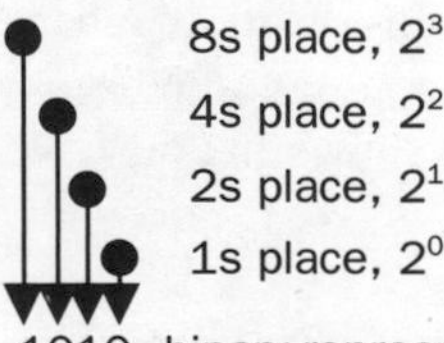

As usual we multiply the digit times the place value and add the results. The example evaluates to ten, which is $0 \times 1 + 1 \times 2 + 0 \times 4 + 1 \times 8$.

> **2nd Base**. The "base" of a numbering system, 10 for decimal and 2 for binary, is also called its *radix*.

Because powers of 2 don't increase as rapidly as powers of 10, binary-represented numbers need more digits for a given amount or magnitude. So, for example, representing the decimal number 1,010 as a binary number requires ten digits:

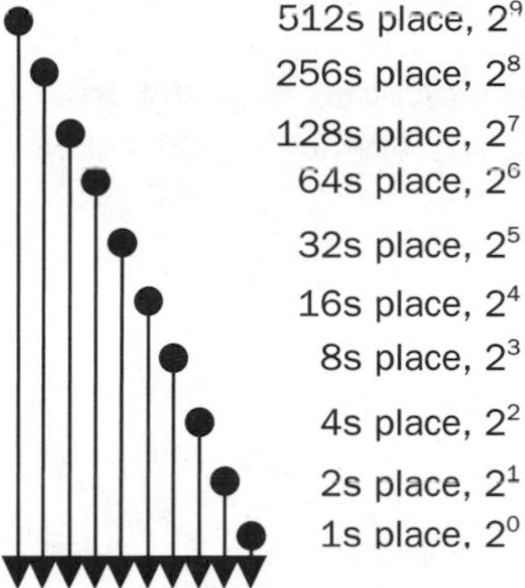

1111110010 binary representing the decimal one thousand ten = 512 + 256+128+64+32+16+2

Because the digit is either 0 or 1, the "multiply the digit times the place value" rule is especially easy—a 1 means include the place value and a 0 means forget it. So, to convert a binary number to its decimal equivalent, just add the place values for the places with 1s.

> **Foursomes**. When writing long decimal numbers, it is customary in North America to separate groups of three digits with a comma for readability. Binary numbers, which are usually even longer, are grouped in four-digit units, separated by a *space*.

Returning to the representation of color. The fact that a byte—eight bits—is allocated to each of the RGB intensities means that the smallest intensity is 0000 0000, which is 0, of course, and the largest value is 1111 1111. Figuring out what decimal number this is, we add up the place values for the 1s,

$$\begin{aligned} 1111\ 1111 &= 2^7 + 2^6 + 2^5 + 2^4 + 2^3 + 2^2 + 2^1 + 2^0 \\ &= 128 + 64 + 32 + 16 + 8 + 4 + 2 + 1 \\ &= 255 \end{aligned}$$

which explains the fact from earlier that the range of values is 0 through 255 for each color.

As we learned, black has no intensity for any color,

0000 0000	0000 0000	0000 0000	*RGB bit assignment for black*
red byte	green byte	blue byte	

whereas white

1111 1111	1111 1111	1111 1111	*RGB bit assignment for white*
red byte	green byte	blue byte	

has full intensity for each. Between these extremes is a whole range of intensity.

Manipulating Intensities

As we've seen, converting a binary number to decimal representation requires adding up the powers of two corresponding to "1 bits." Going the other way, converting a decimal number x to binary representation, is only slightly harder. Start by finding the largest power of 2 that is less than or equal to the number. (Table 11.1 shows the powers of 2 to simplify this task.) For example, for the number 200, the largest power of 2 less than or equal to 200 is $128 = 2^7$ because $256 = 2^8$ is too large. If the largest power of 2 is 2^d, there will be $d + 1$ digits in the binary result. To find those digits, follow this simple procedure shown in Figure 11.1 that constructs the binary number one place at a time from left to right. So, for example, to convert the decimal number 200 into binary, the procedure would produce the following sequence of values

Place Number	x	Power of 2	x ≥ 2d	Digit	Comments
7=d	200	$2^7 = 128$	yes	1	*Leftmost digit, always 1*
6	72	$2^6 = 64$	yes	1	
5	8	$2^5 = 32$	no	0	
4	8	$2^4 = 16$	no	0	
3	8	$2^3 = 8$	yes	1	
2	0	$2^2 = 4$	no	0	
1	0	$2^1 = 2$	no	0	
0	0	$2^0 = 1$	no	0	*Rightmost digit*

The decimal number 200 is binary 1100 1000.

Table 11.1. Powers of 2

Power (*n*)	2^n	Power (*n*)	2^n	Power (*n*)	2^n
0	1	10	1,024	20	1,048,576
1	2	11	2,048	21	2,097,152
2	4	12	4,096	22	4,194,304
3	8	13	8,192	23	8,388,608
4	16	14	16,384	24	16,777,216
5	32	15	32,768	25	33,554,432
6	64	16	65,536	26	67,108,864
7	128	17	131,07	27	134,217,72
8	256	18	262,14	28	268,435,45
9	512	19	524,28	29	536,870,91

1 Is First. When writing numbers without leading 0s, all binary numbers start with, what else, 1.

Returning to our discussion of color representation, the extreme colors of black and white are easy, but what color is

1100 1000	1100 1000	1100 1000
red byte	green byte	blue byte

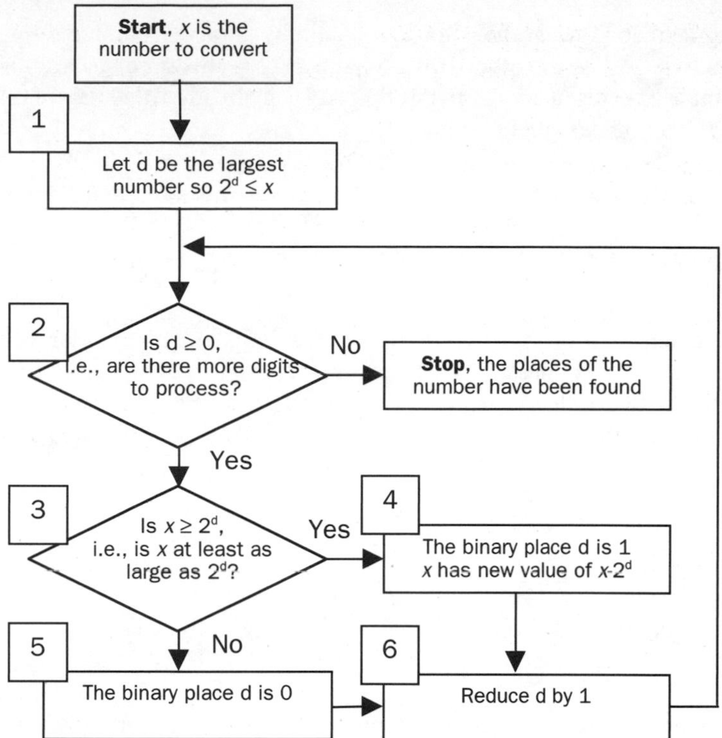

Figure 11.1. Algorithm to find the bits representing a decimal number *x*. Starting at Start, follow the operations in a box.

The first observation is that each byte contains the decimal value 200, which we recognize from the just completed conversion process. So it's the color produced by the color specification RGB(200, 200, 200). To guess at the color, notice that, like black and white, it specifies equal amounts of the three constituent colors, and it is closer to white than black. In fact, it is a medium gray. All colors with equal amounts of RGB are gray if they are not black or white. It's just a question of whether they're closer to black or white. To make a *lighter* color of gray, we obviously change the common value to be closer to white. We propose to do this by increasing each of the RGB values by 16, that is, to add 16 to each byte. In this case, adding 16 is

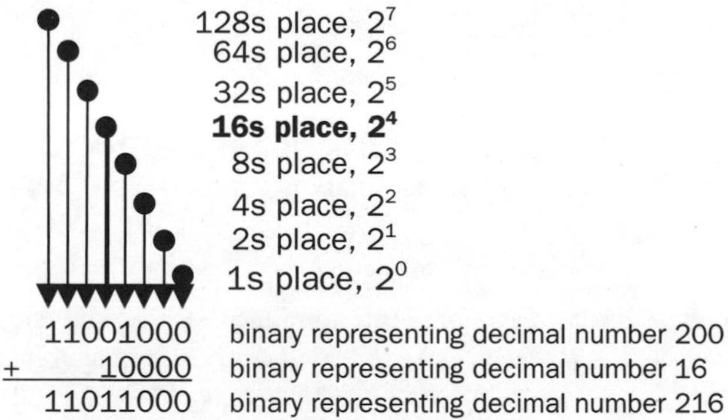

which is simply setting the 16s place value, that is, changing it from 0 to 1. The result

1101 1000	1101 1000	1101 1000
red byte	green byte	blue byte

is a lighter shade of gray.

Imagine that we want the color lighter still by another 16 units of intensity for each RGB byte. Adding another 16 isn't quite as easy this time because the 16s position in the binary representation 1101 1000 of 216 is already filled. But it only requires us to "carry" to the next higher digit. Thus,

```
    1          ← carry
1101 1000      binary representing decimal number 216
+  1 0000      binary representing decimal number  16
1110 1000      binary representing decimal number 232
```

Like decimal addition when the sum of the digits in a place is larger than any digit (1 in binary!), we must reduce the sum by the radix (2) and carry to the next higher digit. The two 1s in the 16s position sum to 2, an amount larger than 1, which forces us to reduce it by the radix (2), producing 0 for the 16s place and a carry into the 32s place.

```
1110 1000  1110 1000  1110 1000
   red       green      blue
   byte      byte       byte
```

Notice that if we'd simply added 32 to 200 originally, we'd have ended up with the identical result, the gray with each intensity set at 232 .

The process just illustrated is binary addition, and in general it works just like decimal addition, except with the usual limitation of just two digits. Specifically, for every place there will be two digits and possibly a "carry-in" from the previous digit place. (See Table 11.2.) We can find the sum of two binary numbers by starting at the right, where the carry-in will be zero, and proceeding to the left, applying the rule given earlier: sum the digits and if the result is larger than 1 reduce the sum by the radix (2) and "carry out" to the next higher digit place.

For example, consider adding the two binary numbers 0000 0101 1000 1100 and 0000 0011 1000 1010. These two quantities handily illustrate all of the cases shown in the table.

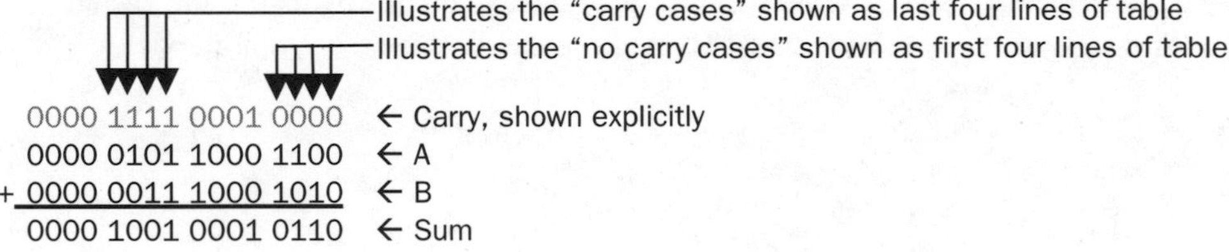

Illustrates the "carry cases" shown as last four lines of table
Illustrates the "no carry cases" shown as first four lines of table
0000 1111 0001 0000 ← Carry, shown explicitly
0000 0101 1000 1100 ← A
+ 0000 0011 1000 1010 ← B
0000 1001 0001 0110 ← Sum

(Usually the carries are shown only when they are 1, if at all. But showing both 0 and 1 helps with reading the table.) Of course, counting in binary is simply the process of repeatedly adding 1.

> **Fingers or Fists.** It is thought that the reason decimal numbers became standard is that people count with their 10 fingers. By that logic, computer scientists must count with their fists.

Because computers use fixed size bit sequences, for example, a byte is 8 bits long, an interesting question is what happens when there is a carry-out of the most significant bit, that is, the leftmost bit. For example, 255 + 5 in binary is

```
  1111 1111
+ 0000 0101
1 0000 0100
```

as can be easily verified. But 260 requires 9 bits to represent, one bit too many to fit into a byte. Such situations are called *overflow exceptions*. Computers report when the computation they're told to perform overflows, and it is up to the programmer to plan for that eventuality. Usually programmers try to avoid the situation by choosing large bit fields.

Table 11.2. The Cases for Binary Addition

Binary Addition of A+B				
A digit	**B digit**	**Carry-In**	**Sum**	**Carry-Out**
0	0	0	0	0
0	1	0	1	0
1	0	0	1	0
1	1	0	0	1
0	0	1	1	0
0	1	1	0	1
1	0	1	0	1
1	1	1	1	1

Computing on Representations

Though we have seemingly been focused on binary representation, conversions between decimal and binary, and binary addition, the previous sections have also introduced another fundamental concept of digital representation—the idea of *computing on a representation*. That is, when we made gray lighter, we were illustrating how digital information—the RGB settings of a pixel, say—could be changed through computation because we could have made every shade of gray in the image lighter by the same process. Consider a more involved example for a deeper understanding of the idea.

Imagine that you have scanned into your computer a black-and-white photo you took of the moon (Figure 11.2(a)). This is a memento from last weekend when you were out with your friends, and you tried connecting your camera to Jaime's telescope. Unfortunately you only had black-and-white film loaded, causing you to miss the gorgeous orange of the close-to-the-horizon moon. In the computer, the pixels of your photo form a long sequence of RGB triples. What values do they have?

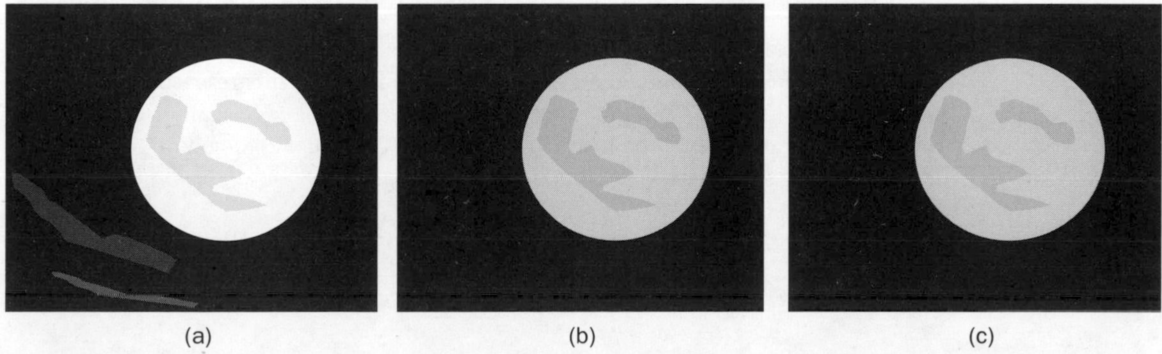

(a) (b) (c)

Figure 11.2. Schematic diagrams of (a) the original black-and-white picture, (b) tinted version of original, (c) with boosted highlights.

Because they are all black, white, or gray, it's easy to guess. There is the (0,0,0) of the black night sky, the (255,255,255) of the brightest part of the moon, some light gray values very close to white, for example, (234,234,234), of the craters and *marae* of the moon, and some dark gray values very close to black, for example, (28,28,28), from the smudge left on the glass when someone scanned in a burrito. What you would like to do is email a colorized version of your photo to your friends (Figure 11.2(c)).

To accomplish this, you must remove the smudges and transform the pixels of the black-and-white image into the colors that you remember. The first task is easy because any value "close" to black can be changed to be true black by replacing it with (0,0,0). But what does *close* mean? The example dark gray value (28,28,28) is represented in binary as

(0001 1100, 0001 1100, 0001 1100)

Though other dark gray values may be somewhat larger or smaller, it is a safe guess that any dark gray pixel will have the most significant bit of each of its RGB bytes set to 0. That's because from the binary representation, a byte whose most significant bit is 0 is less than 128, that is, is less than half the magnitude of full intensity, and any pixel all of whose colors are less than half magnitude must be a darker color.

To convert the smudges to pure black simply requires that we go through the image looking at each pixel and testing to see if the first bit of each of its bytes is 0, and if so, setting the entire byte to 0. Recalling our substitution arrow from Chapter 3, we describe this operation as

0*xxx xxxx* 0*xxx xxxx* 0*xxx xxxx* ← 0000 0000 0000 0000 0000 0000

where *x* is a standard symbol for "don't care" or "wildcard," that is, a symbol matching either 0 or 1. So the substitution statement says "Any three RGB bytes each of whose first bits is 0 are replaced with all zeros." Making that substitution throughout the image removes the digitized smudge.

Similarly, turning the moon to orange involves changing the white pixels (255,255,255). You decide that the moon must have been about the orange color (255,213,132). Changing all of the white pixels to this color requires the substitution

1111 1111 1111 1111 1111 1111 ← 1111 1111 1101 0101 1000 0100

or, equivalently in decimal,

255 255 255 ← 255 213 132

to produce an orange moon. But it will not change the gray of the craters because they are not pure white and therefore won't be modified by this replacement. If, like the dark gray, the very light gray were changed to this orange too, all of the beautiful detail of the craters would be lost. How do we get the white changed to orange and the gray changed to the appropriate orange-tinted gray?

The technique that we'll use, though there are many very sophisticated ways to adjust color, is to transform any light gray into orange by the following three-part transformation

Red byte—leave unchanged

Green byte—subtract 42 from the green value; that is, modestly reduce the green

Blue byte—subtract 123 from the blue value; that is, substantially reduce the blue

Thus the light gray color (234,234,234) would be changed into (234,192,111), and the slightly darker light gray (228,228,228) would change into (228,186,105), a slightly grayer orange. The numbers of the transformation were found by noting how white (255,255,255) changed into the chosen orange (255,213,132): the red byte was unchanged, the green byte was reduced by 42, and the blue byte was reduced by 123. If all pixels having the most significant bit of each RGB byte equal 1 (that is, the white pixels and all the light gray pixels) are transformed by this three-part process, the white areas will become orange and the gray parts will be transformed into the corresponding grayish orange.

You have cleaned up the smudge and colorized the moon (Figure 11.2(b)).

After making those transformations, you inspect your work and decide that the gray parts of the moon are really not as luminous as you remembered. So, you decide to boost the red. If the red in all of the orange pixels is shifted to 255, the moon's craters look too red and "unnatural." But a compromise might be to "split the difference." That is, if the current value of the red byte in an orange tint is 234, say, half the difference between it and pure red—(255 – 234)/2 = 10.5—could be added on to get 244. (You need whole numbers, so drop the "point 5.") Thus the two example tints (234,192,111) and (228,186,105) become (244,192,111) and (241,186,105), respectively. This process brightens the craters without making them unnatural (Figure 11.2(c)). The resulting image looks great, and you can attach it to email to your friends.

Summarizing, we have computed on a digital representation. We manipulated a real photograph scanned into the computer to create an artificial image. First, we improved it by removing the smudges, artifacts of the scanning process. Then we colorized it by changing white and light gray into orange and corresponding shades of orange-gray. Finally, we boosted the red in the orange-gray tints to make them a little brighter. We discussed these transformations as if you were writing a program to make the changes, which you could do, but image processing software like Photoshop performs such transformations through user control of properties like Saturation, Brightness, Hue, and so forth. Such software manipulates the pixels with transformations as described here, as well as in much more sophisticated ways. The result is not the photograph we would have taken had there been color film in the camera, but rather a different image, a synthetic formulation closer to what we remember or prefer. It's definitely not reality . . . because we could have just as easily made "the man in the moon" smile.

Making Waves

Once the picture is digitized, it is easy to manipulate it, as just described. But how does it become digitized in the first place? In this section we consider digitizing, though we focus on digitizing sound rather than images because it is slightly easier. The principles are the same when digitizing any continuous information.

An object—think of a cymbal—creates sound, as we know, by vibrating in some medium such as air. The vibrations push the air causing pressure waves to emanate from the object, which are detected by our eardrums and transmitted by three tiny bones to the fine hairs of our cochlea stimulating nerves that allow us to sense the waves and perceive them as sound. The force or intensity of the push determines the volume, and the frequency with which the pushes beat is the pitch. Figure 11.3 shows a graph of a sound wave, where the horizontal axis is time and the vertical axis is the amount of positive or negative sound pressure. The key aspect of this process from a digitization point of view is that the object vibrates *continuously* producing a continuously changing wave. That is, as the wave moves past a detector—microphone

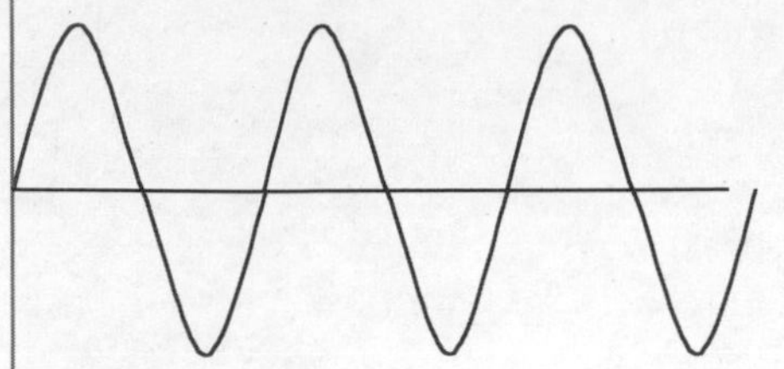

Figure 11.3. Sound wave. The horizontal axis is time; the vertical axis is sound pressure.

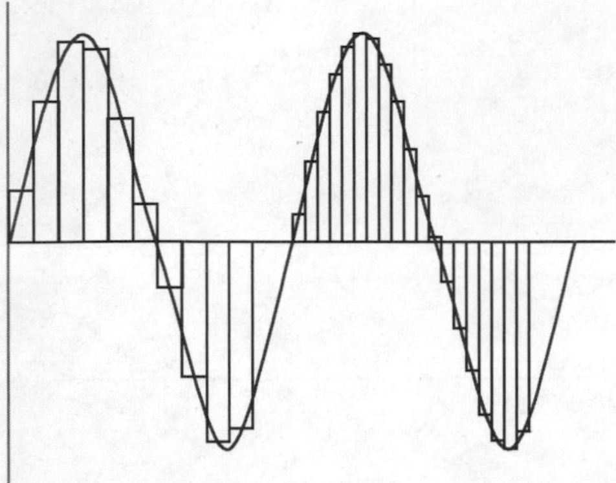

Figure 11.4. Two sampling rates, the rate on the right is twice as fast as that on the left.

—the measured pressure changes smoothly. When this pressure variation is recorded directly, say, as Edison originally did with a scratch on a wax cylinder or the more recent vinyl records, we have an *analog* representation of the wave. In principle, all of the continuous variation of the wave has been recorded. Digital representations work differently.

To digitize, we must convert to bits, of course, and the obvious bit-representation for the sound wave would be to record, as a binary number, the amount by which the wave is above or below the 0 line at a given point. But at what point? There are infinitely many points along the line, which prevents us from recording every position of the wave. So, we *sample*, which means to take measurements at regular intervals. The number of samples in a second is called the *sampling rate*, and the faster the rate, the more accurately the wave is characterized. (See Figure 11.4.) Obviously the sampling rate required for a decent characterization of a wave is related to the wave's frequency. For example, a fast frequency could "fit" between the samples of a slow sampling rate. In electrical engineering, the Nyquist Rule says that a sampling rate must be at least twice as fast as the fastest frequency. And what is the fastest frequency we should expect? Because human perception can detect sound up to roughly 20,000 Hz, a 40,000 Hz sampling rate fulfills Nyquist's Rule for digital audio recording. For technical reasons, however, a somewhat faster-than-two-times sampling rate was chosen for digital audio, 44,100 Hz.

The digitizing process works as follows: The sound is detected by a microphone, known in engineering terms as a *transducer* because it converts the sound wave into an electrical wave. This electrical signal is fed into an *analog-to-digital converter* (ADC), which takes the continuous wave and samples it at regular intervals, outputting for each sample binary numbers to be written to memory.

The process is reversed to play the sound: The numbers are read from memory into a *digital-to-analog converter* (DAC), which is a device that creates an electrical wave by *interpolating* the digital values, that is, smoothly moving from one value to another. The electrical signal is then input to a speaker, which converts it into a sound wave, as shown in Figure 11.5.

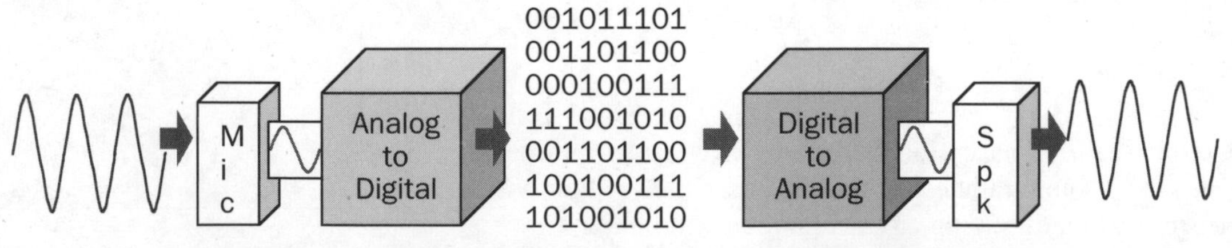

Figure 11.5. Schematic for analog-to-digital and digital-to-analog conversion.

The problem is solved except for describing how accurate the samples must be. To make the samples perfectly accurate, we would need an unlimited number of bits for each sample, which is impossible. First we observe that the bits must represent both positive and negative values. Second, we note that the more bits there are, the more accurate the measurement will be. For example, with only three bits, one of which is allocated to indicate whether the sign is + or –, we could encode one of four positions in either direction (they align at 0). With so few bits, it will be typical for the wave to be sampled at an inexact point, yielding only an approximate measurement. (See Figure 11.6.) With another bit, the sample would be twice as accurate. (In Figure 11.6, each interval would be half as wide, making the illustrated crossing in the "upper" interval.) Thus the sample—though still inexact—would be more accurate. More bits yields a more accurate digitization. The digital representation of audio CDs uses 16 bits, meaning that $2^{16} = 65{,}536$ levels are recorded—$2^{15} = 32{,}768$ for positive and 32,768 for negative directions.

> **Unforgiving Minute**. How many bits does it take to record a minute of digital audio? There are 60 seconds of 44,100 samples of 16 bits each times 2 for stereo. That's 84,672,000 bits, or 10,584,000 bytes, more than 10 megabytes! An hour is 635 MB!

A key advantage of digital information (as demonstrated in the last section) is that we can compute on the representation. One computation that would be valuable is to compress digital audio, that is, reduce the number of bits required to represent the information. For example, an orchestra produces many sounds that the human ear cannot detect—some too high and some too low. Our ADC still encodes these frequencies, not to annoy our dog, but simply as an artifact of the encoding process. By computing special functions on the digital audio representation, it is possible to remove these waves without harming the way the audio sounds to humans. This is the sort of compression used for the famed MP3 representation, and it tends to achieve a *compression ratio*—the factor by which a representation is reduced—of more than 10:1, implying that a minute of MP3 music typically takes less than a megabyte to represent. This makes MP3 a favored format for Internet transmission because it has lower *bandwidth* requirements. *Bandwidth*—the rate at which bits are transmitted—is discussed shortly.

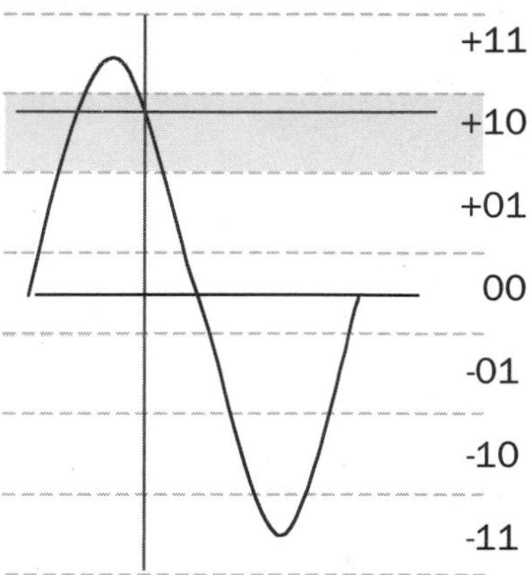

Figure 11.6. Three-bit precision for samples requires that the indicated reading be approximated as +10.

Other applications of computing on the representation can "fix" a recording in the same way we "fixed" our moon picture. If someone coughs during a quiet moment of Verdi's *Requiem*, the offending noise can be removed. Performances can be sped up or slowed down without affecting pitch, and so on. Though digital audio is rarely a direct record of the bits that stream out of an ADC, the modifications surely add to our enjoyment.

> **MP3**. The "sound track" of a digital video in the MPEG representation is known as *MPEG level 3* and gives its name to MP3.

Another key advantage of digital representations over analog is that they can be faithfully reproduced. So, by copying the file of bits that make up an audio performance, it's possible to have an exact reproduction of it. Further, when the original and the copy are played by the same system, they will produce the identical sound. With analog storage, there is typically a loss in quality between both an original and a copy because the imprecision of reading the original is replicated in the copy, and between earlier and later plays of the same version because of wear. Such problems do not arise with digital representations as long as the bits remain stable.

> **Word Search.** Searching digital audio for a segment of sound, though possible in principle, is difficult because of the need to specify the search string. Thus, in Chapter 6, we searched Fuller's *What I Know* recordings not by searching the audio, but by searching the textual transcript.

PEG of My Art

Recall from our discussion of the moon picture, that an image is a long sequence of RGB pixels. Of course, the picture is two-dimensional, but we think of the pixels stretched out one row after another in memory, which is one-dimensional. How many pixels are there? For an 8 × 10 image scanned at 300 pixels per inch, there are 80 square inches, each requiring 300 × 300 = 90,000 pixels for a grand total of 7.2 megapixels. At 3 bytes per pixel, it takes 21.6 MB of memory to store one standard 8 × 10 color image. That's more memory than personal computers came with until the late 1990s and would still be cumbersome to manipulate. Sending such a picture across a standard 56 Kb/s modem—that's kilobits per second—would take at least 21,600,000 · 8 / 56,000 = 3085 seconds, or more than 51 minutes, that is, longer than the average college class. Obviously, if screen-size pictures were so ponderous, surfing the Web would be a much slower experience.

The first observation is that if the picture is for display on a computer screen as part of a Web page, there are not 300 pixels per inch on any computer monitor. A typical LCD display has about 100 pixels per inch, which is a factor of 9 savings in memory. But this isn't quite the simplification we need, first because it still takes more than five and a half minutes to send, and second because once received, we might want to print the picture out, requiring the resolution again. Luckily, electrical engineers invented the JPEG compression scheme.

> **Joint Experts**. *JPEG* stands for "Joint Photographic Experts Group," a nickname for an International Standards Organization team guiding the development of digital representation of still photographs. There's also *MPEG,* the "Motion Picture Experts Group" of the ISO.

Compression means to change the representation of information so that fewer bits are required to store or transmit it. For example, faxes are usually long sequences of 0s and 1s encoding where the page is white or black. Rather than sending all of the 0s and 1s, run-length encoding can be used in which binary numbers are sent describing how long the first sequence (run) of 0s is, then how long the following sequence of 1s is, then how long the following sequence of 0s is, and so on. Though short sequences of 0s and 1s are not efficiently encoded this way, most of the time run-length compression is a big win. Run-length encoding is a *lossless compression* scheme, meaning that the original representation of 0s and 1s can be exactly reconstructed. The opposite of lossless compression is *lossy compression*, meaning that the original representation cannot be exactly reconstructed from the compressed form.

JPEG is a compression scheme for still images that takes advantage of the fact that the human eye is not very sensitive to small changes in hue (chrominance), though it is quite sensitive to small changes in brightness (luminance). Accordingly, it is possible to store a less accurate description of the hue of a picture (fewer bits), and though such a compression scheme is lossy, the human eye won't notice. JPEG easily achieves a 20-to-1compression ratio compared to an uncompressed still image without humans perceiving a difference. For example, if there is a large area of very similar hues, for example, sky, they can all be "lumped together" as the same hue without our noticing. Then run-length type compression, which wouldn't have worked well with many slight variations, can be applied. The handy aspect of JPEG from a user's point of view is that the amount of compression can be controlled: Image compression software can offer the user a control—a slider or dial, say—specifying the amount of compression. Fiddling with the control allows us to determine visually how much more compression can be applied without seriously affecting the look of the image.

MPEG is the analogous idea applied to motion pictures. On the one hand, it seems like an easier task because each image will not be seen for very long, so even greater levels of single-image compression might go undetected. On the other hand, the problem appears much more daunting because so many stills are required to represent motion. In MPEG, JPEG-type compression is applied to each frame, but then "interframe coherency" is exploited. That is, because two consecutive video images will usually be very similar, MPEG can, in essence, keep track of the "differences" between frames and only record or transmit them. This results in tremendous amounts of compression, making MPEG video realistic, requiring only moderate amounts of bandwidth.

Optical Character Recognition

On toll roads now, computers watch cars going by, read their license plates, find accounts for the car in a database, and deduct the toll from the "car's" account. It sure beats stopping every few miles to pay a few more coins! The interesting aspect of this technology is that there is no machine-readable identification for the car such as a bar code or electronic transponder; the machine simply recognizes the letters of the license plate. Reading license plates is pretty easy for humans, but it's a big deal for computers.

Consider some of the difficulties. First, the computer needs an image of the license plate, but the camera is pointed at the highway getting many images that are not license plates—the scene, parts of cars, trailers, litter, road-kill before it is road-kill, and so on. An electronic device called a *frame grabber* recognizes when to "snap" the image and ship it to the computer for processing. Assuming a frame with a license plate in it has been snapped, the computer must next figure out where in the image it is because there is no standard location for a license plate on a vehicle, and even if there were, the vehicle could be changing lanes. Looking for letters and numbers doesn't work because the backs of some vehicles display advertising. Once the region of the license plate is found, however, recognizing its characters is the most significant challenge because they're not yet characters, but thousands of pixels.

Happily, license plate colors are chosen to be "contrasty," for example, dark letters on a light background. The computer scans groups of pixels looking for "edges" where the color changes. It forms these into "features." A *feature* is a constituent part of a character to be recognized. For example, a *P* might be described by the features of a "vertical stroke," and a "hole" at the top of the stroke because lines and holes are patterns that could be recognized by noting where color changes. Given the features, a *classifier* matches the features to the alphabet to determine which are close, perhaps finding a strong correlation with *P*, a weaker one with *9,* and a still weaker one with *D.* Finally, having determined a good guess for the characters, an optical character recognizer usually checks the *context*, trying to decide if the proposed combination makes sense; for example, has a license been issued with the conjectured combination of letters? Finding the number in the database, the computer figures it has read the plate right and duns the account.

> **Beginning Reader**. In 1954, J. Rainbow demonstrated an optical character reader that could recognize uppercase typewritten characters at the rate of one letter per minute.

Optical character recognition (*OCR*) is a very sophisticated technology, but one that adapts the computer to our needs—we prefer to read printed characters rather than barcodes and want the computer to do so, too. The economic applications for OCR are in mail and banking. The U.S. Postal Service uses a system that locates the address block on an envelope or card, reads it in any of 400 fonts, identifies its ZIP code, generates a 9-digit barcode, sprays the bars on the envelope, sorts it, and with only a 2% error rate can process 45,000 pieces of mail per hour. In this instance, the context for street names might be whether they are in a given ZIP code. In banking, where the magnetic numbers at the bottom of the check have been read by computers since the 1950s, OCR is now used to read the *handwritten* digits of the "courtesy amount" (the numeral version of a check amount) to verify that a data entry person has interpreted the amount correctly.

Perhaps the most significant application of optical character recognition, however, is Raymond Kurzweil's text-to-speech reading machines developed for the blind and partially sighted. Produced in 1976, the reading machine uses a flatbed scanner—a technology originally developed by Kurzweil—to scan reading material, recognize it as text, and then speak it using a voice synthesizer. Scanning, font-independent optical character recognition, large-vocabulary dictionaries, and speech synthesis are by now standard technologies that Kurzweil had to create for his devices. For the disabled, the reader—and its inverse, the speech-to-text machine—are applications of technology that have dramatically improved their personal lives and career opportunities. Says the blind musician Stevie Wonder, who credits the reader with changing his life, "It gave blind people the one life goal that everyone treasures, and that is independence."

Inventor, Humanitarian, Entrepreneur. Raymond Kurzweil received the National Medal of Science and the Lemelson–MIT Award for Innovation, which is like a Nobel Prize for inventors.

Virtual Reality

The ultimate form of digital representation is to create an entire digital world. The idea has become known as *virtual reality*, but so far it has less to do with representing the world and more to do with fooling our senses into perceiving something that doesn't exist. Rapid display of still images is a standard way to fool our eyes and brain into perceiving motion. Virtual reality applies that idea to our other senses and attempts to eliminate the cues that keep us grounded in reality. For example, when we see a TV scene of a train coming toward us, we know by various cues, such as peripheral vision, that we're watching a TV; we perceive the motion but we're not deceived. When we look away we see a room. However, if we're wearing a helmet with a TV in front of each eye that shows the train in a complete scene, gives us three-dimensional vision, and fills in our periphery so that when we move our head we can look at other parts of the scene, the cues are reduced or eliminated. Add to that high-quality audio in each ear and a treadmill giving the ability to walk or run through the scene, and it's easy to imagine how a computer could effectively deceive us into thinking the train is chasing us.

Certain deceptions are more useful. *Haptic devices* are input/output technology for interacting with our sense of touch and feel. For example, a haptic glove allows a computer to detect where our fingers are and to apply force against them. When we bring our fingers close enough together, the glove stops their movement leaving us with the sensation of holding something. With haptic gloves and the helmet described earlier, a computer can show us Legos in space, which, when we grab them, gives us the sensation of holding them and perpetuates the illusion as we assemble them. If the glove pulls down on our fingers, we receive the signal that the Legos are heavy, perhaps made of metal. Though the world is virtual, it is credible to us. Such technology can be used to train surgeons for complex operations, for example.

Virtual Meaning. The term virtual is used frequently in IT, for example, virtual memory, because a computer can often produce a credible illusion of something that doesn't exist. *Virtual* in these contexts means "not actually but just as if."

The key challenge with virtual reality and other sophisticated output devices like video is for the system to operate fast enough and precisely enough to appear natural. We know that when the rate at which stills are presented in an animation is too slow, the illusion of motion is lost. When that happens in a VR system—when we turn our head but the scene doesn't smoothly change—the person wearing the helmet gets dizzy, maybe even sick. Our sensation of touch and feel actually operates faster than the 30 Hz standard for visual perception, closer to 1000 Hz. Thus, when we "see" our virtual hand going to pick up a virtual Lego, we must perceive its presence by touch before we perceive it visually if the illusion is to work.

This phenomenon is *latency*—the time it takes for information to be delivered. We are familiar with long latencies when Web pages are not delivered instantaneously, but the phenomenon arises wherever information must be transmitted or generated. In most instances, as with Web pages, long latencies just cause us to wait, but in video, VR, voice communication, and so on, long latency can ruin the medium. Reducing latency is a common engineering goal, but there is an absolute limit to how fast information can be transmitted: the speed of light. Eventually, the virtual world is constrained by the physical world.

A closely related phenomenon to latency is *bandwidth*—information transmission capacity per second. Bandwidth is related to latency in that a given amount of information, for example, 100 KB, transmitted with a given bandwidth, for example, 50 KB/s, determines the (best) latency by dividing the amount by the bandwidth, for example, 2 seconds. Other delays can extend the latency beyond this theoretical best. Higher bandwidth implies lower latency in *most* practical situations. (The rule eventually fails for speed-of-light and switching-delay reasons.) So, faster modems imply that Web pages load faster.

Virtual reality is a developing technology. It is still challenged by both latency and bandwidth limitations—It takes many, many bytes to represent a synthetic world. Creating them and delivering them to our senses is a difficult technical problem. Nevertheless, it is an exciting future application of IT.

Bits Are It

Looking back over this and previous chapters, we have seen that four bytes, say, can represent many kinds of information from four ASCII keyboard characters to numbers between zero and about 4 billion. (See Figure 11.7.) This remarkable versatility of bits is not an accident, but a fundamental property of information, which we will summarize in this principle:

> **Bias-free Universal Medium Principle:** Bits can represent all discrete information; bits have no inherent meaning.

The first half of the principle—all discrete information can be represented by bits—is the universality aspect. Discrete or separable things can be represented by bits—at the very least, by assigning numbers to each one and representing those numbers in binary. But, as we saw with color, it is possible to be far smarter. We assigned the colors so that the intensity of an RGB constituent could be increased or decreased using binary arithmetic. This scheme is much more organized than simply saying: "Black will be 0, purple will be 1, yellow will be 2, puce will be 3, . . ." As a result of organizing the representation in a rational way, we can *easily* compute on it, making uniform changes like brightening the image. (In principle, it would be possible to compute on the arbitrary representation, too, but it would be hopelessly difficult.) Of course, if the information is continuous, that is, analog information like sound, it must first be made discrete by an ADC. But once digitized, it can be represented by bits.

The second half of the principle—bits have no inherent meaning—is the bias-free aspect. Given a bit sequence

0000 0000 1111 0001 0000 1000 0010 0000

there is no way to know what information it represents. The meaning of the bits derives entirely from the *interpretation* placed on them by the computer through our programs. If the four bytes are treated as a zero byte followed by the RGB intensities (241,8,32), it produces a color ■,but if they are interpreted as an instruction, the computer is directed to add two binary numbers. As a binary number, the bits work out to 15,796,256.

So, bits are bits. What they mean depends only on how the software interprets the representation, which means they work for representing any kind of information. Storage media need only store one pair of patterns: 0 and 1. The principle explains why, for example, a single transmission medium—the TCP/IP packet—is sufficient to deliver any kind of information across the Internet to your computer: text, photos, MP3 tunes.

Since computers first came into the public's consciousness, it's been "common knowledge" that computers represent information as binary *numbers*. Experts reinforce this view, but it's not quite right. Computers represent information as bits. Bits can be *interpreted* as binary numbers, as we've seen, which is why the experts are not wrong. But the bits are not binary numbers. They can be interpreted as ASCII characters, RGB colors, or an unlimited list of other things. When programs manipulate the bits, they often perform arithmetic on them as we saw when we modified the moon image; but often they do not because doing so is incompatible with the intended interpretation of the information. Computers represent information with bits. They're an amazing medium.

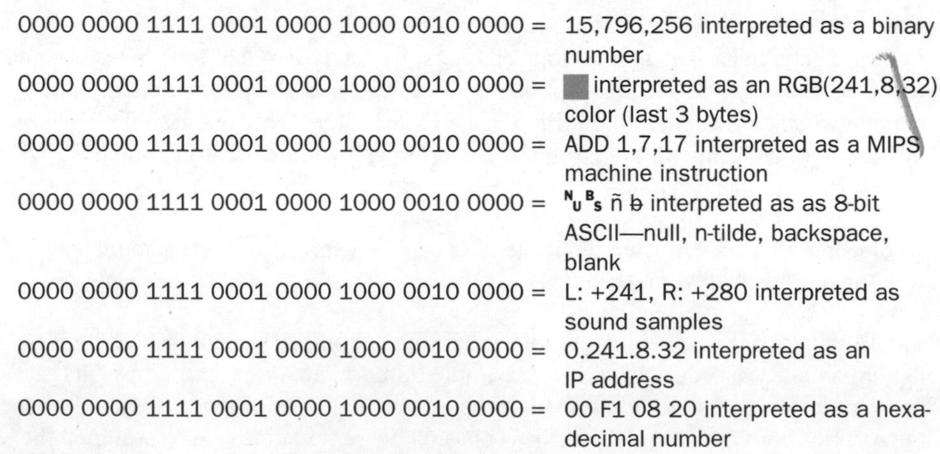

0000 0000 1111 0001 0000 1000 0010 0000 =	15,796,256 interpreted as a binary number
0000 0000 1111 0001 0000 1000 0010 0000 =	■ interpreted as an RGB(241,8,32) color (last 3 bytes)
0000 0000 1111 0001 0000 1000 0010 0000 =	ADD 1,7,17 interpreted as a MIPS machine instruction
0000 0000 1111 0001 0000 1000 0010 0000 =	NUBS ñ ƀ interpreted as as 8-bit ASCII—null, n-tilde, backspace, blank
0000 0000 1111 0001 0000 1000 0010 0000 =	L: +241, R: +280 interpreted as sound samples
0000 0000 1111 0001 0000 1000 0010 0000 =	0.241.8.32 interpreted as an IP address
0000 0000 1111 0001 0000 1000 0010 0000 =	00 F1 08 20 interpreted as a hexadecimal number

Figure 11.7. Illustration of the principle that "bits are bits." The four bytes shown are interpreted with some of the representations covered in this book.

SUMMARY

In this varied chapter we have considered how different forms of information are represented in the computer. In the case of RGB color, we learned that each intensity is a one-byte numeric quantity represented as a binary number. Binary representation and arithmetic work exactly like decimal but are limited to two digits. We found the decimal equivalent of binary numbers by adding up their powers of 2 corresponding to 1s, and using a simple algorithm we did the reverse to find binary from decimal. Performing arithmetic on the intensities allowed us to "compute on the representation," making gray lighter and colorizing the moon. Much more exotic computations on images are possible in photographic software, but the principles are the same.

Next we considered how to digitize sound as an illustration of all analog to digital conversion. Sampling rate and measurement precision determine how accurate the digital form is; uncompressed audio requires more than 80,000,000 bits per minute. That audio, video, and motion all take so many bits motivated consideration of the "PEG" compression schemes: JPEG for compressing stills, and MPEG for compressing video. These alternative representations demonstrated that removing information people don't miss makes lossy approaches work. Our discussion of virtual reality illustrated the complexities of conveying information to all of our senses at once. Finally, we emphasized that all of the magic of which computers are capable derives from the universality of bit representations and the unbiased way they encode. The Bits Are Bits principle encapsulates that idea.

EXERCISES

1. What is the principal difference between decimal and binary?
2. What decimal number does the binary number 1100110 represent?
3. What are the 16 binary digits for the hexadecimal number FADE?
4. How many binary digits are there in the decimal number 1,000,000?
5. Convert the decimal number 35 to binary representation.
6. The text showed the addition of binary numbers [illegible] and 0000 0011 1000 1010. Show that the binary result 0000 1001 0001 0110 is correct by converting all numbers to decimal and verifying the addition in decimal. (You will need the Powers of 2 table.)
7. Add the binary numbers 1101 0001 0111 and 1 0011 0100.
8. Describe how to change the moon to be the color of green cheese, say, (193,249,143) , from a scanned-in black-and-white image.
9. Define sampling rate.
10. Simon and Garfunkel's famous song "Bridge Over Troubled Water" is 4:54 minutes long. How many bits does it take to digitally encode it?
11. Redraw Figure 11.6 showing the digital sampling using four bits.
12. Give two advantages of digital recording.
13. JPEG exploits what feature of human visual perception?
14. What is interframe coherency?
15. What is the limiting constraint on latency?
16. How are latency and bandwidth related?
17. Find the ASCII representation of TINY. Demonstrate computing on this representation by adding 32 to each byte. What is the result?

Part III

Communication and Data

CHAPTER 12

Using Computers in Polite Society

Learning Objectives

- Learn the dos and don'ts of email.
- Understand the rules and rationale for netiquette.
- Become familiar with the idea of expecting the unexpected.
- Learn to create good passwords and manage them.
- Understand viruses and worms, and their risks.
- Learn the basics of copyright law and its application.
- Learn the limits of software in safety-critical applications.

When computers moved out of the lab and onto our desks, laps, palms, and into thin air, they became part of our social interactions. Usually they are passive tools, being a medium of communication and an aid to our work. But a tool can be used crudely or skillfully. By using it skillfully, we smooth our social interactions and make life more pleasant for one another. In this chapter, we break from our usual theme of becoming more effective computer users to become more considerate computer users.

The chapter begins with three sections considering email. Our first goal is to understand the limitations of email, so that we may apply it in the right situations and express ourselves in the most effective ways. Next, we consider a group of guidelines that are collectively known as *netiquette*, etiquette for the Internet. We continue with the email theme by using it to introduce a deep problem in applying IT—the problem of expecting the unexpected. Unexpected things can happen in any situation, of course, but email is so familiar that it gives a good context for discussing the issues. The next three topics concern familiar matters that arise when interacting with computers and information. The Passwords section discusses the basics of creating good passwords as well as managing them. The Viruses section explains how viruses and worms work, and what to do to protect yourself from them. And the Copyright section concerns itself with the law, answering questions about when you can and cannot copy programs and information. The final section deals with the matter of how completely we can trust computer systems, especially their software, in safety-critical applications. If a computer runs a life-support system, how do we know there are no bugs in the program?

THE PROBLEM WITH EMAIL . . .

For many, email has become as routine and ubiquitous as telephone communication, often replacing the telephone or face-to-face conversation as the medium of choice. Is this progress? Certainly the fact that email is asynchronous—the other person doesn't have to be receiving the communication while it is being created and sent—makes it very convenient. And its multicast property—many people can be sent a message with little more effort than sending to one—has its value. So, we use it for much factual communication, "`The next meeting has been postponed until Tuesday at 1:30`," but should we use it for everything, "`Your brother died at 4:00 this morning`"?

When is email appropriate and when is it not? We cannot give an algorithm for deciding, so our approach will be to identify some of the weaknesses with email. The five problems considered here are

- Conveying emotion
- Emphasis
- Conversational alternation
- Ambiguity
- Flame-a-thons

Keeping these weaknesses in mind can help you decide if you should use email for your communication.

Conveying Emotion

It is difficult to convey sympathy, grief, and other subtle emotions using email. The problem is not the medium of writing per se because sympathy cards convey emotional content as text (and graphics). Rather, it seems that email is too informal, too impersonal, and often too casually written. But often even feelings like happiness or sadness fail to be expressed in email because it is treated as a chatty conversation. We type words that in conversation would be accompanied by cues such as tone of voice, inflection, stress, pacing, intensity, volume, pauses, and incidental sounds such as chuckling, and though the words may have those cues in our heads, they don't on the screen. Without the cues, the meaning we intend may be lost. Indeed, the words can convey a meaning we do not intend. This problem explains why so-called *emoticons*—for example, characters forming smiley faces :) —have proliferated in email. The emoticon tags a sentence with an icon for the intended emotion. It is probably more effective to rewrite the sentence so the emotion is clear from the text. The lessons are that (1) expressing sympathy, grief, and so on with email is so difficult that it is inappropriate in almost all cases, and (2) in regular email we should be sensitive to emotional content, perhaps being more complete or rephrasing the text to make our feelings clear.

Emphasis

At an even more primitive level, the simple act of typing for emphasis can convey the wrong message. Readers could interpret text in all capitals as yelling. For example, "Do you know you forgot my birthday?" has a different sense than "DO YOU KNOW

YOU FORGOT MY BIRTHDAY?" It may be impossible to capture the right nuance for this sentence in any form, but uppercase is almost surely the wrong choice. Generally, stress must be used with care because email is still largely text-based and often does not make the standard indicators of emphasis like italics or underlining available to the writer. A common way to express emphasis is with special symbols like *asterisks* or _underscores_ on both sides of the word. Thus you could write, "Do you know you forgot my _birthday_?" to convey some emphasis. Certain email reading programs convert such embellished words into bold or italics, respectively, but others do not. Because you probably don't know what mail reader your correspondent uses, it's best to avoid uppercase letters unless you intend to yell.

Conversational Alternation

It is cumbersome to have a dialog, that is, rapidly alternating communication asynchronously. This is one of several reasons why chat room "conversations" are often so inane. If the purpose of the communication is interactive, say, a negotiation, the telephone is preferable because it replaces the asynchronous compose/send/wait/receive cycle of email with synchronous conversation that switches quickly. The ability to alternate rapidly not only speeds up the pace of the communication, but it can also allow us to detect confusion or misunderstanding through audio cues from the listener, such as the feedback of long pauses (cluelessness) rather than periodic "uh huhs" (comprehension). Of course, email is useful for setting the time for a phone conversation and exchanging phone numbers.

Ambiguity

Expressing ourselves is difficult, but it's even worse when our text is construed in a way that we did not intend. Ambiguity is a problem with natural language generally, and therefore all writing that is not programming or mathematics. But ambiguity arises even more in email, it seems, because it is more casual than most other writing. Some people apparently don't even proofread what they write, much less take time to consider carefully how their writing might be misinterpreted. If you write, "I cannot recommend saffron rice too highly," your intent may be to say that the dish is so good that you will not overstate your praise. But your reader may interpret the sentence as saying that there is little that you can say that is good about the food. If there are no other cues, the wrong idea could be received. As a result it is wise to proofread carefully and to look carefully for possible ambiguities.

> **Universal Mistake** It is nearly impossible to be sarcastic in email and not be offensive to some readers. Many writers try to be funny by being sarcastic, but it rarely works unless you know the recipient well. A good rule: No sarcasm in email sent to more than one person.

Flames

Perhaps the worst abuse of email is the phenomenon known as a *flame-a-thon* or *flame war*, an email battle named after the computer slang *flame* for "inflammatory email." It's hard to generalize on how flame-a-thons begin, but they are likely perpetuated by the same mentality that perpetuates war in some parts of the world, which is that no one wants to quit without getting revenge for the most recent attack. The main reason that flame-a-thons occur and continue seems to be email's immediacy. Email written in anger and sent immediately, gives no time for reflection. And we make it worse by including a cc list. If like snail mail email had to be addressed to only a single recipient and transported to the post office, most of us would probably cool down before completing the process and think better of it. It is almost universally true that no one wins a flame-a-thon. Clearly the best response when you are angered by email is to delay answering it and consider an alternative form of communication with the other person.

Generally, email is a very handy medium. It is most effective when it is used with a sensitivity to its weaknesses.

NETIQUETTE

There are a few rules, popularly known as *netiquette*, that promote effective and civilized email usage. The world won't end if you don't follow them any more than it will end if you chew with your mouth open, but you'll be considered less boorish when you do observe these guidelines:

- Address one topic at a time.
- Include context.
- Use your vacation message facility.
- Answer a backlog of email in reverse order.
- Get the sender's permission before forwarding email.
- Use more targeted distribution lists for broadcasting email messages.

Address One Topic at a Time

An email message that requires a response from the receiver should treat only one topic. For example, don't ask your parents for money in the same email that you ask if you left your brown sweater at home. Because most of us handle one matter at a time, the recipient of a one-topic message can respond to the matter appropriately, and then delete or archive the mail. With multiple topics, it is likely that one will be dropped or ignored. For example, you'll find out you did forget the sweater, but the money request might be ignored. Further, the subject line of the email can describe that one topic. Email is cheap, and it costs no more to send two messages than one containing the same information, but managing one-topic messages is much easier for everyone.

Include Context

An all too common email reply, unfortunately, is "Yes." Of course, we all like to get positive email, but what is our correspondent affirming? The subject line reads, "`Re: Question`". "`Question`" is the name we gave our querying email, but now we've forgotten what the question was. So, we need to search through Sent Mail for the original message that asked the question. Any email reading software worth two bits provides a means of including the message to which a reply is sent. Including the question with the reply is a courtesy. It provides the context for your answer, allowing you to give a terse reply without leaving the receiver clueless. One of the problems with always including the message in a reply, however, is that an email conversation quickly accretes to a significant size. If every character is typed by one of the two correspondents, there is little chance that this history will become gigantic. But as a courtesy to those whose connection to the Internet is "narrow," it is thoughtful to trim the history to the most recent message or to the most salient point of a long conversation.

Use Your Vacation Message Facility

When you will not be answering email for an extended period, it is a courtesy to set up an *automated reply* to correspondents saying so, and perhaps indicating when you expect to be reading email again. Such a facility, originally called a vacation message in the earliest mailers, is generally available from your mail server. The benefit of using the vacation message is that recipients can know that your nonresponse is a result of your absence. Otherwise, they may interpret it as a snub or incompetence.

Nor Rain, Nor Heat, Nor Gloom of Night. Email does get lost occasionally, but it is generally quite reliable. If an Internet destination is not responding for a given period of time, typically four hours, the sender is usually notified. Attempts to deliver the message continue for three days, but if they fail, the sender is then notified. "I never got the message," is usually a very suspect excuse.

Answer a Backlog of Emails in Reverse Order

When we keep current with our email, we usually answer messages in the order received. But if we've not been answering email for a while and our inbox is brimming, it is a courtesy to our correspondents to answer email in *reverse* order of its arrival. The rationale is simple. Many of the oldest messages will have, in computer jargon, "timed-out." That is, we may have messages that no longer need to be answered because a follow-up message resolves the issue. Or we may receive a "forget it" sent by someone who sent mail, received our vacation message, and realized that they couldn't wait for our reply. Not answering such mail saves us time and saves our correspondent aggravation. For example, when your boss sends a message trying to set up a meeting and asking for everyone's availability next week, it is unnecessary and somewhat embarrassing to reply when a later message sets the time for the meeting. Answering email in reverse time–order allows us to see these resolution messages before seeing the original. The only cautionary note about reverse processing a large inbox is to avoid the temptation to quit and never finish the backlog. After all, one of those unread messages may be telling you that you have won a new car in that $1 raffle you entered.

Get the Sender's Permission before Forwarding Email

As a general rule, most people assume that when they send email to one or a few people it is a private communication. Accordingly, it is inappropriate to forward someone's email without getting the sender's permission. If you want to forward it ask for permission. Asking gives the sender a chance to review the mail to decide if there is something in it that should not be passed along. The sender's opinion is important because although the mail may look innocuous to us, other readers my react differently and the sender may know that. It is the sender who should decide how widely his or her email is to be disseminated. Notice that most email in the United States is *not* a private conversation, and companies, colleges, or other parties can (under most circumstances) review the email sent or *received* by the members of their organization; that is, *your* personal email account might be private, but your recipients' may not be. (See Chapter 16.)

Use More Targeted Distribution Lists for Broadcasting Email Messages

There are many good reasons, such as changing your address, for mailing dozens of people the same email message. But maintaining a single list of all people you've exchanged email with and then forwarding to them the latest lame joke off the Internet is just a bad idea. Not only is it an abuse of one of the benefits of email—that a group of people can be informed simultaneously—but they've doubtless already heard it. It doesn't take long for the recipients of such mass mailings and forwards to start deleting all messages *unread.* Your correspondents will appreciate it if your mailing lists have a rational and limited basis. So, having short lists like Brothers and Moms_Kin is better than a list like Relatives. Not everything you'd send your brother would be of interest to every member of your family. Smaller, more specific lists promote more effective communication.

By observing such rules and general courtesy, our interactions using email can be more pleasant and effective.

Expect the Unexpected

To be alert to the unexpected is a valuable survival skill both in life and in IT. When something unexpected happens, we should not only notice it, but also ask ourselves "Why did that happen?" or "What's going on?" By wondering about the unexpected event, and analyzing what might have caused it, we may discover an advantage, or avoid harm, or learn something new, or perhaps most important, save ourselves from looking like total dummies! Because it is difficult to discuss "the unexpected" in general terms, consider a specific situation in which analyzing the unexpected is beneficial.

Occasionally—meaning every one to two years in my experience—an email handler for a large mailing list, for example, 5000 recipients or more, fails. (Another name for a mailing list application is a list-server.) The problem could be a bug in the mailing list software, or the list's *moderator*—the person responsible for deciding what is sent out to the mailing list—could have misconfigured it. Whatever the cause, there is a more-or-less typical sequence of messages to everyone on that mailing list that reveals that some people don't expect the unexpected.

The event begins innocuously enough with a message such as

```
From:    "Sue Marie Acker" <smacker@thermalmail.com>
Subject: Re: Topic of most recent mailing to this list
To:      Mondo_list

Remove me from this list, please.
```

A few similar messages of this same type follow. This is an unexpected event. Mailing lists are for sending information from one source, say, an organization, to many receivers. This kind of mail looks like communication from a receiver back to the source. Unexpected. Though there are many systems for managing mailing lists and we probably don't understand at all how they work, no software for handling mailing lists should send requests for removal from the list to the entire list. They should probably be sent to the moderator, or intercepted by someone else managing the list. Something is wrong here. It could be in the protocol for removing from the list, or it could be something else. *Everyone* on the mailing list should have noticed this and given it some thought. The moderator, especially, should have noticed, and fixed it if that is the problem.

But because he or she didn't fix it, the next message is . . .

```
From:    "A. S. King" <new2net@coolmail.com>
Subject: Re: Re: Topic of most recent mailing to this list
To:      Mondo_list

Why am I getting these messages??
> From: "Sue Marie Acker" <smacker@thermalmail.com>
> Subject: Re: Topic of most recent mailing to this list
> To: Mondo_list
>
> Remove me from this list, please.
```

From this mail we can conclude that the problem is not simply with the "unsubscribe" feature, that is, the facility that removes people from a mailing list. Rather, it is that the mailing list handler is apparently reflecting all of the mail it receives. If we send anything to this list, everyone will get it. The moderator is not intercepting replies to the list. Consequently, until someone fixes the problem, the only way to avoid getting more email is if everyone stops sending to this list. At this point the situation should be evident to everyone, and there should be no further traffic. That is, if everyone were expecting the unexpected. (It would be good if a civic-minded individual sent a private email to the moderator pointing out the problem.) Nevertheless, there follow several more messages of the form

```
From:     "Jackie S. Low" <dipsy_fan@tepidmail.com>
Subject: Re: Re: Topic of most recent mailing to this list
To:       Mondo_list
Yeah, why am I getting this mail? I don't even know why I'm on
this list. Remove me too.
> From: "A. S. King" <new2net@coolmail.com>
> Subject: Re: Re: Topic of most recent mailing to this list
> To: Mondo_list
>
> Why am I getting these messages??
>
> > From: "Sue Marie Acker" <smacker@termalmail.com>
> > Subject: Re: Topic of most recent mailing to this list
> > To: Mondo_list
> >
> > Remove me from this list, please.
```

After a dozen of these "`Yeah, what's up with this?`" types of messages, someone gets completely frustrated with those who don't seem to be figuring out that continuing to send email to the list prolongs everyone's agony. That person—actually there are usually several—writes,

```
From:     "M. St. Eamed" <code_ranger@infernomail.net>
Subject: Busted Mailing List Handler
To:       Mondo_list
Hey, dummies, the list handler's broken. Don't send anything
more to it.
```

This will be immediately follow by a message of the form

```
From:     "Fran K. Lee" <fleet@coldmail.net>
Subject: Re: Busted Mailing List Handler
To:       Mondo_list
You just did what you told everyone not to do! - Fleet
> From: "M. St. Eamed" <code_ranger@infernomail.net>
> Subject: Busted Mailing List Handler
> To: Mondo_list
>
> Hey, dummies, the list handler's broken. Don't send anything
more to it.
```

Or perhaps the message will read, "`I find it offensive getting messages calling me a dummy.`" Then other frustrated recipients will jump in with comments pointing out that any person who sends email to a broken email list claiming to be offended at being called a dummy probably is, and so on. This literally can go on for dozens of messages before the person responsible for the mailing list finally gets it fixed. The surprise, perhaps, is that the people sending these messages are on the mailing list because they share some common characteristic, implying, possibly, that many of them know each other. How embarrassing!

The key point about this email history is that it should have been evident very quickly (with A. S. King's message) that something unusual was happening. With a moment's thought, people should have realized—even though they had no possible way of knowing exactly what was wrong—how to act in a rational manner. Clearly most of the people involved in the event did so or there would have been *much more* such email. The lesson to be learned is not simply to be alert to mailing list handler bugs, but to be alert to unusual events of any kind at any time, and to think about them. At the very least, it could save some embarrassment.

PASSWORDS

One day electronic hardware may reliably detect who we are when we come in contact with a computer, and there will be no need for passwords. Meanwhile, passwords are an integral part of our daily interaction with computers. Selecting, changing, and managing passwords sensibly simplify our IT interactions. This section considers those three topics as well as password principles in connection with routine, everyday computer usage. Chapter 16 deals with the related topic of computer security.

Principles

Of course, the point of a password is to limit computer or software system access to only those people who know a not-likely-to-be-guessed sequence of keyboard characters. So, obviously, it is necessary to select such a sequence, and choosing a good one is discussed next. But couldn't one computer break into another if we programmed it to try all passwords in an algorithmic way until the true password is found? Computers must surely be fast enough. They probably would be. But they're not that dumb. Or, rather, the software running on them won't let potential users (computers) try zillions of passwords. The software for the login protocol may incorporate a delay when notifying the user that the password is wrong. The delay is not particularly noticeable to a human user, but it slows down the login protocol to the point that it is too slow to try zillions of passwords. Alternatively, software may notice long sequences of failed attempts to type the correct password and take some action. Of course, humans sometimes produce a sequence of failed attempts because they are agitated or groggy or try to log in using a pencil held in their teeth while holding a coffee cup in one hand and a Danish pastry in the other. So, login protocols allow several password failures before deciding they constitute an attempted break-in.

Another curiosity about passwords is that if we should forget ours and go to the system's administrator to find out what it is, he or she can't usually tell us. How could that be? Don't they have complete access—known as superuser or administrator status—to all of the computers, and so aren't they able to look up passwords? Yes, but the actual password is not stored on the computer. Rather, when a new password is created, it is scrambled or encrypted and then stored in that form. The new password is thrown away. Then, at login, the text given as the password is scrambled using the same algorithm used originally when the new password was set. The two scrambled sequences are then compared. If they are the same, the right password must have been given.[1] If not, the password must have been wrong. This technique is used so that passwords are not stored in "clear text" that someone could steal. How the scrambling is done is explained in Chapter 16. What the superuser does when you ask for your forgotten password is to create a new password, and force its scrambled form to replace your old one. You then use the new password.

[1] The scrambling algorithm should be one-to-one, that is, no two passwords should scramble to the same sequence.

Selecting Passwords

When we receive a new computer account, we are usually given an automatically generated password that is a scramble of letters and digits and possibly special characters: rU4Uw2?gR8. And we are told to change it. Of course, the motive for asking us to change it is so that we'll select something we can remember. Changing it to our boyfriend's name wouldn't be a good idea because that's too easily guessed, at least by our friends. (And, besides, how long will he last?) But what is a good choice?

Passwords are better if they are longer, at least six characters, and if they contain a mix of upper- and lowercase letters, numbers, and if allowed, punctuation characters. They are better if they have no "obvious" association to us, such as our name. And they are better if we can remember them immediately. Though these seem to be significant constraints, it's still pretty easy to come up with a good password with a few moments' thought.

Here are a few *heuristics*—guidelines to help solve a problem but that are not guaranteed to produce a solution—that should give good results:

- Select a personally interesting *topic*, such as a parent, favorite movie, or best travel destination, and *always* select passwords related to that topic. Because you will use many passwords, selecting from one topic area will help you to remember them.
- Develop a password from a phrase rather than a single word. The phrase must be memorable to you. It will be compressed according to the next rule.
- Encode the password phrase, trying to make it short (6–12 characters) by abbreviating, and by replacing letters or syllables with alternative characters, spellings, or encodings.

The goal is to generate letter strings that are not in dictionaries and are a mixture of numbers and letters.

Examples make this process clear. If you are using your father as the topic and your chosen phrase is his alma mater, Oxford University, then

Oxford University	⇒ OxfordU	Standard abbreviation and compress
	⇒ Ox4dU	Replace *for* with "4"
	⇒ Ohx4dU	Replace *O* with "Oh"

The result doesn't make much sense to someone who hasn't seen the process of construction, but it wouldn't be difficult for the creator to remember.

If your topic is your favorite movie, *Gone With The Wind*, proceed as follows:

Gone With The Wind	⇒ GWTW	Standard abbreviation and compress
	⇒ G2uTW	Replace *W* with "2u"
	⇒ G2uT2U	Replace *W* with "2U"
	⇒ G2uTdosU	Replace *2* with Spanish "dos"

The last replacement is not really needed because the password is already sufficiently obscure and varied, but the use of Spanish emphasizes that passwords can build on any aspect of our knowledge, heritage, or background.

Finally, if you are using your vacation to Australia as your topic, and your phrase is Surfing in Australia, you might modify it as follows

Surfing In Australia	⇒ SurfingInOz	Australia is often abbreviated Oz
	⇒ SurfininOz	Drop *g* as in slang
	⇒ Surf2inOz	Replace *inIn* with "2in"
	⇒ sirf2inOz	Replace *Sur* with "sir"
	⇒ sirF2inOz	Introduce a capital for variety

It is possible to be too clever, so terminating such modifications before they become excessively obscure is advisable. After all, you must be able to remember it!

Total Recall. It might seem that remembering such obscure passwords would be difficult, but it usually is not. If you type them daily, they come to mind quickly. It's almost as if your "fingers memorize them." If you use them, say, only monthly for your credit card account, being able to reconstruct them as illustrated assures that they're memorable.

Notice the importance of the topic. The topic provides context to narrow the possibilities for us personally, serving as a memory aid. If we're changing from having used G2uT2U for a year, a password based on phrases like "Frankly, my dear" or "Rhett and Scarlet" suitably transformed, should be easy to remember. And even if (foolishly) we tell someone our password, and (more foolishly) explain to them what it means, and (most foolishly) describe the topic from which we select passwords, the topic is probably rich enough to allow us to continue to use it. There are likely to be sufficiently many phrases and transformations that we could still produce obscure passwords providing reasonable protection.

The foregoing process is intended to produce an obscure password that should be easy to recall without having to write it down. But should it be written down anyway? It's personal choice. Some people would never be comfortable not having a password written down somewhere. Others are confident they'd be able to remember it under any circumstances, even after an all-night party at a brewery.

Changing Passwords

Passwords should be changed periodically. Organizations often have a policy as to how frequently a password must be changed, and there are occasionally security intrusions that cause administrators to request that passwords be changed. As a guideline the frequency with which a password should be changed is related to how likely it is that the password has become known and how important it is to keep the information secure. If you haven't changed your password in a year, it's probably time to consider changing it.

Every system that uses passwords provides software for changing them, though we usually don't notice its presence when we don't need it. Check the GUI where you enter your password for the option to change it. Failing that, do a search for "password" with the online Help facility. These systems typically ask for your current password, your new password, and a second copy of your new password. The second copy is simply to check that the two versions are identical as a test for a typing error. If they match, the password is changed.

Managing Passwords

People who make extensive use of computers can be required to present passwords in dozens of situations. Obviously, if they are all different, it can become a serious intellectual challenge to remember them all. But using a single password might also be burdensome if some of them must change frequently because of the hassle of visiting all accounts frequently to update to a new password. One strategy is always to have two current passwords, only one of which you change frequently. That way you would typically only ever have to try three or four times to get the right password: the slowly changing one, the quickly changing one, and perhaps the last versions of each in case you hadn't yet gotten around to updating it.

Finally, it is possible to recycle passwords in two ways. First, if you have a good and memorable password, change it slightly using the process described above to produce a new one. So, if you've been using the *Gone With The Wind* password, G2uT2U, and need to change it, go for the Spanish version, G2uTdosU. This works well for routine changes, but if there is a security concern related to your password, picking a totally new one from your topic area is essential. Second, if you have a series of good passwords, it is probably safe to reuse them over time, especially if they are not variants of one another as just described. Security experts do not like this idea, but most of us don't have Top Secret files on our computers either.

Freedom to Choose. It's sensible to use judgment when choosing passwords. For a personal computer kept at home that only you use, even a single letter password is probably too much. For your online bank account, a password of the type just discussed is advisable. Assess the risk in each case. Even your girlfriend's name can work in some instances.

VIRUSES AND WORMS

In the 1950s, shortly after computers were invented, scientists demonstrated programs with the ability to make exact copies of themselves. Though these programs generated philosophical discussions about the nature of life, computability, evolution, and so forth, they largely remained curiosities. Self-replication was hardly the most interesting application of programs. Then on November 2, 1988, Robert Tappan Morris, Jr., a computer science graduate student apparently lost control of a program he wrote, and the general public learned for the first time that programs could replicate themselves. Morris's program was supposed to embed in a computer once and then propagate itself to other machines. It propagated itself to 6000 machines, or about 10% of the Internet at the time. Though it was not designed to do any harm, it had an unfortunate bug in it that caused it to continue to replicate itself on each machine it infected. This quickly filled each machine's memory and hard disk, crashing the machines. The machine had to be manually "cleaned up" at the cost of millions of dollars in wages and downtime. As a result, new security organizations were created to monitor and quickly react to such malicious programs.

Crime and Punishment. Morris was prosecuted and convicted under the United States's Computer Fraud and Abuse Act of 1986, sentenced to three years' probation and 400 hours of community service, and fined $10,000. A similar conviction today would doubtless draw a much stiffer punishment.

A *virus* is a program that "infects" another program by embedding a (possibly evolved) copy of itself so that when the infected program runs, the virus replicates itself infecting other programs. A virus is transmitted when an infected program or floppy is transferred to another computer. A closely related phenomenon is a *worm*, which is an independent program that replicates from machine to machine across network connections. Morris's program was a worm. From a user's point of view, the distinction is less important than the fact that both viruses and worms have the *potential* to cause irreparable harm to your computer, such as erasing your files and trashing your software installation.

Viruses embed in software, so the common way to infect a computer is to copy software from some infected computer. Thus, if a friend's computer is infected, and you copy software from that machine onto your machine—either by using a portable medium like a floppy disk or a direct transfer—the virus may come with the software. Once you run that software, the virus will then infect your machine. For example, suppose you get your friend's very cool screen saver, which is infected. Then, when your computer is quiescent, the screen saver runs, infecting your computer.

> **More Than Meets the Eye**. A Trojan Horse is useful and apparently innocent software containing additional hidden code allowing the unauthorized collection, exploitation, or destruction of data. Screen savers are good hosts for Trojan Horse code because they run regularly.

Notice that any software distribution from *freeware* (software available on the Web at no cost) to *shareware* (software available on the Web that you pay for on the honor system) to standard commercial applications (software you can pay a bundle for) is a *potential* source of virus-infected code. However, the people who distribute software are extremely aware of the risks and take extreme precautions to ensure that the software they publish is clean. Because computers are pretty useless unless we use software other people wrote, we inevitably take a tiny risk when loading new software, but usually too tiny to worry about.

Recently viruses have been propagated in email attachments. For example, if you and a friend both use the same software, say, for word processing, an easy way to work together on a report is to exchange the document file by attaching it to email. When it's your turn to work on the report, your friend attaches the latest version, you receive it, and open the document with your software. It's very convenient. Viruses can exploit this process by embedding themselves in documents for widely used software like a word processor. When an unthinking email recipient opens such a document, the software "runs" the virus commands—often in the form of macroinstructions—enabling it to do its work. A common behavior for the virus then is to locate the user's email address book and to send email to people on the list with attachments into which it has embedded itself. When the next person opens the attachment, the virus infects their computer and can continue its spread. The Melissa virus used this process; see Figure 12.1.

Obviously the process doesn't work if no one opens the attachments, but attachments are very useful. It also doesn't work if the software manufacturer takes greater diligence in creating software that cannot be so easily compromised. But the best deterrent is the attentive user who is not "trigger happy" about opening attachments and who reads email with a slight skepticism. Is the message a sensible follow-on to the last message from the sender? Is the content of the message something the sender would say to me? Is there a reason for the sender to include an attachment? If such considerations raise concern about the authenticity of email, be cautious. Do not open the attachments. You can send return email telling the sender you didn't understand his or her last email and request clarification. If you believe the email is infected—new worms and viruses are usually reported in the media with much fanfare—simply Trash it. The infected mail usually need not be *expunged*—permanently deleted— because viruses are generally harmless as long as the proper software does not open them.

Looking at Melissa

The Melissa virus, known in security circles as W97M/Melissa, burst onto the Internet on Friday March 26, 1999, embedded in Microsoft Word documents attached to email messages. The original Melissa virus's email message had the form

```
From:     <Name of infected user>
Subject: Important Message From <name of infected user>
To:       <50 names from infected user's email address book>

Here is that document you asked for ... don't show anyone else ;-)
Attachment: LIST.DOC
```

The virus was so virulent that many companies, including Microsoft, had to shut down their email servers to limit the spread of the virus. Would this look like a suspicious email if it came from someone you knew?

Viruses mutate—hackers who get a copy change them and start them up again—causing variations to propagate. For example, later versions of Melissa had a different attachment file name rather than LIST.DOC. Also, a variation, known as W97M/Melissa.I, used a random number generator to choose among a variety of different subject lines and email bodies, trying to fool people who were alert for the preceding form of the virus. The eight variations are shown in Table 12.1.

Table 12.1. Variations of the Melissa Virus Email

Subject Line	Email Body
Question for you ...	It's fairly complicated so I've attached it.
Check this!!	This is some wicked stuff!
Cool Web Sites	Check out the Attached Document for a list of some the Web
80mb Free Web Space	Check out the Attached Document for details on how space. It's cool, I've now got heaps of room.
Cheap Software	The attached document contains a list of web sites Cheap Software
Cheap Hardware	I've attached a list of web sites where you can ob
Free Music	Here is a list of places where you can obtain Free
* Free Downloads	Here is a list of sites where you can obtain Free

* A randomly selected digit

Figure 12.1 Looking at the Melissa virus.

> **It's a Jungle Out There**. Though viruses and worms may not be much in the news at any particular time, they are circulating around the Internet all the time. At www.wildlist.org find a list of the currently active viruses, worms, and other malicious programs that are still known to be "in the wild." Three years later the Melissa virus was still at large.

Suppose you do propagate a virus to the world, what should you do? Having been duped into opening the attachment and assisting the virus's spread is embarrassing to most of us, so we'd like it to go away. But if we discover quickly enough what we have done, there are some useful responses. If we discover it immediately, that is, if our mailer is still sending out virus-infested mail, we may be able to disconnect the computer, say, if the connection is via a modem, and limit the number of messages sent. If the messages have been sent, but very recently, it may be possible to send follow-up email quickly alerting the recipients to the infected mail. (The victims are in the Sent Mail file.) It is best if the subject line calls attention to itself somehow, perhaps by being in caps: ALERT! I SENT A VIRUS. This will assist email readers who look over their Inbox before beginning to process the mail. If as is likely the damage has already been done, there is little to do, except perhaps to commiserate with those who got it and passed it along, too—you'll likely get infected mail back from them! Finally, you will have to disinfect your computer by running commercial antiviral software.

Admission. David L. Smith pleaded guilty to creating and propagating the Melissa virus.

Because viruses, worms, and other unsavory critters are at large, it is mandatory that each computer have up-to-date virus checking software loaded and running. Various vendors produce effective products: McAfee, Norton, and Sophos Inc. are three of the many companies that sell antivirus software. These programs check for the known viruses, worms, and so on, but like biological organisms, new creatures are being created all the time. So, it is necessary to get updates periodically. Typically, owning software from a vendor entitles you to updates to keep the diagnostics current. The task of keeping your computer free of malicious software is yours and it's never ending.

Colorful Language. Computer security uses many other colorful terms (see the NSA Security Glossary). An *ankle-biter* is an aspiring cracker (hacker attacking a system) with very little knowledge, and so is ineffective but annoying like a little dog. *Derf* is to use a terminal or computer someone absent-mindedly left logged in. A *Nak Attack—nak* is engineering slang for "negative acknowledgment"—exploits a certain OS weakness to make a computer vulnerable. The *Ping of Death* is a huge message sent to another machine to see if it replies, but instead it chokes.

Copyright and Intellectual Property

Like land or Rover or a Land Rover, information is something that can be owned. Information, including photographs, music, textbooks, and cartoons, is the result of the creative process. The act of creation bestows on the creator ownership of the result in the United States and most of the world. Sometimes there are multiple forms of ownership. If on her new CD Mariah Carey sings a song written by Paul Simon, he owns the words and music, and she owns the performance. If a person creates something while working for a company, the company generally owns the information. All such human creations are called *intellectual property* to distinguish them from real estate, pets, cars, and other stuff that can be owned.

The two important aspects of intellectual property for this chapter are software and copyright on the Web. Each affects your flexibility in using information technology.

Software

When you buy software, you load it onto your machine without giving much attention to the tiny, legal mumbo jumbo that you agree to by opening the package or downloading the file. (Sure, lawyers probably read it, but the rest of us don't.) If you read it, you'd discover a remarkable fact: You didn't buy the software—you're effectively renting it. That is, software licenses tend to give you the use of the software whose ownership remains with the company that is marketing it.[2] Why this is true is probably an interesting story if we had the proper legal and business background to understand it, but the "why" is not the issue for us. Rather, it's the implications of such agreements that matter.

If the agreement allows us to use the software, we can use it on any of our computers, assuming we have more than one. Thus we should be able to install the software on all of our computers. The fact that we use it personally generally implies that we use one instance at a time. Installing several instances to make our use of it more convenient should be OK. An analogous situation exists in companies. If a company has several engineers who need a certain specialized software package, they might buy x "site licenses" for that software. The site licenses authorize x engineers to use the software simultaneously. The point is not how many hard disks contain a copy of the software, but rather how many people can *use* the software at once.

Because you don't own commercial software, you cannot give it to your friend. If you were to do this, you would be violating the terms of the contract that you agreed to when you opened the software package. But even if you simply bought software from a friendly hacker you met in the computer lab, you probably still can't give it away. The hacker created the software—it's his or her intellectual property—and creating it confers full copyright protection. Like a photographer who creates a stunning picture, the hacker's ownership of the software allows copies to be made and sold to people like you. You buy a photograph to frame and enjoy it; you buy software to run and enjoy it. Unless the hacker gave you the explicit right to make copies and distribute them, you cannot sell the software or even give it away.

For the Record. "Hacker" is used here in its original, correct usage to mean expert programmer. The news media has needlessly tainted the word, but it retains its original meaning in the profession.

Finally, there is shareware, which is software that is typically distributed over the Internet. You can download a copy for free, and you can copy it to your friends. The idea of shareware is that you can try out the software, and if you like it and use it, you are to pay the creator for it. (The price is listed.) It's a great system both because it allows craftsman programmers to distribute their often well-built and effective software and because you can try it out before paying. But it is an honor system, and if you do use it, you should pay. It would be unethical to download software on the implied promise of paying for it if you use it, and then to use it without paying. Prices are generally very modest, and the software is often exceptionally good.

Copyright on the Web

When a person creates a document such as a term paper, Web page, or a sculpture, the action creates a copyright in the United States and most nations of the world. The document is referred to as a "work" and includes many more forms of creation than those listed. The creator typically owns the copyright, unless the creation is "work for hire," in which case, the owner is the person who paid the creator, usually, a company. For example, if you create a personal Web page, you own the copyright, but if you built the Web page as part of your job, the company owns it. Posting information on the World Wide Web is a form of publishing, and though the copyright and other law has not been fully developed yet, it is a good assumption that if you find information on the WWW, someone else owns it.

[2] Of course, every license is different, forcing this section to discuss the topic generally. To be sure, check your software license.

No © 'em. It was once necessary to claim copyright with the phrase "**Copyright** *dates* **by** *author/owner* **All Rights Reserved**" but it's no longer necessary for works produced after March 1, 1989. However, the "© <dates> **by** <author>" is still used as a reminder and reference.

What rights does copyright of intellectual property bestow? Obviously the right to copy it, but surprisingly, there are others. Copyright protects the owner's right to

- Make a copy of the work
- Use a work as the basis for a new work, called creating a derivative work.
- Distribute or publish the work, including doing so electronically
- Publicly perform the work, as in music, poetry, drama, or to play a video or audio recording or CD-ROM
- Publicly display the work, as in to display an image on a computer screen

And it is the very act of creating the intellectual property that creates these rights. No application or approval is required. The work need not carry the © symbol. It's copyrighted the moment it's finished.

Notice the second item, using the work to create a derivative work. This is an important aspect of copyright because it prevents someone from, for example, changing each of the Simpsons characters in some small way and claiming to have created a new dysfunctional cartoon family. If the characters are to be different, for example, to age, it's Matt Groening who has the right to do it. We might be tempted to bypass copyright law by restating a work in our own words, but if the result follows the original closely, restating probably produces a derivative work rather than new intellectual property. Thus, for example, if someone restates this book in different words, I could sue them—and might.

Of course, just because someone else owns it doesn't mean that you cannot use and enjoy it. Obviously the fact that they've published it on the Web means that you are free to read, view, or listen to it as you wish. Printing it so that you can read it on the bus would be OK, as would filing away a copy on your computer for future *personal* enjoyment. You can mail the URL to your friend, notifying them of the information. Such applications, presumably, motivated publishing the information on the Web in the first place.

Many sites state an explicit copyright policy. Often the information is placed in the *public domain*, meaning that it is free for use by anyone in any form. This is convenient because it means that we can treat the information as if it were our own. We could even sell it to someone else, if we could find a buyer. Another frequent situation is that the owners explicitly state that they allow the information to be republished or used in other forms provided that the source is cited. They keep ownership, but we get to use it. Again, this is a very flexible policy, which simply requires that we take care to follow the guidelines. And, of course, some sites—all of them that don't state otherwise—retain all rights to the Web-published information under the applicable copyright laws. Generally, this means that if you want to use works from such a site in one of the five ways listed earlier, you must get permission from the owners of the information to do so. Using such copyrighted property without receiving permission is illegal, of course. But the fact that a site retains the rights to its information should not deter you from asking for permission. Many sites routinely give permission; their purpose in requiring you to ask for permission is to retain control over the dissemination of the works. It takes only a little effort to ask.

> **No Harm in Asking**. When asking for copyright permission, state what works you are interested in, e.g., "the photograph on your page ../greatpix/elvis/"; how you would like to use them, e.g., "put copies on my personal Web page at . . ."; and any other relevant information, e.g., "I want to colorize his suede shoes so they are actually blue."

Between the free personal use and the need to get permission there is a gray area in which limited use of copyrighted materials is allowed without getting permission. This is known as the "Concept of Fair Use." Fair Use is recognized in copyright law to allow the use of copyrighted material for educational or scholarly purposes, to allow limited quotation of copyrighted works for review or criticism, to permit parody, and a few other uses. For example, I can quote Stanley Kubrick's *2001, A Space Odyssey* in

> One of the most widely known computer instructions is David Bowman's command, "Open the pod bay doors, HAL."

without getting the permission of Warner Brothers, the present owner, because I am using the quotation for the educational purpose of instructing you about Fair Use. This is true even though this book is a commercial application of the quoted material. And you would be allowed to use similar brief quotations in class assignments. Indeed, Fair Use provides many opportunities for using copyrighted material for socially beneficial purposes. The problem is that it is very fuzzy when Fair Use applies.

The following four questions are applied to determine whether a given use of copyrighted information constitutes Fair Use:

- What is the planned use?
- What is the nature of the work in which the material is to be used?
- How much of the work will be used?
- What effect would this use have on the market for the work if the use were widespread?

The factors that figure into deciding whether the answers to these questions constitute Fair Use are complex and subject to disagreements by fair-minded people, lawyers and even judges. Indeed, a recent two-year Conference on Fair Use (CONFU) struggled mightily with the interpretations and failed to clarify the matter fully. It is beyond the scope of this section to delve into the nuances of deciding Fair Use. But the University of Texas publishes easy-to-apply rules of thumb that serve as a very useful guideline:

```
www3.utsystem.edu/ogc/IntellectualProperty/copypol2.htm
```

Finally, many people say that it is all right to use copyrighted material for noncommercial purposes, but that's false. You violate the law whether you sell the material or not, though commercial use usually results in larger fines or damages when you get sued. Because the penalties for copyright infringement are substantial—up to $100,000 per act—it pays to be careful. By far the best approach is to think things up on your own—that is, create intellectual property with your own intellect. Not only are you not required to ask for anyone else's permission, you enjoy copyright protection too!

> **Uncopyrightable Fact**. Facts cannot be copyrighted. For example, "*Uncopyrightable* is the longest English word without repeated letters" is a fact, and so is uncopyrightable.

What's Right?

If there is a bug in the credit card billing program and it makes a mistake, you'll immediately call the credit card company to say you owe them more money. Right? Right. So, some computer errors[3] go undetected or unreported. Most errors are harmless. But computers control life-support and other medical apparatus, airplanes, nuclear power plants, weapons systems, and so on. Errors in these systems are potentially much more serious. How do we know the software running safety critical systems is perfect? We don't and we can't! It's a sobering thought.

We must demand that any system, whether mechanical or electronic, that supports life or controls potentially hazardous devices or materials work flawlessly. Anything less is reckless and immoral. But it is easier to assert that we must have perfection than it is to achieve it. To understand the issues, distinguish first between hardware failures and software failures. In general, hardware failures can be resolved using techniques such as redundancy. For example, three computers can perform all the computations of a safety-critical system and make all critical action decisions based on majority vote. If a failure in one computer causes it to come up with a different answer, the other two overrule it. Another technique, dubbed *burn in,* exploits the so-called "infant mortality" property of computer hardware failures caused by fabrication problems: Most errors are revealed after only a few hours of operation. A computer that has run for a while has a record of successful operation, and is likely to continue to do so. Overall, such techniques can give us confidence that the fetch-execute cycle and other hardware will work properly.

Software is another matter. Compared with mechanical and electronic systems, software is amazingly complex. The number of possible configurations that a typical program can define grows exponentially and quickly becomes unimaginably large even for small programs. It is a fact that all states that the software can get into, known as *reachable configurations*, cannot be examined for their correctness. This reality poses a daunting problem for programmers and software engineers: How can they be sure their programs work right?

Like all engineers, programmers begin with a specification—a precise description of the input, how the system is to behave, and the output to be produced. The specification doesn't say how the behavior is to be achieved necessarily, just what it should be. Using various design methods, the programmers produce a program, an implementation. The implementation is tested by providing sample inputs and then verifying that the resulting outputs match the specification's dictates. If they do not, there is a bug and the program must be fixed. *A program is said to be correct if its behavior exactly matches its specification.* Unfortunately it is not possible to establish correctness by testing. Through extensive and thoughtful testing, however, it is possible to gain confidence that the program closely approximates the specification. Confidence, but not certainty, is the best that can be done.

> **Hard Fact of Software.** Programming pioneer Edsger Dijkstra first stated this fundamental fact: Program testing reveals only the presence of bugs, never their absence.

With absolute correctness an all but unattainable technical goal, what should our response as users be to the fact that the software we use cannot be known to be correct? There are two aspects to consider:

---

[3] Though it's actually a software bug, the billing problem is termed a "computer error" in accordance with popular usage. As mentioned repeatedly, computers per se make few errors.

1. We must accept that software is very likely to contain bugs despite even Herculean efforts by programmers and software engineers to get it right. Accordingly, we must monitor all software usage, alert to unusual behavior that may indicate a bugs, and prepared to limit the harm that it can inflict on our work.
2. Because programmers and software engineers are well aware of this challenge to producing correct software, poorly tested software is simply evidence of poor professionalism; users should demand software of the highest quality, refuse buggy software, and be prepared to change to better software.

Thus we must be wary and informed users and take our business to those who produce the best product.

The alternative to correct is *reliable*, a quantitative measure indicating how likely it is that the software works correctly under normal circumstances. The way to measure reliability depends on what the software does, of course, but for a word processor, say, failures per thousand hours of normal use might be appropriate. The term *failures* needs to be defined appropriately and will include general conditions like system crashes and lost files as well as application-specific faults like "broken" edits and "unavailable" operations.

The real difficulty is in defining what "normal use" is. Is it the most common operations repeated many times, or is it every capability performed on the easiest inputs, or what? Most users use the common operations most of the time, as we all know, so these invariably work well. Repeating them a zillion times gives no information because the computer (assumed to be reliable) faithfully follows the instructions for them each time. Nothing new happens. Mixing these with more complex operations is sensible, but what combination and with what inputs? The problem is a tough one. A good solution might be to use complete keystroke histories from a diverse set of users—students writing term papers, businesspeople creating form letters and mailing labels, authors writing IT textbooks with many figures, and so on.

The key point is that although reliability is a quantitative measure, it is not a statistical measure in the same sense as testing light bulbs. Product life for light bulbs describes a normal "bell curve," with some short-lived, some long-lived, and most about average. Program reliability is different. A given period of error-free operation can be extended in principle forever by simply remaining within the range of the operations already demonstrated to be working. Moving on to untested configurations may reveal bugs, but doing so doesn't typically require hours of error-free operation to reach. The test could begin with those configurations. There need not be a "bell curve" describing average behavior.

If correct software is effectively impossible to produce, how much confidence can we have in software-controlled life support systems or nuclear power plants? Clearly, the software must be reliable in the sense just described—quantitatively correct under normal use. But most of our concerns are with unusual or unexpected events. *Software is said to be* robust *if it performs according to specification under unusual circumstances.* Thus, when operations at a nuclear power plant deviate from normal, say, an earthquake occurs, will the software perform as the specification requires, that is, correctly? By definition it is difficult to test software under unusual circumstances, so robustness poses significant challenges to system designers.

There are two responses to unusual circumstances, known as fail-soft and fail-safe. *Fail-soft* means that the program continues to operate, providing a possibly degraded level of functionality. *Fail-safe* means that the system stops functioning to avoid causing harm. The basic strategy, therefore, is to continue to operate as long as productive service can be safely provided, but when that ceases to be possible to avoid negative results by stopping entirely. Perfectly safe software is usually achieved by the useless solution of doing nothing—don't allow the nuclear power plant to start up in the first place—but there will be risk in virtually every *useful* solution. Like most safety issues, it is not possible to avoid risk entirely.

SUMMARY

The chapter began with a discussion of the weaknesses of email. Among the limitations we recognized email's shortcomings in expressing emotion and ideas unambiguously. Problems arise in stressing words, alternation, and using email in anger. But netiquette makes email usage more pleasant. Refined email users limit messages to one topic, include context, don't forward private correspondence or thoughtlessly broadcast email to every acquaintance they ever met. As a courtesy they use a vacation message when they will not be processing email for a while, and they answer a backlog of email in reverse time order.

Expecting the unexpected is a difficult, but useful survival skill. The opportunity to apply it arises in IT. It requires that one first recognize the unusual situation, and then think about its implications. "Why is it happening?" "What's going on?" The challenge is to think about the unexpected event, and correctly determine whether and how you should respond.

The next topic was passwords. We gave a set of heuristics for constructing an easy-to-remember password. The approach emphasized selecting all of your passwords so they are connected to a common topic. This will assist in remembering them. It is also advisable to use passwords sensibly, choosing simple passwords where little security is needed, and selecting a more obscure password for those cases where there is greater risk.

Risk is also present with viruses and worms, but the chances that such a threat could harm our computer usage is reduced when we install and run antivirus software. Copyright infringement poses a legal risk, causing us to take care not to share software or pirate copyrighted information from the Web. Finally, we discussed the reliability of computers and software. Unfortunately it is practically impossible to have bug-free software. This doesn't mean that we quit using computers, or accept bugs in software. Rather we must be vigilant for unusual behavior that might be caused by the presence of bugs, and to take precautions to limit the harm that software bugs can cause.

EXERCISES

1. What is the rationale for answering email in reverse time order after returning from a vacation?
2. What does it mean to "expect the unexpected"?
3. Why does A. S. King's mail give more information than we had originally?
4. Superusers have complete access to a computer. Why do they not know your password?
5. If you forget your password, how can the superuser remind you of it?
6. How many eight-character passwords can be created from the ASCII letters and digits?
7. What are heuristics?

8. Using the guidelines for creating good passwords and the topic "Fluency Class," generate a good password. Explain how you derived it as was done in the illustrations.
9. What is the role of the "topic" in creating a memorable password?
10. If a program running on one computer starts itself up on another computer and continues propagating itself from there, is it a virus or a worm?
11. Is it true that a virus can infect a computer not connected to the Internet? Why or why not?
12. What is a Trojan Horse?
13. What does it mean to "create a derivative work"?
14. What are the four questions asked in deciding Fair Use?
15. Explain the procedure required to copyright a work.
16. Why can't software be checked for correctness?

CHAPTER 13

Databases

Learning Objectives

- Appreciate the difference between the informal and DB concepts of "table."
- Learn the basic terms of (relational) databases.
- Understand why redundancy is bad and how to avoid it.
- Know how to use entity/relationship diagrams.
- Learn the five fundamental operations on tables.
- Learn how Join creates tables.
- Understand how to create tables with queries.
- Appreciate the relationship between the chapter's concepts and SQL.

Most people understand *database* to mean a "collection of information." That's correct, as far as it goes, but it allows almost anything to be a database, including the neighborhood newspaper recycling bin. That fails as a database for at least two reasons. First, it doesn't record data about any particular thing—we are rarely interested in amorphous collections of text or documents. Second, it is not organized—information must be arranged and structured if it is to be useful so that specific items can be found. This chapter introduces the theory and practice of organizing information into a database. After that introduction a more precise definition will be possible.

The chapter begins by contrasting *tables* as we know them informally with *tables* as the idea is formulated for the purposes of building a database. With the idea of database table motivated, we next introduce the appropriate ideas and terminology from the study of relational databases, allowing us to construct sample database tables. We next introduce the subject of redundancy, a surprising topic that once understood saves us from creating poor databases. To simplify creating databases we introduce entity-relationship diagrams, a notation that abstracts the important ideas in a database design. Next the five fundamental operations of DB tables are introduced, followed by a sixth, Join, that simplifies practical table construction. Finally, we introduce the concept of a query, the mechanism with which the most sophisticated and refined manipulations of databases can be expressed. All of these ideas are demonstrated with a rich set of examples.

"You Can Look It Up"

Baseball legend Yogi Berra coined the phrase "you can look it up" as a challenge to the disbelieving listener to check the record book to verify a claimed fact. A "record book" is a database, and we can imagine—even if we've never seen one—that it is organized as a collection of tables like most other archives of factual information. For example, the Olympic record book contains a table for each Olympic event, giving the gold, silver, and bronze medal winner's names and nationalities for each year. (Find them online at `www.olympic.org`.) There are also tables of host countries, participating nations for each games with the number of athletes competing, and so on.

To "look it up" involves locating the right table(s) containing the sought-after information and then finding the appropriate entry or entries. For certain kinds of information, multiple tables may be needed. So, to find all of the athletes from African nations who have won medals in the marathon, we must consult the tables of marathon medalists for all Olympics and select those from Africa. The answer to this more complex question will likely be a table itself. The challenge "you can look it up" is not difficult if the information is organized properly. The essence of databases is to organize information into tables properly and to extract the answers to questions.

But there are two important differences with everyday tables.

The first distinction between everyday tables and tables as they exist in the world of databases is perhaps the most significant. Everyday tables show a *picture* of the information, whereas database tables describe the *structure* of the information. Knowing the structure, we can produce a picture, but the opposite is not possible. The distinction is roughly the same as the one we encountered in Chapter 8 with the digitization of the *Oxford English Dictionary*. Using a word processor, we could type the definition of *byte*, for example, as it appears in Figure 8.7, including all of the proper formatting to produce a printed version of the definition. Or we could specify the structure of dictionary definitions, as has been done for the *OED*, and provide all of the information for the definition of *byte* in that form. A computer could then produce the formatted document of Figure 8.7. But it could also help us search because it would know which text is the word being defined, which text is the pronunciation, which text is the first example of its usage, and so. By providing structural information, the computer can help to a greater extent than simply printing the definition. Our goal with database tables is the same as with the *OED*—to explain to the computer how the information is structured so that it can help us manipulate the data.

To emphasize the distinction and to motivate our database abstraction, consider the HTML table shown in Figure 13.1. Though this is a computer specification of a table that *appears* to describe its structure, it is still only a table in the everyday "picture" sense. The HTML specifies how the table entries are arranged, but it doesn't describe the nature of the data. For example, we know that countries are usually referred to by their names, which are strings of ASCII letters. We should expect to find that kind of data in the first column headed Country. But there is no way in HTML to require such a characteristic of a table—that is, to specify a property of the data in a column. Thus an equivalent HTML table (Figure 13.2) could replace the first column entries with numbers, colors, currency amounts, images, exclamations, and so on. It's still a well-formed HTML table despite being completely meaningless. Therefore, among the structural features of a table that a database specifies is the kind of information that will appear in each column.

```
<table border>
   <caption>Country Data</caption>
   <tr>
      <th>Country</th>
      <th>Capital</th>
      <th>Language</th></tr>
   <tr>
      <td>Ecuador</td>
      <td>Quito</td>
      <td>Spanish</td></tr>
   <tr>
      <td>Bolivia</td>
      <td>La Paz</td>
      <td>Spanish</td></tr>
   <tr>
      <td>Brazil</td>
      <td>Brasilia</td>
      <td>Portuguese</td></tr>
</table>
```

Country Data		
Country	Capital	Language
Ecuador	Quito	Spanish
Bolivia	La Paz	Spanish
Brazil	Brasilia	Portuguese

Figure 13.1. HTML specification for a table—but not a database table—giving country information.

The second difference between everyday tables and tables used in databases concerns the distinction between the structure of the information and the data itself. We separate the two in databases. One consequence of this separation is that it is possible to have a table—that is, the structure—but with no data in it. What would such a table look like? It would have a name and column headings, called *fields*, but no rows, see Figure 13.3(a). This is an *empty table*, and though it's pure structure, it's not such an unusual idea.

Country Data		
Country	Capital	Language
$54.40	Quito	Spanish
	La Paz	Spanish
Eureka!	Brasilia	Portuguese

Figure 13.2. HTML table made meaningless by replacing table data entries in the first column.

If it's possible to think of the structure in isolation, is it possible to think of the data in isolation? Yes. In database terminology, information is a set of *entities*. *Entity* is about as vague a word as *thing* or *stuff*. But databases should be able to contain *any* kind of information, so the inventors of relational databases chose a very inclusive term. When we think of a database containing data, the sorts of information most people have in mind are entities.

What are entities like? They're things with *attributes*; see Figure 13.3(b). Attributes can be any features people observe about things. Each entity's attributes have *values*. Often, attributes are features such as weight that can be measured; 36,000 kg might be a value for the attribute weight for a given type of whale. But attributes are very general and can include relationships, such as aunt, beliefs like Buddhism, and estimates like lifetime earning capacity. The key point is that entities are synthetic; that is, they are invented by people, so they can have any attributes we want. If it's possible to identify a set of things, the features that separate those things from everything else, and from each other, are their *attributes*.

Whales					
name	scientific_name	food	weight	length_range	photo

(a)

Name GRAY
Food Crustaceans
Weight 36,000 Kg
Scientific Name *Eschrichtius robustus*
Length 13.7–14 m
Photo

Name KILLER
Weight 5,400 Kg
Scientific Name *Orcinus orca*
Food Salmon, Seals
Length 6.7–8.2 m
Photo

Scientific Name *Balaenoptera musculus*
Food Krill
Name BLUE
Length 23–24.5 m
Weight 100,000 Kg
Photo

Length 15–18 m
Name SPERM
Food Squid
Weight 40,000 Kg
Scientific Name *Physeter macrocephalus*
Photo

Name HUMPBACK
Food Krill
Weight 36,000 Kg
Scientific Name *Megaptera novaeangliae*
Length 13–15 m
Photo

(b)

Whales					
Name	**Scientific**	**Food Source**	**Wt. Kg.**	**Length Range**	**Photograph**
Gray	*Eschrichtius robustus*	crustaceans	35,000	13.7–14	
Killer	*Orcinus orca*	salmon,seals	5,400	6.7–8.2	
Blue	*Balaenoptera musculus*	krill	100,000	23–24.5	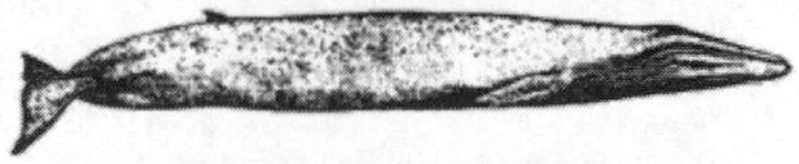
Sperm	*Physeter macro-cephalus*	squid	40,000	15–18	
Humpback	*Megaptera novaeangliae*	krill	36,000	13–15	

(c)

Figure 13.3. The constituents of a database table; (a) the table structure, (b) unordered entities with their unordered attributes, (c) the tuples for the whale entity structured by the table.

> **A Bright Idea.** Though many people contributed to the creation of relational databases—the kind of databases discussed here—E. F. Codd of IBM is widely credited with the idea and received ACM's Turing Award for it, the field's "Nobel Prize."

Once a table's structure has been defined as in an empty table and the entities with their attribute values have been made available, the entities become the rows of the table, called *tuples*, producing our familiar conception of a table (Figure 13.3). We prefer the terms *tuples* and *fields* to *rows* and *columns* because the latter pair can suggest an ordering. There is no ordering to either tuples or fields, though we often define one for printing.

> **Tuples**. The sequence of terms *singleton, pair, triple, quadruple, quintuple, sextuple, septuple, . . .* for groups of things motivates the word *tuple*. A group of *n* things could be called an *n-tuple*, or just *tuple*. It conveys the idea of *n* things, grouped together, but without order.

Defining Tables

In this section, we explain how to define the structure of database tables. We also describe pitfalls to avoid when building a definition.

The definition of a database table requires three essential parts:

Name: Although we informally call a table's name its *caption,* the name in the database world is not just text; it *describes* the kind of things that are collected together in the table and is the entity's name. So, we prefer descriptive nouns like *whales* rather than phrases like "Rita's Five Favorite Whales," which might contain irrelevant text. *Five,* for example, is inappropriate because the number of entities collected together by a table is variable.

Field Specifiers: Fields give the values of an entity's attributes. Field specifiers give names to the attributes—essentially column headings—and describe the type of information (in a computational sense) that will appear in the columns. Field specifiers are said to *declare* a column of a table using the syntax

field_name data_format optional_comment

where *field_name* describes the attribute, *data_format* specifies the type of information to be expected in that field, and *optional_comment* is any explanatory information that should be recorded about the attribute. The available *data_formats*, which ultimately depend on the implementing database software, are usually quite rich, including numbers, ASCII strings of a given length, dates, currency amounts, JPEG or GIF images, Boolean values (i.e., a single bit), and so on. (Because the present discussion is independent of an implementing system, we use any convenient *data_formats*.) By specifying the *data_format,* problems of the kind illustrated in Figure 13.2 are prevented.

Primary Key: A primary key is one or more fields that uniquely identify any row in the table, as explained later in this chapter.

Notice that although a database table has a single name and a single primary key, it will typically have several field specifiers.

> **For the Record**. We use *tuples* for actual entities and use *rows* as a synonym; the term *records* is also a synonym. *Record* is a holdover from computing's punch-card days but is still common.

To apply the concepts just described, consider the specification of the database table shown in Figure 13.3(a).

Whales

name	character 15	The common English name
scientific_name	character 30	Genus and species
food	character 12	Primary food source
weight	number	Typical max. adult weight, kilograms
length_range	character 20	Lower-upper adult length range, meters
photo	GIF	Picture of mature adult

Primary Key: name

In this specification, the data format character dd has been used to refer to a sequence of ASCII symbols—not just letters—of length dd, number specifies a numerical quantity, and GIF specifies a value represented in the Graphic Interchange Format.

> **DOT COMmunication**. Databases typically contain many tables, which must all have different field names. It's convenient and legal to reuse field names, however, because different tables may record similar kinds of data, for example, photos. Reuse motivates the "dot" notation for fields, *table_name . field_name*, as in Whales . photo.

Three aspects of the Whales specification warrant further explanation: descriptive field names, atomic field data, and keys.

Descriptive Field Names. The field names *describe* the attribute in the same sense that the table name should describe the entities of the table. They are nouns, not the text that would label a column as the heading when the table is printed. For example, weight describes the attribute, whereas "**Weight, kg**" might be used as the printed heading for its column. Notice that we use the comment field to remind ourselves that the measurements are in kilograms. As might be expected, the names have meaning only to us; the computer doesn't know what they mean and would be just as happy with field0001, field0002, and so on.

Atomic Field Data. One essential rule in database design is that the information in the fields must be atomic, meaning that it cannot be further subdivided into smaller units. (We called such items *tokens* in the searching sections of Chapter 3.) For example, the scientific name is made up of two words: the genus and the species. Our specification of scientific_name was a single 30-character string of letters, sufficient to give both components of any scientific name. Because fields must be atomic, the scientific_name can be used only in its entirety, not by its two component parts. We can search on the whole entry (e.g., Orcinus·orca) but not on a part of it (e.g., orca).

If we had wanted to treat the genus and species separately, we should have replaced the original specification

scientific_name	character 30	Genus and species

with

genus	character 15	Genus
species_name	character 15	Species

allowing searches or grouping based on either the genus or the species name. Though separating the two has its advantages, keeping the scientific name together has its advantages, too, because we will probably treat the names as a monolithic unit and do not plan to change either name separately. Predicting the usage is a difficult aspect of database design. Notice that the length range could also have been broken into two fields: the lower and upper ends of the range. If the limits are stored separately to allow manipulating them separately, each will be stored as a number.

Finally, there is the problem of data types such as dates (e.g., 14 July 2002), time (e.g., 12:57:21), and money (e.g., $199.95), which are constructed out of parts (days and months) or have special characteristics (only two decimal places) or both. Strictly speaking, such data should be kept in separate fields, stored in its most primitive unit—seconds or pennies—and specially maintained to preserve the necessary characteristics. Doing so is tedious, so database systems create special data types—dates, time, currency—that automatically preserve these properties and allow the subfields to be referenced when necessary. This is a safe way to "cheat" on the atomic property for those few types of information. The problem of atomicity still arises frequently, however, with such data as addresses.

Keys. Entities must be distinguishable. That is, if like rice grains or amoebas you can't tell the data items apart, they're not entities. A further database requirement is that the fields chosen for the table are sufficient to distinguish the entities of the table; that is, every row is different. Usually one or a few of the fields make this property true. A field for which all rows have a different value is known as a *key*. For example, because the English names for whales are unique, the name field is a key for the table in Figure 13.3. The scientific_name is also a key. Keys are used to identify a row. For example, we can look up the second row either by the value Killer in the name field or Orcinus·orca in the scientific_name field because either one uniquely specifies a row. It is common for a table to have more than one key, so we designate one of the keys as the *primary key*, which tells the database system that among the possible keys, this field is the one to use as the key. The uses for keys will be described later in this chapter.

Being Assertive. Specifying a key states that *as a property of the data* all tuples for all time will have different values for that field. Sometimes we notice a column with different values, for example, Whales.weight, but if it is not a requirement of the data—whales could weigh the same—it's not a key. Thus saying a field is a key is an assertion, not an observation.

Let's summarize the important points of the last two sections. Tables in databases are not simply an arrangement of text, that is, a picture, but they have a structure that is specified. The structure of database tables is separated from their contents. A table represents a set of entities—any things distinguishable by their attributes—by naming fields for the attributes' values and giving the data types for those fields. The instances of the entities of the table are represented as tuples. We use *rows* as a synonym for tuples and *column* as a synonym for field, but understand that both rows and columns are unordered in databases. (Of course, when defining a table or displaying it, we must list the fields in some order, and we can always sort the tuples when printing them out.) Tables and fields have names that should be descriptive, the fields must be atomic (i.e., indivisible) and one field—the primary key—has the property that it will have a different value for every row in the table.

DB Redundancy Is Bad, Very, Very, Very Bad

Though a database can be formed from a single table, the more typical case is for it to be composed of several tables. The collection of entity (and other) descriptions defining a database is known as a *database schema,* or *database scheme*. Interactive software often assists in defining a database schema, but as seen in the last section, declaring the entity's structure is not particularly difficult. Of course, if a database has multiple tables, they are probably not unrelated. In this section we consider how to relate them.

A fundamental rule of database design can be informally stated as: *Never duplicate information.* It's common sense that avoiding duplication, or *redundancy,* as it's known, is good because storing multiple copies of the same information must require more resources, for example, disk storage, than storing only a single copy. But, saving disk space is not the motivation—it is so inexpensive that there is little economy in saving it.

The main reason to avoid duplication is to avoid *inconsistency*. That is, the "same" value stored in different tables of the database could differ in its different locations. For example, we might change one and forget to change the other. If the values stored in one database table indicate that, say, your home address is 1011 Passing Lane, and another table indicates your home is 4 Wheel Drive, the database is inconsistent. Which, if either, is correct? The database yields no information. Inconsistent data, known as *garbage*, is actually worse than having no data at all because with no value for the address, the tuple could be flagged and someone could contact you to find out your address. Inconsistent data "looks good" in each table. Because duplication opens up the opportunity for inconsistency, which has the potential of converting perfectly good data into garbage, we adopt the rule: *Never duplicate information.*[1]

Why is duplication such a problem? Consider the campus organizations that need your permanent address:

- Administration—to send tuition bills
- Dean—to send notification of your outstanding grades
- Library—to send notices of your outstanding books
- Sports center—to send your Outstanding Athlete trophy

And many more campus units from the parking office to the theater may need your permanent address.

Typically these campus units each ask you to fill out a form or a card with your home address, and they may even go to the effort to record it in a database. But doing so is a waste of everyone's time—especially yours! These multiple copies can become inconsistent if one, but not all, are changed. You might remember to tell the administration that your address changed, but will you remember all the rest?

There is a better way, and it's familiar:

> **Data Reference.** The college should keep a table recording permanent addresses together with each student's Student ID number; the other campus units should record only the Student ID numbers and whatever data is pertinent to their purposes. When a

[1] Of course, just because data is in a database doesn't guarantee that it's accurate. It could have been entered incorrectly, or not revised when it changed. Our concern here is in maintaining a database's internal consistency.

home address is needed, they simply locate the address in the permanent address table using the Student ID as a reference.

When permanent addresses change, they can be corrected in one place and all campus units will have the current, accurate copy thereafter.

The Student_ID, which is unique for each student, is a primary key for the college's student records including the permanent address table. Thus the solution to redundancy—and therefore the way to avoid inconsistency—is to store the data in only one table and in all other tables store a key to the information rather than duplicating the information (i.e., *refer* to the information instead of replicating it). But there is more to the problem.

Physical and Logical Tables

An important distinction when organizing a database is the difference between how it is organized into tables to be stored on the hard disk of our computer system—the *physical* representation—and how it is to be organized for viewing by the users—the *logical* representation. For example, considerations such as avoiding inconsistency, using only a small amount of disk space, providing rapid access, and so on—and other technical design guidelines that we will not consider—influence how the physical database is arranged. It has nothing to do with how we would like to *look* at the data.

On the other hand, how users see the data of the database—the most important aspect of the design—should be determined by what information they contribute to it, what information they need to do their work, whether they have the authority to access certain information, and so on. It is unlikely that the tables of the physical database will match these requirements. More significantly, because different people have different uses, different levels of authority, and so forth, they cannot all use the same tables anyway. Therefore, we think of a logical database—tables separate from the physical tables—that is customized to each user group. These tables are *virtual tables*, meaning that we define them and use them as if they actually exist, but they do not. Logical tables are constructed on the fly by the computer from the information stored in the physical database. Logical databases are often referred to as *database views*, a term that conveys the idea of *looking at the database* in a certain way.

To illustrate these ideas, imagine a college has at least two entities defined in its physical database schema:

Student

Field	Type	Description
Student_ID	Number	8 digits
First_Name	Character 25	Single name, starting with a capital
Middle_Name	Character 25	All other names
Last_Name	Character 25	Family name
Birthdate	Date	
On_Probation	Boolean	0 = good standing; 1 = academic trouble

Primary Key: Student_ID

Home_Base

Field	Type	Description
Student_ID	Number	8 digits
Street_Address	Character 100	All address info before city
City	Character 25	No abbreviations like NYC
State	Character 25	Or province, canton, prefecture, etc.
Country	Character 25	Standard postal abbreviations OK
Postal Code	Character 10	Most including ZIP+4 are not numbers

Primary Key: Student_ID

The intent of the Student entity is to associate a student with his or her Student_ID. The information stored is basic to the person's identity. The Home_Base entity records a student's permanent address. Though these two entities are separate, the intent is that the Home_Base entity records student addresses and connects them to the Student_ID. We say that there is a *relationship* between the two entities. Specifically, there is a direct correspondence between tuples of the Home_Base table and the tuples of the Student table. Each address in the Home_Base table refers to exactly one student because a student couldn't have two addresses in the Home_Base table without both rows having the same Student_ID field, which is not legal because it is a key. (Keys must be unique.) If it is also true that every student has an address—most colleges won't admit a person without a complete application form containing a permanent address—there is a one-to-one relationship between Student and Home_Base; each student in Student refers to exactly one address in Home_Base. These relationships are extremely important as we now see.

> **Key Idea.** Notice that the Student_ID allows people and computers to locate and record information on students. It greatly simplifies a college's database design to have a unique number, which is why it is assigned, of course. Names wouldn't work because they're not unique, as anyone named Bill Clinton—who's not the former president—well knows.

Because there is such a close correspondence between the information in the Student and Home_Base tables, we can *imagine* constructing a single table containing the combined information from both tables.

Student_ID
First_Name
Middle_Name
Last_Name
Birthdate
On_Probation
Street_Address
City
State
Country
Postal_Code

This combined table would not actually exist, but we could display it by showing the first six attributes from the Student table, looking up the corresponding tuple in the Home_Base table using the Student_ID value, and retrieving the last five entries. (The Student_ID field need not be repeated.) Such a logical table could be the school administrator's view of the data. The table doesn't exist, but the administrator might think it does because anytime he or she requests it, it is reconstructed. (It is constructed using the Join operation, explained in a later section.)

This keeping-a-table-in-two-parts-but-showing-it-as-one seems silly. Would there be any harm in storing it as one table? Probably not if everyone needing the address information is authorized to see the entire student record—including, for example, the On_Probation status. If not, separate tables are best because access to the address can be wider than access to the Student table.

Consider other entities in the college's database schema that need address information, say, for the Dean's office and the sports center:

```
Top_Scholar                      Good_Sport
    Student_ID                          Student_ID
    Nickname                            Locker Number
    Major                               Deposit_Amt
    GPA                                 Sport
Primary Key:  Student_ID         Primary Key: Student_ID
```

(We dispense with defining the field information while we are designing the database.) The Top_Scholar and Good_Sport tables have a one-to-one relationship with the Home_Base table, based on the Student_ID attribute. For each scholar, there is a unique address in Home_Base, as there is for each athlete. Thus a combined table can be created on the fly for the Dean's office and for the sports center, drawing on data from the Student table, the Home_Base table, and from the specific tables stored by those offices—Top_Scholar or Good_Sport (see right).

Student_ID	Student_ID
First_Name	First_Name
Middle_Name	Middle_Name
Last_Name	Last_Name
Birthdate	Birthdate
Street_Address	Street_Address
City	City
State	State
Country	Country
Nickname	Locker Number
Major	Deposit_Amt
GPA	Sport

As before, these are logical tables that don't exist but are created. They have the data pertinent to the office, but they also have the name, which wasn't stored, and the correct address information. Organizing the data into a separate Home_Base table removed duplication of address data, allowing us to avoid the hazards of redundancy.

The essential requirement for constructing the logical tables from the physical tables was the availability of the relationship between the tables based on the Student ID. It said how to use information in a table (e.g., the Student_ID field of Good_Sport) to find information in another table (e.g., address information in Home_Base).

ER Without Trauma

Obviously relationships are important. One aspect of relationships not discussed in the last section is that relationships have names, like everything in computing. Familiar named relationships that we encounter everyday are

- Father Of relationship between a male parent and his child
- Daughter Of relationship between a female child and her parent
- Employee relationships between people and companies
- Stars In relationships between actors and movies

There are hundreds. Names of database relationships should be meaningful as an assist to people working with the database, but like all names in computing, the computer doesn't know whether the name makes sense or not.

The original one-to-one relationship between the Home_Base and Student entities discussed in the last section might be called Home_Of. When we agreed that no student would be admitted unless he or she had a permanent address, we introduced the opposite relationship, Lives_At from Student tuples to Home_Base tuples. The one-to-one relationship between Top_Scholars and Home_Base might be called Resides_At because it is a different relationship than Lives_At and anyone on the Dean's List probably has a larger vocabulary. The reason Lives_At and Resides_At are different (even though they seem to express the same informal connection) is because they relate different entities.

With many entities, attributes, keys, and relationships in a large database, the design can get confusing. For this reason, database administrators and others who work daily with databases employ a shorthand notation for visualizing relationships using an arrow between boxes representing entities.

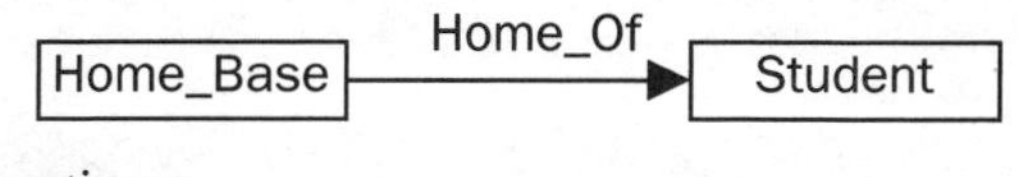

Such a diagram is known as an *Entity-Relationship Diagram*, or more briefly, an *ER Diagram*. It visually indicates that tuples of the Home_Base entity (addresses) are associated with tuples of the Student entity in a relationship that the DB designer is calling Home_Of. The relationships and entities of the last section can be expressed as the ER Diagram in Figure 13.4. As we shall see, ER Diagrams help us make sense out of the relationships among the entities.

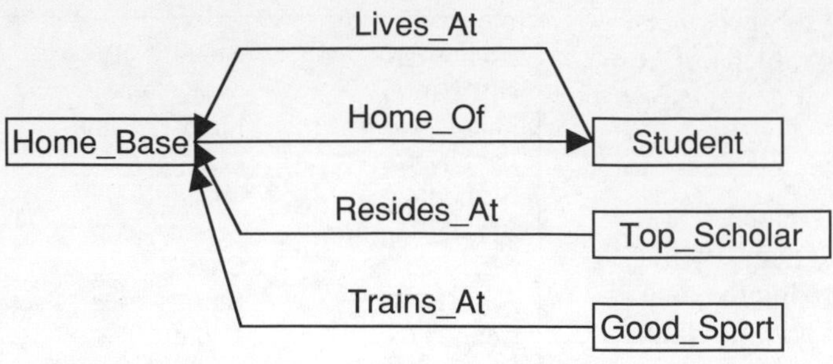

Figure 13.4. ER Diagram for the entities and relationships involving Home_Base.

The ER Diagram displays relationships among a set of entities. In its simplest form, it uses arrows to represent the relationships between the boxes that represent the entities. That's the form just given. But, slight variations on this form can also be helpful. One form shows the entity name outside the box and lists the attributes of the entity inside the box.

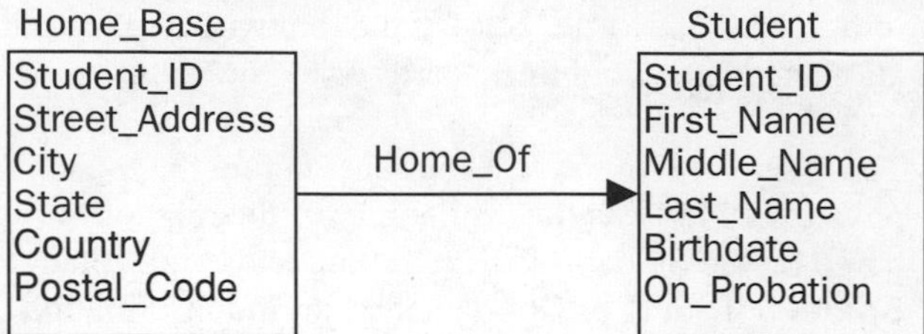

The formulation is the same, but more information is given. More embellishments are possible, but they all capture the same idea.

Operations on Tables

A sensible and convenient use of tables is to construct other tables from them. This is also how the logical tables are created from the physical tables. In this section, we explain how this process works using a database table of the countries of the world from a travel agency. Its structure and sample entries are shown in Figure 13.5. To build a personal archive of places we'd like to travel to, we must transform the travel agency's table, as we now explain.

Nations

Name	Character 15	Common rather than official name
Domain	Character 2	Internet domain name
Capital	Character 20	Nation's capital
Latitude	Number	Approx. latitude of capital
N_S	Boolean	Latitude is N(orth) or S(outh)
Longitude	Number	Approx. longitude of capital
E_W	Boolean	Longitude is E(ast) or W(est)
One_Word	Character 50	A word describing the country

Primary Key: Domain

Name	Dom	Capital	Lat	NS	Log	EW	Word
Ireland	IE	Dublin	52	N	7	W	History
Israel	IR	Jerusalem	32	N	34	E	History
Italy	IT	Rome	41	N	12	E	Art
Jamaica	JM	Kingston	17	N	77	W	Beach
Japan	JP	Tokyo	35	N	143	E	Kabuki

Figure 13.5. The Nations table definition and sample entries. Notice that the text labels for the columns are not the field names.

Five basic operations can be performed on tables: Select, Project, Union, Difference, and Product. Most students will not have encountered these before, but they are nevertheless very intuitive.

Select

The operation of taking rows from a table to produce a new table is known as Select. Generally the selection operation is specified by giving the (single) table from which rows are to be selected and the criterion for selection. These components can be expressed using the syntax

Select_from *Table* On *Criterion*

The *Criterion* gives a test to be applied to each tuple of the existing table to decide if it's included in the new table. The *Criterion* is a short formula that tests field values written using field names, constants like numbers or letter strings, and the relational operators $<, \leq, =, \neq, \geq, >$. The relational operators just test whether the field has a particular relationship, for example, Word = 'Beach' or Latitude < 45. If the *Criterion* is true, the tuple is included in the new table; otherwise, it is ignored. Notice that the information used to create the new table is a copy, so the original table is not changed by Select (or any of the table building operations discussed here).

Thinking that you would like the basis for your travels to be beaches, you formulate a query to extract a list of all of the countries that have Beach as their one-word description. The query would be

```
Select_from Nations On One_Word = 'Beach'
```

which produces a new table that is shown in part in Figure 13.6. Notice that the information in the final column is constant because the *Criterion* required that specific field entry.

Name	Dom	Capital	Lat	NS	Log	EW	Word
Australia	AU	Canberra	37	S	148	E	Beach
Bahamas	BS	Nassau	25	N	78	W	Beach
Barbados	BB	Bridgetown	13	N	59	W	Beach
Belize	BZ	Belize	17	N	89	W	Beach
Bermuda	BM	Hamilton	32	N	64	W	Beach

Figure 13.6. A portion of the table resulting from selecting Nations with the criterion that the One_Word description be "Beach."

The *Criterion* can be more complex than testing a single value. For example, the logical operations of AND and OR can be used in the same way they were used to search in Chapters 5 and 6. So, for example, to find countries whose capitals are at least 60° north latitude, we write

```
Select_from Nations On Latitude ≥ 60 AND N_S = 'N'
```

which should produce a four-row table formed from Greenland, Iceland, Norway, and Finland.

Project

If it is possible to pick out rows of a table (using Select), it must be possible to pick out columns as well. Project is the operation that constructs a new table out of the columns of an existing table. The name of the existing table and columns to be included in the new table, indicated by their field names, are all that must be specified. The syntax

Project *Field_List* From *Table*

specifies the components of Project. For example, to create a new table from the Nations table without the capital and position information, that is, to keep the other three columns, write

```
Project Name, Domain, One_Word From Nations
```

The resulting table will have as many rows as the Nations table, but just three columns. See Figure 13.7 for a portion of the result.

Name	Dom	Word
Nauru	NR	Beach
Nepal	NP	Mountains
Netherlands	NL	Art
New Caledonia	NC	Beach
New Zealand	NZ	Adventure

Figure 13.7 Sample entries for a Project operation on Nations.

Project does not require that the resulting table have the same number of rows as the original table. When, as in the last example, the new table includes a key from the old table, the key makes each row distinct, all rows will be present, and both tables have the same number of rows. But if some of the table's rows, when restricted only to the Project columns, are identical, they will be merged together into a single row, reducing the number of rows in the result, and causing the two tables to have different numbers of rows. Merging is required because of the rule forcing the tuples of any table to always be distinct. So, for example, to see what the single-word descriptions travel agents use to describe countries, we create a new table of the last column of Nations

```
Project One_Word From Nations
```

which produces a one-column table with a row for each descriptive word, for example, History appears once and Art appears once. Thus the table has as many rows as unique words, not as many rows as Nations.

Most often Select and Project operations are used together because base tables are often "trimmed" to keep only some of the rows and some of the columns. To illustrate, name the table of the countries with northern capitals Northern and define it with the command

```
Northern = (Select_from Nations On Latitude ≥ 60 AND N_S = 'N')
```

which is the four-element subtable of Nations constructed earlier. To throw away everything except the name, domain, and latitude, write

```
Project Name, Domain, Latitude From Northern
```

Name	Dom	Lat
Finland	FI	64
Greenland	GL	72
Iceland	IS	65
Norway	NO	62

Figure 13.8. Trimmed table of the countries with northern capitals.

to produce the items in Figure 13.8. An equivalent way to achieve the same result simply combines the two operations

```
Project Name, Domain, Latitude From
        (Select_from Nations On Latitude ≥ 60 AND N_S = 'N')
```

Because it avoids creating and saving the intermediate table, the latter might be a slightly more efficient solution if the Northern table is not needed for any other purpose, but generally either solution is fine.

Union

Besides picking out rows and columns of a table, another obvious operation on tables is to combine two tables. This only makes sense if they have the same set of attributes, of course. The operation is known as Union, written as though it were addition

*Table*1 + *Table*2

It can be read "combined with." So, if the table of countries with capitals at least 45° south latitude are named Southern with the command

```
Southern = (Select_from Nations On Latitude ≥ 45 AND N_S = 'S')
```

then countries where the Northern or Southern Lights should be visible—call it Aurora—would be

```
Aurora = Northern + Southern
```

Name	Dom	Capital	Lat	NS	Log	EW	Word
Falkland Is	FK	Stanley	51	S	58	W	Nature
Finland	FI	Helsinki	64	N	26	E	Nature
Greenland	GL	Nuuk	72	N	40	W	Nature
Iceland	IS	Reykjavik	65	N	18	W	Geysers
Norway	NO	Oslo	62	N	10	E	Vikings

Figure 13.9. The Aurora table created with Union.

and is shown in Figure 13.9. This table could have been created with a complex Select command. A more typical case for Union is to combine separate tables, say, Nations with Canada_Territories. (The Domain field would be CA for all of them.) For example, had the Northern table been defined by

```
Select_from (Nations + Canada_Territories) On Latitude ≥ 60 AND N_S = 'N'
```

then Yukon would be included because its capital Whitehorse is north of 60°.

Difference

The opposite of combining two tables with Union is to remove from one table the items also listed in a second table. The operation is known as Difference and it is written with the obvious syntax

*Table*1 – *Table*2

Like Union, Difference only makes sense when the table's fields are the same. For example,

Nations – Northern

produces a table identical to Nations but without the countries having northerly capitals, that is, without Finland, Greenland, Iceland, and Norway. Interestingly, this same command works just as well if Northern had included Canadian territories like the Yukon. That is, in a Difference command the items "subtracted away" do not have to exist in the original table.

Product

Adding and subtracting tables are easy. What would multiply be like? The Product operation on tables, which is written as

*Table*1 × *Table*2

creates a super table. The table has all the fields from *both* tables. So, if the first table has five fields and the second table has six fields, the Product table has eleven fields. The rows of the new table are created by concatenating each row of the left table to each row of the right table, that is, putting the tuples together. The result is the "product" of the rows of each table. For example, if the first table is Nations with 230 rows, and the second table has 4 rows, the "all combinations" aspect of Product implies there will be 230 × 4 = 920 rows because each row of the first table would be concatenated with each row of the second table to produce a row of the result.

For example, suppose there is a table of your traveling companions as described in Figure 13.10(a) containing the information shown in Figure 13.10(b). Then the Product operation

Nations × Travelers

creates a new table with ten fields—eight fields from Nations and two fields from Travelers—and 920 rows. Some of the rows of the new table are shown in Figure 13.11. The "all combinations" property means that for each country, there is a row for each of your friends. Notice that the field name Name occurs in each table, so for the Product table, some change is necessary to keep the field names unique.

Travelers
Name
Homeland
Primary Key: Name

(a)

Name	Homeland
Isabella	Argentina
Brian	South Africa
Wen	China
Clare	Canada

(b)

Figure 13.10. The definition of the Travelers table and its values.

The Product operation may seem a little odd initially because its "all combinations" approach associates information that may not "belong together." And it's true. But most often, Product is used to create a super table that contains both useful and useless rows, and then it is "trimmed down" using Select, Project, and Difference to contain the exact information desired. This is a powerful approach that we will see many times.

Name1	Dom	Capital	Lat	NS	Log	EW	Word	Name2	Homeland
Cyprus	CY	Nicosia	35	N	32	E	History	Clare	Canada
Czech Rep.	CZ	Prague	51	N	15	E	Pilsner	Isabella	Argentina
Czech Rep.	CZ	Prague	51	N	15	E	Pilsner	Brian	South Africa
Czech Rep.	CZ	Prague	51	N	15	E	Pilsner	Wen	China
Czech Rep.	CZ	Prague	51	N	15	E	Pilsner	Clare	Canada
Denmark	DK	Copenhagen	55	N	12	E	History	Isabella	Argentina

Figure 13.11. Some rows from the product of Nations and Travelers; for each row in Nations and each row in Travelers, there is a row in the product table that combines them.

To illustrate, suppose your traveling companions volunteer to tutor students preparing for the National Geographic Society's Geography Bee. Each friend agrees to tutor students "on their part of the world," that is, in the quadrant of the world from which they come. So, Isabella, coming from Argentina in the Southern and Western Hemispheres, agrees to tutor students on the geography of that part of the world, and so on. Then you can produce a master list of who's responsible for each country with the commands

```
Super  = Nations × Travelers
Assign =   ( Select_from Super On N_S = 'S' AND E_W = 'W' AND Name2 = 'Isabella' )
          +( Select_from Super On N_S = 'S' AND E_W = 'E' AND Name2 = 'Brian' )
          +( Select_from Super On N_S = 'N' AND E_W = 'E' AND Name2 = 'Wen' )
          +( Select_from Super On N_S = 'N' AND E_W = 'W' AND Name2 = 'Clare' )
Master= Project Name1, Name2 From Assign
```

How do these commands accomplish the goal? The Super table is the product table discussed earlier with a row for each nation paired with each friend. Then the Assign list is created by the Union operation (+) that combines four tables each created by a Select operation from Super. The first Select keeps only those countries from Super with Isabella's name that are also in the Southern and Western Hemispheres. The second Select keeps only those countries from Super with Brian's name that are in the Southern and Eastern Hemispheres. And similarly for Wen and Clare. The resulting Assign table has 230 rows—the same as the original Nations table—with one of your friends' names assigned to each country.

We know that all of the countries are in the Assign table because every country is in one of the four hemisphere pairs and each has a row for each friend. When the right combination "comes up," the nation will be selected. In addition, Assign has the property that each person is given countries in "their" part of the world. (Wen seems to have been assigned the greatest amount of work!) Finally, we throw away all of the location information for our Master list, keeping only the names. Part of the result is shown in Figure 13.12.

Name1	Name2
Chad	Wen
Chile	Isabella
China	Wen
Christmas Is.	Clare
Cocos Is.	Brian

Figure 13.12. A portion of the Master table.

> **Quotient Intelligence**. There *is* a divide operation on tables, but it's complicated and rather bizarre. Because it doesn't provide any new capabilities, we leave it to the experts.

Summary

We have introduced the five fundamental operations on tables. Though we may not have been familiar with "adding" two tables together or have known about projection, these transformations on tables were straightforward. It is surprising, therefore, that these five are sufficient to create any table that is possible in the relational database world. In practice, we will rarely use the operations directly. Rather, they will be incorporated into database software in ways so natural that if we are thinking about creating tables from other tables—the point of learning them—we will hardly be aware they are being used.

Join the Team

Join is a powerful and useful operation for creating database tables. Indeed, it is so useful that although Join can be defined from the five primitive database operations of the previous section, it is usually accorded the status of a separate operator. In concept, Join combines two tables like the Product operator does, except that if the two tables have a common field, the new table produced by Join includes only rows from the given tables that match on that field, not all pairings of rows like the Product. We write the Join operation as follows

*Table*1 ⋈ *Table*2

The "bow tie" operator is to suggest a special form of Product in which the two tables "match up."

We have already seen Join in an earlier section, when we were manipulating the college database. Recall that we introduced the Dean's table, Top_Scholar, that didn't contain home addresses, and the Home_Base table that did. We observed that by matching the Student_ID fields of both tables, it is possible to create a table for the Dean that contains the information from both Top_Scholar and Home_Base. That action was the Join of the two tables, that is

Top_Scholar ⋈ Home_Base

An example is shown in Figure 13.13.

So, Join is a "look-up" operation on tables that have one or more attributes in common. A result row is created out of the fields of each pair of rows from the given tables that match on their common attributes. Another way to understand the Join of two tables, TableA ⋈ TableB, is to think of the computer as first forming the Product of the two tables, that is, TableA × TableB, which creates an intermediate table of all pairs of rows from the two given tables, and then saving all rows in which the common fields match using a Select. Finally, a Project is used to keep all of the columns except the duplicates—those in common. The computer doesn't actually do this, of course, but the outcome is the same as if it did.

> **It's Natural**. Join, as described, is actually the Natural Join because the natural meaning of "to match" is for the fields to be equal. But databases being IT, it's possible to use any relational operator (<, ≤, =, ≠, ≥, >) not just = to compare the common field. Unnatural or not, a Join where T1.tupleID < T2.tupleID is handy.

As a second example, what does the Join

Nations ⋈ $_{\text{(Nations.Name = Travelers.Homeland)}}$ Travelers

produce? Here the Join has been written so that the "match" between the rows of Nations and Travelers is stated explicitly. Thinking for a moment about a row in Nations (say, Afghanistan's row) and a row in Travelers (say, Isabella's row), we see that they don't match because she's from Argentina. In fact, the only rows from Nations that will match rows in Travelers are the four rows for the home countries of the Travelers. Thus the result is a four-row, nine-column table—the duplicated column (Name or Homeland) is removed—where each person's name is appended to the Nations entry for their home country.

Student_ID	Nickname	Major	GPA
1006616	Candy	PoliSci	3.82
1007250	Jake T	Chem	3.79
1010043	Broadway Joe	PoliSci	3.80
...	...	...	...

Student_ID	Street_Address	City	State	Country	Postal_Code
0998185	1 Rocky Rd	Burnaby	BC	Canada	V6N 4T4
1006616	61 Peekaboo St	Vail	CO	USA	71021
1006681	1011 Passing Ln	Ames	IA	USA	50502
1007250	4 Wheel Dr	Daytona	FL	USA	32330
1010043	302 Second Pl	New York	NY	USA	10011
...	...	...	...	...	...

Student_ID	Nickname	Major	GPA	Street_Address	City	State	Country	Postal_Code
1006616	Candy	PoliSci	3.82	61 Peekaboo St	Vail	CO	USA	71021
1007250	Jake T	Chem	3.79	4 Wheel Dr	Daytona	FL	USA	32330
1010043	Broadway Joe	History	3.80	302 Second Pl	NewYork	NY	USA	10011
...	...	...	...	...	...	...	...	...

Figure 13.13. Sample values for Top_Scholar, Home_Base, and the result of TopScholar _ Home_Base. Notice that only one copy of the common field (Student_ID) is included.

Queries: Putting It All Together

Having warned against redundancy, introduced the fundamental operations on database tables and showed how Join could be used to look up information in two tables to create another table, we are ready to put the whole picture together.

Imagine that our physical database has been organized so that the information is stored in tables to minimize redundancy, along the lines of the college database tables introduced earlier. Relationships exist among these tables and, using an ER Diagram, the relationships can be displayed as shown in Figure 13.4. Specific users such as the Dean will want to have their own view of the data being stored. In that spirit, imagine that the Dean wants to see a table, known as the Dean's View, containing the following information:

Deans_View		
Nickname	Used by the Dean to seem "chummy" toward students	Top_Scholar
First_Name	Name information required because	Student
Middle_Name	the dean forgets the person's	Student
Last_Name	actual name, being so chummy	Student
Birthdate	Needs to know if the student is of "drinking age"	Student
City	Hometown (given by city, state) is important for small talk,	Home_Base
State	but actual street address not needed by Dean	Home_Base
Major	Indicates what the student's doing in college besides hanging out	Top_Scholar
GPA	Need to know how the student is doing gradewise	Top_Scholar

This is a table specification, of course, but not for any table that actually exists in the physical database. Rather, it is composed of information that is stored in several tables, as indicated by the final column. What we want to do is to specify to the computer how to create the Dean's View—a logical table—from the tables that are actually stored in the database—the physical tables. To do this, we define a *query*, a computation to produce a table using the operations on tables explained earlier. The computer creates the logical or virtual table, by evaluating the query operations and creating the Dean's View. The Dean thinks the table actually exists. Consider how this is done.

The first step is to note that the Dean's View contains information from three tables: Top_Scholar, the table actually storing the data the Dean wants kept; Student, the college's permanent record of the student; and Home_Base, the college's current address list. The information for each student must be associated to create the Dean's View table and the Join operation is the key to doing this. The expression

Top_Scholar ⋈ Student ⋈ Home_Base

makes a table that has a row for each student in the Dean's Top_Scholar table, but it has all of the information from all three tables. The association of each student's row in each table is accomplished by matching on the Student_ID attribute. (Of course, the operations are performed in pairs; for example Student ⋈ Home_Base might be performed first, producing an intermediate table, say, T1, and then Top_Scholar ⋈ T1 is performed. The order of operations doesn't matter with Join.)

The resulting table contains too much information, of course, because it has all columns from the three tables, except for the repeated Student_ID. The Dean doesn't want to see so much. So, the second step is to retrieve only that information of interest to the Dean. Retrieving columns is performed by Project, and all that is needed is to specify which columns the Dean wants:

Project Nickname, First_Name, Middle_Name, Last_Name,
Birthdate, City, State, Major, GPA
From Top_Scholar ⋈ Student ⋈ Home_Base

In English, the query says "Save out the Nickname column, First_Name column ande so forth, from the table that is formed by joining, that is, associating on Student_ID, the three tables Top_Scholar, Student and Home_Base." This is precisely what the Dean wants. Therefore, the Deans_View table is not at all a new table stored in the computer, but rather a query to the database specifying how to construct the required table based on tables already stored. The Dean thinks we've set up a special table for his or her purposes. In reality, we store the data the way we must to reduce redundancy and improve convenience, and when the Dean wants to look at the data, we simply construct the Dean's View on the fly. Notice that the Dean doesn't even want to view the Student_ID, so it's not displayed. But it is essential to creating the table.

Database Systems

The relational database concepts just introduced are abstract and independent of any specific database system. As a result, the syntax for operations such as Select has been invented for use here and does not match any particular implementation. Learning the principles abstractly ensures that we are learning the foundations on which every vendor's software is based. But to use a database, you must use some vendor's software.

Fortunately there is a standard language in wide use, SQL, the Structured Query Language. As the name suggests, SQL doesn't expect that you will create arbitrary queries using the full power of the five fundamental relational database operators of the previous sections. Rather it provides a specific query structure that users must follow. This format is expressive, so it suffices for defining a rich set of tables, and because it has a particular structure, the software can implement the operations efficiently. This is important because databases are usually large, and because they are stored on (relatively slow) hard disks, they can potentially be time consuming to manipulate.

Though vendors have their own dialects of SQL—and SQL is complicated to begin with—it is still possible to give the flavor of its structured queries. SQL's query structure begins with the keyword SELECT and typically includes a FROM clause and a WHERE clause. (Confusingly, SELECT in SQL means *select fields*, and very closely approximates Project of the abstract presentation given earlier; unfortunately these two standard sets of terms conflict.) FROM gives the table(s) that the fields are to be taken from, and WHERE specifies any additional conditions that must be met. If multiple tables are given in the FROM clause, they are combined using Product, but a common technique is to combine the tables into a single table with a Join. SQL has multiple kinds of Joins, but the INNER JOIN type corresponds to Join as given earlier. The main difference is that the "match fields" must be specified explicitly using an ON clause (and so they don't need to have the same name).

Thus the Dean's View constructed in the last section using our conceptual query

```
Project Nickname, First_Name, Middle_Name, Last_Name,
    Birthdate, City,State, Major, GPA
From Top_Scholar _ (Student _ Home_Base)
```

can be created in SQL using the query

```
SELECT    Top_Scholar.Nickname, Student.First_Name,
          Student_Middle_Name,    Student.Last_Name,
          Student.Birthdate, Home_Base.City, Home_Base.State,
          Top_Scholar.Major, Top_Scholar.GPA
FROM      Top_Scholar INNER JOIN
      (Student INNER JOIN Home_Base
          ON Student.Student_ID=Home_Base.Student_ID)
          ON Top_Scholar.Student_ID = Student.Student_ID
```

where the tables have been color coded blue and the fields color coded purple to improve readability. Notice first that following the SELECT is the list of fields that form the Dean's view. Then the FROM field has two Joins that have been grouped as shown in the preceding abstract form. First Student and Home_Base are joined ON equal Student_IDs, and then the Top_Scholar is joined with the result, again ON matching Student_IDs. There is no WHERE clause because the Dean's View doesn't require further limiting. However, if the Dean wanted to view only students whose GPA is greater than 3.7, a WHERE clause can implement that criterion:

```
SELECT Top_Scholar.Nickname, Student.First_Name,
       Student_Middle_Name, Student.Last_Name, Student.Birthdate,
       Home_Base.City, Home_Base.State,  Top_Scholar.Major,
       Top_Scholar.GPA
FROM Top_Scholar INNER JOIN
  (Student INNER JOIN
       Home_Base ON Student.Student_ID=Home_Base.Student_ID)
WHERE Top_Scholar.GPA > 3.7
```

Interestingly, the WHERE constraint implements the behavior of our abstract Select operator. Though the SQL query is longer because the table must be specified with each field using the dot notation and the fields ON which the match is based must be specified, the result embodies the abstract principles quite well.

This SQL example is only the tip of an enormous query language iceberg. Many very handy embellishments can be included in SQL queries. And learning the dialectical differences of your system will be necessary—though not particularly difficult—now that the abstract ideas are well established.

SUMMARY

That's it. The secret of modern databases is that many of the tables we see don't actually exist, but rather are logical tables constructed for us on the fly based on queries from the physical tables that do exist. An underlying structure of tables and relationships has been carefully designed by the database administrator—that's a professional database manager, or us if we create our own databases. The design for the physically stored tables is optimized to avoid problems such as redundancy and enhance convenience, performance, and other benefits. If the physically represented tables have been set up properly, it is a straightforward matter to give users whatever view of the data they may want using a query. To ensure that the data is correct and fresh, this view is created each time it is needed.

To achieve these qualities, computer scientists created the abstraction of a relational database. We motivated their ideas and terminology for tables by contrasting an informal table with one whose structure was explicit and useful to a computer. Tables of relational databases have names, and fields that describe the attributes of the entities contained in the table. The data quantitatively recording each property has a specific data type and is atomic. When multiple tables explicitly record the same information, like mailing address, the entries in the different tables could differ, producing garbage. Garbage is worse than no data at all. We showed how such redundancy could be avoided by a careful table organization and the use of keys to support relationships among the tables. Operations such as Join allow the separate tables to be combined to form the logical views that database users want to see, while preserving the stored-once property of the computer's representation. Join is an especially useful composite operation built from (some of) the five fundamental operations on tables: Select, Project, Union, Difference, and Product. Queries are the general mechanism for using these five operations to create and customize new tables. In practical databases, queries are expressed in SQL, the structured query language.

EXERCISES

1. What two differences distinguish everyday tables from database tables?
2. What sorts of things are stored in database tables?
3. List the three items required to define a table.
4. Why is redundancy so bad in a database system?
5. Compare and contrast Select and Project.
6. List the operation(s) to make a table of the names and domains of Southern Hemisphere countries.
7. If Table1 and Table2 are tables with the same attributes and Table1 + Table2 = SumTable, explain why their sharing common tuples causes Table1 ≠ SumTable – Table2.
8. Eliminate the Homeland and Capital from the Assign table.
9. Express the Aurora table using a single select.
10. Give a Select command for the table Nations – Northern.
11. If Table1 has 6 fields and 1000 tuples and Table2 has 8 fields and 70 tuples, how many fields and tuples does Table1 × Table2 have?

12. Using the analogy to numerical multiplication, what is the result of Table × TableEm if TableEm is empty, that is, has zero rows?

13. Write T1 ⋈ T2 using any of the five fundamental operations, assuming T1's attributes are A, B, C, D, and itemID, and T2's attributes are E, F, G, H, and itemID.

14. What characterizes a Natural Join?

15. In SQL, `SELECT` and `WHERE` are equivalent to what abstract database operators?

CHAPTER 14

HAI! Adventure Database Design

Learning Objectives

- Understand the problem solving strategy to be used.
- Learn by example how to design a database.
- Know how to perform a Needs Analysis.
- Understand the rationale for the physical DB tables.
- Know why Rentals must be redesigned.
- Understand the relationships of the Snow Machine tables.
- Learn how to formulate conceptual queries for logical views.
- Know how to express queries in SQL.
- Understand the problems of Class_List and the advantages of Activities and Apply.

This chapter concerns three college friends, Hon, Amanda, and Ian, who wasted way too much time hanging out together. During their senior year, while jogging in a last-ditch effort to get in shape before spring break, the three hatched a plan to go into business together. Their idea was to rent sports equipment to rich people at resorts in ski areas, tropical islands, and in the mountains, including lessons and guided activities such as dives and climbs. What would distinguish their business from others is that the employees—they plan to call them *adventure specialists*—will be very well trained, knowledgeable, "up," and helpful, giving their customers complete satisfaction so they return again and again to the business. To maintain their positive attitudes and dedication to the company, the adventure specialists will rotate among several resorts, in both the northern and southern hemispheres, working at different rental shops. And hanging out. The trio planned to call their business HAI! Adventure, knowing that *hai* is Japanese for "yes." Whether HAI! Adventure is a realistic business idea or not is irrelevant—it presents great opportunities for database design.

The major goal of the chapter is to work out the conceptual design of a database, using the ideas and principles from Chapter 13. To limit the problem to a manageable size initially, we focus on designing the database for a ski rental shop. That design will be created by a "needs analysis," that is, understanding the nature of the business activity, and then following the workflow of the shop, asking at each step what the information needs are for that activity. From the analysis will emerge a conceptual design. The next goal is to convert the conceptual design to an operational database using standard database software. Having completed the initial design, we consider how the design applies to other HAI! Adventure rental shops. The final goal of the chapter is to extend the database design to handle business activities such as lessons and guided tours. As before, the conceptual database is designed before trying to implement it, but with the lessons and guided tours extension, certain pitfalls of alternative designs will be discussed. The practical implementation follows. The overall objective is to illustrate how a significant database design activity can be conducted at a high conceptual level before considering all of the details of an implementation.

Strategy

Though this chapter focuses on the design for the HAI! Adventure database, the strategy to be followed has general applicability. Pay attention to the "big picture" of this specific example to learn how to create your own databases. Like most design activities, however, it is not possible to give an algorithm for creating a database. The steps used here can only be guidelines for other designs because the circumstances of each case are always different.

Though database design is not algorithmic, constructing databases follows a reasonably consistent pattern:

- **Needs Analysis**—Understand the context in which the database will be used, and list the kinds of data that must be captured from the users and the kinds of data that must be delivered to the users. It is often helpful to study the information "flow" through the organization or business that will use the database as it conducts its activities. The goal of the Needs Analysis is to understand what the goals of the database design should be.
- **Approximate and Revise a Conceptual Physical Design**—One approach to creating any design is to construct a rough solution and then to revise it. Once created, the solution can be assessed for its ability to fulfill the needs developed earlier, and where it fails, the solution can be revised. Because it is difficult to create the perfect design the first time, this iterative approach is often very effective. The criteria for evaluation include goals such as avoiding redundancy, and the ability to meet the user needs. For databases, the conceptual physical design is all "on paper"—often using ER Diagrams—making it easy to revise.
- **Fix the Physical Design and Define Relationships**—At some point, the revisions stop and the resulting design is "optimal" to this point in the design process. For databases, the physical tables will have been defined, and a series of relationships will have been established. If the process has been done thoughtfully, the physical design is finished and can be implemented. It is often a good idea to take the trouble to implement the physical tables at this point and fill them with some sample values. The process often reveals oversights or errors.
- **Design and Revise Conceptual Views of the Logical DB**—With the physical DB defined, the creation of the logical database is next. For this task consider who must interact with the database. Identifying the groups of users will define the (maximum) number of views needed. For each group determine what data they will enter into the database, and what data they must see from the database. The view will generally be the combination of these two types of infor-

mation. Assess how the groups will be served by the views, and possibly revise the designs.

- **Fix the Logical Database**—At some point, the views are defined. Next the queries that will create the views can be written down using the conceptual notations of Chapter 13. The process is easy: Determine what physical tables are required for the information included in the view, build a composite table using Join(s), and then trim for the desired rows and columns.
- **Implement the Database**—Finally, with the logical views defined, it is time to complete the implementation. This amounts to translating the views into the SQL dialect of your database software system and creating the GUIs with which the users will interact. Though the process can be tedious and detail oriented, the software makes significant efforts to assist.
- **Evaluate for Usefulness and (Possibly) Revise**—Like all designs, the database must be evaluated to be sure it fulfills the user's needs as far as possible. Though the design process just described should produce a very useful database, it is almost always possible to think of improvements. This is especially true once we've understood the value of having a database to support our activities. It seems to be a fact of human nature that there is no limit to people's wishes for software. The design can be revised to add more functionality.

The Problem

The database to be designed supports a business called HAI! Adventure, founded by three college friends. The business, when it is fully up and running, will be composed of many shops at various resort locations around the world. Each shop will offer equipment for a single activity such as skiing, wind surfing, scuba diving, mountain climbing, and kayaking. The focus is on renting high-quality equipment, but where appropriate the company plans to run "organized activities" such as lessons and guided tours. These activities—dives, climbs, bungee jumping, paragliding—will involve one or more customers and a responsible person such as a guide, leader, or instructor. Though the business will have other data processing needs such as payroll, receivables, taxes, and equipment management, they may be contracted. Our interest in the database design concerns supporting the customer-employee interactions in the direct transaction of the rentals and other business activities.

The ideal employees working for HAI! Adventure will be active, "outdoors" type people who like to travel. They will have some sort of training in an active sport to qualify them to competently rent sophisticated equipment such as scuba gear, and to serve as an instructor, guide or other responsible role. HAI! Adventure's employees are known as *adventure specialists*, and it is a benefit of the job that they will periodically change locations and activities. (It's clear what motivated our three entrepreneurs to come up with this business idea!)

Acknowledging that any business needs to start small, and as a simplification for the initial database design, assume the first HAI! Adventure business is a ski rental shop at a resort in the Canadian Rockies, The Snow Machine Ski Rental Shop (Snow Machine). The shop rents downhill skis and snowboards. The physical premises of Snow Machine are composed of four rooms—a large Entry Room through which the customers enter and leave, a large Fitting Room adjacent to it in which the customers get their equipment, an Equipment Room behind the Fitting Room where the gear is stowed and maintained, and a small Staff Room. A typical customer proceeds through the following stages:

- **Selection:** The customer comes to the store and is greeted by the receptionist. The equipment and services available and their prices are posted on the wall. When the customer has decided to rent equipment, he or she gives basic personal data to the receptionist, such as name, address, and local contact information. This information is entered into the database and forms the initial data for a rental.
- **Fitting:** The customer proceeds to the Fitting Room, where a specialist will get additional information needed to set the bindings of the skis, for example, weight and skiing ability. The equipment is selected and its equipment identification numbers are recorded. The equipment is adjusted, the settings are recorded, and the gear is given to the customer.
- **Payment:** On the way out, the client returns with the equipment to the Entry Room to sign the rental agreement—a legal contract stating the personal data about the person, what gear the person rented, the specialist's name who set the gear, and all of the legal mumbo-jumbo required to rent equipment for a life-threatening activity like skiing. The receptionist also collects payment from the customer, who is asked to leave a document such as a driver's license as collateral for returning the equipment.

When the skis are returned, they are inspected by the specialist and stowed in the Equipment Room.

Needs Analysis

The task at hand is to decide how to organize the database to support HAI! Adventure's ski rental shop. Perhaps the best way to approach the question is to consider what information is *created* and what information is *needed* to transact the business. The information that is being created is the documentation on the customer (personal information), and the data on the equipment rented and adjustments set (technical information from the specialist). The information needed to transact the rental is the content of the rental agreement document, which the customer must sign before taking the equipment. In essence, the rental is the association of the customer's personal data with the technical data of the equipment expressed in the rental agreement.

The first idea might be to define a Rentals table containing a field for each kind of the information needed for the contract. Then, in principle, each row of the table would represent one rental. This is a good place to begin the design, but the Rentals table as described may not be perfect. So, before adopting it, we must think about the design's usefulness.

Specifically, the contract needs to contain the customer's name, address. and phone number, implying that this information will be in the table. But if the HAI! Adventure business plan works out, customers will return repeatedly to the shop, implying that their names, addresses, and phone numbers will be repeated in the Rentals table multiple times. As we learned in Chapter 13, having the same information stored in multiple locations in a database is called *redundancy*, and it should be avoided. Consequently we decide that we need a table of customers, Clients, so that when we record their personal data, it will be in the database only once.

There is a similar problem with adventure specialists. The Rentals table needs to record which specialist adjusted the bindings for legal reasons. (The bindings hold the skis to the ski boots, and release when the skier falls in order to avoid injuries such as broken legs. The setting specifies the amount of force required to cause the bindings to release; it is affected by the skier's weight and ability.) Because making such adjustments requires training, the specialist's credentials for performing the operation should be available online. The credentials don't have to be in the contract—

only the specialist's name—so they shouldn't be stored in the Rentals table. This implies there should be another table for this purpose, the Adventure Specialist Team table, or ASTeam for short.

With the customer and specialist's data moved to their own tables, and being referenced by keys, what remains in the Rentals table? Plenty. The table still records the date of the transaction, equipment rented, adjustments, and a record of any special information that the specialist gave the customer.

Summarizing, the database as it has been designed so far includes three tables

- Clients—the table of customers giving their personal information
- ASTeam—the table of adventure specialists, including their training records and certification, as appropriate
- Rentals—the table of rentals giving the gear rented and the customer information such as level of skiing ability, weight, and settings

Further, relationships will exist between the Clients and Rentals tables, and the ASTeam and Rentals tables, reflecting the fact that a customer and a specialist participate in the rental, but that their specific information is stored in other tables.

TABLE DESIGN

Next we specify the details for the tables required by the HAI! Adventure's Snow Machine database. By being explicit about the design, we can work out additional details conceptually before trying to implement them.

Clients Table

The Clients table is straightforward. It includes the customer's name, home, and local addresses, and contact information, most of which is required for contractual purposes. Although we expect repeat customers, we do not have to worry about the problems that colleges do of keeping track of their students' frequent address changes. A client will probably not be changing addresses while on vacation, so a single record will suffice for a single season. If the customer returns the following year, a new record will be created.

Accordingly, all of the personal information about a customer will be stored in this table. We recognize the following fields, data types, and field sizes:

```
Clients
   Customer_ID            Integer          Unique Identifier
   First                  Character, 20    Given name
   Middle                 Character, 15    Middle name
   Last                   Character, 30    Family name
   Birthdate              Date             Date of birth
   Street                 Character, 30    Home address
   City                   Character, 20
   State                  Character, 2     State/Province Abbreviation
   ZIP                    Character, 10    Postal Code
   Country                Character, 10
   Home_Phone             Character, 20    Phone at residence
   Mobile_Phone           Character, 20
   Email                  Character, 40
   Local_Contact [Hotel]  Character, 40    Where staying locally
Primary Key: Customer_ID
```

The key for this relation is Customer_ID, since none of the other fields is guaranteed to give uniqueness to the rows of the table.

AS Team Table

The employees of HAI! Adventures do move around, and they have both local addresses and permanent addresses, the latter being recorded for tax purposes. Accordingly we will manage these addresses by setting up an employee contact schema. Recall that a schema is the abstract structure of an entity.

Contact		
Contact_ID	Integer	*Unique identifier*
Street	Character, 30	
City	Character, 20	
State	Character, 2	*State/Province Abbreviation*
ZIP	Character, 10	*Postal Code*
Country	Character, 10	
Phone	Character, 15	*Phone at this address*
Primary Key: Contact_ID		

The schema will be used to set up two tables, AS_Home and AS_Local, recording permanent and local address information, respectively. The tables are, therefore, two instances of the schema, that is, separate tables with the same structure.

The contact schema could have been used for the customers as well, but it's not necessary. The customers will not likely move in one season, and because we will probably archive and delete all of the Clients records after each season, the addresses don't have to be carried across multiple years. The employee data must be kept over a longer period of time. Such differences in the characteristics of the data motivate keeping the employee addresses separate.

The full ASTeam table will record relevant employment information, such as Social Security number, and relevant professional information, such as certification data. All employees will use the same table, though some like the receptionists may not need the certification fields. The table contains the following fields:

ASTeam		
Nickname	Character, 10	*Unique Identifier*
First	Character, 20	
Middle	Character, 15	
Last	Character, 30	
Birthdate	Date	
SS_Number	ddd-dd-dddd	
Home_Addr	Number	AS_Home.Contact_ID
Local_Addr	Number	AS_Local.Contact_ID
Mobil_Phone	Character, 20	
Email	Character, 40	
Certified	Y/N	*Is the specialist certified?*
Cert_Expire	Date	*When does certification expire*
Cert_Detail	Character, 255	*Description of certification type*
Primary Key: Nickname		

The HAI! Adventure team is an informal but very cohesive group, who know each other by nicknames like Sissy and Chip. They prefer to use these names around the office rather than an Employee_ID. So the database software will use the Nickname field as a key, even though the uniqueness requirement forces any two employees who go by the same name—say, Chip—to adopt different versions of that name—ChipR and ChipS. The Social Security number field also makes the entries unique, but that will be used primarily for payroll and tax purposes.

Because there will be different kinds of certification, the ASTeam table has fields for whether the person is certified at all, when the certification expires if it's time dependent, and the specifics of the certification, such as where, when, what type, and certifying organization. This information must be recorded, but it will probably not be frequently accessed.

Rentals

The Rentals table fields are straightforward. They include both the customer's and the specialist's keys to refer to the Clients and ASTeam tables, and details about the gear rented. If the customer rents skis and therefore must have bindings set, the Ski? field is checked. If this field is checked, the Weight must be filled in, Ability must be filled in, and the two settings fields must be filled in. The implementation will enforce these constraints.

The table that records a rental has the following fields:

Rental

Rental_ID	Integer	*Unique idenfier*
Date	Date	
Customer	Number	Clients.Client_ID
ASTeamer	Number	ASTeam.Nickname
Boot_Serial	Character, 10	*Serial number of boots rented*
Gear_Serial	Character, 10	*Serial number applies to skis and boards*
Ski?	Y/N	*Yes, specifies skis and bindings*
Ability	Character 12	*Beginner/Intermediate/Expert*
Weight	Integer	*Skier weight*
Binding_Set_L	Character, 5	*Setting for left binding*
Binding_Set_R	Character, 5	*Setting for right binding*
Poles	Character, 5	*Mfr abbrev and length*
Out_Remarks	Character, 255	*Cautions or directives to customer*

Primary_Key: Rental_ID

The Out_Remarks field can be used for any comments that the specialist thinks are relevant to the rental, such as comments made to the skier or observations about the equipment.

Summarizing, we have designed five database tables of the physical database to support the activity of the ski rental shop. Two of the entities—Clients and ASTeam—record information about people, and two—AS_Home and AS_Local—record information about places. These tables record facts about physical phenomena. But the Rentals table records information, not about a physical object, but about an event. The event occupies time in the same way the physical objects occupy space. Entities are flexible enough for this purpose: We must identify the properties that the event has (attributes), decide what type and how much data describe each property (field specifications), and determine which information uniquely describes the records that will be stored (primary key selection). The fact that rentals are not as tangible as whales is no limitation—they're still entities.

The Relationships

The Rentals table references the Clients and ASTeam tables. That is, Rentals has fields, Customer and ASTeamer, which contain keys for Clients and ASTeam tables. Additionally, ASTeam has fields with keys referencing the AS_Home and AS_Local tables. These references establish relationships, and though they have been expressed clearly in our logical database, we must specify their characteristics for the implementation, too.

The relationships are all "one-to-many" relationships. That is, each relationship associates the key of one table (the "one" side) with rows in the other table (the "many" side). We name the relationships for our own benefit.

- *Contracts*, the Clients:Rentals Relationship—In the Rentals table each customer is referred to by its key (CustomerID) in the Clients table.
- *Serves*, the ASTeam:Rentals Relationship—In the Rentals table specialists are referred to by their key (Nickname) in the ASTeam table.
- *Home_Of*, the AS_Home:ASTeam Relationship—In the ASTeam table the specialist's permanent address is referred to by its key (Contact_ID) in the AS_Home table.
- *Sleeps_At,* the AS_Local:ASTeam Relationship—In the ASTeam table the specialist's local address is referred to by its key (Contact_ID) in the AS_Local table.

By specifying these relationships, we make our intent clear as to how the information of the tables is interconnected.

At this point, the conceptual design of the Snow Machine database's physical components is complete. The entities and relationships have been defined. The design could be implemented using any of the many database software systems, all of which support the relational database concepts used here. But before investing our time in the detailed and time-consuming work of implementing the design, we should assess it.

Assessment

As with any design, we assess this table organization to determine how effectively it fulfills the needs of the Snow Machine shop. We notice that there is little redundancy because of the use of the Clients, ASTeam, AS_Home, and AS_Local tables. As a result, the fields of the Rentals table concern only the details of a ski rental, plus links to the customer and specialist that participated in it. The design is sound. Is this the best design?

From the point of view of The Snow Machine Ski Rental Shop, the design will probably meet their needs well. But from the point of view of HAI! Adventure, it might not. Why? The entrepreneurs who formed HAI! Adventure expect to grow, renting sports gear of many kinds at many sites. The ideas behind the Snow Machine database design can apply to scuba diving, wind surfing, kayaking, and mountain climbing equipment rentals as well because these sports all have a similar set of requirements. How would the five tables and four relationships of the design translate to another business unit?

Table	**Changes**
Clients (Customer data)	None
AS_Home (Employee addresses)	None
AS_Local (Employee local digs)	None
ASTeam (Employee profile)	None, though the info *entered* in Cert_detail will differ
Rentals (Transaction)	Revise equipment detail to specialize to the activity
Relationships	
Contracts (Clients:Rentals)	None
Serves (ASTeam:Rentals)	None
Home_Of (AS_Home:ASTeam)	None
Sleeps_At (AS_Local:ASTeam)	None

Though Rentals changes because a different kind of equipment is being rented, it is only the ski equipment-related fields that change.

Imagine that another HAI! Adventure business unit, say Fat Daddy's Dive Shop on Grand Cayman Island, modifies the Rentals table for renting scuba diving gear. Only the first four fields would be the same, and possibly the last. All others change. Though this is not a hard technical task, it means that the Fat Daddy's Rentals table and the Snow Machine Rentals table are different. Specifically, the rentals of the scuba shop and rentals of the ski shop cannot be part of the same table because of these different fields. It's not a problem for the two shops—they're thousands of miles apart and never interact. But from the point of view of the main company, HAI! Adventure, they're all rentals. The fact that different equipment is being rented is unimportant in many circumstances. It would be desirable to be able to regard all such transactions as *rentals*, each of a different kind of equipment. Is this possible? Of course, anything's possible.

What is the solution? Obviously, in the same way that customer information has been recorded in a separate table, the details of the equipment rental can also be recorded in another table. Each transaction will include the key of a record that specifies the details of the rented equipment. The newly revised Rentals table has the following form:

Rentals

Shop_ID	Character, 10	*Short name of the shop*
Rental_ID	Integer	*Unique idenfier*
Date	Date	
Customer	Number	Clients.Client_ID
ASTeamer	Character, 10	ASTeam.Nickname
Gear_facts	Number	*Reference to* Equip_ID *of a* Gear table
Payment	Currency	*Amount received for rental*

Primary_Key: Shop_ID, Rental_ID

Notice that the four key fields of the earlier version of Rentals has been augmented with the Gear_facts field to link to the specifics of the equipment rented. A Shop_ID field has also been added to identify which shop transacted the rental. Entries in this field might be `SnoMachine` or `FatDaddys`, though store numbers would be an unimaginative alternative. The reason for this field is to create unique records when the rentals of multiple stores are unioned together. (Recall from Chapter 13 that union combines the rows of two tables that have the same fields.) That is, each store uses its own sequence of Rental_ID numbers, but to avoid disaster if two stores use the same number, the rows are made unique by prefixing them with the store name. Thus the primary key is the composition of Shop_ID and Rental_ID. Finally we've added a Payment field because the HAI! Adventure's founders may be interested in that information, too.

For the purposes of the Snow Machine's ski rentals, we need to define Ski_Gear, which serves as their Gear table,

Ski_Gear

Equip_ID	Integer	*Unique identifier*
Boot_Serial	Character, 10	*Serial number of boots rented*
Gear_Serial	Character, 10	*Serial number applies to skis and boards*
Ski?	Y/N	*Yes, specifies skis and bindings*
Ability	Character, 12	*Beginner/Intermediate/Expert*
Weight	Integer	*Skier weight*
Binding_Set_L	Character, 5	*Setting for left binding*
Binding_Set_R	Character, 5	*Setting for right binding*
Poles	Character, 5	*Mfr abbrev and length*
Out_Remarks	Character, 255	*Customer/Specialist Conversation*

Primary_Key: Equip_ID

which simply records the remaining data from the first version of Rentals.

By splitting up the original Rentals table into the core activity of executing a rental (the new version of Rentals) and the detail of the specific equipment rented (Ski_Gear), we introduced a fifth relationship

- *Rents*, the Ski_Gear:Rentals Relationship—In the Rentals table, the specific equipment is referred to by its key (Equip_ID) in the Ski_Gear table.

This is a one-to-many relationship just like the others.

With these revisions, it will be possible for all equipment rentals of any HAI! Adventure shop to use the Rentals table unchanged, though different recreations will refer to different Gear tables. For example, Fat Daddy's rental will refer to a Scuba_Gear table. Of course, all shops renting the same kind of gear can use the same Gear table.

IMPLEMENTATION – BUILDING THE DB

The revised design can be implemented in any of the commercial database systems because they support the concepts used in the foregoing conceptual database design. The specifics used below are for the Microsoft Access system.

The first step in the implementation is to define the tables. Defining tables is essentially transcribing the information outlined above into the database system. It is tedious, but easy. We go to the trouble of implementing the tables at this stage to fill them with sample data in hopes of noticing errors or oversights. Some of the Snow Machine tables are shown in Figure 14.1.

Clients : Table

Field Name	Data Type	
Customer_ID	AutoNumb	Unique identifier
First	Text	First Name
Middle	Text	Middle Name
Last	Text	Last Name
Birthdate	Date/Time	Date of Birth
Street	Text	Street address
City	Text	City
State	Text	State/Province/Canton/Prefecture
ZIP	Text	Postal Code
Country	Text	Country of Residence
Home_Phone	Text	Phone at Residence
Mobile_Phone	Text	Cell
Email	Text	Email Address
Local_Contact	Text	Hotel or local phone number

ASTeam : Table

Field Name	Data Type	
Nickname	Text	Unique Identifier
First	Text	First Name
Middle	Text	Middle Name
Last	Text	Last Name
Birthdate	Date/Tim	Date of Birth
SS_number	Text	ddd-dd-dddd
Home_Addr	Number	Key into AS_Home
Local_Addr	Number	Key into AS_Local
Mobile_Phone	Text	Cell
Email	Text	Email address
Certified	Yes/No	Any relevant certification?
Cert_Expire	Date/Tim	Expiration date
Cert_Detail	Text	Details of when, where, et

Rentals : Table

Field Name	Data Type	
Store_ID	Text	Unique store name
Rental_ID	AutoNumber	Unique number for each rental
Date	Date/Time	Transaction Date
Customer	Number	Key into Clients
ASTeamer	Text	Key into ASTeam
Gear_facts	Number	Key into Ski_Gear or other
Payment	Currency	Amt received for rental

Ski_Gear : Table

Field Name	Data Type	
Equip_ID	AutoNumt	Unique Identifier
Boot_Serial	Text	Serial Number for boots
Gear_Serial	Text	Serial Number for skis or board
Ski?	Yes/No	Are bindings involved?
Ability	Text	Beginner/Intermediate/Exper
Weight	Number	Weight of skier
Binding_Set_L	Text	Binding setting, left
Binding_Set_R	Text	Binding setting, right
Poles	Text	Mfr Abbrev + length
Out_Remarks	Text	Comments about rental or to custo

Figure 14.1. Four of the six tables required for the revised Snow Machine database. The AS_Home and AS_Local are identical and are composed only of address fields, like fields 6–11 of Clients.

The next step is to define the relationships to connect the parts of the database into the unified whole that we intend. Again, the database systems provide easy-to-use software tools for defining the relationships. The specification of these relationships is shown in Figure 14.2.

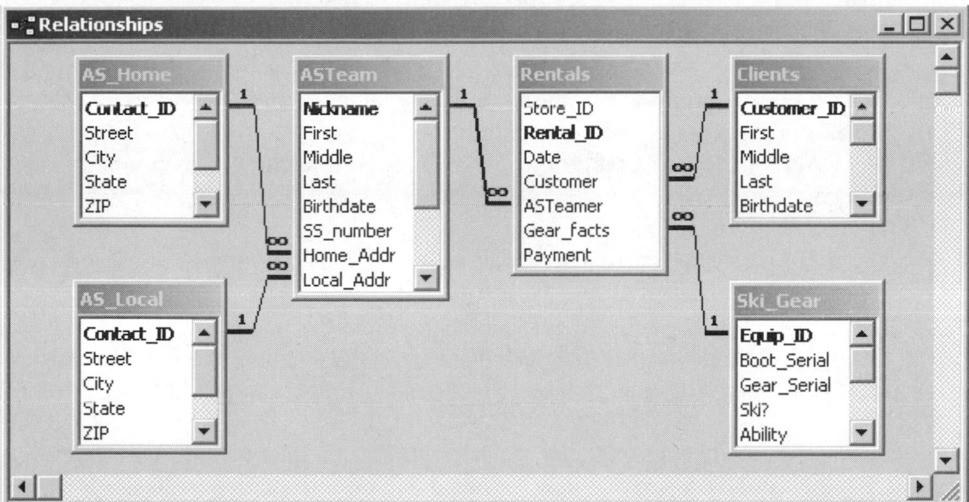

Figure 14.2. The five relationships of HAI! Adventure's Snow Machine database. The relationships are one-to-many where the "one" side is a primary key to the relationship, and the many side (shown as a small infinity symbol) is a position where the key is used as a reference. Notice keys are shown in bold.

VIEWING THE DATABASE

Having defined the database, it is time to make it useful. Though we have stored the information in a particular way, say, to avoid redundancy, it is likely that users will want to look at it differently. Recall that how users look at a database for a particular purpose is called their *view* of the database. The Snow Machine database will be typical: Users will want to view a different set of tables than the ones we've defined, and in fact, only we will ever want to look at the tables in the form we've defined them. So, it's time to design the logical database.

Providing users views of the database is easy by applying a rather obvious five-step process:

1. Analyze the business activity to identify the information inputs and outputs—these are the needed views.
2. Determine what information the specialists need from each view, and where it is stored in the tables.
3. Define a conceptual query for a new table as a merge-and-extract process from existing tables.
4. Implement the conceptual query by expressing it in SQL.
5. Define a GUI to display the information in a pleasant form for the specialists.

Executing this process requires the remainder of this section, plus three more.

To begin, formulate the views of the database by analyzing the business activity. The adventure specialists interact with the Snow Machine database at essentially three times:

- **Sign-in:** After the receptionist has greeted the customer and the customer has decided on what to rent, the receptionist records the customer's personal information. That is, the receptionist enters data into the Clients table.
- **Fitting:** When the personal data has been entered, the client moves to the Fitting Room where an adventure specialist helps the customer select and fit the gear. The specialist must enter information into the Ski_Gear table.
- **Agreeing**: After the equipment has been fitted, the customer takes the gear and stops at the receptionist's station to sign the rental agreement and pay for the rental. For the rental agreement contract, the information in the Clients, Ski_Gear, and Rentals tables must be composed together into a contract and printed.

In addition to these three customer-related views, there is one employee-related view:

- **Hiring:** When a new adventure specialist is hired, their professional information and addresses must be entered into the database. That is, information must be entered into ASTeam, AS_Home, and AS_Local.

Notice that the first two and last are "input views," when the specialists are entering data, and the third is an "output view," when database information is displayed.

To present these four views of the database, it is necessary to create the tables that correspond to them. These will not be stored tables, but rather tables computed by queries. What data is in the new tables depends on what information the specialists must see. Analyze the four cases:

- **Sign-in:** Requires all of the fields from the Clients table. Since Sign-In initiates a transaction, it requires fields from Rentals as well, including Rental_ID and Customer. It should also include the ASTeamer field so that the receptionist can assign the customer to a particular specialist, if one is requested.
- **Fitting:** Requires all the fields from Ski_Gear. It also requires fields from Rentals, specifically the Rental_ID, ASTeamer, so the specialist can sign in, and the Gear_facts fields. In addition, so that the specialist can call the customer by name rather than by the decidedly impersonal Client_ID number, the two fields First and Last from the Clients table are also required.
- **Agreeing:** Requires all of the fields from Rentals, Clients, Ski_Gear and the legal name of the specialist from the ASTeam table.
- **Hiring:** Requires all of the fields from ASTeam, AS_Home, and AS_Local for signing in new specialists or updating their records.

This information is summarized in Table 14.1.

Where do the new tables for the views come from? Clearly we do not what to define more tables like those of the previous sections. They're the physical tables to be stored on the hard disk. Rather, as we explain in Chapter 13, we assemble the data fields needed for these hybrid tables by constructing queries. Queries create "computed" tables out of "stored" tables of the physical database in order to give users their preferred view of the database. Of course, this was our plan all along because when we split information out into separate tables, referencing it by keys and defining the relationships, we knew we would eventually want to reassemble it so it would be useful to the Snow Machine personnel.

Table 14.1. Summary of the Fields Required for the Snow Machine Database Views

Fields Required for the Views of the Snow Machine **Database**						
View	Clients	ASTeam	Ski_Gear	AS_Home	AS_Local	Rentals
Sign-In	*All*					Rental_ID Customer ASTeamer
Fitting	First Last		*All*			Rental_ID Customer ASTeamer Gear_facts
Agreeing	*All—except* Email Local_Contact	First Middle Last	*All*			*All*
Hiring		*All*		*All*	*All*	

Creating the View Queries

The views will be created using queries, commands formed from the basic table-manipulating operations described in Chapter 13. The process will always use the same basic approach: *Combine the base tables, and then retrieve the fields needed for the view.* The tables will be combined using the natural join operator and the fields will be retrieved using the project operator. (Refer to Chapter 13.) Consider each query in turn.

Sign-In. The Sign-In View requires fields from the Clients and the Rentals tables. All fields of Clients are used, but only Rental_ID, Customer and ASTeamer are used from Rentals. The formula for the query is

> **Project** Customer_ID, First, Middle, Last, Birthdate, Street, City, State, ZIP, Country, Home_Phone, Mobile_Phone, Email, Local_Contact, Rental_ID, Customer, ASTeamer
> **From** Clients ⋈ Rentals

The join relies on the *Contracts* relationship between Clients and Rentals. It will combine a row of each table whenever Customer_ID = Customer.

Fitting. The Fitting View requires data from three tables, Rentals, Ski_Gear, and Clients. From Rentals only the Rental_ID, ASTeamer, Gear_facts, and Customer fields are needed. The latter field is needed to retrieve the customer's name from Clients. All of the fields of Ski_Gear are needed. Clients will provide only the First and Last fields of the customer's name. The query is

> **Project** Rental_ID, ASTeamer, Customer, Gear_facts, First, Last, Equip_ID, Boot_Serial, Gear_Serial, Ski?, Ability, Weight, Binding_Set_L, Binding_Set_R, Poles, Out_Remarks
> **From** (Rentals ⋈ Clients) ⋈ Ski_Gear

Like the Sign-In view, the Rentals ⋈ Clients join relies on the *Contracts* relationship, combining rows whenever Customer_ID = Customer. Further, the resulting table will be joined with Ski_Gear using the *Rents* relationship, combining rows whenever Gear_facts = Equip_ID.

Agreeing. The contract will require information from the Rentals, Clients, Ski_Gear, and the ASTeamer. It requires all of the fields (except Clients' Email and Local_Contact) from the first three tables, and the name fields from ASTeamer. Though straightforward in concept, listing off all of the fields is rather lengthy.

Project Shop_ID, Rental_ID, Date, Customer, ASTeamer, Gear_facts, Payment, Customer_ID, Clients.First, Clients.Middle, Clients.Last, Birthdate, Street, City, State, ZIP, Country, Home_Phone, Mobile_Phone, Equip_ID, Boot_Serial, Gear_Serial, Ski?, Ability, Weight, Binding_Set_L, Binding_Set_R, Poles, Out_Remarks, NickName, ASTeamer.First, ASTeamer.Middle, ASTeamer.Last
From (((Rentals ⋈ Clients) ⋈ Ski_Gear) ⋈ ASTeamer)

The three relationships used for the earlier joins are *Contracts*, *Rents,* and *Serves*, respectively. We've seen the *Contracts*- and *Rents*-based equality tests for the joins. The join based on *Serves* composes rows whenever ASTeamer = NickName.

Hiring. Unlike the customer-related queries, the *Hiring* query is more direct. It uses all of the fields form the three tables, ASTeam, AS_Home and AS_Local. Because all of the fields are of interest, no project operation will be required. The query is simply the three joins

(ASTeam _ AS_Home) _ AS_Local

The first join relies on the *Home_Of* relationship, combining rows whenever Home_Addr = AS_Home.Contact_ID. The second join relies on the *Sleeps_At* relationship, forming rows whenever Local_Addr = AS_Local.Contact_ID. All of the fields are retained.

Having defined the views that the Snow Machine personnel will use to interact with the database, it's time set up the interfaces to the Views.

VIEW IMPLEMENTATION

Naturally the view queries can be implemented in the database system software. There are several different ways of doing so. In the process of implementing the queries, two methods will be illustrated: query-by-example, and direct SQL. We begin with the personnel-centric view, that is, the *Hiring* query, because specialists must be added to the database before any customers can be processed.

Hiring

The *Hiring* query is especially easy because it is just the join of three tables: ASTeam, AS_Home, and AS_Local. All the fields are needed, though there is a little duplication between Home_Addr and AS_Home.Contact_ID, and between Local_Addr and AS_Local.Contact_ID, because of the equality test. (The conceptual join that we used for the *Hiring* query earlier would eliminate one of the duplicates, but practical database system software usually doesn't.)

Figure 14.3 shows a display of the query-by-example facility for defining the Hiring_Q query. Notice that there are two windows: The upper window recapitulates the Entity-Relationship diagram for the tables used in the query, and the relationships used for the joins. Commands allow tables to be added and deleted from this window; the defined relationships are automatically imported. In the lower window can be sccn (part of) the display of the fields of the intended table. This is an "example" of how the table should look. Each position corresponds to a field of the desired table with the source table and source field given. It is possible to order the items of the table's column (Sort), include them, but not display them (Show), or impose conditions on them (Criteria, Or). (Consult software documentation for further information.)

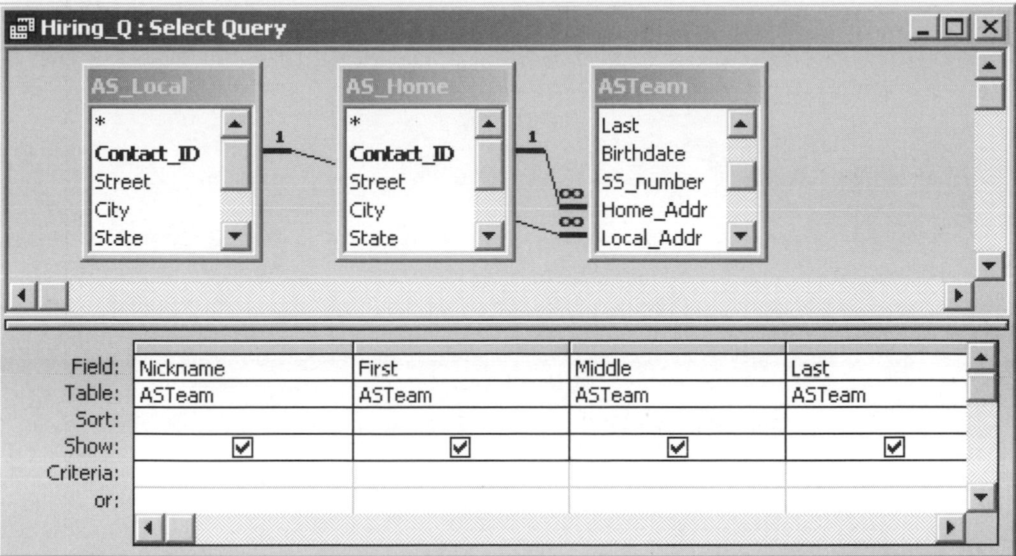

Figure 14.3. Query-by-example display (from MS Access) showing the tables with the relationships and the first four fields of the Hiring_Q query.

Our use of this facility is limited to listing all of the fields of the three tables. The result is the Hiring_Q query.

Query-by-example queries are translated by the software into SQL, which is used by the "backend" part of the database system to perform the actual query processing operations. It is informative to look at the SQL because it is only a minor variation on the theoretical form used earlier. The SQL for Hiring_Q is

```
SELECT ASTeam.Nickname, ASTeam.First, ASTeam.Middle, ASTeam.Last,
   ASTeam.Birthdate, ASTeam.SS_number, ASTeam.Home_Addr,
   ASTeam.Local_Addr, ASTeam.Mobile_Phone, ASTeam.Email,
   ASTeam.Certified, ASTeam.Cert_Expire, ASTeam.Cert_Detail,
   AS_Home.Contact_ID, AS_Home.Street, AS_Home.City,
   AS_Home.State, AS_Home.ZIP, AS_Home.Country, AS_Home.Phone,
   AS_Local.Contact_ID, AS_Local.Street, AS_Local.City,
   AS_Local.State, AS_Local.ZIP, AS_Local.Country, AS_Local.Phone
FROM  AS_Local INNER JOIN
   (AS_Home INNER JOIN ASTeam ON AS_Home.Contact_ID = ASTeam.Home_Addr)
ON AS_Local.Contact_ID = ASTeam.Local_Addr;
```

At first glance, we might think that SQL's form is *not* a minor variation of the conceptual version, but then we recall the annoying fact that SQL and the concepts use different terms, for example, `SELECT` is Project. So, the `SELECT` clause is simply listing all the fields of the three tables using the *table name.field name* syntax. These were implied in the conceptual formulation. Further, the SQL form has to explicitly specify the equality test of the relevant relationship, which is also implied in our conceptual join. Notice that although the order of the `INNER JOIN`'s operands is different than our conceptual expression, the parentheses ensure that the operations are actually done in the intended order; that is, ASTeam ⋈ AS_Home is first, though order doesn't matter when giving joins.

Sign-In

With the example of the *Hiring* query expressed in SQL, it is straightforward to transcribe the *Sign-In* query developed earlier directly into SQL. Recall that the query is

Project Customer_ID, First, Middle, Last, Birthdate, Street, City, State, ZIP, Country, Home_Phone, Mobile_Phone, Email, Local_Contact, Rental_ID, Customer, ASTeamer
From Clients ⋈ Rentals

The three key points to remember about the translation from our conceptual form of the query to the SQL form are

1. Rather than the keyword pair Project . . . From, use the keywords SELECT ... FROM.
2. Rather than the join operator ⋈, use the operator INNER JOIN.
3. It is necessary to explicitly give the equality test that is the basis for the INNER JOIN.

In addition, all references to fields use the *table name.field name* syntax. Making those syntactic changes yields the Sign-In_Q

```
SELECT Clients.Customer_ID, Clients.First,
        Clients.Middle,Clients.Last, Clients.Birthdate,
        Clients.Street, Clients.City, Clients.State,
        Clients.ZIP, Clients.Country, Clients.Home_Phone,
        Clients.Mobile_Phone, Clients.Email,
        Clients.Local_Contact, Rentals.Rental_ID,
        Rentals.Customer, Rentals.ASTeamer
FROM Clients INNER JOIN Rentals ON Clients.Customer_ID =
        Rentals.Customer;
```

which is exactly the query required for the *Sign-In* view.

Fitting

The Fitting_Q query is also an easy command to program directly in SQL. Recalling the conceptual version of the query

Project Rental_ID, ASTeamer, Customer, Gear_facts, First, Last, Equip_ID, Boot_Serial, Gear_Serial, Ski?, Ability, Weight, Binding_Set_L, Binding_Set_R, Poles, Out_Remarks
From (Rentals ⋈ Clients) ⋈ Ski_Gear

notice that the only challenge is that there are three tables involved, as there were in the Hiring_Q query. So the challenge can be answered by analogy to that query. The Fitting_Q query is therefore,

```
SELECT Rentals.Rental_ID, Rentals.ASTeamer,
        Rentals.Customer,Rentals.Gear_facts, Clients.First,
        Clients.Last, Ski_Gear.Equip_ID, Ski_Gear.Boot_Serial,
        Ski_Gear.Gear_Serial, Ski_Gear.Ski, Ski_Gear.Ability,
        Ski_Gear.Weight, Ski_Gear.Binding_Set_L,
        Ski_Gear.Binding_Set_R, Ski_Gear.Poles,
        Ski_Gear.Out_Remarks
FROM Ski_Gear INNER JOIN
        (Clients INNER JOIN Rentals
         ON Clients.Customer_ID = Rentals.Customer)
ON Ski_Gear.Equip_ID = Rentals.Gear_facts;
```

Transcribing queries directly into SQL can be somewhat more complicated that these two examples, but not a lot. Because SQL is the standard language for database queries in production database systems, anyone expecting to build or be responsible for one, that is, be a database administrator, should plan on spending a few more minutes to learn all of the details.

Agreeing

Finally, the view query for the rental agreement contract seems to be the most complex of all because it involves four tables. But because it uses all of the fields (but two) of three tables, and only three fields of the other, it isn't so difficult in concept. Nevertheless, we will use the query-by-example technique to define Agree_Q.

Figure 14.4 shows the two windows of the query-by-example editor, with the tables/relationships and example table windows. Notice the three relationships that enable the query to assemble the needed information. All fields of Rentals are required. All fields of Clients are required, too, except Email and Local_Contact. Three fields, the specialist's name, are used from ASTeam.

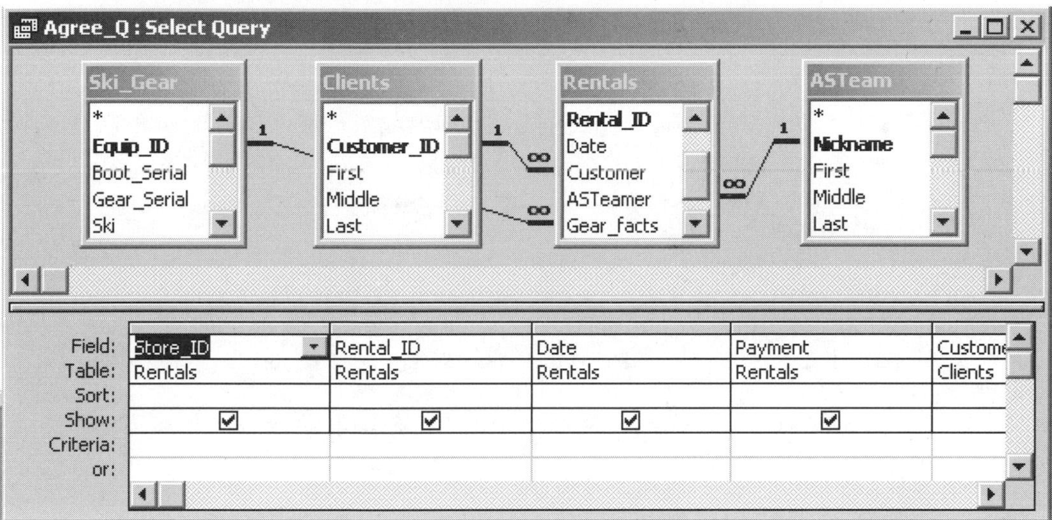

Figure 14.4. Agree_Q query in the query-by-example window.

The SQL form generated by the query-by-example specification is

```
SELECT Rentals.Store_ID, Rentals.Rental_ID, Rentals.Date,
       Rentals.Customer,Rentals.ASTeamer, Rentals.Gear_facts,
       Rentals.Payment, Clients.Customer_ID, Clients.First AS
       Clients_First, Clients.Middle AS Clients_Middle,
       Clients.Last AS Clients_Last, Clients.Birthdate,
       Clients.Street, Clients.City, Clients.State,
       Clients.ZIP, Clients.Country, Clients.Home_Phone,
       Clients.Mobile_Phone, Ski_Gear.Equip_ID,
       Ski_Gear.Boot_Serial, Ski_Gear.Gear_Serial,
       Ski_Gear.Ski, Ski_Gear.Ability, Ski_Gear.Weight,
       Ski_Gear.Binding_Set_L, Ski_Gear.Binding_Set_R,
       Ski_Gear.Poles, Ski_Gear.Out_Remarks, ASTeam.First,
       ASTeam.Middle, ASTeam.Last
FROM Ski_Gear INNER JOIN
      (Clients INNER JOIN
         (ASTeam INNER JOIN Rentals ON ASTeam.Nickname = Rentals.ASTeamer)
      ON Clients.Customer_ID = Rentals.Customer)
   ON Ski_Gear.Equip_ID = Rentals.Gear_facts;
```

It's an imposing command to be sure, but when it's decomposed into its components, it's far less menacing.

DATA ENTRY

Data can be entered directly into the "tabular sheet" form of the tables, but users expect to be provided a GUI to make data entry more palatable. Such GUIs are also known as *forms*. The goal in constructing the GUIs is to make them clear and convenient to use, and pleasant to look at. Though designing pleasing and effective GUIs is a definite art—making it a career specialty for those who are sufficiently talented at it—there are some obvious guidelines:

- **Arrange Information Sensibly.** Cluster the fields appropriately—names go together, address fields go together, and so on. Also, orient the fields intuitively—perhaps arranging name information horizontally, address information vertically, to follow the most common orientation in which the information is written.
- **Avoid Clutter.** Eliminate duplicate fields and unnecessary text, lines, and visual effects. Many believe that sans serif fonts are generally to be preferred.
- **Preload Fields.** Where possible, fill a field with a default value, or if there is a specific format expected, fill the field with the guidelines for its form, as in DD/MM/YY for dates.

Probably, most people who must use a data entry GUI quickly become oblivious to it, not noticing either its pleasant or annoying features. Still we should make it the best possible. Use the facilities of the database system to build the GUIs.

Ta DAH! It's done. The Snow Machine Ski Rental Shop has its database, designed and implemented. See Figure 14.5. HAI! Adventure is in business.

LESSONS, DIVES, AND CLIMBS

The Snow Machine database has been designed to anticipate the other rental businesses of HAI! Adventure, such as scuba and mountain climbing gear. It will be a simple matter to develop new tables for the different equipment types required for those sports.

The problem for this section is to consider what modifications are required for the HAI! Adventure team to move into the lessons and tours business. That is, how do the shops also support the possibility that some of the adventure specialists will serve as instructors, guides, or leaders for activities related to the shop's sports specialty? The common thread among these activities is that each is composed of a set of customers and a leader or instructor. The question is, "How should the present database be extended to handle these new activities?"

When thinking about how to design the tables to incorporate lessons and tours, it is natural to make analogies to familiar situations. We visualize a ski instructor and a retinue of students, and naturally think about organizing the table design around the concept of a class list. Because the lessons and tours will have an upper limit of participation, that is, a maximum size, it would seem that a Class_List table with the following schema should suffice:

```
Class_List      CAUTION – NOT A GOOD DESIGN
   Class_ID          Number          Unique identifier
   Date              mm/dd/yy        Date of event or first lesson
   Type              Character, 50   Description of the lesson or tour
   Leader            Character, 10   ASTeam.Nickname value
   Participant1      Number          Clients.Customer_ID
   Participant2      Number          Clients.Customer_ID
```

Participant3	Number	Clients.Customer_ID
Participant4	Number	Clients.Customer_ID
Participant5	Number	Clients.Customer_ID

Primary Key: Class_ID

The idea is that each group has a leader or instructor as well as a set of participants, up to some maximum. By using the keys for the Leader and the Participants, we avoid the mistake of storing redundant information. But we make a different mistake. This is *not* the way to extend the database to include lessons and tours, even though the analogy seems apt.

The Class_List table idea has several problems, but mostly the error is in binding together data that should be independent. Specifically, participation in the class is not ordered. The Class_List definition implies, for example, that because we've assigned a numbered attribute to each student, we are interested in tuples in a table that are the same in all respects except that the participants are ordered differently, as in Table 14.2. But we don't want to recognize such distinctions. Students in a class should be unordered. This design is faulty.

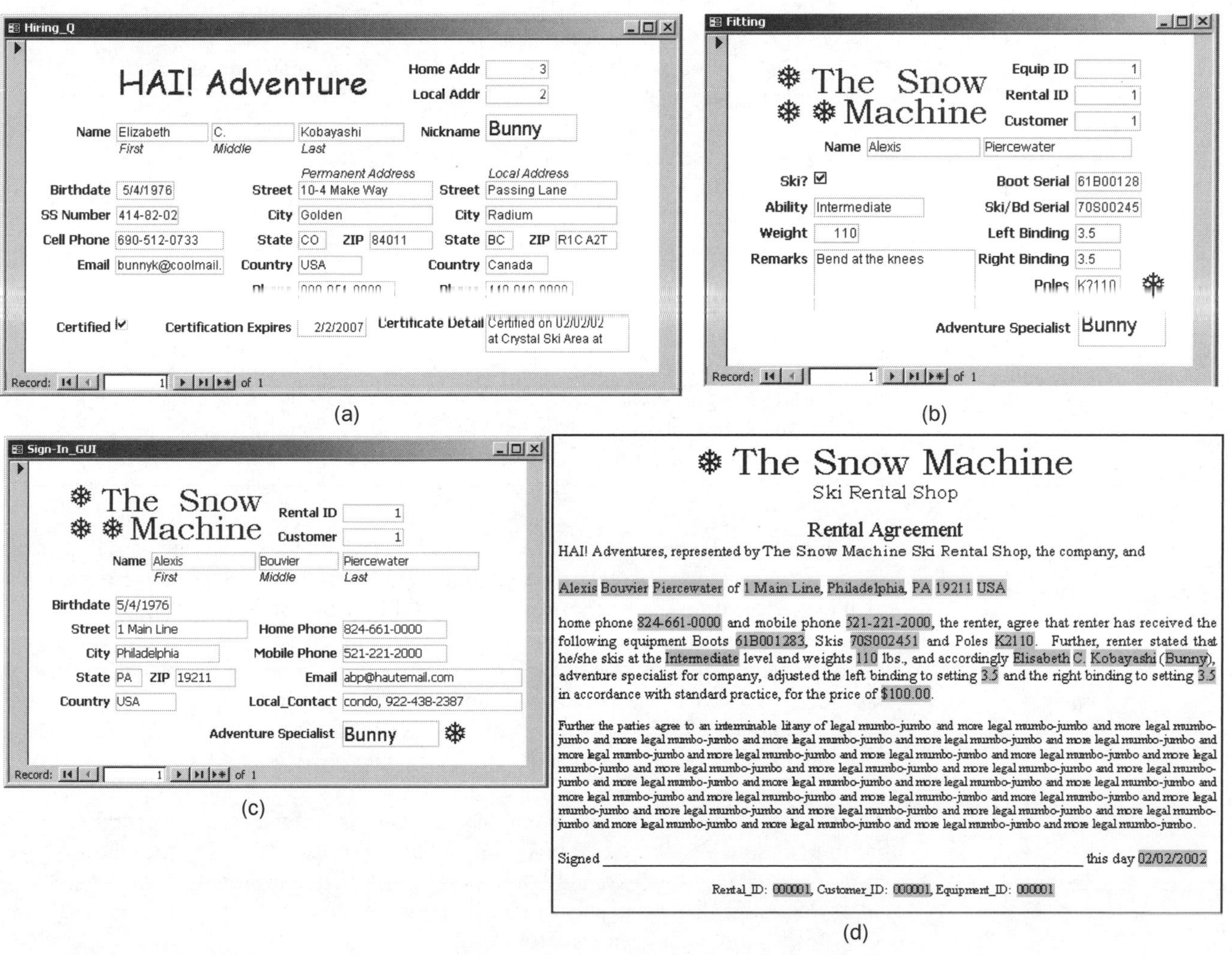

Figure 14.5. Sample GUIs for the four Snow Machine views, (a) Hiring view, (b) Fitting view, (c) Sign-In view, and (d) Rental agreement (the entries of a database instance are shown in gray).

Table 14.2. Possible Tuples Based on the Class_List Table Definition

Class_ID	Date	Type	Leader	Partic_t1	Partic_2	Partic_3	Partic_4	Partic_5
223	2/2/02	Beg'g Skiing	Thor	Jan	John	Jon	Ian	Juan
223	2/2/02	Beg'g Skiing	Thor	Juan	Jan	John	Jon	Ian
223	2/2/02	Beg'g Skiing	Thor	Ian	Juan	Jan	John	Jon

A better way to formulate the lessons and tours extension to the database is to create an entity that expresses their common features and properties. The "thing" we're trying to describe is a scheduled activity—a lesson at a given time or a dive on a given morning or a climb on a specific day—and a collection of such things would form a table of instances in which each would have the fields

Activities		
Activity_ID	Number	*Unique Identifier*
Date	Date	*Date of activity*
Leader	Character, 10	*Specialist value* ASTeam.NickName
Description	Character, 50	*Statement saying what the activity is*
Limit	Number	*The upper limit on participation*

Primary Key: Activity_ID

HAI! Adventure plans to offer these activities. Essentially this is the Class_List schema, but without the participants. The design not only resolves the problem of "ordering the participants," but it regularizes lessons and tours for all sports because the nature of the activity is embodied in the Description field. Having all lessons "look alike" in the database tables is a feature that will be important to the HAI! Adventure founders, just as it was with rentals.

Thinking abstractly about the database design for a moment, how *will* we create a class list or tour-participants list? After all, even if it is unwise to implement the class list metaphor directly as a table in the database, it's nevertheless a useful document. The purpose of thinking about that question before the design is completed is that the answer might guide us to a more effective solution. And it does.

Building on our earlier experience with the HAI! Adventure database, we will probably construct the class list by creating a query that combines some of the base tables such as ASTeam for the leader. From the resulting super table, we will extract the fields needed for the class list. That's the way we solved all of the earlier situations when the view of the database didn't exactly match the tables of the physical database. So, what should we store so we can create the class list in this way? Obviously, we need a table of students. But we already have that. It's simply our Clients table. Perhaps the activity the customer signs up for could be added to the Clients records. When thinking about how we might extend the Clients table to include "sign-up" information, however, we realize that the customer might register for several tours or multiple lessons. And as we're imagining adding a series of fields to the Clients records—Activity1, Activity2, and Activity3, say—in which to store the Activity_ID keys, we realize that we're about to make the same mistake as with the class list! The activities should be independent, too.

To solve the problem, recall another very familiar analogy. Colleges have students (analogous to Clients) and they have classes (analogous to Activities), but for a student to take a class, he or she must *register*. That is, the binding of Clients to Activities can be done using the concept of registration. What form would the registration take? Because it's binding customers with activities, it will be very similar to

Rentals, but without an equipment reference. It would likely have the following schema:

Apply

Field	Type	Description
Shop_ID	Character, 10	*Short name of the shop*
Regist_ID	Number	*Unique identifier*
Date	Date	
Activity	Number	*Class or tour key:* Activities.Activity_ID
Participant	Number	Clients.Customer_ID
Skill	Character, 255	*Skill level description*
Payment	Currency	*Amount paid for activity in case of refund*

Primary_Key: Shop_ID, SignUp_ID

The fields are self-explanatory except perhaps for Skill, which is a textual description of the participant's qualifications for the activity. The leader will evaluate this field. That is, registration is an application to participate, hence the table name Apply. Some activities like skiing require routine information, "Intermediate Skier;" some like mountain climbing require detailed information, "Climbed the 4 highest peaks in the Bugaboos as follows . . ."; and some like bungee jumping require little information, "Has Mass." Like college, you have to have the prereqs.

Notice that everyone registered for any activity will be in the Apply table; that is, the design suffices for participants of any class or tour. If a person is registered for more than one activity, there will be multiple rows for them in Apply, and they're independent, that is, unordered. If two Clients are signed up for the same class, they are also unordered. If participants cancel their registration, they are given a refund and removed from the table, but they don't leave "holes" in a schedule, as would have happened with Class_List, because there is not yet any schedule. And, finally, a participants list or class list can be created by joining Apply, Clients, and Activities as explained later in this chapter. The solution has virtually every positive feature imaginable except one. Specifically, even though there is a limit for each of the activities, this registration scheme doesn't automatically cap the enrollment at that number. Any number of people could register for a three-person trek to Acuncagua. Because this problem is easily solved with database software systems, it will not concern us further.

The creation of the Activities and Apply tables naturally defines some relationships:

- *Leads*, the ASTeam:Activities relationship—In the Activities table, specialists are referred to by their key (Nickname) in the ASTeam table.
- *Offers*, the Activities:Apply relationship—In the Apply table, lessons and tours are referred to by their key (Activity_ID) in the Activities table.
- *Registers_for* Clients:Apply relationship—In the Apply table, the participants are referred to by their key (Customer_ID) in the Clients table.

These are all one-to-many relationships. Figure 14.6 shows the existing relationships.

With the relationships defined, constructing the participants list for a given activity, that is, the Class List, is straightforward. As mentioned earlier, the Activities, Apply, and Customers tables are joined, and the appropriate fields are extracted. For the Class List, we want all fields from Activities and the participants' names from Clients. No information is actually required from Apply because the instructor or leader will have already looked over the participants and decided who is qualified. (This requires another view, of course.) Thus the Class List uses the registration table Apply, but only for associating Activities table entries to Clients table entries, as planned. The required Class List view is implemented by the table created by the Attends_Q query

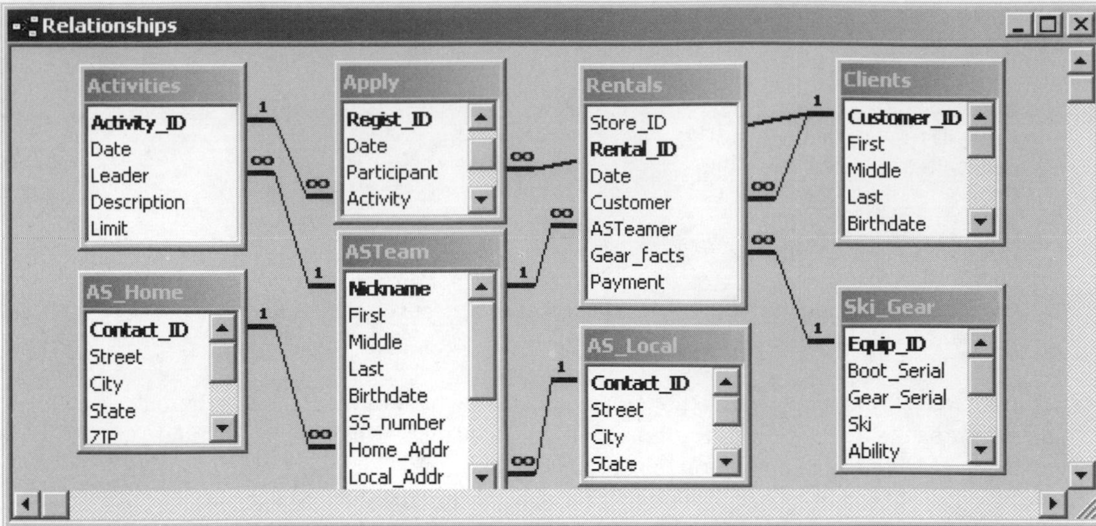

Figure 14.6. The relationships of the Snow Machine database after adding the Activities and Apply Tables, and their induced relationships.

Project Activity_ID, Date, Leader, Description, Limit, Activity, Participant, Customer_ID, First, Last
From (Activities ⋈ Apply) _ Clients

Converting this conceptual query to SQL is direct because it amounts to recapitulating the field list and testing equality on the fields of the *Offers* and *Registers_for* relationships. The result is

```
SELECT Activities.Activity_ID, Activities.Date,
       Activities.Leader,Activities.Description,
       Activities.Limit, Apply.Participant, Clients.First,
       Clients.Last
FROM Clients INNER JOIN
   (Activities INNER JOIN Apply
       ON Activities.Activity_ID = Apply.Activity)
ON Clients.Customer_ID = Apply.Participant
```

by now a familiar structure.

One additional twist is relevant for the Class List view, but hasn't concerned us so far. Attends_Q will create a table of *all* the students signed up for *all* of the classes, which isn't quite what we want. What we actually need is the list for a given class, or perhaps a list for a given day, if there are few enough classes in a day. We can easily achieve this using Activity_ID or Date to select the necessary rows from the Attends_Q table. Using the conceptual Select_from . . . On . . . operation discussed in Chapter 13, the Attends_Q query is revised to form the Class_List_Q query

Select_from
  Project Activity_ID, Date, Leader, Description, Limit, Activity, Participant, Customer_ID, First, Last
  From (Activities ⋈ Apply) ⋈ Clients
On Date = current_date

where current_date is a system-defined constant. Select_from keeps only those rows that satisfy its On criterion, implying that Class_List_Q produces the list of students taking lessons or participating in other activities on a given day. To select on

Activity_ID, the user would be queried for the specific activity and the On clause would have to be appropriately modified.

The SQL equivalent for the Class_List_Q query requires only that we add a `WHERE` clause to the Attends_Q query, which saves only those rows that meet the `WHERE` criterion. Therefore, the Class_List_Q query has the SQL form

```
SELECT Activities.Activity_ID, Activities.Date,
        Activities.Leader,Activities.Description,
        Activities.Limit, Apply.Participant, Clients.First,
        Clients.Last
FROM Clients INNER JOIN
        (Activities INNER JOIN Apply
        ON Activities.Activity_ID = Apply.Activity)
ON Clients.Customer_ID = Apply.Participant
WHERE (((Activities.Date)="Date"));
```

An example document produced by the Class_List_Q query is shown in Figure 14.7.

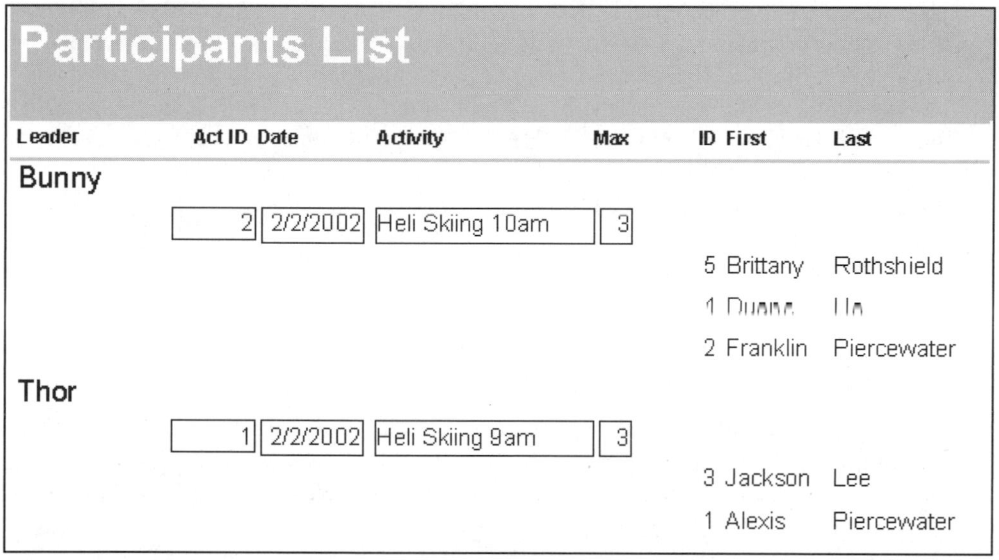

Participants List

Leader	Act ID	Date	Activity	Max	ID	First	Last
Bunny							
	2	2/2/2002	Heli Skiing 10am	3			
					5	Brittany	Rothshield
					1	Duane	Ha
					2	Franklin	Piercewater
Thor							
	1	2/2/2002	Heli Skiing 9am	3			
					3	Jackson	Lee
					1	Alexis	Piercewater

Figure 14.7. A participants list document displaying the results of the Class_List_Q query.

SUMMARY

Our HAI! Adventure database design proceeded like most design efforts. Conceptually it began with our best guess at a workable minimal solution, followed by an analysis of how well the solution satisfied our needs. That led to revisions, which were followed by further analysis, and so on. That iterative process of design-then-refine continued until eventually we produced a quality solution. We immediately considered how it could be improved! The result, a long way from our first idea about how the database should be organized, resulted from careful thought about what would make the solution better.

Less abstractly, our design process began by studying the structure and operation of the Snow Machine Rental Shop. Though we used the physical structure of the shop to help us visualize its operation, the components that affected the database design were the rental process and the allocation of tasks among the employees. The receptionist began the rental process with an information processing activity. The adventure specialist then contributed additional critical data. Finally, the information had to be brought together in a form of a rental agreement contract. This originally motivated a "mega" Rentals table in which all of the relevant information would be stored. But such an arrangement introduced the dreaded problem of *redundancy*, so smaller tables were created that collected together information in logically related units. There is no algorithm for how to formulate the tables. It is simply a matter of thinking about the rental process and the types of information created. Before finally implementing the tables in a commercial database system, we considered whether the Snow Machine database design perfectly fulfilled HAI! Adventure's plans to branch out into other forms of equipment rental. We found that it did not, and revised the design one more time before implementing the tables and relationships.

When the tables and relationships are defined, the physical database is set as it will be stored on the hard disk. But it will not likely match the needs of the users, and so we designed database views needed for the operation of the Snow Machine shop. Three views were identified as being essential for transacting business: *Sign-In*, *Fitting,* and *Agreeing*. After analyzing what information is needed and where in the physical database it comes from, we worked out the conceptual queries required to create these view tables. There was a (not surprising) consistency to the task. A few tables were combined using Join, and then the needed fields were retrieved. Once the conceptual queries were created, it was a simple matter to encode those in SQL for use by a commercial database system. Finally, a GUI for the view was created to complete the task and make the database convenient for the Snow Machine's adventure specialists. At that point, the basic rental database was complete and ready to have the GUIs customized to any of HAI! Adventure's rental endeavors.

Finally, we addressed the question of how the HAI! Adventurers could extend the rental version of their database to be suitable for offering lessons and guided tours. The task was not difficult, but it gave an opportunity to illustrate that although reasoning by analogy is a very powerful design and problem-solving technique, it is not perfect. It is possible to invoke the wrong analogy or metaphor. The class list was used as an illustration. Quickly, however the weaknesses of that metaphor were revealed, and the registration analogy was adopted to lead us to an effective design, yielding the Activities and Apply extensions. Finally, the Class List view—still a useful output from the database, even if it doesn't provide good guidance for how to construct the physical database tables—was implemented within the Activities, Apply structure.

Though the focus has been on solving the database problems for HAI! Adventure and their Snow Machine shop, the ideas and approaches used in this case study are fully general. The approach—consider the workflow and information inputs and outputs—works for other database design situations. Moreover, the details of the approach—tables and relationships first, views second, implementation dead last—also apply to most other design situations. We were successful here simply by working through the process carefully. It's a powerful strategy.

EXERCISES

1. The ASTeam table gives the specialists birthday. Why instead doesn't it include the specialist's age, which is probably the information a database user might want?
2. Revise the Clients table to refer to a customer's address in another table based on the Contact schema, helping families in which several renters all reside at the same address.
3. Assign the names given in the text to the five relationships shown in Figure 14.2.

4. Why does the GUI for the *Hiring* view use the name of HAI! Adventure instead of the name of the ski shop, Snow Machine?

5. The Snow Machine shop wants to send out paychecks to the adventure specialists that work there. Construct the query that creates the mailing list table containing the specialist's legal name and *local* address.

6. Construct a view query for a view that allows leaders to look over the Skill levels of the students who have applied for a given class.

CHAPTER 15

eCommerce and Interactive Networking

Learning Objectives

- Appreciate eCommerce's challenge of variation.
- Know the structure of networked interactions.
- Understand the implications of the *discrete event problem.*
- Learn how cookies can give interaction continuity.
- Learn the role of transactions and serialization.
- Understand the importance of interoperability.
- Know how to protect from disasters recover from failures.

At the end of the second millennium, electronic commerce was white hot. Known as eCommerce, it was an application of technology to business that "was revolutionizing the economy" so dramatically that "old business rules no longer applied." Amazon.com, whose founder Steve Bezos was *Time* magazine's "Man of the Year for 2000," was a model for such businesses. Happily, the hype has died down. What remains are three facts: ECommerce will continue to grow as a significant commercial mechanism; eCommerce is extremely complex from both technical and business points of view; and the methods and techniques of eCommerce have not yet been fully worked out. That is, it's here to stay; it's too complex to learn in one chapter; and it's a moving target. Our best hope is to learn the fundamentals. Then, when the day comes that eCommerce sites are so good that we don't even notice them, we'll at least appreciate the tremendous obstacles these pioneers overcame.

ECommerce means conducting business using electronic data communications. Usually the Internet and World Wide Web come to mind because we think of "shopping on the Web." But the term is broader, including also electronic funds transfer (cash machines), point of sale transactions (credit and debit cards), business-to-business activities, networked meetings, and so on. Essentially any activity using network communication with a computer at one or both ends for the purposes of conducting business is eCommerce. We study eCommerce for Fluency because it embodies all aspects of serious networked interactions. People and organizations need not conduct business to use the same ideas or encounter the same problems. ECommerce, besides being interesting, focuses our study.

Using network communication for transacting business and other forms of interaction is a topic under active development. Though the process can at times seem very chaotic, certain fundamental properties of interacting over a network define the context in which the developers work. Understanding those features of eCommerce is the goal of this chapter. Specifically, we consider the following topics:

- Complexity of variation—the people, products, and interactive experiences are extremely diverse.
- Structure of the setting—interacting with computers across a communication network has a standard form.
- Discrete events are the medium—unlike person-to-person or phone, eCommerce happens in quanta.
- Transactions do the work—many operations happening simultaneously without colliding.
- Interoperability—orchestrating all of the specialists to solve a problem requires an established interface.
- Unreliability—life is uncertain, so how does "life go on" after disaster strikes?

Though eCommerce is often criticized for its shortcomings, it faces many difficult challenges, which, when we understand them, leave us amazed that eCommerce exists at all.

> **Don't Accept Crummy**. ECommerce is new and difficult, but it is also competitive. Companies that should know better put up poor sites that are hard to use, slow, repetitive, and crash or fail. Don't accept it! Take your business to sites that work well. Reward those who are trying to make eCommerce a success. After all, consumers have the power.

Complexity of Variation

When compared to traditional businesses—the so-called "bricks and mortar" enterprises—eCommerce confronts a significantly greater range of variation. Four types of variation are important:

- Customer diversity
- Business constraints
- Product variation
- Shopping experiences

In each case, the contrast with the bricks and mortar alternative is striking.

Customer Diversity

When Americans visit a greeting card shop, they probably do not notice that it sells cards for birthdays, graduations, Mother's Day, condolences, and so forth because these are the occasions for which Americans send cards. Nor does it come to their attention that the cards are written in English, use "beached whale" humorously, generally open on the right, are priced in dollars, are printed on recycled paper, meet the local postal regulations, and so on. But others would notice the absence of cards designed for Children's Day, written in Farsi, using "beached whale" respectfully, opening on the left, priced in dracmas, printed on new paper, preprinted with postal code squares, and so on. Enterprises with a physical location can and do specialize to the local population, its language, customs, biases, and needs. Electronic businesses, which can trivially reach customers across the planet, are challenged to accommodate the enormous variation of the people of the world. It is not enough to have a Web page in a foreign language; it is necessary to respect all of the cultural differences that impact business.

Business Constraints

The countries of the world exercise their power to define a currency and set import and export controls, tariffs, taxes, and other conditions of business operation. Though crossing a border is easy electronically, the complexity of being informed of and respecting all of these constraints is challenging. An apparently obvious simplification that could be used, especially when getting started, is to limit business to only one country, say, the United States, and refuse to honor orders from clients without a mailing address in the country. The tactic reduces the currency to dollars and eliminates import/export controls and tariffs. But it doesn't eliminate taxation as a problem, for example. There are about 7000 taxing authorities in the United States, so collecting the right amount of tax is complicated, but then paying the proper amount to each authority is perhaps a greater complication. There has been a moratorium on collecting taxes on net business when a company doesn't have a physical presence in the locality, but it won't last forever, and in any case, the moratorium simplifies only one aspect of conducting business on the World Wide Web.

Product Variation

Physical stores are usually constrained in the number of products they offer by their display space, and catalog businesses are typically constrained by page space. Because eCommerce's display space is virtual, there is no upper limit on the number of products that can be offered. This motivates some businesses to offer a large number of products, especially of different types. But for a customer to buy, shopping must be informed. With no clerks, eCommerce must rely on a computer to provide the proper information customized to each product. The representation and presentation of factual information about shirts, textbooks, and computers varies widely, and though there are common principles, a one-size-fits-all software approach will not satisfy the customer. Thus, no sale. Even within a single product type—clothing or books— there is still considerable variation that challenges the eCommerce site to deliver all the useful, relevant information for each product.

Shopping Experiences

Though shoppers enter a physical store distracted by their phones, friends, children, and packages, they are essentially there to shop. And clerks can observe them, deciding when to offer assistance as they proceed through a more-or-less standard protocol of looking, selecting, deciding, paying, and leaving. Visitors to an Internet site may have those distractions too, but they could also be eating breakfast, fixing dinner, trying to work, watching *Jeopardy*, playing with a pet that might be pawing at the keyboard, communicating over a slow connection, or have any of hundreds of other distractions. There is no "standard protocol" under these circumstances, no standard navigation path through the site. There isn't even a guarantee that a single person is doing the navigating. Besides distractions, there is the problem that customers cannot inspect the product beyond seeing a photograph of it or hearing a clip of it. Catalogs have this same problem, but there is always an 800 number that a customer can dial to get informed assistance. Online there's just a computer at the other end.

Each of these differences poses a significant challenge, but taken together they are truly daunting. They explain some of the struggles that eCommerce sites have confronted as they have developed the idea.

Structure of the Setting

The eCommerce settings considered here share a common form. A customer is poised before a personal computer's display using a Web browser and interacting by Internet with a business's computer at an unknown location. Speaking only of the two computers, this situation is known as the *client/server structure*, wherein the customer's computer is the client and the remote computer is the server. Though the "client" is the customer's computer, the term isn't motivated by eCommerce. It predates eCommerce, and refers to any situation where one computer, the *client*, gets services from another computer, the *server*. Whenever you are browsing, your computer is in a client/server relationship with the remote Web server—it "serves" the Web pages that your browser client requests in response to your clicks. And, it's called a "Web server" because of this relationship. *Caution:* Though you may think of your browser as *serving* you, that's not the relationship of interest here. Rather it is the relationship of your client computer (and browser software) interacting with the server computer (and its software) that is important. Figure 15.1 displays this familiar setup.

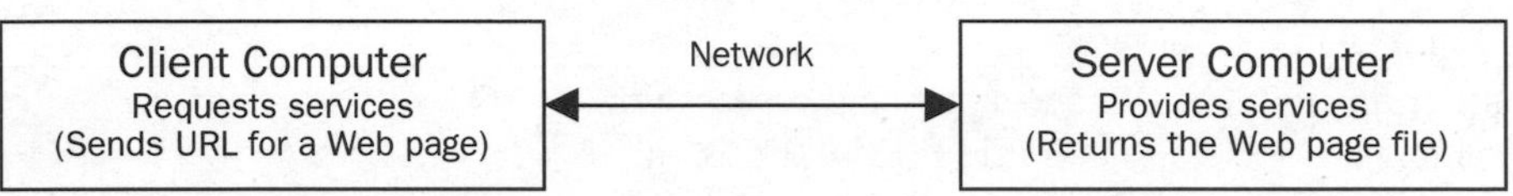

Figure 15.1. The basic client/server structure, as illustrated by the browser (client) requesting Web pages provided by the Web server.

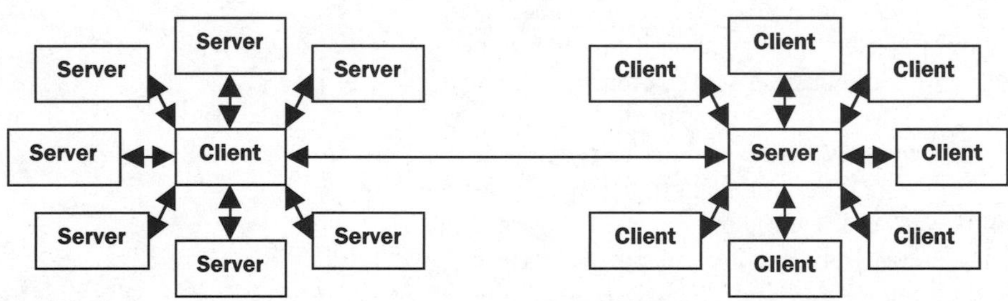

Figure 15.2. Clients and servers evolved over time in many client/server relationships with other servers and clients, respectively.

The client/server abstraction is the workhorse of the Web. A key aspect of the idea is that in Figure 15.1 only a single service request and response are shown. It is a very brief relationship, coming into existence at the moment the request is sent and ending the moment the service has been provided. Specifically, unlike a telephone call in which a connection is made and held by the participants for as long as the session lasts, and wherein there may be many alternating exchanges, the client/server relationship is transient. It only entails the client asking for a service and receiving it. An important advantage of this arrangement is that the server can handle many clients at a time. Typically between two consecutive client events from your browser—between getting a Web page and requesting the next one from the same site—that server could have serviced hundreds or perhaps thousands of other clients. This is a very efficient system because the server is engaged in your service for only as long as it takes to perform it. Once it's done, the relationship is over from the server's point of view. But the relationship is over from your client's viewpoint, too. Your next click could be on the URL for a different server. Between that click and the next time you visit the site, if ever, you and your browser could be clients to hundreds or perhaps thousands of other servers. Accordingly Figure 15.2 shows a more suggestive view perhaps of the client/server relationship over time.

> **Staying Connected**. With the conventional telephone, callers remain connected, even if no one is talking. In a client/server structure, there's no connection. There is a client-to-server transmission for requests, and a server-to-client transmission for replies. But doesn't your computer stay connected to the Internet? Yes, but only to your ISP—that is, the Internet—not to any Web server.

The client/server abstraction was a useful starting point for developing Web technology, and it continues to be an excellent tool for understanding eCommerce, but it is not sophisticated enough to solve all the problems. The basic client/server abstraction is fine for serving up static Web pages in HTML, say, as the college's Web server might do, but in order to handle the kinds of variety discussed in the last section, it is necessary to create customized Web pages on the fly. For example, a Web page that is to give real-time flight arrival and departure times for an airline cannot be based on static, preprogrammed HTML pages. Almost all eCommerce applications require created-for-the-situation Web pages because

- Some or all of the information changes frequently—once a month or faster.
- The huge volume of information prohibits building separate Web pages for each item—think of a dictionary.
- The combinations of information groupings that potentially go together grows geometrically—model, engine size, transmission type, number of doors, body color, interior color, interior fabric, wheels, tires, and so on.

Though servers can and do create Web pages on the fly, the standard scenario involves other components, such as a database system where all of the information that goes into the Web page is stored. The addition of other components requires that we extend the client/server structure. Though the extensions are conceptually reasonable, the terminology is rather curious.

To extend the client/server abstraction, the techies who create Web software began calling it a *two-tier system*, where the client and the server are each a *tier*, synonymous with *layer*. (Think of them as being drawn as a vertical stack. Also note that given all the grief such systems can create, the spelling *tear* might have been better!) Then, the case where the database is added onto a two-tier system can be called a *three-tier system*. The third tier doesn't necessarily have to be a database management computer. It only needs to be another logical system component dedicated to the fulfillment of client requests. Given that two-tier and three-tier systems are useful abstractions, it is inevitable that the term n*-tier system* would emerge, meaning systems with several layers devoted to serving client needs. Finally, the amazing term *middleware* refers to the programs running at the center of the three-tier or *n*-tier system. It is middleware that produces the created-on-the-fly HTML pages by getting information from the database and assembling it into Web pages to fulfill the client's request.

> **Where Ware?** A tech document on the Web describes "middleware" as "software running on the middle end of the system."

Discrete Events Means Cookies for All

As already noted the client/server relationship is a transient one. That characteristic allows a server to handle many clients, fulfilling each request in a brief time quantum, and then moving on to the next. It's very efficient. But there's a very serious disadvantage, too. No continuity exists across a series of requests produced by one client. If you request a biography of Serena Williams, the tennis star, and then in your next request ask for a biography of Venus, everyone—though not a Web server—would know that you're asking about Venus Williams, her sister, not the goddess of Roman Mythology. The Web server is unaware of the connection between the two requests. Although your requests were consecutive from your point of view, the server handled many others in between. It may be that your Serena request wasn't even in the last thousand requests, and that a request for Aphrodite was. That is, the more recent relevant context from the server's point of view may not be yours.

The biography server assembles biographies from its database as a series of unrelated events responding to client requests because there is no (apparent) commercial value in knowing which biographies you've asked for recently, that is, in knowing your context. (After all, how hard is it to type "Venus *Williams*"?) But many eCommerce businesses do need continuity because, for example, they must correlate your request to purchase a product with your credit card number to pay for it, information likely to be in separate client/server events.

Before considering how this problem is solved, consider another compounding factor: The server cannot be sure that two requests came from the same person or session. Imagine requesting the Serena Williams biography in the lab, reading it, deciding it's time to go to class, and logging out. Your friend logs into the same machine and requests a biography of Venus. He doesn't want Venus Williams, but the goddess. From the point of view of the biography server, the two requests come from the same IP address, that is, the same client. In a related situation, if you request Serena's bio at home, and then log out, your ISP will assign the IP address you were using to someone else. Whoever receives it could be similarly surprised if the bio server tried to maintain continuity with your request based on the IP address. The problem of relating consecutive requests, which we will call the *discrete event problem*, is clearly difficult.

One solution is the mechanism of storing and retrieving cookies, a computer science concept not widely known before the WWW. A *cookie* is information stored on a Web client computer by a server computer. Cookies were introduced into Netscape 1.0 to solve the "discrete event problem" as explained momentarily. Cookies are stored in a file (Netscape) or directory (IE) called cookies and have a standard structure for each browser. Netscape's cookies have the form

domain dom_flag path secure_flag exp_date name value

where the three fields of interest to us are *domain*, the server that wrote the cookie, *name* is the cookie's name, and *value* is the information that the cookie is storing. Cookies are typically exchanged between a client and server on all exchanges. For example, while researching Buckminster Fuller's life in Chapter 6, WNET-TV's Web site server placed the following cookie on my computer:

```
www.WNET.org FALSE / FALSE 1027192661 thirteen_uid 64.10.140.253.171119956565334
```

domain   *name*   *value*

and a related Web server stored

```
www.thirteen.org FALSE / FALSE 1026961838 thirteen_uid 64.10.140.161.28198995425707131
```

domain   *name*   *value*

The two different domains identify two different servers, but they are apparently part of the same site because they use a common cookie name, `thirteen_uid`. The two different values, which seem to begin with four-digit IP addresses, identified my client to these two different servers.[1]

The *value* of a cookie is anything that the *domain* server needs to store on the client, but typically the value is simply a unique identifier for the client. It solves the discrete event problem as follows. When a client first visits a site, there is no stored cookie from the server, so the server—if it needs to maintain continuity—creates a

---

[1] The expiration date is a "UNIX date," counting milliseconds since 1 January 1970, 00:00:00 GMT; see Chapter 19.

cookie and sends it to the client in the header of the Web page. The client records it, and with each subsequent exchange between the server and the client, the cookie will be passed. The server records in a database whatever information it needs to remember as the interaction proceeds, each time using the unique value as the key (Chapter 13) to find the client among its records. In this way, the server can maintain the coherent thread of the client's requests and visits, as shown in Figure 15.3.

> **Finding Cookies**. Locate the cookies stored on your computer by searching for files and folders containing the string `cookie` or `cookies`. The files can be opened using a basic ASCII text editor like Notepad or SimpleText. College computers are often "wiped" clean after each session, so you may have to surf for a few minutes before any cookies are stored.

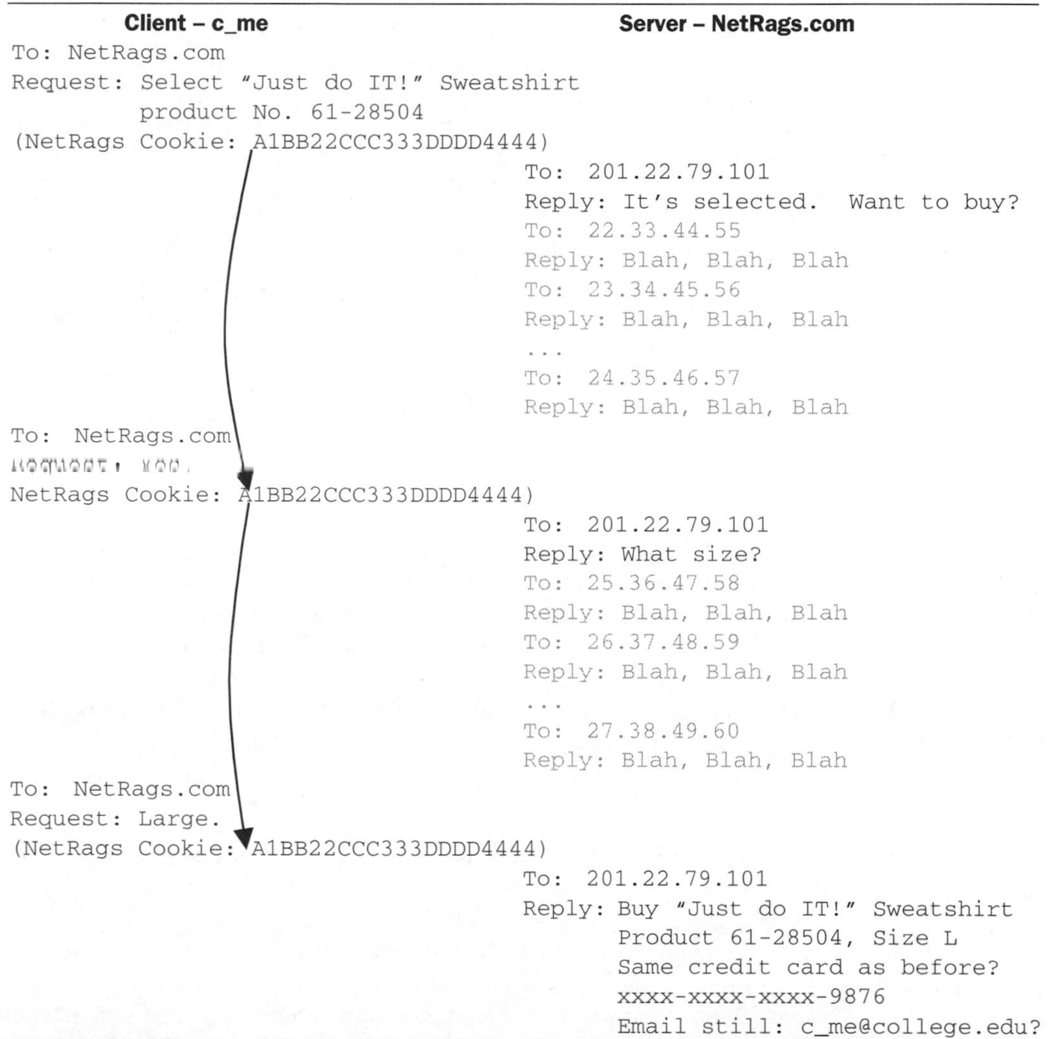

Figure 15.3. An idealized interaction between client and server in which a cookie stored at the client allows the server to connect independent events into a coherent dialog. Notice that the cookie also connects to an earlier session when the customer gave the email address, credit card number, and probably mailing address.

Servers could try to keep the whole history of a session, but doing so might record too many extraneous events of little significance. For example, customers might make many requests to the server just to browse the site. The server could try to infer some characteristics of the customer's wanderings, but it's probably too difficult.

Consequently only certain significant events would typically be recorded in the database, for example, the `Select` request of Figure 15.3. The "shopping cart" abstraction has been used to assist customers in conceptualizing the idea of having designated some product as one of interest. In such a situation, the server would only bother to record a "put in the shopping cart" request (in addition to a "buy" request, of course, and the subsequent requests needed to "close the sale").

The original idea of the Netscape engineers who adopted the cookie solution was that clients would store the shopping cart, credit card, and mailing address information rather than having the *server* store it in its database. The approach is smart, for example, because storing on the client relieves the server of various responsibilities like keeping credit card numbers secure. The idea requires that severs be allowed considerable latitude to set any value on the client. However, the use of cookies has largely evolved to the approach described earlier, where a cookie is basically a unique identifier that the server uses as a key to find client information it keeps in its own database. Meanwhile, privacy experts have become alarmed because there are many ways to abuse cookies, and some companies have apparently done so. The potential problems with storing cookies are topics discussed more fully in Chapter 16, *Privacy and Security.* For now, cookies solve the difficult problem of maintaining continuity across many discrete events.

Surviving Without Cookies

Between the extremes of processing completely unrelated requests and knowing the entire history of the client's contact with the site using cookies, there is a middle ground solution in which continuity is maintained, but not the exact identity of the client. This is perhaps the most common setting for WWW interactions and eCommerce. While explaining this solution, which involves looking a bit more closely at the three-tier system organization, we will clear up some major mysteries of the Web.

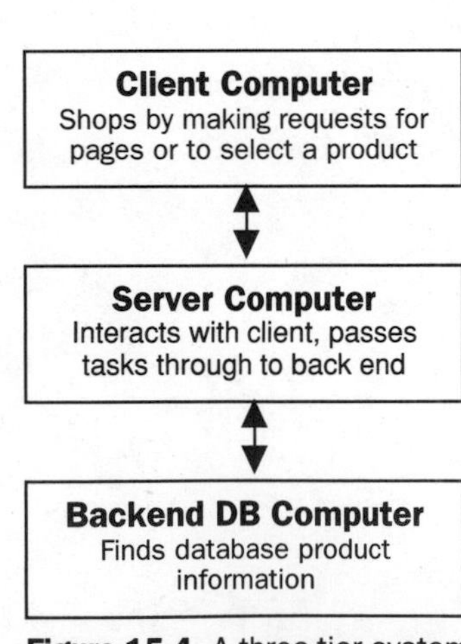

Figure 15.4. A three-tier system in which backend tasks are performed by CGI programs.

Imagine the server configuration that supports interactions like Figure 15.3. Because it must access a database to get information about the clothing products, it is probably organized as a three-tier system, as shown in Figure 15.4. To create the pages that the client sees, the server applies the following standard sequence of actions:

1. The server receives the client's request and figures out what to do, asking a middleware program to do it.
2. The middleware program runs, accessing the database and building a Web page containing the requested information.
3. The server receives the synthesized page back from the middleware and returns it to the client.

This processing sequence—in which the middleware program is in the *middle*—explains the mystery of how middleware got its name. It is in the middle of the processing activity for cases in which the server needs to request additional services, like accessing a database. Notice that the system organization in Figure 15.4—showing who communicates with whom—places the computer added as the third tier at the end farthest from the client. Thus there are two ways to look at the situation. In the processing view, the middleware is in the middle, hence its name. In the communication view, the third computer is at the end because it's farthest removed from the client. (See Figure 15.5.) Seen from these two points of view, the description "middleware is at the middle end of the system" doesn't seem so bizarre, perhaps.

We postulate that the middleware program uses the Common Gateway Interface (CGI) mechanism, though there are many other alternatives. The CGI program,

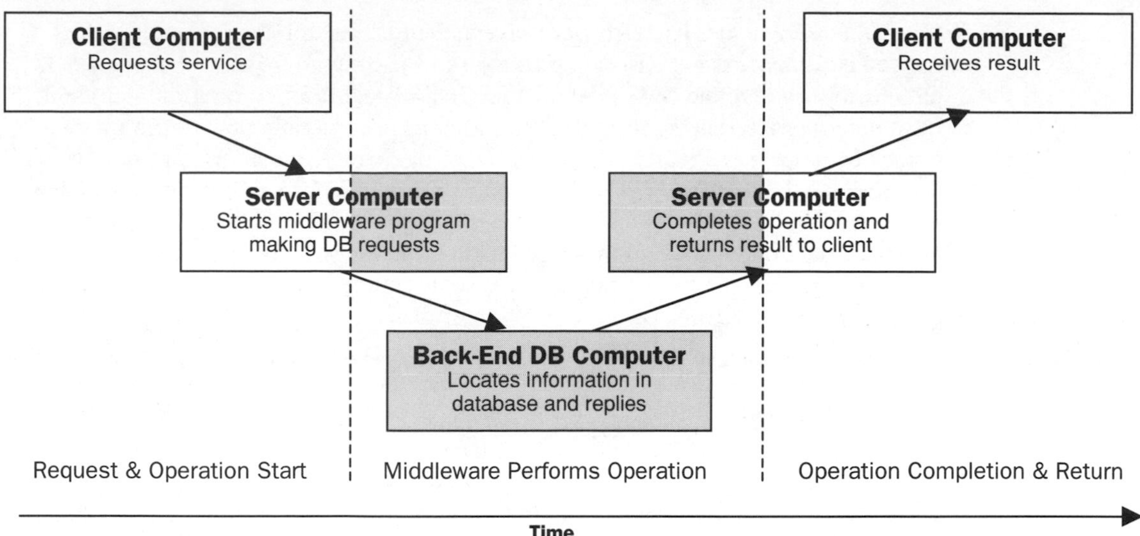

Figure 15.5. Middleware performs an operation on a three-tier system; time moves to the right; the Client Computer boxes represent one computer at different points in time; similarly for the Server Computer boxes.

running on the Server, queries a backend database telling it what product information to retrieve in response to the client's request. The database system looks up the information and returns textual, image, and other forms of information back to the program. Typically the program then fills in the information on a predefined page form, or *template*, containing standard structural information like headings and other page layout specifications, but with placeholders for the content. The server returns the newly constructed page, which has a consistent "look and feel" because of the template, but is customized to the client's requested content. This approach goes a long way to solving a problem such as product variability mentioned earlier. Notice that when the CGI program requests information from the backend database system, those two computers are in a different client/server relationship, wherein the former server has become the client and the database computer is the server.

Now it is possible to clear up a mystery of Web usage. The CGI program is servicing many clients' requests. How does it know that the client wants pricing information for a round-trip flight between Cairo and Bangkok? The client typed in Cairo or chose it in a pop-up menu of departing cities, and similarly for Bangkok. (Such capabilities are not expressible directly in HTML, but are using the JavaScript capabilities explained in Chapters 17–20.) When the client sends its request to the server, it doesn't request an HTML page, but rather directly calls the CGI program that will find the route information in the DB. The call gives the parameters, that is, the two cities and other information, to the program as part of the request string as if it were a long URL. The typical form is

```
.../cgi-bin/find_flights?DEP=CAIRO&ARR=BANGKOK&RET=Y&FARE=ECON&DEP-DATE=...
```

where `find_flights` is the program, and the text following the "`?`" gives the data for the request. The data is a list of parameters separated by "`&`" and having the form *data_name* = *data_value* in this example. Each CGI program can define its own format as long as it adheres to a few simple rules, for example, use "+" instead of blank. Such long strings of semi-readable text are familiar in the location window of our browsers when using many Web sites, including, for example, Google—the query being searched is encoded after the question mark. These are requests to the specific middleware program that performs the service.

When the reply comes back from the server, the information may result in the client's making more decisions, say, picking a specific departure time. This new data will be appended to the end of the next request, so that the CGI program has the data from both queries. And so forth. By returning the accumulating data from many rounds of request and reply, the CGI mechanism enables the program to stay in context because the data list effectively contains the whole history of the dialog. When the client finally decides to buy the ticket, the assembled information can be passed off as the data list to the CGI program handling purchases, giving it the context of the previous interactions, too. Notice that this solution doesn't require storing or retrieving cookies.

TRANSACTIONS

When the middleware is interacting with the database, caution must be exercised in order to maintain the integrity of the information. For example, while one instance of a CGI program is replying to a customer about selecting seat 14C on a given flight, another instance of the same program may be simultaneously assigning 14C to a different customer on that flight. If the customers are not to be stacked to the ceiling, the interaction with the database cannot be haphazard. The method for avoiding such problems is to be found in the long-studied topic of distributed databases. When independent *transactions* on a database—operations like finding information and making changes—are performed so that they overlap in time, there is the potential for the low-level changes to the database to come in a sequence so they produce erroneous results or corrupt the database producing garbage. Consider an example.

Imagine two people—perhaps husband and wife—with a joint bank account, who have traveled to a distant city, realized they're short on cash, try to use the nearest cash machine, and find it is broken. They decide to split up to look for a working machine and agree to return to the hotel in 15 minutes. If neither is successful, they'll develop a plan B; if one is successful, they've got their cash; and if both are successful, they'll have twice as much cash, but the bellman deserves a big tip after struggling with all their bags. Naturally they both find a machine at about the same time. The ATMs send their requests to withdraw $100 from the same account, and two middleware programs, W and H, process the requests (see Figure 15.6). These are two instances of the same program that must get from the database the current balance in the account, check that the balance is more than $100, subtract $100, and store the new balance back in the database. (Of course, if the balance is less than $100, the ATMs are notified, and the request is denied.)

W	DB Acct Bal	H
	$500	
Req. balance of Acct 02468HW		
Recv. reply that it's $500		
Compute. NewBal = $500 – $100		
Req. Chng Acct 02468HW Bal to $400		
Tell ATM to give $100 to customer	$400	Req. balance of Acct 02468HW
		Recv. reply that it's $400
		Compute. NewBal = $400 – $100
		Req. Chng Acct 02468HW Bal to $300
	$300	Tell ATM to give $100 to customer

Figure 15.6. Correct processing of two withdrawals from a bank account.

The W and H programs and the database serving their requests *should* operate as shown in Figure 15.6. However, the transactions are implemented as multistep operations with two requests to the database server: one to get the balance, one to change the balance. They might have been interleaved in time as shown in Figure 15.7. That is, the ATMs dispensed $200 in cash to the lucky depositors, but their account was charged only $100. Maybe they should have gotten even more cash! What happened?

W	DB Acct Bal	H
	$500	
Req. balance of Acct 02468HW		
Recv. reply that it's $500		Req. balance of Acct 02468HW
Compute. NewBal = $500 – $100		Recv. reply that it's $500
Req. Chng Acct 02468HW Bal to $400		Compute. NewBal = $500 – $100
Tell ATM to give $100 to customer	$400	Req. Chng Acct 02468HW Bal to $400
		$400 Tell ATM to give $100 to customer

Figure 15.7. Two withdrawal transactions interleaved in time to produce the wrong balance, that is, corrupt the database.

In the second scenario, the H program's request for the account balance came before the W program had completed its transaction and updated the balance. So, instead of receiving a balance of $400, it received the original balance of $500 in response to its request. Obviously the bank isn't going to be too happy about this, and because this is a well-understood phenomenon in distributed databases, it is safe to assume that it doesn't happen with ATMs. But similar phenomena do happen in other situations. Without getting too deeply into technical discussions, they can be handled by assuring that any transactions that use common data—the balance, in this case—run so that one completes before the other starts. The property is called *serialized behavior.*

Serialized behavior says that the operations are done as if they take place one at a time in some order, which ensures that no two programs are ever working on the same information at the same time. Thus, from the point in time of the first reference to any data involved in the transaction until the point at which the last modification of any data has been returned to storage, there can be no references to any of the data involved in the transaction—neither reading nor writing—except by the program performing the transaction. The W and H transactions of Figure 15.7 were not serialized because H referenced the balance before W had completed its transaction. Serialized behavior doesn't prevent references or modifications to other parts of the database from taking place simultaneously, as long as they reference independent data. So, other people can be getting money from their accounts from other cash machines as long as they are all separate accounts.

Uncooperative. A common case where transactions are not serialized, but should be, is when a group of people works cooperatively on a project. Someone finishes a draft of the work and sends it around. Then two or more people work on it without signaling the others that they are doing so. If they work on separate parts, it's OK; if not, the draft may have incompatible changes; that is, the document is corrupted. The solution: Treat the draft like a library book; send email "checking it out" to change it, and "checking it in" to give someone else a chance.

Recalling the example of assigning seat 14C on the airplane, we infer that the two instances of the seat-assignment middleware programs, which had to have checked for the availability of the seat and then made the assignment, must not have been serialized either. That is, they must have each checked for availability before either of them made an assignment. We will return to this problem later when we consider the reliability of computer systems.

The Standards Case

Many commentators have marveled about the changes wrought by the World Wide Web, but few have considered the truly miraculous part of it. Every use of a network is a dialog between two computers, and like people *they must both speak the same language to communicate*. The people of the world have an almost impossible time communicating even though most of them speak one of only a dozen different languages. What's the problem?

> **Common Language:** In a population of speakers of one of *n* languages, there are n^2 ways to pair people, but only *n* ways to do it so they speak the same language. For example, with 12 languages, there are 144 different pairs of speakers, but only 12 can communicate. The other 132 cannot. Having a common language is essential to communication. (Some people speak multiple languages, of course, but still most of the people of the world cannot communicate with most of the others—we need a world language!)

There are millions of different computers using thousands of different hardware computer configurations and thousands of different operating system configurations. If each server had to customize its interaction with each client according to the kind of computer it is and its operating system peculiarities, the Web would never have happened. Period. The enabling concept was the standard representation of the Hypertext Markup Language, HTML, and the processing method of the Hypertext Transport Protocol, HTTP. Having these standards meant that client computers only had to "understand" HTML to display an image to the user, and server computers only had to "understand" HTTP to fulfill the client's request. Each end of the networked connection can be constructed of any hardware, run any operating system, use any file structure, and adopt myriad other system specifics. As long as each end can process the information it receives and send the right information back—that is, understand HTML/HTTP—everything works. It is the common language. Using hypertext for networked communication was brilliant, but the genius of the Web was that everyone adopted it as the standard. Standards are fundamental to networking.

> **IT's Standard**. HTML/HTTP is actually one in a long sequence of standards used in networking. TCP/IP—the packet-level communication of Chapter 4—was the first and most basic of these.

As important as the HTML/HTTP standard is, it only really got the World Wide Web started and defined its baseline capability. For the WWW to provide more functionality—splashier media, more dazzling graphic affects, less stilted interaction—both the client and the server have to be upgraded. This has already happened. For example, the HTML/HTTP client/server relationship supports the CGI mechanism, mentioned earlier. CGI is an extension of the HTTP protocol, making it another standard. The key point is that standards are essential to the present and future of networked communication. They allow the client and server to be independent, but to communicate in a way that allows both ends to interpret the information being transferred correctly.

Java is an important standard that provides a general means for dynamically upgrading a browser's capability. Java is a programming language that browsers can interpret. A server can send a client a small Java program, known as an *applet*, so named to convey a diminutive *app*lication. The client computer runs the applet because browsers know how to do that. The applet might display data from the server in a splashy way or perhaps assist the user in gathering and packaging data to send back to the server. Because Java is a general programming language capable of expressing any algorithm, the server can add any capability to the client side of the interaction so long as it's consistent with the security and other limitations purposely imposed on Java.

> **What Side Are You On?** Facilities like Java enable the server to move portions of its work to the client, introducing the need for terms like *client-side* and *server-side.* The advantage of client-side services like applets is that Internet delays cannot slow them, whereas delays can slow delivery of a server's services.

In effect, the server can improve its dialog with a client by extending their common standard of communication. Java gives flexibility to both sides of the client/server relationship. The server tells the client how it wants the client upgraded for the specific situation at hand by giving the client the applet program. Then, rather than doing the server work and sending the result to the client, that is, supporting the interaction from the server side, the server simply directs the applet to do the work on the client's side. The client gets better service because doing the work locally eliminates the (potentially) slow network and (possibly) overloaded server. Over time, as programmers improve the applet, the subsequent interactions get even better. Further, each server can customize to its own business needs.

Though it is probably true that every aspect of eCommerce benefits from standards, there is one other place besides the basic Web client/server relationship where standards are critical for interoperability. In the three-tier system, we noted that when the server interacts with the backend database it was in a new client/server relationship, being the client to the database's server role. In an *n*-tier system, such relationships are quite numerous, and often the server in these cases is some other company's product. For example, an eCommerce site might decide not to try to keep track of 7000 tax rates, but to buy a tax rate server from a vendor specializing in taxation. Thus we have many client/server relationships *inside* the site's middleware system, and as before *both ends of each of these client/server pairs* must "speak" the same language to understand the communication. Accordingly, they must use the same encodings and protocols, and if different companies produced the software, the companies must agree on the standard. Though fundamental, the problem of interoperability is potentially a huge drag on business flexibility.

One standard addresses a most critical aspect of this middleware client/server interoperability, the task of encoding complex data structures so that they may be exchanged. For basic Web pages, HTML performs this encoding. But HTML focuses only on the presentation and is both rigid and limited. Middleware needs to know how to find specific information in the data sent between a client and server, so describing the presentation is less important than describing the *content*. But content is extremely variable. The new standard is called the *Extensible Markup Language* or XML. XML, whose precursor was used for digitizing the *Oxford English Dictionary* in Chapter 8, uses tags just like HTML. What makes XML significant is that it is a *self-describing* encoding of information. The tags are invented for each client/server relationship. That is, XML files specify the information to be exchanged by using matched self-identifying tags defining the meta-information about the components of the exchange. Accordingly XML can be adapted to the structural needs of any information flowing among the middleware subsystems, making it essentially universal.

For example, in Figure 15.8, the order information, perhaps to be sent to the order processing subsystem as a result of the dialog in Figure 15.3, shows the key information in human-readable and machine-understandable form. When the middleware order-processor gets it, it looks through for the `<ClientCode>` tag and knows that all of the information between it and the `</ClientCode>` tag is the client code. The tag was invented for this specific client/server interaction.

```
<?xml version="1.0"?>
<Order>
   <OrderNum>71442</OrderNum>
   <ClientCode>A1BB22CCC333DDDD4444</ClientCode>
   <PurchaseList>
     <ItemCode color="Blue">64-28741</ItemCode>
       <ItemCode size="L">61-28504</ItemCode>
   </PurchaseList>
</Order>
```

Figure 15.8. An example XML encoding of order information that might result from the session in Figure 15.3. Notice that it is possible to include attributes that further specify the tag information.

So, who decides on the standards? In some cases, a standard achieves acceptance because many people independently decide to follow it. The original HTML became standard that way. Many people got a copy of a free browser program, called Mosaic, which displayed HTML. That allowed them to read HTML that others published, and they quickly decided to set up their own Web site. Naturally they chose to follow the HTML/HTTP protocol. But such an anarchic process only works at the beginning. Soon the process must become much more organized. Today a group known as the World Wide Web Consortium (W3C) decides on standards like CGI and XML. By having broad representation among the interested parties, the process of creating a standard receives wide input, and the resulting standard is thus likely to be widely adopted.

SURVIVING DISASTERS

As the saying goes, "Life is uncertain; eat dessert first." Uncertainty in the physical world results from lightning strikes that cut power, earthquakes and other natural disasters, terrorist attacks, accidents, as well as simple entropy—the tendency of things to "run down." To the list of physical risks, add the potential logical problems of program bugs, operator errors, and malicious mischief by those intent on causing harm. Obviously, at any moment, parts of the World Wide Web and the Internet are "down," that is, out of service. Being completely decentralized, however, means that most of it is "up and running" most of the time. What does this uncertainty mean for eCommerce? There are three basic aspects to consider:

- Maintaining multiple copies
- Picking the right protocol
- Eternal vigilance

Though not exhaustive, these topics are critical to eCommerce and to us personally.

Redundancy is Very, Very, Very Good

The software-crash-before-the-work-is-saved experience is a common frustration for everyone. We know we should save, but we forget until it's too late. Usually not more than one session's work is lost. On a longer time scale, periodically backing up files to a secondary device or alternate medium is the companion to periodically saving. We know we should back up, but we forget until it's too late. The difference is that the consequences of negligence are much more serious. When the hard disk starts screeching or smelling like burning plastic, much more than one session will be lost. A week or a month or a year's worth of work can be gone, and it is irreproducible and often irreplaceable. In eCommerce, daily backups, off-site storage, a system recovery team, and possibly system redundancy are equivalent to our personal periodic backups and saving. But responsibility to prepare for disaster cannot be left to memory. It must be an integral part of the business operation.

> **Replacing Superstition**. People can be superstitious, believing, for example, that thinking about a disaster can make it happen. Naturally, repressing such thoughts is sensible. But believing a different superstition—that taking precautions against disasters, like saving often, prevents them—may be better in IT. They're both superstitions, of course, but the second one reduces the harm when it turns out to be wrong.

It is impossible for a company to remain in business if it ever loses more than a negligible amount of information. Thus, any eCommerce site expecting to remain in business long enough to make money must work the "backup and fault recovery problem" immediately. The solutions quickly become technical, beyond the scope of this book, but the basic idea is to keep a full copy of everything written on the system as of some date and time. This is a *full backup*. Then moving into the future, periodically record all new information written—called a *partial backup*—since the last full or partial backup. The period of partial backups is daily or every eight hours or some frequency determined by the cost and grief caused by loss of all information since the last partial backup. If disaster strikes, beginning with the full backup copy of the system, progressively re-create the state of the system up to the last backup by remaking all the changes of the successive partial backups! It's tedious, but disaster doesn't often strike, either. It would be easier to have full backups everyday, but that's usually too much information to copy and save.

> **A 3-Line Sermon.** Disasters don't always happen to someone else. Backups are truly important. Furthermore, it's wise periodically to store a full backup somewhere away from your computer.

Picking the Right Protocol

The serialized transaction is an important principle for maintaining high-quality information. But what happens when disaster strikes in the middle of performing a serialized transaction? Referring to our earlier example, we need not worry about a power failure bringing the ATM down because dispensing the money is the last action. In this case, the accounting part of the transaction would normally complete. Any customer that didn't get his $100 would be in the bank immediately complaining. Counting the money in the machine determines if there's $100 too much, verification enough to repay the customer and apologize with a (truthful) "it was beyond our control" explanation. Rather the problem concerns internal systems without the physical check that the cash gives.

Imagine that a Web customer has chosen a product, given the credit card information, had it verified, entered the mailing address, and confirmed the whole purchase. Then some transactions run to record the purchase, charge the credit card, and send the order to shipping:

Transaction 1: Charge the credit card and receive confirmation.

Transaction 2: If confirmed, enter record of purchase in the database; otherwise, send email to customer.

Transaction 3: If confirmed, send order to shipping and record in the database; otherwise, skip.

This seems like a solid solution. Nothing happens until the company gets its money, which it should because the card has already been verified; there's an email "safety valve" if something goes wrong; finally with everything in shipshape, ship. But a nearby fire brings down power to the computer room—there's time to worry about battery backup power on Monday—but meanwhile there's a problem. Four possibilities exist:

- Transaction 1 doesn't complete: No credit card charge made; it's as if nothing happened; customers will be very annoyed, and if they ever check back, the company looks clueless with no record of anything.
- Transaction 1 completes, but Transaction 2 doesn't complete: There's a credit card charge, but no record of a purchase; now the company looks fraudulent; customers are extremely annoyed and threaten legal action
- Transactions 1 and 2 complete but Transaction 3 doesn't complete: There's a charge and a record, but no order in shipping; eventually the irate customer calls, the company looks deceptive, but it can at least ship the product with an apology and bonus or other attempt at contrition.
- All complete: Everything is in order; but the company can't know for sure that this is the last transaction . . . is everything really OK?

No company wants any of these outcomes, even if some don't actually result in legal action. What to do?

The solution is to record everything the middleware is doing on a persistent medium, like a hard disk. "Everything" here means every part of every transaction. For each, a record of the transaction and all of its data are written before it starts, and when the transaction is finished, its completion is recorded, all with timestamps. Then when the power is restored, a record of the events immediately preceding the power failure can be reconstructed. It will be possible to identify those that were completed, and then only the ones started, but not completed, need be checked. Thus, if the credit card has been charged, this will have been noted, as will the product the customer intends to purchase, mailing address, and so on. It would be tedious, but the whole situation can be unraveled, avoiding any of the earlier outcomes.

> **Note Taking**. Analogously to the illustrated transactions, we often navigate a long chain of sites on the Web, find a great page, and for various reasons (including crashes) "lose our place." Keeping our own transaction history—outside the browser—can allow us to reconstruct the preceding navigation events.

Eternal Vigilance

Though the transaction history solves the scenario, total disasters are rare. Minor disasters are somewhat more frequent. For example, suppose Transaction 1 tries to charge the card, but the credit card company's computers are down. Transaction 1 cannot complete until it gets the credit card charged, so it puts the task on its to-do list, periodically trying again. Steadily, the unavailability of the credit card company's server will cause uncompleted Transaction 1s to build up in the system. This is probably not good. For example, there is no final acknowledgment to the clients that shipping has been requested—though they've probably left the site anyway figuring the transaction is over from their point of view. The "real problem" is that no one is aware that there is any risk. The many partially processed charges in the system could be lost if the system crashes. Though it might be possible to reconstruct them, it could take a while, and would probably be a tedious task. If the "problem" were known, an alternative might be to capture all of the information and retry if the credit card people ever get their act together. But the lights are flashing, the disks are humming, and everything seems all right . . . how do you know that there is any risk to your system?

The bad performance of the credit card company, though not surprising perhaps, illustrates the general phenomenon of a system problem causing performance to slowly degrade and probably eventually fail. Has your bathtub drain ever clogged up? Did it happen instantaneously or progressively? The solution for computers is the same as for everyday life. Pay attention. In a well-designed middleware system, special programs periodically wake up, check around for some unusual condition, like many pending Transaction 1s, and either report or resolve them if found, or go back to sleep if not. Such programs are called *daemons*, and they are the computational equivalent of "paying attention." The computer has to be explicitly programmed to do everything, of course, including paying attention. Daemons allow computers to monitor and regulate themselves.

Possessed. It is difficult to benefit from daemons in normal computer usage, but *we* can be demonic ourselves, noticing an application's strange behavior, such as slowing down, "forgetting" changes, or failing in other ways. Software behaves this way regularly, and the faults are usually precursors to an application or system failure. Recognizing such peculiarities, we should act immediately: save, exit, and restart.

SUMMARY

ECommerce is an interesting topic to think about while we're waiting for a page to download. It is also a challenging business paradigm to implement. Web-based enterprises are like any business, except that customers can "walk in" from around the world, and all of the clerks are fast, but rather slow-witted—that is, computers. And interaction with customers comes not from continuous contact typical of shopping, but in brief events, as if the store were all dark and the clerk and customer used a camera's flash attachment to conduct business.

We learned that the standard mechanism for handling eCommerce activities is the client/server structure, wherein one computer, the client, requests that some task be performed on its behalf by another computer, the server. This structure is used directly to solve activities like serving Web pages. It is also used as a constituent of much more complex processing structures—3-tier and *n*-tier organizations—where a given computer might at one time be the server and at another time be the client. The client/server interaction is an event or transaction whose duration spans the request, the needed processing by the server, and the reply. When the Internet provides the network connection anonymously, as it does on the World Wide Web, the server has a challenging problem of maintaining the context with any given client. (Not all client/server interactions are handicapped in this way.) Two solutions were introduced. In the cookie solution, the server places a unique identifier on the client, which is exchanged on all client/server interactions, effectively allowing the client to identify itself and the server to associate that identity with a record of the transactions that it keeps in its database. The other solution—the CGI approach—has the client remotely calling a program of the server and passing it the accumulated information of the successive events. We learned the distributed transaction processing can trash a database unless the operations are serialized, and that standards are truly the essence of communication generally and network communication specifically. Finally, we learned that the uncertainties of the world require backups, transaction logs, and daemons to maintain the integrity of the information and processing of an eCommerce site.

There is much more to say about eCommerce-related topics. In Chapter 16 we return to the question of using cookies to maintain the context in a client/server interaction. The possibility that your privacy will be invaded by unscrupulous Web sites exists, just as there is the possibility of being gypped by unscrupulous businesses. As always, vigilance is essential.

EXERCISES

1. Define *eCommerce.*
2. Name four kinds of variation that challenge eCommerce businesses.
3. In the typical client/server relationship of the WWW, which participant are you and your computer?
4. Referring to the client/server relationship between a lab computer and the class Web server, what would be examples of a typical request and service relative to the Fluency class?
5. Measuring from the time that you arrive at a Web site until the time you visit the next site, how much of that time are you connected to the Web server?
6. Between the time a Web server completes sending your browser a page and the time it gets the request for the next page from your browser, what is the server doing?
7. Give a characteristic that differentiates a three-tier system from a standard two-tier system client/server system.
8. Find three cookies on your computer and identify the domain, name, and value. For Netscape Navigator, the format is given in the text. For Microsoft Internet Explorer, they are the first three items in the file.
9. Using the calculator application, compute the number of milliseconds in a year (365.25 days) to determine in what year the cookies given in the text expired or will expire.
10. What would be the advantage of using a cookie to identify a customer rather than an IP address?
11. When is a Web server not a server?
12. Why do we need standards for network communication?
13. Why can you shop online at home and on campus, but the sites you frequent seem to be unaware of your existence at the other location?
14. What is serialized behavior for a transaction?
15. When registering for a course, you must consult the registration database at two times: to check if there is space (Has the class limit been reached?) and to enter the registration information into the database (Enter the student ID and class number into the database). Explain how a class could become oversubscribed if registration is not a serialized transaction.

Chapter 16

Privacy and Security

Learning Objectives

- Appreciate the issues in the privacy debate.
- Know the definition of privacy.
- Know the OECD principles for privacy.
- Understand the risks with third party cookies.
- Learn encryption terminology and system structure.
- Understand the PKC system scenario.
- Learn how the RSA system works.
- Understand whether the RSA is likely to be compromised.

Privacy is a fundamental human right. The United Nations' Universal Declaration of Human Rights recognizes privacy in Article 12. The constitutions of Australia, Hungary, and South Africa among others state a right to privacy. Though privacy is not explicitly mentioned in the U.S. Constitution, the U.S. Supreme Court has accepted privacy as a right implicit in other constitutional guarantees. And privacy is a right that matters to us all. No matter how exemplary our lives may be, all of us have aspects of our story that we would prefer no one else found out about, and which rightfully are no one else's business. When those aspects interact with information technology, the issues of electronic privacy and security become important. We have much more than our password that we want to keep to ourselves.

In this chapter we discuss privacy and security. To begin, we consider a business transaction scenario as a basis for understanding the topic of privacy, and who has an interest in private information. With the issue described, we consider different formulations of privacy, adopting a clear, but abstract definition. Using the definition, we observe that maintaining privacy in the modern world is difficult, given the many situations in which we are required to or choose to reveal information about ourselves. This leads to the matter of keeping private information private, and we enumerate the various principles, including the now-standard principles from the Organization for Economic Cooperation and Development. We then explore how widely these principles are adhered to, discovering a difference between the principles followed in the United States and those of other countries of the world. A disagreement between the United States and the European Union over these principles is the context for exploring the differences. Finally, we consider the practical implications of the principles by analyzing how cookies can be abused to compromise Web users' security.

The next topic is encryption. After the standard vocabulary is introduced with a simple encryption example to illustrate, the concept of a Public Key Cryptosystem (PKC) is studied as a means of achieving more convenient security for Internet-related situations. PKC systems seem at first to offer almost no protection, and then they seem to offer so much protection that it's impossible to decrypt what was encrypted. The dilemma is resolved by explaining the RSA public key system and the details of its operation. Examples make the whole process clear. Finally, the matter of compromising the RSA's security is explored with the outcome that 100 billion computers wouldn't really help! The chapter concludes with a summary discussion.

PRIVACY—WHOSE INFORMATION IS IT?

Buying a product at a store generates a transaction, which is information. The data includes the date and time of the purchase, the product, the cost, and possibly an association with other products in the same "market basket." Is this information connected to a specific buyer? Paying with cash generally assures anonymity; that is, the buyer is not connected with the purchase, though cash payments in a small town or even in a neighborhood store where "everyone knows everyone" probably aren't anonymous. However,

- Paying by check, credit, or debit card,
- Purchasing through mail order or on the Internet,
- Providing a "preferred customer number," or
- Buying a product that must be "registered" to validate a service agreement or warranty

effectively guarantee that the transaction record will associate the product with the buyer. If you're buying socks, you probably don't care. If you're buying *Dating for Total Dummies*, you probably do. You want the information to remain private.

But what is private? It's not so easy to define. Certain information—your health records, your religion, or how much you've paid in parking fines this year—is clearly private. Only you should decide whether someone else is permitted to know that information. But as the scenario of the last paragraph makes clear, some information involving you arguably belongs to others, too. The book merchant who accepted your check for *Dating for Total Dummies* and thus can relate you to the book, can reasonably claim that gathering this information was part of normal business activities, and so belongs to the store, or at least doesn't belong to you alone. If the bookstore decides, based on the information from this transaction, to send you an advertisement for the upcoming "The *Improve Your Love Life* Spring Sale"—"All Whitman books and Samplers half price"—the merchant is using the information for the standard business practice of generating more business. You may even be happy to receive it. But even if not, such applications of "buyer profiles" are so established—they've probably been used since merchandizing began—that few would claim the store misused the information. If the merchant sells your name and lovelorn status to the local florists, movie theaters, restaurants, cosmetic surgeons, and so forth, has the information been misused? They're only trying to generate more business, too. Is it misused if the information gets to the campus newspaper, where it is published? Has the store violated the law? (The United States differs from Europe.) Can't you just be left alone to upgrade your dating skills in peace?

Famed Supreme Court Justice Louis Brandeis would have sympathized with your wish. He formulated privacy as the individual's "right to be left alone." He also wrote with Justice Earl Warren,

> The narrower doctrine [of privacy] may have satisfied the demands of society at a time when the abuse to be guarded against could barely have arisen without violating a contract or a special confidence; but now that **modern devices** afford abundant opportunities for the perpetration of such wrongs without any participation of the injured party, the protection granted by the law must be placed upon a broader foundation. [Emphasis added]

which argues in essence that, in the past, it was hard for people's privacy to be violated without their knowledge, but using *modern devices,* people's privacy can be violated without their being aware of it. The amazing thing about Warren and Brandeis's comments is that as appropriate as they seem for IT, they were written in 1890. The modern devices referred to were portable cameras and the faster film permitting short exposure photographs. They continued,

> While, for instance, the state of the photographic art was such that one's picture could seldom be taken without his consciously "sitting" for the purpose, the law of contract or of trust might afford the prudent man sufficient safeguards against the improper circulation of his portrait; but since the latest advances in photographic art have rendered it possible to take pictures surreptitiously, the doctrines of contract and of trust are inadequate to support the required protection.

What would Warren and Brandeis have thought about the ubiquitous surveillance camera? Their important point is that your image—and more generally information about you—deserves "sufficient safeguards against improper circulation." It's a 19th-century formation of a 21st-century concern.

The *Dating for Total Dummies* problem comes down to, "Who controls the subsequent use, if any, of the transaction information?" There are four possibilities:

1. The information ought to be expunged when its transactional role is complete, for example, when the check has cleared the bank, because there can be no further use of it.
2. The store can use it for other purposes beyond its transactional role, but only if you approve the use.
3. The store can use it for other purposes beyond its transactional role, but not if you object to a use.
4. The information can be used however the store chooses.

The four choices span a spectrum of permissibility and could be summarized as No Uses, Approval, Objection, No Limits. There is a fifth possibility, call it Internal Use, wherein the store can use the information for purposes of conducting business with you, but for none other. "Conducting business with you," might mean keeping your address on file so that you can be sent announcements about book readings. It would not include giving or selling your information to another person or business.

If the transaction took place in Europe, New Zealand, Australia, Canada, Hong Kong, or several other countries, the prevailing law and standards would place it between (1) and (2), but very close to (1). If the transaction occurred in the United States, the law and standards would place it between (3) and (4), but very close to (4). Perhaps of greater concern, many Americans apparently *assume* that there is a privacy law that approximates the fifth case, Internal Use. We return to these different standards in a later section, but first we must clarify the concept of privacy.

> **Australian Perspective**. The Preamble to the Australian Privacy Charter states, "A free and democratic people requires respect for the autonomy of individuals, and limits on the power of both state and private organizations to intrude on that autonomy. . . . Privacy is a basic human right and the reasonable expectation of every person."

A Privacy Definition

For as important as it is, privacy is difficult to define. It is more than Brandeis's right "to be left alone." Generally, privacy discussions concern compromising four spheres of our lives: our bodies, territory, personal information, and communication. Of these only the last two domains—personal information and communication—are of concern here. We adopt the definition

> **Privacy**, the right of people to choose freely under what circumstances and to what extent they will reveal themselves, their attitude, and their behavior to others.

The definition emphasizes first that it is the person who decides the "circumstances" under which and "extent" to which information is revealed, not any other party. Thus the person has the control. Second, it emphasizes that the range of features over which a person controls the information embodies every aspect of the person—themselves, attitudes, and behaviors. Adopting such an inclusive definition is essential to cover situations of importance. For example, the purchase of *Dating for Total Dummies* was an act, covered by behavior, and therefore relevant to a privacy discussion by our definition. Notice that it doesn't automatically imply the No Use classification for the information. We may decide in our analysis of the privacy implications of the transaction that the fact that the book was paid for with a check rather than cash—that is, an identifying as opposed to an anonymous form of payment—was evidence of an intent to reveal the fact of the purchase. Alternatively, we could decide that the form of payment has no bearing on whether the information should be revealed; permission to reveal it must be explicit.

With the definition established, what are the threats to privacy? There are only two basic threats: government and business. A third class of threats, private parties snooping to discover information or gossiping to circulate ill-gotten information, will be handled here by security, that is, keeping the information private until one chooses to reveal it. (See later sections.) Historically the governmental threat—regimes spying on their citizens—has been the greater concern to privacy advocates, probably because the instances have been so numerous and the abuses so egregious. The business threat is a more recent concern, and its IT aspects even newer still. The business concerns separate into two types: surveillance of employees and the use of business transaction information for other purposes.

A person could in principle have pristine privacy relative to these threats by simply deciding not to reveal anything to anyone, that is, to be a recluse or hermit, though it's probably difficult to implement the idea without living alone on a remote oceanic island surviving on coconuts and clams. The complicating aspect of privacy is that, in our daily lives, we interact with many people and organizations—businesses, our employer, and governments—with whom it is in our interest to reveal private information. That is, we freely choose to reveal information in exchange for real benefits.

- We tell our doctors many personal facts about ourselves for their assistance in keeping healthy.
- We allow credit card companies to check our credit record for the convenience of paying with a card.
- We permit our employer to read the email we send at work knowing that it's the employer's computer, Internet connection, and time we are using to send it, that it's there for use in our job, and that we have no need or intent to send personal mail.
- We reveal to the government—though not in the United States—our religion, our parent's names and birthplaces, race, ethnicity, and so on for the purposes of enjoying the rights of citizenship.

How private can we be revealing so much about ourselves, our attitude, and our behavior?

It is possible to reveal information about ourselves and still retain considerable privacy, but it depends on what happens to the information after we've revealed it to other people and organizations. If they hold the information in confidence, restrict its use to only the purposes for which it was revealed, and hold it secure from all threats, our privacy has not been seriously compromised. We derive the benefits and preserve our privacy. It's a good deal. But if the receiver is free to give or sell the information to anyone else, they are also engaged in "revealing," not just us. Our privacy is compromised. It's not enough to trust the recipient of the information to keep it secure. There must be explicit guidelines adopted for handling private information, so we have some standard by which to judge whether the trust is warranted. For that we have the Fair Information Practices guidelines.

Fair Information Practices

The first clear statement of the principles underlying the collection and use of private information came in 1972 from a report of the Advisory Committee on Automated Personal Data Systems for the U.S. Department of Health, Education and Welfare (HEW). The report listed five principles, called the Code of Fair Information Practices:

1. There must be no personal data record-keeping systems whose very existence is secret.
2. There must be a way for a person to find out what information about the person is in a record and how it is used.
3. There must be a way for a person to prevent information about the person that was obtained for one purpose from being used or made available for other purposes without the person's consent.
4. There must be a way for a person to correct or amend a record of identifiable information about the person.
5. Any organization creating, maintaining, using, or disseminating records of identifiable personal data must ensure the reliability of the data for their intended use and must take precautions to prevent misuses of the data.

These principles were an excellent start, coming at a time before personal computers and when the ARPANet—precursor to the Internet—connected only a handful of U.S. universities. Though they covered core issues, they needed to have their scope broadened. For example, the principles do not address the matter of what happens if the principles are not followed, that is, compliance and enforcement.

In 1980 the Organization of Economic Cooperation and Development (OECD)—an organization of 29 countries that foster international trade—enunciated an eight-point list of privacy principles that incorporated the five HEW principles and assumed the mantle of Fair Information Practices. They have become a widely accepted standard, forming a reasonably complete solution to the problems of retaining privacy while simultaneously revealing information to businesses and governments. For that reason, the public has an interest in these principles becoming law. But they also describe a standard that governments and businesses can meet as a "due diligence test" for protecting citizens' or clients' rights of privacy, thereby protecting themselves from criticism or legal action. The OECD principles are a practical implementation of privacy protection.

The OECD Fair Information Practices principles are

Limited Collection Principle: There should be limits to the personal data collected about anyone; data should be collected by fair and lawful means; and it should be collected with the knowledge and consent of the person in so far as is appropriate and possible.

Quality Principle: Personal data gathered should be relevant to the purposes for which it is used, and should be accurate, complete, and up-to-date.

Purpose Principle: The purposes for collecting personal data should be specified at the time of collection, and the uses should be limited to the fulfillment of those purposes.

Use Limitation Principle: Personal data should not be disclosed or used for purposes other than specified in the Purpose Principle, except with the consent of the data subject or the authority of law.

Security Principle: Personal data should be protected by reasonable security measures against risks of disclosure, unauthorized access, misuse, modification, destruction, or loss.

Openness Principle: There should be general openness of policies and practices relative to personal data collection, making it possible to readily establish its existence, kind, and purpose of use, as well as the identity and contact information for the data controller.

Participation Principle: An individual should be able to determine (a) whether the data controller has information about him or her, and (b) to discover what it is in a timely manner, in a reasonable and intelligible form, and at a charge (if any) that is not excessive. If the enquiry is denied, the individual should be allowed to find out the reasons and be able to challenge the denial. Further, the individual can challenge the data relating to him or her, and if successful, have the data erased, eradicated, completed, or amended.

Accountability Principle: The data controller should be accountable for complying with the aforementioned principles.

Thus the OECD principles fill out the original HEW Five. An important added concept in the OECD principles is the notion of the *data controller*, a specific person or office that, by the last three principles, sets the policies, must constructively interact with individuals regarding their information, if any, and be accountable for those policies and actions. In 1981 the Council of Europe's Convention for the Protection of Individuals produced similar rules.

Despite being a fundamental human right, however, much of the world does not enjoy privacy by the OECD standard in both public and private spheres. This is somewhat surprising considering that the topic is well understood, the IT implications are clear, and little remains but to enact OECD-grade laws and to enforce them. What's the problem?

The Atlantic—What Side Are You On?

Privacy often comes in conflict with private or governmental interests. For example, it can be presumed that the United States doesn't adopt the OECD principles, despite being a major player in the OECD and having created the earlier HEW principles in the first place, because many U.S. businesses make their profits gathering and collating information, or by buying and using information in ways that are inconsistent with the OECD principles. Similarly, the Chinese government isn't going to protect the fundamental right to privacy when it denies other fundamental human rights. The rights to privacy for these countries' citizens are thus diminished. Globalization may change that.

In a landmark advancement for privacy the European Union in 1995 issued the European Data Protection Directive, a benchmark law incorporating the OECD principles. The member countries have implemented this law giving a consistent level of privacy across the EU. (Another directive handles privacy for telecommunication.) Many non-EU countries have also adopted laws based on OECD principles, such as Australia, New Zealand, Canada, Hong Kong, and non-EU countries of Europe. This is significant because one provision in the Directive requires that data about EU citizens be protected by the standards of the law even when it leaves their country. Non-EU countries must get approval to receive information on EU citizens by showing that they have privacy laws consistent with the Directive, which effectively means consistent with OECD principles. Switzerland, a non-EU country, applied and was approved. The United States was not. What sorts of laws protect U.S. privacy?

The United States has the Privacy Act of 1974, which strongly limits the government's ability to compromise people's privacy, giving its citizens high-quality protection for "half" of the privacy problem—interactions with *government*. But the reason it failed to meet the requirements of the Directive concerns information stored by *businesses*. By contrast to the "omnibus" solutions of the OECD-subscribing countries, the United States uses an approach often described as "sectoral," meaning that it passes laws to deal with specific industries (business sectors) or practices. For example, there are the

- Electronic Communication Privacy Act of 1986,
- Video Privacy Protection Act of 1988,
- Telephone Consumer Protection Act of 1991,
- Driver's Privacy Protection Act of 1994,

and others. To illustrate, this last law ends the specific practice in which motor vehicle registration departments made information publicly available, where mass marketers used it to create mailing lists and demographic data. (Driving an expensive car may imply that you have a large income.) Now, the DMVs must *get permission from the registrant* before making the information available for any purpose other than registering cars.

Don't Ask. When the Supreme Court upheld the constitutionality of the Driver's Privacy Protection Act, the *Wall Street Journal* quoted a mass marketing industry spokesman as saying it was "death to us . . . If you can't use information about a person without permission, that generally means you're not going to have a list of any great substance." That is, using information without permission is essential to mass marketing.

The sectoral approach, though it often provides strong privacy protections in specific narrow cases, leaves much information unprotected. For example, the *United States has no federal law protecting the confidentiality of medical records*. Americans generally believe their medical records are secure, but they're for sale. Naturally, then, when an EU resident allows a drug company access to his or her medical records for purposes of evaluating the efficacy of a new treatment, that information cannot be transferred to the company's subsidiary office in New York.

The problem becomes extremely serious for multinational companies, and Internet and Web-based businesses. Any company wanting to move data from an EU country to the United States is prohibited from doing so until the United States meets the OECD principles. (Non-EU states subscribing to the OECD principles would probably object, too.) Think of a plane ticket bought from KLM in Holland for a Northwest flight in the United States—how does KLM tell Northwest the customer data? What is a business to do?

The Federal Trade Commission and the EU have been negotiating for years to resolve the matter. A tentative agreement was founded on a concept called a Safe Harbor, which effectively means a U.S. company that follows the rules of the agreement is safe to receive information from the EU. Though the FTC Safe Harbor guidelines incorporate privacy principles, they're weaker than the original HEW principles that predated the OECD. There are two glaring points of disagreement—Opt-in/Opt-out and compliance/enforcement—that are causing most of the difficulties in resolving the matter.

- **Opt-in/Opt-out** is jargon referring to the distinction between approval and objection laid out in the *Dating for Total Dummies* scenario. That is, what are the circumstances under which an organization can use information it collects for one purpose for a different purpose? "Opt-in" means the business "cannot use" it unless the person explicitly allows the new use. "Opt-out" means the business "can use" it unless the person explicitly prohibits the new use. Privacy principles as far back as the HEW Five have consistently required Opt-in for all changes in use because otherwise the person does not control the dissemination of private information.[1] It was the Opt-in requirement of the motor vehicle registration act that caused predictions of "death" by the mass marketing spokesman. The FTC guidelines, however, require Opt-in only for highly sensitive information like medical data; Opt-out is the norm for most information.
- **Compliance/Enforcement** means that some mechanism exists to assure that organizations comply with the principles, that is, fulfill the role of the data controller. The EU and other OECD-subscribing countries have introduced bureaucratic offices to perform the duties of the data controller. There is no such person or office in the United States, of course. The FTC proposes that U.S. companies be subject to voluntary compliance with "market pressure,"

[1] Notice that Opt-in is actually a longer-standing principle than stated. Warren and Brandeis's concept of a "special confidence" between photographers and their subjects protecting their privacy amounts to Opt-in. That is, the photographer would violate the confidence unless he or she asked for and received permission from the subject first.

private firms like TRUSTe and private sector agencies like the Better Business Bureau performing the monitoring. These private mechanisms would then report any verified violations to the FTC, but privacy advocates assert that such a voluntary process amounts to no enforcement at all. See the Voluntary Compliance Report Card, Figure 16.1.

What: The Georgetown Internet Privacy Policy Survey Report
For Whom: Federal Trade Commission
Purpose: Assess "extent to which commercial Web sites have posted privacy disclosures based on fair information practices."
Sample: 361 `.com` Web sites, (describing 98.8% of the population as of January 1999)
Sampling Dates: March 8-12, 1999
Results:

Sites collecting ...	
Personal identifying information (name, email, postal address):	92.8%
Demographic information (gender, preferences, Zip Code):	56.8%
Both personal and demographic information:	56.2%
Sites posting ...	
Either a privacy policy disclosure or information practice statement:	65.9%
Both privacy policy disclosure and information practice statement:	36.0%
Sites collecting information and posting a privacy policy following Fair Information Practices . . . On the five elements examined in the survey (notice, choice, access, security, contact):	9.5%

Figure 16.1. Voluntary Compliance Report Card. Fewer than a tenth of .com Web sites gathering personal information as of March 1999 posted a privacy statement that included five of the Fair Information Practices components. Source: Mary Culnan, Georgetown Internet Privacy Policy Survey, 1999.

Both issues are critical to both sides. Without Opt-in and Enforcement, the OECD principles are badly eroded. But with those requirements, industries like direct marketing are by their own description mortally affected. At last check, the stalemate continued.

> **Voluntary Compliance?** Privacy consultant Richard M. Smith discovered in November 1999 that Real Networks' JukeBox software was sending users' unique IDs back to the company servers with each personal CD they played, allowing Real to profile users' musical tastes. The company had a privacy statement, but it didn't mention the unique ID, *until they got caught.* Further, Real had engaged the audit firm TRUSTe.

The Cookie Monster

Cookies are perhaps the most controversial aspect of Internet privacy. As described in Chapter 15, cookies are a standard computing concept originally adopted by Netscape engineers to connect the identity of a client across a series of independent client/server events. The mechanism they adopted was to allow Web site servers to store six-item records on the clients. Though the engineers assumed servers would use cookies to record information like the client's mailing address, credit card number, and shopping cart contents—information that is private and rightly should be stored on the client's computer—that's not the way it developed. Universally, cookies are simply serial numbers chosen by the server to identify the client uniquely. Every time a client visits the server, whether within a single session or at different times separated by years, the server gets its cookie from the client, and thus can connect the latest visit with any information gathered and saved from earlier visits based on the serial number. From the point of view of the intended purpose of cookies, as explained in Chapter 15, the serial number variation is entirely equivalent. But there are other more questionable ways to use a serial number.

Obviously, if two companies can correlate the serial numbers they have stored on a client, they can share the information they've gathered. Correlating would seem not to be possible, however, at least not based on our earlier explanation of the Netscape browser because it only allows Web servers to store and retrieve *their own cookies*.[2] In principle this would seem to imply that the cookies are private information shared between you and the site you visit, and the information they have you gave them voluntarily, say, to buy a product. But if you check the cookies on your computer, you will probably find cookies from many sites you've never visited or even heard of. How could they get there?

A loophole in the plan works as follows. If you visit site B that displays advertisements, B might contract with another site A to place the ads. While your browser is constructing the Web page sent from B, it goes to A's site to get the ads. At that point, A is in a client/server relationship with your computer and is allowed by the only-the-server-can-store-and-receive-its-own-cookies policy to store its cookie on your client. Site B contracting with site A, a third party, enabled it to place a cookie on your computer. But so what? The cookie uses a few bytes of disk space, sure, but if you never visit A's site, they'll never again see the cookie. Right? Probably wrong.

Enter Your Salary. In a widely reported incident in 2000, the Internet `.com` Intuit was sued by customers of its Web-based Quicken mortgage software for disclosing to mass advertiser DoubleClick private information gained when Web users computed mortgages. Cookies were blamed in the press, which would imply Doubleclick was A and Intuit was B in the preceding scenario. At the time DoubleClick's ads were displayed on more that 11,000 Web sites.

Another site C can also contract with A to place ads on its page, enabling the same scenario to unfold, although this time A's cookie is already on the client. In both cases, A has the chance to associate its unique cookie with the cookie of the site for which it's providing advertising services, that is, B or C. There is an opportunity for a B–A link and a C–A link, and because it's the same unique A serial number, B's information can be linked to C's information, that is, A can make a B–C link. If this were to happen—actually, it almost certainly is happening—the linking takes place on the "server side," out of sight or control of you, the client. And, of course, A's potential connections don't stop at two. Summarizing, the threat to privacy is not the cookie per se, but the third-party cookie placement and the opportunity for the second and third parties to link their serial numbers, and hence the associated information.

Many Double Clicks. Richard M. Smith, the privacy consultant, testified to Congress in June 2000 that in the previous six months his computer had logged 250,000 net transactions, roughly 10% of which was traffic to DoubleClick, tracking the URLs of the sites he visited.

One rationale for A to place its cookie on the client is so that it can be paid for its advertising. That is, suppose when you visited site B, A was advertising for site D, and later you buy a product from site D. Site D may be obligated by its advertising contract to pay A because you saw the ad. No one knows whether you looked at the

[2] A bug in Microsoft's Internet Explorer allowed a server to look at other servers' cookies, but the bug was reportedly fixed in mid-2000.

ad, but the existence of A's cookie on your client may be evidence that A placed some ad on your machine and may be enough for D to pay A a commission. It's not much different from including coupons with print ads, a standard business practice for demonstrating the effectiveness of an ad placement.

Plugging a Loophole. The third-party cookie loophole is a serious flaw in the cookie mechanism that browser manufacturers could easily fix. Privacy advocates have been lobbying for a fix, but strong public support is needed.

Though this discussion has focused on the potential problems with third-party cookies, cookies are hardly the only way to connect your identity between the B and C sites. Even if there were no cookies, your email address is effectively a unique serial number, and so the scenario described earlier applies. Companies can connect their information on you to information others have on you based on that unique identifier. The core issue is not cookies. It is the same issue that concerned us with *Dating for Total Dummies* and the Opt-in/Opt-out discussions: Do you have control over the information you created in a business transaction? Is the law that the business cannot use it for other purposes unless they receive your approval, or can the business use it for other purposes unless they receive your objection? The issue is privacy policy, not the technology of collating user information.

Identity Crisis. Chipmaker Intel introduced a unique ID for each Pentium III processor chip, but removed it under intense criticism. The ID would have greatly simplified the task of collating Web-collected data—it's like all `.coms` using the same cookie on a given machine.

What is to be done about cookies? As noted, they are not the culprits per se. Many organizations without information gathering goals—WNET, the *Oxford English Dictionary,* even the EU Secretariat—place cookies because they can help to give a higher quality of Web interaction. All recent browsers provide the ability to disable cookies, as well as to set other levels of "cookie acceptance," including stopping third-party cookies. Many users choose to turn them off. But to benefit from online banking, securities trading, or other similar services, your browser client will usually have to accept cookies. It's possible to delete the cookies files—be sure your browser is closed because while it's running, the cookies are stored in the RAM—but that's equivalent to starting over with a new computer. In particular, any "good" cookies that you want for applications like online banking will also be lost. Despite browser warnings not to, it's possible to selectively edit the cookies files, deleting those you do not want, though it is a rather delicate operation better left to the experienced.

The best response when concerned about cookies is to visit privacy Web sites, which can advise you on managing cookies for your browser or direct you to software that will help contain cookies. (Make sure to assess the legitimacy of such sites!) By remaining aware of both the risks and the benefits, you can receive useful network services and perhaps preserve some privacy.

Encryption and Decryption

The way to keep electronic information secret is to *digitally encrypt* it—that is, to transform the representation so that the information cannot be readily discerned. We have already seen encryption applied to passwords in Chapter 12. We noted that if we forget our password, the superuser usually cannot tell us what it is because the software stores it in encrypted form—we described it at the time as being scrambled. In *cryptography*—the study of encryption and decryption methods—the password is the *cleartext* or *plaintext*, that is, the information before encryption. The encrypted password would be the *cipher text*, that is, the text's encrypted form. Passwords use a *one-way cipher*—an encryption technique that cannot be easily reversed—because there's really no need ever to decrypt them. It's possible to encrypt the password the user enters and compare it to the stored version, which is also encrypted. If they don't match as cipher text, they don't match as cleartext either. So, for the special application of password scrambling, the simple one-way encryption works.

Information is encrypted so it can be transmitted or stored. These are two times when someone who has no need to view the information could snoop. When encrypted for this purpose, the cleartext must eventually be recovered by reversing the encryption process, or *decrypting* the cipher text. In the schematic diagram of the cryptosystem shown in Figure 16.2, the sender and receiver agree on a key K_{SR}. The sender uses the key to encrypt the cleartext, and the receiver uses it to decrypt the cipher text. The key can be applied to the letters of the cleartext in various ways, but a common way is as follows: ASCII letters are treated as numbers using their bit representation and transformed by some mathematical operation with an inverse, say, multiplication, to produce the cipher text bits. That is, a few letters of the ASCII text are multiplied times the key and the resulting number is sent or stored. The cleartext can be recovered by applying the inverse operation (division by the key, in this case) to the number.

Exclusive or, known as XOR, is an interesting case for applying a key to cleartext. XOR, which can be described as "*x* or *y* but not both," is written like an addition symbol in a circle, ⊕ and combines two bits by the rule: If the bits are the same, the result is 0; if the bits are different, the result is 1. Thus, if 0101 is the cleartext and 1001 is the key, then

```
 0101   Cipher text
⊕1001   Key
 1100   Cleartext
```

XOR produces 1100 for the cipher text. Applying the key to the cipher text again with XOR produces the original cleartext

```
 1100   Cleartext
⊕1001   Key
 0101   Cipher text
```

Thus XOR is its own inverse.

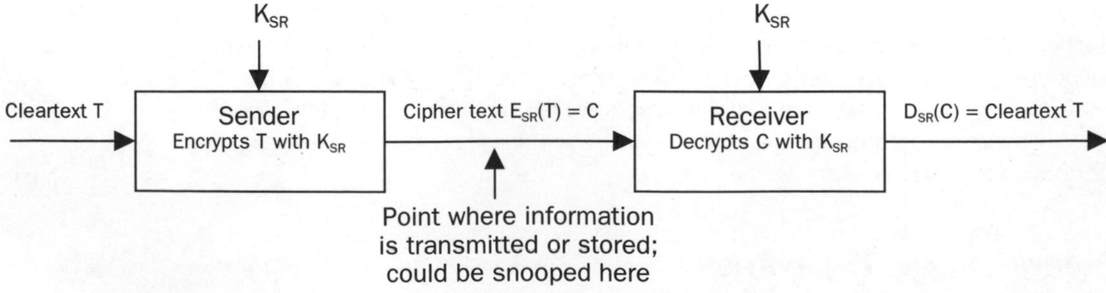

Figure 16.2. Schematic diagram of a cryptosystem. Using a key K_{SR} known only to them, the sender encrypts the cleartext information to produce a ciphertext, and the receiver decrypts the cipher text to recover the cleartext.

To illustrate encryption, imagine two students who have been communicating by writing messages to each other on the white board in the computer lab, but now worry that others may be reading them, and so decide to encrypt them. They agree on a key `0110 0101 1001 1010`, and plan to encode pairs of ASCII letters by transforming them with the key using XOR. Here's what they do. (See Figure 16.3.) Using the cleartext `Meet @ 12:15 XOX`, they first write down the ASCII representation of these letters in pairs. (The ASCII representation is shown Table 8.4.) Next, they XOR each of these 16-bit sequences with their key sequence to produce the cipher text, which in this case has the ASCII equivalent of (ÿᴺᵤîEÚE«WᴬₙT¯EÂ*Â. This is the cipher text—a very strange sequence that should be secure to the causal observer in the computer lab. The cipher text can be easily decrypted using the same technique: XOR each of the ASCII equivalents of the cipher text with the key to produce the cleartext bits of the pairs. Then, look up the letters in the ASCII table. We can see that this scheme must always work by reviewing Figure 16.3 and using two facts:

- If any bit sequence is XORed with another bit sequence (the key) and the result is also XORed with the key, that result is the original bit sequence.
- With XOR, it makes no difference whether the key is on the left or the right.

The facts mean that encrypting is moving from left to right in the figure, whereas decrypting would move from right to left.

	Cleartext		Key		Cipher Text	
Me	0100 1101 0110 0101				0010 1000 1111 1111	(ÿ
et	0110 0101 0111 0100				0000 0000 1110 1110	ᴺᵤî
␢@	0010 0000 0100 0000				0100 0101 1101 1010	EÚ
␢1	0010 0000 0011 0001	⊕	0110 0101 1001 1010	=	0100 0101 1010 1011	E«
2:	0011 0010 0011 1010				0101 0111 1010 0000	Wᴬₙ
15	0011 0001 0011 0101				0101 0100 1010 1111	T¯
␢X	0010 0000 0101 1000				0100 0101 1100 0010	EÂ
OX	0100 1111 0101 1000				0010 1010 1100 0010	*Â

Figure 16.3. Encrypting the cleartext `Meet @ 12:15 XOX`, using ASCII encoding of letter pairs, the key 0110 0101 1001 1010, and the operation of Exclusive Or to produce the cipher text (ÿᴺᵤîEÚE«WᴬₙT¯EÂ*Â. (Decryption works in the opposite direction, as if the "⊕" and "=" symbols of the figure were exchanged.)

How secure is the code? Probably not too secure. It is possible, knowing that XOR is the operation, to guess 6 of the 16 bits of the key in about three minutes (see Exercises), and it probably wouldn't take much fooling around to deduce the others. And this is with only a 16-character cleartext. The longer the text, the easier the task becomes because once enough letters have been used, it is possible to notice what bit patterns show up frequently. With a large volume of English text, we might notice the patterns

```
0000 0000 xxxx xxxx
xxxx xxxx 1111 1111
```

which correspond to *e* in the first letter position and *e* in the second letter position. (Our key just happened to use the ASCII bit sequence for *e* as the first half of the key, and its complement—the opposite bits—as the second half of the key, but the code breaker won't use that information.)

Statistically, *e* is the most frequently occurring letter in English. Seeing these patterns as the most numerous, and guessing that they correspond to *e* bytes, we can begin constructing the cleartext from the cipher text by replacing each occurrence with *e*. The frequency ordering for English's twelve most common letters is: e t a o i n s h r d l u.[3] Each language has its own characteristic distribution, of course. These dozen letters represent about 80% of the letters occurring in the average English text. Using these letters, we proceed to replace the dozen most frequently occurring (left and right) patterns. Decrypting that many letters of a cipher text would make decrypting the remainder a simple Wheel-of-Fortune endgame. We would have broken the code without ever knowing that the two students had used XOR as the encryption scheme, or what the key was. The only property we exploited was that their code consistently replaced each letter with one of two patterns. Clearly they'd better be smarter next time!

Tse Beht of Tnmeh". The frequency count for English is not fixed, of course. Different sources produce somewhat different results, even for large documents. For example, *A Tale of Two Cities* contains more than half a million letters that are distributed: e t a o n i h s r d l u That is, n, i interchange, and s, h interchange from the commonly quoted frequency distribution.

Being smarter about byte-for-byte substitutions is easy to do. Grouping more than two bytes will help. The harder problem is that the sender and the receiver have to agree on the key *ahead of time*. That is, they had to meet or at least communicate for the purpose of selecting the key. Of course, if they don't meet, but communicate instead, that communication couldn't be made secure because by hypothesis there is no agreed upon key yet. Key exchange would be a showstopper for applications like Internet commerce, where credit card numbers should be kept secret, but the customer and the company cannot meet, being perhaps on opposite sides of the planet. The problem is beautifully solved using public key encryption.

Public Key Encryption Systems

Public key encryption is a very ingenious idea in which people who want to allow others to send them information securely—receivers—publish, for example, post on a Web page, a key that senders should use to encrypt messages. Imagine that the key is 129 digits long and the senders are told to proceed as follows: Cube 32-byte groups of ASCII letters—yes, treat the bits as a 256-bit number and raise it to the third power—divide the result by the key, and send the remainder, that is, the bits smaller than the key that are left over from the division. The key was chosen so that the receiver, but not the general public or a cracker, can decrypt it. Revising Figure 16.2 to reflect this new scenario, we have Figure 16.4 of a public key cryptosystem.

Public Spirited. Computer scientists Whitfield Diffie and Martin Helman invented public key cryptosystems in 1976.

Thinking about it, it seems a little surprising that secrecy's possible. The cracker—the bad guy who is trying to snoop the communication by intercepting the cipher text and decrypting it—knows the key, too, because it's published on the Web page. And it would seem the cracker has the same ability to perform arithmetic on the cipher text that the receiver does. But cracking isn't so easy. All that was sent was the *remainder*—the bits that were left over from the division.

Recall from elementary school that the actual definition for division, *a/b*, is to satisfy the equation

$$a = b \cdot c + d$$

[3] Curiously, most people who remember this sequence do so by pronouncing it!

for *divisor b*, *quotient c*, that is, the result of the division, and *remainder d*. Further, d will be smaller than b. For example, 30/8 becomes

$$30 = 8 \cdot 3 + 6$$

which is equivalent to saying, "30 divided by 8 is 3 with a remainder of 6." This is called the *quotient-remainder* form of division. Substituting the variables of our encryption situation, the equation becomes

$$T^3 = K_R \cdot c + d$$

for cleartext T and some quotient c that doesn't interest us. Only d, the remainder, is sent.

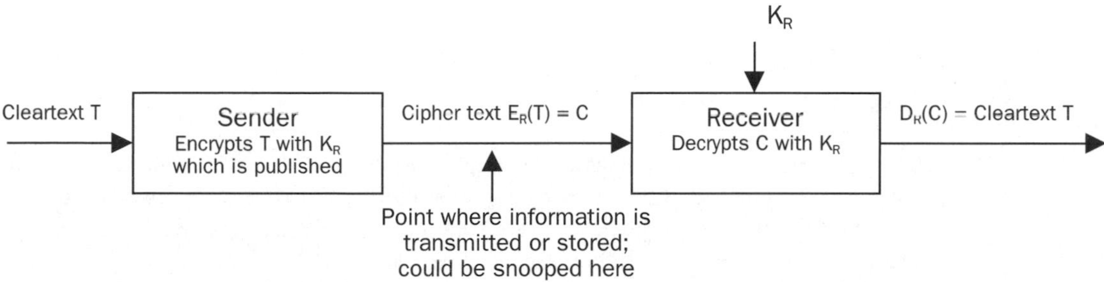

Figure 16.4. Public Key Cryptosystem. The sender uses the receiver's public key K_R to encrypt the cleartext, and only the receiver is able to decrypt it to recover the cleartext.

If the cracker had the quotient c *and* the remainder d, he or she could simply multiply the quotient by the key ($K_R \cdot c$) and add in the remainder to produce T^3. Using a calculator to find the cube root gives the binary number of the 32-byte sequences. Presto! There's the original cleartext, T. But the cracker didn't get both the quotient and the remainder, only the remainder. So snooping's a lot tougher.

But now it doesn't look so good for the receiver. The receiver didn't get the quotient either, only the remainder, so how is he or she supposed to figure out what was sent? Public key encryption looks astonishing in the other direction: It seems that the message is so well encrypted *no one* can figure it out! Happily, Leonhard Euler, an 18th-century mathematician, and a few enterprising computer scientists, came to everyone's rescue—except, of course, that of the cracker.

The RSA Public Key Cryptosystem is the best known of the PKC systems, and the one discussed here. Named for its inventors, Ron Rivest, Adi Shamir, and Len Adleman, the RSA scheme is basically the PKC scheme just outlined. We need to learn enough about how it works to retrieve the original cleartext. *Why* it works relies on very deep mathematics and computer science that will not be described here. But it does work. It has withstood formidable attacks and will continue to as computers get faster. The assaults on RSA are described after we give it a try.

Looking at RSA Encryption

Besides the familiar operations of multiplication, division, and raising a number to a power, understanding the RSA scheme and finding out how the receiver retrieves the cleartext rely on only one more easy topic, prime numbers. Recall from middle school that some whole numbers, called *prime numbers*, have the property that the only numbers that divide them evenly—that is, without a remainder—are 1 and themselves. So, the first few prime numbers are 2, 3, 5, 7, 11, 13, 17, 19, 23, 29,

31, . . . Mathematicians adore studying prime numbers because they have amazing properties. The rest of us only know that prime numbers are the basic "atoms" of a whole number: Any number can be *factored* into one sequence of primes. The factors of a number x are just numbers that multiply together to give x. So, factors of 30 are

$1 \times 30 = 30$
$2 \times 15 = 30$
$5 \times 6 = 30$
$2 \times 3 \times 5 = 30$

but only {2,3,5} are the prime factors of 30.

The secret of the RSA scheme, of course, is that the receiver didn't publish any random 129-digit sequence as the public key, K_R. The key has some special properties. Specifically the public key must be the product of two different prime numbers, p and q,

$$K_R = pq$$

Because multiplying two numbers of roughly equal size produces a number twice as long, p and q must be about 64 or 65 digits long to produce the 129-digit public key. Additionally, p and q, besides being long enough and prime, must also be 2 greater than a multiple of 3. It's a rather strange requirement, but essential as we'll see in a moment. Many primes have this property such as 5 and 11, being 2 larger than multiples of 3, namely, 3 and 9. As a running example, take

$p = 5$
$q = 11$
$K_R = pq = 55.$

To encrypt a cleartext, divide it up into blocks—we'll use 6-bit blocks of the ASCII encoding for the running example, but they're usually many bytes long—cube the blocks, divide them by the public key, and transmit the remainders from the divisions.

Thus, to encrypt the amount of a credit card transaction,

```
****$0.02
```

the ASCII characters are expressed in their binary representation

0010 1010 0010 1010 0010 1010 0010 1010 0010 0100 0011 0000 0010 1110 0011 0000 0011 0010

and grouped into blocks,

0010 1010 0010 1010 0010 1010 0010 1010 0010 0100 0011 0000 0010 1110 0011 0000 0011 0010

shown in white and gray.

Recalling from Chapter 11 that bits can be interpreted in any way that is convenient, the groups are interpreted as numbers

T = 10, 34, 40, 42, 10, 34, 16, 48, 11, 35, 0, 50

cubed,

T^3 = 1000, 39304, 64000, 74088, 1000, 39304, 4096, 110592, 1331, 42875, 0, 125000 divided by the key $K_R = 55$, and expressed in quotient, remainder form,

$1000 = 55 \cdot 18 + 10$
$39304 = 55 \cdot 714 + 34$
$64000 = 55 \cdot 1163 + 35$
$74088 = 55 \cdot 1347 + 3$
$1000 = 55 \cdot 18 + 10$
$39304 = 55 \cdot 714 + 34$
$4096 = 55 \cdot 74 + 26$
$110592 = 55 \cdot 2010 + 42$
$1331 = 55 \cdot 24 + 11$
$42875 = 55 \cdot 779 + 30$
$0 = 55 \cdot 0 + 0$
$125000 = 55 \cdot 2272 + 40$

And finally only the remainders are kept to yield the cipher text

$C = 10, 34, 35, 3, 10, 34, 26, 42, 11, 30, 0, 40$

These numbers are the encrypted message to be sent.[4]

How does the receiver reconstruct the cleartext? First, we must compute the quantity

$s = (1/3)(2(p–1)(q–1) + 1)$

For the quantities of our running example, this curious number is

$s = (1/3)(2 \cdot 4 \cdot 10 + 1) = 81/3 = 27$

It was to make *s* come out right that we added the requirement of "2 greater than a multiple of 3" when choosing *p* and *q*.

The amazing fact is that if the cipher text numbers *C* are each raised to the *s* power, C^s—that's right, C^{27} in our example—and divided by the key K_R, the remainder is the cleartext! That is, for some quotient *c* that we don't care about

$C^s = K_R \cdot c + T$

which is *truly* the key to the RSA scheme.

To demonstrate this amazing fact, take the first number of our cipher text

$C = 10$

and compute

$C^s = C^{27} = 10^{27} = 1{,}000{,}000{,}000{,}000{,}000{,}000{,}000{,}000{,}000$

which is not a binary number, but the huge decimal number of 1 followed by 27 zeros. Divide by $K_R = 55$ and express the result in the quotient-remainder form

$1{,}000{,}000{,}000{,}000{,}000{,}000{,}000{,}000{,}000 = 55 \cdot 18{,}181{,}818{,}181{,}818{,}181{,}818{,}181{,}818 + 10$

[4] It is pure coincidence that some of the cipher text numbers happened to be the same as their corresponding cleartext. The result is still incomprehensibly scrambled (see Exercises).

Thus, $T = 10$, so the first six bits of the clear text must be 10 in binary, 001010, as can be checked.

The numbers can get very large for us—encryption algorithms actually use several techniques such as modular arithmetic to avoid the large intermediate numbers—but let's try another example. The fourth term of the cipher text is

$$C = 3$$

which we can raise to the 27th power with a calculator to get

$$3^s = 3^{27} = 7{,}625{,}597{,}484{,}987$$

Dividing by the public key, K_R and expressing the result in the quotient-remainder form yields

$$7{,}625{,}597{,}484{,}987 = 55 \cdot 138{,}647{,}226{,}999 + 42$$

implying that the fourth block of the text is binary for 42, or 101010, as can be verified. As a third example, we notice that everything works out right for the cipher text $C = 0$.

Why *does* the RSA work? Euler proved the following theorem[5] in 1736,

Theorem: Let p and q be distinct primes, $K = pq$, $0 \le T < K$, and $r > 0$. If $T^{r(p-1)(q-1)+1}$ is divided by K, the remainder is T.

For our use of Euler's formula, $r = 2$, because

$$\begin{aligned}(T^3)^s &= (T^3)^{(1/3)(2(p-1)(q-1)+1)} \\ &= T^{2(p-1)(q-1)+1}\end{aligned}$$

Thus, when the cipher text—that is, the remainders—are raised to the s power and divided by the key, the cleartext is recovered.

Attacking Public Key Encryption

To summarize, the RSA public key crypto scheme distills to the following steps.

- **Publishing**: Select two different prime numbers, p and q, which are 2 larger than a multiple of 3, and define $K_R = pq$, the public key. Compute $s = (1/3)(2(p-1)(q-1) + 1)$. Keep p, q and s secret. Publish K_R where senders can find it.
- **Encrypting**: Get the public key from the sender, break the cleartext bit-sequence into blocks according to the sender's instructions, but less than K_R. Cube each block, divide each of the results by K_R, and transmit the remainders to the sender as the cipher text.
- **Decrypting**: Using the secret value s, raise each number in the cipher text to the s power, divide each result by K_R and assemble the remainders into the blocks of the bit sequence of the cleartext.

[5] This is the only occurrence of mathematics in this book. It isn't necessary to understand it. Simply accept that Euler's formula makes the RSA scheme work out.

Of course, humans don't do all of this calculating. Software does. And though the software is extremely sophisticated to perform these operations fast, the principles that the programs implement are embodied in these three bullets.

How impervious is the scheme to attacks? Could a cracker actually break the code? As far as is known scientifically a cracker would have to determine s to break the code. Constructing s is easy if the two primes p and q are known, so the problem reduces to factoring the public key K_R to discover p and q. But factoring large numbers is a computationally difficult problem, meaning that even for the world's fastest computers, it's extremely time-consuming to factor numbers that are hundreds of bits long. It is that fact—factoring large numbers is computationally difficult—that keeps the public key encryption schemes secure. Stated differently, if the key is sufficiently large, it can be published because there is no known way to factor it into its two prime components in any reasonable amount of time.

In 1977, shortly after inventing their scheme, Rivest, Shamir, and Adleman issued a challenge to the world: Break the small cipher text they encrypted with their public key RSA129—the 129 refers to the number of digits of their key. This was a bold challenge because although there was no known way to factor a 129-digit key quickly, maybe someone could invent a better factoring algorithm. The best-known method at the time wasn't much better than the grammar school technique of dividing consecutive prime numbers into the number looking for one that divides evenly. If computer scientists were clever enough to come up with public key encryption in the first place, they could probably come up with better ways to factor.

In fact, in 1981 Carl Pomerance did invent a new factoring method that gave some hope, though all the while other computer scientists were trying to prove that the factoring process could never be improved much. Pomerance's algorithm was better, but it didn't crack the code. Eventually in 1994, exploiting better algorithms, the Internet, and the improved speed of computers, the RSA129 cipher was cracked over an eight-month period using nearly 1000 computers from around the world. But this doesn't sound the death knell for public key cryptosystems. It only revealed the factors of a single public key. Most of us don't have 1000 computers or eight months to spend trying to snoop a credit card transaction. Even if the secret is extremely important—a missile code, for example, or the outcome of the final episode of a TV show—and the cracker has the resources of the U.S. government, the RSA scheme is still secure because all it takes to make things harder for crackers is to increase the size of the key. The complexity of the factoring task increases dramatically as the key length grows. It has been estimated that increasing the key length to 250 digits would increase the cracking time 100,000,000 times. So, even if you're willing to use 1000 computers for 800 million months, or maybe use 100 billion computers for 8 months, the key can be increased to 300 digits or 400 or whatever, and thwart your efforts. Larger keys do not seriously complicate the problem for the encryption and decryption processes compared to their tremendous impact on increasing the factoring time.

> **Big Secret**. When RSA129 was cracked, an effort dubbed the largest computation of all time, everyone was doubtless waiting breathlessly to know what the secret message was. It turned out to be THE MAGIC WORDS ARE SQUEAMISH OSSIFRAGE.

Public key encryption techniques are known as *strong encryption*. The term is intended to convey the fact that a communicating party can use the technology to protect their communication so that it is effectively unknowable by anyone else. From a national defense or crime fighting perspective, complete secrecy is of great concern. Agencies that protect the society from internal and external threats have routinely snooped on those people and organizations that may cause harm. Because surveillance would be impossible if the "bad guys" got such technology, the U.S. government has fought a long-running battle since the invention of PKC technology to keep it contained and out of the hands of "bad guys." This has never been a very realistic goal because papers describing the scientific foundations of the technology—including Diffie and Helman's original paper, "New Directions in Cryptography"—are published in freely accessible scientific journals (*IEEE Transactions on Information Theory* IT(22):644–654), enabling anyone with a respectable computer science education to build his or her own encryption software. On the other hand, security professionals probably have a point. It could be valuable to spy on people who are in the process of planning crimes or attacks.

Of course, most people don't produce their own software—they buy it—and that observation probably applies to most "bad guys." If cryptography software vendors were required to provide a means for breaking such codes when there was a demonstrated need-to-know by the authorized security or law enforcement personnel, perhaps the conflicting goals of security and defensiveness could be reconciled in the presence of strong encryption. How could that be? Doesn't breaking the code require earth-shaking discoveries in factoring? Not from the software vendor's point of view. Two techniques that could be used are known as *Trapdoor* and *Key Escrow*.

- **Trapdoor**. The idea is that while encryption software is encrypting the cleartext, ways might be provided to bypass the security. One obvious possibility is that along with sending cipher text to the receiver, the cleartext could also be sent to law-enforcement or security officials. The trapdoor would work like a telephone wiretap in that the "bad guys'" encryption software would be configured without their knowledge, and legal safeguards (court-approved warrant) would be required to do so. Other trapdoor techniques exist.
- **Key Escrow**. Because knowing the key allows for trivial code breaking, a key escrow system would require encryption software to register the keys it uses with a third party, which would hold them in confidence. Then, if there was ever a need to break a code—law enforcement personnel having a court-approved warrant, or your computer being toasted in a fire—the escrow agent could provide the key.

Though perhaps solving the security specialist's problem, these two schemes have obvious potential for abuses: Couldn't anyone with (legal or illegal) access to your computer open the trapdoor? Isn't the escrow company a tantalizing target for criminals because it contains everyone's PKC keys? Neither of these schemes has satisfied security and other experts, and the battle continues. It is an important matter of public policy, and worthy of our continued vigilance.

SUMMARY

This chapter has covered deep philosophical topics as well as deep scientific topics. After discussing a privacy scenario, we adopted a definition for privacy, as the right of individuals to choose freely under what circumstances and to what extent they will reveal themselves, their attitudes, and their behaviors to others. Unfortunately the dilemma between privacy and life in the modern world is that the latter presents numerous opportunities to compromise the former for tangible and valuable benefits. So the people and organizations that receive the information we reveal must keep it private. The guidelines for keeping data private have been formulated by several organizations, including the Organization for Economic Cooperation and Development. Next, we observed that such guidelines might conflict with the interests of business and government, preventing nations from adopting them. The member states of the European Union and other countries around the world have nevertheless embraced them as the guidelines for business or government or both. Moreover the EU countries have further required that information on any of its member state's citizens must enjoy the same level of data privacy when it moves beyond their borders. Because the United States takes a sectoral approach to privacy, adopting laws only for specific business sectors or practices, much of the information collected on U.S. citizens is not protected to OECD standards, causing long-running negotiations between the EU and the United States regarding privacy standards. The dispute's two main sticking points are Opt-in/Opt-out and Compliance/Enforcement. Finally, we completed the privacy discussion by revisiting the subject of cookies. Because of the "third-party cookie" loophole, advertisers can place cookies on your computer, which enables them to correlate data they receive from different Web servers. Though cookies are not the only culprits—simple email addresses constitute a decent "unique identifier"—plugging the third-party cookie loophole would improve Web privacy considerably. The best solution is to have OECD-grade privacy laws.

Digital security uses digital encryption, a topic that seems to require considerable new vocabulary. After introducing the vocabulary and detailed example using XOR, we introduced the concept of public key cryptography. Though it is at times intricate, PKC is a straightforward idea built entirely on familiar concepts. We showed a complete example of the RSA scheme. Though computer scientists have not yet proved the invincibility of the RSA scheme, it can be "made more secure" simply by increasing the size of the key. This has little affect on the encryption and decryption processes, but it greatly increases the problem of finding the prime factors that make up the key. Such strong encryption methods are a concern to defense and law enforcement officials, but to date the conflict between balancing those concerns with the interests of peaceful, law-abiding citizens has not been reconciled.

The summary is, then, that both privacy and security are topics that have not been fully resolved in the public forum. Laws and policies regarding both are still under construction. Privacy, it would seem, awaits the broad adoption of the OECD safeguards for both business and government information gathering. Security, it would seem, awaits a means for parties to communicate securely by mechanisms fully within their control, yet that can be compromised in extraordinary circumstances of public importance. Both pose daunting challenges.

EXERCISES

1. What conclusion can be drawn from Justices Warren and Brandeis's writings on privacy?
2. Write a paragraph that distinguishes between the bookstore's use of the information to announce their sale and their having sold it to a video rental store.
3. What is the tension between privacy and living in the modern world?
4. Do a Google search and find five recent stories about privacy abuses in the United States that would be covered by OECD principles.
5. What is a possible reason that the United States has not adopted the OECD principles for information gathered in connection with business transactions?
6. Explain the two main points of contention between the United States and the EU regarding privacy.
7. Explain how a third party can place a cookie on your computer.
8. Does the Real Networks example show that "self-policing" works or doesn't work?

9. Note that there are two particular bytes in the cipher text of Figure 16.3—one is all 0s and the other is all 1s. Guessing that the text is English, and thus would likely use ASCII encodings in which the first half byte (nibble) is from 0010 to 0111, determine the first 3 bits of the key, and the 9th, 10th, and 11th bits.

10. Using the opening phrase from *A Tale of Two Cities* "It was the best of times and the worst of times" rewrite the sentence keeping only the 12 most frequent letters and replacing the others with an underscore (_). Show the sentence to three friends and describe their experience trying to guess the phrase.

11. Find the opening paragraph from *A Tale of Two Cities* (it's on the Web) and compute frequencies for the 12 most frequent letters.

12. Explain the difference between Figures 16.2 and 16.4 and why it is significant.

13. What are the prime factors of 10, 50, and 61?

14. The RSA example uses 55, the product of 5 and 11, as the public key. Find the other primes under 60 that could be used to form keys.

15. If the cipher text numbers 10, 34, 35, 3, 10, 34, 26, 42, 11, 30, 0, 40 of our example are considered to be 6-bit blocks of ASCII, what would it translate to? That is, convert the cipher text to ASCII.

16. If $K_R = 55$ and $C = 2$, what does $T = ?$ [Hint: Table 11.1.]

17. What brands of cookies do you get? Check the cookies on your computer by doing a file/search on cookie, and then looking at the file using an ASCII text editor like NotePad or SimpleText. Are there cookies from third parties like the advertiser `DoubleClick.com`, whose sites you've never visited? Record the serial number of three cookies.

PART IV

Problem Solving

CHAPTER 17

Foundations of Programming

Learning Objectives

- Understand the distinction between name, value and variable.
- Learn why and how variables are declared.
- Learn the basic data types of JavaScript.
- Understand how assignment changes a variable's value.
- Know how to form expressions using arithmetic, relational, and logical operators.
- Learn the syntactic structure of if-statements and understand their flow of control.
- Understand how the JavaScript operations combine to produce a simple pricing computation.

Programming is a profession, yet we need to know something about it to be effective computer users. This is analogous to medicine. Doctors and nurses are professionals, but we need to know something about their specialties—our bodies, disease symptoms, nutrition, first aid, and so forth—to care for ourselves and benefit fully from their care. In neither case do we need an expert's knowledge, and in both cases we could probably survive with near total ignorance. But knowing some of what the professionals know is of unquestionable benefit and worth learning despite its technical nature.

What we need to know about programming is a fuller elaboration of the concepts already discussed in Chapter 10 on algorithms. The reason is that the concepts are deep and subtle. We cannot expect to encounter them once and comprehend them fully. Indeed, the end goal is to change our thinking habits to be more "abstract." Just as we need experience writing, reading, and speaking a foreign language in order to acquire it, so too do we need experience writing, reading, and executing algorithms and programs to acquire the thought processes of computation.

REVIEW AND PLAN OF ATTACK

Recall that programming is the act of formulating an algorithm or program. It entails developing a systematic means of solving a problem so that an agent—someone other than the programmer and usually a computer—can produce the intended result for every input, every time. Furthermore, the agent must perform or execute the program autonomously without any intervention from the programmer. This implies that all of the steps must be spelled out precisely and effectively, and that all contingencies must be planned for.

Programming actually requires thinking. But relying on thinking alone would make programming very difficult indeed. Instead, in this and other chapters, fundamental programming concepts developed over the past fifty years will be introduced. These are basic, essential tools needed for formulating any computation. They are used daily by professional programmers. They not only simplify common programming tasks, but they also promote clarity and completeness, assisting the programmer in managing the complexity of writing a program. When the constructs have all been introduced, programming should be manageable and accessible, an interesting intellectual exercise similar to working a crossword puzzle or deducing whodunit in a murder mystery. It's really no harder than that.

Trying to program an algorithm precisely using English is hopeless. Natural languages are too ambiguous for directing anything as clueless as a computer. So, programming languages have been developed that greatly assist programmers in two ways: They are perfectly precise, and they are specialized in using the concepts mentioned in the last paragraph. Using a programming language is actually easier than writing in English. We will use JavaScript, a recently developed programming language that is especially effective for World Wide Web applications. Though you will not become a JavaScript expert, it is possible that one day you might use JavaScript to make your personal Web page fancier.

The plan for this chapter is to introduce the following programming concepts:

- Variables, Names, and Values
- Declarations
- String Literals, Booleans, and Data Types
- Assignment
- Expressions
- Conditionals

With just these few concepts, enough programming ideas will have been presented to write actual programs. The program in Figure 17.1 is an example. It probably reads as complete gibberish at this moment, but by the end of the chapter it will become comprehensible. It is presented now to make it clear where we are headed, but it should be skipped now if it appears intimidating.

Finally, in introducing the deep ideas of the chapter, we must set down the practical details needed when actually programming. These rules can be burdensome as a chapter-long list of dos and don'ts. So, the more obvious rules—the ones you would guess intuitively—are skipped, relegated to Appendix B. This allows us to emphasize the few rules that are unintuitive. When in doubt, refer to Appendix B. All of the rules are listed there.

At the Espresso Stand

Espresso is concentrated liquid coffee produced by passing steam through finely ground coffee beans. Some people enjoy drinking espresso straight, but others prefer a café latté, espresso in steamed milk, a cappuccino, espresso in equal parts of steamed milk and milk foam, or an Americano, espresso in near-boiling water. Espresso drinks are sold in three sizes: short (8 oz.), tall (12 oz.), and grande (16 oz.). These drinks come with a single unit of espresso, called a *shot*, but coffee addicts often order additional shots. The price of additional shots is added to the base price of the drink, and tax is figured in to produce the charge for the drink. The program to compute the price of an espresso drink is:

Input:

```
drink, a string with one of the values: "espresso", "latte", "cappuccino", "Americano"
ounce, an integer, giving the size of the drink in ounces
shots, an integer, giving the number of shots
```

Output:

```
price in dollars of an order, including 8.7% sales tax
```

Program:

```
var price;
var taxRate = 0.087;
if (drink == "espresso")
      price = 1.00;
if (drink == "latte" || drink == "cappuccino") {
      if (ounce == 8)
            price = 1.55;
      if (ounce == 12)
            price = 1.95;
      if (ounce == 16)
            price = 2.35;
}
if (drink == "Americano")
      price = 1.10 + .30 * (ounce/8);
price = price + (shots - 1) * .70;
price = price + price * taxRate;
```

Figure 17.1. Sample JavaScript computation to figure the cost of espresso drinks.

Variables, Names, and Values

Though we are familiar with the concepts of a *name*, the letter sequence used to refer to something, and a *value*, the thing itself, we tend in normal conversation not to distinguish carefully between the two. Thus, when we use the letter sequences "Michele Pfeiffer" or "Harrison Ford," we mean those specific movie stars. There are many people with those names, of course, and if your friend from Geology class is also named Harrison Ford, that name has one value for you in the context of that class, and another in the context of the movies. However, humans disambiguate so easily that this distinction is ignored in everyday conversation. We treat names as inextricably bound to their values.

Names and values are separable in programming.

The best way to think of names and values in the context of programming is to ignore everyday usage and to think of names as if they were offices, titles, or other designations purposely selected to have changing values. Examples are abundant:

Name	Current Value (1/1/2002)	Previous Values
U.S. President	George W. Bush	Bill Clinton, George Washington
U.S. Supreme Court Chief Justice	William Rehnquist	Warren Burger, Earl Warren
James Bond	Pierce Brosnan	Sean Connery, Roger Moore
Queen Of England	Elizabeth II	Victoria I, Elizabeth I
UN Secretary General	Kofi Annan	Butros Butros-Ghali, U Thant

The names used in the right two columns are, of course, the informal usage of names from everyday conversation.

The reason to focus on the case where the values associated with a name can change is because they change in programs. A program is a fixed specification of a process. As the process evolves and the program transforms data, the names must refer to different values. This is a natural result of the fixed specification of the process. So, for example, the U.S. Constitution contains this specification of a process: "The President-elect will be sworn into office by the Chief Justice on the January 20 following the election." The intent of this command is to describe a process that applies no matter which people happen to be winner of the election, that is, the value of "President-elect", and the senior justice of the Supreme Court on that date, that is, the value of "Chief Justice." We naturally interpret the U.S. Constitution this way. The names "President-elect" and "Chief Justice" have changing values.

Names used in this way—a single letter sequence with a varying value associated with it—are an already familiar concept from our previous computing experience. The file with the name `EnglishPaper` has its value changed every time a version of the composition is saved. The names used in computing always have the property that the name is separable from the value and can be changed. It's a basic idea worth thinking about.

In programming terminology, the names just discussed are called *variables,* a reminder that the expectation is that their values will *vary*. In the *Alphabetize CDs* program in Chapter 10, two variables, *Alpha* and *Beta*, were used. Nearly every step in that program changed the value of one or the other of those variables. That's typical. The most commonly used programming language operation is the command to change the value of a variable. That command is called *assignment*, and it is discussed in a later section.

> **Names and Values:** We've seen one other example of names having multiple values over time. Memory locations—their names are called *addresses*—have the same property. This is not a coincidence. Variables are memory locations in the computer. Their names are simply a more readable and convenient way to reference computer memory than are the actual numerical addresses. The value of the address is the current contents of the memory location, and it is the value of the corresponding variable.

The letters of a variable's name are called the *identifier*. Identifiers in every programming language are required to have a particular form, though the form differs somewhat from language to language. Generally, identifiers must begin with a letter and can be composed of any sequence of letters, numerals (the digits 0 through 9) or the underscore symbol (_).[1] Identifiers are not allowed to contain spaces, so they must be consecutive symbols. Example variable names include

```
X           x
ru4it       nineteen_eighty_four
Time_O_Day  Identifiers_can_B_long_but_if_so_typing_them_can_be_a_pain
o00000      elizaBETH
```

Notice two features of identifiers: The underscore symbol can be used as a word separator to promote readability, taking the place of a space while "keeping the identifier together." Identifiers in most programming languages, including JavaScript, are case sensitive, meaning that the uppercase and lowercase letters are different.

> **Form Rules.** User IDs, our login and email names, follow similar rules, but with different constraints. So, login or email names often allow dash (-), but variable names cannot because it could be confused with the minus sign.

Declarations

Programs are usually written "starting from scratch." That is, when beginning to program, you can think of the computer as if it were newly manufactured; it knows nothing but how to understand the programming language. Accordingly, the first order of business in any program is to state what variables will be used in the computation. Saying what variables will be used is called *declaring variables*, and it is accomplished with a command called a *declaration*. In JavaScript, the declaration command is the word `var`, short for *variable,* followed by a list of the identifiers to be declared separated by commas. For example, to write a computation that computes the area of a circle given its radius, we would need variables `area` and `radius`. So we declare,

```
var radius, area;
```

This command *declares* that in the program we will use these two identifiers as variables. Notice that the first command in the espresso computation in Figure17.1

```
var price;
```

is a variable declaration of this type. (The program uses other variables that will be explained momentarily.)

The declaration was called a *command*, which is a true description because it is commanding the computer to record which identifiers will be used as variables. But everything we tell a computer is a command, so we should call the declaration by its proper term, *statement*.

A *program* is simply a list of statements. Because it's not always possible or desirable to put one statement per line as in a normal list, the statements are often run together, which requires that each statement be *terminated* by some punctuation symbol. The statement terminator in JavaScript is the semicolon (`;`). It's the same idea as terminating sentences in English with periods, question marks, or exclamation marks. The main difference is this If I forget to terminate an English sentence, like I just did,

[1] JavaScript permits slightly more general identifiers than suggested here, but throughout the book, tiny limitations to JS are implied to smooth language acquisition and help avoid errors. There is no loss of expressiveness.

you still understand—both from the meaning and from the capital letter on the next sentence—that the sentence is over, that is, terminated. The computer isn't that clever. It *needs* the semicolon. So, the rule is: Terminate every statement (including the statements introduced below) with a semicolon.

First Mistake. *Everyone* makes mistakes when programming. One of the most common mistakes for beginners is to forget the semicolon. When the semicolon is missing the computer becomes confused. Debugging is necessary. Training ourselves to remember semicolons eases programming.

Every variable used in a program must be declared. JavaScript allows declaration statements to be placed anywhere among the list of program statements. But because variable declarations announce what variables *will* be used in the program, programmers like to place them first in the program. It's like saying, "Here's the list of variables I'll be using in the program that follows." We will adopt that convention of declaring variables first.

The declaration states that the identifier is the name of a variable. But what is the name's value? It has no value yet! More precisely, the value of a declared variable is initially undefined. It's a name that doesn't yet name anything. The situation is analogous to when a group of people forms an intramural basketball team, say, Crunch. The intramural sports office can refer to the Crunch Captain, even if the person who is to be captain hasn't been chosen. The name is declared—it will be meaningful when the season is under way—but there is no value assigned yet. The value is *undefined*.

The most common case is that we know an initial value for the identifiers we declare. So JavaScript allows us to set the initial value as part of the declaration. To declare that `taxRate` and `balanceDue` are to be variables in the program, and that their initial values are .087 and 0, respectively, we write

```
var taxRate = .087;
var balanceDue = 0;
```

The `var` statement need not be limited to declaring and initializing just one variable at a time. Any number of variables can be declared and optionally initialized by separating the items with commas

```
var taxRate = .087, balanceDue = 0;
```

The computer doesn't care which is used. They're equivalent. Typically programmers include several variables in a single declaration statement when the variables are logically related. The only purpose is to remind themselves that the variables are related. For example, variables describing a person's features might be declared

```
var height, weight, hairColor, eyeColor, astrological_sign;
```

If the variables are not related, they are usually specified in separate statements. All approaches are equivalent and there is no "proper" way.

The values assigned to the variables `taxRate` and `balanceDue` are numbers. Like everything in programming there are rules for writing numbers, but basically the rules require numbers to be written in the "usual way." (Details are in Appendix B.) One "unusual" aspect of numbers in programming is there are no "units." So `33%` and `$10.89` are wrong, and we must write `0.33` and `10.89`. This explains why there are no dollar signs (`$`) in the program of Figure 17.1 even though it is a computation to figure the price of a coffee drink. In addition to normal numbers, JavaScript understands scientific notation, as in `6.022 e+23`, where "e" means "times 10 to the power of" and can also be "`E`". Standard computer numbers[2] can have about ten significant digits and range from as small as 10^{-324} to as large as 10^{308}.

String Literals, Booleans, and Data Types

Though computers frequently compute on numbers, they compute on other kinds of data as well. For us, strings will be the most common kind of data. *Strings* are sequences of keyboard characters. For example,

```
"abcdefghijklmnopqrstuvwxyz"          "May"     '!@#$%^&*()_+|}{:][''
"strings are surrounded by quotes"    "   "     "M&M's"
'strings can contain blanks'          ""        '"No," she said.'
```

are strings. Like numbers, strings can be used to initialize variables in declarations. For example,

```
var hairColor = "black", eyeColor = "brown", astrological_sign = "Leo";
```

Strings are essential when manipulating text, as is common in building Web pages. The program in Figure 17.1 uses several string constants: `"espresso"`, `"latte"`, `"cappuccino"`, and `"Americano"`.

The rules for writing strings in JavaScript, most of which are obvious from the examples, are:

- Strings must be surrounded by quotes, either single (`'`) or double (`"`).
- Most characters are allowed within quotes except New line, Backspace, Tab, \, Formfeed, and Return.
- Double quoted strings can contain single quotes, and vice versa.
- The apostrophe (`'`) is the same as the single quote.
- Any number of characters is allowed in a string.
- The minimum number of characters in a string is zero(`""`), which is called the *empty string*.

Notice that the empty string is a legitimate value. That is, writing

```
var exValDef = "";
var exValUndef;
```

results in two quite different situations. After these two statements, asking the computer what kind of value `exValDef` has, the answer would be "String," while the answer for `exValUndef` would be, "Undefined." We could also ask what the length of `exValDef` is (0), but this question makes no sense for `exValUndef` because it has no value. As we will see later, the empty string is very handy.

The third rule enables us to include quotes in a string. To use double quotes in a string, for example, enclose the string in single quotes, as in `'He said, "No!"'`. For a string containing single quotes, enclose it in double quotes, as in `"Guide to B&B's"`. Because the apostrophe is common in English's possessives and contrac-

[2] Numbers and computer arithmetic are unexpectedly subtle. Our uses of numbers will be trivial and avoid any difficulties. As a general rule, the "safe zone" is the range from ±2 billionths to ± 2 billion. Outside that range, learn more.

tions, it's a good idea to use double quotes as the default. Doing so allows free use of apostrophes. Change to single quotes only when the string contains double quotes. But both work, and the computer doesn't care.

The numbers and strings discussed are known as *constants* or *literals*, values *typed literally* in the program. So, the rules given concern how to express such values explicitly in a computation. However, when literals become the values of variables and are stored inside the computer the representation changes slightly, especially for strings. First, the surrounding quotes or double quotes disappear. That's why the length of the empty string is 0 rather than 2. Second, prohibitions against certain characters like New-line and Backspace don't apply. Specifically, though a Tab or other prohibited characters cannot be *typed*, they can be the value of a string inside the computer. How so? The "escape" mechanism, which we encountered in Chapters 4 and 8. For JavaScript, the escape symbol is backslash (\) and the escape sequences are shown in Table 17.1. Thus we can write declarations such as

```
var fourTabs = "\t\t\t\t", backUp = "\b"; bothQuotesInOne = "'\"";
```

which give values to the variables that cannot be typed literally. The escape sequences are converted to the single characters they represent when stored internally in the computer's memory. So, the lengths of the values of these three string variables are 4, 1, and 2, respectively.

Another kind of value is the Boolean value. Unlike numbers and strings, there are only two Boolean values: `true` and `false`. Boolean values have their obvious logical meaning. It should be emphasized that although `true` and `false` are letter sequences they are *values*, like 1 is a value, not identifiers or strings. Although Booleans are used implicitly throughout the programming process, as we'll see, they are used only occasionally for initializing variables. Examples might be,

```
var foreignLanguageReq = false, mathReq = true, totalCredits = 0;
```

This last declaration illustrates that variables appearing in the same declaration can be initialized with different kinds of values.

> **It's True**. Boolean values get their name from George Boole, the English mathematician who invented them. No. True and false have been around since humans began to reason. Boole invented an algebra based on these two values that is essential to computer engineering and other fields.

The different kinds of values of a programming language are called its *value types* or simply its *types*. We have introduced three types for JavaScript: numbers, strings, and Booleans. There are several other types, but these will be sufficient for most of what we will do in JavaScript. JavaScript is very kind to programmers with respect to types, as we will see later in this chapter.

Table 17.1. Escape Sequences for Characters Prohibited from String Literals

Seq.	Character	Seq.	Character
\b	Backspace	\f	Form feed
\n	New-line	\r	Carriage return
\t	Tab	\'	Apostrophe or single quote
\"	Double quote	\\	Backslash

> **Meta-Brackets:** In discussing programming languages, we often need to describe a syntactic structure, such as declaration statements. To separate the language being defined from the language doing the defining, we enclose terms of the defining language in "angle brackets," (<, >) known as meta-brackets. So, the general form of the preceding JavaScript declaration would be `var` *<variable name>* = *<initial value>*—where the symbols not in meta-brackets are written literally and the meta-brackets are variables standing for things of the sort indicated. Notice that despite looking similar, these are *not* tags.

ASSIGNMENT

If variables must change values in an algorithm or program, there should be a convenient way to command the computer to do so. An assignment statement accomplishes that operation, and it is the workhorse of programming. An assignment statement has three parts that always occur in this order:

<variable> *<assignment symbol>* *<expression>* ;

where *<variable>* is any declared variable in the program, *<assignment symbol>* is the language's notation for the assignment operation, discussed next, and *<expression>* is a segment of legal program like a formula defining how to compute the new value that is to be assigned to the variable, explained in a moment. Because it is a statement, it is terminated by a semicolon. JavaScript's *<assignment symbol>* is the equal sign (=), and we've already seen the assignment operation as the initializer for variable declarations.

Different programming languages use different symbols for indicating assignment. The three most widely used symbols are the equal sign (=); the colon, equal sign pair (: =), and the left pointing arrow (←). There are others, but these three are in widest use. The : = is considered a single symbol even though it is formed from two keyboard characters. Like JavaScript most languages use =. Pascal uses : = and more mathematical languages like APL use ←. Regardless of which symbol they use, assignment is a standard and heavily used operation in every programming language.

An example assignment statement is

weeks = days / 7;

Semicolon terminator
<expression>
<assignment symbol>
<variable>

where the variable `weeks` is the variable whose value is being changed, the = is the assignment symbol and `days/7` is the expression. Therefore, this assignment statement fulfills the requirements of the standard form shown earlier.

To understand the workings of assignment, it is *essential* to think of a value flowing from the right side (expression side) of the assignment symbol to the left side (variable side). (This view makes the left arrow (←) perhaps the most intuitive assignment symbol.) The assignment symbol should be read as "*is assigned*" or "*becomes*" or even more economically, "*gets*." Therefore, the foregoing example can be read

> "the variable `weeks` *is assigned* the value resulting from dividing the value of the variable `days` by `7`"
>
> "the value of `weeks` *becomes* the value resulting from dividing the value of the variable `days` by `7`"
>
> "the variable `weeks` *gets* the value resulting from dividing the value of the variable `days` by `7`"

Terms like *is assigned, becomes* and *gets* emphasize the role that the assignment = plays, namely, to change the value of the variable named on the left side.

> **Get with the Program.** Programmers mostly prefer *gets* to verbalize assignment. It conveys the idea of filling a container, as in a "mailbox gets a letter" or a "flour tin gets refilled." The variable is the container.

In an assignment statement, the expression, that is, everything to the right of the assignment symbol, is computed or evaluated first. If there are any variables used in the expression, their current values are used. This evaluation produces a value, which then becomes the new value of the variable named on the left side. So, the effect of executing the example assignment statement

```
weeks = days / 7;
```

is that the current value of the variable `days` is determined by looking in the memory; suppose it is `77`, and that value is divided by `7` producing a new value, `11`. This is a new value that then becomes the new value of the variable `weeks`, that is, `weeks` is assigned 11.

> **Assignment to Memory.** In the computer, an assignment statement causes the value in the memory location(s) corresponding to the variable to be replaced by the new value resulting from the expression.

There are three key points to remember about assignment statements. First, all three of the components must be given; if anything is missing, the statement is meaningless. Second, the flow of the value to the name is always right to left. Thus the two variable names in the assignment statement

```
variable_receiving_new_value = newly_computed_value;
```

properly reflect the motion of information. Notice that the expression can simply be some other variable; it doesn't have to be a complicated formula. Third, the values of any variables used in the expression are their values prior to the start of execution of the assignment. This point is extremely important because the variable being changed in the assignment statement might also be used in the expression.

For example, a program simulating a basketball game would probably use the assignment statement

```
totalScore = totalScore + 3;
```

to reflect the result of a basket from outside the three-point circle. When the expression on the right side of the assignment statement, `totalScore + 3`, is evaluated, the value of `totalScore` used in the computation will be its value before starting this statement, that is, the score before the shot. When the assignment statement is completed, `totalScore` will then have the updated value reflecting the three-point shot.

Similarly, the program might contain the code

```
shotClock = shotClock - 1;
```

to implement the "tick" of the shot clock. Again, when evaluating the right expression, the values used for variables are those before the statement is executed.

Repeating, because this is the most important of all of the ideas of this chapter, the role of = is to *assign* the value computed on the right side to be the new value of the variable named on the left side.

> **Programming Is Not Algebra:** Like algebra, many programming languages use an equal sign in assignments. In programming "=" is read "becomes", which suggests the dynamic meaning of right-to-left value flow. In algebra "=" is read "equals", which emphasizes the static meaning that both sides are identical. In programming, the statement "$x = x + 1$" means the value of x becomes one larger; in algebra, the equation "$x = x + 1$" is meaningless because there is no number that is identical to itself plus 1. The unknowns in algebra are names whose values do not change.

EXPRESSIONS

Programming is not mathematics, but it is closely related, and it traces its intellectual roots to higher math. Accordingly, it is not surprising that one of the primitive concepts in programming should be an algebra-like formula called an *expression*. Expressions are the means of performing the actual computation. As we've already seen, they are built out of variables and *operators*, which are standard arithmetic operations as found on the keys of a calculator, such as addition or subtraction. The actual symbols used for the more exotic operators vary somewhat with the programming language, so we limit ourselves here to those of JavaScript. Examples include

```
a * (b + c)
height * width / 2
pi * diameter
(((days * 24) + hours) * 60 + minutes) * 60 + seconds
```

Expressions usually follow rules similar to algebraic formulae, but not quite. Multiplication must be given explicitly with the asterisk (`*`) multiply operator; that is, write `a * b` rather than `ab` or `a · b` or `a × b`. As with algebra, multiply and divide are performed before add and subtract—we say multiply and divide have *higher precedence* than add and subtract—unless parentheses group the operations differently. Therefore, `a*b + a*c` is equivalent to `(a*b) + (a*c)` because multiplication is performed first. Also, because expressions must be typed on a single line, superscripts as in x^2 are prohibited. Some languages have an operator for exponents or powers, but JavaScript doesn't. If we want to compute the area of a circle, we must multiply R times itself because we can't square it. So

```
pi * R * R
```

is the expression for computing the area of a circle, assuming that `pi` has the value 3.1415962.

Operators like "+" and "*" are called *binary operators* because they operate on two values. The values they operate on are called *operands*. There are also *unary* operators, like negate (-), having only one operand. (Language parsers can easily figure out whether any use of minus is the unary negate or the binary subtract.) One very useful operator in future chapters will be mod (`%`). The result of `a%b` for integers `a` and `b` is the remainder from the division `a/b`. So, the result of `4%2` is `0` because `2` evenly divides `4`, whereas `5%2` is `1` because `2` into 5 leaves a remainder of `1`.

Expressions involving addition, subtraction, and so on are similar to algebra, but programmers use other kinds of expressions. *Relational operators* are used to make comparisons between numerical values, that is, test the relationship between two numbers. The outcome of the comparison is a Boolean value, either `true` or `false`. The operators are illustrated here with sample operands `a` and `b` that should be replaced with variables or expressions:

```
a <  b   is a less than b
a <= b   is a less than or equal to b
a == b   is a equal to b
a != b   is a not equal to b
a >= b   is a greater than or equal to b
a >  b   is a greater than b
```

Notice that the "equal to" relational operator (==) is a double equal sign, making it different from assignment.

Examples of relational expressions include

```
bondRate  > certificateDeposit
temperature <= 212
drink == "espresso"
```

Notice that relational tests can apply to string variables as in the last example, which is taken from the program in Figure 17.1. Both equal and not equal can be applied to string variables.

> **One Lump or Two?** Several operators, such as "<=", ">=", "!=", and others, are composed of two keyboard characters. Such compounds may not contain a space and are considered a single character. They were adopted years ago to make up for the limited number of characters on a standard keyboard. Were programming language research started today, compounds would not be necessary because it is now easy to introduce symbols not represented on the keyboard, such as "≤", "≥", and "≠".

The relational test results in a `true` or `false` outcome; that is, either the two operands are related to each other as the relational operator asks, making the test outcome `true`, or they are not, making the test outcome `false`. It is common to test two or more relationships together, requiring that relational expression results be combined. For example, teenagers are older than 12 and younger than 20. In programming, "teenagerness" is determined by establishing that the relational tests `age > 12` and `age < 20` are both true. This is specified by the expression

```
age > 12 && age < 20
```

The `&&` is the *logical and* operator, playing the same role AND plays in query expressions seen in Chapters 5 and 13. The outcome of *a* `&&` *b* is true if both `a` and `b` are true; otherwise, it is false. (The operands *a* and *b* can be variables, in which case they have Boolean values, or expressions, or a mixture.) Thus, in the teenager expression, the current value of `age` is compared to 12, which yields a `true` or a `false` outcome. Then the current value of `age` is compared to 20, yielding another `true` or `false` outcome. Finally, these two outcomes, the operands of `&&`, are tested and if they are both `true`, the entire expression has a `true` outcome; otherwise, it is `false`. For example,

Value of `age`	`age > 12`	`age < 20`	`age > 12 && age < 20`
4	false	true	false
16	true	true	true
50	true	false	false

Notice that the operands for relational expressions must be numeric, whereas the operands for logical expressions must be Boolean, that is, `true` or `false`.

> **Programming Is Still Not Algebra:** In algebra, the notation *12 < age < 20* would be used to assert "teenagerness," the static condition of an age within the indicated limits. In programming, both tests must be specified and the two results "anded" to produce the final answer. The difference, again, is that in algebra we assert a static condition, whereas in programming we are *commanding* the computer to perform the operation of testing the two conditions.

Not surprisingly, there is also a *logical or* operator given by `||`. The outcome of `a || b` is true if either *a* is `true` or *b* is `true`, and it is also true if they are both `true`; it is false only if both are `false`. A "preteen" test expression

```
age == 11 || age == 12
```

illustrates the use of the logical operator `||`. Because `&&` and `||` have lower precedence than the relational operators, the relations are always tested first. To include 10-year-olds as preteens, write the expression

```
age == 10 || (age == 11 || age == 12)
```

which states that either the person's age is 10 or it satisfies the previous preteen definition. Notice that the subexpression in parentheses produces a `true` or `false` value when evaluated, just like a relational test does. It matters not how the operands of `||` are produced; it matters only that they are `true` or `false` values. An equivalent way to achieve the same result would be

```
(age == 10 || age == 11) || age == 12
```

Of course, it is also possible to test this definition of preteen with the expression

```
age >= 10 && age <= 12
```

which takes a bit less typing, and is analogous to the teenager test. All of these expressions seem equally clear to a person, and the computer doesn't care which is used.

An equivalent "teenagerness" expression can be written using `||` and the *logical not* operator, given by, `!`. Logical not is a unary operator—it takes only a single operand—and its outcome is opposite of the value of its operand. Thus an alternate teenager expression is

```
! (age <= 12 || age >= 20)
```

which works as follows. The subexpression in parentheses tests if a person is outside the range of being a teenager, that is, 12 or younger or 20 or older. If `true`, the person is not a teenager; if `false`, the person is a teenager. Then the *logical not* operator changes the outcome. Thus, the whole expression tests whether a person's age is not outside the range of being a teenager. If a person is not outside the range of being a teenager, the person is a teenager. The original formulation is probably clearer to a person, but they both produce the same result. And again, the computer doesn't care.

Finally, we've reached "operator overload." That might sound like the description of trying to learn too many new operators at a time—a state the reader has no doubt achieved!—but it is a technical term meaning the "use of an operator with different data types." The case of interest is +. Operators usually apply to a single data type like numbers. So, we expect `4 + 5` to produce the numerical result of `9`. And it does when the operands are numbers. But if the operands are the strings `"four" + "five"` the result is the string `"fourfive"`. That is, when + is applied to strings it joins them together, an operation called *concatenation*. In everyday writing, we simply place two strings together if we want them joined, but in programming, we are commanding the computer to do the work, so we need the operator concatenation. We have "overloaded" the meaning of + to mean addition when operands are numerical and concatenation when the operands are strings. Though overloading is common in some programming languages, + is the only example we'll see with our use of JavaScript. When manipulating strings, as in the statement

```
fullName = firstName + " " + middleName + " " + lastName;
```

which composes a name from its parts using blanks as separators, it's easy to interpret + as concatenation. But for a statement like

```
colt = "4" + "5";
```

the variable `colt` will be assigned the string `"45"`, not `9`, because the operands are (length 1) strings. Thus we must be alert for quotes that reveal the use of strings rather than numerical values.

CONDITIONALS

The *Alphabetize CDs* program given in Chapter 10 required many tests. For example, there was a test to determine if the titles of two CDs were in alphabetic order. Testing frequently is typical of most computations, so a specific statement type, called a *conditional statement*, has been invented to simplify making tests. The conditional statement has the form

```
if (<Boolean expression>)
      <then-statement>;
```

where the *<Boolean expression>* is any expression evaluating to the Boolean `true` or `false` outcome, such as relational expressions. For example,

```
if (waterTemp < 32)
      waterState = "Frozen";
```

is a typical conditional statement. The operation of a conditional is as follows: The *<Boolean expression>*, called a *predicate*, is evaluated producing a `true` or `false` outcome. If the outcome is `true`, the *<then-statement>* is performed. If the outcome is `false`, the *<then-statement>* is skipped, that is, not performed. Therefore, in the example the value of the variable `waterTemp` is determined and compared to 32. If it is less than 32, the value of the variable `waterState` is changed to `"Frozen"`. Otherwise, the statement is passed over, and `waterState` remains unchanged. As another example

```
if (waterTemp >= 32 && waterTemp <= 212)
      waterState = "Liquid";
```

tests a range of values.

Some programming languages use the word *then* to separate the predicate from the *<then-statement>* that follows, but JavaScript does not, because it is unnecessary.

Writing the *<then-statement>* on the following line indented is actually only a convention; the *<then-statement>* could be on the same line as the predicate,

```
if (waterTempC >= 0 && waterTempC <= 100) waterState = "Liquid";
```

It has the same meaning because white space is ignored in JavaScript. But programmers write the *<then-statement>* indented on the following line as a way of setting it off and emphasizing its conditional nature for themselves. By the way, when reading a conditional statement it is convenient to *say* "then" following the predicate.

Conditionals are extremely useful, but sometimes it is necessary to perform more than one statement on a `true` outcome of the predicate test. It is possible just to repeat the test for each statement to be executed, as in

```
if (waterTemp < 32) waterState  = "Frozen";
if (waterTemp < 32) description = "Ice";
```

but repeating becomes tedious quickly. Accordingly, programming languages allow for a sequence of statements in the so-called `Then`-clause. The problem is that if there are several statements, how will we know how many to skip in case the predicate has a `false` outcome? The solution is easy: Group the statements by surrounding them with "curly braces" `{ }`, which collects them together to become a single statement known as a *compound statement*. Then they fulfill the requirements of the definition given above because now *<then-statement>* refers to the (single) compound statement; it is skipped when the predicate outcome is `false`. For example,

```
if (waterTempC < 0) {
        waterState  = "Frozen";
        description = "Ice";
}
```

Notice the location of the curly braces. One immediately follows the predicate to signal that a compound statement is following and the other is placed conspicuously on its own line below the *i* of `if`. This is a standard programmer convention adopted so that compound statement grouping symbols—which are easily overlooked by a person if placed at unexpected locations in a program—are sited at the positions where we will need to know the information. As always the computer doesn't care where the curly braces are placed. But compound statement braces have a huge impact on program behavior, so they are always located at a consistent place where they will be found and where they can be noticed. This is an excellent habit to adopt!

> **An Exception**. The "exception proving the rule" that every statement must be terminated by a semicolon is the compound statement exception. The closing curly brace } should *not* be followed by a semicolon.

Another example from the espresso computation of Figure 17.1

```
if (drink == "latte" || drink == "cappuccino") {
    if (ounce == 8)
          price = 1.55;
    if (ounce == 12)
          price = 1.95;
    if (ounce == 16)
          price = 2.35;
}
```

shows an `if` with a compound statement containing three simple `if` statements. If `drink` is neither a `"latte"` nor a `"cappuccino"` the three statements will be skipped. Otherwise, if `drink` equals `"latte"` or drink equals `"cappuccino"`, the three statements will be performed. Notice that at most one predicate of the three statements of the compound statement can be true because `ounce` has only one value: 8, 12, 16, or something else. So, `price` will be changed at most once.

Of course, performing statements when a condition is true is handy, but how can statements be executed when the condition's outcome is false? There is a secondary form of the `if`-statement known as the `if/else`. It has the form

```
if (<Boolean expression>)
    <then-statement>;
    else
<else-statement>;
```

The `if/else` operates as follows. The *<Boolean expression>* is evaluated. If the outcome is `true`, the *<then-statement>* is performed and the *<else-statement>* is skipped. If the *<Boolean expression>*'s outcome is `false`, the opposite happens, namely, the *<then-statement>* is skipped and the *<else-statement>* is performed. For example,

```
if (day == 'Friday' || day == 'Saturday')
     calendarEntry = "Party!";
else
     calendarEntry = "Study";
```

The *<then-statement>* and *<else-statement>* are single statements, but several statements can be grouped into a compound statement with curly braces when necessary. For example,

```
if ((year % 4)== 0) {
      leapYear = true;
      febDays = febDays + 1;
}
else
      leapYear = false;
```

This example uses the *mod operator* `%`, so the outcome of `(year%4)` is the remainder of `year / 4`; that is, the result is 0, 1, 2, or 3.

A typical example sets the same variables in both parts of the conditional. Consider a coin toss at the start of a soccer game, which can be expressed as

```
if (sideUp == sideCalled) {
      coinTossWinner = visitorTeam;
      firstHalfOffensive = visitorTeam;
      secondHalfOffensive = hostTeam;
}
else  {
      coinTossWinner = hostTeam;
      firstHalfOffensive = hostTeam;
      secondHalfOffenive = visitorTeam;
}
```

Notice that the opening curly brace for the *<else-statement>* is placed by convention right after the `else`, and the closing curly brace is placed conspicuously on its own line directly below the *e* of `else`.

Either the *<then-statement>* or the *<else-statement>* can contain an `if/else`, but if so care must be exercised. This is because it can be ambiguous which `if` an `else` is associated with. The rule in JavaScript and most other programming languages is that the `else` associates with the (immediately) preceding `if`. For example, the code

```
if (Spot == "dog")
    if (Puff == "dog")
        report = "Spot and Puff are the same kind of animal";
else
        report = "Spot is not a dog";        Caution this code is deceptive
```

has been *deceptively* indented so that it *appears* that the `else` associates with the first `if`. But white space is ignored. The JavaScript rule means that the `else` associates with the "inner" `if`, implying that the following indentation matches the actual meaning:

```
if (Spot == "dog")
    if (Puff == "dog")
        report = "Spot and Puff are the same kind of animal";
    else
        report = "Spot is not a dog";        Caution this conclusion is wrong
```

In fact, assuming Spot is a dog and Puff is cat or any other animal, `report` gives the wrong conclusion. The best policy—followed by successful programmers—is to enclose the *<then-statement>* or *<else-statement>* in compound curly braces whenever it contains an `if/else`. Thus the proper way to express the statement would have been

```
if (Spot == "dog") {
    if (Puff == "dog")
        report = "Spot and Puff are the same kind of animal";
    else
        report = "Spot is not a dog";        Caution this conclusion is wrong
    }
```

The braces explicitly group the `else` with its `if`. The policy saves a lot of grief.

As one final example of conditionals, consider the four outcomes from flipping two coins expressed by nested conditionals:

```
if (flip1 == guess1) {
    if (flip2 == guess2)
        score = "win win";
    else
        score = "win lose";
}
else {
    if (flip2 == guess2)
        score = "lose win";
    else
        score = "lose lose";
}
```

Inner `if` for `true` outcome of Outer `if`

Inner `if` for `false` outcome of Outer `if`

Outer `if`

This example shows clearly the logic of the true and false outcomes of the predicates.

The Espresso Program

After studying basic programming concepts in this chapter, we now return to the program mentioned in the introduction. Recall that the program computes the price of four kinds of espresso drinks based on the type of drink, size of drink and number of additional shots, plus tax. The input variables are listed at the start of the program, as is the output.

Input:

```
drink, a string with one of the values: "espresso", "latte",
       "cappuccino", "Americano"
ounce, an integer, giving the size of the drink in ounces
shots, an integer, giving the number of shots
```

Output:

```
price in dollars of an order, including 8.7% sales tax
```

Program:

```
1.  var price;
2.  var taxRate = 0.087;
3.  if (drink == "espresso")
        price = 1.00;
4.  if (drink == "latte" || drink == "cappuccino") {
4a.      if (ounce == 8)
             price = 1.55;
4b.      if (ounce == 12)
             price = 1.95;
4c.      if (ounce == 16)
             price = 2.35;
    }
5.  if (drink == "Americano")
        price = 1.10 + .30 * (ounce/8);
6.  price = price + (shots - 1) * .70;
7.  price = price + price * taxRate;
```

The input variables are assumed to be given; see Chapter 18 for details on how this is done with a GUI. Because the program will create the output, we declare it to be a variable as the first statement of the program.

Statements 3 through 5 determine the kind of drink and establish the base price. These statements have been written to exhibit different programming techniques.

- **Line 3.** If the order is straight espresso, the first shot is priced at a $1.00. This is an example of a basic conditional statement. The `ounce` variable does not apply to straight espresso because it is served in special small cups. So, there is nothing more to computing the base price. Even so, lines 4 and 5 will be performed.
- **Lines 4–4c.** These statements establish the base prices for lattes and cappuccinos using an `If`-statement with conditionals in the `Then`-clause compound statement. Thus the three conditionals 4a–4c apply to either lattes or cappuccinos. The three conditionals test for the different sizes and set the base price accordingly. A short latte or cappuccino has a base price of $1.55, talls are $1.95 and grandes are $2.35. Only one of these conditionals will perform its *<then-statement>* because `ounce` has only one value, but all three tests will be made.
- **Line 5**. This line uses a basic `If`-statement to compute the base price for Americanos. And, like Lines 4–4c, it computes base prices for each of the three sizes. But, unlike the latte/cappuccino case, the three base prices are not computed as separate `If`-statements. Instead, the base price is $1.10 plus an increment determined by the drink size. Here's how it works: The `ounce` value, which has one of three values (8, 12, or 16), is divided by 8 in the subexpression (`ounce / 8`). This yields one of three values (1.0, 1.5, or 2.0), depending on what the value of `ounce` is. This result—it's called a *scaling*

factor—is multiplied by .30, yielding one of the values 0.30, 0.45, or 0.60. This increment is added to the $1.10. Therefore, an Americano has a base price of $1.40, $1.55, or $1.70, depending on the value of `ounce`. Thus, rather than treating the three different `ounce` cases separately as was done in the latte/cappuccino case, Line 5 computes the proper base prices by incorporating the `ounce` into the computation. Neither approach is better; they are simply different ways of achieving the same result.

Notice that the `If`-statements on Lines 3, 4, and 5 will always be executed, but because they apply to different drinks, the statement(s) of their `Then`-clauses will be executed in only one of the cases.

Finally, the total `price` is computed in Lines 6 and 7. In Line 6, the cost of additional shots is added to the base price. If a person does not order additional shots, the value of `shots` will be 1, and because reducing shots by 1 results in multiplying by 0 to produce a 0, nothing extra is added in. When this line is completed, the total price has been computed. In Line 7 the tax is added in. This is accomplished by multiplying the total price by.087, to compute the tax and then adding that to the total price computed so far.

Execution for a Double Tall Latté

To see this program in action, compute the price of a double tall latté, the second most common phrase used in Seattle after "it's still raining." A "double" means a total of two shots in the drink, that is, one extra shot. Thus the input variables to the program are

```
drink ⇔ "latte"
ounce ⇔ 12
shots ⇔ 2
```

where the notation "⇔" is read as "has the value of" or "contains." This notation allows us to say the value of a variable without using the equal sign, which would look like an assignment statement.

The first statements are declarations, and as such are thought of as definitions. In particular, we should treat `price` as not yet having any value. The following lines are executed:

- Line 3 is executed first. The test `drink == "espresso"` fails, so its `Then`-clause is skipped.
- Line 4 is executed next. The test `drink == "latte" || drink == "cappuccino"` has a `true` outcome because the subexpression `drink == "latte"` is true; the relational test `drink == "cappuccino"` is false, of course, but because one of the operands of the `||` is `true`, the whole expression is `true`. This means that the `Then`-clause containing the conditionals 4a–4c will be executed.
- Line 4a is executed next. The test `ounce == 8` has a false outcome, so its `Then`-clause is skipped.
- Line 4b is nexecuted.[3] The `ounce == 12` test is true, so the `Then`-clause is executed, giving `price` its initial value, `price ⇔ 1.95`.

[3] Isn't *nexecuted* a great word for "next executed"?

- Line 4c is nexecuted. The `ounce == 16` test fails, so its `Then`-clause is skipped.
- Line 5 is nexecuted. The `drink == "Americano"` test fails, so its `Then`-clause is skipped.
- Line 6 is nexecuted. This causes the value of `shots` to be multiplied by .70, resulting in the value .70, which is added to `price`, yielding `price` ⇔ `2.65`.
- Line 7 is nexecuted. The current value of `price` is multiplied by `taxRate` whose value was initialized on line 2 (`taxRate` ⇔ `0.087`) resulting in `.23`, which is added to `price` to compute the final value of `2.88`, which is assigned to `price`.

Thus, with the pricing structure implemented in the program, `price` ⇔ `2.88`, so a "double tall latté" costs $2.88. Is this cheaper or more expensive than a "triple grande Americano"?

Summary

In this chapter, we introduced enough programming concepts—and their JavaScript syntax—to read and understand nontrivial programs. Though it has been intense, the ideas are generally intuitive, when seen from the right perspective. Only a few concepts remain for later chapters. Mostly what we need is practice with these ideas. They are surprisingly powerful.

The chapter began by introducing the idea that a name can be separated from its value. Captain is a name for the team leader, but its value, that is, the person who is the captain, can change. In fact, the name exists, though with an undefined value, as soon as a team is formed. Names with changing values is a familiar idea. Filenames work this way as we progressively update a file with, say, a word processor. Variables in programming languages have changing values, too. The reason is simple. A program is a fixed, finite specification for a computation written out in a few pages of code. Yet, when the computation is executed, many values may be created to produce the final answer. In the espresso computation, for example, the variable `price`, which is initially undefined, has three different values: the base price, the total price before tax, and the final price. At any point, the value of `price` is the price as computed so far, but the process of computing `price` continues until the program is finished. The separation is an important idea and is a feature of programming that distinguishes it from algebra.

Next we introduced identifiers, the letter sequences that make up a variable's name. Their structure was explained, as was the fact that they must be declared. Optionally variables can be initialized when they are declared. With their structure defined and the need for declaring them explained, we introduced the idea of changing the value of a variable using assignment—the main workhorse concept in programming. It's subtle. An assignment statement has a variable on the left side of the assignment symbol, and an expression on the right side. The operation is to compute the value of the expression and make that result the new value of the variable. This makes information flow from right to left in an assignment statement. Statements like

```
x = x + 1;
```

make sense in programming. They are commands to the computer to find out the current value of the variable `x`, to add 1 to it, and to make the result of the addition the new value of `x`.

Having previously introduced the concept of a data type and defined three JavaScript data types—we need numbers, strings, and Booleans—we explained how to build expressions to compute values of these types. We have the standard arithmetic operators and relationals to compute on numbers, concatenation for combining strings, and logical operations for Booleans. (See the table in Appendix B for a full listing.) In defining concatenation, we introduced the idea of "operator overload." Expressions "do the computing" in our programs, and are a generally familiar idea.

As a rule, all of the statements of a program are executed, one after another, starting at the beginning. The conditional statements allow for a variation on the rigid "execute everything first-to-last." JavaScript's two conditional forms are `if` and `if/else`. These allow statements to be selectively executed depending on the outcome of a Boolean expression called a *predicate*. Using conditionals, we can organize our computations so that operations are performed when "the conditions are right." Care must be exercised to group statements within a compound statement to make plain which statements are optionally skipped or executed. Also, using `if/else` within a conditional requires caution to make certain that the statement components associate correctly.

Finally, we reviewed most of the ideas of the chapter by analyzing the espresso computation of Figure 17.1. Both numeric and string data types were used, as were the declaration, assignment, and conditional statement forms. The program illustrated that certain parts of the computation—figuring the base price of a drink as determined by its size—could be computed in different ways. There were few surprises.

All that prevents us from actually running the program and demonstrating our knowledge is setting up the input to acquire the values for `drink`, `ounce`, and `shots`, and outputting the `price`. This will require a GUI written in HTML, and is the topic of Chapter 18.

EXERCISES

1. How do names of everyday usage differ from names as used in programming?
2. What is a *variable* and what are two examples from *Alphabetize CDs*?
3. How are variables related to a computer's memory locations?
4. What is an *identifier*?
5. Which are legal variable names: (a) `OhZero`, (b) `Oh0`, (c) `Ozero`, (d) `O0` and why?
6. Which are legal variable names: (a) `Catch22`, (b) `Catch-22`, (c) `Zerotolerance`, (d) `0tolerance`?
7. Explain the difference between the identifier `OhZero` and the string `"OhZero"`.
8. Which of the following are legal assignment statements:
   ```
   OhZero = "OhZero"
   "OhZero" = OhZero
   ```
9. What are the three key features of assignment statements?
10. What is the purpose of a variable declaration?

11. Suppose a program has two statements in a row:
```
x = 4;
x = 8;
```
Is this (a) illegal, (b) legal, but meaningless, or (c) legal, but inefficient? Explain your choice.

12. Explain the difference in meaning of $x = x + 1$ in programming and in algebra.

13. List the six relational operators of JavaScript.

14. Give the expression that defines an octogenarian.

15. Using the program given in this chapter, is a "triple grande Americano" more than $2.88, and if so, by how much?

16. How much is a double espresso?

CHAPTER 18

The Bean Counter: A JavaScript Program

Learning Objectives

- Learn the mechanics of writing and running JavaScript programs.
- Acquire experience with HTML tables.
- Learn the concepts of `form` and `input` controls.
- Understand the idea of event-based programming.
- Learn the process of writing event handlers.
- Know how to reference a component in one control from another.
- Adopt the program-change/program-test paradigm.
- Distinguish between a program's logic and its GUI.
- Learn the importance of design assessment.

Much of modern programming requires two activities. The first is the creation of the logic that directs the computer to solve a problem. The second is the construction of a user interface to assist in the human/computer interaction; specifically to create a mechanism by which the input can be entered and the computed output can be displayed. In Chapter 17, we formulated a program to charge for espresso drinks as an illustration of basic programming concepts. That program is the logical component of our solution. In this chapter, we focus on the creation of a user interface and connecting the two parts together.

Because JavaScript is designed for Web applications, the graphical user interface will be a Web page written in HTML. The initial goal is the page in Figure 18.1.

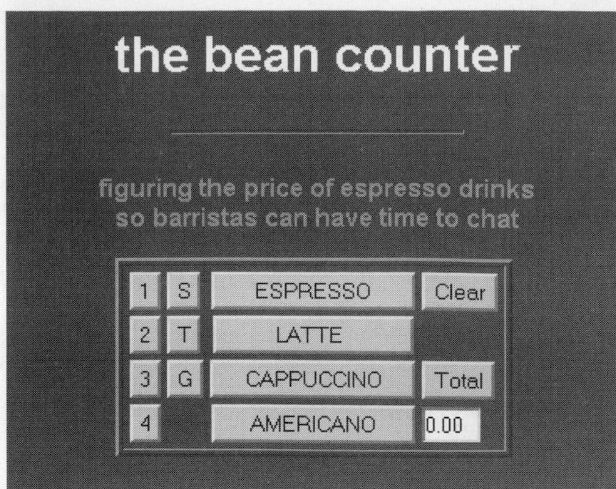

Figure 18.1. Initial Web interface for the Bean Counter program.

The Bean Counter program shows a series of buttons, and a window in the right corner with which to display the total price of the espresso drink. The first column of buttons with numbers on them specifies the number of shots. The second column specifies the size of the drink, where S, T, and G stand for short, tall, and grande. The next column specifies the type of espresso drink. The last two buttons are obvious.

The main task of this chapter is to construct the Bean Counter application by building the user interface and connecting it to the logic of Chapter 17. After covering two preliminaries, the steps required are as follows:

- Review Web page programming, recalling some of the HTML basics, and introduce the idea of the HTML `input` specifications.
- Construct the Web page components, so that the graphic is "right." Only the picture will be complete; the buttons will not work at this point.
- Introduce the idea of "event programming" and connect the buttons to the program logic.
- Try out the Web page, evaluating it for its usefulness.
- Revise the page and the logic so that it more effectively solves the problem.

When the Web page is complete, we will have created our first complete JavaScript program. *The best way to learn both the ideas and the practical skills of this chapter is to construct the computation while reading the text.*

Preliminaries

Recall from Chapter 4 that HTML files are simple ASCII text. The fancy formatting included by state-of-the-art word processors like WordPerfect, MS Word, or Claris Works simply confuses Web browsers, and so must be avoided. Accordingly, the programming of this chapter will use a basic text editor such as NotePad, SimpleText, WordPad, or BBText. The file format must be `text` or `txt`, and the filename's extension (the characters following the last dot) must be `.html`. So, `bean.html` would be a good name. In this way, the operating system will know that the file is to be processed by a Web browser, and the browser will be able to understand everything in the file without becoming confused.

To create your program, you will construct a file whose first line is `<html>` and whose last line is `</html>` using the text editor. To include JavaScript in an HTML file, the JS text must be enclosed in `<script language="JavaScript">` `</script>` tags. The information that you include between these tags is the subject of this chapter, of course. When it's time to test your program, save it. Remember that the file format must be `text` and the file extension `.html`, though if you've specified this information already, a simple `Save` should suffice. Then, find the file on your computer, and double-click on it. Your standard Web browser[1] should open the file and display the Web page you've constructed. It's that simple.

To work through the mechanics of running a JavaScript program, we will ignore the user interface for the moment and simply run the computational part of the program

[1] The JavaScript in this book requires a "contemporary" browser such as Internet Explorer 4 or higher, or Netscape 6 or higher. Because of browser inconsistencies, the text's pictures may differ slightly from yours.

from Chapter 17. This is mostly an exercise because we will not be able to interact with the result, and all that we will see is one number printed out. We begin this way to make sure the code of the basic Bean Counter computation is working. This code will be used later in the chapter. The program structure needed to run just the computation is shown in Figure 18.2. It should be *accurately* typed into a file named `beanV0.html`, and run.

```
<html>
  <head><title>Version 0</title></head>
<body>
<h1>Here's Version 0 of the Bean Counter</h1>
  <script language = "Javascript">
  var drink = "latte";            //Temporary Decl. for Version 0; to be removed
  var shots = 2;                  //Temporary Decl. for Version 0; to be removed
  var ounce = 12;                 //Temporary Decl. for Version 0; to be removed
  var price;
  var taxRate = 0.087;
     if (drink == "espresso")
          price = 1.00;
     if (drink == "latte" || drink == "cappuccino"){
          if (ounce == 8)
                price = 1.55;
          if (ounce == 12)
                price = 1.95;
          if (ounce == 16)
                price = 2.35;
      }
      if (drink == "Americano")
            price = 1.10 + .30 * (ounce/8);
      price = price + (shots - 1) * .70;
      price = price + price * taxRate;
      alert(price);               //Temporary statement to print result; to be changed
  </script>
</body>
</html>
```

Figure 18.2. Version 0 of the Bean Counter program without the user interface, and with fixed inputs: drink="latte", shots=2, ounce=12.

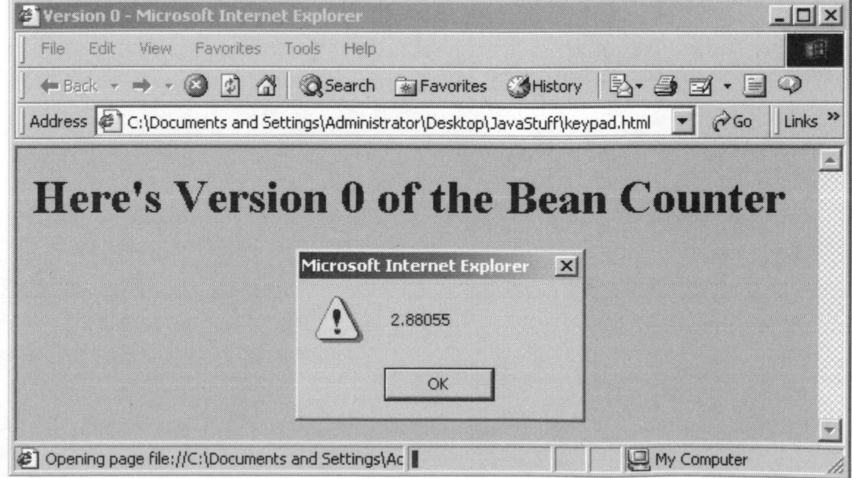

Figure 18.3. Web page displayed by Version 0 of the Bean Counter program of Figure 18.2.

Because we have not yet built the user interface, we have no way to give inputs. So we "fake" the input. Declare and initialize three new variables—`drink`, `shots`, and `ounce`—as the first three statements of the JavaScript code. These will be removed later when buttons are added. These initializers are for a "Double tall latté," that is, a 12-ounce café latté with two shots of espresso. Typing and running the program yields the result shown in Figure 18.3.

The `alert(price)` command prints out the amount that the program computed for the `price`. We verify that the program did produce the same price for a "double tall latté" that we computed in Chapter 17. (The answer isn't rounded to a "whole penny," but we'll solve that problem later.) With the computation working, the next step is to construct the graphic user interface.

GETTING STARTED

This section covers two introductory topics that we will need to create the JavaScript user interface. We present a quick review of HTML, but if it is insufficient, consult Chapter 4 and its appendix. Next we explain a new HTML tag, the `<input...>` tag. This will allow us to create buttons and print output.

HTML Review

Recall from Chapter 4, that HTML is a markup language describing how a Web page should appear on a computer monitor using tags that surround the relevant text, images, and so on. An HTML file is enclosed in `<html> </html>` tags. It requires a heading, which has the form

```
<head>
<title>The Bean Counter</title>
</head>
```

and its body is surrounded by `<body> </body>` tags. All of the programming of this chapter is concentrated in the body of the document.

HTML provides several levels of heading, such as the `<h1> </h1>` tags, paragraphs are surrounded by `<p> </p>` tags, and text can be forced to a new line using the `<br>` tag. Text can be made italic using `<i> </i>` tags, or bold with `<b> </b>`. A horizontal line can be drawn with the horizontal rule `<hr>` tag. The `<a href="`*fn*`"> </a>` tags place a link to another Web page with filename *fn*. The tag `<img src="`*fn*`">` places an image contained in the file *fn* into the document. Most tags have attributes that customize the document to the situation. For example, the background color for a page can be specified, as can its font color and typeface. Thus

```
<body bgcolor="#804000" text="#FF9900" align="center">
<font face="Helvetica", "Arial">
<h1 align="center"><font color="#FFFFFF">the bean
counter</font></h1>
<hr width=50%>
<p align="center"><b>figuring the price of espresso drinks<br>
   so barristas can have time to chat </b></p>
```

gives a coffee brown background color (`#804000`), a terracotta text color (`#FF9900,`) and a sans serif font (`Helvetica`). All of the HTML just presented is part of our Bean Counter program in the file `bean.html`.

It is common when constructing interfaces for JavaScript programs to organize the design around a table. This is because tables give the programmer some control over where information is displayed on a page. Recall that table definitions are enclosed by `<table></table>` tags, and are formulated as a sequence of rows. Each row is surrounded by table row tags, `<tr></tr>`. Within each row, a sequence of table data items is given, each surrounded by `<td></td>` tags. There are several embellishments, but our use of tables requires only these basic concepts. Consult Appendix A for further information.

Input Controls

Curiously the input facilities like buttons and checkboxes are known as *controls*. When controls were introduced into HTML, they were formulated to assist with activities like ordering products or answering survey questions. This is the view of a person filling out a form by clicking buttons and filling in boxes. When the form is complete, it is sent to the computer for processing. Accordingly the designers of the input facilities introduced the concept of a *form*, which must surround all of the input controls. Though the form tags `<form> </form>` have several attributes, we will use only the `name` attribute. Thus, to allow us to use input buttons, the next item in our HTML program is the pair

```
<form name=Bean>
</form>
```

The remainder of our programming will be placed between these two tags. The file ends with

```
</body>
</html>
```

By the way, the name like everything in JavaScript is case sensitive. See Figure 18.4 for the page so far.

```
<html>
 <head>
     <title>The Bean Counter</title>
 </head>
  <body bgcolor="#804000" text="#FF9900" align="center">
   <font face="Helvetica", "Arial">
      <h1 align="center"><font color="#FFFFFF">the bean counter</font></h1>
   <hr width=50%>
      <p align="center"><b>figuring the price of espresso drinks<br>
      so barristas can have time to chat</b></p>
  <form name = "Bean" >
  </form>
 </body>
</html>
```

Figure 18.4. The Bean Counter Interface to this point, and the HTML that produced it.

The `<input . . .>` control is the one tag for all of the various input types, buttons, text boxes, check boxes, and so on. The easiest way to learn them is simply to study an example of each. The three Input controls used in this book are button, text, and radio controls.

- `Button`: The form of the button control is
```
<input type=button value="label" onClick="JS text">
```
where `value` gives the text to be printed on the button, and `onClick` is an event handler composed of JavaScript instructions. When the user clicks the button, the JavaScript code of the event handler is performed. Event handling will be discussed momentarily. The image for the button control is placed in the next position in the text of the HTML program.

- `Text`: The text box can be used either to input or output either numbers or words. Its general form is
```
<input type=text name="identifier" size=6 onChange="JS text">
```
where *identifier* is the name of the control, and the `onChange` is the event handler. After the user has changed the contents of the text window, the JavaScript program instructions in *JS text* are performed. Event handling will be discussed momentarily. The image for the text control is placed in the next position in the text.

- `Radio`: Radio buttons give a selection of preprogrammed settings. Their general form is
```
<input type=radio name="identifier" onClick="JS text">label text
```

where *identifier* is the name of the control, *label text* is shown beside the control, and `onClick` is an event handler. When the user clicks a radio button, the center darkens to indicate that it is set, and the JavaScript instructions in *JS text* are performed. If there are other radio buttons with the same `name`, they are also cleared. The image is placed in the next position in the text.

For the Bean Counter application, we only need the text and button controls; we will use radio buttons later.

Creating the Interface Page

Constructing the Bean Counter interface shown in Figure 18.1 is well underway. The HTML given in Figure 18.4 contains the heading information, the horizontal line, and the slogan beneath. "All" that remains is to create a table and fill in the entries. It should be placed between the form tags to ensure that the browser understands the input controls.

Focus Point. When faced with a task, it is a good idea to "think it through" before starting. List the steps required in the order you will do them. Then attention can be focused on only one step at a time. This process—a topic of Chapter 21—is illustrated here by writing down our plans before starting.

Notice that the table is a 4-row, 4-column table with two empty cells. (The columns are not all the same size, but the browser will take care of making them the right size.) Buttons appear in all of the occupied cells but one, so our table will mostly be a table of buttons. This suggests the following strategy for building the table:

1. Program the HTML for a 4-row, 4-column table with a generic button in each cell. This is a good strategy because we can build such a table quickly using copy and paste.
2. Kill the buttons, but not the cell, in the two cells that should be empty.

3. Replace the button control for the last cell, making it a text control.
4. Pass through the table setting the `value` attribute of each button so that the label on the button is right.
5. Check the interface and primp it as necessary.

Once these five steps are complete, the picture of the Bean Counter interface will be finished. Consider each step in turn.

1. Creating a Button Table

The easiest way to build a copy-and-paste table is from the inside out. That is, we produce a cell first. Then we replicate it and surround it by `<tr></tr>` tags to make a row. Then we replicate that and surround it by `<table></table>` tags to create the table. Of course, using this strategy means that the cell entry must be generic.

Given the information about the button input control, we conclude that the generic cell can have the form

```
<td>
  <input type=button value="b" onClick =' '>
</td>
```

where `"b"` is a placeholder for the button label that will be fixed up in Step 4, and `' '` is a place holder for *JS text* of the event handler that will be inserted in a later section.

We replicate the cell to produce four instances and surround them by row tags. We replicate that to produce four instances and surround them by table tags. We save the page and look at it, and immediately notice that the buttons are left justified. Wanting them centered, we surround our table tags with `<center> </center>` tags. The result is shown in Figure 18.5(a).

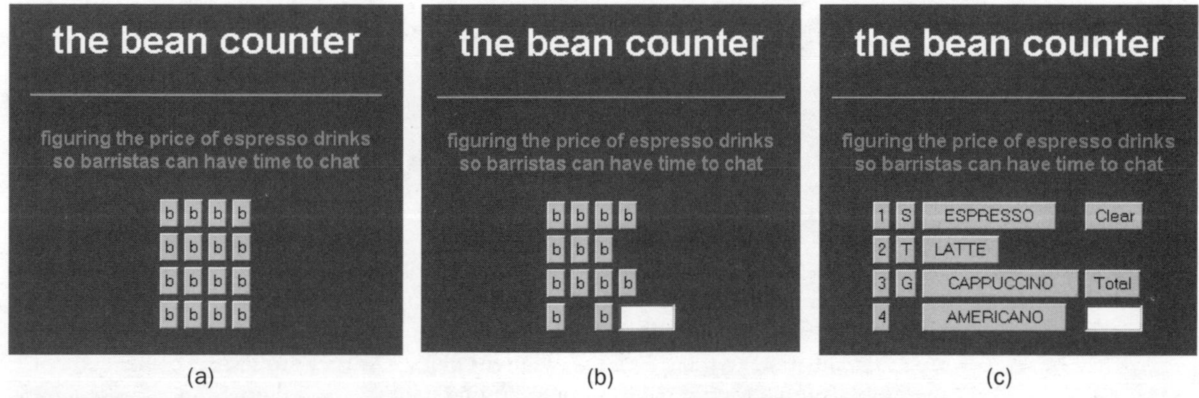

Figure 18.5. Intermediate stages in the construction of the Bean Counter interface. (a) After Step 1, (b) after Step 3, (c) after Step 4.

2. Kill Buttons in Empty Cells

In row 2, fourth column, and row 4, second column, we remove the `<input...>` control because these cells are to be empty. HTML is happy to leave a cell empty, but it still needs the `<td> </td>` tags to be a cell.

3. Text Control

Consulting the last section to decide on the proper text control, we conclude that it should be named "`price`" because that is the information that will be printed, that the window should be 4 digits in size because no combination of drink characteristics will result in a price of more than 4 digits, and that `onChange` needs a placeholder. Thus the present button control should be replaced by

```
<input type=text name="price" value="0.00" size 4 onChange=' '>
```

which produces the result in Figure 18.5(b). This looks a little lopsided at this point, but the true labels are not on the buttons yet.

4. Label Buttons

The next task is to pass through the table cells changing the `value` attribute of each button from `"b"` to its proper button label. Recall that the first column is the number of shots (1, 2, 3, 4), the second column is the sizes (S, T, G), and the third column is the drinks (espresso, latte, cappuccino, Americano), which will be given in all upper-case letters

Because of the row formulation of HTML tables, it is easiest to proceed row-wise through the table rather than column-wise as the data was just presented. The result is shown in Figure 18.5(c). The results are close but need to be fixed up some.

5. Primp the Interface

Our guess that the form of the form wouldn't be quite right was right. Critiquing the design in 18.5(c), we notice that the number buttons are a little wimpy. If the `value="1"` text included a space before and after the numeral, the button would be larger. A similar change for the sizes will make the second column buttons wider as well. Spaces will have to be added to the drink buttons to equalize their sizes, but this will require a little experimentation. Even so, when the drink buttons are approximately the same size, they will look nicer if they are centered in the column. This can be accomplished by adding the `align` attribute to each cell in the third column. For example,

```
<td align="center">
   <input type = button value = "   ESPRESSO   " onClick=' '>
</td>
```

These changes will arrange the buttons so that they match the organization in Figure 18.1.

The only remaining difference is that the table in Figure 18.1 is bordered. Adding the `border` attribute to the `<table>` tag will place a border around all of the cells of the table. But we want the border only around the table as a whole. So, we use a trick common in such designs: We make a table with only a single cell and make the existing table be the table data for that cell, that is, we put the table we've just developed into a one-cell table. To do so, we write

```
<table border=2>
  <tr><td>
    existing table goes here
  </td></tr>
</table>
```

With that addition the structure in Figure 18.1 has been replicated.

EVENT-BASED PROGRAMMING

How should the Bean Counter program operate? Like a calculator, something should happen as each button is clicked. And, the rest of the time, nothing should be happening. Programming the Bean Counter application amounts to defining in JavaScript the actions that should be performed when each button is clicked. Writing that code is the task for this section.

The greatest part of the programming task is already complete because the action for the `Total` button is to compute the final price, and that computation, shown between the `<script>` and `</script>` tags in Figure 18.2, has already been programmed. Because this code defines the action we want the computer to perform when the `Total` button is clicked, we make it the `onClick` event handler for the `Total` button. Specifically the input control for the `Total` button is now

```
<td>
   <input type = button value = "Total" onClick =' '>
</td>
```

where `onClick` is the event handling attribute for the `Total` button. We place the price computation code inside the quotes for the `onClick` attribute as shown in Figure 18.6, and it becomes the `onClick` event handler.

Here's what happens. When the barrista clicks the `Total` button, it causes a *click-event* in the browser. The browser, needing to perform an action in response to the click-event, looks for the `onClick` event handler in the `Total` button input control. What the browser should find there is JavaScript instructions to perform the intended action. The browser runs those instructions, implementing the action, and then it waits for the next event. That's why we move the price computation instructions—the JavaScript text of Figure 18.2 with the temporary assignments removed—to between the quotes of the `onClick` attribute. In this way we have specified what action the browser is to perform on the click-event and how it is to be performed. The browser can now *handle* the click-event. (One additional instruction is required, as explained at the end of this section.)

```
<td>
  <input type = button value = "Total" onClick =
   'var price;
    var taxRate = 0.087;
       if (drink == "espresso")
            price = 1.00;
       if (drink == "latte" || drink == "cappuccino"){
            if (ounce == 8)
                 price = 1.55;
            if (ounce == 12)
                 price = 1.95;
            if (ounce == 16)
                 price = 2.35;
        }
        if (drink == "Americano")
             price = 1.10 + .30 * (ounce/8);
        price = price + (shots - 1) * .70;
        price = price + price * taxRate;
        //one more assignment is required here
   '>
</td>
```

Figure 18.6. The Total input control with the price computation inserted as the event handler. Notice that the three temporary declarations of Figure 18.2 have been removed as has the temporary "alert" command.

Handling the click events for the other buttons is even easier. In each case, we ask what action should be performed when this button is clicked? For the first column of buttons—the shots buttons—the answer is to specify the number of shots the customer requests. For example, clicking the "1" button should cause the shots variable to have the value 1. So, to handle the click-event for the 1 button input control, we need to assign shots as follows

```
<td>
   <input type = button value = " 1 " onClick = 'shots = 1'>
</td>
```

Obviously the 2 button assigns shots the value 2, and so on. Thus the event handlers for the shots buttons only require a single JavaScript command each, an assignment of the right number to shots.

The buttons in the size and drink columns are similar. The action to be performed on a click-event for the size buttons is to assign the ounce variable the appropriate value, 8, 12, or 16, depending on the size, as in

```
<td>
   <input type = button value = " S " onClick = 'ounce = 8'>
</td>
```

For the drink column, the action is simply assigning the drink variable the name of the drink quoted.

```
<td align="center">
   <input type = button value = "  ESPRESSO  " onClick =
         'drink = "espresso"'>
</td>
```

Notice that the single quote surrounds the assignment statement, which uses double quotes. Planning for the use of double-quoted string literals is why we chose the single quote for the event handler placeholder in the generic button of the last section.

> **Match Point**. Care is required when typing string literals like "espresso" because when the computer compares this value with the string literal in the Total button's event handler (Figure 18.6, line 3), they must match *exactly*. Misspellings ("expresso"), case differences ("Espresso"), or even unintentional blanks (" espresso") will fail to match. Care is essential!

The action of clicking the Clear button is to reset all of the variables (drink, ounce, and shots) to their initial values. When we think about what those initial values are, we realize that we haven't initialized them yet. In fact, we haven't even declared the variables yet. (Recall that the temporary declarations included in Figure 18.2 were removed when the code became the Total event handler in Figure 18.6.) As is common in programming, working on the solution to one task—setting up the Clear event handler—reminds us that we have another task to do. So, first we handle the declaration with initialization, and then we return to the Clear event handler.

The declarations should be placed at the beginning of the program, but we don't really have a single program. Rather we have many little program pieces in the form of event handlers. So, referring to Figure 18.3, we place the declarations for the three variables at the start of the body just after the <body> tag. As usual, the declarations must be enclosed in <script> tags,[2] as in

```
<script language = 'JavaScript'>
  var shots = 1;
  var drink = "none";
  var ounce = 0;
</script>
```

The initial value for shots is 1 because every espresso drink will have at least one shot. The initial values for drink and ounce are chosen to be illegal values, so that if the barrista forgets to specify either one, an erroneous result will be produced, indicating that an input has been forgotten. Finally, the Clear button should make these same assignments, resulting in its onClick event handler being

```
<td>
  <input type = button value = "Clear"
  onClick = 'shots = 1;
             drink = "none";
             ounce = 0;
             document.Bean.price.value = "0.00"'>
</td>
```

completing both the initialization and Clear event handler specifications.

The last assignment statement of the Clear event handler

```
document.Bean.price.value = "0.00"
```

is important. It places 0.00 in the price window (lower right corner of the table). Here's how it works. The document that is displayed by the browser can contain one or more forms. Our document has a form named Bean. Forms can contain one or more elements such as input controls. Our Bean form has an input control named price. Input controls can have several attributes. The price input control has a value attribute, which was initially assigned "0.00". (See Step 3 of Creating the Interface.) The dot operator

object.property

gives us the ability to tell the computer how to locate that value so it can be changed. It selects the *property* of the *object* and is most conveniently read right-to-left as "of," that is, "*property* of *object*." So, the assignment in the Clear button event handler reinitializes the window with a statement that can be read "the value attribute *of* the price control *of* the Bean form *of* the document is assigned 0.00." Because the value attribute is the content displayed in the price window, the assignment has the effect of displaying the assigned value, that is, acting as an output.[3] In this way, the event handler of one control can refer to an attribute of another input control. (We'll have more to say about this idea.)

There is one other case where the event handler of one control must refer to the value attribute of price. The Total event handler, the one we constructed first,

[2] <script> tags are not needed for the event handlers because the controls *expect* JavaScript.

[3] The idea that something called an *input* control is used for output is strange, but because both the user and the computer can put information into the window, it is an input control from each side's point of view. But because of the "other side's action," it also delivers output.

must output the computed price. It does this in the same way as the `Clear` event handler clears the price window—by assigning to the `value` attribute of `price`. Thus the final line of the `Total` event handler—the one that is a comment promising a revised statement—should be replaced by

```
document.Bean.price.value = price;
```

in order to display the final price. That modification completes the `Total` event handler, completing the task and completing the Bean Counter application. Run it!

CRITIQUING THE BEAN COUNTER

Every design must be critiqued when it is completed to ensure that it meets the requirements of the problem and to determine if it can be improved. Therefore, the next task is to experiment with the Bean Counter application, trying a dozen or more sample values to observe how well it works. *It is recommended that you not proceed further without experimenting with the Bean Counter page.*

Does our design fulfill the barrista's needs? Perhaps the best way to proceed is to organize our analysis by topic.

Numbers versus Money

The most obvious and annoying problem with the Bean Counter application is that the final price is shown as a decimal number with several digits of precision rather than as currency with only two digits to the right of decimal point. This problem can be almost completely fixed by changing the last line of the `Total` button event handler to be

```
document.Bean.price.value = Math.round(price*100)/100;
```

which works as follows: The `price` is first multiplied by 100. This changes the price from a "dollars amount" to a "cents amount," that is, the price is expressed as the total number of pennies. That result is then rounded to eliminate any fractional digits that are less than a penny using a built-in JavaScript program `Math.round` provided for the purpose. Finally, that result is divided by 100 again to convert back to a "dollars amount." This doesn't quite solve the problem because trailing zeros are dropped; that is, \$3.00 would print as 3. But, this is a small problem that does not arise with the values we have chosen and will be ignored.[4]

Organization

The organization of the buttons is generally consistent with how the application will be used. Because espresso drinks are typically named with syntax of the form

<*shots*> <*size*> <*kind*>

as in "double tall latté," the buttons are properly arranged to have a left-to-right cursor flow. It might make sense to put the `Clear` button on the left side to start the process off, but because there is no obvious place for it and because the cursor will generally be positioned on the `Total` button at the end of the previous pur-

[4] The full solution requires some advanced concepts, resulting in the assignment statement:
```
document.Bean.price.value=(Math.round(price*100)/100).toString().match
(/[\.\d]{4}/);
```

chase—that is, on the right side of the table below the `Clear` button—the design is not inconvenient. We will leave the page organized as it is.

Feedback

One problem with the design is that there is no feedback to the barrista regarding the current settings of the variables. One principle of user interfaces from Chapter 3 is that there should always be feedback for every operation. There is some feedback because buttons are automatically highlighted when they are clicked. But once another button is clicked, the automatic highlighting moves to that button. Adding feedback would be a definite improvement to the interface and is a topic for the next section.

Completeness

Does the Bean Counter fulfill the needs of the barrista? Clearly there could be a much more extensive list of products, requiring that we add more buttons, but the application approximates the needs of a barrista with an espresso cart. As an illustration of extending the design, however, we postulate that the espresso business sells flavorings for the drinks such as vanilla, hazelnut, and raspberry. Patrons would then order a "double tall vanilla latte," and receive a shot of flavoring syrup in their drink as well as steamed milk and espresso. We decide that the syrup costs $.40 and add a button for it in the open position at the end of row two.

REVISING THE BEAN COUNTER

In this section, we make useful improvements to the Bean Counter application as a means of reviewing and practicing the concepts introduced earlier. We will add feedback, and we will add a "flavor" key to charge for the addition of flavoring syrup. We'll add flavor to our project first.

As with most computational tasks, we need to plan out a strategy before beginning to modify the Bean Counter application. What must be done? Reviewing the steps that got us to this point, we obviously need to

1. Add a `Flavor` button as table data at the end of row two.
2. Declare a new variable, `flavor`, indicating the amount to be charged for syrup (0 for no flavor, or .40 for flavor).
3. Initialize the `flavor` variable to 0 in its declaration.
4. Initialize the `flavor` variable to 0 in the `Clear` button event handler.
5. Set the value of `flavor` to .40 in the `Flavor` button event handler.
6. Add in the value of `flavor` in the computation of total `price` before tax in the (next to last line of the) `Total` button event handler.

Keep in mind, especially for steps (2) and (4), that semicolons are required to terminate statements. The resulting page will look like Figure 18.7, after a little fiddling with the sizes of table entries. Rather than working through these changes here, we ask the reader to perform them for the experience and review of the preceding sections that it provides. The changes, which parallel the programming in the "Event-based Programming" section, are evident in the final version of the Bean Counter shown in Appendix C.

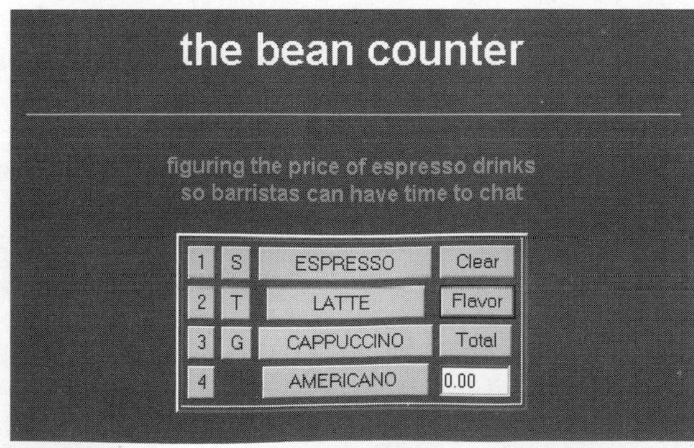

Figure 18.7. Bean Counter page after inclusion of the Flavor button.

Turning to the task of providing feedback to the barrista, we ask, "What form should the user feedback take?" One possibility is to change the label on the button in response to a click, say, from "2" to "-". Other variations are possible, of course. Changing the button to have a new label is easy. Changing it back to its original form, however, when some other button is clicked, is slightly messy, motivating us to consider other solutions.

Another possibility—and the one we will choose—is to add windows at the top of each column to show the label of the most recently clicked button in that column. For the last column, the window displays either `Flavor` or blank. When the application is cleared, the feedback windows are made blank. As usual, we form a list of the steps needed to make the change:

1. Add a new first row to the table containing input controls of type text, each having a name, and an initial value of blank, that is, `" "`, and adjust the `size` attribute of each input control so the window's width matches the standard width of the column.
2. Change the event handler for each button, except `Clear` and `Total`, to set the window value.
3. Expand the event handler for the `Clear` button to set all of the feedback window values to blank.

We perform these steps in sequence.

Add New Row

The new top row contains four instances of the data cell text

```
<td>
   <input type=text name="temp1" value=" " size=temp2>
</td>
```

which can be replicated as usual with copy/paste. The result must be surrounded by `<tr> </tr>` tags, of course. For each cell *temp1* is the name of the window, a new identifier describing the role of the buttons in that column. For example, using "`fb`" as an abbreviation for "feedback," we might choose `shots_fb`, `ounce_fb`, `drink_fb`, and `flavor_fb` as the new names. For each cell, *temp2* is the size of the window needed to make the column look attractive. Typically this requires some fiddling around. And unfortunately this attribute has different behaviors in different browsers.

Change Event handlers

Each button's event handler must be modified to place text in the feedback window indicating that it was selected. The button's value, that is, the text on the button, is a good choice. Writing that to the feedback window requires the same technique used earlier to set the `price` window. That is, to refer to the `value` property of another input control requires that we describe how to find that control within the `document`, that is, dot notation. This is why each control was given a new name—so it could be referred to. Thus, for example, the event handler for the `1` button would become

```
onClick =    'shots = 1;
              document.Bean.shots_fb.value = " 1 "'>
```

indicating that the `value` attribute *of* the `shots_fb` control *of* the `Bean` form *of* the `document` is to be assigned the text `"  1  "`. That change to the `value` of the control causes it to be displayed, giving feedback to the barrista that it was clicked. (Notice the addition of the semicolon to terminate the first statement of the event handler.) Every event handler except `Clear` and `Total` will have to be modified in an analogous way.

Revise the Clear Event handler

The `Clear` event handler must initialize all four windows to blank. Again, this requires that one event handler of one control write to the `value` attribute of another control, so the assignment statements have the same form as the modifications just completed. Specifically the `Clear` button event handler now looks like

```
onClick="shots = 1;
       drink='none';
       ounce=0;
       flavor=0;
       document.Bean.price.value      = '0.00';
       document.Bean.shots_fb.value   = ' ';
       document.Bean.ounce_fb.value   = ' ';
       document.Bean.drink_fb.value   = ' ';
       document.Bean.flavor_fb.value = ' '"
```

which restores the feedback windows to blank and completes the modifications to the Bean Counter program.

As our final changes, we propose to color the row of feedback window cells terracotta, and to color the price window cell red. Further, we will center the controls in these fields. The intent is simply to make the new form more esthetically pleasing. The changes are simple. The row tag for the first row is revised to be

```
<tr bgcolor="#FF9900" align="center">
```

which has the effect of coloring and centering each of the cells in the row. And, the table data tag for the last table item is revised to be

```
<td bgcolor="red" align="center">
```

The final version of the Bean Counter computation is given in Figure 18.8. The program that produced this result is shown in Appendix C.[5]

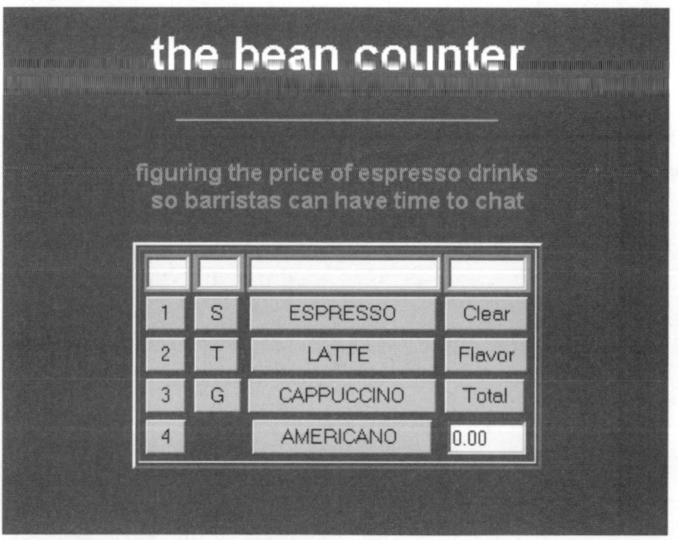

Figure 18.8. The final version of the Bean Counter application.

REVIEW

The sample program of Chapter 17 has been converted to a useful application. In the process we have learned the basics of event-based programming using JavaScript. Because this chapter focused primarily on achieving the goal of building the application, little time was devoted to discussing the ideas more generally. We now review the major ideas of the chapter and elaborate them further.

---

[5] Because of differences between Netscape's and Internet Explorer's handling of the size attribute, the program given in Appendix C may differ slightly form its appearance in Figure 18.8.

The main activity of this chapter was to create a graphic user interface for the Bean Counter application by first creating the HTML text to produce the picture of the interface, and then adding JavaScript—mostly in event handlers for input controls—to perform the actions needed to make the application "work." Though we discussed programs in Chapter 17 as if they were single, monolithic sequences of statements, the Bean Counter application is actually many tiny code segments that are one or two statements long. This is a characteristic of event-based programming. Other less interactive forms of computing exhibit the more monolithic program form.

The only problem that the many-tiny-code-segments characteristic caused is that we didn't immediately know where to place the declarations for the variables, `shots`, `ounce`, `drink`, and later, `flavor`. Declarations are usually placed at the start of the program. With many event handlers, it's as though we have many program "starts." We placed the declarations right after the `<body>` tag, which is not the start of a JavaScript program, but rather the start of the body of the HTML program. That's why the declarations had to go inside of `<script> </script>` tags. But this position makes sense for two reasons. First, the declarations came before any of the code segments using the variables, so the variables were known by the time they were encountered in any event handler. Second, if we'd placed them in an event handler, say, the `Total` button event handler, they'd only be available for use within that handler. (This is the case for the `price` and `taxRate` variables of the `Total` button event handler. They are available only within that routine.) By being declared outside any event handler—we say they are *global* to the event handlers—they are known to all of them and therefore can be used by all of them. (This is the concept of *scope*, discussed in Chapter 19.)

Though any event handler can reference the globally declared variables, the same was not true for the values of the text controls such as the `price` or feedback windows. The `value` property of these windows is local to the control. So, for an event handler of one control to place a value in the window of another control, it must in effect describe how to navigate to the item it wants to change. That was the purpose of the code of the form

```
document.Bean.price.value = 0;
```

It uses the dot operator to navigate from the enclosing document to the target control value, by naming the appropriate item at each step along the path. The dot operator is best read right to left and can then be pronounced "of." Thus the foregoing statement reads, "assign 0 to the `value` attribute *of* the `price` control *of* the `Bean` form *of* the `document`." Thus the Bean Counter application illustrates three different ways to reference data values in an event handling program: as variables local to a routine (`taxRate`), as variables global to the routines (`drink`), and as a variable in another control (`document.Bean.price.value`). The first two can be referenced by their simple variable name because they are defined in the routine in the case of locals, or in the "enclosing" routine in the case of globals. Only cross-control references require navigation.

The process used to program the Bean Counter application was very incremental. We began by producing a minimal fourteen-line HTML program (Figure 18.4), and then we tested it. We added a skeleton table and tested it. We improved the table one feature at a time, testing as we went. We wrote JavaScript to solve one event handler at a time. And, recognizing similarities among the various events, we developed their event handlers together. Finally, we critiqued the result, improved it and tested it further. The result is a 136-line program of 3600+ characters. As compared to other first programs, that's huge! This strategy—the result of decomposing the task into tiny pieces and testing after each small milestone—had two advantages: At no point did we have to solve any complex tasks that would tax our brains, and the continual testing meant that we immediately knew where any errors were located, namely, in the part we just added. Though the program in Appendix C looks impressive, it is not difficult to produce by the program-and-test method. Obviously the approach works generally, as we'll see in Chapter 21.

When the initial design was completed, we critiqued the result. We were not critiquing the programming. Rather, we were critiquing how well our solution fulfilled the task for which it was designed. Evaluation is an essential aspect of any design effort, but it is especially critical for software because software is "perfectly malleable"—it can do anything—so it should perfectly match the requirements. We found that our design had not provided feedback to the barrista and so violated one of the principles listed in Chapter 3. This shortcoming was remedied by adding feedback windows, though there are numerous other, probably more esthetically pleasing, ways to fulfill that requirement.

Summary

The Bean Counter application has been created using the price computation of Chapter 17 and a GUI developed in this chapter. The result is a substantial program that performs a useful computation, at least if you are a barrista. The application is analogous to the calculator applications provided by operating systems in that the user commands the application by clicking or typing. The requested computation is performed immediately in response to the input events.

Part of the activity of the chapter was to write HTML to set up a context in which event handlers perform the actual work. The setup involved placing buttons and other input controls on a Web page, enabling users to enter the data to be processed and to receive the results from the complicated computation. It is the input/output portion of the application and it is principally written in HTML. The other activity was to write JavaScript code for the event handlers. This is the processing activity of the application. It used the event-based programming style and the basic instructions learned in Chapter 17. The style, which is ideal for interactive applications, will be used throughout the remainder of this book. Though HTML and JavaScript are separate languages, the distinction will not matter much. Generally, HTML will simply be the input/output part of a program that we think of as being written in JavaScript.

Exercises

1. Explain in words how to build a table "inside out with copy-paste." What advantage does inside/out construction have over building the table directly?
2. The `<input . . .>` control tags cannot be placed anywhere in an HTML document. Where is the only place that they can be placed?
3. Users interact with input controls to request the computer to perform some action. How does the computer know what action to perform?
4. The `name` of a button input control is not the text printed on it. How is the text shown on the button specified?
5. Why when we want to change the value of `shots`—as in the event handlers of the first column of Bean Counter buttons—do we just refer to it as `shots`, but when we want to change the value of the `price` window, we need to refer to it as

```
document.Bean.price.value
```

6. Why is it better to program by starting out with a very small solution and adding to it incrementally—testing after each addition to make sure that the new code is working properly—rather than writing an entire program completely and testing it later?

7. Add the `Flavor` button and the accompanying programming changes to the Bean Counter

8. Change the Bean Counter application to remove the feedback windows and revise it so that the label on the keys changes when the key is clicked. Change the numbers to `'-ƀ'`, sizes to `'-ƀƀ'`, drinks to lowercase (with blank padding), and flavor to start with a lowercase letter. This exercise emphasizes the use of the `document.Bean.`*name*`.value` construction, which must be used extensively.

9. When programming a button event handler, what question should you ask?

10. Popcorn of three types—"white," "yellow" and "radioactive alien orange"—is sold in three sizes of containers: large (200 g), giant (300 g), and humongous (400 g). "Butter" can be sprayed on the popcorn and is charged per spray. Tax is charged on the whole purchase. To assist the popper-azzi, develop a program and GUI for computing the price of a popcorn purchase. You should decide on the prices and taxation rate for the popcorn.

CHAPTER 19

Abstraction and Functions

Learning Objectives

- Understand abstraction.
- Learn naming, encapsulation, and parameterization.
- Know the two main purposes of abstraction.
- Understand the distinction between declaring and invoking a function.
- Learn the JavaScript's function mechanism.
- Build a Web page containing functions.
- Learn about random numbers by flipping virtual coins.
- Acquire practice with HTML forms and JavaScript programming structures.

The practical goal of this chapter is to explain and demonstrate the concept of functions, the most fundamental idea in software. But as important as functions are to programmers, they are simply the computational form of a more general thinking process known as *abstraction.* So we will study abstraction as an aid to understanding functions. As a result, the benefits will be broader than programming knowledge. You will notice abstraction in other situations and in other classes—architecture, geology, business, and so on. Our clearer understanding of abstraction may make you a better observer and thinker beyond the Fluency class. It's a terrific bonus from learning the useful idea of functions.

The chapter begins by introducing the idea of abstraction and its key features of naming, encapsulation into a definition, and parameterization. The two main computational advantages of abstraction—managing complexity and promoting reuse—are identified and explained. Next, we walk through an example of creating a function, relying heavily on intuition to take us through to the end of the whole process.

Having created a function definition, we show how to apply it in several Web applications, illustrating the write-once-use-repeatedly advantage to creating functions. Our intuitive introduction to functions skipped over all of the nitty-gritty details that we need to know, but having the whole picture in mind, we easily describe the details and give more examples. Next we create the Memory Bank, a Web page of useful computations, including the Body Mass Index, allowing us to monitor our weight. Embellishing this page is the basis for writing more functions and gaining more experience. Among the additions, we explain random numbers and show how to flip an "electronic coin." Finally, we summarize the deep ideas of the chapter.

ABSTRACTION

As we programmed the Bean Counter application in Chapter 18, we steadily changed from thinking about it simply as a long sequence of HTML and JavaScript commands and began to think about its components more abstractly. What do we mean by "more abstractly"? Portions of the computation—features of the graphic image, groups of HTML commands, JavaScript statements, or actions of the solution—began to have a coherent identity in our minds worthy of being named. Thus, rather than just being an amorphous table with undifferentiated data entries, there were

- *feedback windows*, the top row feature of the graphic image
- *button input controls*, a group of HTML commands
- Total *button event handler*, a sequence of JavaScript statements
- `shots` *click-events*, a set of actions

These italic terms name components of the Bean Counter design that made sense to us, and that we referred to by name while solving the problem. Assigning a name is natural because the abstractions have an identity in our minds. HTML and JavaScript do not dictate these abstractions, nor did they emerge for mystical or magical reasons. They are simply a result of our thinking and reasoning processes. When parts of the design become coherent because of similar form, behavior, structure, or other types of commonality, they have an identity in our minds, and we give them a name. Abstraction is what humans do when they understand and recognize something significant.

Abstraction has other aspects besides identifying a coherent form or behavior and giving it a name. For one thing, we must be specific about what the name names, that is, we must define the name. We say that the abstraction *encapsulates* the phenomenon when we are specific about what exactly the name stands for. Often, especially when the significance is based on the commonality of several instances, the features of each instance will not be quite the same. Though similar for the most part, the instances vary in substantive ways. So, in addition to naming, we must enumerate the variations and describe how they contribute to each instance. These are the *parameters* of the abstraction. And they are essential to explaining the range of instances that the abstraction encapsulates.

Though abstraction is important far beyond computing—in a sense, it embodies one aspect of being intelligent—it is extremely important to computing for two reasons. First, it allows humans to handle complexity. By abstracting a computation and giving it a name, we no longer need to think about it as the sequence of operations. For example, naming the `Total` button event handler as, say, `figurePrice`, allows us to stop thinking about it as a sequence of declarations, `if`s, and assignment statements for computing the price, and we replace them with the name for its action. The name "stands" for the operations. We replace how it works with what it does. This is a significant simplification. With the name replacing the operations, we eliminate detail. A long sequence of instructions can be reduced in our mind to a short sequence of descriptive names for the actions implemented. It's less complex to remember and understand.

The second reason abstraction is so important in computing is that it allows us to reuse our work and build upon it. Not only do we give a name to an abstraction, programming languages allow us to "package" the operations the abstraction names into *functions*, also known as *procedures*. The function's name is the name of the abstraction. Then, to perform the operations, we give the name and the computer performs the operations of the package. That is, we program using the abstraction's names, not the actual instructions that implement them. In this way, very sophisticated and complex software can be built by first building functions for simple abstractions, then using those to implement more complex abstractions, which are also packaged into functions and given names, becoming the building blocks for the next layer of sophistication, and so on.

Because abstraction helps us to handle complexity and promotes the reuse of our thinking, it is a fundamental tool of computing. It's a deep idea, but not a difficult one to use.

> **Gift Wrapped**. Functions are packaging for algorithms.

FUNCTIONS

When we exchange email with our friends in other countries, they often mention their weather, knowing that it's a topic Americans talk about. But the temperatures are always given in Celsius. Is 38°C cold or hot? The United States should join the rest of the world in using Celsius, of course, but because that is unlikely, we must convert Celsius to Fahrenheit. The conversion process is a coherent, well-defined process, an abstraction. It is ideal for packaging into a function. Recall from school that the formula for the relationship between the Fahrenheit and Celsius temperature scales is:

$$\text{Fahrenheit} = {}^{9}/_{5}\,\text{Celsius} + 32$$

This is an equation, of course, not an assignment statement. With it we can "solve for Celsius" deriving a second equation

$${}^{5}/_{9}\,(\text{Fahrenheit} - 32) = \text{Celsius}$$

To command the computer to perform the Celsius to Fahrenheit conversion, we must encode the first equation into a JavaScript function. (We will write the second equation in JavaScript later so we can convert back.)

A function "packages" computation. JavaScript defines the packaging syntax as

```
function <name> ( <parameter list> ) {
      <function definition>
}
```

where the text not in meta-brackets must be given literally. Functions, being abstractions, have names, of course. The *<name>* is given immediately after the keyword `function`. Next comes a parenthesis pair containing the *<parameter list>*. Parameters are the inputs to the computation, and if there are several, they are separated by commas. Finally, enclosed in a pair of curly braces, is the function definition, which is the sequence of JavaScript statements that performs the computation. Notice that the closing curly brace is located conspicuously on its own line so that we notice it when reading the program.

To formulate the Celsius to Fahrenheit conversion as a function, we first decide on a name. We choose "`convertC2F`" because it briefly summarizes what's to be done. For input parameters, we'll need only one, and it is the temperature in Celsius. We'll name it `tempInC`. The computed answer will be called `tempInF`, making it a variable that must be declared. Writing the statements for the body is straightforward given the preceding equation. The entire function definition, with one detail missing, becomes

```
function convertC2F ( tempInC ) {
   var tempInF;
   tempInF = (9 / 5) * tempInC + 32;          //Incomplete
}
```

We notice that the `convertC2F` function matches the function syntax given earlier. Also, we notice that the input parameter isn't declared. That's because the variables of the <*parameter list*> are automatically declared to be variables in JavaScript, saving some typing.

The purpose of functions is to package computation so that when someone provides the input parameter(s), for example, 38, the computation is performed for us, and the result is returned. Thus, when we write `convertC2F(38)`, we expect to get the Fahrenheit temperature back because the computer will follow the instructions packaged in the function, thereby computing the answer. Because our conversion function computes only one value, it's pretty obvious what value to return as the answer, `tempInF`. But in general function definitions compute many values, and the computer must be told which one is the answer. Thus, there is a statement in JavaScript

```
return <answer>;
```

that says "the computation is now complete, and this is the answer." The <*answer*> can be either a variable or an expression, so we can complete our conversion function with one additional line, and for good measure, a comment

```
function convertC2F ( tempInC ) {
  // Converts its parameter, assumed to be a Celsius
  // temperature, into the equivalent Fahrenheit
   var tempInF;
   tempInF = (9 / 5) * tempInC + 32;
   return tempInF;
}
```

The function, which will be used by giving the name with values for the parameters in parentheses, for example, `convertC2F(38)`, is defined and ready for use.

APPLYING FUNCTIONS

Because JavaScript is meant to assist with writing useful Web pages, we write a simple page as a means of running the `convertC2F()` function.[1] Specifically, Figure

[1] It is customary to write functions with their parameter list parentheses, even when the parameters are not given.

19.1 shows the text for running the program within an HTML document, and the resulting output. Notice that the JavaScript code in Figure 19.1 is surrounded by `<script></script>` tags. In addition to the function definition as given earlier, there is a `document.write` command. This special JavaScript function outputs text directly into the HTML document. Most important, `document.write` is performed before the page is created, allowing us to create HTML commands on the fly. The HTML created is a second-level header (<h2>) line that is composed of three pieces joined together with the concatenate (+) operator. The three parts are the string literal `'38 degrees C is '`, the returned value from running the function `convertC2F(38)` with its input value of 38, and the string literal `' degrees F'`. The result of the function is computed, the three parts are joined to make the second-level header, and the page is composed and displayed as shown.

```
<html>
 <head><title>Converter Usage Example</title></head>
 <body><font face='Helvetica'><b><center>
   <script language = 'JavaScript'>
        function convertC2F ( tempInC ) {
        // Converts its parameter, assumed to be a Celsius
        // temperature, into the equivalent Fahrenheit
         var tempInF;
         tempInF = (9 / 5) * tempInC + 32;
         return tempInF;
        }
   document.write('<h2>38 degrees C is ' + convertC2F(38) + ' degrees F</h2>');
   </script>
 </body>
</html>
```

Figure 19.1. An HTML page showing the use of the `convertC2F()` JavaScript function to find the Fahrenheit equivalent of 38°C.

Here's what happens when a file containing the text of Figure 19.1 runs. The browser starts out processing the HTML as usual. When it reaches the `<script>` tag, it calls on the JavaScript Interpreter to process the file until the next `</script>` tag. The JavaScript interpreter works like a sophisticated Fetch/Execute Cycle, fetching JavaScript statements and executing them. The JS Interpreter records the fact that a function by the name of `convertC2F` is being defined, that it has a single parameter, and that its definition is the JavaScript code given. The function doesn't run at this point; the JS Interpreter just makes a note of its definition.

Once past the closing curly brace, the Interpreter comes to the `document.write` function. Recognizing this as a built-in JS function—that is, provided by the system—the Interpreter does what the function commands. Specifically, it sees that it must combine the string literal `'<h2>38 degrees C is '` with the result of the computation `convertC2F(38)`. Referring back to the definition of `convertC2F()`, the JS Interpreter assigns the value 38 to the parameter variable `tempInC`, declares `tempInF`, computes the value of `tempInF`, and returns that value as the result of running the function. It then (converts the number to a letter string and) combines it with the first string literal, and then with the second string literal, `' degrees F</h2>'`. Having produced a line of text, the Interpreter performs the `document.write` operation, placing the text into the HTML document at the next position, namely, at the beginning of the document because nothing else has been defined for the <body> so far. Finally, the JS Interpreter seeing the </script> tag, returns back to the browser. The browser, finding that the document (now) contains the single <h2> line, displays it.

Now that we know that 38°C is hot—at least as air temperatures go—we might consider other ways to use our newly created `convertC2F()` function. One possibility is to apply it to construct a list of representative Celsius-to-Fahrenheit equivalents. Then, we could try to learn the pairs as an aid to estimating the temperature equivalents when there is no computer handy. Figure 19.2 shows the HTML and JavaScript for creating the list and the Web page they produce. The behavior is completely analogous to the description of the last paragraph, and the reader is advised to work through it.

> **Hot Tip.** Notice it's not so difficult to estimate C temperatures in F. Remember an equivalent or two, e.g., 20°C is 68°F or 30°C is 86°F, and for each 10° in C up or down, add or subtract 18° in F.

The page in Figure 19.2 is not esthetically pleasing, and we realize that the list should have been a two-column table. Revising the HTML and JavaScript to produce such a table is straightforward and is shown in Figure 19.3. (Again, working through the logic of the computation is advisable.)

```
<html>
 <head><title>Conversion List</title></head>
 <body><font face='Helvetica'><b><center>
   <script language = 'JavaScript'>
       function convertC2F ( tempInC ) {
         // Converts its parameter, assumed to be a Celsius
         // temperature, into the equivalent Fahrenheit
          var tempInF;
          tempInF = (9 / 5) * tempInC + 32;
         return tempInF;
       }
   document.write('<h2> Celsius Equivalents in Fahrenheit</h2><P>');
   document.write('-10 degrees C = ' +  convertC2F(-10) + ' degrees F<br>');
   document.write('  0 degrees C = ' +  convertC2F(0)   + ' degrees F<br>');
   document.write(' 10 degrees C = ' +  convertC2F(10)  + ' degrees F<br>');
   document.write(' 20 degrees C = ' +  convertC2F(20)  + ' degrees F<br>');
   document.write(' 30 degrees C = ' +  convertC2F(30)  + ' degrees F<br>');
   document.write(' 40 degrees C = ' +  convertC2F(40)  + ' degrees F<br>');
   </script>
 </body>
</html>
```

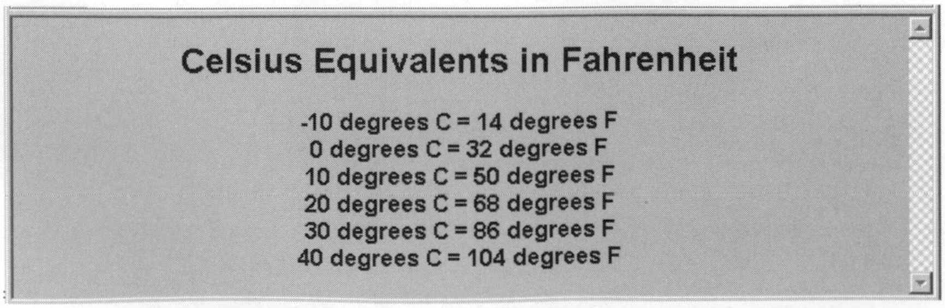

Celsius Equivalents in Fahrenheit

-10 degrees C = 14 degrees F
0 degrees C = 32 degrees F
10 degrees C = 50 degrees F
20 degrees C = 68 degrees F
30 degrees C = 86 degrees F
40 degrees C = 104 degrees F

Figure 19.2. The HTML and JavaScript to display a list of equivalent temperatures.

```
<html>
 <head><title>Conversion Table</title></head>
 <body bgcolor="maroon", text=white>
   <font face='Helvetica'><b><center>
   <script language = 'JavaScript'>
        function convertC2F ( tempInC ) {
          // Converts its parameter, assumed to
          // be in C, into the equivalent F
           var tempInF;
           tempInF = (9 / 5) * tempInC + 32;
           return tempInF;
        }
   document.write('<h2> Table of Celsius-<br>Fahrenheit Equivalents</h2>');
   document.write('<table border=1><TH> C </TH><TH> F </TH>');
   document.write('<tr align=center><td>-10</td><td>' + convertC2F(-10) + '</td></tr>');
   document.write('<tr align=center><td>  0</td><td>' + convertC2F(0)   + '</td></tr>');
   document.write('<tr align=center><td> 10</td><td>' + convertC2F(10)  + '</td></tr>');
   document.write('<tr align=center><td> 20</td><td>' + convertC2F(20)  + '</td></tr>');
   document.write('<tr align=center><td> 30</td><td>' + convertC2F(30)  + '</td></tr>');
   document.write('<tr align=center><td> 40</td><td>' + convertC2F(40)  + '</td></tr>');
   document.write('</table>');
   </script>
 </body>
</html>
```

Table of Celsius-Fahrenheit Equivalents

C	F
-10	14
0	32
10	50
20	68
30	86
40	104

Figure 19.3. HTML and JavaScript to produce a table of equivalents.

All three of these Web pages have been different in terms of their HTML, but they have all used the *same* `convertC2F()` function. And this is the main point of all of the examples: Once we take the trouble to work out a function, it can be used over and over again. The logic has been thought through and packaged. There is no further fuss with the computation—any time a conversion is needed, we ask for the function to be run by giving its name and the number we want converted. The computer does the rest. In this way, we can focus on tasks of importance to us—the esthetics of the page, for example—rather than programming operations like conversion. The write-once-use-repeatedly property of procedures is a principal reason why functions are so important to us.

RULES FOR FUNCTIONS

We have shown how functions package computation, and the idea is reasonably intuitive. But like everything related to computers, the details must be exactly right. In this section, we explain the details of JavaScript functions carefully so you can meet the computer's exacting standards when writing your own functions. Though the rules are specific to JavaScript, most programming languages impose a similar set of rules. The topics to be covered are:

- Function Declarations
- Selecting Names
- Parameter Variables
- Return Value
- Scope of Reference
- Local Variables
- Global Variables
- Multiple Parameters
- Parameters versus Arguments
- Parameter Reference

Along the way we give numerous examples of functions.

Function Declarations

The construction used to define the function "package"

```
function <name> ( <parameter list> ) {
      <function definition>
}
```

is known as the *function declaration*. Its parallel to an initializing variable declaration is clear: The keyword `function` corresponds to `var`, the *<name>* is the identifier being declared, and the *<parameter list>*–*<function definition>* pair is the initial (and only) value of the *<name>*. The only difference is that rather than assigning a number or letter string or Boolean value to the *<name>*, the declaration assigns a computation and its list of inputs. But it's the same idea.

Selecting Names

The function *<name>* is an identifier, just like variable names are identifiers. The main implication of this fact is it follows the same formation rules: The function *<name>* must start with a letter and can contain any combination of letters, numerals, or underscore; it is case sensitive. It is essential that JavaScript's reserved words, listed in the Appendix B, not be used so as to avoid *name conflicts*. Selecting a name descriptive of the function's function is also smart.

Parameter Variables

A function isn't required to have parameters, but because parameters provide the input to the computation, they're common. (There are other ways to give input, as explained later.) When there are parameters, they can be thought of as *implicitly declared variables*. So, like function names and explicitly declared variable names, parameter names must follow the usual rules for identifiers.

Return Value

A JavaScript function can have any number of `return` statements, but when the Interpreter is running the function and encounters one, it will treat the function as complete. (Also, functions need not have any `return` statements, as explained later.) Because the return value can be either a variable or a computed expression, it is common to make the last computation of a function part of the `return` statement. Accordingly, the Fahrenheit to Celsius conversion function

```
function convertF2C ( tempInF ) {
// Convert temps from Fahrenheit to Celsius
   return (5 / 9) * (tempInF - 32);
}
```

exhibits this technique, saving a declaration compared to the `convertC2F()` function. The approaches are equivalent, and the computer doesn't care which is used.

Scope of Reference

As we saw with the Bean Counter program, it is common to assign a value to a variable at one place in a program and to use the value at another place. When there are no functions, it's generally possible to assign to variables anywhere and use their values anywhere else. With functions there are limits on where in the program this is possible. The *scope* of a variable describes where and when it can be referenced—that is, assigned to and used. The two scopes of interest are local and global scopes.

Local Variables

If a variable is declared in a function, it is known only within that function, that is, only inside the curly braces. Thus `tempInF` can be used within `convertC2F()`, but not outside. Such a variable is said to be *local* to the function, or have local scope. The main consequence is that if two or more functions use the same name for a variable, there is no conflict. They are each local to their respective functions. So, for example, the `tempInF` of `convertC2F()` will not conflict with the parameter—recall parameters are implicitly declared variables—`tempInF` of the function `convertF2C` just defined, should they both be used in the same Web page. Being local to their respective functions, they don't conflict.

Global Variables

Variables declared outside of a function declaration are said to be *global* to the function. We saw an example of global variable declarations in Chapter 18, when `shots`, `ounce`, `drink`, and `flavor` were declared in the Bean Counter example. Though it didn't appear as if we used any functions in that program, the Interpreter treated our event handlers as functions, so the effect was the same. Variables like `shots` had to be declared outside of the event handlers if they were to be known by several of them. Global variables are another way to get input into a function.

Very Global. An HTML file can have several blocks of JavaScript text within pairs of `<script> </script>` tags. All global variables declared within each pair are known in all of the other pairs.

Multiple Parameters

The parameter list of a function can have any number of items separated by commas. Thus the Body Mass Index (BMI) calculation—an index of a person's weight in proportion to their height—will have two parameters, weight and height.[2] The formula for BMI when weight and height are given in metric units is simply

$$\text{Index} = \text{weight} / \text{height}^2$$

leading to the simple two parameter function

```
function bmiM ( weightKg, heightM ) {
   // Figure Body Mass Index in metric units
   return weightKg / (heightM * heightM);
}
```

For weight and height given in English units, BMI is defined as

$$\text{Index} = 4.89\ \text{weight} / \text{height}^2$$

where *weight* is in pounds and *height* is in feet. Because a height given in feet and inches is a little messy to work with, we take the input in inches and convert it to feet. The function declaration for the English BMI is

```
function bmiE ( weightLBS, heightIn ) {
   // Figure Body Mass Index in English units
   var heightFt = heightIn / 12;              // Change to feet
   return 4.89 * weightLBS / (heightFt * heightFt);
}
```

[2] "Normal" is generally accepted as a Body Mass Index in the range 18.5 to 25.

If we desire a single function that takes `"metric"` or `"English"` as its first parameter, describing the units of the measurements, and the height and weight as the next two parameters, we can solve the problem generally

```
function BMI (units, height, weight ) {
   // Compute BMI in either metric or English
   if (units == "English")
      return bmiE(weight, height);
   else
      return bmiM(weight, height);
}
```

with a three-parameter function. Notice that the `BMI()` function is building on the earlier `bmiE()` and `bmiM()` functions—that is, reusing them—saving us from having to work out those details again.

Parameters versus Arguments

The act of using a function to compute an answer, that is, causing the computer to perform the function's instructions, is known as *calling* or *invoking* the function. When we call a function, we must supply values for the parameters, that is, the inputs to the function. These input values are known as *arguments*. The key point about arguments is that there are the same number of them as there are parameters, and they correspond. So, to use the `BMI()` function to compute the index for a person standing 5 feet 6 inches (66 inches or 1.65 m) and weighing 125 lbs. (55 kg.), we must supply three arguments corresponding to the three parameters, yielding

```
BMI ("English", 66, 125)
```

And, because the arguments correspond to the parameters, we must give them in that order. Specifically, the 66-inch height is the second argument because `height` is the second parameter. Presenting the arguments in the wrong order produces the wrong result because the computer has no way of telling that arguments don't correspond to the parameters. The function's definition determines how the arguments must be given. Period. So, for example, `weight` is the third parameter of `BMI()`, making 125 the third argument to the call. But because `weightLBS` is the first parameter of `bmiE()`, the arguments of its call have been customized to the situation, making

```
bmiE (125, 66)
```

the proper call. The answer is 20.2 by the way.

Wrong Arguments. Calling a function with the arguments given in the wrong order is an extremely difficult bug to find in a program because it goes unnoticed so easily. The advice is to take extreme care when listing arguments in the first place.

Parameter Reference

The final topic concerns assigning argument values to the parameters to which they correspond. Calling a function causes the arguments to be assigned to the parameters just as if they were assignment statements. Thus, calling the `BMI()` function

```
BMI ("English", 66, 125)
```

has the same effect as if we had explicitly written in its place the code

```
var units  = "English";          //Assign value to 1st param
var height = 66;                 //Assign value to 2nd param
var weight = 125;                //Assign value to 3rd param
if (units == "English")          //Code of function def
   return bmiE(weight, height);
else
   return bmiM(weight, height);
```

As we said before, the parameters are like implicitly declared local variables, and they can be used as such. In each case, the initial assignment is the corresponding argument value. The best part about this view is that we can, if we wish, assign to them. Thus, comparing it with its previous definition, the `bmiE()` function could have been written

```
function bmiE ( weightLBS, height ) {
   // Figure Body Mass Index in English units
   height = height / 12;      // height is inches; change to feet
   return 4.89 * weightLBS / (height * height);
}
```

That is, we do not declare a separate `heightFt` variable as we did before, but simply change the `height` parameter from inches to feet.

> **Easy Test.** JavaScript must run in an HTML Web page definition. Thus to test JS functions, it is smart to keep a text file handy with all the necessary HTML already in it, called, say, `eztest.html`. Then the JavaScript can be copied into it, making function testing easy. One such template is
>
> ```
> <html><head>EZ</head><body><script>
>        function definition goes here
>        alert(function call with arguments goes here);
> </script></body></html>
> ```
>
> where the italicized text must be replaced with the function to be tested.

The Memory Bank

Remembering useless trivia is fun. For example,

Q: Who was the fifth Beatle?
A: Stuart Sutcliffe was a founding member of the Beatles with Lennon, McCartney, and Harrison.

Remembering useful stuff seems to be more difficult for some reason. So, in this section, we create a Memory Bank Web page of useful computations. It will provide a means of practicing programming with functions, which is why we're doing it. But we can also save the page in our Web space and perhaps add to it. It's a handy place to "park" computational things we want to remember.

Figure 19.4 shows the HTML image for the initial Memory Bank Web page. Here is how it is supposed to work. Each table row is a computation. Each window in the row except the last is an input to the computation; the last window is the output. The user types inputs into the window(s), and when they are all entered, gets the answer back in the output window. Inspecting the HTML, we notice that each row has two or more input controls requiring event handlers. What remains for us is to program the JavaScript to implement the computations and to define the event handlers.

```
<html>
   <head><title>Fact Page</title></head>
   <body bgcolor="#000000" text="#FF9900" >
     <font face="Helvetica", "Arial">
     <h1 align="center"><font color="#FFFFFF">Memory Bank</font></h1>
     <hr width=50%>
     <b><P align="center"> <font color="#FF0000"> a convenient table of all
         the computations I can never remember </font></p>
     <form name="memory">
     <table align="center" border=2>
     <tr>
       <td><b>Celsius to Fahrenheit</b></td>
       <td> Celsius:
          <input type = text name = "cTemp" size = 4
              onChange='  C-to-F Event Handler    '> Fahrenheit:
          <input type = text name = tempInF size = 5></td></tr>
     <tr>
       <td><b>Fahrenheit to Celsius</b></td>
       <td> Fahrenheit:
          <input type = text name = "fTemp" size = 5
              onChange='  F-to-C Event Handler    '> Celsius:
          <input type = text name = tempInC size = 4></td></tr>
     <tr>
       <td><b>Body Mass Index </b>
          <input type = radio name = "pick1" checked = TRUE
              onClick='  The English Event Handler   '>English
          <input type = radio name= "pick1"
              onClick='  The Metric Event Handler    '>Metric</td>
       <td>Height:
          <input type = text name = "howtall" size = 4
              onChange = '  The Tall Event Handler   '> Weight:
          <input type = text name = "howwide" size = 4
              onChange = '  The Wide Event Handler   '> BMI:
          <input type = text name = "shape" size = 5></td></tr>
      </table></b>
      </form>
      <script language = "JavaScript">

      </script>
    </body>
   </html>
```

Figure 19.4. The HTML schema for the initial Memory Bank interface and its image.

Before starting on the programming, notice the two new features in this page. All of the rows take text *input*, and the Body Mass Index row uses radio buttons.

Text Input

We are familiar with using the `input` control for output. Using it for input introduces only two differences. First, the `value` attribute need not be explicitly mentioned. The `value` property is still part of the control, and we will refer to the contents of the window using `value` as before. But if we are satisfied to have the window blank when the page loads, `value` need not be explicitly mentioned. Second, we need an event handler to perform whatever action is to take place when the user enters information into the window. Filling in a window is not a click-event; it is a change-event. So, we specify the handler using `onChange`.

Radio Buttons

As introduced in Chapter 18, radio buttons are like regular button controls with a `name` attribute and an `onClick` event handler. Rather than having a label on the button, however, the button's identification is just the text following the input control. There are two main differences with standard buttons. First, several radio button controls are usually used together, and only one of them should be set at any time. To achieve this effect requires that all of the radio controls have the same name. Then, when one button is clicked, any other set radio button with the same name is cleared automatically. Second, it is often handy to preset one of the buttons. This is done with the `checked = TRUE` attribute.

Turning now to programming the Memory Bank Web page, notice that most of the work is done. The functions developed in the last section, `convertC2F()`, `convertF2C()`, `bmiE()`, `bmiM()`, and `BMI()`, provide the majority of the computation. So, the first step is to insert the definitions for these five functions between the `<script> </script>` tags of the Memory Bank page.

The remainder of the programming involves specifying event handlers. Considering the *C-to-F Event Handler* in the Celsius to Fahrenheit row of Figure 19.4.

```
<td><b>Celsius to Fahrenheit</b></td>
<td> Celsius:
   <input type = text name = "cTemp" size = 4
       onChange='    C-to-F Event Handler    '> Fahrenheit:
   <input type = text name = tempInF size = 5></td></tr>
```

we ask, "What should happen when the user enters a Celsius temperature?" Obviously we must call the `convertC2F()` function with the entered temperature as the argument and place the result from the computation in the output window. With the function already defined, the only questions are how to get the input out of the `cTemp` window, and how to place the answer in the `tempInF` window. The one answer to both questions is that the event handler will use the dot notation, as seen in Chapter 18. For example,

```
document.memory.tempInF.value = convertC2F(document.memory.cTemp.value)
```

does the job. However, because both windows are part of the same document, and they are part of the same form, we can drop the first two specifiers. Accordingly, the *C-to-F Event Handler* is

```
onChange = 'tempInF.value = convertC2F(cTemp.value)'
```

which can be read in English as "on a change to the `cTemp` window, use its value as the argument to the `convertC2F()` function, compute the result, and assign the result as the value of the `tempInF` window."

Obviously the *F-to-C Event Handler* is only trivially different. Only the three names differ. Thus the appropriate event handler is

```
onChange = 'tempInC.value = convertF2C(fTemp.value)'
```

which completes the first two rows of the Memory Bank page.

The Body Mass Index row has four event handlers that must be written. The first two handle the clicking of the radio buttons. As with all event handlers, we ask, what should be done when the event happens? Clearly we need to remember which unit is set, `English` or `metric`. We'll use a variable to record this information, and because the variable will be used in all of the event handlers of this row, it should be a *global* variable, that is, defined outside of any function or handler. We'll call the variable `measure`, and declare it

```
var measure = "English";
```

just after the `<script>` tag. Giving `measure` the initial value of `English` makes it the default measurement and is equivalent to having "preclicked" the English radio button. For this reason, we preset it using the `checked = true` specification. (The English default is correct for the United States, but elsewhere initializing to `metric` and presetting its radio button may improve the convenience of the page.)

With the global variable `measure` declared, defining the event handlers for the `pick1` radio buttons

```
<td>Body Mass Index
 <input type = radio name = "pick1" checked = TRUE
 '   onClick=' The English Event Handler '>English
   <input type = radio name= "pick1"
     onClick=' The Metric Event Handler '>Metric</td>
```

is simple. They assign the correct value to `measure` in a single JavaScript assignment statement. Thus

```
onClick = 'measure = "English"'
```

is the *English Event Handler*, and

```
onClick = 'measure = "metric"'
```

is the *Metric Event Handler*. Notice that although `English` is the initial value for `measure`, we still need an *English Event Handler*. This is because the user might click on the Metric button, and then click the English button. The *English Event Handler* resets `measure` back to `English`.

The last two event handlers, the *Tall Event Handler* and the *Wide Event Handler,* are straightforward now that everything has been set up.

```
<td>Height:
  <input type = text name = "howtall" SIZE = 4
    onChange = '   The Tall Event Handler    '> Weight:
 <input type = text name = "howwide" SIZE = 4
    onChange = '   The Wide Event Handler     '> BMI:
 <input type = text name = "shape" SIZE = 5></td>
```

(The `shape input` control doesn't require an event handler because its window is used as an output.) What should happen on a change to the `howtall` window (height specification)? It might seem that nothing should happen because the weight hasn't been specified yet. But maybe it has. There is no requirement that the windows be filled in in left-to-right order. There are two ways to solve the problem. The easiest is to run the `BMI()` function in response to a change in either window. In this case

```
onChange = 'shape.value=BMI(measure,howtall.value,howwide.value)'
```

is *both* the *Tall Event Handler* and the *Wide Event Handler*. Notice that the global variable `measure`, known to all functions and event handlers, is the argument for the first parameter position, the value from the `howtall` window is the argument for the second parameter position, and the value from the `howwide` window is the argument for the last parameter position.

What happens if the `BMI()` runs when only the height has been specified, that is, the `howwide` window is blank, which would be interpreted as 0? The two functions `bmiE()` and `bmiM()` both run and produce 0, so that's what will be set in the `shape` window. What happens if `BMI()` runs when only the weight has been specified? The two functions `bmiE()` and `bmiM()` both run and divide by 0, an illegal operation in arithmetic, so `INFINITY` will be displayed in the `shape` window. Either way, there is an indication that the result is invalid, and in any event the user knows that one window hasn't been filled yet. So, it is an adequate solution, but it is not a very elegant solution.

If only one of the inputs to a multi-parameter function is set, it seems that nothing should happen. So the proper solution is for the *Tall* and *Wide Event Handlers* is to test to see if the value from the other window has been set. If it hasn't, do nothing. If it has, call `BMI()`. Accordingly, the *Tall Event Handler* is

```
onChange = 'if (howwide.value != 0)
            shape.value = BMI(measure,howtall.value,howwide.value)
```

which tests to see if the weight has also been changed from 0, and, if so, it calls `BMI()`. Otherwise, nothing happens. The *Wide Event Hander*

```
onChange = 'if (howtall.value != 0)
            shape.value = BMI(measure,howtall.value,howwide.value)'
```

is the opposite, checking the value in the `howtall` window. The inclusion of these two event handlers ensures that nothing happens until nonzero data is in each window.

Notice that the "test for 0 input" conditional statement placed in the event handlers might have been placed in the `BMI()` function. Though possible, this is not a good choice. The reason is that the problem of not-yet-specified arguments is not caused by the way we are using the `BMI()` function and is not a property of the computation itself. Rather, it is because we are getting the values one-at-a-time in some order that we must protect the `BMI()` function from computing with only partial data. It's a problem for the event handler not the Body Mass Index computation. So that's where it should be handled.

Having completed the initial development of the Memory Bank page, we consider next how to make it more useful.

ELECTRONIC COIN FLIPPING

From deciding who kicks first in soccer matches to who buys coffee after class, making decisions by flipping coins is common. Of course, when everyone is using electronic money, it will be necessary to use electronic "coins" to make these decisions. So, we will add a row to our Memory Bank page to flip an electronic "coin." And, because we often pick one from several choices by a "think of a number between 1 and *n*" process, we'll add a facility to do that, too. Both additions will allow us to discuss random numbers, an important IT topic, as well as gain further experience with functions.

A Random Definition. The question of what constitutes a random number is an interesting philosophical question. For our purposes, a *random number* is defined operationally by counting particle emissions from the decay of a radioactive substance, say U_{238}, over a fixed time period.

As has been stated repeatedly, computers are deterministic. That is, given a fixed input and instructions, they produce the identical result every time they run the instructions with the input. Thus computers technically cannot generate random numbers. Any program to produce random numbers will have a completely predictable output. So, instead, they generate something called *pseudo-random numbers*. Computer scientists have developed sophisticated algorithms to generate pseudo-random numbers, and though they are created by a deterministic process, they pass statistical tests for randomness. This means that for all practical purposes, they are as good as flipping fair coins. Therefore, from here on we'll drop the "pseudo" part and just call them random numbers.

Flipping Out. The mathematician John von Neumann, one of the pioneers of computing, once said, "Anyone who attempts to generate random numbers by deterministic means is, of course, living in a state of sin."

Because random numbers are important, programming languages provide a built-in random number generator. JavaScript is no exception with its `Math.random()` function. Every time `Math.random()` is called it returns a new random number. To simplify their use, all random number generators produce a random decimal number strictly between 0 and 1. That is, the number is a fraction like 0.541507552309933 that will never be exactly equal to 0 or 1. So, to "flip an electronic coin" we can generate a random number and then round to the nearest integer,

```
Math.round(Math.random())
```

which produces either 0 if the fraction is less than 0.500000000000000, or a 1 otherwise. By treating 0 as tails and 1 as heads, we have flipped an electronic "coin."

There is another way to choose between two whole numbers, 0 and 1, and we are interested in it because it is more general, solving the coin flipping problem as well as other problems that have more than two outcomes. Here is the idea: Suppose we want to choose among four outcomes. Thinking about it, we notice that a decimal number from `Math.random()`, say, 0.3333 . . . , is just a fraction of the interval from 0 to 1, and that by multiplying by an integer *n*, we get the same fraction of the larger interval from 0 to *n*. (See Figure 19.5 for a schematic.) So, $4 \times 0.3333\ldots = 1.333\ldots$, meaning that 0.3333 is one-third of the way across the 0 to 1 interval, and 1.333 is one-third of the way across the 0 to 4 interval. Thus if `Math.random()` produces a random number in 0 to 1, *n* * `Math.random()` produces a random number between 0 and *n*, and additionally, the two numbers are in the same proportional position in their respective intervals.

Converting the resulting fraction to an integer cannot use `Math.round()`, however, because it changes a decimal number to the *closest* integer, which is not what we want. This can be seen by the relationships

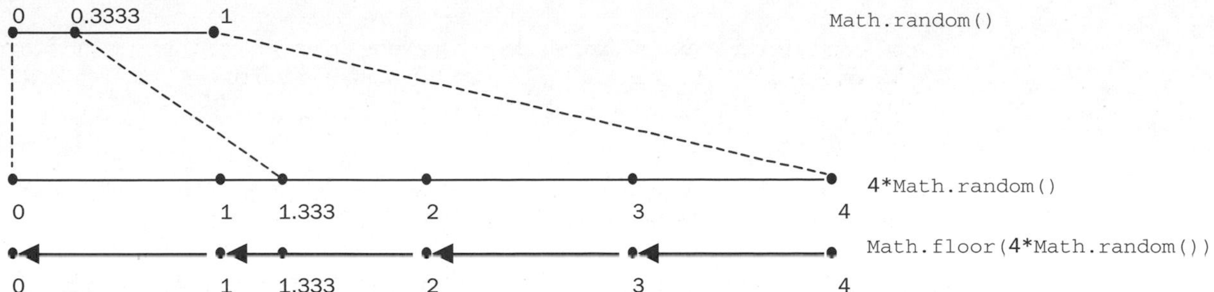

Figure 19.5. Schematic diagram of the output `Math.random()` translated by 4 to expand to a larger interval, followed by the application of floor to convert to integer values.

```
0.0 < Math.round(4 * Math.random()) < 0.5 become 0
0.5 ≤ Math.round(4 * Math.random()) < 1.5 become 1
1.5 ≤ Math.round(4 * Math.random()) < 2.0 become 2
2.5 ≤ Math.round(4 * Math.random()) < 3.5 become 3
3.5 ≤ Math.round(4 * Math.random()) < 4.0 become 4
```

which not only produces "too many" numbers (we're only choosing among four things), the highest and lowest integers are assigned only a "half unit." The right solution is just to drop the digits to the right of the decimal point. This "rounding down" operation is called *floor*, and has exactly the right outcome as these relationships show:

```
0.0 < Math.floor(4 * Math.random()) < 1.0 become 0
1.0 ≤ Math.floor(4 * Math.random()) < 2.0 become 1
2.0 ≤ Math.floor(4 * Math.random()) < 3.0 become 2
3.0 ≤ Math.floor(4 * Math.random()) < 4.0 become 3
```

Of course, a 4.0 will not be created because `Math.random()` never produces a 1.0. Notice that `Math.floor(2 * Math.random())` is the alternative way to produce the "electronic coin flip." Also, notice that given the 0 to 4 interval, we can change it to another interval, say, 1 to 5, by adjusting the output, for example, adding 1.

Having worked out how a random number chosen in the interval 0 to 1 can be converted into an integer from a range 0 to *n*, we write a JavaScript function to implement the idea. The function will be called `randNum` and will have one parameter, called `range`, which is the upper end of the interval. The code is

```
function randNum ( range ) {
   // Produces a random integer from 0 to range-1
   return Math.floor (range * Math.random());
}
```

Clearly `randNum(4)` yields a random choice from among four items, though they will be numbered 0 to 3. We can use this function in our Memory Bank page by adding a line of the form

The user can specify an interval size, which is preset to 10. Then clicking the `Pick` button results in an application of the `randNum()` function. The HTML for the controls is by now familiar.

```
<tr>
  <td><b>Pick A Random Number From 1 To </b>
   <input type = text name = "topEnd" size = 2 value = "10"> </td>
  <td>
    <input type = button value = "Pick"
       onClick = "choice.value = 1 + randNum(topEnd.value)">
       Outcome from the range:
    <input type = text name = "choice" size = 2></td></tr>
```

The `value` field is used in the `topEnd` control to preset the range. Also, 1 is added to the result of the `randNum()` function because the interval it returns is 0 to `range-1`, but the user wants a range 1 to `range`.

Though the just completed Memory Bank row can be used as a coin flip, by making range 2, we will develop a somewhat more user-friendly Memory Bank application for coin flips. First, it will print `Heads` or `Tails` for the outcome, which is better than 1 or 2. Further, it will keep track of how many heads and tails are generated, on the assumption that anyone losing a flip will want to see the e-coin flipped a few times to be assured that it is producing an approximately equal number of heads and tails. The window we have in mind has the form

The HTML controls for this row of the Memory Bank page are

```
<tr>
  <td><b>Electronic Coin Flip </b></td>
  <td align="center">
    <input type = button value = "Flip" onClick = "runTrial()">
         Outcome:
    <input type = text name = coin  SIZE = 5> Totals: H
    <input type = text name = heads SIZE = 3 VALUE = 0> T
    <input type = text name = tails SIZE = 3 VALUE = 0></td></tr>
```

We could have embedded all of the JavaScript programming for the `Flip` button click-event handler inside the `input` control, but it is clearer to package it all into a function and simply call it. We will name the function `runTrial()`.

The `runTrial()` function handles click-events, and so as always we ask, "What action should happen on a `Flip` click?" Clearly `randNum(2)` must be run, the outcome window must be assigned `Heads` or `Tails`, and either the H or T count must be incremented by 1. The required function is straightforward

```
function runTrial() {
   if (randNum(2) == 1) {
      document.memory.coin.value = "Heads";
      headCount = headCount + 1;
      document.memory.heads.value = headCount;
   }
   else {
      document.memory.coin.value = "Tails";
      tailCount = tailCount + 1;
      document.memory.tails.value = tailCount;
   }
}
```

provided we declare two global variables (right after the earlier `measure` declaration) to keep the counts,

```
var headCount = 0, tailCount = 0;
```

No local variables are required. Rather, `randNum(2)` is called in the predicate of a conditional statement. Then, depending on which outcome results, three parallel statements are executed in either the `Then`-clause or the `Else`-clause. The first sets the `coin` window; the second increments the appropriate global variable, keeping track of the total count; and the third statement updates the appropriate `heads` or `tails` window. Notice that, unlike the earlier abbreviated uses of the dot operator, the full path `document.memory.heads.value` is required because the reference within a function is a nonlocal reference relative to the form.

Finally, `runTrial()` is different from our earlier functions. It differs in that it has no `return` statement. The function just finishes when it reaches the end of the definition. That is, it does not use the return mechanism to report the outputs from the call. The function does have outputs—three to be exact: It changes the `coin` window, updates one of the two counts, and changes either the `heads` or `tails` window. But it does these operations by making direct references to the variables involved. What makes it different is not the missing `return` statements, but that it is customized to a very specific situation, rather than being a general solution.

All of our previous functions—`convertC2F()`, `BMI()`, `randNum()`, and so on—are general. We wrote them for our application, but we hope that we will have a chance to use them again. Think of them as building blocks to more complex programs that we may write in the future. But `runTrial()` is not a building block. It contains explicit references like `document.memory.heads.value` that require it to run within a document that has a `memory` form and, within that form, to have input controls named `coin`, `heads`, and `tails`. We do not expect this to ever happen again. Instead we wrote the function to encapsulate the complexity of handling the `Flip` click event, removing it from the HTML form. Giving the event handling operation a name allowed us to write a function for it and get it out of the way. Thus we've seen two reasons to write functions: Name a computation that may be useful, package it, and hope to use it again. Name a computation that is bulky, package it, and move it to somewhere out of the way. These are both legitimate reasons for abstraction.

Final Embellishments

To wrap up our discussion of functions and the Memory Bank page development, we add two final embellishments: a date, and Web links. Both features are simple, but they make the page more useful. Also, we add one bonus feature.

Date

The date can be added at the top after the red motto text, centered. JavaScript provides many programming resources for manipulating dates, but we use only the `Date()` function. We could write a function to insert the date into the HTML document, but it is only a single line, so we write the code

```
<script language = 'JavaScript'>
   document.write('<center>' + (Date().toString()) + '<center>');
</script>
```

placing it inline just after the motto line. The `document.write` operation, being a JavaScript statement, must be surrounded by `<script>` tags as usual. Like all JavaScript commands, `document.write()` will be performed while the browser is inputting the HTML file, that is, before the page is created. The JS Interpreter composes the string—recall that the + is the concatenate operator for strings—and inserts the result at the present position in the HTML file, that is, just after the motto.

The expression in the center of the string `(Date().toString())` references the date object, which contains the current date and time in numeric form. The numeric form can be converted to a printable form using the `toString()` facility. So the expression says, "Get the current date and time converted to a printable string."

Web Links

Our Memory Bank page has concentrated on programming computations, but it's a Web page, so we can include useful links, too. These links are probably bookmarked in your browser, but by placing them on the Memory Bank page, they are available even when you're using a different computer or browser. What should the links be? Anything that is useful. An online dictionary and thesaurus for writing term papers, a link to the Fluency class' home page, a periodic chart for Chem class, and maybe the State Department's list of country information for Geography.

Where should the links be located? We could add another column to the table, placing one link per row. Because the links are highlighted with a different color, they would appear to be their own, coherent column. But, why should the number of links match the number of rows of the table? Also, it's cumbersome to add columns to HTML tables. An alternative is to add another row at the bottom of the table that spans across both columns and fill it with the links. We choose this solution for two reasons. First, it gives us a free-form region in which to list the links and to organize them by topic. Second, we can set up such an area simply so that adding more links is very easy, encouraging us to include new ones. The HTML is shown in Figure 19.6, and the completed page is shown in Figure 19.7.

```
<tr>
<!--  The standard form for the links is...
 <br><b>___topic name___...</b>
   <img src='bullet.gif'>
     <a href='http://___url goes here___'>
        _______anchor term(s)here_____</a>
       -->
<td colspan = 2> <center>IMPORTANT LINKS</center>
 <br>Resource Links ...
   <img src='bullet.gif'>
     <a href='http://dictionary.cambridge.org'>
         Cambridge Dictionary</a>
   <img src='bullet.gif'>
     <a href='http://www.wordsmyth.net'>
         Thesaurus</a>
 <br>Classes...
   <img src='bullet.gif'>
     <a href='http://www.cs.washington.edu/100'>
         Fluency Class</a>
   <img src='bullet.gif'>
     <a href='http://www.chemsoc.org/viselements/pages/pertable_j.htm'>
         Periodic Table</a>
   <img src='bullet.gif'>
     <a href='http://www.state.gov/r/poa/gbn'>
         Countries for Geography</a>
</td>
</tr>
```

Figure 19.6. HTML for the link area of the Memory Bank Web page.

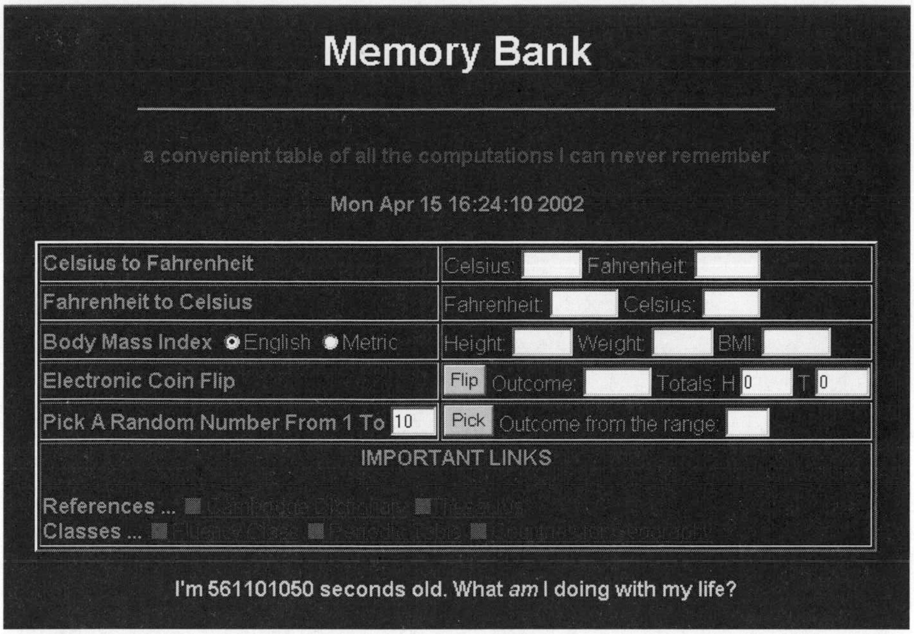

Figure 19.7. Final version of the Memory Bank page.

Notice first that to get the table data to span two columns, HTML's `colspan = 2` attribute is included with the `<td>` tag. Second, the links are grouped by topic, which uses the standard text color to stand out from the differently colored links. Third, a red bullet—a `.gif` image—is used to separate the entries because some of them are multiword. (Of course, a file named `bullet.gif` must be in the same directory as this page, as explained in Chapter 4.) Finally, and most important, the link area has a very neat structure that makes adding new links almost trivial. The headings and entries all have a standard structure, and a schema has been developed and placed in a comment, allowing simple copy-and-paste modifications. This approach should encourage us to keep the content current.

Finally, to close, we add a bonus feature to the page. It applies slightly more advanced concepts, so will not be completely explained. We exploit the fact that JavaScript has extensive support for working with dates. One feature that makes it easy for computers to work with dates is that they mostly keep track of dates and time with "UNIX dates." (Recall that UNIX dates were used in cookies as explained in Chapter 15.) The UNIX operating system began recording dates as the number of milliseconds since 1 January 1970 at 00:00:00 Universal Time, that is, New Year 1970 in Greenwich, England. Thus the number of milliseconds between any two dates can be found by subtracting the two UNIX dates, making it much easier to compute than if time were recorded in days and hours. JavaScript uses UNIX dates, but it provides functions to refer to time as if it were recorded in days and hours when that is convenient for us. We use these features to compute your age in seconds. (Of course, your age in milliseconds is just 1000 times more.)

The proper JavaScript code, to be placed just before </script> tag at the end of the Memory Bank program, is

```
var today = new Date();      // Get today's date
var myBdate = new Date();    // Get a date object to modify
var difference;              //
myBdate.setFullYear(1984);   // Set my birth year to 1984
myBdate.setMonth(6);         // Set my birth month to July (mo.s start at 0)
myBdate.setDate(4);          // Set my birth day to 4th
myBdate.setHours(11);        // Set my hour of birth to noon
myBdate.setMinutes(0);       // Set my minute of birth to o'clock
myBdate.setSeconds(0);       // Set my second of birth on the hour
difference = today.getTime() - myBdate.getTime();
difference = Math.floor(difference/1000);
document.write("<center><font color=yellow> I'm " + difference
   + " seconds old. What <i>am</i>I doing with my life?</font><center>");
```

The program creates two date objects, one for today and one for your birthday. (Objects are a complex subject and will not be covered.) In the six statements following the declarations, we set your birthday as if it were exactly noon, July 4, 1984. To do this, we use functions that are provided by JavaScript and that allow us to refer to the time using the familiar months and hours concepts. Once your birthday has been set, we compute `difference`, the difference between the present time and that date. This computation uses UNIX dates. We then divide the result by 1000 to convert it to seconds and print it out at the bottom of the Memory Bank page.

With these additions, the Memory Bank page is complete for the moment. (An HTML and JavaScript listing is given in Appendix C.) It is possible to make extensive additions, adding to the page throughout college.

SUMMARY

This chapter began by introducing the concept of abstraction. Abstraction is identifying significant components of a process, design, or other phenomenon based on form or behavior. We *name* the abstraction and define it, and when its significance is based on commonality of structure or behavior among different instances, we *parameterize* the variation. Abstractions are important to computing because they help *manage complexity* in that we can refer to the name rather than its definition. And abstractions are important because they *promote reuse* by being packaged into functions, which can be a building blocks to more complex computations.

After thinking about abstraction abstractly, we made the whole idea specific by describing how to encapsulate a computation into a function. We learned the JavaScript structure for function declarations and illustrated it with temperature conversion operations. The declaration is the defining part of a function, but there is also an application part, the function call. Using several small HTML programs, we illustrated calling the function for different purposes: to find a single Celsius temperature in Fahrenheit, to make a list of equivalents, and to make a table of equivalents. This write-once-use-many-times characteristic demonstrates the reuse feature of functions. We then devoted a section to getting the details right, including such distinctions as local and global variables, parameters and arguments, definitions and calls.

Armed with a clear understanding of the details we developed the Memory Bank Web page, a combination of programming in JavaScript—mostly event handlers, because the functions were already written—and HTML. The Memory Bank illustrated how useful content could be added to a Web page through programming

JavaScript. After discussing random numbers, we extended the page to flip an electronic "coin" and to choose among a sequence of integers. Both extensions provided additional programmng opportunities. Finally, we added a few more routine features—links and date—to the Memory Bank to make it more useful. Many more additions to the page can be contemplated.

Looking back on the function programming of the chapter we notice two distinct cases. Most of the functions of this chapter like `convertC2F()` and `randNum()` are general, written for one purpose, but of use in the future. These functions illustrate how abstraction promotes reuse. One of the functions of the chapter, `runTrial()`, was written for a situation that is so specialized it will probably never arise again. We gave a name to the computation simply to encapsulate it so as not to think about it anymore, that is, to "get it out of the way." This function illustrates how abstraction helps us manage complexity. Both uses of abstraction—reuse and complexity management—made our thinking easier.

Though the topics of this chapter are deep and important, they are also reasonably intuitive. For example, abstracting from processes or other complex phenomenon and giving them names is something humans do naturally. By strengthening our ability to identify commonality and patterns we become more incisive thinkers. Add to that the ability to package abstractions into functions to help manage complexity or promote reuse—the idea applies even when the abstractions are not computations—and we have added significantly to our ability to understand the world.

Exercises

1. Abstraction is identifying a significant structure or common feature in a process, design, or other phenomenon. What are the three aspects of abstracting?
2. What are the two reasons abstraction is important in computing?
3. A JavaScript function declaration has three parts, the name, parameter list, and definition, which must be given in that order. What punctuation symbols surround these three items?
4. Why are `else`, `return`, and `Boolean` not good names for functions or parameters?
5. What does it mean to say "Functions impose a scope of reference on variables"?
6. Compare and contrast the concepts of local variables and global variables.
7. In the JavaScript

```
var sampleVarX = 10;
function example (sampleVarY) {
  var sampleVarZ = 11;
  ...
}
```

   say which of the variables are global and which are local.
8. Compare and contrast the concepts of parameter and argument.
9. The JavaScript function

```
function BMI (units, height, weight ) {
   // Compute BMI in either metric or English
   if (units == "English")
      return bmiE(weight, height);
   else
      return bmiM(weight, height);
}
```

contains three variables. State for each occurrence of each variable whether it is a parameter, an argument, both, or neither.

10. Build the `eztest.html` file and test the `bmiE()` or `bmiM()` using your weight and height.

11. Compare and contrast the concepts of function definition and function call.

12. Compound interest for one year is defined by the following equation

$$\text{principal and interest} = p0(1+r/4)^4$$

for a deposit of *p0*, an interest rate, *r*, and quarterly compounding. Write a JavaScript function to figure compound interest given those two parameters.

13. The volume of a sphere is defined by the equation

$$Volume = {}^4/_3\, \pi\, r^3$$

where *r* is the radius of the sphere. Write a JavaScript function to figure the volume of a sphere given its radius. Recall that π is approximately equal to 3.14159.

14. Show the "managing complexity" advantage of functions, by creating the `figurePrice()` function and revising the `onClick` event handler for the `Total` button of the Bean Counter application in Chapter 18.

CHAPTER 20

Once Is Not Enough

Learning Objectives

- Learn the JavaScript `for`-statement.
- Understand the parts of an iteration and their range of variability.
- Learn the Fundamental Principle of Iteration.
- Learn the World Famous Iteration and acquire experience using it.
- Know how to use indexing and arrays.
- Know the concept of regularizing indices and how to apply it.
- Understand the principles of online animation.

The topic of this chapter is iteration—the process of repetition. We are familiar with the English word *reiterate*, which means to repeat something, as in "The attorney reiterated his client's position." Because *iterate* already means to repeat, *reiterate* sounds redundant. But repetition *is* redundant; that's what it's about. So, English has both words, and maybe it needs a third, *rereiterate*, an even more redundant form meaning, perhaps, "repeated *ad nauseum*," as in "Beer commercials are rereiterated." Though repetition is usually tiresome, learning about it is not. And, iteration is the source of considerable computational power, making it a very important topic. By learning how to use iteration, we can make the computer do the tiresome parts of computing.

In this chapter, we conclude our coverage of programming concepts by studying iteration and applying it to computational problems. We begin by explaining the `for`-statement, one of JavaScript's iteration statements, and the main workhorse of all iterative computation. Learning the `for`-statement without a deep discussion of iteration is possible because it is quite intuitive. Then, with the syntax for `for` clearly in mind, we explore the iteration concept more deeply by discussing how its components can vary. The key to understanding iteration is to focus on how the iteration variable changes values. We mention the Fundamental Principle of Iteration and its main corollary. As a context for practicing iterative statements, we return to the topic of random numbers. After this iteration practice come the companion topics of indexing and arrays. Together indexing and arrays can be used with iteration to perform almost unlimited amounts of computation, making them a major source of computing power. Finally, to bring all of these topics together, we study online animation, which allows us to add action to our Web pages. We work through the animation of the familiar waiting icon as a precursor to more interesting animations.

PLAY IT AGAIN, SAM

The first fact to learn is the slight difference between *iterate* and *repeat*. When your mother said, "I've repeated myself four times," she meant, strictly speaking, she'd said the same thing five times. Usually, the first time isn't considered a "repeat." Only numbers 2 through *n* are. If she'd actually said it only four times, she should have used *iterate*. (Pointing this out to her would *not* have been smart.) We often ignore this fact in common speech. For example, "reps" in weight training count the total number. To avoid confusion use *iterate*. When something is iterated five times, there are five instances; you can't be off by one. In this book, we follow common usage and use *repeat* and *iterate* interchangeably, except where precision is essential and then we use *iterate*.

Iteration—probably the fourth most important programming idea after assignment, conditionals, and functions—is a process for looping through a series of statements to repeat them. In JavaScript, the iteration statement begins with `for` and has the structure

```
for ( <initialization>; <continuation>; <next iteration> ) {
     <statement list>
}
```

where the text not in meta-brackets must be given literally. (Notice the prominent position of the closed curly brace.) The statement sequence to be repeated is in the *<statement list>*, and the constructs in parentheses—to be explained momentarily—control how many times they are iterated. The statement sequence is performed in its entirety in each iteration. So, if the `for`-loop

```
for ( <initialization>; <continuation>; <next iteration> ) {
     document.write('→');
     document.write('–→');
     document.write('—→');
}
```

iterates three times, it will produce

That is, the computer completes the statement sequence of the *<statement list>* in its entirety before beginning the next iteration.

The trio of operations in the parentheses of the `for`-loop, *<initialization>*, *<continuation>*, and *<next iteration>*, control the number of times the loop iterates.

They control the loop by using a variable known as an *iteration* variable. Iteration variables are just normal variables, so they must be declared. They are known as iteration variables only while they are serving to control the loop. Here's a typical example in which the iteration variable is `j`,

```
for ( j = 1 ; j <= 3 ; j = j + 1 ){
    <statement list>
}
```

To see how these statements work, imagine that the `for`-loop has been replaced with the schematic form

General

```
<initialization>;
if (<continuation>) {
    <statement list>;
    <next iteration>;
}
```

Specific Example with j

```
j = 1;
if ( j <= 3 ) {
  <statement list>
  j = j + 1;
}
```

where the arrow means to go back to do the `if`-statement again.

Here's what happens. The first operation of a `for`-loop is to perform the *<initialization>*. It sets the iteration variable's value for the first (if any) iterations through the loop. Next, the *<continuation>* test, which has the same form as the predicate in a conditional statement, is performed. If the *<continuation>* test has a `false` outcome, the loop terminates, the *<statement list>* is skipped, and it is as though nothing happened except that the iteration variable got assigned its initial value.

However, if the *<continuation>* test has a `true` outcome, the *<statement list>* is performed. When the statements are completed, the *<next iteration>* operation is performed, which will change the iteration variable. That completes the first iteration. The next iteration starts with the *<continuation>* test, performing the same sequence of operations. All subsequent iterations proceed as the first did until the *<continuation>* test has a `false` outcome, terminating the loop. In this way, the statement sequence can be performed many times without having to write out all of the statements explicitly.

Terminator, Too. The second item among the control operations is named the *<continuation>* test here, because if its outcome is `true`, the iteration *continues*, and if its outcome is `false`, it ends. But the proper programming term for this test is the *termination* test because it is viewed as checking to determine if the loop should terminate. However, as a termination test, the outcomes are backwards—`true` means continue, `false` means terminate! Both terms are useful, but to remember the meanings of the outcomes, think of the test as asking "Continue?"

In the `for`-loop with iteration variable `j`, and in all `for`-loops, the story is fully embodied in the operations involving the iteration variable. Consider the sequence of operations on `j` shown in Table 20.1.

Table 20.1. The Sequence of Operations on `j` from the `for`-loop with Control Specification `(j=1; j <= 3; j=j+1)`

Operation	Operation Result	Role
`j = 1`	`j`'s value is 1	Initialize iteration variable
`j <= 3 true`	`j` is *less than*	First <*continuation*> test, continue
`j = j + 1`	`j`'s value is 2	First <*next iteration*> operation
`j <= 3 true`	`j`is *less than*	Second <*continuation*> test, continue
`j = j + 1`	`j`'s value is 3	Second <*next iteration*> operation
`j <= 3 true`	`j`is *equal to*	Third <*continuation*> test, continue
`j = j + 1`	`j`'s value is 4	Third <*next iteration*> operation
`j <= 3 false`	`j`is *greater than*	Fourth <*continuation*> test, terminate

Thus the loop iterates 3 times by beginning at 1, and after assigning a new value to `j`, testing to see if it should continue. The statements of the <*statement list*> are executed between the <*continuation*> test and the <*next iteration*> operation. Notice that `j` counts from 1 to 4, but at 4, the test finds out that `j` has counted too far, so it quits before performing the <*statement list*> again. Thus the <*statement list*> is performed the right number of times.

> **No Planning.** The `for`-loop *might have been* designed to figure the number of iterations to perform before starting out, and then doing them. But iteration doesn't work that way. Instead, the computer just methodically plods along, testing to see if it should continue before starting an iteration, doing the statement sequence if so, changing the iteration variable, and repeating. Plodding is more powerful because it's not always possible to predict the number of iterations.

To solidify our understanding of how `for`-loops work, consider a computation on declared variables `j` and `text`,

```
text = "She said ";                        //Set text to a string
for (j = 1; j <= 3; j = j + 1) {           //Define a 3 cycle loop
    text = text + "Never! ";               //Concatenate on a string
}                                          // ... end of loop
alert(text);                               // Show result
```

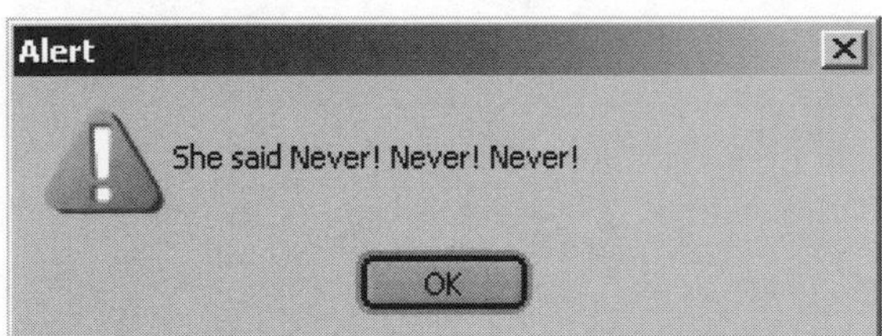

which produces the box shown at left.

The preceding `for`-loop, which iterates three times, was used with two assignment statements to produce the value of `text` by appending three copies of the word `"Never! "`. To check the code's operation, notice that prior to the four continuation tests, the values of the variable `text` are the following strings

`"She said "`	*Before the loop is entered*
`"She said Never! "`	*After one iteration*
`"She said Never! Never! "`	*After two iterations*
`"She said Never! Never! Never! "`	*After three iterations*

Thus the `for`-loop allowed us to progressively construct the phrase one word at a time. Of course, this phrase could have been typed out explicitly, `"She said Never! Never! Never! "`. But the more emphatic phrase in which she says `"Never!"` 1000 times would be much harder to type; it can be accomplished by simply changing the 3 in the preceding `for`-loop to 1000. It's easy to be emphatic with `for`-loops.

Range of Variation

A programmer would say that the `for`-loop just illustrated "iterates from 1 to 3 by 1." This is different from saying the `for`-loop iterates three times. The programmer's description is preferred because the most relevant feature of a `for`-loop is its control, and the key aspects of the control—the starting point (1), the ending point (3), and the step size (1)—are significant because they can be so varied. In this section, we consider some of the possibilities. We consider the

- Iteration variable
- Starting point
- Continuation/termination test
- Step size
- Reference to the iteration variable
- A world famous iteration

each in its turn.

Iteration Variable

As mentioned, iteration variables are normal variables called into service to help with an iteration. Accordingly, they must be declared, and they follow the usual rules for identifiers. Programmers tend to choose short or even single-letter identifiers for iteration variables because they tend to be typed frequently, as we'll see. By far, `i`, `j`, and `k` are the most common.

Starting Point

An iteration can begin anywhere, including with negative numbers. So, for example, in

```
for ( j = -10; j <= 10; j = j + 1) { ... }
```

the iteration variable `j` spans the 21 values from `-10` to `10`, that is, including 0. And, similarly,

```
for (j = 990; j <= 1010; j = j + 1) { ... }
```

`j` assumes the 21 values around `1000`. And finally, it's possible to start at a fractional number. So, in the loop

```
for (j = 2.5; j <= 6; j = j + 1) { ... }
```

`j` enumerates the values `2.5`, `3.5`, `4.5`, and `5.5` because the *<continuation>* test will finally fail at `6.5`.

Continuation/Termination Test

Obviously, if it is possible to begin an iteration anywhere, it must be equally possible to end it anywhere. The *<continuation>* test follows the rules for predicates as seen in conditionals, that is, any well-formed expression resulting in a Boolean value.

For example, it is possible to have an iteration end on an even number, say, `limit` or `limit + 1` if `limit` is odd. To illustrate, the operator `%` is the modulus operator—the remainder after dividing—allowing us to compute `j%2`, which is 0 if `j` is even (meaning there is no remainder), and 1 if it's not. The expression `((j%2) == 0)` is `true` when `j` is even, implying that the loop

```
for (j = 0; (j <= limit) || ((j%2) == 0); j = j + 1) { ... }
```

terminates under the circumstances required. (Recall that `||` is *or* and notice that the left and right *clauses* of `||` have been parenthesized so we can more easily recognize them.) If `limit` is a positive number, then as long as `j` is less than or equal to it, the first clause of the *<continuation>* test is `true`, which makes the test true. For `limit+1`, the clause will be `false` as will the second clause if `limit` is even, making the test false. But if `limit` is an odd number, `limit+1` is even, making the second clause `true` and continuing the iteration for one more cycle. Odd or even, both clauses will fail on the next iteration, terminating the iteration.

Step Size

The *<next iteration>* component also allows considerable freedom. It usually specifies an amount of change, known as the *step* or *step size*. For example, it is possible to step by units of 2, say, to iterate through the even numbers from 0 to 20,

```
for (j = 0; j < 20; j = j + 2) { ... }
```

which is 10 numbers because `20` is not included. The *<next iteration>* computation is often called the *increment* computation by programmers because, as we've seen, it is almost always *increasing* the value of the iteration variable. But it doesn't have to. The step can be negative, resulting in a decrement, and so we call it the *<next iteration>* computation. For example, to reprise the enumeration of the 21 integers around `0`, but to do so from positive to negative this time, we have

```
for (j = 10; j >= -10; j = j - 1) { ... }
```

The successive values of `j` are `10`, `9`, `8`, . . . , `-9`, `-10`. Notice that reversing the direction of the enumeration of the values required the *<continuation>* test to be adjusted, too.

Pluses and Minuses. Because incrementing and decrementing by 1 are so common, JavaScript has adopted the special "post increment/decrement" syntax to save a bit of typing. Thus `i++` means `i = i + 1`, and `i--` means `i = i - 1`. (The variable can be anything, of course.) This notation is handy for the *<next iteration>* component of a `for`-loop.

Reference to the Iteration Variable

As we will soon see, it is common to use the iteration variable in the computations of the *<statement list>*, which is why we focus so on the values that the iteration variable assumes during the looping. We care what they are because we compute with them. So, for example, the iteration variable `j` is used in the statement of

```
fact = 1;
for (j = 1; j <= 5; j = j + 1) {
    fact = fact * j;
}
```

which computes 5! Specifically, it computes `((((1 * 1) * 2) * 3) * 4) * 5` ⇔ `120`. Using the iteration variable in the computation is necessary and useful. Though changing it *is* possible,

```
j = ... ;          // Not recommended in <statement list>
```

it is a very bad programming practice. That is, only assign to iteration variables in the control section of the `for`-loop for *<initialization>* and computing the *<next iteration>* value.

World Famous Iteration

Because JavaScript adopted the same `for`-loop statement structure common to the most popular programming languages (e.g., C, C++, and Java), thousands of `for`-loops with the form just described are written every day—millions in the past decade. Not surprisingly, a stylized form has emerged through extensive use and familiarity. Without a doubt, the most commonly written `for`-loop is

```
for (j=0; j<n; j++) { ... }
```

where `n` is often some other limit variable, although `n` itself is quite common. It is worth taking a moment to study this form because you will encounter it again and again. It may even come in handy.

Notice first that the iteration variable starts at 0. Why starting at 0 should be more advantageous than starting at 1 will be seen shortly. The iteration counts up from 0 in steps of 1 because the post-increment `j++` is used. And the iteration ends when the iteration variable is no longer strictly less than `n`, that is, the loop's last iteration is for `j = n-1`. Thus the `for`-loop *<statement list>* is performed `n` times. When used in this stylized form, the variable or expression following the < symbol—the `n` in this case—is exactly the number of times through the loop, making it possible for us to recognize the iteration count in an instant without thinking hard about it. And this form saves on typing, which is not an inconsequential consideration if you remember how difficult it is to type programming symbols. When you see JavaScript in the SOURCE listing of the Web pages you download, chances are you will see this World Famous Iteration. Nearly every iteration in the remainder of this book has this "World Famous" form.

> **Off Again.** An extremely common error in computing—you've probably made it several times in *this* section—is to miscount by one. It's so common it has a name, *Off By One Error*. "Exam week is from the 3rd to the 10th," so how many days is it? We tend to subtract to get seven, but it's eight because it includes the end points. Figuring iterations is similarly fraught with error, thus the importance of knowing that the `n` following < in the "World Famous" form is the iteration count.

THE PRINCIPLES OF ITERATION

Because looping is so fundamental to computing—we get a lot of computation for a little writing—iteration statements have many variations. Some loop constructs test at the end rather than the beginning as the `for`-loop does. Others leave the *<initialization>* and *<next iteration>* computations to the programmer to do explicitly in the *<statement list>*, and so on. Learning the catechism of iteration is for professional programmers. We are interested here only in the fundamental ideas about iteration. The most basic of these is the

> **Fundamental Principle of Iteration:** All iterations have a test to determine whether the iteration continues or terminates.

The principle's obvious truth is based on the observation that if there is no test, the iteration runs forever. That is, it is an infinite loop, and we would have to wait infinitely long for the computation to yield an answer. Our interest is only in finite algorithms—see the fifth property of Algorithms, Chapter 10—so every iteration must end. Thus, `for`-loops include the *<continuation>* test as a standard element of the control trinity.

The Fundamental Principle of Iteration has an important corollary, which is significant when programming.

> **Corollary**: Some variable on which the iteration's test depends must be changed during each iteration.

Suppose there are two consecutive iterations during which no variable on which the *<continuation>* test depends changes. How will the second iteration vary from the first? It may vary in many ways, but by hypothesis, the *<continuation>* test will have the same outcome as after the first iteration, which caused the second iteration. So, the loop will execute a third time. Because there is no variation in the outcome of the third test, the outcome will again be the same. And so on. The iteration will continue forever. That is, some variable on which the test depends must change, or we again have an infinite loop. The corollary explains the presence of the *<next iteration>* component as a standard part of the `for`-loop statement structure.

The reason that the corollary is so important is that it's not too difficult to make a mistake when programming `for`-loops and create an infinite loop. For example,

```
for ( j = 1 ; j <= 3; i = i + 1) { ... }
```

looks almost like our earlier emphatic `for`-loop, but it is broken and will loop forever. (Very emphatic, indeed!) The problem is that the variable being compared in the *<continuation>* test (`j`) is not the one incremented in the *<next iteration>* operation (`i`). Unless the iteration variable is changed in the loop—we've already said that's a bad idea—the iteration will loop forever. Obviously anyone carefully analyzing this `for`-statement will spot the problem, but it's easy to miss. It's also easy enough to create, say, by making incomplete edits. (Imagine that the statement had previously used `i` as an iteration variable.) Though it's tough for humans to get every detail right when writing programs, we should be especially vigilant when programming the *<continuation>* and *<next iteration>* components of a `for`-loop to avoid infinite loops.

> **Infinite Loops.** Infinite loops happen. It's a fact of programming. Luckily, JavaScript is kind to programmers making this mistake. Microsoft's Internet Explorer tells you that the script is running slowly and asks if you want to terminate it. Netscape and other browsers can simply be forced to close. In the past, it was necessary to turn off the computer to stop an infinite loop.

Purposely write an infinite loop, run it, and force the browser to terminate so that you recognize the behavior.

EXPERIMENTS WITH FLIPPING ELECTRONIC COINS

As an opportunity to practice `for`-loops, we experiment with flipping electronic coins. Recall that in Chapter 19 we wrote a function `randNum()` taking an argument that is the range of integers from which to select. So, `randNum(2)`, which returns either 0 (tails) or 1 (heads), can be used for the experiments.

The first experiment is to find out how many heads and tails are produced in 100 flips. We expect the numbers to be roughly equal. To run the experiment, we obviously must set up an iteration in which our `randNum()` function is performed 100 times and statistics are gathered along the way. The code

```
<html><head><title>Coin Flips</title></head>
  <body><script language='JavaScript'>
  var heads=0, tails=0;                    //Counters
  var i;                                   //Iteration variable
  for (i=0; i<100; i++ ){
   if (randNum(2) == 1)
        heads++;
      else
        tails++;
  }
  alert("Heads: " + heads + " and Tails: " + tails);
  function randNum(range) {
    return Math.floor(range*Math.random());
  }
</script></body></html>
```

does the task. (Because the output will be reported using `alert()`, the page is irrelevant, motivating us to compress the HTML.) The `for`-loop, which uses the "World Famous Iteration" form mentioned earlier, loops 100 times—`i` ranges from 0 through 99—and it uses a conditional statement to check and record the outcomes of the random number generation. The post-increment (++) notation has been used three times, allowing us to replace statements like `heads = heads + 1` with the briefer `heads++`. Running the program yielded the box shown at right the first time I tried it on my computer. But you should experiment on your computer.

Running the program several times produces a range of answers. My five runs ranged from a 50–50 outcome to a 57–43 outcome. This motivates us to run several trials.

A *trial* will be the 100-sample iteration just described. To run several trials, we obviously want to iterate them. That is, we will iterate an iteration. Think of the earlier iteration

```
for (i=0; i<100; i++ ){                               //Trial line 1
 if (randNum(2) == 1)                                 //Trial line 2
      heads++;                                        //Trial line 3
    else                                              //Trial line 4
      tails++;                                        //Trial line 5
}                                                     //Trial line 6
alert("Heads: " + heads + " and Tails: " + tails);    //Trial line 7
```

as a unit.[1] To iterate these statements, we construct another `for`-loop with the *<statement list>* containing this trial unit and a couple of additional statements needed to make the whole process work out. The additional statements must reinitialize the counters because they should begin at 0 for each new trial. The result is

```
var i, j;                                  //Iteration variables
for (j = 0; j < 5; j++){                   //Outer loop start
   for (i=0; i<100; i++){                  //Trial line 1
      if (randNum(2) == 1)                 //Trial line 2
        heads++;                           //Trial line 3
```

[1] Notice that thinking of the loop as a unit is *abstraction*, as discussed in Chapter 19. We have named it *trial* and could convert the iteration into a function, but that would be a distraction at the moment.

```
        else                                            //Trial line 4
          tails++;                                      //Trial line 5
      }                                                 //Trial line 6
      alert("Heads: " + heads + " and Tails: " + tails); //Trial line 7
      heads = 0; tails = 0;                             //Additional
}                                                       //Outer loop end
```

This structure—a loop within a loop—is called a *nested loop*. Notice that another iteration variable, `j`, had to be declared because the outer loop cannot use the same iteration variable as the inner loop.

The behavior of the nested loop should be clear: The outer loop on `j`, which also uses the "World Famous" form, iterates 5 times, that is, `j` assumes the values `0` to `4`. *For each of these* `j` *values*, its *<statement list>* is executed in its entirety; that is, the inner loop on `i` iterates 100 times, the alert is printed out, and the counters are reinitialized. That will be a total of 5 trials of 100 flips each, or 500 total flips. Run the program, and see the range of results.

Rather than printing out one result per `alert()`, we could print them all out with one `alert()`. The way to do this is to accumulate the results like the "emphatic loop" above accumulated `Never!`. Declare a new variable,

```
var text = '';
```

which is initialized to the empty string. The place to accumulate the information is at the position where the `alert()` call is located, so replace it with

```
text = text + "Heads: " + heads + " and Tails: " + tails + "\n";
```

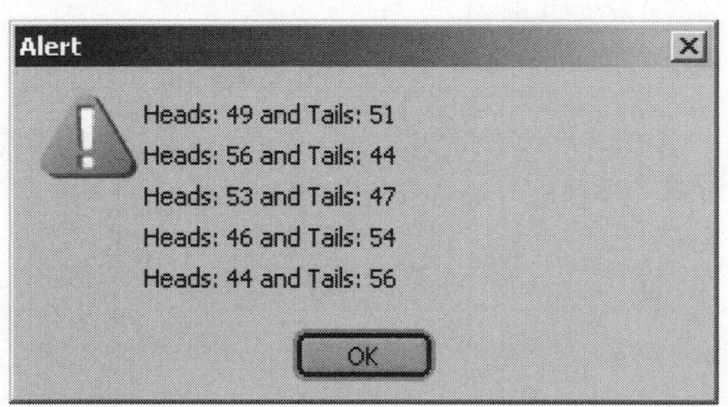

At the end of each inner loop this statement concatenates the results of a trial to the end of the text variable. The `"\n"` string is a New-line character, so that each pair of trial results is printed on its own line. (Recall that New-line cannot be typed explicitly.) A sample result is shown at left.

Though there are statistical methods for evaluating the randomness of the coin flipping, our only interest is in how far off from a perfect 50–50 score a trial is. So, rather than displaying the raw results of the outcomes, we will display a diagram embodying the information. We compute the difference of the coin flip from 50–50 and show that number using asterisks. For example, the first of the previous trials, 49–51, would be represented by a single asterisk because it differs from perfect by one coin flip. Either of the quantities `heads-50` or `tails-50` gives us the right number of asterisks, but one expression will be positive and the other one will be negative. JavaScript has a function `Math.abs()` for the absolute value; that is, it makes all numbers—positive or negative—positive, implying that `Math.abs(heads-50)` is the number of asterisks to display.

As with the raw data, the line of asterisks will be added to `text` at the end of the inner loop. But how do we include a variable number of asterisks? With another iteration, of course. Specifically, replace the previous `text` assignment statement with the statement sequence

```
text = text + 'Trial ' + j + ': ';
for (i = 0; i < (Math.abs(heads-50)); i++) {
  text = text + '*';
}
text = text + '\n';
```

The line for the jth trial result begins with the text `"Trial j:  "`. Then, an iteration is performed in which asterisks are added one at-a time up to a total of `Math.abs(heads-50)`. We are at liberty to reuse the iteration variable `i` because its previous use as an iteration variable is complete. It is also fine to put the math function in the *<continuation>* test. (Notice that the WFI form tells us immediately that we have the right number of iterations.) Finally, after the iteration, the new-line character is added. My program generated the output shown at right.

In the sample output, we notice that the successive values of `j` are, indeed, 0 through 4, that Trial 2 evidently resulted in a 50–50 outcome, and that Trial 1 had the widest variation, being 6 away from perfect, that is, either 44–56 or 56–44.

We can revise the program to print the trials 1 through 5 by changing the `text` assignment to become

```
text = text + 'Trial ' + (j + 1) + ': ';
```

This is a very unusual statement because the + has two different meanings. The third + is addition, while the other three are concatenation. How does the computer know which one we mean? It looks to see if we are combining numbers (in which case, it adds) or strings (in which case, it concatenates). The special rule is that if there is one number and one string, it concatenates. So, the parentheses are required to cause the addition.

The final version of the coin-flipping program (Figure 20.1) uses three iterations, all of the "World Famous" form.

Though it is a mere 21 lines, the program embodies hundreds of statements' worth of computation. We could easily change to 1000 sample trials, and have much more computation performed for no additional lines of program. And that's the value of iteration: It allows very few lines of code to command the computer to do a lot of work.

INDEXING

If you're familiar with Elizabeth II, Super Bowl 25, *Rocky 3,* and Apollo 13, you are acquainted with indexing. *Indexing* is the process of creating a sequence of names by associating a base name with a number. When a new name is needed, the next number in sequence is used. Each indexed item is called an *element* of the base named object. Naturally, in programming, indexing has a special syntax. Indices are enclosed in square brackets in JavaScript, making `Apollo[13]` a syntactically correct indexed name. Having just learned about iteration, it is obvious why indexing might be an important idea in computing: Iterations can be used to refer to all elements of a name, that is, a finite specification like `A[j]` can, on successive iterations over `j`, refer to different elements.

> **Index Origin.** When indexing Super Bowls, monarchs, popes, Congresses, and so on, we usually start counting at 1, though often the first item doesn't initially get an index, for example, Queen Elizabeth I wasn't so named until Elizabeth II came along, but now she is. Yard lines in football begin indexing with 0 (goal = 0). Movie sequels start at 2 because there can't be a *sequel* to nothing. The point at which indexing begins, that is, the least index, is known as the *index origin.*

```
var heads=0, tails=0;                              //Counters
var i,j;                                           //Iteration variables
var text = '';                                     //Output accumulator
for (j=0;j<5; j++){                                //"Trials" iteration
  for (i=0;i<100; i++){                            //"Flips" iteration
    if (randNum(2))
      heads++;
    else
      tails++;
  }
  text = text + 'Trial ' + (j + 1) + ': ';
  for (i = 0; i < (Math.abs(heads-50)); i++) {     //"Star" iteration
                text = text + '*';
  }
  text = text + '\n';
  heads=0; tails=0;
}
alert(text);
function randNum(range) {
   return Math.floor(range*Math.random());
}
```

Figure 20.1. The final version of the coin-flip trials program.

An indexed base name is called an *array* in programming, and of course, arrays must be declared. In JavaScript, arrays are declared with the syntax

var <*variable*> = new Array(<*number of elements*>)

Notice that unlike queens—Elizabeth I became an array element when Elizabeth II came along—variables either are or are not arrays; they don't change. In the example declaration

```
var week = new Array(7);
```

`week` is the identifier being declared, and `new Array(7)` specifies that the identifier will be an array variable. The number in parentheses gives the number of array elements. *JavaScript uses index origin 0,* meaning that the least index of any array is 0, and the greatest index will be the number of elements minus 1. Thus the array just declared has elements `week[0]`, `week[1]`, ..., `week[6]`, that is, 7 elements. The number of elements in an array is its *length.* To refer to an array's length, use <*variable*>`.length`. For example, `week.length` ⇔ `7`. To summarize, here are the properties of arrays in JavaScript:

- Arrays are normal variables initialized by `new Array(`<*number of elements*>`)`.
- <*number of elements*> in the declaration is just that—the number of array elements.
- Array indexing begins at 0.
- The number of elements in an array is its *length.*
- The greatest index of an array is <*number of elements*> – 1 because of the 0-origin.

An array reference is the array name together with an *index*—a constant, variable, or expression—enclosed in brackets and evaluating to a nonnegative integer, the *index value*. The value must be less than the array's length. Thus statements

```
var  dwarf = new Array(7);            //Declarations use parentheses
var deux = 2;                         //Create value for examples
dwarf[0] = "Happy";                   //References use brackets
dwarf[1] = "Sleepy";                  //Index by a constant
dwarf[deux] = "Dopey";                //Index by a variable
dwarf[deux+1] = " Sneezy";            //Index by an expression
dwarf[2*deux] = "Bashful";
dwarf[3*deux-1] = "Grumpy";
dwarf[10-(2*deux)] = "Doc";
```

assign values to the array elements using a variety of index alternatives.

> **Sub Standard**. The index is also known as a *subscript*. In mathematics indices, being written below the line as in x_1 and y_2, are referred to as subscripts. Programming inherits the terminology but writes them in brackets.

When introducing the World Famous Iteration, we said the motivation for indexing from `0` to `n-1` would soon be evident. Now it's clear. The 0-origin iteration facilitates 0-origin indexing. Study the following version of the WFI

```
for (j = 0; j < week.length ; j++) {
   week[j] = dwarf[j] + " & " + dwarf[(j+1)%7] + " do dishes";
}
```

The variable `j` ranges over all of the elements of the array `week`. By using *<array name>*`.length` in the *<continuation>* clause of the control, everything is set up to enumerate all of the array's elements. This iteration creates entries of the form

```
week[0] ⇔ "Happy & Sleepy do dishes"

week[6] ⇔ "Doc & Happy do dishes"
```

by referring to a consecutive pair of elements from `dwarf`. To construct the final pair—Doc & Happy—which must "wraparound," we use *j+1 mod 7* to index the second reference to the `dwarf` array, that is, `(j+1)%7`, results in index value of 0 because (6+1) divided by 7 has a 0 remainder, which is Happy.

REGULARIZING ARRAY REFERENCES

An important concept was just illustrated in the *<statement list>* of the last `for`-loop.

```
for (j = 0; j < week.length ; j++) {
   week[j] = dwarf[j] + " & " + dwarf[(j+1)%7] + " do dishes";
}
```

The concept might be called *regularizing the array reference process*. Specifically, in a `for`-loop, a stream of consecutive numbers will be generated, which are the values of the iteration variable. In programming, our goal is to formulate index expressions using those numbers (and others) to reference the array elements making each repetition "work the same way." We *regularize* the referencing process.

For example, the `for`-loop will generate the numbers `0, 1, . . . , 6`, which will be the values of the iteration variable `j`. Using these numbers, we must reference each element of the `week` array, and because they correspond directly to indices needed, the `j` index in `week[j]` is correct. Similarly, for referencing the `dwarf` array with `dwarf[j]`. Because the next array reference is also to the `dwarf` array, though not to the `j`th element, but the `j+1`st element, we need to compute that index value using the iteration variable. Initially `dwarf[j+1]` looks to be satisfactory, but then what happens at the end of the array? In that case, `j+1` should be `0`, that is, wraparound, but instead it's `7`. There is no `dwarf[7]`, so `7` is an illegal index value. Thus `j+1` is part of the answer, but we need to handle the case of the last element.

One solution is to do this in two steps, iterating over all but the last element (`week.length-1`) referencing the next element as `j+1`, and then handling the last case separately and explicitly,

```
for (j = 0; j < week.length - 1 ; j++) {
   week[j] = dwarf[j] + " & " + dwarf[j + 1] + " do dishes";
}
week[6] = dwarf[6] + " & " + dwarf[0] + " do dishes";
```

The other approach is the "mod" solution as illustrated originally. It is more regular. Both schemes work, and the computer surely doesn't care which is used. Most programmers prefer the "mod" solution because it embodies a succinct statement of the entire process: Refer to the next element, with wrap-around. But they are equivalent.

To advance the regularization idea one more click, imagine that it's boring to wash dishes with the same helper each week. So, we decide to set up a rotation. In this case, the helper is not the next element of the `dwarf` array, that is, `j+1`, but rather some larger offset further down the list, for example, two down the list is `j+2`. In general, there will be a variable, `offset`, that is greater than 0 and gives the "distance" to the helper. Our original solution

```
for (j = 0; j < week.length ; j++) {
  week[j]=dwarf[j] + " & " + dwarf[(j + offset)%7] + " do dishes";
}
```

with `offset` replacing `1` still works, but the alternative two-step approach is not so easily modified. This easy conversion to the more general situation is a tangible benefit of our earlier "mod" approach that expressed the relationship as "refer to the next element, with wraparound." Now it expresses it as "refer to the element `offset` distance away, with wraparound." Such situations explain why programmers prefer the "mod" approach, and it illustrates the benefits of regularization.

Finally, if the array `week` corresponds to the days of the week, why should Grumpy always be stuck washing dishes on Friday nights? No wonder his disposition isn't as sunny as it might be. So, perhaps the rotation should shift the days of the week. That is, `week[0]` should be assigned two different washers according to some variable `rotate`, giving the place in the `dwarf` array to begin picking the primary washer, that is, the first of the two names. The `offset` should be the distance from this point on to the second name, with wrap-around of course. Again the "mod" solution can be trivially modified to incorporate the rotation idea because `j+rotate` takes the place of `j` in the previous solution, that is,

```
for (j = 0; j < week.length ; j++) {
  week[j] = dwarf[(j + rotate)%7] + " & " +
                dwarf[((j + rotate) + offset)%7] + " do dishes";
}
```

Of course, `j+rotate` can be larger than the maximum index, 6, and so requires the mod operator, too. Figure 20.2 illustrates some of the assignments using these various forms looping.

Original Statement: `week[j] = dwarf[j] + " & " + dwarf[(j+1)%7] + " do dishes";`

```
Happy & Sleepy do dishes
Sleepy & Dopey do dishes
Dopey & Sneezy do dishes
Sneezy & Bashful do dishes
Bashful & Grumpy do dishes
Grumpy & Doc do dishes
Doc & Happy do dishes
```

With `offset: week[j] = dwarf[j] + " & "+dwarf[(j + offset)%7] + " do dishes";`

```
offset ⇔ 2                              offset ⇔ 4
Happy & Dopey do dishes                 Happy & Bashful do dishes
Sleepy & Sneezy do dishes               Sleepy & Grumpy do dishes
Dopey & Bashful do dishes               Dopey & Doc do dishes
Sneezy & Grumpy do dishes               Sneezy & Happy do dishes
Bashful & Doc do dishes                 Bashful & Sleepy do dishes
Grumpy & Happy do dishes                Grumpy & Dopey do dishes
Doc & Sleepy do dishes                  Doc & Sneezy do dishes
```

With `rotate: week[j]=dwarf[(j+rotate)%7]+" & "+dwarf[((j+rotate)+offset)%7]+" do dishes";`

```
offset ⇔ 2, rotate ⇔ 2                  offset ⇔ 2, rotate ⇔ 4
Dopey & Bashful do dishes               Bashful & Doc do dishes
Sneezy & Grumpy do dishes               Grumpy & Happy do dishes
Bashful & Doc do dishes                 Doc & Sleepy do dishes
Grumpy & Happy do dishes                Happy & Dopey do dishes
Doc & Sleepy do dishes                  Sleepy & Sneezy do dishes
Happy & Dopey do dishes                 Dopey & Bashful do dishes
Sleepy & Sneezy do dishes               Sneezy & Grumpy do dishes
```

Figure 20.2. Example outputs from the three iterations of the Regularization section.

In summary, using iteration and arrays effectively involves regularizing the array references so that given the base set of values from the iteration variable, the indices needed for each iteration can be computed by a fixed expression. It is not always easy, and in some instances, it is so complicated that it is better to break the problem apart into separate loops. But generally, focusing on regularizing references using a given set of index values smoothes programming.

> **Why So Famous?** Our focus on computing the index with an expression explains why the "World Famous Iteration" is so popular. Because it's common to have to program *some* expression for the index values, it doesn't matter much whether the iteration variable counts starting at 0 or at 1 or at 14. The index expression can adjust the value as long as the *total* number of values is correct. The WFI does so, and it is more succinct than other iterations.

ANIMATION

As we know, movies, cartoons, and flipbooks animate by the rapid display of many still pictures known as *frames*. Human visual perception is relatively slow—presumably because of the amazingly complicated tasks it performs—so it is fooled into observing smooth motion when the *display rate* is about 30 frames per second, that is, 30 Hz. In this section, we learn the principles of online animation—like the Dymaxion Map of Chapter 6—and practice the concepts of indexing, arrays, and iteration.

Figure 20.3. The `.gif` images for the Busy Animation. These files are available at `www.aw.com/snyder/chapter20/framepix.html`

The animation we plan to construct is the familiar "busy" indicator, as shown in Figure 20.3. The eight frames contributing to the animation are shown with their indices. The rapid cyclic display of the frames makes the circle appear to revolve. Creating this Busy Animation is the goal of this section. (As always, it is recommended to write the program with the text both because it gives experience and speeds learning.)

Before you can successfully program an animation in JavaScript, you must understand three concepts:

- Using a timer to initiate animation events
- Prefetching the frames of the animation
- Redrawing a Web page image

As the ideas are introduced, we program the Busy Animation.

Timers to Initiate Animation

The animation we produce will be displayed by a Web browser. As we know, Web browsers are *event driven.* That is, they are told to perform some task, they do it, and then they sit idle waiting for some event to tell them to do the next task. If browsers are idle when they are not working on a task, how could they animate anything? Animations require action every 30 milliseconds. The obvious solution is to turn the activity of drawing the next frame into an event. The event will be the regular "ticking" of a clock. Use a timer analogy. We set a timer to wake up the browser to tell it to display the next frame, and then set it again for 30 milliseconds into the future. In 30 milliseconds, we repeat the process. In this way, we draw the frames at regular intervals creating an animation. Such a scheme is for *online animations.* Animations like *Toy Story* work differently. Not surprisingly, JavaScript comes equipped with all of the features, for example, timers, needed to implement online animation.

Though computers have extremely fast internal clocks, they're too fast for most programming purposes. Instead, programmer's timers typically "tick" once per millisecond. Timers are pretty intuitive. In JavaScript, the command to set a timer is

```
setTimeout("<event handler>", <duration>)
```

where *<event handler>* is a string giving the JavaScript computation that will run when the timer goes off, and *<duration>* is any positive number of milliseconds. For example, to display a frame in 30 ms using the function `animate()` as an event handler to display it, write `setTimeout("animate()", 30)`. Thirty milliseconds later, the computer will run the `animate()` function, displaying the frame. Of course, the last step for the `animate()` function must be to set the timer so that it "wakes up" again. Otherwise, the animation stops.[2]

Unlike mechanical timers, computer timers can keep track of many different times at once. How does the computer keep the settings straight? When we perform `setTimeout()`, we get back a special code—it's called a *handle*—that the computer uses to identify our timer. We can use the handle to refer to our timer, say, to

[2] "Every 30 milliseconds" is different from 30 times a second, of course, because 1000/30 = 33.333 ms. We can set the timer to 33 ms, but animation is not an exact science and 30 is close enough.

cancel it. For example, if we declare a variable, `timerID` with which to save the handle, and write

```
timerId = setTimeout("animate()", 30);
```

we can cancel the timer by writing

```
clearTimeout(timerID);
```

and the computer will know which of the timers it's keeping track of should be canceled.

Accordingly we will include two buttons to start and stop our animation. Their definitions will be

```
<input type=button value=Start onClick='setTimeout("animate()",30);'>
<input type=button value=Stop onClick='clearTimeout(timerID);'>
```

The Start button will set the timer for the first time. The animation keeps going on its own thereafter. Each time it is set, the handle is stored in `timerID`. Then, when the Stop button is clicked, it can clear the timer stopping the animation.

Prefetching Images

The next topic to consider is displaying images. Recall from Chapter 4 that to keep our Web pages tidy, we like to keep the `.gif` and `.jpg` images in a separate directory or folder. Accordingly, assume that the graphics files shown in Figure 20.3 are in a folder `gifpix`. Then the first of the images would be displayed on a Web page with the HTML

```
<img src="gifpix/Busy0.gif">
```

Toward the goal of writing our animation, we begin with the skeleton HTML page

```
<html><head><title>Busy Animation</title></head>
   <body><center>
     <img src=gifpix/Busy0.gif>        <!-- Intial Frame -->
   <form>
     <input type=button value=Start onClick='setTimeout("animate()",30);'>
     <input type=button value=Stop onClick='clearTimeout(timerID);'>
   </form>
   </center></body>
</html>
```

which includes the `<form>` tags and the two buttons.

We would like to overwrite that single image with all of the other `.gif` files in `gifpix` in sequence, one every 30ms. But we cannot do so directly. The problem is that loading the images will generally be too slow to allow us to show a new image so quickly. Web images must be transferred from the Web server across the Internet, where they encounter all sorts of delays. (We don't notice this while we're developing a Web application on our computers because all of the files are stored locally.) Consequently the strategy is to get the images first, store them locally so they will all be available in the computer memory, and then display them. The process of loading the images ahead of time is called *prefetching*.

Where will the eight images (`Busy0.gif` through `Busy7.gif`) of the `gifpix` folder be put? Because they are indexed already, it's logical to use an array. We'll name the array `pics`, and declare it

```
var pics = new Array (8);
```

indicating that it will have 8 elements. In order for the elements of the array to store an image, they must be initialized to an *image object*. Think of the image object as a skeleton that provides places for all of the information needed to store an image, such as its name, size of its 2 dimensions, and its actual pixels. To initialize the eight array elements to image objects requires an iteration and the `new Image()` operation,

```
for (i = 0; i < pics.length; i++) {
   pics[i] = new Image();
}
```

Among the places in the image object is a field called `src` where the image's source is stored, that is, the filename of the file containing the image. This is the string that we give in the `<img src="...">` tag. When we assign to the `src` field using dot notation, the browser saves the name and gets the file, storing it in memory, just as we require. Accordingly,

```
pics[0].src = "gifpix/Busy0.gif"
```

parallels our earlier explicit fetch of the initial frame. Because there are eight images in total, we use a loop,

```
for (i = 0; i < pics.length; i++) {
   pics[i].src = "gifpix/Busy" + i + ".gif";
}
```

which constructs the filenames on the fly. That is, we build up filename Busy*i*.gif using the iteration variable.

There is an important difference between the prefetching by assigning to the `.src` field of an image variable, and using `<img src="...">` in HTML. The former is not visible on the screen, whereas the latter is. This works to our advantage both ways The image variable, which is just a part of our JavaScript program, is not visible because it hasn't been placed on the page. But that's fine because we don't want the user to see the prefetch happening anyway. The `<img src="...">` tag places an image on the page, and so is visible. We need both.

Redrawing An Image

To animate the initial frame that we placed earlier with `<img src="...">`, we need to overwrite it with the images that we just prefetched at a rate of one every 30ms. How do we refer to the initial frame so as to overwrite it? Interestingly, Web browsers keep an array of the images in the HTML document that is just like our `pics` array. As the `<img src="...">` commands are encountered, the browser fills its `images` array just like we did. So, `document.images[0]` is the name of the first image, that is, our initial frame. Any additional `<img src="...">` images are indexed with higher numbers in sequence. The browser's `images` array elements have the `src` property too, and assigning to it overwrites the image. Thus, to change the initial frame, we write the assignment

```
document.images[0].src = pics[i].src;
```

which replaces the initial frame with the `i`th element of the `pics` array. All that needs to happen is to sweep through all of the `i` values, cyclically, one every 30 ms.

The `animate()` event handler overwrites the image, sets up for the next frame, and sets the timer to call itself again.

```
function animate () {
   document.images[0].src = pics[frame].src;
   frame = (frame + 1)%8;
   timerID = setTimeout ("animate()", 30);
}
```

With the concepts explained the whole Busy Animation, including the familiar Start and Stop buttons, is shown in Figure 20.4.

As a postscript to Busy Animation, the reader is encouraged to press Start several times, followed by an equal number of Stop clicks. Can you explain the behavior?

```
<html><head><title>Bars</title></head><body bgcolor=white><center>
<img src=gifpix/Busy0.gif>
<script>
   var i, frame = 0;                              //Iteration vars
   var timerID;                                   //Timer handle
   var pics = new Array (8);                      //Array to prefetch into
   for (i=0;i<pics.length ;i++) {                 //Init. array for images
       pics[i] = new Image();
   }
   for (i=0;i<pics.length;i++) {                  //Prefetch images
       pics[i].src = "gifpix/Busy" + i + ".gif";
   }
   function animate () {                          //Draw pic, call self
       document.images[0].src = pics[frame].src;  //Change pic
       frame = (1+frame)%8;                       //Move to next frame
       timerID = setTimeout("animate()", 30);     //Schedule next tick
   }
</script>
<form>
  <input type=button value=Start onClick='setTimeout("animate()",30)'>
  <input type=button value=Stop onClick='clearTimeout(timerID)'>
</form>
</center></body></html>
```

Figure 20.4. The Busy Animation, assuming that the eight `.gif` files are stored in a directory `gifpix`.

SUMMARY

Our interest in studying the fundamentals of programming has been to understand the sources of power in computation. The concepts of this chapter—iteration, indexing, and arrays—account for much of it. There is much more to say about programming, but we leave the rest of it to the experts.

The basics of `for`-loop iteration have been covered in detail. The `for`-statement has a control part in parentheses, and a <*statement list*> enclosed in curly braces. With each iteration, the entire statement list is iterated. The number of iterations is determined by assignments to and tests of the *iteration variable* as specified in the control part. In the JavaScript `for`-statement, the <*initialization*> component is executed first. Then, prior to each iteration, including the first, the <*continuation*> predicate is tested. If it is `true`, the <*statement list*> is performed; otherwise, it is skipped, and the `for`-statement terminates. After each iteration, the <*next iteration*> operation is performed. The principles of iteration ensure that every iteration contains a test, and that the test is dependent on variables that change in the loop.

The `for`-statement is capable of a large range of variation. The <*initialization*> can begin anywhere, the <*continuation*> test can stop the loop anywhere, and the <*next iteration*> operation can step by various amounts as well as count upward or downward. Though for-loops of many forms can be written, programmers have gotten into the habit of using the World Famous Iteration—a stylized iteration, that begins at 0, tests that the iteration variable is strictly less than some limit, and increments by 1. There is no obligation to use the WFI, but doing so has the advantage that you can quickly determine the number of times around the loop—it's the limit to the right of <. Because it is common to make errors figuring out the number of iterations, programmers get in the habit of using the WFI. Ultimately, after we studied the topic of regularization, we realized that the starting and ending points for a loop are less important than the total number of iterations because the index value can be adjusted with an expression, further encouraging the use of the WFI.

Indexing is the process of creating a sequence of names by associating a number with a base name. Need more names? Count out more numbers. Indexed variables are known as arrays in programming. Like ordinary variables, arrays must be declared, but they use the `new Array(`<*length*>`)` syntax, where <*length*> is the number of elements of the array. Array elements—referenced by giving the name and a nonnegative index in brackets—can be used like ordinary variables. Using many examples, we showed how arrays and iteration could be effectively used together. In particular, regularizing array computations—figuring out how to refer to related array elements using the successive values of an iteration variable—is a key programming activity.

Random numbers were used as an interesting context in which to practice iterations. Though computers cannot create true random numbers, they can produce pseudo-random numbers, which can pass the same statistical tests as random numbers. Random numbers are used extensively in programming.

Finally, we introduced some basic concepts of online animation. All animations achieve the appearance of motion by rapidly displaying a series of still frames. For animating information displayed by a Web browser, it is advisable to prefetch the images so that they are readily accessible for rapid display. The key idea is to use a timer to create events, and then use the timer-event handler to redraw an image that has been placed on the Web page by the `<img src="...">` tag. These are referenced as the elements of the document's `images` array.

EXERCISES

1. How does an iteration variable differ from a standard variable in JavaScript?
2. What are the three components of a `for`-loop? In what order does the `for`-loop specification require them to be given?
3. Following the example of the "emphatic `for`-loop" of the text, write a `for`-loop that prints `"I Love You! \n"` 12 times followed by the text `"If I've said it once, I've said it a dozen times, I Love You!"` (Recall that `"\n"` is the New-line character.)
4. What changes are required in Ex. 3 to iterate the phrase 24 times?
5. Define a variable `count` initialized to 1000. Write a `for`-loop that prints *on a Web page* the "I Love You!" phrase `count` number of times. Print the phrase to a Web page—don't use `Alert()`, it's not appropriate now—by using `document.write("I Love You!  ")`. Add the phrase, "If I've said it once, I've said it 1000 times, I Love You!" but use the value of the `count` variable rather than the specific value of 1000.
6. How would Ex. 5 have to be changed to print "I Love You!" 10,000 times?

7. Using the World Famous Iteration form, write three `for`-loops, iterating `12`, `count` and `lower_limit + 20` times, respectively, and with iteration variables `j`, `k`, and `tic`, respectively.
8. Change the iteration for 5! given in the Reference to Iteration Variable subsection to use the World Famous Iteration form.
9. How does the phrase "You will practice that over and over until you get it right!" meet the requirements of the Fundamental Principle of Iteration?
10. In a pair of nested loops, why must the outer loop use a different iteration variable than the inner loop?
11. What changes are required for the program in Figure 20.1 to increase the sample size from 100 to 1000?
12. Following the example in Figure 20.2, compute the results of the `for`-loop when `rotate` ⇔ 4 and `offset` ⇔ 2.
13. If the array `week` has been initialized to the names of the weekdays, what does

    ```
    week[numRand(7)] = "Party Day!";
    ```

    compute ?
14. Why does pressing start multiple times cause the Busy Animation to go faster?

CHAPTER 21

Algorithmic Problem Solving

Learning Objectives

- Learn the Decomposition Principle.
- Understand how the Decomposition Principle is applied to the Smooth Motion task.
- Acquire experience with time-driven animations.
- Learn how mouse events are generated and handled.
- Acquire experience with key-driven animations.
- Learn how to recognize continuity across events.
- Understand when and how to use iteration statements.
- Learn to use functions to reduce complexity.

The programming that we've learned indicates how computers solve problems and what the source of their speed and versatility is. Further, we've learned enough programming that we could embellish our Web pages, making them more adaptive and dynamic. But the great value of the knowledge we've acquired is neither insight nor embellishments. Rather we can apply the programming ideas to general problem-solving situations. Processes, procedures, instructions and directions, decision-making, and so forth are phenomena we meet in daily life beyond the sphere of computers. Our knowledge applies in all of those cases, making us more effective at learning, performing, and planning tasks. Practicing these skills by solving a more substantial task is the topic of this chapter.

Though the ideas have broad application, our interest and preparation are still with IT. Accordingly, the task we will solve is a Web application, Smooth Motion, for testing a user's coordination at manipulating the mouse. How smooth are you? The application will use event programming, including "mouse events," animation, controls, more sophisticated HTML, functions, iteration, indexing, and arrays. Smooth

Motion is a generic application that allows us to focus on the problem solving activity. By patiently following this fully worked example, we will have opportunities to discuss when and how to apply the ideas we have learned. When the chapter is complete, you will be prepared to work on a complex project of your own. And it is recommended that you do because problem solving benefits most from experience.

THE TASK

Step 0 in solving any problem is to understand what must be accomplished. (Almost everything in this chapter is 0-origin!) The Smooth Motion application is a coordination test. The user interface is shown in Figure 21.1. Naming the components from top to bottom as an aid to discussing them, we have

- **Heading**: the text "Smooth Motion"
- **Grid:** the 7 × 20 grid of squares
- **Keys:** the row of seven brown/orange boxes
- **Controls:** the buttons and radio settings
- **Instructions:** the text at the bottom

Further, the components are enclosed in a one-column table with a border and a colored background.

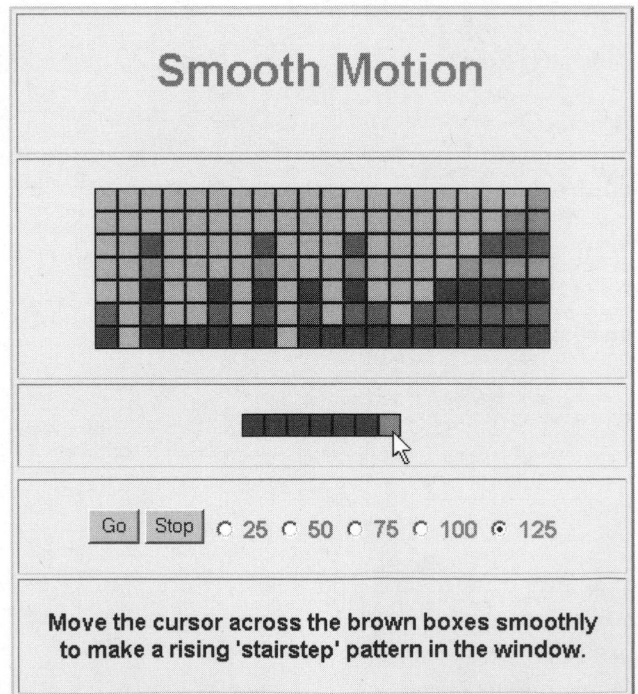

Figure 21.1. The Smooth Motion application user interface. Try it at `www.aw.com/snyder/chapter21/smooth.html`.

Smooth Motion works as follows. The application starts up automatically five seconds after it is loaded. It begins filling the Grid from the right with random height stacks of blocks. The blocks move steadily to the left at a rate determined by the Controls. Examples of the random stacks of blocks are shown in the left half of the Grid in Figure 21.1. The random stack generation continues until the user places the mouse cursor over one of the Keys. At that point, the user is in control of the stacks of blocks displayed in the Grid. If the mouse is over Key *n*, a stack of *n* blocks appears in the Grid, leftmost Key = 1, rightmost Key = 7. Figure 21.1 shows the 7-block stack being selected by the cursor on Key 7. When the user has created a perfect staircase rising to the right, the action stops. The process can be started or stopped at any point using the Go and Stop buttons. The speed selections are given in milliseconds and describe the rate at which the Grid moves left. The test requires a smooth mouse motion across the Keys from left to right at a rate corresponding to the frame rate of the Grid animation.

The task is to create the Smooth Motion application. It is a substantial project, though surprisingly it requires only a modest amount of HTML and JavaScript.

Note: Before reading about problem solving in this chapter, spend five minutes thinking about how you would solve this problem. Truly, thinking about your own solution first will speed understanding the chapter.

A STRATEGY FOR PROBLEM SOLVING

The goal is to design and construct the Smooth Motion application. Achieving such a goal entails a substantial design with several functions and some intricate logic. A complicating factor is that we have both timer events for the animation and mouse events for the controls taking place simultaneously. Most of us would never succeed with such an effort by trying to "brain it out." The complications of the project would overwhelm us. Instead, we will succeed by approaching it in a methodical step-by-step way, applying an important divide-and-conquer technique to simplify our work. By breaking the project into convenient, manageable pieces, we will succeed.

A fundamental strategy for solving complex problems is the following principle:

> **Decomposition Principle**: Divide a large task into smaller independent subtasks that can be solved separately and then be combined to produce the overall solution.

Of course, the subtasks may not be small enough to be worked out easily, so the Decomposition Principle can be applied again to each of the subtasks, producing even smaller subtasks, and so on. Eventually the components become small enough that it is possible to figure out how to solve them directly. When the subtasks are all solved, we begin the assembly process, combining the most primitive components to produce the more complex components, and so on until the overall problem is solved. The Decomposition Principle is little more than common sense, but when applied judiciously, it is a powerful technique for achieving large results.

The Smooth Motion application has several parts that provide an obvious beginning point for applying the Decomposition Principle:

Task	**Description**
Graphic User Interface (GUI)	Creating a Web page with the table and its constituent parts: Title, Grid, Keys, Controls, and Instructions
Animation of the Grid	Moving the block stacks to the left
Sensing of the Keys	Handling the mouse events and transferring the control information to the Grid animator
Detecting Staircase	Recognizing when among a stream of events the user has "met the test"
Control Construction	Implementing the actions to control the application
Overall Design	Building the automatic random start-up, handling the starting and stopping, setting the speeds, and interconnecting the other components

Only the GUI task is simple enough to be solved directly, and even it is fancier than the pages we've constructed so far. All of the other tasks require further decomposition when we start to solve them.

Decomposing the problem into parts is Step Number One in solving it. Step Number Two is to strategize how to solve each of the parts.

The strategy concerns mostly in what order to solve the parts. For example, because JavaScript programming usually needs a Web page to host the computation, it makes sense to begin with the GUI Task rather than any of the others. Such an approach gives us a place to test and save the solutions to the other tasks. The page becomes an organizing structure, a location where we record our progress by adding our JavaScript code to it. One pitfall to avoid, however, is spending hours constructing a splashy Web page only to discover that it doesn't fit well with the solutions to the other tasks. Such a mistake won't happen here—this is a "textbook example" after all—but it is an error to avoid on other projects. Nevertheless, in recognition of this pitfall, we only build a basic page and delay embellishing it until the final step.

So, our strategic decision is to build the host page as a first step, but only the basic primitive page, and wait to embellish the design until all of the parts are working. Thus we're splitting the GUI construction into two parts.

Basics First. Though our problem is too small to illustrate it, there is a problem solving strategy that creates a working prototype first before completing the whole design. This is smart because it is easier to add to an already-working design. Our plan to focus on the core solution and leave the cosmetic features to the end is in the spirit of this approach.

Deciding the order in which to solve the other tasks requires considering the *task dependencies*. That is, some tasks—for example, Detection of the Staircase—*rely on* or *depend on* the solution of other tasks such as Sensing the Keys. Tasks that do not rely on the solution of any other tasks are *independent*. Independent tasks should be done first. Tasks that depend on the independent tasks can be done next, tasks that depend on them can follow, and so on. All of the tasks could be mutually dependent, though this is rare. In that case the dependent tasks are started, pushed as far as possible until they absolutely need the results of another task, and then are interrupted to work on the other task. For us, GUI construction is the independent task, and the Grid Animation task is dependent only on it. So, we'll schedule it second. Key Sensing is also dependent only on the GUI, but it is easier to test with the Grid Animation task complete. It will be our third task.

It Depends. Keeping track of many dependencies can be confusing, so systems engineers and managers draw a *task dependency graph*, or PERT chart. Standing for Program Evaluation and Review Technique, PERT charts were developed by the U.S. Navy in the 1950s. There are several ways to draw them; we place tasks in circles and use arrows to show dependencies.

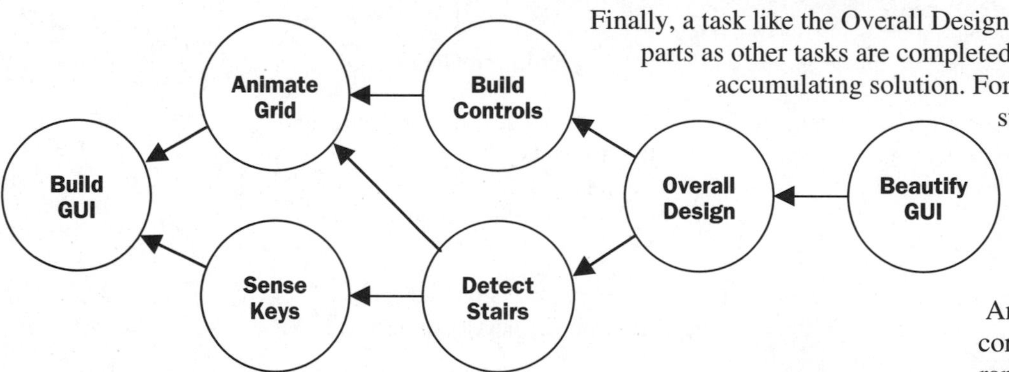

Figure 21.2. A task dependency diagram, also known as a PERT chart, drawn so that tasks are in circles and arrows can be read as "task at tail of arrow depends on task at head of arrow."

Finally, a task like the Overall Design task is often solved in parts as other tasks are completed and fitted into the accumulating solution. For example, one of the steps in the Overall Design task is to set up the automatic start with the randomly generated block stacks. We will find that when the Grid Animation is complete, it is convenient to set up the random generation of blocks as a means of testing the animation. So that step will be solved ahead of time. Nevertheless, it is wise to keep the Overall Design task in the To Do List because even if many of its subtasks have already been solved, it will still be the point at which the loose ends are tied up. See Figure 21.2.

Summarizing our strategy:

- Construct the basic structure of the Web page for the GUI.
- Solve the Grid Animation task, which is dependent only on the GUI.
- Solve the Key Sensing task, which is dependent only on the GUI.
- Solve the Staircase Detection task, a task dependent on Animation and Key Sensing.
- Solve the Control Construction task, a task dependent on Animation.
- Solve the Overall Design task, wrap up those parts not yet complete.
- Embellish the Web page.

Usually each of these tasks would be further simplified using the Decomposition Principle until all of its subtasks were simple enough to solve directly. Doing so ensures that the decomposition has produced a practical solution technique. For our purposes, we will use a slightly different strategy, choosing instead to assign a section to each task and applying the Decomposition Principle at the start of the section.

BASIC STRUCTURAL WEB PAGE TASK

Writing the HTML for a Web page is by now routine. The form of the Smooth Motion application page is fancier than is needed to work out the programming details. So, we create the basic structure and plan to embellish it later when the application is completely working. Call this the Structural Page. For present purposes, the "basic" features include the background color, font style and color, and the centering of the application on the page.

The Structural Page will contain a five-row, one-column table; the text for the Heading and Instructions; and the buttons of the Control section. As we learned making the Memory Bank Web page in Chapter 19, it is easiest to build tables "inside out," using copy and paste. That is, we construct a generic table cell with `<td>` tags, replicate that to make a row enclosed in `<tr>` tags, and then replicate the row to make the whole table enclosed in `<table>` tags. Then we fill it in. Because the table has only one column, it's not necessary to replicate the cells to make a row for the present situation. For us, the "generic" table cell is centered and contains a single blank character. The "basic" table has a border.

For the Heading text we use an `<h1>` heading and for the Instructions, a paragraph tag. Because the Instructions have a different text color than the other text on the page, we must set its font color.

The graphic and the HTML for the Structural Web page definition are shown in Figure 21.3. Notice that the middle three rows contain only white space, so they do not show. However, they are defined in the HTML, providing a site for our next programming, the Grid Animation.

GRID ANIMATION TASK

The Grid Animation task must animate the $7 \times 20 = 140$ grid of blocks moving from right to left. This task is much too complicated to "brain out" directly, so we apply the Decomposition Principle again. Luckily, the Busy Animation of Chapter 20 illustrated the basic steps of animation:

- Define the initial image.
- Prefetch the frames for updating the image.
- Set a timer with an event handler that updates the image.

These then are our starting decomposition for the Grid Animation. But these three don't solve the problem. We need to think and strategize further.

How will we organize the rapid redrawing of 140 images, keeping track of each block's trajectory? Reviewing how the application is supposed to work, we notice first that it only discusses "stacks" of blocks. This implies that there is no "motion" of images vertically, only horizontally. (This is obvious by the color scheme, too.) And, the horizontal motion is limited only to moving from right to left. From these observations we can conclude that we don't have to animate individual squares at all. The images can be whole columns. That simplification reduces the total number of images on the Web page to 20, that is, the number of columns. Of course, we will need a frame image for each stack of blocks, that is, a 0-stack, a 1-stack, . . . , and a 7-stack, resulting in a total of eight frames. So, one new subtask is to define and organize the column frames

```
<html>
    <head><title>Smooth Motion Application</title></head>
    <body bgcolor="white" text="#FF6600"><font face='Helvetica'><center>
      <table border=2>
       <tr> <td align="center">
      <h1>Smooth Motion</h1>
            </td></tr>
       <tr> <td align="center">
            </td></tr>
       <tr> <td align="center">
            </td></tr>
       <tr> <td align="center">
            </td></tr>
       <tr> <td align="center">
      <p><font color='black'><b>
              Move the cursor across the brown boxes smoothly <br>
              to make a rising 'staircase' pattern in the window.</b></font></p>
            </td></tr>
     </table></center>
     </body>
</html>
```

Smooth Motion

Move the cursor across the brown boxes smoothly
to make a rising 'staircase' pattern in the window.

Figure 21.3. Image and HTML for the Structural Web page; the formatting has been compressed to save space.

The next inference we can draw based on the decision to treat whole columns as a unit concerns the "motion of an image." The image in column *i* of the Grid at a given time step is replaced on the next time step by the image in column *i+1*, assuming that the 20-column images are indexed from left to right. See Figure 21.4. (They will be indexed from 0, left to right, because as was mentioned in Chapter 20, when browsers place images on the page, they record them in the array `document.images` in the order encountered; that order is the construction sequence of an HTML page, top to bottom, left to right. So, the leftmost column of the Grid is `document.images[ 0]` .) Thus the action is to replace the contents of `document.images[ i]` with the contents of `document.images[ i+1]` . That is slightly different from our Busy Animation from Chapter 20 where we always assigned one of the prefetched frames. Nevertheless, shifting each column to the left is quite easy, and it leaves only the last column to be handled differently.

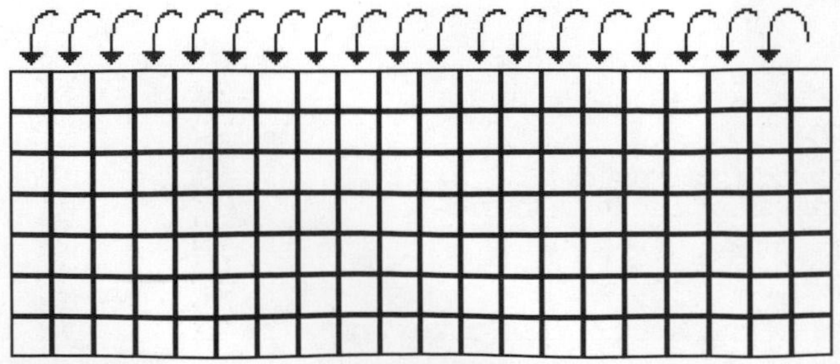

Figure 21.4. With column 0 at the left, the image in column i should become the image in column i+1 to implement the left moving motion for the Grid Animation event handler.

Handling the 19th column (last) is easy because we only need to assign a new image, that is, one of the eight frames. Which frame do we assign? If we are in the random start-up phase, it should be a random frame. If we are in user-controlled phase, it should be whichever frame the user has specified. We will leave this choice of the frame open for the time being because the Overall Design Task will set the frame selection properly.

Because the image shifting and the end frame selection activities are part of the event handler, they don't require a new subtask. In effect, we just figured out how to solve the event handler subtask. It doesn't require a new subtask; it only requires that we use this solution when we construct the event handler we originally planned. So our subtask list for the Grid Animation Task is:

- Define and organize the eight columnar frames.
- Define the initial images, 0 through 19.
- Prefetch the eight frames for updating the image.
- Set a timer with an event handler that shifts the images in columns 1 through 19 to columns 0 through 18, respectively, and introduces a new frame into column 19.

We'll assign a subsection to each subtask.

Define and Organize the Frames

The eight frames for the Smooth Motion application are shown in Figure 21.5. The files are available online[1] and need not be created. Notice that they have names indexed in accordance with the block height. Also, the images have the necessary colors and lines to be placed densely side-by-side to construct the Grid.

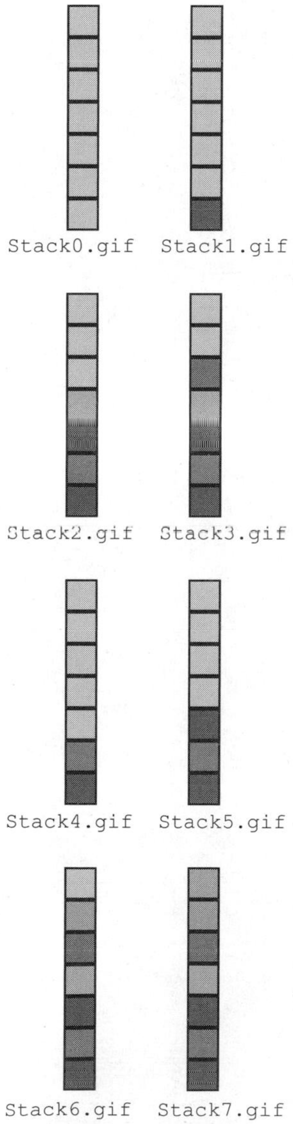

If the `gif` frames had not been available, they would have had to be created. Numerous tools are available for this purpose, from simple paint programs to sophisticated image editing facilities. Though the tools vary in capabilities, convenience, and sophistication, there are only two guidelines to follow when creating frame images for animations with any of these tools:

- Ensure that all images overwriting one another have the same dimensions in pixels; an easy way to meet this constraint is to create an initial "blank" frame, save it, and use it as the base for creating all of the other frames.
- Ensure that all files are saved using either the `.gif` or `.jpg` formats, and that they are used consistently, that is, only overwrite `.gifs` with `.gifs`.

Try creating frame files for your own animations.

To use images in HTML, it is recommended that they be placed in a separate directory, simply as an organizing technique. Following that advice, the stack `gifs` of Figure 21.5 will be saved in a directory called `gifpix`, meaning that their names relative to the HTML file are `gifpix/Stack0.gif`, `gifpix/Stack1.gif`, etc.

Define Initial Images

This subtask constructs the Grid in the second row of the Structural Page. The initial state of the Grid is created from 20 copies of `Stack0.gif`. As usual, to place an image on a page, the `<img src="...">` tag is used. But the 20 images will require

Stack0.gif Stack1.gif

Stack2.gif Stack3.gif

Stack4.gif Stack5.gif

Stack6.gif Stack7.gif

Figure 21.5. The eight frames required for the Smooth Motion application.

[1] `www.aw.com/snyder/chapter21/framepix.html`

20 such tags. This obviously calls for loop. To use JavaScript's `for`-statement, we place the `<script>` tags inside of the second row's `<td>` tags, and within them write the necessary JavaScript. Of course, to have the images appear on the Structural Page, we must place them using the `document.write()` facility.

The iteration can use the World Famous Iteration form and must declare an iteration variable. The necessary code to implement these objectives is

```
<script language='JavaScript'>
   var j;                                      //Declare iteration var
   for (j = 0; j < 20; j++) {                  //Initialize Grid images
     document.write('<img src="gifpix/Stack0.gif">');
   }
</script>
```

which completes the image initialization.

Prefetch the Frame Images

As explained in Chapter 20, animating with images fetched from across the Internet is not likely to work because of delays that the `gif` files might encounter during transfer. So, prefetching is necessary, and it is the goal of this subtask. (Review prefetching from the Busy Animation, if necessary.)

Relative to the creation of the Web page, the prefetching activity can be performed at any time prior to the start of the animation. Because the prefetching also requires JavaScript code, we decide to place it with the code from the initialization subtask just completed, say, after the declaration. This is a good location because to prefetch the frames, we need an eight-element image array to prefetch into, and so we will need another declaration for that array.

The three steps of prefetching are as follows:

1. Declare the array into which the images will be fetched.
2. Initialize the array elements to be image objects, that is, define the image structure for each array element using the `new Image()` constructor.
3. Assign the names of the files to the `src` fields of the image objects, causing the browser to record the names and get the files and thus implementing the prefetch.

The filenames are those given in Figure 21.5, of course. We will call the array `pics`, and use a separate iteration for the second and third tasks, though combining the two operations into a single iteration is equivalent. The resulting code

```
var pics = new Array(8);            //Declare array for frames
for (j = 0; j < 8; j++) {           //Make the elements images
   pics[j] = new Image();
}
for (j = 0; j < 8; j++) {           //Name source file & prefetch
   pics[j].src = "gifpix/Stack" + j + ".gif";
}
```

is inserted within the previous `<script>` tags, after the declaration. Notice that the filename is constructed on the fly to save us from typing separate statements.

Set Timer and Build Timer Event Handler

The subtask is mostly concerned with writing the event handler to move each of the Grid's images left one position, obliterating the 0th image and assigning a new frame to the 19th image. So we begin by constructing that event handler, called `animate()`. As we work on it, several additional details will arise that will require our attention.

The timer event handler `animate()` has three operations:

1. To move all images left one position.
2. To assign a new frame to the 19th image.
3. To schedule itself for sometime in the future.

The mechanism for choosing the new frame is not yet worked out, but the Overall Design Task will resolve it. For the moment, we simply assign a random frame as an easy way to have something different happening on each tick. And, assigning random frames is the way the application is to begin anyway.

Recalling that browsers store the details of the images they display in an array called `images`, that the array is referenced as `document.images`, and that the source field, `src`, is the relevant one to change if we want a new image displayed, we program the `animate()` operations as

```
function animate() {
  for (j = 0; j < 19; j++) {                              //Shift L 1
       document.images[j].src = document.images[j+1].src;
  }
  document.images[19].src = pics[randNum(8)].src;         //New image
  timerId = setTimeout("animate()", duration);            //Set timer
}
```

where the `randNum()` function developed in Chapter 19,

```
function randNum (range) {
    return Math.floor(range * Math.random());
}
```

must also be included, and a variable `duration`

```
var duration = 125;
```

must be added to the accumulating list of declarations.

To get the process started automatically after five seconds, we include before the function definitions the additional statement

```
timerId = setTimeout("animate()", 5000);
```

setting the `animate()` function to be run 5000 ms after the browser starts. As with the Busy Animation, we save the handle received from the `setTimeout` function in a variable `timerId` (it must be declared!) so that the animation can be stopped. And, with that code, the Set Timer subtask is completed, completing the Grid Animation task. Figure 21.6 shows the state of the Structural Page at this point.

```
<html>
    <head><title>Smooth Motion Application</title></head>
    <body bgcolor="white"
           text="#FF6600"><font
           FACE='Helvetica'><center>
      <table border=2>
       <tr> <td align="center">
          <h1>Smooth Motion</h1>
             </td></tr>
       <tr> <td align="center">
     <script>
        var j;
        var duration = 125, timerId;
        var pics = new Array(8);
        for (j = 0; j < 8; j++) {
           pics[j] = new Image();
        }
        for (j = 0; j < 8; j++) {
           pics[j].src = "gifpix/Stack" + j + ".gif";
        }
        for (j = 0; j < 20; j++) {
           document.write('<img src="gifpix/Stack0.gif">');
        }
     </script>
             </td></tr>
       <tr> <td align="center">
             </td></tr>
       <tr> <td align="center">
             </td></tr>
       <tr> <td align="center">
         <P><font color='black'><B>
            Move the cursor across the brown boxes smoothly <BR>
            to make a rising 'staircase' pattern in the window.</B></font></P>
             </td></tr>
      </table></center>
     <script language='JavaScript'>
        timerId = setTimeout("animate()", 5000);
        function animate() {
           for (j = 0; j < 19; j++) {
              document.images[j].src = document.images[j+1].src;
           }
           document.images[19].src = pics[randNum(8)].src;
           timerId = setTimeout("animate()", duration);
        }
        function randNum (range) {
           return Math.floor(range * Math.random());
        }
     </script>
    </body>
</html>
```

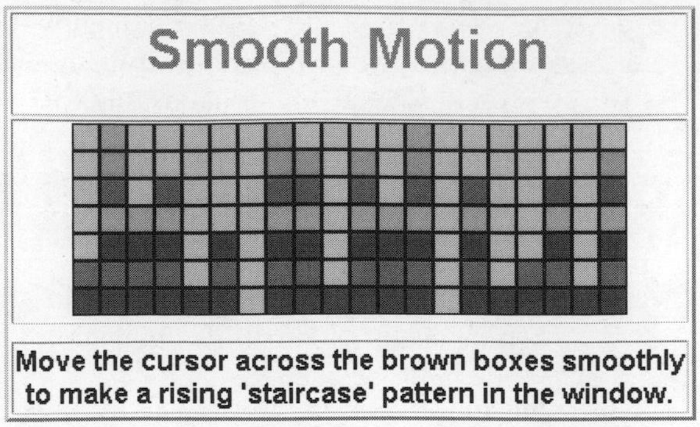

Figure 21.6. Status of the Smooth Motion implementation after the completion of the Grid Animation task.

THE BEST LAID PLANS . . .

The third and next step in our task decomposition strategy is to solve Key Sensing. However, now that we have the Grid Animation worked out, we find it very cumbersome not to be able to start and stop the animation on demand. It would be very helpful to have the Controls available to stop the animation so we don't have to kill the browser application. But the Control Construction task is planned for later. Perhaps it makes more sense to solve it now to simplify our subsequent development. As Robert Burns noted, our plans don't always work out no matter how thoughtfully we developed them.[2] Adjusting the order of tasks is very typical of large projects because it isn't possible to figure out all of the relevant interactions ahead of time. So, we proceed to Control Construction.

Inspecting the GUI in Figure 21.1, we see that the Controls entry of the table contains seven input controls. Thus the fourth element of the table must contain `<form>` tags enabling us to specify the controls. After the two previous chapters, the physical form of the controls should be routine. The only challenge is in how to handle the click-events. As always, we ask, "What should happen when the control is clicked?" There are three cases:

- Go button click-event: Start the animation with `setTimeout()`, keeping track of the handle.
- Stop button click-event: End the animation by clearing the timer using the handle.
- Radio button click-event: Set the timer interval by assigning to `duration`.

None of these activities is more than a single statement, so rather than creating functions for the event handlers, we simply place the code in the control specification.

Implementing these plans for the Control section of the application, we write

```
<form>
   <input type=button value=Go
      onClick='timerId=setTimeout("animate()",duration)'>
   <input type=button value=Stop
      onClick="clearTimeout(timerId)">
   <input type=radio name=speed onClick="duration=25"> 25
   <input type=radio name=speed onClick="duration=50"> 50
   <input type=radio name=speed onClick="duration=75"> 75
   <input type=radio name=speed onClick="duration=100"> 100
   <input type=radio name=speed
      onClick="duration=125" checked=true> 125
</form>
```

and place the code in the fourth row of the table of the Structural Page. We could have used a `for`-loop to place the radio buttons, but only the first four are amenable to a loop because the last one must be `checked` to indicate that `duration`⇔125 is the default. But with the required `<script>` tags, building the text as part of a `document.write`, and so on, it seemed more straightforward just to use Copy-Paste-Edit.

Having completed the Control Construction Task, we can start and stop the animation. "We now return to our originally scheduled program."

[2] Burns put it more poetically, of course, *The best laid plans of mice and men gang aft agley.*

Key Sensing Task

The Key Sensing task implements the ability to recognize when the mouse is over a given Key. The task requires us to understand how mouse motions are sensed, a topic that has not yet been introduced. But, it's typical when solving a large problem not to know all of the constituent ideas and to have to learn about a new idea, system, or operation to solve the task. That's our situation with respect to sensing mouse motions. So, before attempting the task decomposition, we find out about mouse motions.

Actually, sensing mouse motions is very easy. Browsers recognize events on the objects of a Web page like images just as they recognize events caused by controls. For example, if we click on an image, we cause a click-event, which we can process with an event handler specified by the onClick attribute of the image tag, as in <img src="..." onClick="doSomething()">. Thus objects other than controls can have events. Mouse motions are events of exactly this type.

The browser, with the help of the operating system, is keeping track of where the mouse pointer is at any moment. (After all, it's the operating system that is drawing the mouse pointer in the first place.) When the mouse pointer moves over an image or other Web page object, a *MouseOver*-event is recognized. When the mouse pointer moves off of the object, a *MouseOut*-event is recognized. These are the two events that we need to follow the mouse cursor across the keys. The keys are images, so all we do is write an event handler for each of the two mouse events and specify them to the browser by the onMouseOver and onMouseOut event handler specifications in the <img src=""> tag defining the key's image.

With that information, we can decompose the Key Sensing task by asking, "How should Key Sensing work?" First, we notice that there are no keys yet (see Figure 21.6), so we'll have to define them. Second, after thinking about their operation—they change their color from brown to orange on MouseOver and then change back to brown on MouseOut—it's clear that the Keys are effectively another animation. The difference between the other animations we've written and the Keys is that the others are updated by a timer, whereas the Keys are updated by mouse motions. This observation is a tremendous help to our planning because we have solved animation problems before. So, we begin our problem decomposition with the standard animation decomposition used for the Grid Animation:

- Define and organize the necessary frames.
- Place the initial images, creating the keys.
- Prefetch the frames.
- Build the event handlers.

This is a sufficient strategy to solve the problem.

The first subtask involves only two images, and , available on the Web with the Stack images. They are known as BrownBox.gif and OrangeBox.gif and will be stored in the gifpix directory with the Stack images. Moving the files to that directory completes the first subtask.

Placing the images creates the Keys. Seven images will be placed in the center of the third row of the Structural Page's table. They are all the BrownBox.gif. As before, we write a JavaScript loop to iterate the document.write of the <img src=""> tags. The resulting code, which is still incomplete—but will be fixed momentarily—is

```
for (j = 0; j < 7; j++) {                                    //Incomplete
    document.write('<img src="gifpix/BrownBox.gif">');
}
```

which completes the placement subtask for the time being.

Prefetching the frames is also completely analogous to our earlier animations, and by now its three-subtask sequence is becoming familiar. There are only two frames to prefetch, leading to the declaration of a small array

```
var keypix = new Array(2);
```

simple code for image initialization

```
keypix[0] = new Image();
keypix[1] = new Image();
```

and prefetching

```
keypix[0].src = "gifpix/BrownBox.gif";
keypix[1].src = "gifpix/OrangeBox.gif";
```

because it isn't worth writing loops. These lines complete the prefetch subtask.

Finally, the two event handlers, `here()` for MouseOver and `gone()` for MouseOut, pose the most interesting aspect of Key Sensing though they're still not difficult. As with any event handler, we ask, "What should happen when the mouse moves over a key?" First, the key must change color to give feedback to the user that the mouse is on or off the key. This is simply updating the key's image with the `OrangeBox.gif` or the `BrownBox.gif` image. But how do we refer to the key's image? We know that it will be listed in the `images` array that the browser keeps of the images on the page. Because the Keys come after the Grid, the Key images will obviously be stored in the array after the Grid images. The Grid images are `images[ 0]`, . . . , `images[ 19]`, so by the preceding loop, the Keys must be `images[ 20]`, . . . , `images[ 26]`. Of course, if we know the position of the key, say, `pos`, we can refer to the image as `images[ 20+pos]`. We conclude that we need to record the position of each key in the sequence.

Next the mouse sensing event handlers must tell the Grid Animation event handler which new Stack image to draw in the last position of the Grid. All that that event handler needs is the key's position, so if we assign it to a global variable, say, `frame`, we've done the job. These observations lead us to declare a variable `frame` and to define

```
function here (pos) {
   document.images[20+pos].src = "gifpix/OrangeBox.gif";
   frame = pos + 1;
}
function gone (pos) {
   document.images[20+pos].src = "gifpix/BrownBox.gif";
   frame = 0;
}
```

as the two mouse event handlers. We have made the key's position a parameter. Notice that when we assign to the variable `frame` in `here()`, the `MouseOver` handler, we set frame to `pos+1` because the 0-origin of the keys is one less than the number of blocks in the stack, that is, the position with index 0 must cause `Stack1.gif` to be drawn. Also, notice that for `gone()`, the `MouseOut` handler, `frame` is set to 0. This is right because the mouse may be moving off the keys entirely, which should draw the `Stack0.gif`. If the mouse moves to another key, its `MouseOver` event handler will be called immediately, setting `frame` to the right number.

With the two mouse event handlers defined, we return to the image initialization subtask to add the event handler specifications to the `<img src="">` tags. The revised and final form of the initialization is,

```
for (j = 0; j < 7; j++) {
    document.write('<img src="gifpix/BrownBox.gif" ' +
      'onMouseOver = "here(' + j + ')" ' +
      'onMouseOut  = "gone(' + j + ')">');
}
```

The two mouse event handler functions have their position parameter specified by the `for`-loop's iteration variable `j`. To test the Key Sensing task solution, we make one tiny change in the Grid Animation event handler, `animate()`, namely, to change the frame assigned to the 19th column from the random choice to the `frame` variable. The new line has the form

```
document.images[19].src = pics[frame].src;
```

allowing us to test the code.

Having thus completed the Key Sensing task, Figure 21.7 shows the code entered into the Structural Page in the third row. (The two declarations—`keypix` and `frame`—are included with the earlier declarations, and the event handling functions are included with the previously defined functions.)

STAIRCASE DETECTION TASK

When the user has manipulated the mouse in such a way as to create a rising "staircase" of blocks in the Grid, the animation should stop. How do we recognize the "staircase"? It's not possible to look at Grid, of course, so we must identify it by other characteristics. Observe that the user will have created a staircase when the `frame` values for seven consecutive `animate()` calls are 1, 2, 3, 4, 5, 6, 7. This is true because the value of `frame` tells the `animate()` event handler which `Stack` frame to display, and if it is directed to display the seven frames in order on seven consecutive ticks, there will be a staircase in Grid.

How do we recognize the seven consecutive `frame` values? There are many techniques. Some involve keeping an array of the seven most recent frame values and checking each time to see if the desired sequence occurs. Another involves looking at the `src` fields in the last seven images of the Grid—it's almost like looking at the picture—to see if they have the right sequence of filenames. But the one we will program requires slightly less programming and seems cleverer. The idea is to keep predicting the next `frame` value.

To see how to identify the staircase sequence, notice that we are trying to recognize continuity across a sequence of events, that is, seven events in which the value for `frame` is 1,2,3,4,5,6,7. By analogy, imagine sitting at the bus stop trying to determine if seven consecutive buses ever come by with the last digit of their license numbers making the sequence 1 through 7. But you have no paper to write down the data and your memory isn't so good. (There are more interesting things to think about!) But, you do have seven coins—your bus fare—and you put one coin in your left pocket. Whenever any bus arrives, you check to see if the last digit of its license plate is equal to the number of coins in your left pocket. If so, and you still have coins, add another coin to your left pocket. If not, put all the coins, but one, back in your right pocket. If you ever try to add a coin, but have run out, it happened! What you are doing with the coins in your left pocket is predicting the number on the next bus's license plate. If it's right, you make the next prediction by adding another coin; but if not, you start back with 1. It's an easy idea for keeping the continuity of a series of events.

```
<script language = 'JavaScript'>
 var keypix = new Array(2);
 for (j = 0; j < 7; j++) {
    document.write
      ('<img src="gifpix/BrownBox.gif" ' +
        'onMouseOver = "here(' + j + ')" ' +
        'onMouseOut  = "gone(' + j + ')">');
 }
 keypix[0] = new Image();
 keypix[1] = new Image();
 keypix[0].src = "gifpix/BrownBox.gif";
 keypix[1].src = "gifpix/OrangeBox.gif";
</script>
```

Figure 21.7. JavaScript for the Key Sensing task; two declarations and the two event handlers, not shown.

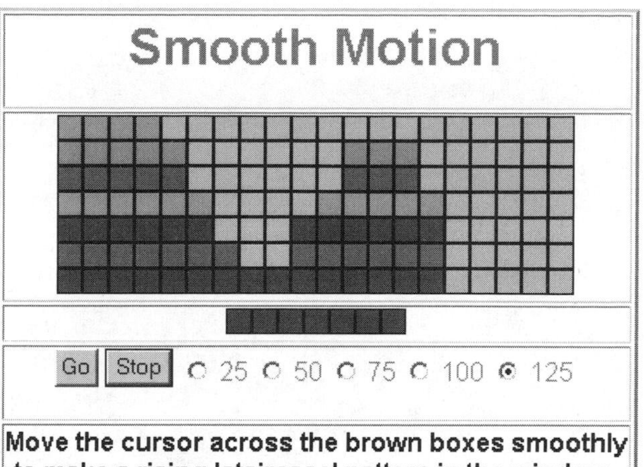

Implementing the bus analogy, we modify the `animate()` function at the point where it is about to set the timer for the next tick because if the staircase is found, there should be no next tick. Additionally, we'll declare another variable, `next1`, that corresponds to the coins in your left pocket, that is, the prediction. Implementing the steps of the process

```
if (frame == next1)                              //Is the prediction correct?
   next1 = next1 + 1;                            //Yes, make next prediction
else                                             //No
   next1 = 1;                                    //Go back to the start
if (next1 != 8)                                  //Are we still looking?
   timerId = setTimeout("animate()",duration);   //Yes, set timer
```

Notice that the test in the last `if`-statement compares to 8 rather than 7 because `next1` was already incremented previously, and so the condition of "no more coins left" is equivalent to `next1`⇔8. With that addition to `animate()` we have completed the Staircase Detection task.

OVERALL DESIGN TASK

With the Construct Controls task performed out of order and parts of the Overall Design task performed ahead of time, there is not much left to do to complete the programming of the Smooth Motion application. Nevertheless, this is the point at which we make sure that the whole application works as planned.

Reviewing the description at the start of the chapter, we notice that the display of randomly selected stacks of blocks isn't presently working. Originally we generated random stacks when we solved the Grid Animation task. But we took that feature out to test the keys. Now we want to put it back in. Basically we should set image 19 to `frame` or `randNum(8)`, depending on whether the user has touched the mouse on the Keys or not. How will we know? The MouseOver event handlers will recognize the situation, but at the moment, they are programmed only to return a `frame` value from 1 through 7. So, if we started out with `frame` initialized to some erroneous number, say, –1, and test it in the `animate()` event handler before using the frame value, we could recognize the two situations. Thus we must change the initialization of frame in its declaration to

```
var frame = -1;          //Set for initial random generation
```

and rewrite the assignment to the last column of the Grid one more time:

```
if (frame == -1)
   document.images[19].src = pics[randNum(8)].src;
else
   document.images[19].src = pics[frame].src;
```

This last change to animate() makes it quite cluttered with if-statements, as can be seen in Figure 21.8. The clutter obscures the simple two-part logic of shifting the Grid and checking for the staircase. So, we relegate both operations to functions. The resulting solution is no shorter, in fact, it is longer by four lines, but it makes the workhorse animate() event handler clearer, making the exercise worthwhile.

After checking the operation of the Smooth Motion application, it seems that we've taken care of all of the design elements, except the fancy GUI, which is the last remaining task.

Embellish the Web Page Task

The Structural Page we've built our application around can be made more attractive. In fact, the task of improving the aesthetics of Web pages is probably an unending task. We recognize the following changes that produce the page shown in Figure 21.1.

- Table background color
- Padding

These are all considered advanced features of HTML and will not be taught here because at the stage when a page is being enhanced, we usually have to familiarize ourselves with the advanced features again, having forgotten them since the last time a page was enhanced. For the record, the two enhancements can be programmed using attributes of the <table> tag

```
<table border=2 cellspacing="3" cellpadding="20%"
bgcolor="#FFFF99">
```

An explanation of how cellpadding and cellspacing work is found at www.w3c.org/TR/REC-html40/struct/tables.html#h-11.3.3 and nearby pages. We leave it to the interested reader to explore alternative styles.

Assessment and Retrospective

When we are asked to design a solution to someone else's problem, we are usually finished when we've verified that we've done what we've been asked to do. If the design is to achieve a goal of our own choice, however, an assessment step remains. When *we* pick the goal, we usually do not have a fixed target like Figure 21.1 to work toward. Rather, we will have designed a solution to our original "best guess" and should now consider whether the result is the best possible. (We have used such assessments in Chapters 14 and 18.) Generally, having a working solution suggests many worthwhile improvements.

Of course, in this chapter, the first case applies, and so we are finished. Instead of an assessment, consider the ideas from earlier chapters applied in this chapter. There are three obvious topics:

- Loops
- Parameterizing functions for reuse
- Managing complexity with functions

Applying these ideas has produced a better program. Consider how.

```
function animate() {
   for (j = 0; j < 19; j++) {
     document.images[j].src = document.images[j+1].src;
   }
   if (frame == -1)
      document.images[19].src = pics[randNum(8)].src;
   else
      document.images[19].src = pics[frame].src;
   if (frame == next1)
      next1 = next1 + 1;
   else
      next1 = 1;
   if (next1 != 8)
   timerId = setTimeout("animate()",duration);
}
```

becomes

```
function animate() {
   shiftGrid ();
   checkStairAndContinue ();
}
function shiftGrid() {
   for (j = 0; j < 19; j++) {
     document.images[j].src = document.images[j+1].src;
   }
   if (frame == -1)
      document.images[19].src = pics[randNum(8)].src;
   else
      document.images[19].src = pics[frame].src;
}
function checkStairAndContinue() {
   if (frame == next1)
      next1 = next1 + 1;
   else
      next1 = 1;
   if (next1 != 8)
   timerId = setTimeout("animate()",duration);
}
```

Figure 21.8. Revision of animate() to encapsulate portions of the computation into functions.

Loops

The Smooth Motion application used several `for`-loops. These saved us from tedious activities like writing 20 <`img src=""`> statements in a row. Such loops simplified the programming. But at times—when we might have used loops—we chose not to. For example, we explicitly wrote the instructions for defining the radio buttons and for Prefetching the Key images. When defining the radio buttons, we had a chance to use a four-iteration loop, but the complexity of setting up that loop was significant—for example, to set the time amounts. We decided not to use a loop, but rather to use Copy/Paste/Edit. Had there been more iterations, or had the specification been slightly simpler, we might have used a loop. In the case of the Prefetch of the Key images, only two iterations were required. Two is too few to justify thinking through the operation of a loop, even the standard World Famous Iteration. In both cases, the decision is one of making the program easier to write and easier for other people to understand. The computer doesn't care.

Many programmers take the view that at least five to seven iterations are required to justify using a `for`-loop for a statement or two; fewer iterations can be expressed explicitly. However, if the instruction sequence to be repeated is more than a few instructions, programmers will use a loop even for *two* iterations. Using a `for`-loop for a long sequence of instructions says, "These instructions are repeated," and it is better to say so than to force someone else to compare the sequences to determine how they are different. Programming may be commanding a computer, but it is also composing for any human who reads the program. Such a consideration guides our use of loops.

Parameterized Functions for Reuse

The `here()` and `gone()` functions each use a single parameter that is the position of the Key in sequence. The actual value is passed to the functions in the event handler specifications. For example, the third Key from the left is defined by a `document.write` that produces

```
<img src="gifpix/BrownBox.gif"
           onMouseOver = "here(2)" onMouseOut = "gone(2)">
```

where the "2" indicates the Key's 0-origin number. The parameter customizes the event handler for each Key. We could have written separate functions in which the Key's position was used explicitly everywhere `pos` occurs, but this would create a proliferation of almost-identical functions. The parameter says where and how the event handlers differ from each other, and their use produces a more abstract—and easier to understand—solution. Any function that is used more than once will generally have one or more parameters.

Managing Complexity with Functions

The functions `shiftGrid()` and `checkStairAndContinue()` shown in Figure 21.8 are examples of creating functions to manage complexity. Both functions "package" program logic allowing us to *name them* and *move them* out of the way, revealing the simple two-part logic of the `animate()` function.

```
function animate() {
   shiftGrid ();
   checkStairAndContinue ();
}
```

As with loops and parameters, this use of functions is intended to clarify to humans how the animation function works; it's all the same to the computer. Humans will see our choice of function names—for example `shiftGrid()`—and correctly interpret them as describing what the function does. If people need to know how the program shifts the Grid, they can check the function; otherwise, it is out of the way, replaced by a succinct statement of what it does (name). This role of shifting the Grid might have been expressed as a comment at the start of the code sequence, but the comments are often ignored. The abstraction—naming the function and giving its definition—creates a new concept in our minds, raising our level of understanding of

Smooth Motion's animation process. Though these two functions will never be used again, the goal of simplifying the program justifies our effort of defining them.

Thus our retrospective look at Smooth Motion indicates that programming is as much about instructing the computer as it is teaching any viewer of our program how we solved the problem. Even for programs that are not part of textbooks, helping humans understand the program is essential. It helps with debugging—an important concern for us—and it instills confidence in others by organizing the solution in an understandable way.

SUMMARY

We have programmed a substantial application that would have been too complicated had we tried simply to "brain it out." To be successful, we applied the Decomposition Principle, first to create the high-level tasks that guided our overall solution, and then, when it came time to solve those tasks, we applied Decomposition again when a task was still too complicated to solve. Though it is mostly just common sense, the Decomposition Principle gives us a strategy that will work to solve hard problems.

Once the tasks were defined, we strategized about the order in which to solve them. Because there usually are dependencies among the tasks, it is essential to determine a feasible plan for solving them. A dependency diagram shows visually which tasks depend on others and can assist us in strategizing. Any order that is consistent with the diagram—that is, no task is scheduled ahead of the tasks it depends on—produces a workable plan. But it is also wise to consider features such as ease-of-testing, and try to adjust the schedule to address these other aspects as well.

The actual solution of the Smooth Motion program was direct. Each task was decomposed further into four to five subtasks. There was similarity among these for similar tasks. For example the timer-driven animation and the key-driven animation used a similar set of subtasks. Unexpectedly we decided to solve the tasks out of order from our original schedule in order to give ourselves the ability to start and stop the animation. It was convenience that motivated us to depart from our original schedule, but originally it would not have been possible to predict the benefits of the alternative plan. Finally, we had to learn about mouse events, a topic that had not been encountered previously. Mouse events are not a difficult concept, and they illustrated a common feature of any large task—that it is often necessary to learn new information to solve a complex problem.

In our retrospective look at our solution, we noted how programming ideas from previous chapters were illustrated in the Smooth Motion application. Consistently we used the programming facilities—loops, functions, parameters, and so on—as tools to instruct both the computer and anyone looking at the program. Those facilities clarified the program, making it plain how the problem was being solved. Understanding *why* a program works is essential for getting it to work in the first place—that is, in debugging and testing—and for giving ourselves and others confidence that it solves the problem. The more abstract the components of the solution and the more straightforward the manner in which they are assembled, the greater will be our appreciation of the solution.

Though this chapter has presented an IT application, the techniques have wide application. Expect to use decomposition in other problem solving, to abstract the components of your solution by giving them names and precise definitions, and to reduce the complexity of your solution to an understandable level. They are powerful problem-solving techniques.

EXERCISES

1. Suppose you are asked to build the Memory Bank Web page shown in Figure 19.6. Decompose the problem into a set of primary tasks, and list them in the order in which you would solve them.
2. Of the tasks in Ex. 1, which are independent?
3. Draw a PERT chart for the tasks given in Ex. 1.
4. The tasks of a PERT chart can be scheduled in any order as long as they follow a simple rule: for any task, the tasks it points to must already be scheduled. Find an alternative order from the one given in the text for performing the tasks of Figure 21.2.
5. We planned to assign a section of the chapter to each of the design tasks. Why is there no section entitled Control Construction Task?
6. What causes the MouseOver and MouseOut events?
7. The `here()` and `gone()` functions have as a parameter the Key position number expressed in 0-origin. Change the Smooth Motion solution so that the value of the Key position in `pos` is 1-origin.

CHAPTER 22

Computers Can Do Almost {❑ everything, ❑ nothing}

Learning Objectives

- Know the structure and purpose of the Turing Test.
- Understand how a game tree works.
- Understand the issues of machine intelligence.
- Understand the issues of computer creativity.
- Know what universality is and why it is beneficial.
- Know when more speed improves computation.
- Understand what it means for a problem not to be solvable by a computer.

Computers have achieved sustained speeds of over ten trillion additions per second. At one operation per second on a pocket calculator, it takes 1000 lifetimes (assuming 60 years of daily calculating for 14 hours each day) to perform a trillion operations. But so what? Everyone knows computers are amazingly fast at arithmetic. Shouldn't we be more impressed if a computer ever had an original thought, no matter how trivial? Absolutely! But it won't happen. As we have learned, for a computer to do anything, it must be programmed to do it, and so far "thought" in the sense we usually mean the term has eluded researchers. So, we have a curious situation. Computers can be truly awesome at some tasks and completely hopeless at others. Because they're so different from humans, it's reasonable to wonder what computers can and cannot do.

This chapter addresses philosophical issues that arise in computing. The first issue considered is whether a computer can think. Thinking about thinking leads us to the famed Turing Test. Using that test to orient ourselves, we distinguish between the appearance of intelligence and the fact of intelligence. Playing chess requires intelligence, intuition, imagination, and analysis. Chess became a de facto goal of Artificial Intelligence research during the last half of the twentieth century. We explore how computers play chess, summarize the advancements, and report the victory of Deep Blue. After intelligence, we turn our attention to creativity and ask whether a computer can be creative. The discussion further serves to clarify the capabilities of humans and computers. Next, we consider the easy-to-understand but deep concept of universality, which asks how different computers can be from each other. Understanding universality explains why computers are so useful now, but it also implies they won't become more capable in the future. Any "new and improved" computer will be faster or larger, but not more capable. How important is more speed? We explore the question of how fast computers can solve various problems by revisiting the *Alphabetize CDs* algorithm from Chapter 10. The discussion characterizes the problems computers solve easily and for which a faster computer will deliver noticeable improvements. There are, however, many important problems that we would like to solve but that are too complex: A computer could solve them in principle, but not in practice. We'll give examples. Finally, there are problems that cannot be solved by computer even in principle, not because they are too nebulous to specify for a computer, but to do so would be a contradiction.

Can Computers Think?

The inventors of electronic computers thought that they were discovering how to "think with electricity." And to the extent that operations like addition and multiplication require *humans* to think, it's easy to see their point. Previously electricity had been used directly as an energy source for driving motors and powering light bulbs. With the digital computer, electricity switched complex circuits implementing logical operations. The power was applied to manipulate information. The phenomenon was truly new.

Today electronic devices manipulating information are so ubiquitous we have a less awestruck view of them. It is difficult to regard a pocket calculator as "thinking." But our view of what constitutes thinking has changed over time, too. In the Middle Ages, when very few people could read or *reckon*, as performing arithmetic was called, anyone who could add and multiply was thought to have special powers, divinely or perhaps mystically conferred. Reckoning was a uniquely human activity. It took centuries for addition and multiplication to be codified into the algorithms that we all learn in elementary school. Is a capability, once classified as thinking and believed to be a divine gift, no longer thinking when it turns out to be algorithmic? It required thinking when we learned it. Maybe all thought is algorithmic. Maybe it's thinking only as long as no one understands how it's accomplished.

> **Sub Text.** Computer scientist Edsger Dijkstra is quoted as saying, "The question of whether a computer can think is no more interesting than the question of whether a submarine can swim," but he seems to be in the minority.

The problem of defining thinking for the purposes of deciding whether a computer thinks troubled Alan M. Turing, one of the pioneers of computation. Turing was aware of definitions like "Thinking is what people do," and the tendency for people to call an activity "thinking" until it turns out to be algorithmic. So, he decided to forget trying to define what thinking is and simply proposed an experiment that would demonstrate intelligence. Turing designed the following experimental setting, which has since become known as the *Turing Test*.

Turing Test: Two identical rooms labeled A and B are connected electronically to a judge who can type questions directed to the occupant of either room. A human being occupies one room, and the other contains a computer. The judge's goal is to ascertain, based on the questions asked and the answers received, which room contains the computer. If after a reasonable period of time the judge cannot decide for certain, the computer can be said to be intelligent.

Turing's experiment not only sidestepped the problem of defining thinking or intelligence, but it also got away from focusing on any specific ability such as performing arithmetic. The judge can ask any questions, so as to explore the entire range of thought processes. Apparent stumpers for the computer like

"In Hamlet's famous soliloquy, what metaphors does Shakespeare use for 'death'?"

might not be so hard if the computer has access to online sources of Shakespearean criticism. Apparent "gimmes" for the computer like

"What are the prime factors of 72,914,426?"

might be answered in more human-like ways such as being slow or refusing to answer such questions at all. When Turing proposed the test in 1950, there was little prospect that a computer could deceive the judge. Nevertheless, it emphasized the important point that thinking is a process, and it's the same process no matter how it is accomplished—with synapses or transistors.

Advances in the last half-century have definitely improved the computer's prospects at "passing" the Turing Test, though perhaps they are still not very good. Researchers reading Turing's paper in 1950 might have conceded that computers could be better than people at arithmetic, but probably all of them would have believed that "natural language"—a true human invention—was beyond the abilities of computers. For example, when Turing thought up the test, no algorithmic process was known for parsing English into its grammatical structure, as word processors' grammar checkers do today. Nor was "machine translation"—converting text from one language into its semantic equivalent in another language—anything more than science fiction. Nor was recognizing semantically meaningful information like Google does thought to be computable, that is, a task a computer could perform. Admittedly computers are still a long way from being perfect at any of these tasks, but they are pretty good at all three—at least good enough to be the basis for useful applications. More important, they are good enough at these language tasks that we can imagine a day when computers *are* better than most humans. And then, like reckoning, the tasks of parsing, translation, and semantic recognition in natural language will have been reduced to algorithmic form. Does it add to our admiration of computers that they are closer to passing the Turing Test? Or does it detract from our opinion of ourselves, suggesting that instead of computers being more like people, perhaps people are just computers. The questions are truly profound.

Motto mot: IBM, the dominant computer manufacturer of the 1950s–1970s, used "Think" as its corporate motto. It was common to see the command in computer rooms and on programmer's desks. Perhaps one of the best signs employed "negative space" to get the reader's brain going.

Acting Intelligently

Anyone with even passing experience with grammar or spell checkers knows that they don't "understand" the sentences. They know the parts of speech such as prepositions and verbs, concepts like subject/object agreement, passive voice, and so on, but they don't understand. Such concepts are not trivialities. It takes tremendously complex software and substantial dictionary resources to implement grammar and spell checking, and they're occasionally good enough to be helpful. But they definitely do not "understand" English. What would a computer have to do to demonstrate that it "understands" something?

The distinction between being intelligent and being programmed to appear intelligent concerned researchers in the 1950s and 1960s. The Doctor program by MIT researcher Joel Weisenbaum demonstrated this difference clearly. Doctor was programmed to ask questions in a dialog like a psychotherapist:

User: `I'm depressed.`
Doctor: `Why are you depressed?`
User: `My mother is not speaking to me.`
Doctor: `Tell me about your mother.`
User: `She doesn't want me to major in engineering.`
Doctor: `No?`
User: `No, she wants me to go into medicine.`

Doctor was programmed to keep the dialog going by asking questions and requesting more information. It would take cues from words like *mother,* including a reference to them in its next response. It would also notice uses of negative sentences, but the dialog was essentially preplanned. It may have appeared to be intelligent, but definitely was not.

As the research field of Artificial Intelligence came into existence, a consensus grew that to exhibit intelligence, a computer would have to "understand" a complex situation and reason well enough to act on its "understanding." Moreover, the actions could not be scripted or predetermined in any way. Most complex situations require the ability to understand natural language and/or require much real-world knowledge. Both properties badly handicapped computers of the day. Playing chess, however, was much cleaner. It offered a challenging task that humans were both good at and interested in. The rules were clear, and success could be easily defined: Beat a grandmaster in a tournament. Indeed, in the initial exuberance over computing, it was predicted as early as 1952 that a computer would beat a grand master "sometime in the next decade." Though it took more than a decade before computers could do much more than know the legal moves of chess, the problem was well established as a litmus test for AI.

How does a computer play chess? First, like all computational problems the information must be represented in bits. The chess "world" is especially easy because it is completely defined by an 8×8 checkered board, 32 pieces of two colors and six different types, and a single bit indicating whose turn it is to move. Because details are unimportant, think of the graphic of a chessboard as printed in game books or newspapers, and call it a *board configuration*, or simply a *board*.

Next the computer must decide on a move. It does this in roughly the same way we do, by exploring moves along the lines of,

"Will a move of this piece to that position, make me better off or worse off?"

"Better off or worse off" are determined with respect to winning, of course, but it is very difficult to "compute" such information. Humans use intuition and experience. A computer uses an *evaluation function*, a procedure that assigns a numerical value to each piece and, taking into account things like captures and board position, computes a score for the board. If the score is positive, it's better; if it's negative, it's worse. Then, starting from the current board configuration, the computer checks the evaluation function on the result of every possible single legal move, as shown in the game tree of Figure 22.1. One of these moves—suppose there are 28 legal moves—will give the highest score, which might be the one that the computer should pick.

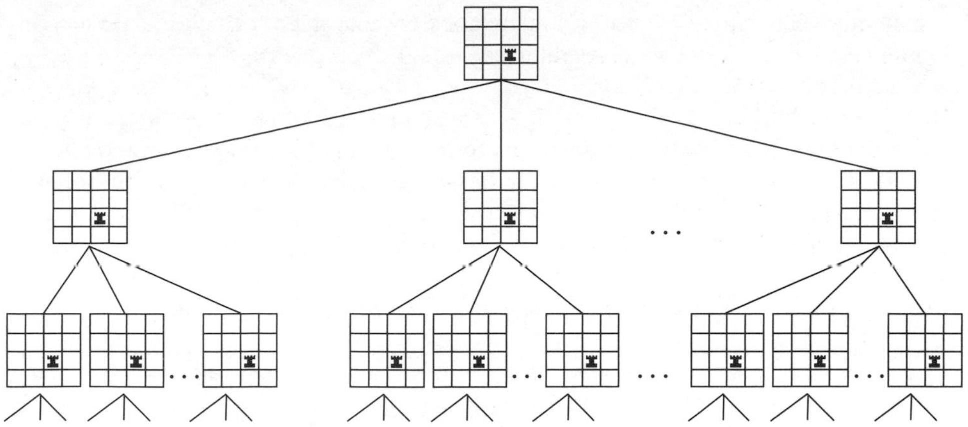

Figure 22.1. A schematic diagram of a game tree for chess. The current board position is at the top (root). The boards produced in a single move are on the layer below, those reachable in two moves are on the layer below that, and so forth.

But before picking, the computer should consider what the opponent will do. So for each of these "1-move" board configurations considered so far, the computer considers every possible next move from each and evaluates them. These are two moves away from the current board configuration. Furthermore, because the opponent makes the second move, the interpretation of the evaluation function is *reversed.* That is, the best move for the opponent is presumably the worst move for the computer, so the computer assumes the opponent will choose the move with the most negative evaluation. This process is known as "look ahead," and clearly the further ahead the computer looks—it's described as *deeper* in chess because of the game tree formulation—the more complete is the computer's knowledge about possible outcomes of the game.

Disoriented. Trees in computing are always thought of with their roots at the top and leaves at the bottom. Motion in the tree is always relative to that orientation. So, a "deeper search" moves further form the root. Perhaps computational trees are not so much like real trees as they are like roots.

It would seem that the computer, being very fast, could look all the way to the end of the game, find a winning path, and follow that. But checking the whole game tree is generally impossible because of the geometric increase in the number of boards that must be considered. For example, if there are 28 moves possible from the current position, and an average of 28 from each of those, and each of their descendents, and so on. then considering only *six* moves deep generates

$$28 + 28^2 + 28^3 + 28^4 + 28^5 + 28^6 = 499{,}738{,}092$$

which is a half billion boards. It's clear that the computer is not going to look 50 moves into the future.

Which move should the computer select? Picking the best move at the first level is not the best strategy because the evaluation function is generally a static assessment of the board configuration. If in that one move the computer could reach a checkmate, the evaluation function would be very positive and the computer should pick it. But if not, the situation needs more strategy because the most positive evaluation might come from a capture that would give the computer a piece advantage, whereas another choice, though less desirable at the moment, might lead in a few moves to a win. To play an intelligent game, that is, to strategize, to sacrifice pieces, to force the opponent into specific behaviors, requires the computer to analyze the game tree much more carefully. Doing so would embody the intelligent behavior to be demonstrated, and successful chess programs do.

Finally, in addition to representing the game and making moves, the computer needs some knowledge. In chess, this takes the form of a database of openings and endgames. Because chess is interesting and has been studied for so long, much is known about how to start and finish chess games. Providing this database is like giving the computer chess experience. Because learning is probably even harder than being intelligent, loading the database saves the computer the need to "learn from experience." It's analogous to aspiring chess players reading books by grandmasters.

Slowly, as the basic logic just discussed got worked out, chess programs got better and better. Eventually they were beating duffers, then serious players, and eventually masters. Progress came as a combination of faster computers, more complete databases, and better evaluation and "strategizing" functions. In time, parallel computation—the application of several computers to the task—and custom hardware allowed computer researchers to entertain the possibility of beating a grandmaster under tournament conditions. In 1996, reigning grandmaster Garry Kasparov trounced an IBM computer dubbed Deep Blue in six games. But in one of those games, the computer played very well and won. Kasparov saw himself as victorious in defending the human race, but computer researchers were ecstatic. At last a computer had played world-class chess in tournament conditions. A rematch was inevitable. On May 11, 1997, Kasparov lost 3.5 – 2.5 to an improved Deep Blue, achieving the "in the next decade" goal in a mere 45 years.

Blue Lightning. Deep Blue is a parallel computer composed of 32 general-purpose computers (RS/6000 SP) and 256 chess processors, enabling it to consider on average 200 million board positions per second.

Did Deep Blue settle the question of whether computers can be intelligent? Not to everyone's satisfaction. To its credit, it answered one of the greatest technical challenges of the century. To do so required a large database of prior knowledge on openings and endgames, but that's analogous to reading books and playing chess. It also required special-purpose hardware that allowed rapid evaluation of board positions, but that's probably analogous to synaptic development in the brains of chess experts giving them the ability over time to encapsulate whole board configurations as single mental units. But disappointingly—at least to some observers, and probably the AI pioneers who made the predictions in the first place—the problem was basically solved by speed. Deep Blue simply looked deeper. It did so *intelligently*, of course, because the geometric explosion of boards prevents success based simply on raw power. And that may be the strongest message from the Deep Blue/Kasparov matches. Intelligence may be the ability to consider many alternatives in an informed and directed way. Deep Blue surely demonstrated that.

The Deep Blue experience may have demonstrated that computers can be intelligent, or it may have demonstrated that IBM's team of chess experts and computer programmers is very intelligent. In the final analysis, the hardware was simply following the instructions that the programmers and engineers gave it. Such an objection has been raised in the "intelligence" debate since the beginning. It is a weak criticism because we can imagine intelligence, or creativity, or any other intellectual process being encoded in a general form, so that once started on a body of information, the program operates autonomously, responding to new inputs and realizing states not planned by its designers. Deep Blue operates autonomously in this sense and thus transcends its designers.

The main cautionary note regarding Deep Blue is that it is completely specialized to chess. That is, the 256 chess processors only evaluate board positions and are not useful for any other purpose. The 32 general-purpose processors can run other programs, of course, but none of Deep Blue's "intelligence" would be transferable to another computation unless a programmer abstracted the ideas from Deep Blue and incorporated them into that computation. The "intelligence" isn't formulated in any general-purpose way. Thus Deep Blue speaks only indirectly to the subject of general-purpose intelligence.

> **Another View**. John Searle, an outspoken critic of AI, offers a widely quoted criticism, The Chinese Room Argument. A monolingual English speaker is locked in a room, given rules in English for correlating symbols in three batches of Chinese text. Ignorant of Chinese, the occupant follows the rules. The format is designed to mirror AI programs. The occupant is amazingly good, but unaware of his role. Amazed Chinese believe he's a native speaker. Is he intelligent? Or only following rules like a computer? Much has been said on both sides.

CREATIVITY

An alternative approach to understanding the limitations and potentialities of computers is to consider whether they can be "creative." For example, could a computer create art? It's not a question of whether they can be the art medium—artists have manipulated computers to produce art for decades. Rather the question is whether a computer could prevail in, perhaps, a "graphic version" of the Turing Test: A judge visits an art show and decides whether a person or a computer produced the art. Could a computer be successful? The task may be more daunting even than the original Turing Test because creativity is by definition a process of breaking the rules, and computers only follow rules. How could they ever succeed? Perhaps there are rules—metarules—that describe how to break the rules, or perhaps, transcend existing rules. A computer could follow those. To see how this might be, first analyze the forms of creativity.

Consider writing a program to create fine art. There has been something of a fad recently in writing Java Applets to create graphic designs after the famed cubist Piet Mondrian (1872–1944), whose paintings are exhibited in the great art collections of the world. [1] See Figure 22.2. The programs display a new "Mondrian" with each mouse click. Inspecting the code, we find that the programs use random numbers to steer a deterministic process for placing lines and filling regions with color. That is, the program encodes a set of rules for creating graphics in the style of Mondrian, using what looks to the casual observer to be the same design elements, same colors, and so on. The graphics are new in the sense that they have never before existed, but as art critics love to say, "The work is derivative."

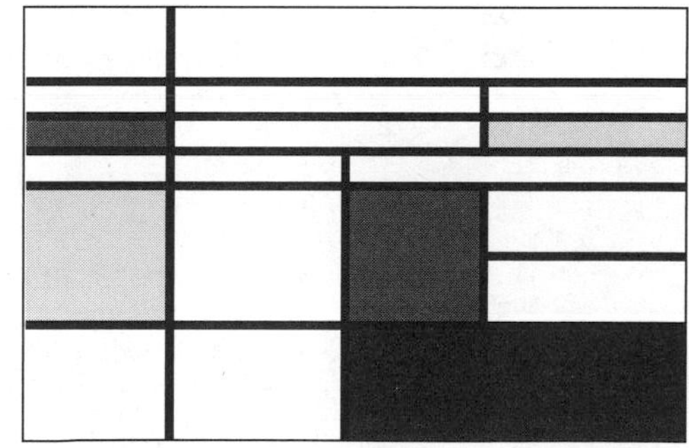

Figure 22.2. Example of a computer-generated graphic in the style of Piet Mondrian.

Mondrian is famous not because he created pleasing pictures with strong lines and bold primary colors, but because he had something to say about his world that could be expressed through paintings. That is, he's famous for a body of work from which the program's rules have been reasonably faithfully abstracted. The program only produces variations on the application of the rules using random numbers. But to many, creativity means *inventing* the rules in the first place, that is, producing the body of work.

[1] Finding current examples only requires a Web search on terms like *mondrian* AND *java*. Other geometrically regular graphics, for example, Moorish designs, can also be found.

Inspiration and Work. Computer scientist Bruce Jacob distinguishes between the "flash out of the blue (inspiration)" form of creativity, and the "incremental revision (hard work)" form. The former remains a mystery; the latter is algorithmic in Jacob's view. The dichonomy is reminescent of Edison's description of invention: 1% inspiration, 99% perspiration.

So, at the Flash end of the spectrum, the computer would have to step outside of the "established order," inventing its own rules, where as at the Applet end of the spectrum, it just randomly assembles parts by the rules, never extending or modifying them. Between those two extremes, there are still alternatives. The Hard Work forms. Canons have the incremental-variation-on-a-theme property. And Jacob has a music composition system, *variations,* which attempts to extend a repertoire of base themes by (randomly) generating new themes, assessing them as "good" or "bad," and discarding the "bad" ones. Interestingly, Jacob points out that because the program must work within the underlying characteristics of the base themes, getting a random variation to "fit" within those constraints "sometimes requires creativity!" That is, forcing a random variation on the constraints imposed by a set of rules produces new techniques.

Calling Jacob's work *computer creativity* may feel strained because the program seems to embody much of the designer—the test for "bad" for instance—and there is a certain "stumbling onto a solution" quality from the randomness. Nevertheless, this and similar efforts, which span creative pursuits from inventing typefaces to making analogies, focus on the rule-making aspect of creativity and demonstrate that incremental revision is algorithmic.

Classical Question. At a recent University of Oregon demonstration, three pianists played music in the style of Bach composed by Bach, Steven Larson (a professor), and EMI, a computer program. The audience voted on who wrote which piece. Larson's composition was thought to be the computer's, Bach's composition was thought to be Larson's, and EMI's composition was thought to be Bach's.

So, the conclusion seems to be this. Creativity is a spectrum ranging from the Flash end to the Mondrian-in-a-click end. When the Turing Test was invented, "Draw a picture in the style of Mondrian" would have been a request a computer would have utterly failed at. Today it is a three-page Java program. AI researchers have demonstrated in various contexts that the Hard Work form of creativity is algorithmic. If the matter of whether a computer can be creative is not taken to be a yes/no question, but rather is seen as an expedition into the process of creativity, we find our answer. The more deeply we understand creativity, the more we find ways in which it is algorithmic in nature. Will it be found to be entirely algorithmic at some point in the future? Will there be rules for breaking the rules? Will it become like reckoning? Or will there necessarily be a nonalgorithmic part at the Flash end? No matter how it turns out, aspects of creativity are algorithmic. To the extent that creativity is algorithmic, a computer can be creative. It simply follows the rules of the algorithm. But who needs a computer? If creativity's algorithmic, we can all be creative by following the rules. Progress in understanding creativity can benefit us, too. It shouldn't matter whether the process is accomplished by transistors or synapses.

Fill in the Blank. In an essay in *Science* on creativity, Goldenberg, Mazursky, and Solomon report that in one study 89% of award-winning advertisements contain a use of one of six "creativity templates," that is, follow-the-rules techniques, and that one simple template, Replacement, accounted for 25% of all award-winning ads.

UNIVERSALITY

Another problem that concerned Turing and other computer pioneers was to determine what set of primitive instructions makes the most powerful computer, that is, enables it to compute the greatest range of computations. Astonishingly what they discovered was that it hardly matters. Almost any set of hardwired instructions with a minimum basic functionality enables a computer to compute anything that any computer can compute. This is known as the *universality* principle of computers. In essence, any computation can be expressed with only a half dozen different types of instructions.

Know How. Different fundamental sets of instructions have been formulated, but `Add`, `Subtract`, `Test_For_Zero`, `Load`, `Store`, and `Branch_On_Zero` are sufficient.

It goes without saying that every computer has these primitive instructions and much more. From the commercial point of view, universality means that Intel and Motorola cannot compete with one another to build a computer that can compute more computations. Every computer the two companies have ever made is equivalent to all other computers in terms of what they can compute. Universality says they all compute the same set of computations. It's surprising.

Getting Down to Basics. Universality can also be interpreted as saying that no matter how complex a task seems to be—playing chess or checking grammar—if a computer does it, it has been simplified by programmers to the point where the collective affects of many of these half dozen operations can realize it.

Perhaps the most important aspect of universality is that if we want to do some new information-processing task, we don't need to buy a new computer. The computer we already have is sufficient if we can write or buy the software for the task. This is quite different, say, from wanting to perform a new task in the kitchen or the shop, where we will have to buy a new gadget. Machines that transform material must be specialized to each activity, requiring us—or enabling us, if you like to get new gadgets—to buy a specialized device. By contrast, there is only one information-processing machine, the computer. Because computers are general purpose, people have a greater role in setting them up and configuring them for a specific task—installing software, for example—than they do for single-purpose machines like food processors or table saws. This greater role in customizing the general-purpose device to our needs is a strong motivator for becoming Fluent with IT.

To understand why computers are universal, postulate two computers, the ZAP^2 and the BXLE, and suppose they have the same hardwired instructions, except that ZAP^2 has one additional instruction. Its manufacturer claims the new instruction enables new computations on the ZAP^2 not possible on the BXLE. "Baloney," says BXLE's CEO. "Using the instructions already in BXLE, we will program a function that performs the operation of the special hardwired instruction. Then in any program for the ZAP^2 we will replace every use of the special instruction with a call to the equivalent function. Anything ZAP^2 can do, BXLE can do." (See Figure 22.3.) Notice that in

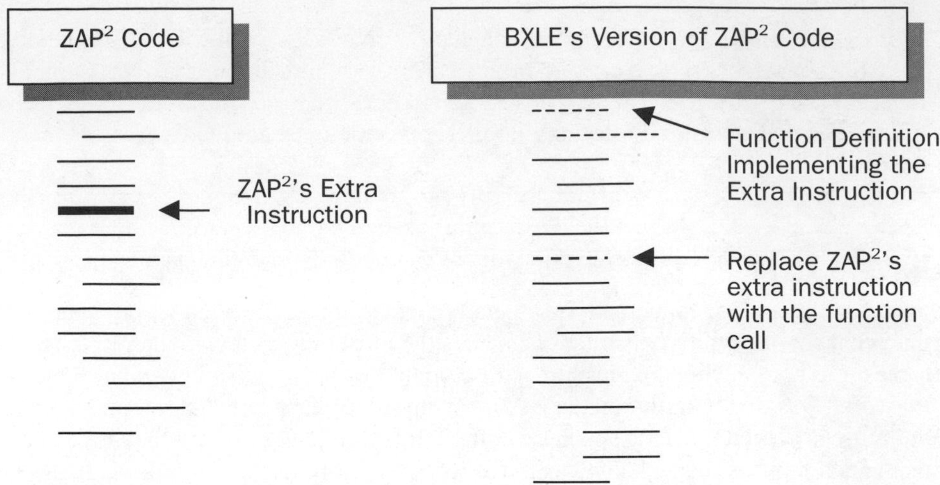

Figure 22.3. Schematic diagram showing a revision of ZAP^2's program to run on the BXLE, in which the special instruction has been replaced by a function call.

effect, BXLE performs the hardwired instruction in software, that is, by using a function. The argument holds up as along as the special instruction can be programmed with the basic instructions of the BXLE, which we can be confident will be possible. But the skeptic needn't accept that on faith. Rather it's possible to write a program for the BXLE to simulate circuits and to simulate the entire circuitry of ZAP^2. Simulating ZAP^2 by the BXLE is possible because ZAP^2 is built from (zillions of) two-input logic gates. There are only 16 different gates, and they can be trivially simulated with the six basic instructions. Because BXLE can duplicate exactly the ZAP^2 operation in the simulator, it is possible to do all of the same computations, too. Notice that this solution also solves the problem in software.

Because all computers do the same computations, the main basis for technical competition among manufacturers is speed.

Practical Consequences of Universality

Universality says computers are all the same in terms of what they compute, and speed is the basis for any differences. The arguments for universality just discussed —implement the special instruction as a function or simulate the whole machine— both have the disadvantage that the BXLE runs slower than the ZAP^2. In the first instance, it might only be slower on the special instruction, which presumably takes several basic instructions to implement. The second case will run much, much more slowly because each instruction of the ZAP^2 may take thousands of logical operations, and the BXLE must simulate each of these. So, although both computers can realize the same computations, they do them at different rates. For that reason, manufacturers *do* include special instructions for tasks such as digital signal processing, graphics, encryption, and others in hopes that their frequent use will make their computer faster.

Universality seems to conflict with our everyday experience, however. Three obvious difficulties are as follows:

- Macintosh software doesn't run on the PC and vice versa; if Macs and PCs are the same, why not?
- People say old machines become outmoded; how so, if they're all the same?
- Is it really true that the computer in my laptop is the same as the one in my microwave oven?

Despite these apparent problems, universality is a practical fact. Consider each objection in turn.

Macintosh versus PC

PC and Mac processors are different, implying each has a different *combination* of instructions, though they include the six most basic mentioned earlier. These instructions sets are encoded differently, they operate slightly differently, each has instructions the other doesn't have, and so on. None of these differences is fundamental. It is possible to write a program for each machine to perform the instructions of the other machine, just as was argued earlier. It is not only possible in principle, computer scientists write such programs frequently.

But consumer software relies heavily on operating system facilities, too. So, to run a user application, the operating system would also need to be available. Running two operating systems—known as *dual booting*—is also possible, but it is not something most users want to worry about. Add to this the fact that the software will run more slowly than on the original platform, and the result doesn't justify the effort of applying the universality principle directly.

The alternative solution, which software companies like Adobe, Microsoft, and Oracle use, is to translate their programs to each computer family, as explained in Chapter 9. The software is written in a programming language like Basic, C, or Java, and then it is compiled—that is, translated—into the machine language of each machine. Special care is taken to ensure that operating system incompatibilities have been removed. The result is that rather than simulating the software of one computer on another computer, there is a separate custom version for each vendor's computer. (And, of course, it won't run on another vendor's computer.) In that way, any application software can run on any computer and not be slowed by simulating another machine. So, universality is used, but not in the way originally discussed.

Outmoded Computers

As noted, speed is the main difference between computers. Users often buy new computers because their new software, which is doubtless loaded with slick new features, runs slowly on their old machines. With the new software doing more, it is not surprising that a faster computer would help. But, for those who are patient, there is no need to change.

The first reason people claim computers become "outmoded" is that hardware and/or software products are often not compatible with older machines. For example, input/output devices like modems or printers are often not compatible with older computers because of other internal parts such as the system bus. (See the Anatomy Diagram, Figure 9.2.) As a result, it is not possible to connect the new devices. These parts are not closely connected with instruction execution. The second reason is that software vendors simply don't support old machines. As just explained, software vendors compile their programs to each platform—usually a processor/OS combination—to sell to customers. But, there are generally too few customers running an old processor/OS combination that the vendor decides it is not profitable to sell and maintain a version for that machine. Thus new software is often not available for old computers. This is a business decision; there is no technical impediment.

The Laptop and the Microwave

The computers embedded in consumer products like microwaves, brakes, and so on are there not because the task of running a microwave is so complex that it needs a computer. Rather, it's cheaper to implement the system with a computer and a read-only memory (ROM) chip containing a fixed program than it is to implement it with custom electronics. It's a matter of economics, not a technical requirement.

But embedded computers have a rich enough instruction set to run any other computer application. Their main handicap as computers is usually neither their instruction repertoire nor their speed. Rather, embedded computers are, well, embedded. They are connected to a very limited set of input/output devices, usually only the sensors and actuators of the system they control. If the embedded computer were connected to a keyboard and a monitor like the personal computer we're accustomed to, it could run the software just fine.

So, universality is not only a theoretical fact, it is a practical fact, too.

Faster and Slower

It's a fact that when we use computers they are simply idling most of the time, waiting for us to give them something to do. For tasks like word processing, even including continuous grammar and spell checking doesn't keep them busy. So we listen to MP3 tunes, too, which is still not stressing them. Eventually, we notice, perhaps when we are manipulating digital images, certain activities like making the image brighter are computed very fast, but others like turning the image on its side are noticeably slower. This is curious when we think about it because the image has the same number of pixels in both cases. What causes some tasks to take longer to compute?

The obvious and correct answer is: It takes more time to do more work. Recall the *Alphabetize CDs* example. If the CD rack were smaller, the algorithm would complete sooner because fewer CDs would have to be considered. The point is even easier to see for a task like making sure the CDs all face forward. The *Face Forward* algorithm requires only that we start at the beginning, inspect each CD to see which way it is facing; if it is not facing forward, reorient it and return it; in either case, move on to the next CD. If the rack holds 24 CDs, the algorithm takes 24 iterations of the inspect-and-reorient sequence because only one pass through the rack is sufficient. If the rack contains 48 CDs, 48 iterations will be required. Cases of this type, where the amount of work is directly proportional to the amount of data, are said to have *work-proportional-to-n* algorithms. That is, the running time is at most the number of basic steps devoted to each item times the number *n* of data items. We say "at most" because not all of the steps may be needed on each data item. If some CDs are already facing forward, there will be no need for a reorient step. In the worst case, all CDs are facing backwards, and it takes the maximum predicted time.

Orienting the CDs to face forward is an easier task than alphabetizing them. Recall that the *Alphabetize CDs* algorithm did not solve the problem in "one pass" through the rack. In fact, for each CD referenced by *Alpha*, all of the CDs after it had to be considered; this was called a *Beta Sweep*. So, if there are 24 CDs in the rack, 23 CDs must be considered to get the first CD into position in the front because *Alpha*'s reference doesn't change, but *Beta* references the 23 other CDs. Thus the "In Order?" test must be made 23 times to locate the alphabetically first CD. Then *Alpha* moves to the second position, referencing the next slot, and *Beta* must visit the 22 CDs after it. This continues until the last step when *Alpha* references the next to last CD and *Beta* references only the last slot, that is, only one interchange of CDs is considered at the very end. Adding these numbers up

$$23 + 22 + \ldots + 1 = 276$$

That is, we test 276 times to see if a pair of CDs is possibly out of order in a 24-slot rack. In the same way if the CD rack contains 48 CDs, locating the alphabetically first CD would require 47 CD references in the first *Beta Sweep*, finding the second 46, and so on. Adding these numbers up we get

$$47 + 46 + \ldots + 1 = 1128$$

which is surprising because the rack is only twice as large, but the number of tests is more than four times larger. Clearly the repeated *Beta Sweeps* of *Alphabetize CDs* require more work than the single sweep of the *Face Forward* algorithm.

> **Brainy Kid**. It's said Johann Karl Friedrich Gauss, a mathematician whose face adorns the 10 Deutsche Mark note, was asked by his teacher to add the numbers 1 to 100. He was done in a jiffy to the teacher's surprise. He explained that adding numbers from 1 to n is always $(n + 1)n/2$ because adding the first and last items gives $n+1$, and similarly for the remaining first and last items, and so forth, and there are $n/2$ such pairs.

Thus, although the *Face Forward* computation took only one pass through the rack, *Alphabetize* took many passes. In the former case, the number of repetitions is proportional to n for an n-slot rack, and in the latter case, the number of repetitions is proportional to $(n+1)n/2 = (n^2 + n)/2$. Whereas *Face Forward* is said to be a work-proportional-to-n algorithm, *Alphabetize CDs* is said to be a work-proportional-to-n^2 algorithm. (Computer people don't worry about the other terms of the equation, only the most significant term, the n^2 here.) Thus, if there are $n = 1000$ pieces of data, and a problem can be solved by a work-proportional-to-n algorithm, it will take about a thousand times the amount of work embodied in the core computation to complete the task. But, if the problem is solved by a work-proportional-to-n^2 algorithm, the amount of work will be about a *million* = 1000×1000 times the amount of work embodied in the basic steps of the repetition. So, when we observe that one computation is taking more time than another despite requiring the same amount of data, it is generally because the algorithm does more work to solve the problem.

Notice that the explanation is that "the algorithm does more work to solve the problem," not that the problem requires more work to be solved. That is, the algorithm the programmer chose to solve the problem may not be the fastest. The fastest known algorithm is rarely the solution of choice. For example, there are faster ways to alphabetize CDs than the solution presented, though none with work-proportional-to-n. And the alternatives are somewhat more complicated. Complexity and other factors contribute to a programmer's decision, and besides the computer is idle most of the time anyway.

How Tough Can It Be?

With algorithms requiring work proportional to n, and proportional to n^2, it is a good guess that there are algorithms requiring work proportional to n^3, and n^4, and so on. There are, and they are all considered practical for computers to solve, though as the example of the last section made clear, the exponent does matter a lot to the user sitting there waiting for the answer. But there are much more difficult computations, many of which are important to business, science, and engineering. In fact, one of the most significant discoveries of the 1970s was that many problems of interest—for example, finding the cheapest set of plane tickets for touring n cities—don't have any known "practical" algorithmic solutions. Such problems are known by the rather curious name of *NP-complete* problems. In essence, the best-known algorithms do little more than try all possible solutions, and pick the best. It seems that there should be cleverer algorithms than that. If there are, the person who discovers one will be extremely famous. In the meantime, such problems are said to be *intractable*—the best way to solve them is so difficult that large data sets cannot be solved with a realistic amount of computer time on any computer. Computers can solve them in principle, but not in practice.

Hard Problems. Steve Cook of the University of Toronto and Dick Karp of UC Berkeley discovered intractability. They also discovered the amazing fact that if anyone finds a better algorithm for certain NP-complete problems, their algorithm will improve *every* NP-complete problem.

Amazingly there are problems computers cannot solve at all. It's not that the algorithms take too long, but that there are no algorithms period! These are not problems like being intelligent or creative, but precisely definable problems with a clear quantifiable objective. For example, it's impossible for an algorithm to determine if a program has a bug in it, like looping forever. Such an algorithm would have been quite useful in Chapter 20 in our study of looping, when we messed up the <*next iteration*> step, causing infinite loops. We'd simply give our program to this imagined Loop-Checker algorithm, and it would tell us whether or not our program loops forever. Notice that the Loop-Checker would be especially handy for computations having, say, work proportional to n^4 because we have to wait a long time for the results. While we're waiting, we'd like to be sure we're going to get a result eventually, rather than have the program caught in an infinite loop, forcing us to wait forever.

But the Loop-Checker can't exist. Suppose it did. That is, suppose there is a program LC(P, x) that takes as its input any program P and input data x, analyzes P, and answers back "Yes" or "No" whether P will loop forever on input x. This actually seems plausible because LC could look through P, checking every loop to see if the <*next iteration*> and <*continuation*> tests are set right. And then it could follow the execution of P on x, looking to see if anything could go wrong. It seems plausible, but it's not. Here's why.

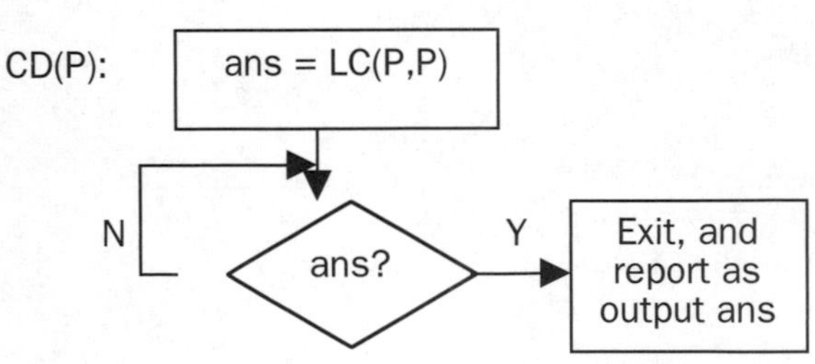

Figure 22.4. The logic of the CD program, given the assumed program LC.

Create another program, CD(P) that also takes as input a program P. CD is mnemonic for "contradiction," and the program works according to this flowchart in Figure 22.4. What does CD(CD) compute? We're not sure what the assumed LC(CD,CD) will answer back, but suppose it says "No," CD does not loop forever when the CD program is its input. In that case, the left arrow out of the diamond is taken and CD loops forever. So, LC would have been wrong. Perhaps LC answers, "Yes," that it will loop forever when CD is its input. In that case, the right arrow out of the diamond is taken, and the program doesn't loop forever, but just stops. The Loop-Checker cannot answer correctly—neither "Yes" nor "No" is the right answer. This problem cannot be algorithmically solved.

The Loop-Checker is trying to solve a famous computation known as the *Halting Problem*. A. M. Turing was the first to recognize the impossibility of the perfect debugger like Loop-Checker. It's too bad because it would have been handy to have such a debugger. Interestingly, debugging—the topic of Chapter 7—is something that humans can do, admittedly with great difficulty sometimes. In fact, it requires considerable intelligence to figure out what has gone wrong when an IT task doesn't work out. It's something that computers won't ever be able to do in any general way. So, maybe we were looking in the wrong place for capabilities that are uniquely human. Making computers do our bidding properly is something only humans can do!

SUMMARY

We have explored the limits of computation. We began by asking a question that has puzzled people since computers were invented—can they think? The question challenged us to define what thinking is. We identified a tendency for people to decide an intellectual activity isn't thinking once it's determined that it is algorithmic. Thinking is probably best defined as what humans do, and therefore something computers can't do. The Turing Test is an experimental setting in which we can compare the capabilities of humans with those of computers. We studied the question of computer chess and learned that computers use a game tree formulation, an evaluation function to assess board positions, and a database of openings and endgames. Deep Blue became the chess champion of the world in 1997, a monumental achievement, but not one that closed the book on the algorithmic nature of intelligence. Next we studied creativity, formulating it as a spectrum from algorithmic variation (Mondrian-in-a-click) through incremental revision to a flash of inspiration. The degree to which the activities along the spectrum are algorithmic has advanced over the years. We presume that there will be further advancement, and we do not know where the "algorithmic frontier" will be drawn. Is creativity like reckoning—entirely algorithmic? It's too early to tell. But however it turns out, computers will be creative in so far as creativity is algorithmic. And so will we all.

Next we considered universality, the property of computers to be equivalent in terms of what they can compute. This is not only a theoretical fact. We use its practical consequences every day. For example, software companies can write a single application program and translate it into the machine language of any computer, making it available to everyone regardless of the kind of computer they own. This implied that computer vendors can only compete on speed, which led us to consider how fast computers solve problems. The many proportional-to-n computations require less work than the proportional-to-n^2 computations even though both require n data values. Such computations are practical and form the large part of computing. But there are important problems—the so-called NP-complete problems—that require much more computational work. Despite including many of the problems we would like to solve, the NP-complete problems are intractable—large instances are solvable by computer only in principle, but not in practice. Finally, we learned the amazing fact that some computations—general-purpose debugging—cannot be solved by computer even in principle. If it existed, it would solve the Halting Problem, and that's not logically possible. They're good computations to keep in mind for those times when it seems computers can do anything.

EXERCISES

1. What was Turing's Test designed to demonstrate?
2. How could a computer deceive the judge in the Turing Test if (a) it was much faster than a human, and (b) if it was much slower?
3. In the game Tic-Tac-Toe (also known as Naughts and Crosses), compute how many boards there are in the game tree if the whole tree were filled out (that is, don't stop at a win)?
4. Assuming the conditions of Exercise 3, and that a game board can be represented in three bytes, can the whole game tree be represented in a megabyte? If yes, how much extra memory is there? If not, how close is it?
5. Write a paragraph defending Deep Blue against the criticism that it isn't exhibiting its own intelligence but rather the intelligence of its creators.
6. Why doesn't Deep Blue answer the question of whether a computer can be generally intelligent?

7. Explain how the following computer-produced "work of art" might have been created.

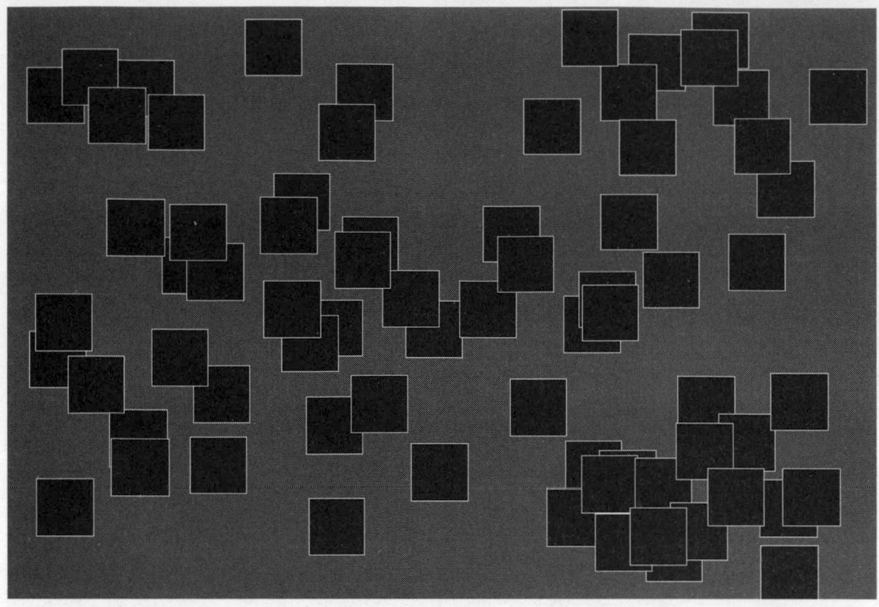

8. What are variations that could be made to the "art" of Exercise 7 that would make new never-before-seen graphics that would still be in the same style?
9. What is *universality*?
10. What does *work-proportional-to-n* mean?
11. Do computations proportional-to-n^3 typically run faster or slower than NP-complete problems?
12. Assuming a JavaScript data type "program," convert the flowchart of the CD program to JavaScript.

CHAPTER 23

Commencement, A Fluency Summary

Learning Objectives

- Understand how knowing concepts allows us to remember fewer details.
- Know the steps of lifelong learning in IT.
- Understand how Fluency enables us to control IT.

We have come to the final chapter. It has been a substantive and, at times, challenging tour. But the barrier of intimidation has collapsed, and our ability to apply IT has dramatically improved. We have studied a very broad spectrum of topics, none thoroughly enough to be considered an expert, but all thoroughly enough to indicate when we need to learn more. So, the study of IT topics is not finished, it has only just started. Fluency is a process of lifelong learning. We have reached a point where greater knowledge converts to greater effectiveness. We have not reached completion, but commencement.

In this chapter, we treat three final topics. The first discusses how our concepts-based study of information technology—though treating many topics—allows us to remember less rather than more. It is a surprise. Next we consider what we must do to keep up with the changes in IT and to continue to improve our uses of IT. Three processes can promote lifelong learning. Finally, we evaluate our new knowledge of IT in the context of driving a car and discover that we can extract the full power today while others must wait.

FLUENCY'S DETAIL SPECTRUM

In reviewing the material covered in this book, it is sobering to realize the enormous amount of detailed information that we've covered. We've learned about anchor tags in HTML, the `if/Else`-statement in JavaScript, the Vacation Message, Nyquist's Rule, SQL SELECT commands, and on and on. How can we ever remember it all?

Curiously our Fluency study allows us to remember less, rather than requiring us to remember more. How could this be?

Recall that the Fluency knowledge is compartmentalized into three classes:

- Skills—competency with contemporary IT applications like word processing.
- Concepts—knowledge of the foundations underpinning IT like the fetch/execute cycle.
- Capabilities—facility with higher level thinking processes like reasoning.

These three kinds of knowledge are co-equal and interdependent. Skills enable us to use computers today. Concepts give us the basics on which to build new knowledge in the future. Capabilities empower us to solve problems, think through the complexities of a situation, manage our work and study, and generally be in control of our IT lives. This Fluency study has covered all three.

When we analyze the three types of knowledge from the point of view of the amount of detail they involve, we realize that they are very much *unequal*. The skills all require much detailed knowledge—are field names in SQL expressed as <*table name*>.<*field name*> or <*field name*>.<*table name*>? It is impossible to write SQL without knowing which. Further, an annoying property of this detail is that the computer demands it be *exactly right*; it is unforgiving. We can't use computers without knowing such facts.

The concepts are quite detailed in their embodiment, but the "basic idea" is less demanding of specifics. We know a computer's fetch/execute cycle is an infinite process for interpreting instructions, but now that we understand the core idea, we don't really need to know that the third of the five steps is called Operand Fetch. It's the concept of an instruction execution engine that is important. IT concepts are like other scientific information. The idea must be explained in full detail for it to be understood, but when it's learned, only the idea, not the particulars, are important for the non-specialist.

And the capabilities are the least detailed of all. Capabilities are mostly approaches to thinking. Problem decomposition, for example, in which a complex task is broken into smaller tasks that are either solved directly, or are themselves broken into smaller pieces still, is simply a rational way to tackle complex problems. Debugging—thinking objectively about a faulty IT application—is mostly a matter of being a good detective. Yes, there are guidelines on how to proceed, but mostly debugging comes down to forcing yourself to look at a situation the way it *is* rather than the way you've been seeing it so far. The capabilities require you to remember almost no detail whatsoever.

So there is a spectrum of detail from skills through concepts to capabilities. But how does the spectrum save us from learning so much detail? Because our knowledge of capabilities and the ideas underlying the concepts can save us from learning any detail required for the skills until it is absolutely necessary to know it, that is, moments before we use it. Then, we need it. Afterwards, we can promptly forget it!

The clearest example—but much of our study of Fluency works this way—was our discussion of what the Digirati know. The chapter seemed to be covering skill-level information about how to use a GUI, what's behind the File and Edit menus, how to use shift-select, and so on. Everyone needs to know this information to use IT. But what the chapter was really about was the capability of *thinking abstractly about technology*, and how we learn it. We asked sweeping questions like,

- "How do we learn technology?"
- "How do software designers, indeed any tool designers, expect users to learn to use their creations?"
- "When we're confronted with a task requiring technology, how do we figure out what to do?"

The answers to these questions turned out *not* to be "Memorize thick, boring manuals." Rather, we pointed out that thinking abstractly about technology implies an adaptive approach to learning. Tool creators exploit consistent interfaces—every tape and CD player uses the same icons—so look for the consistency. Look for metaphors. When presented with a tool, explore it by "clicking around" to see what the inventor provided. Ask, what am I expected to do? And finally, simply "blaze away," trying things out and watching what happens, knowing that the garbage created when making mistakes must be thrown away (at no cost) before starting over. In other words, we don't memorize the tool's details. Rather, we learn them as we need them. If we frequently use the software, we will become adept at the specifics, learning the details through use. If we rarely use the software, we will forget them. But even that's fine. We know abstractly what to do and how to figure them out again.

Thus the higher level capabilities make us rational people, approaching IT tasks thoughtfully, enabling us to proceed in a directed and disciplined way towards the goal, solving problems as they arise, figuring out what to do as required, braining out what's wrong when a bug has us blocked. We've learned how to learn IT. Fluency doesn't require that we use our heads to memorize details. It only requires that we use our heads.

Lifelong Learning

Fluency is a process of lifelong learning, but that doesn't mean you have to read 20 pages of *Programming in XML* every night before going to bed. In fact, it doesn't mean that you have to do much at all. To learn IT throughout life requires only that you engage in three activities:

- Pursuing new uses of IT that fulfill your personal needs
- Being rational about asking for help
- Noticing the invention of new ideas and technology as they arise.

There's no course of study to attend.

Try IT

While studying Fluency, you have had to learn many new and unfamiliar applications. Though learning new skills may initially have been daunting, the process should have become steadily easier as your experience broadened and your facility with "clicking around" and "blazing away" developed. This success and the fact that learning becomes easier the more you know, should give you confidence that you can learn IT on your own. And that's the best way to advance your knowledge. Notice when you are engaged in information processing tasks—addressing envelopes, paying your bills, looking up Manila's time zone in the almanac—whether you should be using information technology to help with them. If so, be confident that you can learn the new application, and take the time to do so. Pushing out the uses you make of IT is the best way to continue to learn.

If you think objectively when you ask the question, "Can IT help in this situation?" the answer will not always be "yes." If the occasions when you address envelopes are limited to Mother's and Father's Day, IT will not help. Besides, do you want address labels on their greeting cards? If the envelope addressing is once-a-year for holiday greeting cards and you have only a modest list, again it may not pay. For the monthly reminders for the members of your book club—even if there are only five of them— it might pay to set up a postcard printing application. You'll send 60 reminders during a year, and once you've set up the announcement document and the address list, running the cards through the printer twice (two sides) might pay. When you're in charge of publicity for your club or other organization, the technology definitely pays. In summary, apply IT only if it helps, but if it can help, don't hesitate to apply it.

Asking for Help

A goal of studying Fluency is to convert you into a self-reliant computer and information user. Does that mean that you should solve all of your problems yourself? Of course, not. In fact, it is certain that there are problems that are beyond your knowledge now, and there always will be. We always need experts. So, eventually we need to get assistance from someone more knowledgeable than we are.

But acknowledging that we need to get help doesn't mean that the moment things go awry we throw up our hands in desperation. Fluency has taught us how to troubleshoot our problems, and our experience has given us some perspective. We should assess whether the problem is probably one of our own stupidity—which we would eagerly fix on our own to save the embarrassment of revealing that stupidity to someone else—or something more fundamental that requires greater expertise. Only after we've applied reasonable efforts to solving our own problem will we need to ask for help. But when we do need it, we should ask. Of course, one factor in limiting our use of professionals is that it usually takes a while, and we'd rather solve our problem ourselves than wait.

As a contributor to lifelong learning, both trying to solve our own problems and asking for help when we're truly stuck, can contribute to a greater understanding of IT. If we figure it out ourselves, we're at least more experienced at troubleshooting. If someone else helps us, we may learn some facts we didn't know. Either way, we come out ahead.

Noticing New Technology

If the technological changes of the last half-century are any guide to the changes to come, IT will be quite different at the end of the next half-century. To learn about and apply the coming advances will require some attention. Is the "advance" being touted in the press a fundamental leap forward that's potentially beneficial to me, or is it just hype about an old product in a different package? The latter is far more common than the former. We must be attentive and skeptical.

When there is a fundamental advancement—it happens more like once a decade than once a month—we need to be willing to learn about it. The media often cover the "science" of new technologies, and following these should be easy given the concepts taught in this book. Using the technology might require taking a class, but more than likely it won't. After all, thinking about technology abstractly, we know that those eager to deploy a new technology will have prepared a "migration path" for those of us who are competent, daily users of the current technology. The new advance will be much harder to use than the mature technologies with which we are familiar, of course, but if being Fluent users isn't background and experience enough to overcome those difficulties, that is, if *we* can't be successful with the new technology, it isn't ready.

It often happens that technologies—small advances as well as large ones—are rushed to market before they're ready, so there is considerable risk in being an early adopter. But waiting has its risks, too. One of technology's defining characteristics is that it steadily improves. Inventing technology is a difficult creative activity, and engineering it to be perfect the first time never happens. So, there are steady improvements—automobiles improved throughout the entire twentieth century. Thus there will always be a next-generation technology that is more convenient, more functional, more versatile with better price performance, and so on. Waiting for perfection might require a hundred-year wait, and all that time you're not benefiting from the technology. The lesson: Adopt a technology as soon as there's a high probability that it will be beneficial to you, but expect it to continue to improve.

License to Drive

Ted Nelson, the inventor of hypertext, tells a story of his first meeting with a software development team for a project he was to direct. He tells how depressed he was to find that *everyone* on the team drove a car with a standard transmission, that is, a car requiring the driver to shift gears manually. Nelson's point in telling the story is that software should be as easy for people to use as automatic transmissions are, and that programmers who enjoy shifting their own gears may not produce such software. Whether his point is correct or not, his story gives us a valuable perspective.

Fluency enables *us* to shift gears. It doesn't give us the ability to build a car, to repair it, or to modify it. But, we can control IT to extract its full power, to be in command, and to get to our goal. Nelson may be right regarding builders, but shifting is not an ability to be deplored for a user.

Fluency empowers us to use technology in a way that those who must have an automatic transmission miss. We'll happily use the convenience of an automatic transmission when it's available—we don't *have* to shift for ourselves. But shifting gives us access now, access to a technology still undergoing significant advancement. Whatever the IT equivalent is of the automatic transmission, it is still on the drawing board. It took automobiles 60 years to come with automatic transmissions. With IT's sixtieth birthday still years away, we can't wait. We'll shift for ourselves.

Exercises

1. Explain why Fluency doesn't require that you memorize more details about IT, but rather allows you to remember fewer specifics.
2. Lifelong learning with Fluency doesn't require an endless stream of short courses. What three features enable one to continue to learn more about IT throughout life?
3. What is the criterion for deciding whether you need a technological solution to an information-processing task?
4. When do you decide that you need someone's help with an IT problem?
5. How will you know about new technology that was not covered in this book?

APPENDIX A

HTML Lists, Tables, and Numerical Colors

A reasonably complete introduction to HTML basics has been given in Chapter 4. Only three basic topics have not been covered: lists, tables, and numerical colors. By briefly treating these subjects, we can complete the HTML introduction.

Lists

Lists take a variety of forms, the easiest being an unnumbered list. The unnumbered list tags <ul> and </ul> surround the items of the list, which are themselves enclosed in list item tags, <li> and </li>. The browser formats the list with the items indented and each starting on its own line, preceded by a bullet mark. As usual, though the form of the HTML doesn't matter to the browser, we write the HTML list instructions in list form. So, for example, the HTML for a movie list would be

```
<ul>
  <li>Luxo Jr.</li>
  <li>Toy Story</li>
  <li>Monsters Inc.</li>
</ul>
```

producing the result

- Luxo Jr.
- Toy Story
- Monsters Inc.

The alternative to an unnumbered list is an ordered list, which uses the tags <ol> and </ol>, and replaces the bullets with numbers. Otherwise, the ordered list behaves just like an unnumbered list. Thus the HTML for the start of the list of chemical elements is

```
<ol>
  <li> Hydrogen, H, 1.008, 1 </li>
  <li> Helium, He, 4.003, 2</li>
  <li> Lithium, Li, 6.941, 2 1 </li>
  <li> Beryllium, Be, 9.012, 2 2 </li>
</ol>
```

producing the result

1. Hydrogen, H, 1.008, 1
2. Helium, He, 4.003, 2
3. Lithium, Li, 6.941, 2 1
4. Beryllium, Be, 9.012, 2 2

It is possible to have a list within a list, simply by making the sublists items of the main list. Applying this idea in the HTML

```
<ul>
  <li>Pear</li>
  <li>Apple</li>
  <ul>
     <li>Granny Smith</li>
     <li>Fuji  </li>
  </ul>
  <li>Cherry</li>
</ul>
```

results in the output

- Pear
- Apple
  - o Granny Smith
  - o Fuji
- Cherry

Finally, there is a handy list form known as a definitional list, indicated by the tags <dl> and </dl>. A definitional list is usually composed of a sequence of definitions made up of a term, surrounded by the tags <dt> and </dt>, and a definition, surrounded by tags <dd> and </dd>. So, for example, a definitional list would be expressed in HTML as

```
<dl>
     <dt>  Man </dt>
     <dd>  <i>Homo sapiens</i>, the greatest achievement
            of evolution. </dd>
     <dt>  Woman </dt>
     <dd>  <i>Homo sapiens</i>, a greater achievement of
            evolution, but
            clever enough not to mention it to man. </dd>
</dl>
```

and would be formatted by browsers as

Man
    Homo sapiens, the greatest achievement of evolution.
Woman
    Homo sapiens, a greater achievement of evolution, but clever enough not to mention it to man.

For especially short terms, there is a more compact form in which the definition is simply continued on the same line as the term, indicated by the `compact` attribute included in the <dl> tag. For example, a definitional list of molecular biology abbreviations would be

```
<dl compact>
    <dt>A</dt>
```

```
      <dd>Adenine </dd>
      <dt>C</dt>
      <dd>Cytosine </dd>
      <dt>G</dt>
      <dd>Guanine </dd>
      <dt>T</dt>
      <dd>Thyamine </dd>
  </dl>
```

is displayed by browsers as

A Adenine
C Cytosine
G Guanine
T Thyamine

Of course, other formatting commands such as italics and bold can be used within any line items.

TABLES

A table is often the most effective way to present certain types of information. Creating a table in HTML is straightforward. In concept it is like defining a list of lists, where each of the main list items, called *rows*, have one or more items, called *cells*. The cells are aligned by the browser to form columns.

The table is enclosed in table tags, `<table>` and `</table>`. If the table is to have a border around it, use the attribute `border` inside the table tag. Each row is enclosed in table row tags, `<tr>` and `</tr>`. The cells of each row are surrounded by table data tags, `<td>` and `</td>`. So, a table with two rows, each with three cells of the form

Canada	Ottawa	English/French
Iceland	Reykjavík	Icelandic

would be defined by

```
  <table border>
    <tr>
       <td>Canada</td>
       <td>Ottawa</td>
       <td>English/French</td>
    </tr>
    <tr>
       <td>Iceland</td>
       <td>Reykjavik</td>
       <td>Icelandic</td>
    </tr>
  </table>
```

Tables can be given captions and column headings. The caption tags, `<caption>` and `</caption>` are given within the table tags and surround the table's caption. The caption is shown centered at the top of the table in bold. Column headings should be given in the first row of the table. In the heading row, the table data tags are replaced by table heading tags `<th>` and `</th>`, which also display in bold. Thus the preceding table can be revised to give it a caption and column headings:

```
  <table border>
    <caption>Country Data</caption>
```

```
    <tr>
      <th>Country</th>
      <th>Capital</th>
      <th>Language(s)</th>
    </tr>
    <tr>
      <td>Canada</td>
      <td>Ottawa</td>
      <td>English/French</td>
    </tr>
    <tr>
      <td>Iceland</td>
      <td>Reykjavik</td>
      <td>Icelandic</td>
    </tr>
    <tr>
      <td>Norway</td>
      <td>Oslo</td>
      <td>Norwegian</td>
    </tr>
  </table>
```

This coding results in the formatted output of

Country Data		
Country	**Capital**	**Language(s)**
Canada	Ottawa	English/French
Iceland	Reykjavík	Icelandic
Norway	Oslo	Norwegian

Notice that the first row uses the `<th>` tag rather than the `<td>` tag to specify the headings.

Numeric Colors

As indicated in Chapter 2, computer colors are often described by the amounts of their base constituent red, green, and blue light. The amounts are specified in a range that spans the interval from 0 through 255. So, for example, a zero amount of all three colors, specified as (0,0,0), produces the color black. Though it makes no difference for black, the order of specification is always red, green, blue—thus motivating the name *RGB color specification.* If all three colors are at full intensity, (255, 255, 255), the color is white because white is a mix of the three colors. And, if there is full intensity of one color and none of the other two, as in

```
(255,   0,   0) Intense Red
(  0, 255,   0) Intense Green
(  0,   0, 255) Intense Blue
```

the three pure colors can be generated. The three numbers are often reported to users by applications that allow "custom" colors to be selected.

Custom colors can be selected for backgrounds and fonts in HTML by giving the three RGB intensity values. The only catch is that they are not specified as a whole number between 0 and 255, but rather as a pair of hex digits between 00 and FF. A *hex digit* is one of the symbols {0, 1, 2, 3, 4, 5, 6, 7, 8, 9, A, B, C, D, E, F} from the base-16 or hexadecimal numbering system, discussed in Chapter 8. But we can use them now without understanding hex. Because the smallest value is 00, corresponding to our normal 0, and the largest value is FF, corresponding to our normal 255, the previous three pure colors are expressed in HTML as

`#FF0000` Intense Red
`#00FF00` Intense Green
`#0000FF` Intense Blue

where the number sign indicates that what follows is a hexadecimal number. The easiest way to find the values for a custom color, say, (255, 142, 42), which is the color of a carrot, is to look up the numbers in Table A.1 to find their two hex digits. To do so, find the intensity in the table and read off the first hex digit on the left end of the row and the second hex digit on the top of the column. Thus the carrot color is

`#FF8E2A` Intense Orange

because 255 translates to `FF`, 142 translates to `8E` and 42 translates to `2A`.

Though numeric colors require two levels of translation—first, the translation of the color into the three RGB intensities, and then the translation of those values into hex digit pairs—they provide considerable flexibility in Web page design. And they work with all browsers. For these reasons HTML programmers tend to prefer them.

Table A.1. Hexadecimal Digit Equivalents

Hex	**0**	**1**	**2**	**3**	**4**	**5**	**6**	**7**	**8**	**9**	**A**	**B**	**C**	**D**	**E**	**F**
0	0	1	2	3	4	5	6	7	8	9	10	11	12	13	14	15
1	16	17	18	19	20	21	22	23	24	25	26	27	28	29	30	31
2	32	33	34	35	36	37	38	39	40	41	42	43	44	45	46	47
3	48	49	50	51	52	53	54	55	56	57	58	59	60	61	62	63
4	64	65	66	67	68	69	70	71	72	73	74	75	76	77	78	79
5	80	81	82	83	84	85	86	87	88	89	90	91	92	93	94	95
6	96	97	98	99	100	101	102	103	104	105	106	107	108	109	110	111
7	112	113	114	115	116	117	118	119	120	121	122	123	124	125	126	127
8	128	129	130	131	132	133	134	135	136	137	138	139	140	141	142	143
9	144	145	146	147	148	149	150	151	152	153	154	155	156	157	158	159
A	160	161	162	163	164	165	166	167	168	169	170	171	172	173	174	175
B	176	177	178	179	180	181	182	183	184	185	186	187	188	189	190	191
C	192	193	194	195	196	197	198	199	200	201	202	203	204	205	206	207
D	208	209	210	211	212	213	214	215	216	217	218	219	220	221	222	223
E	224	225	226	227	228	229	230	231	232	233	234	235	236	237	238	239
F	240	241	242	243	244	245	246	247	248	249	250	251	252	253	254	255

Note: Find the decimal number in the table, and then combine the left column and top row symbols to form the hexadecimal equivalent. Thus decimal 180 is hexadecimal B4.

APPENDIX B

Programming Rules

The "rules" of Chapter 17 are summarized in brief statements. Because the chapter concentrated on the "unintuitive" rules, more rules are listed than were covered in the chapter. Notice the important tables at the end.

PROGRAM STRUCTURE

White space is ignored. Any number of spaces, tabs, or New-line characters can generally separate the components of a program. Avoid breaking up literals such as numbers and strings, and identifiers

Place declarations first. Declarations should appear before other statements.

First-to-last Execution. Program statements are all executed from first to last, unless specifically commanded to skip using conditional statements (or told to repeat as explained in a later chapter).

Terminate statements with semicolons. Every statement, including those on their own line, must be terminated with a semicolon (`;`), except the compound statement, i.e. the `}` is *not* followed by a semicolon.

Slash Slash Comment. Text from `//` to the end of the line is treated as a comment.

Ex. `x=3.1; //Set rate`

Slash Star-Star Slash Comment. All text enclosed by the symbols `/*` and `*/` is treated as a comment. For example, `/* The text in a Slash Star-Star Slash comment can spill across lines of program, but the Slash Slash comment is limited to one line. */`

DATA TYPES

Four rules for numbers. Numerical constants:

1. Keep the digits together without spaces, so `3.141 596` is wrong, whereas `3.141596` is right.
2. Don't use digit grouping symbols of any type, so `1,000,000` is wrong, whereas `1000000` is right.

3. The decimal point is a period, so `0,221` is wrong, whereas `0.221` is right
4. Use no units, so `33%` and `$10.89` are wrong, whereas `0.33` and `10.89` are right.

Six rules for strings. When typing string literals

1. Strings must be surrounded by quotes, either single (`'`) or double (`"`).
2. Most characters are allowed within quotes except New-line, Backspace, Tab, \, Formfeed, and Return.
3. Double quoted strings can contain single quotes, and vice versa.
4. The apostrophe (`'`) is the same as the single quote.
5. Any number of characters is allowed in a string.
6. The minimum number of characters in a string is zero (`""`), which is called the empty string.

Special string literal characters. Table 17.1 gives the escape sequences for the special characters of string literals.

Boolean data type. There are two Boolean values: `true`, `false`.

Variables and Declarations

Identifier Structure. Identifiers must begin with a letter and may contain any combination of letters, numerals, or underscore (_). Identifiers cannot contain white space. For example, `green`, `eGGs`, `ham_and_2_eggs`.

Case Sensitivity. JavaScript identifiers are case sensitive, so `y` and `Y` are different.

Reserved Words. Some words such as `var` and `true` are reserved by JavaScript and cannot be identifiers. Table B.1 lists these words. To use a word in the list as an identifier, prefix it with underscore, for example, `_Date;` but it's safer (and smarter) to think up a different identifier.

Declare variables. All variables must be declared. Do not declare any variable more than once.

Declaration list separated by commas. For example,

```
var prices, hemlines, interestRates;
```

Declaration initializers can be expressions. For example,

```
var minutesInDay = 60 * 24;
```

Expressions

Operators: A selection of JavaScript operators is given in Table B.2.

Use Parentheses: Though JavaScript uses precedence to determine the order in which to perform operators when no parentheses are given, it's for professionals. Parenthesize all complex expressions to be safe.

Operator Overloading: Plus (+) means addition for numerical operands; concatenation for string operands. If + has an operand of each type `4 + "5"`, the number converts to a string and returns a string, that is, `"45"`.

Table B.1. Reserved Words and Property Terms in JavaScript

abstract	eval	moveBy	scrollbars
alert	export	moveTo	scrollBy
arguments	extends	name	scrollTo
Array	false	NaN	self
blur	final	native	setInterval
boolean	finally	netscape	setTimeout
Boolean	find	new	short
break	float	null	static
byte	for	number	status
callee	focus	Object	statusbar
caller	frames	open	stop
captureEvents	function	opener	String
case	Function	outerHeight	super
catch	goto	outerWidth	switch
char	history	package	synchronized
class	home	Packages	this
clearInterval	if	pageXOffset	throw
clearTimeout	import	pageYOffset	throws
close	implements	parent	toolbar
closed	in	parseFloat	top
confirm	infinity	parseInt	toString
const	innerHeight	personalbar	transient
constructor	innerWidth	print	true
continue	instanceof	private	try
Date	int	prompt	typeof
debugger	interface	protected	unescape
default	isFinite	prototype	unwatch
defaultStatus	isNaN	public	valueOf
delete	java	RegExp	var
do	length	releaseEvents	void
document	location	resizeBy	watch
double	locationbar	resizeTo	while
else	long	return	window
enum	Math	routeEvent	with
escape	menubar	scroll	

Note: These words cannot be or should not be used as identifiers.

Statements

Compound statements: A sequence of statements enclosed by `{ }` is a compound statement and is treated as one statement, say, for purposes of `if` and `if/else` statements. The compound statement is not terminated by a semicolon though its constituent statements must be.

Conditional within a conditional: If a conditional's `Then`- or `Else`-clause contains another conditional, make it a compound statement (enclose it in `{}`) to avoid ambiguity as to which `if`-statement the `else` associates with.

Guidelines

Programmer's Rules: Professional programmers have a set of good programming practices including

- Choose meaningful identifiers for variables. For example, `interestRate` is better than, say, `p`.
- Insert white space liberally to improve readability of code. For example,

  ```
  if(input!="")name=first+last;
  ```

  is poor, while

  ```
  if ( input != "" )
   name = first + last;
  ```

  is preferred.

- Comment programs liberally, saying what the variables mean and what the logic is doing.
- Align code—especially when the statements are logically related—and be consistent; it helps locate errors.

  Wrong:

  ```
    able="a;
   baker = 'b';
      charlie   =   "c";
  ```

  Right:

  ```
   able    = "a";
   baker   = "b";
   charlie = "c";
  ```

Table B.2 JavaScript Operators Used in This Text

Name	Symbol	Operands and Data Types	Example	Comment	Result of Example
Addition	+	2 Numerical	4 + 5		9
Concatenation	+	2 String	"four"+"five" 6 + " pack"	1 numeric operand implies concatenate	"fourfive" "6 pack"
Subtraction	-	2 Numerical	9 - 5		4
Multiplication	*	2 Numerical	-2 * 4		-8
Division	/	2 Numerical	10/3		0.33333…
Modulus	%	2 Numerical	10%3	Remainder	1
Increment	++	1 Numerical	3++	See Chapter 20	4
Decrement	--	1 Numerical	3--	See Chapter 20	2
Less Than	<	2 Numerical	4 < 4		false
Less Than or Equal	<=	2 Numerical	4 <= 4		true
Equal	==	2 Numerical 2 String	4 == 4 "a" == "A"		true false
Not Equal	!=	2 Numerical 2 String	4 != 4 "a" != " a"		false true
Greater Than or Equal	>=	2 Numerical	4 >= 4		true
Greater Than	>	2 Numerical	4 > 4		false
Negation	-	1 Numerical	- 4		-4
Logical Not	!	1 Boolean	! true		false
Logical Add	&&	2 Boolean	true && true		true
Logical Or	||	2 Boolean	false || true		true

Note: The examples use literal data for illustrative purposes; generally the operands will be variables.

APPENDIX C

Bean Counter Code

The final HTML and JavaScript code for the Bean Counter application in Chapter 18 (Figure 18.8) is as follows. Notice that variations in Web browsers will affect how closely it matches the sample output in the figure.

```
<html>
 <head>
    <title>The Bean Counter</title>
 </head>
  <body bgcolor="#804000" text="#FF9900" align="center">
<script language = "JavaScript">
  var shots = 1;
  var drink = "none";
  var ounce = 0;
  var flavor = 0;
</script>
   <font face="Helvetica", "Arial">
   <h1 align="center"><font color="#FFFFFF">the bean counter</font></h1>
   <hr width=50%>
   <p align="center"><b>figuring the price of espresso drinks<br>
      so barristas can have time to chat</b></p>
  <form name = "Bean" >
    <center>
    <table border=2>
    <tr><td>
    <table>
     <tr bgcolor="#FF9900" align="center">
       <td>
       <input type=text name=shots_fb value=" " size=1>
       </td>
       <td>
        <input type=text name=ounce_fb value=" " size=1>
       </td>
       <td>
        <input type=text name=drink_fb value=" " size=18>
       </td>
       <td>
        <input type=text name=flavor_fb value=" " size=5>
       </td>
     </tr>
```

```
<tr>
  <td>
    <input type=button value="  1  " onClick = 'shots = 1;
          document.Bean.shots_fb.value = "  1 "'>
  </td>
  <td>
    <input type=button value="  S  " onClick = 'ounce = 8;
          document.Bean.ounce_fb.value = "  S "'>
  </td>
  <td align="center">
    <input type=button value="  ESPRESSO  "
          onClick = 'drink = "espresso";
          document.Bean.drink_fb.value = "Espresso "'>
  </td>
  <td>
    <input type = button value = " Clear "
          onClick = 'shots = 1;
          drink = "none";
          ounce = 0;
          flavor = 0;
          document.Bean.price.value     = "0.00";
          document.Bean.shots_fb.value  = " ";
          document.Bean.ounce_fb.value  = " ";
          document.Bean.drink_fb.value  = " ";
          document.Bean.flavor_fb.value = " "'>
  </td>
</tr>
<tr>
  <td>
    <input type=button value="  2  " onClick = 'shots = 2;
          document.Bean.shots_fb.value = " 2 "'>
  </td>
  <td>
    <input type=button value="  T  " onClick = 'ounce = 12;
          document.Bean.ounce_fb.value = " T "'>
  </td>
  <td align="center">
    <input type=button value="    LATTE    "
          onClick = 'drink = "latte";
          document.Bean.drink_fb.value = "Latte "'>
  </td>
  <td>
    <input type=button value="Flavor" onClick='flavor=.4;
          document.Bean.flavor_fb.value = "Flavor"'>
  </td>
</tr>
<tr>
  <td>
    <input type=button value="  3  " onClick = 'shots = 3;
          document.Bean.shots_fb.value = " 3 "'>
  </td>
  <td>
    <input type=button value="  G  " onClick = 'ounce = 16;
          document.Bean.ounce_fb.value = " G "'>
  </td>
  <td align="center">
    <input type=button value="CAPPUCCINO"
          onClick = 'drink = "cappuccino";
          document.Bean.drink_fb.value = "Cappuccino "'>
  </td>
  <td>
    <input type = button value = " Total " onClick =
```

```
          'var price;
           var taxRate = 0.087;
          if (drink == "espresso")
               price = 1.00;
          if (drink == "latte" || drink == "cappuccino"){
             if (ounce == 8)
                     price = 1.55;
             if (ounce == 12)
                     price = 1.95;
             if (ounce == 16)
                     price = 2.35;
           }
           if (drink == "Americano")
                price = 1.10 + .30 * (ounce/8);
                price = price + (shots - 1) * .70 + flavor;
                price = price + price * taxRate;
                document.Bean.price.value = Math.round(price*100)/100;
         '>
         </td>
      </tr>
      <tr>
         <td>
           <input type=button value="  4  " onClick = 'shots = 4;
                 document.Bean.shots_fb.value = " 4 "'>
         </td>
         <td>
         </td>
         <td align="center">
           <input type=button value=" AMERICANO "
                 onClick = 'drink = "Americano";
                 document.Bean.drink_fb.value = "Americano "'>
         </td>
           <td bgcolor="red" align="center">
           <input type=text name=price value="0.00" size=5>
         </td>
      </tr>
     </table>
     </td></tr>
     </table>
     </center>
   </form>
  </body>
</html>
```

APPENDIX D

Memory Bank Code

The following HTML and JavaScript text produced the Memory Bank in Chapter 19 (Figure 19.7).

```
<html>
<head><title>Fact Page</title></head>
<body bgcolor="#000000" text="#FF9900" >
  <font face="Helvetica", "Arial">
  <h1 align="center"><font color="#FFFFFF">Memory Bank</font></h1>
  <hr width=50%>
  <b><p align="center" > <font color="#FF0000" > a convenient table of all
      the computations I can never remember </font></p>
  <script language = 'JavaScript'>
     document.write('<center>' + (Date().toString()) + '<center>');
  </script>
  <form name="memory">
  <table align="center" border=2>
  <tr>
    <td><b>Celsius to Fahrenheit</b></td>
    <td>
     Celsius: <input type = text name = cTemp size = 4
        onChange="tempInF.value=convertC2F(cTemp.value)">
     Fahrenheit: <input type = text name = tempInF size = 5></td></tr>
  <tr>
    <td><b>Fahrenheit to Celsius</b></td>
    <td>
     Fahrenheit: <input type = text name = fTemp size = 5
        onChange="tempInC.value = convertF2C(fTemp.value)">
     Celsius: <input type = text name = tempInC size = 4></td></tr>
  <tr>
    <td><b>Body Mass Index</b>
      <input type = radio name = pick1 checked = TRUE
        onClick='measure="English"'>English
      <input type = radio name= pick1
        onClick='measure="metric"'>Metric</td>
    <td>Height:
      <input type = text name = howtall size = 4
        onChange = 'if (howwide.value != 0)
               shape.value = BMI(measure, howtall.value, howwide.value)'> Weight:
      <input type = text name = howwide size = 4
```

```
                              onChange = 'if (howtall.value != 0)
                  shape.value = BMI(measure, howtall.value, howwide.value)'> BMI:
         <input type = text name = shape size = 5></td></tr>
     <tr>
       <td><b>Electronic Coin Flip </b></td>
       <td>           <input type = button value = "Flip" onClick="runTrial()">
           Outcome:   <input type = text name = coin size = 5>
           Totals:  H <input type = text name = heads size = 3 value = 0>
               T <input type = text name = tails size = 3 value = 0></td></tr>
     <tr>
       <td><b>Pick A Random Number From 1 To </b>
        <input type = text name = topEnd size = 2 value = 10> </td>
       <td>
         <input type = button value = "Pick"
             onClick="choice.value=1+randNum(topEnd.value)">     Outcome from the range:
         <input type = text name = choice size = 2></td></tr>
     <tr>
       <td colspan = 2> <center><b>IMPORTANT LINKS </b></center>

       <!--  The standard form for the links is ...
           <br><b> ___topic name___...</b>
            <img src='bullet.gif'><a href='http://____url goes here_______'>
                 _____anchor term(s)______</a>
       -->

        <br><b>References ... </b>
           <img src='bullet.gif'><a href='http://dictionary.cambridge.org'>
             Cambridge Dictionary</a>
           <img src='bullet.gif'><a href='http://www.wordsmyth.net'>Thesaurus</a>

        <br><b>Classes ... </b>
           <img src='bullet.gif'><a href='http://www.cs.washington.edu/100'>
             Fluency Class</a>
             <img src='bullet.gif'><a
             href='http://www.chemsoc.org/viselements/pages/pertable_j.htm'>
             Periodic Table</a>
           <img src='bullet.gif'><a href='http://www.state.gov/r/poa/gbn'>
             Countries for Geography</a>
        </td></tr>
   </table></b>
   </form>
   <script language = "JavaScript">
     // Declare a global variable
     var measure = "English";  // The default measure;
     var headCount = 0, tailCount = 0; // Keep score

     function convertC2F( cTemp ) {
        // Figures Fahrenheit equivalent of cTemp
        return Math.round( 9 * cTemp / 5 + 32);
     }

     function convertF2C( fTemp ) {
        // Figures Celsius equivalent of fTemp
        return Math.round(5 / 9 *(fTemp - 32));
     }

     function bmiE ( weightLBS, heightIn ) {
        // Figure Body Mass Index in English units
        var heightFt = heightIn / 12;  // Change to feet
        return 4.89 * weightLBS / (heightFt * heightFt);
     }
```

```
    function bmiM ( weightKg, heightM ) {
       // Figure Body Mass Index in Metric units
       return weightKg / (heightM * heightM);
    }

    function BMI( units, height, weight ) {
       // Calculate Body Mass Index in English or Metric
       if (units == "English")
           return Math.round(bmiE(weight, height)*10)/10;
       else
           return Math.round(bmiM(weight, height)*10)/10;
    }

    function randNum(range) {
       return Math.floor(Math.random()* range);
    }

    function runTrial() {
       if (randNum(2) == 1) {
          document.memory.coin.value = "Heads";
         headCount = headCount + 1;
          document.memory.heads.value = headCount;
       }
       else {
          document.memory.coin.value = "Tails";
         tailCount = tailCount + 1;
          document.memory.tails.value = tailCount;
       }
    }
       var today = new Date();     // Get today's date
       var myBdate = new Date();  // Get a date object to modify
       var difference;             //
       myBdate.setFullYear(1984); // Set my birth year to 1984
       myBdate.setMonth(6);       // Set my birth month to July (mo.s start at 0)
       myBdate.setDate(4);        // Set my birth day to 4th
       myBdate.setHours(11);      // Set my hour of birth to noon
       myBdate.setMinutes(0);     // Set my minute of birth to o'clock
       myBdate.setSeconds(0);     // Set my second of birth to smack on the hour
       difference = today.getTime() - myBdate.getTime();
       difference = Math.floor(difference/1000);
       document.write("<center><b><font color=yellow> I'm " + difference +
            " seconds old.  What <i>am</i> I doing with my life?</font></b><center>");
  </script>
  </body>
  </html>.
```

APPENDIX E

Glossary

Acronyms have their letters spoken, as in H-T-M-L, unless pronunciation is indicated, as in *JAY·peg*.

***1*-way cipher**, see one-way cipher

***2*-tier**, see two-tier

***3*-tier**, see three-tier

absolute pathname, navigation information for locating files in HTML using complete URLs

abstract, to remove an idea, concept, or process from a specific situation

administrative authority, see superuser

algorithm, a precise and systematic method for producing a specified result

alphanumeric, describing characters or text as being composed solely of letters, numbers, and possibly a few special characters like spaces and tabs, but not punctuation

ALU, acronym for arithmetic/logic unit

analog signal, a continuously varying representation of a phenomenon, e.g., a sound wave

anchor, the HTML tag that specifies a link, or the text associated with the reference that is highlighted in the document

applet, a small application program, often written in Java, that is executed on a client

argument, a value provided for a parameter in a function call

arithmetic/logic unit, a subsystem of a computer that performs the operations of an instruction

array, in programming, a variable having multiple elements named by the composition of an identifier and an index

assembly language, a symbolic form of a binary machine language

assignment statement, a programming command expressed with a variable on the left and a variable or expression on the right of an assignment symbol, usually =

asynchronous, in communication, indicates that the actions of senders and receivers occur at separate times, as in the exchange of email

attribute, in HTML, a parameter used within HTML tags to specify additional information; in databases, a property of an entity; also called a field

b, abbreviation for bit, e.g., Kb is kilobits

B, abbreviation for byte, e.g., KB is kilobytes

bandwidth, the bit-transmission capacity of a channel, usually measured in bits per second

binary, having two related components

binary number, a quantity expressed in radix 2 number representation

binary operator, an operator such as addition (+) having two operands

binary representation, any information encoding using symbols formed from two patterns; also called PandA representation in this book

bit, basic unit of information representation having two states, usually denoted 0 and 1

bit-mapped, as in bit-mapped display, indicates that the display's video image is stored pixel-by-pixel in the computer's memory

blaze away, a term used in this book for trying out an application to become familiarized with its operation

bookmark, to record a URL locally to simplify referencing it again

Boolean, having the property of being either true or false

boot, to start a computer and load its operating system

broadcast, a type of transmission of information from one sender to all receivers

bug, an error in a computer, program, or process

byte, a sequence of eight bits treated as a unit

cable, a bundle of wires carrying power and signals between computer components; also called cord or wires

cancel, a command button that stops a dialog or series of operations without penalty or effect

card, a small printed circuit board usually plugged into a socket on a motherboard to provide additional functionality; also called a daughter board

CGI, acronym for Common Gateway Interface

character, an upper- and lowercase Latin letter, Arabic numeral, or English punctuation; can be used more generally to include the alphabet and punctuation for other natural languages

classifier, a component of an optical character recognition system that ranks characters by the probability that they match a given set of features

cleartext, information before encryption or after decryption

click, to press and release a mouse button

click around, to navigate a Web site or file structure; a synonym in this book for exploring the features of an application

click-with-shift, in selection, to maintain the selected status of all items except the clicked item, which is either selected if it is not selected or vice versa; also called shift select

client, a computer that receives the services in a client/server structure

client/server, a relationship between two computers in which the client computer requests services from the server computer

close, to terminate a GUI window and, if the window is the primary or only window, to terminate the application

collating sequence, an ordering for a set of symbols used to sort them; for example, alphabetical ordering

command button, a synthesized image of a GUI appearing to be a 3D button used to cause some operation to be performed; the HTML button input control

Common Gateway Interface (CGI), an extension to HTML allowing browsers to cause a Web server to run programs on their behalf with specific data

compile, to translate a programming language into assembly language

compression, encoding information with fewer bits than a given representation by exploiting properties of regularity or unimportance

compression ratio, the factor by which compression reduces an encoding from its uncompressed size

computable, a task that can be performed by computer, algorithmic

computer, a device that deterministically follows instructions to process information

conditional, a programming statement, usually identified by `if`, that optionally executes statements depending on the outcome of a Boolean test

continuation test, a Boolean expression to determine whether an iteration statement will execute its statement sequence again; also called a termination test

control, a subsystem of a computer that is the hardware implementation of the Fetch/Execute Cycle

cookie, information stored on a Web client computer by an http server computer

copyright, the legal protection of many forms of intellectual property

cracker, a person attempting to break a code

crawler, a program that navigates the Internet, cataloging and indexing the Web pages by the words they contain for use by a query processor

CRT, acronym for cathode ray tube, a video display technology

cryptography, the study of encryption and decryption methods

cycle power, to turn a computer off, wait a moment, and then turn it back on

daemon, a program that periodically "wakes up" to perform some system management task

data controller, in Fair Information Practices, the person who sets policies, responds to individuals regarding their information, if any, and is accountable for those policies and actions

Data Fetch, third step in the Fetch/Execute Cycle, the action of retrieving the instruction's operands from memory

data type, a set of values for which operations are defined, e.g., number

database scheme or **schema**, the declaration of entities and relationships of a database

debugging, the act of discovering why a deterministic system is not working properly

decrypt, to recover the original information from a digitally encrypted representation

definiteness, a property of algorithms that requires a specific sequence of steps be defined

DF, in processor design an acronym for Data Fetch

digital signal, a discrete or "step levels" representation of a phenomenon, varying "instantaneously"

digitally decrypt, see decrypt

digitally encrypt, see encrypt

digitize, originally to encode with decimal numerals, now to encode in bits

directory, a named collection of files or other directories; also called a folder on Mac and Windows operating systems

discrete, distinct or separable, not able to be changed by continuous variation

display rate, in animation, the frequency with which the images are changed

domain, in networking, a related set of networked computers, e.g., `edu` is the set of education-related computers

Domain Name System, the collection of Internet-connected computers that translate domain addresses into IP addresses

dual booting, loading two operating systems at once

eCommerce, use of electronic data communication to conduct business

effectiveness, a property of algorithms requiring that all instructions be performed mechanically within the capabilities of the executing agent

element, an indexed item; also called array element

empty string, a character sequence of zero length

emoticon, any character sequence written to express by its physical form an emotion, common in email; for example, the "smiley face" **:)** to express happiness or humor

encrypt, to transform a digital representation so the information cannot be readily discerned

ER diagram, Entity-Relationship diagram, a visual presentation of some or all of a database schema

escape symbol, a character, often `&` or `\`, prefixing another character or word to enlarge a character encoding, e.g., `&infinity` to encode ∞

EX, in processor design, the abbreviation for Instruction Execution

execute, to perform the instructions of a program, usually by a computer; to run a program

Extensible Markup Language (XML), a W3C standard for structured information encoding

factor of improvement, the amount by which a first measurement must be multiplied to be equivalent to the second measurement when computing scale of change

fair use, a concept in copyright law in which copyright limitations are waived for explicitly listed, socially valuable purposes

feature, a component of a character in a optical character recognition system

Fetch/Execute Cycle, the basic instruction execution process of a computer

field inputs, character input such as telephone numbers with a specific structure

finiteness, a property of algorithms requiring that they terminate with the intended result or an indication that no solution is possible

firmware, instructions incorporated into the hardware, usually changeable by external means with difficulty

flame-a-thon, email battle; also called flame war

floppy disk, a storage device providing persistent memory using (removable) diskettes; also called floppy drive

`for`-statement, a common programming structure for iterating a sequence of instruction over a regular range of index values

formal language, synthetic notation designed for expressing algorithms and programs

frame, in animation, one of many images rapidly redrawn to create the illusion of motion

freeware, software available on the Web at no cost

full backup, a complete copy of a body of information usually as of a specific point in time

function, a programming structure with a name, optional parameter list, and a definition that encapsulates an algorithm

function body, the definition of a function's computation

function declaration, the specification of a function, including its name, parameters, and body

game tree, a conceptualization of the possible future configurations of a multiperson game

generalize, to formulate an idea, concept, or process so that it abstracts multiple situations

GIF, file extension, e.g., `picture.gif`, specifying a graphic image format, pronounced with either soft or hard *g*

giga, prefix for billion; if prefixing a quantity counted in binary, e.g., memory, prefix for 1,073,741,824; pronounced with a hard *g*

global variable, a variable declared outside the scope of a function, usually at the start of the program

graphic user interface (GUI), the synthesized visual medium of interaction between a user and a computer

GUI, acronym for graphic user interface, pronounced *gooey*

Halting Problem, the problem of determining if a computation halts for a given input, a problem that cannot be solved by computer

handle, in programming, a binary value returned by a function or server to be used for subsequent references

haptic device, an input/output technology interfacing with the sense of touch

hard disk, a storage device providing persistent memory, also called a disk or hard drive

hardware, the physical implementation of a computer, usually electronic, including the processor, memory, and usually its peripheral devices

heuristic, a guideline to help solve a problem but one that does guarantee a solution; for example, "when looking for a lost article check the last place you used it"

hex digit, one of the sixteen numerals of hexadecimal, 0, 1, 2, 3, 4, 5, 6, 7, 8, 9, A, B, C, D, E, F

hexadecimal, radix 16 number representation

hierarchical index, a structure for organizing information using descriptive terms that partition the information

hierarchy, an organizing structure composed of a sequence of levels that partition all items so that those of one level are partitioned into smaller groups at the next level

hit, for a Web search, a match to a query; for a Web site, a visit

hop, in networking, the transfer of a packet or message to an adjacent router

HTML, acronym for hypertext markup language

HTTP, acronym for hypertext transfer protocol

hypertext markup language, a common notation for specifying the form of a Web page to a browser

hypertext transfer protocol, the rules governing interaction between client and server on the World Wide Web

Hz, abbreviation for Hertz, cycles, or repetitions per second

ID, in processor design, an acronym for Instruction Decode

identifier, a legal sequence of letters, numerals, or punctuation marks forming the name of variable, file, directory, etc.

IF, in processor design, an acronym for Instruction Fetch

`if`-statement, a programming a structure allowing the conditional execution of statements based on the outcome of a Boolean test

index, in information structures, a organizing mechanism used to find information in a large collection; in programming, the number that together with an identifier forms an array reference

index origin, the number at which indexing begins; the least index

index value, the result of evaluating an index expression; the number of an array element

indexing, in programming, the mechanism of associating a number and an identifier to locate an element

infix operator, a binary operator, e.g., +, whose syntax requires that it be written between its operands, as in 4 + 3

Input Unit, a subsystem of a computer transferring information from the physical world via an input device to the computer's memory

instance, the current values of an entity, table, or database

Instruction Decode, second step in the Fetch/Execute Cycle, the action of determining which operation is to be performed and computing the addresses of the operands

Instruction Execution, the fourth step in the Fetch/Execute Cycle, the action of performing a machine instruction

Instruction Fetch, first step in the Fetch/Execute Cycle, the action of retrieving a machine instruction from the memory address given by the program counter

integer, a whole number; in programming, a data type for a whole number, either positive or negative

integration, in silicon technology, the ability to fabricate both active and connective parts of a circuit using a family of compatible materials in a single complexity-independent process

intellectual property, creations of the human mind that have value to others

Internet, the totality of all wires, fibers, switches, routers, satellite links, and other hardware used to transport information between named computers

Internet Service Provider (ISP), a utility that connects private and business computers to the Internet

interpolation, the smooth movement from one discrete value to another.

intractable, a description for computations solvable by computer in principle, but not in practice

invocation (of a function), to call the function

IP, acronym for Internet Protocol

IP address, the address of an Internet-networked computer composed of four numbers in the range 0–255

IP packet, a fixed quantum of information packaged together with an IP address and other data for sending information over the Internet

ISO, acronym for the International Standards Organization

ISP, acronym for Internet Service Provider

iterate, in programming, to repeatedly execute a sequence of statements

iteration variable, any variable controlling an iteration statement such as a `for`-statement

JPEG, acronym for the nickname Joint Photographic Experts Group, a committee of the ISO; pronounced *JAY·peg*

JPG, file extension, e.g., `picture.jpg`, for JPEG encoding

key, in databases, field(s) that make the rows of an entity (table) unique; in cryptography, selectable code used to encrypt and subsequently decrypt information

kilo, prefix for thousand; if prefixing a quantity counted in binary, e.g., memory, prefix for 1,024

LAN, acronym for local area network, usually pronounced

latency, the time required to deliver or generate information

LCD, acronym for liquid crystal display, a video display technology

length (of an array), the number of elements in an array

lexical structure, a specification of the form of character input; for example, telephone numbers in North America are formed of ten Arabic numerals with a space following the third and a hyphen following the sixth

local area network (LAN), a network connecting computers within a small physical space such as a building

local variable, a variable declared within a function

logical operators, any of the connectives *and*, *or*, or *not*

lossless compression, the process of reducing the number of bits required to represent information in which the original form can be exactly reconstructed

lossy compression, the process of reducing the number of bits required to represent information in which the original cannot be exactly reconstructed

machine language, computer instructions expressed in binary, respecting the form required for a specific machine

mask, in fabrication technology, a planar material similar to a photographic negative containing the pattern to be transferred to the silicon surface in the process of constructing a chip

mega, prefix for million; if prefixing a quantity counted in binary, e.g., memory, prefix for 1,048,576

memory, device capable of storing information, usually in fixed size, addressable units; a subsystem of a computer used to store programs and their data while they execute

memory address, a whole number designating a specific location in a computer's memory

menu, a list of available operations from which a user can select by clicking on one item

metadata, information describing the properties of other information

microprocessor, see processor

middleware, software intermediating between Web clients and databases or other systems for producing online services

mnemonic, any aid to remembering

moderator, a person responsible for deciding what is to be sent out to a mailing list

monitor, a computer's video output device or display; also called a *screen*

mot juste, Anglicanized French, meaning "the right word or phrase"

motherboard, a printed circuit board containing the processor chip, memory, and other electronics of a computer

MPEG, acronym for the nickname Motion Picture Experts Group, a committee of the ISO, pronounced *EM·peg*

MPG, file extension, e.g., `flick.mpg`, for MPEG encoding

multicast, a type of transmission of information from one sender to many receivers

***n*-tier**, a multilayer system design, usually for providing Web services

name conflict, the attempt to give a different definition, e.g., variable declaration, to an identifier with an existing meaning

navigation, in searching, to follow a series of links to locate specific information often in a hierarchy

nested loops, the condition of a loop (inner loop) appearing in the statement sequence of another loop (outer loop)

netiquette, etiquette on the Internet

NP-complete, a measure of difficulty of problems believed to be intractable for computers

Nyquist Rule, a digitization guideline stating that the sampling frequency should exceed the signal frequency by at least two times

OCR, acronym for optical character recognition

one-way cipher, a form of encryption that cannot easily be reversed, i.e., decrypted, often used for passwords

operand, the data used in computer instructions; the value(s) on which operators compute

operationally attuned, in this book the characteristic of thinking about how a system works to simplify its use

operator overloading, a property of some programming languages in which operators like + have different meanings depending on their operand data types, e.g., + used for both addition or concatenation in JavaScript

optical character recognition (OCR), a computer application in which printed text is converted to the ASCII letters that it represents

Output Unit, a subsystem of a computer that transfers information from the computer's memory to the physical world via an output device

overflow exception, an error condition for operations such as addition in which a result is too large to be represented in the available number of bits

PandA representation, in this book, a mnemonic for "present and absent encoding," the fundamental physical representation of information; also called binary representation

parallel computation, the use of multiple computers to solve a single problem

parameter, an input to a function

partial backup, the new information copied to another medium that has been added to a system since the last full or partial backup

PC, acronym for program counter, for printed circuit (board), and for personal computer

photolithography, a process of transferring a pattern by means of light shown through a mask or negative

photoresist, a material used in a silicon chip fabrication process that is chemically changed by light, allowing it to be patterned by a mask

picture element or **pixel**, the smallest displayable unit of a video monitor

pins, stiff wires in a cable's plug that insert into sockets to make the connection

pixel, contraction for picture element

placeholder technique, a searching algorithm in which strings are temporarily replaced with a special character to protect them from change by other substitution commands

plaintext, synonym for cleartext

point-to-point, a type of transmission of information from one sender to one receiver

pop-up menu, a menu that is displayed at the cursor position when the mouse is clicked

precedence, the relationship among operators describing which is to be performed first

prefetching, in online animation the process of loading the images prior to beginning an animation

primary source, a person who provides information based on direct knowledge or experience

privacy, the right of people to choose freely the circumstances under which and the extent to which they will reveal themselves, their attitudes, and their behaviors to others

procedural abstraction, the encapsulation of a sequence of instructions (algorithm) into a function or procedure

processor, the component of a computer that computes, that is, performs the instructions

program, an algorithm encoded for a specific situation

program counter, a register in a computer that stores the address of the next instruction to be executed

public domain, the status of a work in which the copyright owner has explicitly given up the rights

public key, a key published by the receiver and used by the sender to encrypt messages

pull-down menu, a menu positioned at the top of a GUI window, also called a drop-down menu

QBE, acronym for Query by Example

query, database command defining a table expressed using the five database operators

Query by Example, a method for defining queries in a database

query processor, the part of a search engine that uses the crawler's index to report Web pages associated with keywords provided by a user

quotient-remainder form of division, a means of expressing the division of a/b as the solution to the equation $a = b \cdot c + d$, where c is the quotient and d is the remainder

radix, the "base" of a numbering system; equivalently, the number of digits in each place

RAM, acronym for random access memory, pronounced

random access, to reference an item directly; contrast with sequential access

random access memory, memory; a subsystem of a computer used for storing programs and data while they execute

reboot, to restart a computer by clearing its memory and reloading its operating system

reckon, archaic term for performing arithmetic calculations

reference, in HTML, the displayed and highlighted portion of an anchor tag

refresh rate, the frequency with which a video display is redisplayed

relational operator, one of six operators ($< \leq = \neq \geq >$) that compare two values; in JavaScript programming, one of the six operators (`<  <=  ==  !=  >=  >`)

relationship, a correspondence between two tables of a database

relative pathname, local navigation information for locating a file in HTML

replacement string, in editing, the letter sequence that substitutes for the search string

Result Return, the fifth and final step of the Fetch/Execute Cycle, the action of storing to memory the value produced by executing a machine instruction

RGB, acronym for red, green, blue, a color encoding method

ROM, acronym for "read only memory," permanently set memory, pronounced

row, a set of values for the fields of a table, also called a *tuple*

RR, in processor design, an acronym for Result Return

RSA, a public key encryption method invented by Rivest, Shamir, and Adelman

run-length encoding, a representation in which numbers are used to give the lengths of consecutive sequences of 0s or 1s.

sample, to take measurements at a regular intervals as in sound digitization

sampling rate, the number of samples per second

scope, in programming, the range of statements over which a variable or other defined object is known

screen saver, a changing image or animation that displays on a computer's monitor while the computer is idle

scroll bar, a slider control appearing at the side and/or bottom of a window when the information cannot be fully displayed

SCSI, acronym for "small computer system interface," pronounced *scuzzy*

search engine, a software system composed of a crawler and a query processor that helps users locate specific information on the World Wide Web or specific Web site

search string, the information being sought in a text search

seat, to firmly insert a plug into a socket after an initial alignment

secondary source, a person providing information without direct knowledge or experience of the topic; contrast primary source

self-describing encoding, a representation using meta-data tags that embeds its own structure, as in XML

sequential access, a memory reference pattern in which no item can be referenced without passing (skipping or referencing) the items that precede it; contrast random access

serialized behavior, a property of transactions that execute simultaneously stating that only a single result is produced no matter in what order their constituent operations are performed

server, a computer providing the services in a client/server structure

shareware, software available on the Web, paid for on the honor system

shift-select, a GUI command in which the shift key is pressed while the mouse selects an item, to avoid deselecting the items already selected; also called click-with-shift

slider control, a synthesized slot in which a bar can be moved to select a position in a continuous range

software, a collective term for programs

source, in context of the World Wide Web, the HTML or other text description of how a Web page should be displayed

SQL, acronym for Structured Query Language

string, in searching, a sequence of characters; in programming, a data type for a sequence of characters

Structured Query Language, a standard notation for defining tables from tables in a database

subscript, a synonym for index

substitution, in searching, the result of replacing a substring of a character sequence with another string

superuser authority, the capability to access all functions of a computer or software system, including overriding passwords, also called administrative authority

symbol, an information code formed from a specific sequence of base patterns; for example, 01000001 is the ASCII symbol for *A* formed from patterns 0 and 1

synchronous, in communication, indicates that the actions of senders and receivers occur at the same time, as in a telephone call

table, an organizing mechanism for database entities

tag, a word or abbreviation enclosed in angle brackets, usually paired with a companion starting with a slash, that describes a property of data or expresses a command to be performed; e.g., `<italic>You're It!</italic>`

TCP/IP, acronym for Transmission Control Protocol, Internet Protocol

template, the structural information of a document with placeholders for content that is filled in to produce a complete document

tera, prefix for trillion; in prefixing, a quantity counted in binary, e.g., memory, prefix for 1,099,511,627,776

termination test, synonym for continuation test

text, a sequence of characters; in searching, the material being searched

text editor, basic software to create and modify text files; contrast with word processor

three-tier, a three-layer system design, often the client/server structure extended with a backend database

toggling, reversing the state of an item, as in to toggle between selected and deselected

token, a symbol sequence treated as a single unit in searching or languages

transducer, device converting waves of one form into waves of another, usually electrical

translate, as an image, to move an image to a new position unchanged; in programming, to convert a program from one formal language to another, usually a simpler one; a synonym for *compile*

triangle pointers, small triangles indicating hidden information; clicking on the triangle pointer displays the information

Trojan horse, a useful and apparently innocuous program containing hidden code that allows the unauthorized collection, exploitation, or destruction of data

tuple, a set of values for the attributes of an entity, also called a *row*

Turing Test, an experimental setting to determine if a computer and a person can be distinguished by their answers to a judge's questions

two-tier, a two-layer system design, usually the client/server structure

unary operator, an operator such as negation (-) with a single operand

Universal Resource Locator (URL), a two-part name for a Web page composed of an IP address followed by the filename, which can default to `index.html`

universality, a property of computation that all computers with a minimal set of instructions can compute the same set of computations

URL, acronym for Universal Resource Locator

vacation message, an automated reply to email when there is a planned delay in reading it

variable, a named quantity in a programming language

virtual, a modifier meaning not actually, but as if

virus, a program that "infects" another program by embedding a (possibly evolved) copy of itself

volatile, the property of integrated circuit memory in which the stored information is lost when the power is removed

W3C, acronym for World Wide Web Consortium

WAN, acronym for wide area network

Web, short form for World Wide Web

Web client, a computer requesting services from a Web server; a computer running a Web browser

Web server, a computer providing pages to Web clients; a computer hosting a Web page

wide area network, a network connecting computers over a wider area than a few kilometers

word processor, software to create and modify text files that include formatting tags; contrast text editor

work-proportional-to-*n*, a description of the time required to solve a problem with input of size *n*

World Wide Web, the collection of all HTML servers connected by the Internet and their information resources

World Wide Web Consortium, a standards body composed mainly of companies that produce Web software

worm, an independent program that replicates itself from machine to machine across network connections

WYSIWYG, acronym for "what you see is what you get," pronounced *WHIZ·ee·wig*

XML, acronym for extensible markup language

APPENDIX F

Problem Solutions

Solutions to the odd-numbered problems are given when there is a specific answer.

Chapter 1

1. Information technology includes the phenomena of computers, networks, information resources, software and applications, and their use. It encompasses virtually everything encountered when using a personal computer.
3. When figuring the scale of change, the factor of improvement is the number that a first measurement must be multiplied by to compute a value equal to a second measurement.
5. 2.
7. Information that people routinely need—vacation planning information, stock market quotations, sports information, etc.—is available electronically, making it equally convenient from any physical location.
9. One example concerns email. In most companies, email is archived and often reviewed by supervisors. Many employees, without thinking about it, say things in email that they wouldn't say in the elevators. This might lead to negative results such as not getting a raise, promotion, or other forms of recognition.
11. It means that no person or organization censors or limits in any way the information that is communicated.
13. One example is that it enhances privacy because it is possible to find out information via the World Wide Web on topics that might be embarrassing such as information about sexually transmitted diseases.
15. Yes, check out such skills as typing speed, longevity, i.e., the length of life, etc.

Chapter 2

1. IT involves many new ideas, which require new words or the use of old words in new senses to name them.
3. Knowing the right word helps us to remember and understand a concept, and it helps when communicating with others or with an online help system.
5. A TV is passive, displaying the images that are being seen (or were seen) through the lens of the camera, whereas the computer displays an image created in its memory. This difference requires the TV to "see" reality and a computer to "make" reality.
7. P.I.L.P.O.F.—plug in last, pull out first.
9. (Solution varies with computer monitor.) For 10 pt. 5×6; for 24 pt, 11×12.

11. (Solution varies with application and computer chosen.) On some applications, buttons are smoothed on the corners to appear to be more rounded. This is accomplished by not extending the line to the corner and then shading the corner pixels so they appear "rounded." Another technique is to use several shades of gray to give the button a more "3D" look. The Mac uses a complex arrangement of white to make the button appear to be translucent.
13. Save the text and background at the point where the mouse pointer should appear. Draw the mouse pointer and then redraw the black pixels of the text but not the background of the text on top of the pointer.
15. 100, because the screen will be updated $10 = 30 \cdot 1/3$ times in the 1/3 of a second, assuming a 30 Hz refresh rate, or 1000/10.

Chapter 3

1. They are taught how to use it, they read the operator's manual, and they figure it out based on their previous experience with other, similar technologies.
3. The Mac interface emphasizes verisimilitude to a physical device and discreetly hides all auxiliary features, e.g., track names, behind a triangle pointer or in the menus. The Window interface emphasizes usability by placing those features most likely to be needed routinely prominently on the GUI. The Mac creates a special font to be realistic, whereas the Windows player uses routine interface features like underscore shortcuts. The former is perfectly suggestive, emphasizing easy learning; the latter exploits standard interfaces, emphasizing routine use. For routine use the Mac might require customization, whereas the Windows player can probably be used directly.
5. (Answer may vary with machine and application.) Using *Cl* to mean either "clover" for Mac or "control" for PC: new—Cl N, open—Cl O, save—Cl S, print—Cl P, cut—Cl X, copy—Cl C, paste—Cl V, undo—Cl Z, and exit—Cl Q.
7. All operations happen so fast that they are effectively instantaneous. The computer has always finished calculating and has displayed the result before the screen is refreshed again.
9. "Nothing will break!" "When stuck, start over."
11. Change all three to the new color and then change the middle light back to yellow.
13. The task and not the specific software implementation dictates the behavior of a solution.
15. 144, because there are 144 characters up to and including the *c* in *content.*
17. (The answer may be system specific.) Generally, the two pairs will be replaced, yielding · · .

Chapter 4

1. The totality of all of the wires, fibers, switches, routers, satellite links, and other hardware for transporting information between named computers.
3. In synchronous communication, the sender and receiver must participate at the same time, whereas in asynchronous communication, the sender transmits and some time later the receiver receives, i.e., the two sides of a communication are separated in time.
5. A related set of networked computers.
7. Domain Name System. It maps human readable domain names into IP addresses.
9. Seriously. Use this problem as a break from doing Fluency exercises. Your relative will like it.
11. The WWW is a collection of computers, known as Web servers, and the files and databases of information that they can transmit to other computers.
13. A *description* of how to display a Web page.
15. Any sequence of blanks, tabs, or New-lines.

17. Your paragraphs will be different from the following:

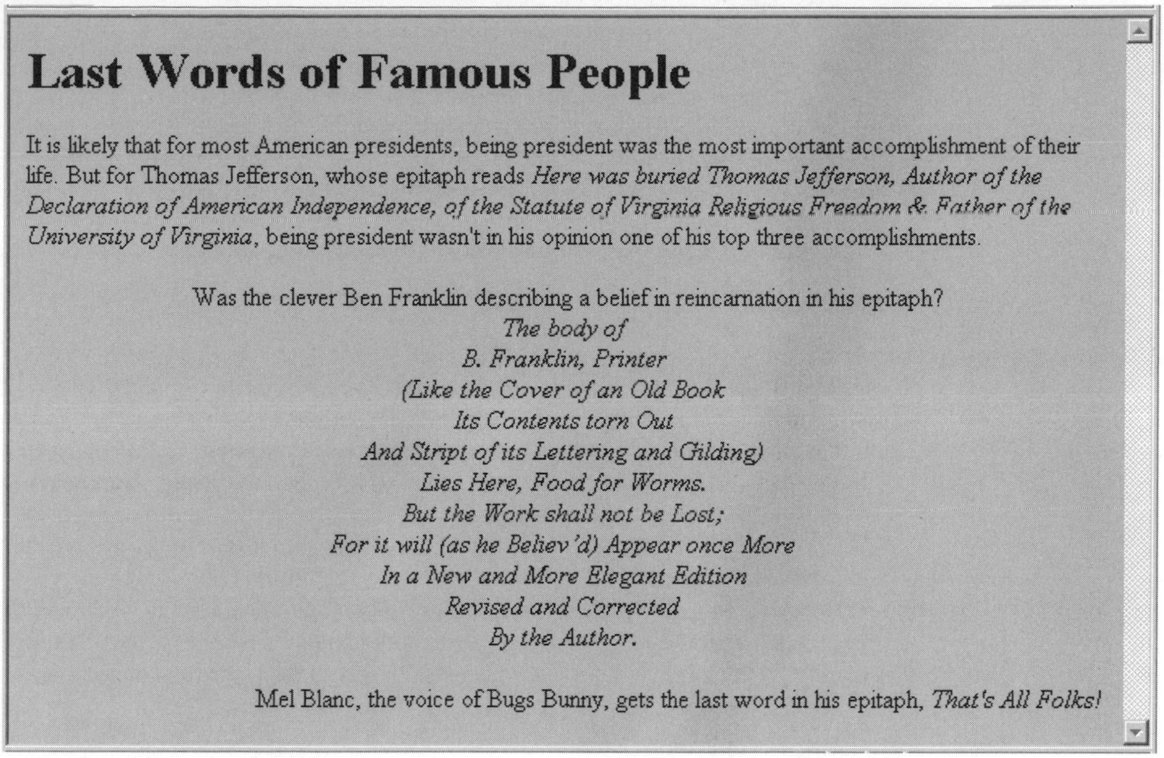

Last Words of Famous People

It is likely that for most American presidents, being president was the most important accomplishment of their life. But for Thomas Jefferson, whose epitaph reads *Here was buried Thomas Jefferson, Author of the Declaration of American Independence, of the Statute of Virginia Religious Freedom & Father of the University of Virginia*, being president wasn't in his opinion one of his top three accomplishments.

Was the clever Ben Franklin describing a belief in reincarnation in his epitaph?
The body of
B. Franklin, Printer
(Like the Cover of an Old Book
Its Contents torn Out
And Stript of its Lettering and Gilding)
Lies Here, Food for Worms.
But the Work shall not be Lost;
For it will (as he Believ'd) Appear once More
In a New and More Elegant Edition
Revised and Corrected
By the Author.

Mel Blanc, the voice of Bugs Bunny, gets the last word in his epitaph, *That's All Folks!*

CHAPTER 5

1. National Geographic, or online at `ngs.org`
3. There are many different ways; an obvious approach is checking a list of the Nobel Prize winners (a link to it is in the Research Reference list at the University of Washington, for example, or guess that because the Nobel Prizes are given in Sweden, a URL like `www.nobel.se` might work).
5. [Your items and classifiers may vary.] milk, eggs, hot dogs, ice cream, soda pop, pickles, orange juice concentrate, carrots, bacon, ice cubes, tomatoes, ketchup, chocolates, pickled ginger, beer, water, white wine, mayonnaise, apples, cabbage, leftover pizza, bell pepper, frozen fish fillet, lettuce, cheese. Groups: frozen/not frozen; frozen/liquid/solid; frozen/liquid/vegetable/non-vegetable; frozen/liquid/vegetable/meat-dairy/other.
7. To the right of Archive would be year, for each year there would be 12 months, for each month there would be 28–31 days, as appropriate, and to the right of each of those days are the programs for that day.
9. The top-level classifications at the University of Washington (Spring 2002) are in quotes followed by the second-level classes: "Come to UW" (Admission, Continuing Education, Employment, Visitor Info, Medical Care, Support UW), "Academic Resources" (Departments, Libraries, Teaching, International, Computing), "For the UW Community" (Student Guide, Administrative Gateway, Human Resources, Research Guide, Alumni Info), "About UW" (President McCormick, Regents, Strategies and Initiatives, Diversity, Campus Info, News, Events, Husky Sports).
11. National Public Radio, 635 Massachusetts Ave., Washington DC 20001 USA.

CHAPTER 6

1. There is no single set of answers, and achieving 0 hits is not easy. The "trick" is to think of two very dissimilar topic areas and then to pick very specialized words in

each area. For example, if mountain climbing is the topic, *carabineer* might be a good search word.

3. Primary sources give information based on direct experience or knowledge and are not biased by other people's opinions or interpretations.
5. In Spring 2002, borlaug AND norman AND nobel gets 5210 hits; but including AND CIMMYT for the International Maize and Wheat Improvement Center gets 606 hits, including the Atlantic article in the first 10 as required.
7. This is a transcript of a TV program produced by Edward R. Murrow and Fred W. Friendly in which they confronted Senator Joseph McCarthy (R-Wisconsin) who was conducting legislative hearings that have since been described as "anti-communist witch hunts."

CHAPTER 7

1. The process of determining why a deterministic system is not working properly.
3. A moth.
5. "Watching yourself" debug causes you to be more directed in the effort because you evaluate your own progress. Asking yourself what assumptions you are making, whether you need more clues, whether you are interpreting the clues correctly, etc.
7. To focus attention on the part where the fault lies. If portions of the system are known to be working, they can be eliminated from further consideration.
9. Working through a process step by step allows you to predict—and—then verify the process; when a prediction is not verified, the faulty step in the process is found.
11. The unnecessary changes were caused by having a mistaken idea of what had gone wrong, i.e., we "fixed" some HTML text that wasn't "broken."

CHAPTER 8

1. "Encode using the ten decimal numerals," becomes "represent information using symbols."
3. Smaller, that is ▲ ‖ ‖ ◀ ▼ ▶ ‖ ▼ ▲ ▲ < ▲ ‖ ‖ ■ ■ ■ ▶ ▼ ▶ ▼ because of the fourth symbol, ◀ < ■.
5. I'M TRAPPED IN MONTE CARLO.
7. *Discrete* means "distinct, separable." It is not possible to transform one into another with continuous gradations.
9. The glasses could be right side up or upside down; they could contain water or not; the glasses could contain water or beer; the glasses could be full or half full of some liquid; the glasses could be more or less than half full, providing "exactly half" is defined to be one state or the other.
11. A bit is the basic unit of the PandA representation, corresponding to the present and absent patterns. It is a contraction for the words "binary digit."
13. 1010 1011 1110 1000 1011 1110 1110 1111.
15. 0010 1000 0011 1000 0011 1000 0011 1000 0010 1001 0010 0000 0011 0101 0011 0101 0011 0101 0010 1101 0011 0001 0011 0010 0011 0001 0011 0010

CHAPTER 9

1. Computers deterministically execute instructions to process information; they are instruction execution engines.
3. Instruction Fetch (IF), Instruction Decode (ID), Data Fetch (DF), Execution (EX), and Result Return (RR). The arrow indicates that the process repeats indefinitely.
5. Discrete locations, Addresses: each location has a unique address; Values: each location records or stores values; Finite Capacity: a location can store a limited amount of information.
7. Arithmetic/Logic Unit and it does the "computation."
9. To process information requires that it be modified (transformed) as in addition, or simply moved, unaltered, from one place to another (transferred) as in alphabetizing a list. Computers do both.

11. Disks, both hard and floppy, are both input and output devices. They are known as storage devices because information written and then later read has been stored for that time period.
13. Modern computers try to start one instruction per tick, but often fail. If they are "multi-issue" computers, they try to start as many instructions as possible, which may be more than one.
15. The first aspect is the integration of the active and connective components of a circuit within a single medium, producing a monolithic electronic system requiring no hand wiring. The second aspect is that integrated circuits are produced by photolithography, which has the property that the cost of producing a chip is independent of the complexity of the chip's design.
17. An operating system is software extending the hardwired functionality of a processor with general-purpose facilities enabling it to start up (boot), manage its memory and applications, and interact with its peripheral devices.

CHAPTER 10

1. A precise, systematic method for deterministically achieving a specific result.
3. Inputs specified, Outputs specified, Definiteness, Effectiveness, and Finiteness.
5. *Effectiveness* means that the steps of the algorithm can be performed mechanically, without additional inputs, using only the capabilities of the executing agent.
7. English is ambiguous—there are multiple meanings for a single sentence or phrase—and it is imprecise—many terms are interpreted differently by people.
9. "Go downhill" isn't influenced by which side of the street one is on when the operation is performed, so in that sense it is different from "go right." However, it is similar in that if a street or road crosses a hill, "go downhill" may have a different interpretation at different points along the road. In that sense, it has similar weaknesses.
11. It tests whether the instructions are to be repeated one more time, or to stop.
13. *Alpha* doesn't have to refer to the last slot because the last *Beta* Sweep covers the last two slots and it is a property (3) of the *Beta* Sweep that the CD in the last slot is later in the alphabet than the CD in the next to last slot. Because they are in order, there is no need to assign *Alpha* to the last slot.
15. **i.** Use the term *Artist_Of* to refer to the name of the group or musician on a given CD.
    ii. Decide which end of the rack is to be the **end** of the alphabetic sequence. Call the end slot at that end the *Alpha* slot.
    iii. Call the slot adjacent to the *Alpha* slot the *Beta* slot.
    iv. If the *Artist_Of* the CD in the *Alpha* slot is **earlier** in the alphabet than the *Artist_Of* the CD in the *Beta* slot, then interchange the CDs.
    v. If there is a slot **preceding** the *Beta* slot, begin calling it the *Beta* slot and go to step iv; otherwise, continue on.
    vi. If there are two or more slots **preceding** the *Alpha* slot, begin calling the slot **preceding** the *Alpha* slot, *Alpha* and the slot **preceding** it the *Beta* slot, and go to step iv; otherwise, stop.

CHAPTER 11

1. Decimal uses 10 digits and binary uses only 2.
3. 1111 1010 1101 1110.
5. 100011 = 32 + 2 + 1.
7. 0000 1001 0001 0110. To verify,
   The A number, 0000 0101 1000 1100 = 4 + 8 + 128 + 256 + 1024 = 1420
   The B number, 0000 0011 1000 1010 = 2 + 8 + 128 + 256 + 512 = 906
   The Sum number, 0000 1001 0001 0110 = 2 + 4 + 16 + 256 + 2048 = 2326
9. The rate at which an analog signal is measured.

11. We have revised the diagram slightly so that 0 is the exact value "zero sound pressure." To give it a wider interval is possible but requires adjusting all the interval sizes rather than simply dividing them in half, which is the best solution when more bits are added.

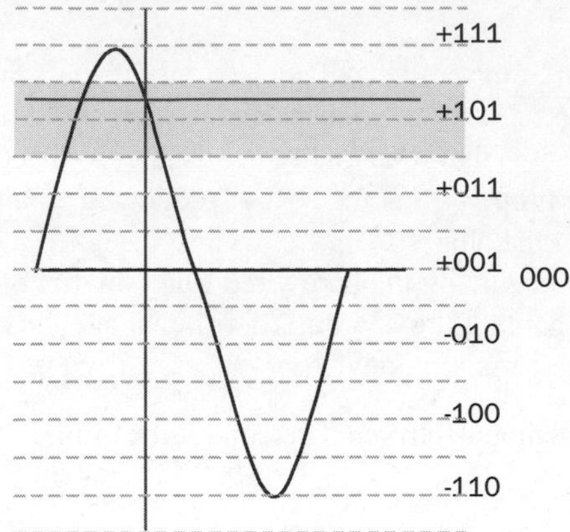

13. The fact that humans do not notice small changes in chrominance.
15. The speed of light.
17. `tiny`.

CHAPTER 12

1. Some message will have been resolved between the time it was sent out and the time we read it. Seeing the resolution first saves us from answering the original message.
3. Before A. S. King, the "please remove me" messages might have been properly intercepted by the moderator, but then re-sent to the whole list for some reason. (There was something definitely wrong, but it could be with the removal process.) King's message was a general query, not involving removal. So, we can conclude that messages are not being intercepted.
5. A superuser cannot tell you your old password, only give you a new one, which he or she does by forcing it to replace the forgotten password.
7. Guidelines to help solve a problem but do not guarantee a solution.
9. The topic is a context in which to select passwords, and recalling the topic area should aid in remembering them.
11. It is true because infected software can be loaded onto the computer from a floppy or CD.
13. To create new intellectual property by transforming an existing work.
15. There is no procedure. The work automatically becomes copyrighted the moment it is finished.

CHAPTER 13

1. Everyday tables are pictures, whereas DB tables describe their structure; unlike everyday tables, DB tables separate the structure from the content.
3. Table name, field specifiers, primary key specification.
5. Both Select and Project are operations on tables allowing a new table to be created from an existing table. They are different in that Select builds a new table from specific rows (and all columns) that meet a selection criterion, whereas Project builds a new table from specific columns (and all rows) specified by attribute name.
7. If each Table1 and Table2 have the same tuple, when SumTable is created, they are merged, leaving only one copy of it in SumTable. The subtraction of Table2 from SumTable ensures that it is not in the result, making the result different from Table1.
9. Select_from Nations (On Latitude ≥ 60 AND N_S = 'N') OR (Latitude ≥ 45 AND N_S = 'S').
11. 6 + 8 = 14 fields, 1000 × 70 = 70,000 tuples.

13. Project A, B, C, D, E, F, G, H, itemID from (Select_from (T1 × T2) On T1.itemID=T2.itemID).
15. Project, Select, respectively.

CHAPTER 14

1. The age changes—as time passes the entry goes out of date. Birthdate does not.
3. Left to right, top to bottom, they are Home_Of, HQ_Of, Serves, Contracts, Rents.
5. The required query draws data from ASTeamers and AS_Local, but only needs information required for a *local* mailing label.

   Project Nickname, First, Middle, Last, Local_Addr, Contact_ID, Street, City, State, ZIP From ASTeamers ⋈ AS_Local.

CHAPTER 15

1. The act of conducting business using electronic data communications.
3. Client.
5. You are never connected to the Web server. There are only independent transmissions between the client and the server.
7. The use of a backend database system in addition to the Web server and client.
9. They both expire(d) in 2002, just after the midpoint of the year, i.e., July.
11. When it is the client of the database in the backend system.
13. The computers at home and school have different cookies, so the server believes you have two identities. Superman has to deal with this problem, too.
15. If students A and B both try to register for a class with one slot remaining, the middleware program instance serving student A could query the database to see if there is a slot, and before it registers the student, B could do the same. Both see a slot, and so register their respective student clients.

CHAPTER 16

1. New technology can create new threats to our privacy.
3. We choose to reveal information to people or organizations that we might wish to keep private in order to enjoy the benefits those people or organizations can provide.
5. U.S. companies gather, sell, buy, and use information in ways that are inconsistent with the OECD principles.
7. When a server places the URL of a third party, e.g., an advertiser, on the page that it is setting up for your client, the third party has the opportunity to place a cookie when it serves the page of the URL.
9. This analysis begins with the first column of nibbles in Figure 16.3. Noting that the leftmost bit of the cipher text is 0 in all cases, it must be that the leftmost bit of the key is 0 because if it were 1, the zeros would imply that every byte of the cleartext falls outside the range 0010 through 0111. Focusing on the all zeros byte, we know that either the 2nd or 3rd bit of the key must be 1, or else this byte falls outside of the range, too. Suppose that bit 2 of the key is 0, then bit 3 of the key must be 1 for the all zeros byte to be in range. But if so, the first byte of the cipher text would imply that the corresponding cleartext byte begins 000 and thus falls outside the range. So, bit 2 must be 1. Because the key begins 01, it must be that the third bit is also 1 because if it were not, all of the nibbles in this column beginning with 01 would also fall outside the range. Thus the key begins 001. . . . Turning now to the third column of nibbles, the fact that these all begin with 1 implies that the key must have a 1 in this position or else the cleartext would be 1 in this position, implying that all bytes fall outside of the range. Considering the next two bits, notice that they must be 00 in the key because if they were any other combination, at least some of these nibbles would correspond to cleartext that begins 000, falling out of range.
11. e[69], t[48], i[45], o[44], s[42], a[28], h[28], r[27], n[22], w[21], f[19], d[14].
13. $10 = 2 \times 5$, $50 = 2 \times 5 \times 5$, $61 =$ is prime.

15. 10, 34, 35, 3, 10, 34, 26, 42, 11, 30, 0, 40 converts to binary as follows 001010 100010 100011 000011 001010 100010 011010 101010 001011 011110 000000 101000 and regrouping into bytes 0010 1010 0010 1000 1100 0011 0010 1010 0010 0110 1010 1010 0010 1101 1110 0000 0010 1000 which can be found in the ASCII table as: *(Ã*&♀-à(
17. There is no single answer to this exercise.

CHAPTER 17

1. In everyday usage, names are inextricably associated with values; whereas in programming, they are separated from the values, which can and do change.
3. Variables are memory locations, with the variable name being a synonym for the address and the value being the contents of the memory location.
5. All of them are legal because they all start with letters and contain only letters or numerals.
7. `OhZero` is a name, whereas `"OhZero"` is a value, meaning that `OhZero` could be a variable that could have the value `"OhZero"` but it could name any other value, too.
9. The three parts must all be given in "variable = expression" order, the flow of information is right to left, and the values of any variables used in the expression are their values prior to executing the assignment statement.
11. Legal but inefficient. The first assignment statement changes the value of `x` to `4`.The second statement changes the value of `x` to `8`. The second statement obliterates the effect of the first statement, and so the first statement is unnecessary.
13. <, <=, =, !=, >=, >
15. More, by $.49.

CHAPTER 18

1. Build a generic table data entry, surrounded by `<td> </td>` tags. Replicate this item the desired number of times (number of columns) and surround the result with `<tr> </tr>` tags. Replicate this item the desired number of times (number of rows) and surround the result with `<table> </table>` tags. Go back and correct any entries that differ from the generic entry. It has the advantage that the difficult-to-type tags are mostly copy-pasted.
3. The action is specified as an *event handler*, one or more JavaScript instructions given as part of the input control. When the event happens, the computer performs the instructions.
5. The variable `shots` is declared outside of any input control and so is global to them all, i.e., `shots` can be referenced directly from any control. But the value attribute of the `price` input control is local to it, and so referring to it from the event handler of some other input control requires that we say how to navigate to it.
7. The needed modifications are visible code in the appendix.
9. "What should happen when this button is clicked?"

CHAPTER 19

1. Naming, defining, and parameterization.
3. The name must be preceded by a space (to separate it from the word function), and it is usually followed by a space, but that is not required. The parameter list is enclosed in parentheses, and the function definition is enclosed in curly braces.
5. "Functions impose a scope of reference on variables" means that the variables declared within a function are restricted to being assigned to or having their values used, i.e., being referenced, only within the definition of the function.
7. Global: `sampleVarX`. Local: `sampleVarY`, `sampleVarZ`.

9. The first occurrences of the three variables are parameters, the next occurrence of `units` is neither, and both of the next occurrences of `weight` and `height` are arguments.

```
function BMI (units, height, weight ) {              //All parameters
   // Compute BMI in either metric or English
   if (units == "English")                           //Neither
      return bmiE(weight, height);                   //Both arguments
   else
      return bmiM(weight, height);                   //Both arguments
}
```

11. The definition says how a function works and what inputs it needs; the call is an application of the function for specific inputs.
13. Choosing `findVol` as the function name and `rad` as the parameter (other legal name choices are okay, of course), the function has the declaration

```
function findVol ( rad ) {
   return = (4 / 3) * 3.14159 * (rad * rad * rad);
}
```

CHAPTER 20

1. Iteration variables are standard variables in JavaScript, but they are called *iteration variables* while they are helping in the definition of a loop, i.e., in the range of the loop definition.
3. The following JS suffices.

```
<script language="JavaScript">
  var j;
  var text="";
  for (j=1; j<=12; j=j+1){
    text = text + "I Love You! \n";
  }
  text = text + "If I've said it once, "
+ "I've said it a dozen times, I Love You!";
  alert(text);
</script>
```

The program produces the output shown at right.

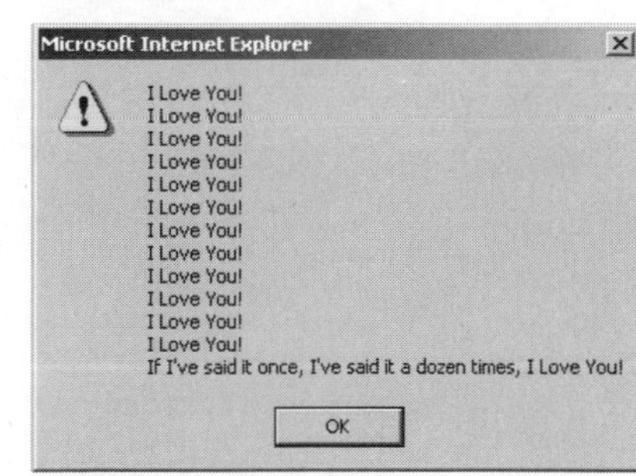

5. The following program suffices.

```
<html><head>
<title>The Sentimental Loop</title></head>
<body><script language="JavaScript">
  var j;
  var count = 1000;
  for (j=1; j<=count; j=j+1){
     document.write("I Love You!  ");
  }
  document.write("If I've said it once, I've said it "
  + count + " times, I Love You!");
</script>
</body>
</html>
```

And it produces the (abbreviated) output shown on the next page.

I Love You! I Love You! I Love You! I Love You! I Love You! I Love You! I Love You! I Love You! I Love You! I
Love You! I Love You! I Love You! I Love You! I Love You! I Love You! I Love You! I Love You! I Love You! I
Love You! I Love You! I Love You! I Love You! I Love You! I Love You! I Love You! I Love You! I Love You! I
Love You! I Love You! I Love You! I Love You! I Love You! I Love You! I Love You! I Love You! I Love You! I
Love You! I Love You! I Love You! I Love You! I Love You! I Love You! I Love You! I Love You! I Love You! I
Love You! I Love You! I Love You! I Love You! I Love You! I Love You! I Love You! I Love You! I Love You! I
Love You! I Love You! I Love You! I Love You! I Love You! I Love You! I Love You! I Love You! I Love You! I
Love You! I Love You! I Love You! I Love You! I Love You! I Love You! I Love You! I Love You! I Love You! I

. . .

Love You! I Love You! I Love You! I Love You! I Love You! I Love You! I Love You! I Love You! I Love You! I
Love You! I Love You! I Love You! I Love You! I Love You! I Love You! I Love You! I Love You! I Love You! I
Love You! I Love You! I Love You! I Love You! I Love You! I Love You! I Love You! I Love You! I Love You! I
Love You! I Love You! I Love You! I Love You! I Love You! I Love You! I Love You! I Love You! I Love You! I
Love You! I Love You! I Love You! I Love You! I Love You! I Love You! I Love You! I Love You! I Love You! I
Love You! If I've said it once, I've said it 1000 times, I Love You!

7.
```
for (j=0; j<12; j++) { ... }
for (k=0; k<count; count++) { ... }
for (tic=0; tic<lower_limit+20; tic++) { ... }
```

9. The iteration—practice, practice, practice . . . —has a termination test, namely, getting it right.
11. Change the 100 in the Flips Iteration to 1000, and change the "–50" in the `Math.abs()` function to "–500."
13. A random day is selected and the weekday name is replaced with the text "Party Day!"

CHAPTER 21

1. The following steps are a logical decomposition, though others are also possible.
   a. Build GUI including title, table, left-side entries, and the important links section.
   b. Build random number generator.
   c. After GUI build CtoF and enter into table.
   d. After GUI build FtoC and enter into table.
   e. After GUI build BMI and enter into table.
   f. After GUI and Random, build coin flip and enter into table.
   g. After GUI and Random, build number pick and enter into table.
   h. After tasks c–g, program date and last line and beautify design if needed.
3. See below.

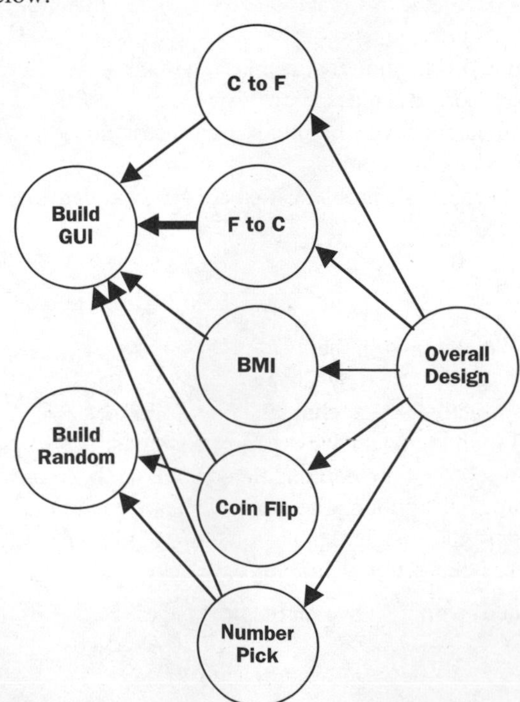

5. The Control Construction was programmed in the Best Laid Plans . . . section, because it was done out of order so that we could more conveniently test the Grid Animation task.
7. There are several ways to do this, but perhaps the easiest is simply reduce the value of `pos` throughout the definitions of the functions

```
function here (pos) {
    document.images[20+pos-1].src = "gifpix/OrangeBox.gif";
    frame = pos;
}
function gone (pos) {
    document.images[20+pos-1].src = "gifpix/BrownBox.gif";
    frame = 0;
}
```

and to increase it by one in the event handler specifications. Notice that parentheses are needed to cause the "+1" to be treated like a number rather than a letter string.

```
for (j = 0; j < 7; j++) {
    document.write('<img src="gifpix/BrownBox.gif" ' +
       'onMouseOver = "here(' + (j+1) + ')" ' +
       'onMouseOut = "gone(' + (j+1) + ')">');
}
```

CHAPTER 22

1. If a computer were successful in Turing's Test, it would demonstrate that a computer could appear as intelligent as a human being to the judge.
3. There is the board at the root plus there are 9 choices for the first move, so 9 boards below it, 8 choices from each of those moves, 7 following each of those, etc., giving $1 + 9 \times 8 \times \quad \times 1 = 362,881$
5. Though Deep Blue is following instructions specified by its creators, the solution takes a more general form so that when it is started on a body of information, namely, the information of a developing game, it works on the problem at a high level, entering states and making decisions that its creators could not predict or anticipate.
7. The background was painted gray. Then in a loop counting out the number of black squares to be produced, pairs of random numbers, *x,y,* were selected between 0 and the number of pixels in each dimension. Then a black square with a white border was painted so that its upper-left corner is placed at position *x,y.*
9. The property that once computers have a minimal set of instructions, they are all capable of computing the same computations.
11. They generally run faster because the problems that are NP-complete are intractable, i.e., they run very slowly.

CHAPTER 23

1. By emphasizing higher-level thinking in the form of capabilities, Fluency teaches you how to learn about IT, as illustrated by Chapter 3, "What the Digerati Know." The topic was thinking abstractly about technology, and from that we learned a process that allows us to familiarize ourselves with new applications when we need to know how they work. It replaced memorizing the manual on an application.
3. Is it likely that the technological solution, after an initial start-up period, produce a more convenient, faster, or higher-quality solution? If not, don't use IT.
5. Follow the media and notice the "science" articles about new technology.

Index